Estuarine Research in
the 1980s

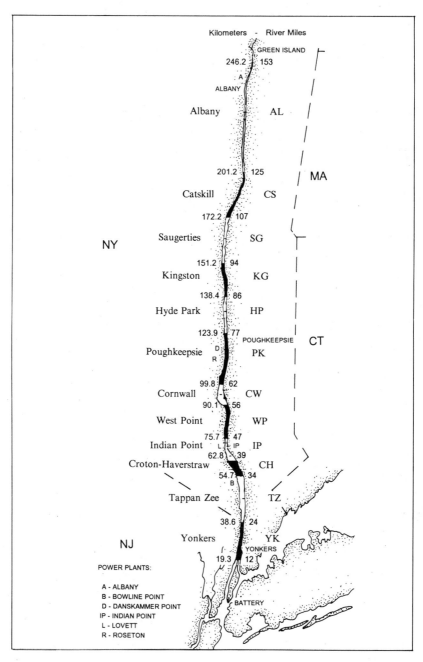

Geographical regions used during field sampling programs in the Hudson River Estuary.

Estuarine Research in the 1980s

THE
HUDSON RIVER ENVIRONMENTAL SOCIETY
SEVENTH SYMPOSIUM ON
HUDSON RIVER ECOLOGY

C. Lavett Smith,
Editor

STATE UNIVERSITY OF NEW YORK PRESS

Published by
State University of New York Press, Albany

© 1992 State University of New York

All rights reserved

Printed in the United States of America

No part of this book may be used or reproduced
in any manner whatsoever without written permission
except in the case of brief quotations embodied in
critical articles and reviews.

For information, address State University of New York
Press, State University Plaza, Albany, N.Y., 12246

Production by E. Moore
Marketing by Theresa A. Swierzowski

Library of Congress Cataloging-in-Publication Data

Symposium on Hudson River Ecology (7th : 1989 : Poughkeepsie, N.Y.)
    Estuarine research in the 1980s : Hudson River Environmental
Society, Seventh Symposium on Hudson River Ecology / C. Lavett
Smith, editor.
    p. cm.
    Symposium held April 5–6, 1989, Poughkeepsie, N.Y.
    Includes bibliographical references and index.
    ISBN 0-7914-0937-6 (alk. paper). — ISBN 0-7914-0938-4 (pbk. :
alk. paper)
    1. Estuarine ecology—Hudson River Estuary (N.Y. and N.J.)—
Congresses. 2. Hudson River Estuary (N.Y. and N.J.)—Congresses.
3. Fishes—Hudson River Estuary (N.Y. and N.J.)—Congresses.
4. Fisheries—Hudson River Estuary (N.Y. and N.J.)—Congresses.
5. Water quality—Hudson River Estuary (N.Y. and N.J.)—Congresses.
I. Smith, C. Lavett, 1927– . II. Hudson River Environmental
Society. III. Title.
QH104.5.H83S94   1989
574.5'26365'087473—dc20   91-11040
                                                                       CIP

10 9 8 7 6 5 4 3 2 1

Contents

Acknowledgments ix

Introduction xi
   C. Lavett Smith

PART I. PHYSICAL AND CHEMICAL ECOLOGY

1. General Evaluation of Hudson River Freshwater Flow Trends   3
   Karim A. Abood, Guy A. Apicella, and Alan W. Wells

2. Long-Term Variability and Predictability of Hudson River Physical and Chemical Characteristics   29
   Alan W. Wells and John R. Young

3. Recent Trends and Patterns in Selected Water Quality Parameters in the Mid-Hudson River Estuary   59
   Wayne J. Mancroni, Martin W. Daley, and William Dey

4. Impacts of Channel Dredging on Dissolved Oxygen and Other Physical Parameters in Haverstraw Bay   82
   Leonard J. Houston, Mark W. LaSalle, and John D. Lunz

5. Evaluation of Induced Sedimentation in New York Harbor   105
   Karim A. Abood, E. A. Maikish, T. B. Vanderbeek, and M. U. McGowan

6. Impact of Withdrawals on Hudson Salinity 134
   M. Llewellyn Thatcher

7. Hudson River Radionuclide Research Revisited: 152
   Watershed Removal of Fallout Radionuclides and
   Long-Term Trends in the Estuary
   Paul Linsalata and Norman Cohen

PART II. FISHERY BIOLOGY

8. Biology of the Shortnose Sturgeon (*Acipenser* 187
   brevirostrum Lesueur, 1818) in the Hudson River
   Estuary, New York
   William L. Dovel, Anthony W. Pekovitch,
   and Thomas J. Berggren

9. Distribution of the Shortnose Sturgeon in the 217
   Hudson River Estuary, 1984–1988
   Paul Geoghegan, Mark T. Mattson,
   and Roger G. Keppel

10. Temporal and Spatial Distribution of Bay Anchovy 228
    Eggs through Adults in the Hudson River Estuary
    Robert E. Schmidt

11. Abundance Trends in Hudson River White Perch 242
    Alan W. Wells, John A. Matousek,
    and Jay B. Hutchison

12. Effects of Year Class Strength on Size of Young-of- 265
    the-Year Striped Bass
    Kim A. McKown and Byron H. Young

13. Movements of Immature Striped Bass in the 276
    Hudson Estuary
    William L. Dovel

PART III. FISHERIES METHODS

14. Quality Assurance and Quality Control Aspects of 303
    the Hudson River Utilities Environmental Studies
    John R. Young, Roger G. Keppel,
    and Ronald J. Klauda

15. Accuracy of Catch per Unit Effort Indices of Atlantic Tomcod Abundance in the Hudson River 323
    Mark T. Mattson, Paul Geoghegan, and Dennis J. Dunning

16. Postjuvenile Striped Bass Studies after the Settlement Agreement 339
    Dennis J. Dunning, Quentin E. Ross, William L. Kirk, John R. Waldman, Douglas G. Heimbuch, and Mark T. Mattson

17. Abundance of Selected Hudson River Fish Species in Previously Unsampled Regions: Effect on Standing Crop Estimates 348
    Susan G. Metzger, Roger G. Keppel, Paul Geoghegan, and Alan G. Wells

18. Post-Yolk-Sac Larvae Abundance as an Index of Year Class Strength of Striped Bass in the Hudson River 376
    Douglas G. Heimbuch, Dennis J. Dunning, and John R. Young

19. Assessing the Effect of Compensation on the Risk of Population Decline and Extinction 392
    Lev R. Ginzburg and Scott Ferson

PART IV. ESTUARINE ECOLOGY

20. Aquatic Studies at the Hudson River Center Site 407
    Roy R. Stoecker, Janet Collura, and Phillip J. Fallon, Jr.

21. Fish Distribution Survey of Newark Bay, New Jersey, May 1987–April 1988 428
    Robert Will and Leonard J. Houston

22. Biomass and Energetics of Consumers in the Lower Food Web of the Hudson River 446
    David Lints, Stuart E. G. Findlay, and Michael L. Pace

23. Dynamics of Larval Fish Populations in a Hudson River Tidal Marsh ... 458
Robert E. Schmidt, A. Barth Anderson, and Karim Limburg

24. A Case for the Restoration of the Estuarine Ecosystem of Croton Bay/Croton River and Associated Tidal Marshes ... 476
Edward H. Buckley

PART V. SUMMARY

25. What Do We Really Know about the Hudson? ... 491
C. Lavett Smith

Abbreviations ... 497

Literature Cited ... 499

Contributors ... 539

Index ... 543

Acknowledgments

The Hudson River Environmental Society thanks the following persons who graciously served as peer reviewers for the papers submitted for this volume: Henry Bokuniewicz, Malcolm Bowman, Mark P. Brown, David R. Bouldin, Deborah Coffey, Robert Daniels, William C. Dennison, William Dovel, Dennis Dunning, Vincent Gallucci, Carl George, Cynthia C. Gilmour, D. R. F. Harleman, Bob Haselvlat, Robert Henshaw, William Kirk, Ronald Klauda, James B. McLaren, Mark Mattson, Ray Morgan, Tavit O. Najarian, Tom Occhigrosso, Curtis Olsen, Anthony Pacheco, John Palmer, Joseph Rachlin, Paul J. Rago, R. Anne Richards, Saul B. Saila, William R. Schell, Robert Schmidt, H. J. Simpson, Loretta Stillman, Don Strickert, Dennis Suszkowski, M. Llewellyn Thatcher, John Tietjen, John Titus, Webb Van Winkle, Charles Wahtola, John Waldman, Peter J. Woodhead, and John Young.

C. LAVETT SMITH

Introduction

With the signing of the Settlement Agreement between Public Utilities and environmental groups in 1980, the Hudson River assumed a unique role as an example of an environment that can be protected and restored when dedicated, concerned citizens work together with commercial interests to resolve conflicts in a fair and equitable way. As the Settlement Agreement ends in 1990, the world will be watching the renegotiation process and its outcome may well point the way to similar agreements the world over.

Research in the Hudson Estuary changed drastically after the settlement. During the controversial decade that preceded the settlement, most of the research was aimed at gathering data to answer specific questions that would aid in predicting the effects of new power plants on the environment and the organisms that depend on that environment. While the data were gathered using the most rigorous methods, state of the art equipment, and the finest analytical techniques, scientists are justifiably disappointed to find that the increase in our understanding of the Hudson ecosystem, and estuarine ecosystems in general, has not been commensurate with the amount of data gathered during the monumental efforts that collectively have been called the Hudson River Ecological Study.

Does this mean that the Hudson River Ecological Study was a badly designed program? Under the circumstances, no. It was designed with the paramount goal of answering specific questions. For example, a large part of the conflict centered on the effects of entrainment of fish larvae. Power plants use tremendous quantities of cooling water and when this water comes from a tidal estuary, it carries with it vast numbers of larvae of fish and invertebrates. Immediately this raises questions of the ability of the larvae to survive entrainment, of the numbers of larvae actually entrained, of the effect of mortality caused by the power plants, and of what measures can be taken to protect the larvae from the power plants. Answering such questions was enormously difficult and costly, and the data had to be collected in ways that would stand intense scrutiny in the courts. The program had to be designed to give precise answers to specific questions of what goes on at specific sites in this river. There simply was no time for broad general studies that would not promise immediate, useful results. As a consequence we have vast quantities of specific data showing what goes on in the river, but we still have little understanding of why it happens in this way.

After the settlement, the emphasis of Utility-sponsored research changed to studies aimed at evaluating the steps being taken to mitigate the effects of the power plants, focusing on such questions as the effectiveness of the release of hatchery raised striped bass fingerlings, and the advantages of different intake and screen designs. But again, the approach is directed at answering questions of what rather than why.

This volume is the published proceedings of the Seventh Symposium on Hudson River Ecology organized by the Hudson River Environmental Society. It presents a selection of estuarine research studies that have been conducted on the Hudson ecosystem, mostly since 1980, and it is a follow-up on a similar conference held in 1981. The 1981 conference brought together a number of biologists who were directly involved in the Hudson River Ecological Study. The resulting published proceedings were focused on fishery studies, since fisheries played a key role and were highly emphasized in the study. The present volume is much less limited in its scope and reflects the broader perspective of research that is being conducted today. Some of the research presented here was funded by the Hudson River Foundation for Science and Research that was established as part of the Settlement Agreement. Some was funded by the utilities as part of their monitoring programs, and the rest was supported by various other agencies and organizations. The fact that more different institutions are supporting research on the Hudson River is as encouraging as the expanded breadth of topics represented. We take both as indications that scientists are now finding it possible to pursue more basic types of research; research aimed at developing a fundamental understanding of how estuarine systems work as well as research aimed at answering specific immediate questions.

Like the previous volume *Fisheries Research in the Hudson River*, this symposium provides a sampling of current projects in the Hudson Estuary. Several of the papers deal with physical and chemical ecology with a strong emphasis on long-term trends and predictability, which is in itself an indication of the maturing of our approach to further understanding of the basics of the system. This is followed by a series of papers on fisheries methods including reviews of quality control and indices, and statistical approaches that are being applied to Hudson River data.

A few of the papers deal with individual species with emphasis on trends and long-term studies, but there are also several surveys that deal with the complete fish fauna instead of a few key species. Certainly this is a reflection of the recognition that estuaries are complex integrated systems and the whole is much more than the sum of its parts. Another indication of the systems approach is the paper on energetics and the lower food web of the river.

Finally, we have included a paper dealing with the restoration of the tidal marshes in the vicinity of Croton Bay, giving us hope that sections of the river can be returned to something near their natural state.

Together these papers provide a cross section of estuarine research as it is being practiced in the Hudson River. They indicate that the trend in estuarine research in general is toward more fundamental research directed toward clarifying the mechanisms of the estuary. A part of this trend is that a wider variety of investigations is being conducted by a greater diversity of specialists. We hope this trend continues.

Basic research is often characterized as uneconomical because it so frequently leads to dead ends or just to more questions instead of to answers that are immediately useful. In fact the opposite is true. The history of environmental impact studies has clearly demonstrated that in our haste to answer immediate questions for specific projects, we have overlooked the larger goal of really understanding the ecosystem. Consequently we have to gather the same kinds of data over again for the next project. If the articles in this book are any indication, the future will see much more emphasis on fundamental principles.

I. PHYSICAL AND CHEMICAL ECOLOGY

KARIM A. ABOOD
GUY A. APICELLA
ALAN W. WELLS

1

General Evaluation of Hudson River Freshwater Flow Trends

ABSTRACT

This background paper presents a brief description of the Hudson River basin and its hydrology, with emphasis on freshwater flow patterns observed at selected gaging stations. Freshwater flow histograms in the Upper Hudson River and in the tidal portion of the river have been developed using data from gaging stations and empirically derived relationships. The periodic variability of Upper Hudson River flows has been analyzed using data from two gaging stations, Spier Falls and Green Island. The drainage area of the former (3882 mi^2) is approximately half of the latter (8090 mi^2). Statistical analyses of flow data for both stations demonstrate a seasonal trend and a long-term cycle of approximately twenty years. Although the freshwater flow in the Lower Hudson (below Troy) cannot be measured precisely because of tidal oscillation, flow histograms may be constructed using travel time and flow relationships between the Green Island gaging station and Lower Hudson locations.

The analysis of the Spier Falls monthly average flows from 1930 through 1987 was used in a periodic regression analysis that revealed a 20-year period removing approximately 20% of the variance and a one-year period removing approximately 24%. Long-term data from Green Island (1918–1988) and from Wappinger Creek (1928–1985) were also evaluated. The Wappinger Creek record displays a strong seasonality in flow, with maximum during March and minimum during August. After removal of the seasonal component, Green Island residuals demonstrate a pattern similar to that observed in the Wappinger Creek data—low flow during the 1960s, high flow during the 1970s, and low flow during the 1980s. No consistent pattern was apparent prior to 1960.

The contribution of the drainage area below Green Island (5277 mi^2) to the lower Hudson River freshwater flow has been empirically determined using USGS estimates of ungaged and gaged tributaries. Based on mean monthly net discharges for the period October 1946 through September 1966, monthly factors relating Lower Hudson flows (Poughkeepsie and the Battery) to their Green Island counterparts have been developed. These factors and an equation relating travel time between Green Island and Indian Point may be used to estimate Lower Hudson River freshwater histograms.

This paper presents results of freshwater flow analyses showing the variation in mean, minimum, and maximum monthly flows at Spier Falls, Green Island, Wappinger Creek, Poughkeepsie, and the Battery.

INTRODUCTION

Knowledge of the hydrology of the Hudson River, particularly its freshwater flow patterns, is an essential component of most aquatic assessment programs. Water movements and mixing processes—and the distribution of salinity as a result of their combined action—are influenced by the magnitude of the flow in the river. These processes in turn influence the movement and dispersion of naturally occurring and introduced substances in the river. A thorough understanding of the aquatic resources of the Hudson River and the effects of human activities on them thus requires knowledge of the temporal and spatial variations in river flows.

This paper provides an overview of the Hudson watershed, its hydrology and flow patterns, beginning with basic background information describing the main stem of the river and its tributaries, key physiographic features of the basin, including its lakes and reservoirs, and the general climate of the basin and precipitation patterns.

A summary of flow patterns measured at three Hudson River gaging stations (Green Island, Spier Falls, and Wappinger Creek) is given next. Lower Hudson flow patterns in the tidal portion of the river (at Poughkeepsie and the Battery) are estimated, using upstream gaging station data and empirically developed relationships. Annual hydrological cycles and long-term cyclical patterns are given last.

Many of the studies summarized in this paper were conducted in recent years by Lawler, Matusky, and Skelly Engineers (LMS). These and other cited studies are used as sources of information for this paper and are duly referenced. In a number of cases the cited data sets have been updated to reflect more recent observations. Flow patterns are only summarized in this paper; the reader is referred to the cited references for additional details.

DESCRIPTION OF THE HUDSON RIVER BASIN

Basin Characteristics

The Hudson River basin, located in the eastern part of New York state, drains an area of 13,366 mi^2. Most of this area lies in the east-central part of New York state, with small portions in Vermont, Massachusetts, Connecticut, and New Jersey. Views of the basin are shown in Figures 1.1 and 1.2.

The Hudson River basin is bounded on the north by the St. Lawrence and the Lake Champlain drainage basins; on the east by the Connecticut and Housatonic river basins and the Connecticut coastal area; on the west by the Delaware, Susquehanna, Oswego, and Black river basins; and on the south by the basins of small streams tributary to the Hudson River in New York harbor. The Hudson River watershed extends 128 miles east to west and 238 miles north to south.

The Hudson River has its source in Lake Tear-of-the-Clouds* in the Adirondack Mountains of northern New York state. It flows generally south for 315 river miles to its mouth at the Battery, where it discharges into upper New York Bay.

The major tributaries entering the main stream are the Mohawk

---

*Lake Tear-of-the-Clouds is in Essex County, on the southwest slope of Mt Marcy, the highest point in New York (elevation 5344 ft).

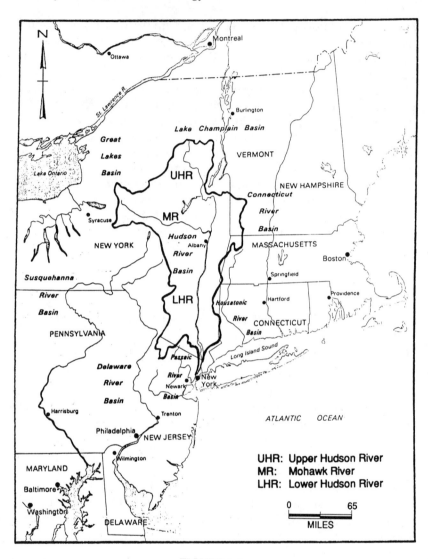

FIGURE 1.1.
Hudson River basin.

River, Hoosic River, Kinderhook Creek, Indian River, Sacandaga River, Esopus Creek, and Rondout Creek. For convenience, the entire Hudson River basin has been separated into three principal drainage areas: the Upper Hudson, the Mohawk River, and the Lower Hudson subbasins.

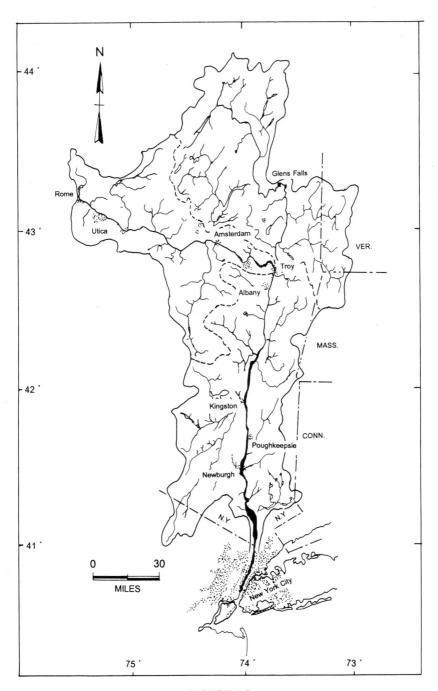

FIGURE 1.2.
Hudson River basin showing tributaries.

8   Physical and Chemical Ecology

The division between the Upper and Lower Hudson basins is at the confluence of the Mohawk River with the Hudson at Green Island. The Federal Dam at Troy, some 154 river miles above the Battery, is the head of tidewater.

The Upper Hudson River flows generally south-southeast to its confluence with the Sacandaga River, where it turns to the east. At Hudson Falls it turns again to the south. The river's total length to Green Island is about 150 miles, and it drains an area of some 4627 mi^2. From its source to Troy Dam the Hudson River drops 1810 ft, an average bottom slope of about 12 ft per mile.

The Mohawk River has its source in the hills near the boundary between Lewis and Oneida counties, New York. It flows in a southerly direction to Rome, then follows a general east-southeast course to its junction with the Hudson River at Cohoes, New York. The river is approximately 155 miles long and drains some 3462 mi^2. The Mohawk River falls irregularly from its source at elevation 1800 ft above mean sea level (m.s.l.) to elevation 14.3 ft, where it joins the Hudson River at Cohoes.

The lower Hudson River commences at the junction of the Mohawk and Upper Hudson rivers at Troy and discharges into Upper New York Bay. All of this section of the river is tidal. The Lower Hudson is approximately 154 miles long and drains an area of some 5277 mi^2. Its average slope, represented by the halftide (mean tide) level, is about 2 ft in 150 miles. The slope is greatest in the section of the river from Troy to Catskill and least between Catskill and Tarrytown. From Tarrytown to New York City the halftide elevation drops about 0.7 ft.

The discharge of the Hudson River to the Atlantic Ocean is somewhat hampered by the constriction of New York Harbor at the Verrazano Narrows. The Lower Hudson River discharges into Upper New York Bay and subsequently through the Verrazano Narrows into Lower New York Bay, an arm of the Atlantic Ocean.

The Hudson River receives a number of tributaries throughout its length. The major ones with their drainage areas are listed in Tables 1.1 and 1.2. Major basin characteristics, including rainfall and runoff data for the three subbasins (Upper Hudson, Mohawk, and Lower Hudson), are summarized in Table 1.3.

Physiographic Features

The major physiographic features of the Hudson River basin are a mountainous terrain (48% of the basin), cultivated lands (42%), lakes and water bodies (2%), and urban developments (8%).

TABLE 1.1
Upper Hudson River and Mohawk River tributaries.

Stream	Drainage Area (mi²)
Upper Hudson River	
Cedar River	164
Indian River	201
Boreas River	92
Schroon River	568
Sacandaga River	1058
Batten Kill	441
Kayaderosseras—Fish Creek	252
Hoosic River	713
Minor streams and direct drainage	1138
Subtotal	4627
Mohawk River	
Oriskany Creek	146
West Canada Creek	562
East Canada Creek	291
Schoharie Creek	926
Minor streams and direct drainage	1537
Subtotal	3462
(*Hudson River at Green Island*	8090)

The major feature of the northern Hudson River watershed is the rugged eastern portion of the Adirondack Mountains. Some of the highest mountains in the eastern United States are found in this portion of the watershed, including Mt Marcy (5344 ft m.s.l.), Algonquin Peak (5112 ft m.s.l.), Mt Skylight (4920 ft m.s.l.), and Mt Haystack (4918 ft m.s.l.).

The Mohawk River Valley, which lies between the Adirondack and Catskill mountains, forms a wide connecting link between the Hudson River Valley and the region of the Great Lakes.

The Catskill Mountains, with peaks exceeding elevations of 4000 ft m.s.l., form the divide between the Lower Hudson River and the Delaware River. The eastern boundary of the Lower Hudson River basin is formed by the Taconic Mountains.

The major physiographic feature of the central part of the Lower Hudson watershed is the Highlands of the Hudson; its cliffs rise close to the edge of the river on both sides, making this river reach a scenic attraction.

TABLE 1.2.
Major freshwater tributaries to the Hudson River below Troy, New York.

Tributary	River Mile (km)	Shore	Drainage Area (mi^2)	Mean Flow (cfs)
Green Brook	16.0 (26)	West		
Crumkill Creek	24.0 (39)	West		
Sparkill Creek	24.5 (39)	West		
Croton River	34.0 (55)	East	378	
Cedar Pond Brook	39.0 (63)	West		
Peekskill Creek	44.0 (71)	East		
Arden Brook	51.0 (82)	East		
Indian Brook	53.0 (85)	East		
Foundry Brook	55.0 (89)	East		
Moodna Creek	58.0 (93)	West		
Fishkill Creek	60.0 (97)	East		
Wappinger Creek	67.0 (108)	East	208	254
Casper Creek	70.0 (113)	East		
Maritje Kill	79.0 (127)	East		
Crum Elbow Creek	82.0 (132)	East		
Black Creek	84.0 (135)	West		
Indian Kill	85.0 (137)	East		
Fallsburg Creek	88.0 (142)	East		
Landsman Kill	89.0 (143)	East		
Rondout Creek (+Wallkill River)	92.0 (148)	West	1197	
Stony Creek	101.0 (163)	East		
Esopus Creek	103.0 (166)	West	425	588
Post Creek	110.0 (177)	West		
Roeliff Jansen Kill	111.0 (179)	East	208	
Foxes Creek	111.5 (179)	East		
Bargett Creek	112.0 (180)	West		
Dubois Creek	113.0 (182)	West		
Catskill Creek	113.0 (182)	West	417	
Mineral Spring Brook	113.0 (182)	West		
Corlaer Kill	115.5 (186)	West		
Murderers Creek	120.0 (193)	West		
Kinderhook Creek	122.0 (196)	East	512	
Coxsackie Creek	128.0 (206)	West		
Mill Creek	129.0 (208)	East		
Hannacroix Creek	132.5 (213)	West		
Coeymans Creek	134.5 (126)	West		

(*continued*)

TABLE 1.2. (Continued)

Tributary	River Mile (km)	Shore	Drainage Area (mi^2)	Mean Flow (cfs)
Schodack Creek	136.0 (219)	East		
Muitzes Kill	136.5 (220)	East		
Baker Creek	137.0 (220)	West		
Vlockie Kill	137.5 (221)	East		
Binnen Kill	138.0 (222)	West		
Moordener Kill	138.5 (223)	East	33	38
Vloman Kill	139.0 (224)	West		
Vierda Kill	140.0 (225)	East		
Cooper Kill	142.5 (229)	East		
Papscanee Creek	143.0 (230)	East		
Island Creek	143.5 (231)	West		
Normans Kill	144.0 (232)	West	168	145
Mill Creek	145.5 (234)	East		

Several reservoirs and many lakes are located in the Hudson River basin. The Sacandaga Reservoir (29,670 million cubic feet) and Indian Lake Reservoir (4692 million cubic feet) are the two major reservoirs controlling flow in the Upper Hudson River. The Hinckley Reservoir (3320 million cubic feet), Delta Reservoir (2808 million cubic feet), and Schoharie Reservoir (2353 million cubic feet) are located in the Mohawk River basin.

Water from the Schoharie Reservoir is diverted by a tunnel to the Ashokan Reservoir and from there via the Catskill Aqueduct to the New York city public water supply system. The Ashokan Reservoir (16,431 million cubic feet) is located on Esopus Creek in the Lower Hudson River basin.

The Ashokan and Schoharie reservoirs constitute one of the three reservoir systems supplying drinking water to the New York metropolitan area. The second system consists of 12 reservoirs and lakes in the Croton River basin with a total storage capacity of 12,653 million cubic feet. The Croton River, a tributary of the Lower Hudson River, discharges into the estuary approximately 30 miles above the Battery. The third system, called the Delaware System, consists of four reservoirs: three in the Delaware River basin and the fourth, Rondout Reservoir, in Rondout Creek in the Lower Hudson River basin.

Most of the natural lakes are found in the northern part of the

TABLE 1.3.
Hudson River basin characteristics.

Subbasin	Drainage Area (mi²)	Channel Length (mi)	Mean Annual Air Temp. (°F)	Mean Annual Precipitation (in.)	Mean Annual Runoff[a] (in.)	Mean Annual Runoff[a] (cfs)	Storage Usable Capacity (acre-ft)
Mohawk River at Cohoes	3,456	155	45	46	22.4	5,691	203,900
Upper Hudson at Green Island (not including Mohawk)	4,627	150	40	40	23.5	8,009	863,000
Upper Hudson at Green Island (including Mohawk)	8,090	—	—	—	22.9	13,700	—
Lower Hudson at Green Island	—	—	—	—	—	13,618	—
Lower Hudson at Poughkeepsie	—	—	—	—	—	18,831(e) 20,750(e)	—
at Battery	13,366	154	48	42	21.1(e)	—	551,000

[a] Mohawk and Upper Hudson River values are as of 1986. Lower Hudson values are estimates based on 1946–1988 Green Island flows and 1947–1965 USGS estimates of Lower Hudson flows.

basin. The largest are Saratoga and Schroon lakes. Other large lakes are Lake Pleasant and Piseco Lake. The other lakes and ponds are small and generally located near the headwaters of streams.

Basin Climate and Hydrology

The general climate of the Hudson River basin may be considered moist continental. The upper Hudson basin has comparatively long, cold, and snowy winters and short, mild summers. In the lower Hudson basin, where the modifying influence of the valley moderates the climate, summers are usually longer and winters milder.

The Mohawk River basin has variable weather conditions with characteristics of both areas. The average annual air temperature within the basin ranges from 50°F in the southern portion to 40°F in the Adirondack Mountains. The corresponding average July temperature varies from 75 to 65°F and the average January temperature from 30 to 15°F, respectively. The maximum and minimum temperatures recorded in the basin are 106 and −42°F, respectively.

The average annual precipitation varies from 34 in. in the center of the basin to more than 50 in. in the Herkimer County vicinity in the Adirondacks. Most of the basin receives an average of about 40 in. In general, precipitation is distributed evenly through the year, with a slight rise during summer. Figure 1.3 depicts the normal annual precipitation for the entire Hudson River basin.

The average annual snowfall for the basin ranges from about 30 in. in New York City to over 130 in. in the Adirondack Mountains.

OBSERVED FRESHWATER FLOW PATTERNS

Freshwater flow histograms in the Upper Hudson River and in the tidal portion of the river have been developed using data from gaging stations. Brief descriptions of the Upper Hudson flow trends (as measured at Spier Falls and Green Island [see Figure 1.4 for location]) and a Lower Hudson tributary (as measured at Wappinger Creek) gaged by the U.S. Geological Survey (USGS) are given below. Lower Hudson River flow patterns are presented in Section 4. The reader is referred to the cited references for additional details (Giese and Barr 1967; Busby and Darmer 1970; QLM, 1970 1974; LMS 1975, 1978, 1979, 1989; and Abood 1974, 1977).

The periodic variability of Upper Hudson River flows has been analyzed using data from two gaging stations, Spier Falls and Green

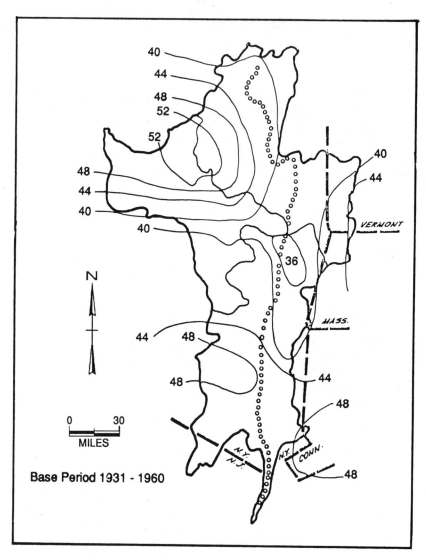

FIGURE 1.3.
Hudson River basin normal annual precipitation.

Island. The drainage area of the former (3882 mi²) is approximately half of the latter (8090 mi²).

The Spier Falls Station, maintained by the Hudson River-Black River Regulating District, has been in operation since 1930. The Green Island Station, operated by USGS, has been in existence since 1947

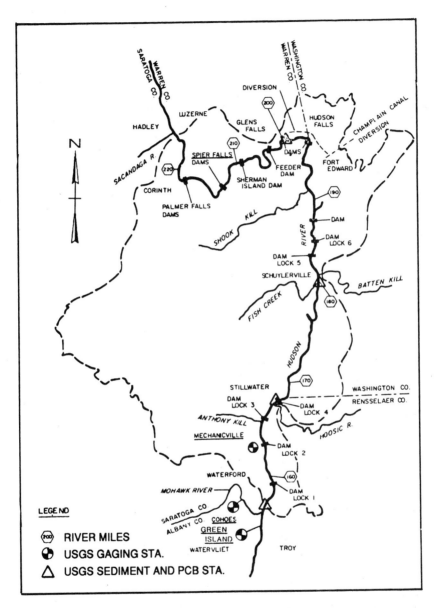

FIGURE 1.4.
Upper Hudson River basin showing gaging stations.

and measures the contribution of the Upper Hudson and Mohawk rivers. For the period from 1918 to 1947 one may obtain comparable Green Island flows from the Upper Hudson measurements at the Mechanicville gage when it was in operation and the Mohawk River measurements at the Cohoes gage (see Figure 1.4).

The Wappinger Creek USGS Station, located in Dutchess County, New York, gages a Lower Hudson drainage area of approximately 181 mi^2 and has been in operation since 1928. This station was selected because of its extensive temporal coverage and is likely more indicative of discharges of the smaller Lower Hudson tributaries.

Figure 1.5 depicts the mean, minimum, and maximum monthly flows at Green Island (1918–1988), Spier Falls (1930–1987), and Wappinger Creek (1946–1984). A summary of these data is given in Table 1.4.

TABLE 1.4.
Summary of long-term monthly mean Hudson River freshwater flow (cfs).

River Drainage Area Area (mi^2) Period of Record	Spier Falls Upper Hudson 3,882 1930–1987	Green Island Upper Hudson and Mohawk 8,090 1918–1988[a]	Wappinger Creek Lower Hudson 181 1928–1985
Jan	4,931	13,210	295
Feb	4,760	14,029	340
Mar	5,604	22,503	579
Apr	9,612	30,490	504
May	7,658	18,592	300
Jun	4,462	10,201	195
Jul	3,397	6,694	119
Aug	3,080	5,734	79
Sep	3,168	6,564	92
Oct	3,832	8,685	103
Nov	4,617	12,263	180
Dec	4,936	14,631	252
Yearly mean	4,993	13,633	253
Min. month	1,408	2,875	4
Max. month	17,738	51,610	1,195
Yield, mgd/sm	0.83	1.09	0.90

[a] Provisional 1988 data.

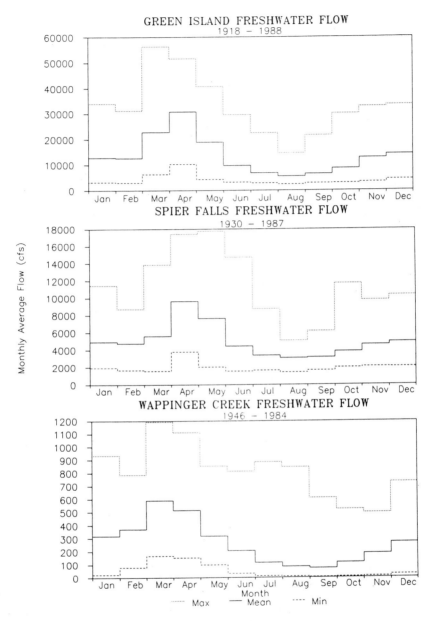

FIGURE 1.5.
Hudson River freshwater flow histograms.

ESTIMATES OF LOWER HUDSON FRESHWATER FLOW PATTERNS

The major portion (about 75% under normal summer conditions) of freshwater flow enters the estuary at its head at Troy. The remaining portion consists of contributions by tributaries flowing largely into the upper reach of the estuary. The freshwater flow in the estuary cannot be measured precisely because of tidal oscillation. Lower Hudson flow histograms in the tidal portion of the river are usually constructed by measuring Hudson River flows at Green Island (the most downstream USGS gaging station above tidewater) and adding measured or estimated flows contributed by the Lower Hudson River Tributaries.

The contribution of the drainage area below Green Island to the Lower Hudson freshwater flow has been empirically determined using USGS estimates of gaged and ungaged (estimated on the basis of drainage area) tributaries for the periods October 1946 through September 1965 at Poughkeepsie and at the Battery (Giese and Barr 1967). A correlation between these values and their Green Island counterparts yielded the relationship summarized in Table 1.5. These relationships do not take travel time into account.

Texas Instruments (TI. 1976) subjected these data (excluding February data) to statistical analysis and developed the following expressions:

$$Q_p = 1.1101 Q_g + 0.0207 (Q_g)^2$$

$$Q'_p = 0.9541 Q'_g + 0.0103 (Q'_g)^2$$

$$Q_m = 1.2078 Q_g + 0.0277 (Q_g)^2$$

$$Q'_m = 1.0445 Q'_g + 0.0114 (Q'_g)^2$$

in which Q_g, Q_p, and Q_m equal freshwater flow in thousand cubic feet per second at Green Island, Poughkeepsie, and Manhattan (February, April, and May excluded), respectively; Q'_g, Q'_p, Q'_m equal freshwater flow in thousand cubic feet per second at Green Island, Poughkeepsie, and Manhattan during April and May, respectively.

The lag time between the head and Lower Hudson locations may be estimated using empirical relationships similar to the following one developed by Abood (1977) to estimate the lag time between

TABLE 1.5.
Relationship between Green Island freshwater flow and Lower Hudson River flow at Poughkeepsie and the Battery.

$$(Q_{LH} = a + b\, Q_{GI})$$
(Oct 1947 to Sep 1965)

Month	Poughkeepsie			Battery		
	a	b	R^2	a	b	R^2
Jan	−413	1.477	0.96	−353	1.648	0.94
Feb	−1179	1.600	0.92	1105	1.600	0.90
Mar	4718	1.319	0.92	5302	1.503	0.88
Apr	1115	1.311	0.93	1626	1.432	0.88
May	−154	1.356	0.98	85	1.483	0.96
Jun	711	1.231	0.91	1228	1.310	0.86
Jul	−12	1.228	0.94	52	1.317	0.95
Aug	−951	1.358	0.96	−1062	1.452	0.93
Sep	−192	1.237	0.87	−319	1.336	0.80
Oct	−1968	1.569	0.96	−2544	1.748	0.94
Nov	−964	1.516	0.95	−1678	1.741	0.92
Dec	−958	1.421	0.90	−1008	1.621	0.94

Green Island and a mid-Hudson location (Indian Point, some 110 miles downstream:

$$t_{LH} = 256.14/Q_{LH}^{0.4}$$

in which t_{LH} equals travel time between Green Island and Indian Point in days; Q_{LH} equals estimated lower Hudson freshwater flow in cubic feet per second. This equation was derived from Manning's equation and is based on the results of a detailed Hudson River flood routing study (QLM 1970).

Figure 1.6 and Table 1.6 present lower Hudson flows estimated using the relationships summarized in Table 1.5, the Green Island long-term record (1946–1988), and the above-presented lag time equation. This table also compares the Upper Hudson subbasin with its Lower Hudson and total basin counterparts. In general, the runoff comparison reflects the overall basin precipitation pattern (see Figure 1.3) with the Lower (Upper) Hudson runoff being about 10% lower (higher) than the entire basin average of 1 mgd/mi².

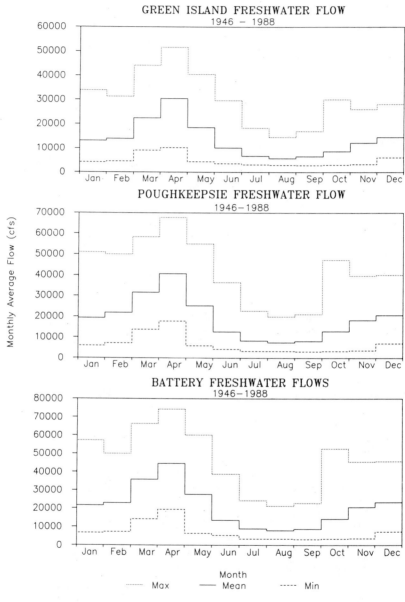

FIGURE 1.6.
Lower Hudson River freshwater flow histograms.

TABLE 1.6.
Hudson River freshwater flow summary.

	Upper Hudson at Green Island	Lower Hudson Green Island to Battery[a]	Total Basin
Drainage area, mi^2	8,909.0	5,276.0	13,366.0
Mean flow, cfs	13,633.0	7,303.0	20,936.0
Runoff, in./yr	22.9	18.7	21.3
cfs/mi^2	1.7	1.4	1.6
mgd/mi^2	1.1	0.9	1.0
Percent contribution	65.0	35.0	100.0

[a] Estimated using 1918–1988 Green Island flows (1988 provisional) and 1946–1965 USGS estimates of Lower Hudson flows. Approximate lag time between Green Island and Indian Point ranges from about 3 to 7 days depending on flow.

Table 1.7 summarizes the long-term, seasonal average flows at Green Island and in the Lower Hudson. Based on these observations and relationships over a period of 71 years (1918–1988), the long-term average freshwater flow in the Lower Hudson at the Battery is estimated at about 20,936 cfs. The maximum flows (about 1.8 the average) occur primarily during the spring months (March–May), while the period of low freshwater flows (about 0.5 the average) usually begins in June and continues until September or October. During the fall and winter months (October through February), the flow in the Lower Hudson River is closer to average conditions.

EVALUATION OF OBSERVED LONG-TERM PATTERNS

Spier Falls

The following analyses of long-term cyclical patterns of Hudson River flows were conducted in 1978 and updated in 1987 in conjunction with modeling the fate and transport of PCB in the Upper Hudson River. Monthly averages of the Spier Falls flow data, as reported by the Hudson River-Black River Regulating District from 1930 to 1977, were used in a periodic regression analysis. An initial examination of the data and time-series analysis of flows at Green Island performed by TI (1976) indicated that a 20-year cycle may explain the variance in flow. Accordingly, a multiple sinusoidal regression equation with a

TABLE 1.7.
Long-term Hudson River mean monthly freshwater flow summary.

	Long-Term Hudson River (cfs) at		
	Green Island	Poughkeepsie[a]	Battery[a]
Spring (Mar–May)	23,862	33,515	37,356
Summer (Jun–Sep)	7,298	9,060	9,794
Fall (Oct–Nov)	10,474	14,643	16,155
Winter (Dec–Feb)	13,957	20,061	22,559
Yearly (Jan–Dec)	13,633	18,854	20,936
Min. Month (Aug)	2,875	3,364	3,522
Max. Month (Apr)	51,610	67,800	74,300

[a] Estimated using 1946–1988 Green Island flows (1988 provisional) and 1946–1965 USGS estimates of Lower Hudson flows. Approximate lag time between Green Island and Indian Point ranges from about 3 to 7 days depending on flow.

20-year harmonic along with five discrete yearly subharmonics (10, 5, 4, 2, and 1 year) proved to be a reasonable fit of the 48 years of flow data.

The multiple periodic regression equation for mean monthly flow, Q(t), is given by:

$$Q(t) = 4591.7 + 1788.8 \sin\left(\frac{2\pi t}{240} + 0.460\right)$$
$$+ 649.7 \sin\left(\frac{2\pi t}{120} - 0.932\right) + 506.4 \sin\left(\frac{2\pi t}{60} - 0.359\right)$$
$$+ 585.5 \sin\left(\frac{2\pi t}{48} - 1.252\right) + 71.1 \sin\left(\frac{2\pi t}{24} + 0.13\right)$$
$$+ 1930.0 \sin\left(\frac{2\pi t}{12} + 2.313\right)$$

where Q is in cubic feet per second and t is in months, with the phase angle in radians.

A total of 50.8% ($r^2 = 0.508$) of the variance in monthly flow is removed by the entire equation. The 20-year period (first sinusoidal term) accounts for about 21% of the variance removed, which is almost as much as the one-year period (last sinusoidal term) that removes about 24%. Subsequently, a multiple periodic regression equation applied to 57 years of monthly average flows yielded similar results. It is important to note that although a 20-year cycle appears to be evident, it is not as significant as the annual hydrological cycle, and that almost half of the variance cannot be explained by the multiple periodic regression. Moreover, it should be noted that the length of flow record for this analysis was limited to less than three long-term periods; ideally, four or more periods should be used.

Green Island

Weekly average discharge values for Green Island from 1947 through 1987, (Figure 1.7) were subjected to time-series analysis using the Box-Jenkins approach (Box and Jenkins 1976; LMS 1989; Wells and Young 1989). The Autoregressive moving average (ARMA) modeling procedure indicated that the data series required deseasonalization, linear trend removal, and a first-order autoregressive component (AR1) to reduce the data to white noise. The final model explained about 58% of the total variance. Table 1.8 indicates the variance contributions of each component.

A flow analysis designed to determine periods of unusual discharge rates (i.e., periods of abnormally high or low flow rates, the residual flow, or deviations from weekly average flow) revealed several distinct periods of high and low flow (LMS 1989). The most pronounced period was from approximately 1960 through 1970, a period of severe drought. This was followed, from 1972 through 1980, by a

TABLE 1.8.
Hudson River flow variance at Green Island.

Source	Cumulative Variance Explained	Additional Variance Explained	Percentage Explained	Cumulative Percentage
Seasonal cycle	48,553,820	48,553,820	37.39	37.39
Linear trend	48,601,250	47,430	0.04	37.42
AR1	75,009,500	26,408,250	20.34	57.76
Residual		54,855,500		

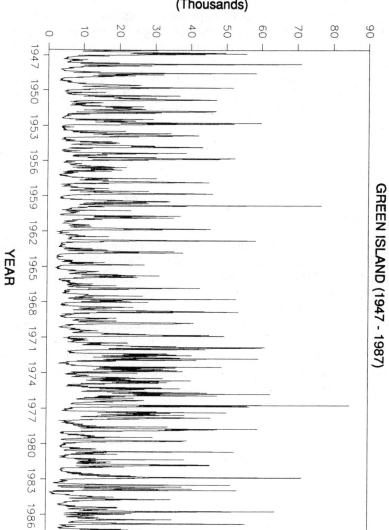

FIGURE 1.7.
Weekly average flow versus time, Green Island (1947–1987).

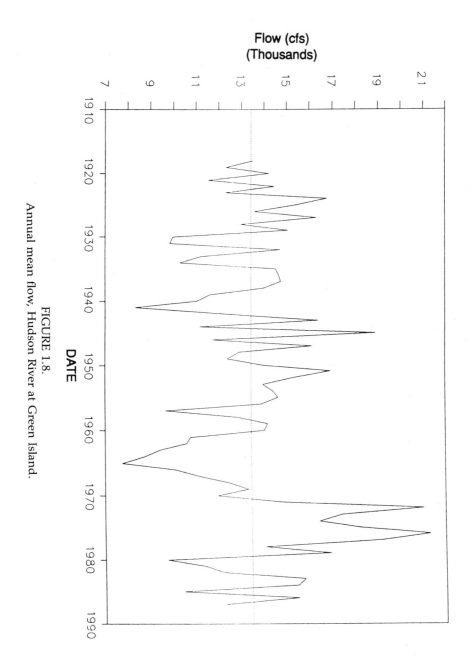

FIGURE 1.8.
Annual mean flow, Hudson River at Green Island.

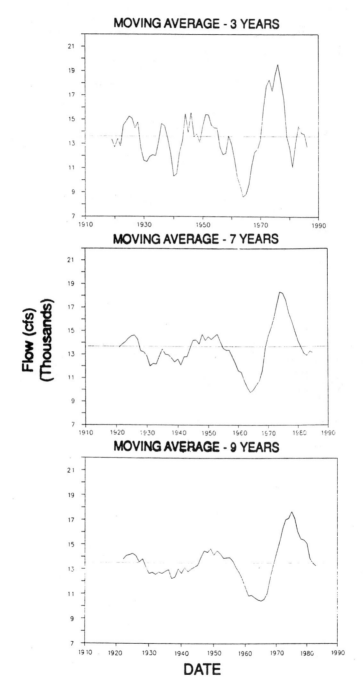

FIGURE 1.9.
Average trends of Hudson River flow at Green Island.

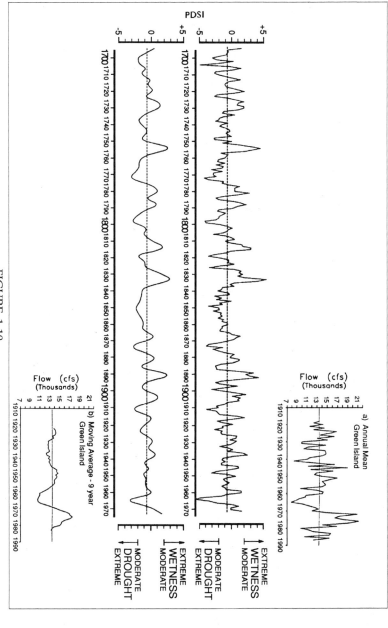

FIGURE 1.10.
Comparison between Hudson River flow patterns at Green Island and drought indices.

period of above-average discharges. The period 1980–1987 saw a return to drought conditions, but not of the same severity.

An ongoing (1989) in-house study being conducted by LMS deals with longer term (pre-1918) Hudson River drought conditions. The study has provided additional information on Hudson River cyclical patterns. Partial initial results are given here. The study involves comparison between the long-term (1918–1988) Hudson River flow patterns and available tree-ring reconstructed drought indices for the Hudson Valley dating back to 1694. Figure 1.8 depicts the annual average freshwater flows at Green Island. Three-, seven-, and nine-year moving average Green Island flow patterns are shown in Figure 1.9. The July Palmer Drought Severity Indices (PDSI) for the Hudson Valley region of New York state developed by Cook and Jacoby (1979) from the annual ring-width variations of old local trees are depicted in Figure 1.10. Based on the PDSI results, Cook and Jacoby concluded that the low frequency of past Hudson Valley droughts was partly quasiperiodic and that these periods might be identified with the 11-year sunspot cycle and a 27-year cycle of solilunar tidal influence on zonal westerly flow.

Figure 1.10 compares the unsmoothed PDSI estimates and a low-pass filtered version that passes all variance at frequencies of once in 10 years or less with the unsmoothed Green Island annual average and the 9-year moving average patterns. In general, the agreement between the PDSI and their Green Island flow counterparts is reasonable, particularly the smoothed PDSI and 9-year running average values since the 1950s. This agreement, given the differences between the two data sets and approaches, is encouraging and warrants further analysis.

ALAN W. WELLS
JOHN R. YOUNG

2

Long-Term Variability and Predictability of Hudson River Physical and Chemical Characteristics

ABSTRACT

The physical and chemical characteristics of an aquatic environment play a major role in influencing reproduction, migration, distribution, growth, and survival of organisms within that environment. Although the average seasonal values are important, often of more importance are the deviations from the average values. As part of an ongoing study by the Hudson River Utilities into the factors influencing the bionomics of Hudson River fishes, the variability and predictability of several physical and chemical characteristics of the Hudson River were studied. Water temperature and freshwater discharge, with its subsequent influence on salinity, appear to be the most important of these characteristics.

An autoregressive moving average (ARMA) time-series procedure was used to model the average weekly water temperature at the Poughkeepsie Water Works (PWW) during the period 1951–1987. A model consisting of seasonal coefficients, a linear trend, and a second-order autoregressive process was required to reduce the series to white noise and indicated that a temperature is highly predictable ($R^2 = 0.9996$). The linear trend, while explaining only a small fraction of the variance, suggests an average warming of 0.51°C over the 37-year period. Examination of the deseasonalized data indicates generally higher than average water temperatures since 1980. PWW temperatures are highly correlated, $r > 0.996$, with 12 river regions from Yonkers to Albany.

The time-series procedure was also used to estimate the variability and predictability of the weekly average freshwater discharge measured at the U.S. Geological Survey (USGS) Green Island gaging station. This model required seasonal coefficients, a linear trend, and a first-order autoregressive process to reduce the series to white noise. Overall predictability was much less than for temperature, $R^2 = 0.5776$. Examination of deseasonalized data indicates a period of low flow from 1960 through 1970 and from 1981 through 1987. The period 1972–1980 was characterized by higher than average discharges. Changes in freshwater discharge are related to changes in salinity distribution. Variation in salinity is greatest in the Yonkers region.

INTRODUCTION

Estuaries are highly variable and productive habitats that serve as spawning or nursery areas for many fish species. One hundred forty fish species have been recorded from the lower Hudson River Estuary (Beebe and Savidge 1988) with at least 38 species utilizing the lower river as a spawning and nursery ground (McFadden et al. 1977). In using the Hudson River either for their complete life cycle or for spawning and nursery purposes, each of these species has adapted its life history characteristics to survive in the physical, chemical, and biological environment present in the estuary.

Two of the most important physical variables for estuarine fish are temperature and freshwater inflow, which is a primary determinant of salinity. These variables have a pervasive influence on distribution, growth, reproduction, migration, and survival. Temperature may determine the timing of migrations, onset of reproduction, rate of embryological development, abundance of food organisms, and growth rates. Faster growth may reduce predation and result in greater survival. The freshwater discharge affects temperature and carbon availability (growth factors) (Gladden et al. 1988) as well as salinity distribution and turbidity (habitat suitability) (Cooper et al. 1988).

The physical and chemical characteristics of the Hudson River, and estuaries in general, have been widely studied in an effort to predict the distribution and reproductive success of a number of fish species. Chadwick et al. (1977) demonstrated flow to be a major determinant of striped bass abundance in a California estuary. Marcy (1976) found that water temperature and river discharge during June significantly influence Connecticut River American shad reproductive success. Klauda et al. (1988) found that Hudson River white perch growth rates were positively correlated with water temperature and negatively correlated with freshwater flows during July and August.

Most studies of the relationships among physical and chemical characteristics, fish distribution, and spawning success have focused on average environmental conditions during the spawning season. Less frequently studied, but potentially of equal or greater import, are the effects of variability and extremes in environmental conditions. In this paper we characterize the variability and predictability of temperature and freshwater flow in a way that may lead to a better understanding of factors influencing year class strength and fish distribution.

MATERIALS AND METHODS

The Hudson River Estuary flows 248 kilometers in a southerly direction from the Federal Dam at Troy, N.Y., to the Battery at New York City (Frontispiece). At its southern end the estuary discharges into upper New York Bay. The bay is connected to Long Island Sound by the East River, to Newark Bay by the Kill Van Kull, and, at its southern end, through the Narrows, to lower New York Bay and the Atlantic Ocean. The estuary between the Federal Dam and New York harbor is under tidal influence. Tidal amplitude, freshwater discharge, and meteorological conditions such as barometric pressure and winds are the primary determinants of the degree to which saline waters enter the estuary.

Although there are several sources of water temperature data for the Hudson River, one of the most complete records is available from the Poughkeepsie Water Works (PWW) located just north of the city of Poughkeepsie, N.Y., at km 122. The daily water temperature readings were recorded from 1951 through June 1982. Thereafter, readings were recorded daily except for weekends and major holidays. To fill in the missing values, we substituted the temperature from the nearest preceding day.

Although the PWW data set provides a relatively extensive temporal description of Hudson River water temperatures, it does so for only one location along the river's length. The most complete data set for riverwide temperatures is from the Hudson River Utilities' biological monitoring programs conducted from 1974 to the present.

The water quality data used in this analysis were collected during ichthyoplankton and juvenile fish surveys conducted each year between km 19 and 248, generally from March or April through November. From 1974 through 1982, temperature, dissolved oxygen, and conductivity were measured in situ with every biological sample collected. Since 1983, water quality measurements were taken at surface, mid-depth, and bottom at approximately 5-km intervals on a weekly or biweekly basis. Additional measurements were taken with each beach seine sample. Details of the sampling programs are given in Klauda et al. (1988b), Cooper et al. (1988), and Young et al. (1988).

Predictability and variability of Hudson River discharge rates were assessed from USGS records at the Green Island gaging station (No. 01372500). This station is located just upstream from the Troy lock and dam, 0.8 km downstream from the fifth branch Mohawk River. The drainage area monitored by this station is approximately 20,953 km^2. The accuracy of discharge records is considered fair above 15,000 cfs and poor below this level (Lumia et al. 1984).

Statistical analysis of temperature and discharge data was accomplished using time-series methodology. The autoregressive moving average (ARMA) approach of Box and Jenkins (1976) was used to fit models of the general form:

$$\phi_p(B)Z_t = \theta_q(B)a_t$$

where

$$\phi_p(B) = (1 - \phi_1 - \ldots \phi_p B^p)$$
$$\theta_p(B) = (1 - \theta_1 - \ldots \theta_p B^p)$$

The ϕs (phis) are the autoregressive parameters to be estimated, the θs (thetas) are the moving average parameters to be estimated, the Zs are the original time-series values, and the a's are a series of unknown random errors (residuals) that are assumed to be normally distributed. The use of seasonal differencing to model systematic, periodic variation in the data and nonseasonal differencing to convert a nonstationary series into a stationary series with a constant mean and variance, as described by Box and Jenkins (1976), was not used. Instead, we followed Brockwell and Davis (1987), using a moving average estimation technique to remove the seasonal component. A first-degree polynomial was then used to remove the long-term trend. This approach closely follows the "classic decomposition" approach, which, while less parsimonious, provided a better statistical fit and was more interpretable than a seasonal and nonseasonal differenced model.

RESULTS

Temperature

Temporal patterns. Weekly average water temperature over the 37-year period of record (1951–1987) is summarized in Figure 2.1. Water temperatures cycle on an annual basis, with the low, averaging approximately 1.0°C, occurring in January and February, the high, averaging approximately 25°C, in August. From April through June temperatures increase at an average rate of approximately 0.2°C per day; from mid-September through mid-December temperatures fall at the same rate. On corresponding days over the 37-year period the daily January and February temperatures ranged from a low of 0°C to a high of 5°C; August temperatures ranged from a low of 21.7°C to a high of 27.8°C (Figure 2.2).

During the period of record the average annual temperature was 12.38°C (SD = 0.51). On the basis of values greater than ± one standard deviation from the mean, the years 1951, 1960, 1962, 1963, 1972, 1974, and 1976 were cooler than average; 1957, 1959, 1964, 1968, 1983, 1984, and 1985 were warmer than average (Figure 2.3).

To further quantify the predictability and variability of Hudson River water temperatures, an ARMA model was fit to weekly average temperatures. The water temperature series was found to be adequately modeled by a second-order autoregressive process (AR2) after seasonal decomposition and removal of a linear trend. The dominant source of variation in Hudson River water temperatures is the seasonal cycle, accounting for over 99% of the total variation (Table 2.1). Autocorrelation analysis indicated a very high degree of correlation among observations at 52-week, i.e., one-year, intervals. The weekly

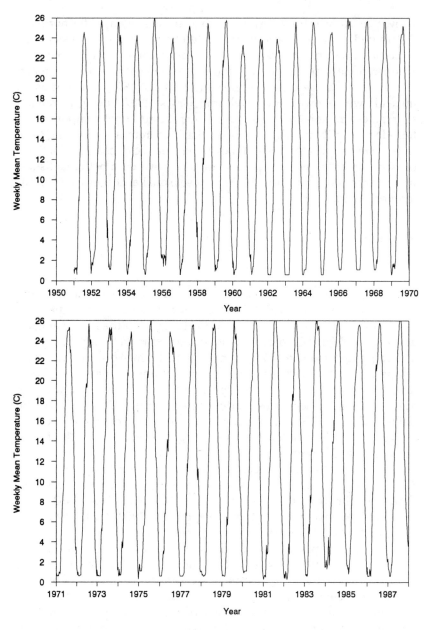

FIGURE 2.1.
Weekly mean Hudson River water temperature measured at Poughkeepsie Water Works, 1951–1987.

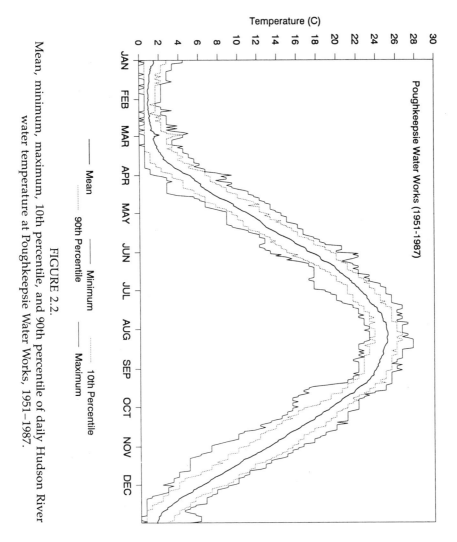

FIGURE 2.2. Mean, minimum, maximum, 10th percentile, and 90th percentile of daily Hudson River water temperature at Poughkeepsie Water Works, 1951–1987.

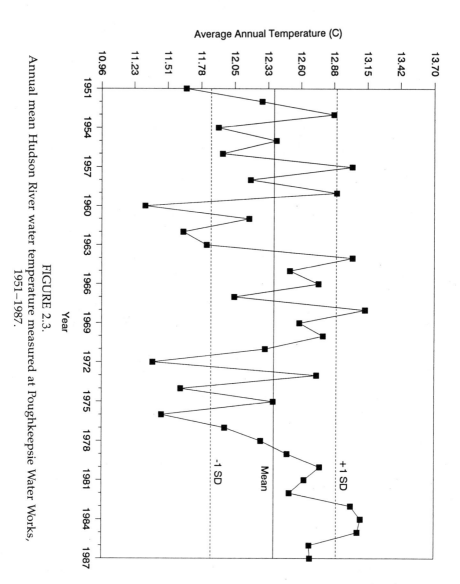

FIGURE 2.3.
Annual mean Hudson River water temperature measured at Poughkeepsie Water Works, 1951–1987.

TABLE 2.1.
Coefficient of determination (R^2) and cumulative variance explained for Poughkeepsie Water Works temperature (1951–1987) and Green Island freshwater discharge (1947–1987) time-series models.

Water Temperature

Source	Variance	Cumulative Variance	Percentage Explained	Cumulative Percentage Explained
Seasonal Cycle	799.0371	799.037	99.7996	99.7996
Linear Trend	0.0213	799.058	0.0027	99.8023
AR2	1.1441	800.202	0.1429	99.9452
Error	0.4388	800.641	0.0548	100.0000

Freshwater Discharge

Source	Variance	Cumulative Variance	Percentage Explained	Cumulative Percentage Explained
Seasonal Cycle	48,553,820	48,553,820	37.3879	37.3879
Linear Trend	47,430	48,601,250	0.0365	37.4244
AR1	26,408,250	75,009,500	20.3352	57.7596
Error	54,855,500	125,865,000	42.2404	100.0000

coefficients describing this seasonal cycle, which are interpreted as expected deviations from the annual mean temperature, are presented in Table 2.2.

The linear trend is described by the relationship $x_i = 12.15 + 0.0002631i$, where i is weeks since January 1, 1951. Although this component accounts for only a small proportion of the total variance, less than 0.01%, it compares favorably with other assessments of recent climatic trends. The coefficient for this component, 0.0002631 per week, indicates that the average water temperature has increased 0.51°C over the 37-year period. Hansen and Lebedeff (1987) indicate an approximate 0.7°C rise in temperature over the last 100 years in the northern hemisphere. This equates to a rise of 0.007°C per year compared to our estimate for the Hudson River Estuary of 0.014°C per year. (We emphasize that this analysis describes past trends. It is not intended to be used as the basis for predicting future trends.)

After removal of the seasonal and linear trends, a significant amount of the remaining variation was explained by the high degree of autocorrelation among observations. The autocorrelation function

TABLE 2.2.
Seasonal coefficients for Poughkeepsie Water Works water temperature (1951–1987) and Green Island freshwater discharge (1947–1987) models.

Week	Temperature	Flow	Week	Temperature	Flow
1	−10.93	1690.7	27	10.47	−3651.8
2	−11.23	2897.4	28	11.19	−4055.0
3	−11.33	913.8	29	11.95	−3825.1
4	−11.45	−102.3	30	12.43	−4312.0
5	−11.46	919.5	31	12.73	−5558.5
6	−11.44	−521.7	32	12.78	−6177.6
7	−11.34	−337.9	33	12.47	−7503.7
8	−11.18	−617.1	34	12.18	−7595.8
9	−10.86	203.0	35	11.81	−7908.2
10	−10.63	511.4	36	11.32	−7843.2
11	−10.15	92.8	37	10.45	−7982.3
12	−9.51	1801.4	38	9.26	−7813.7
13	−8.12	3938.8	39	7.94	−7878.2
14	−6.69	7802.1	40	6.68	−7715.5
15	−5.69	7198.9	41	5.34	−7986.5
16	−4.15	16616.3	42	3.83	−7444.4
17	−2.51	13851.5	43	2.31	−6351.3
18	−0.92	15425.8	44	0.87	−6030.3
19	0.32	16509.1	45	−0.77	−5262.0
20	1.74	13446.2	46	−2.38	−4053.2
21	3.41	12270.2	47	−3.93	−3079.9
22	4.89	7672.2	48	−5.61	−3055.2
23	6.23	7777.8	49	−7.15	−2728.4
24	7.54	5209.2	50	−8.64	−90.0
25	8.68	1843.4	51	−9.82	100.9
26	9.63	−1293.6	52	−10.57	82.2

of the series displayed an exponential dampening with significant correlations at numerous lag periods; the partial autocorrelation function displayed significant correlations only at the first two lag periods. Taken together, this pattern suggests a second-order autoregressive model. This conclusion was further supported by examination of the residual mean sum of squares from various alternative models. The final maximum likelihood AR2 solution was:

$$x_t = 1.0395\, x_{1-1} - 0.2376\, x_{t-2} + a_t$$

where

x_{t-1} = detrended and deseasonalized temperature at time t − 1
x_{t-2} = detrended and deseasonalized temperature at time t − 2
a_t = random shock, residual

This second-order autoregressive model successfully reduced the residual variation to randomness, or white noise (Portmanteau Test X^2_{18} = 16.83, P > 0.05). The small size of the residual variance, 0.4388 from an initial variance of 800.641, indicates that average weekly water temperatures are highly predictable from the time-series model.

To determine periods of unusually high or low temperature, deviations from weekly average temperature were examined. A plot of smoothed (5-point moving average) residuals indicates a period of cooler than average temperatures during the early to mid-1960s and late 1970s (Figure 2.4). Warmer than average temperatures occurred during the mid- to late 1960s and mid-1980s.

Seasonal predictability was determined from the standard deviations of the weekly temperature residuals. A plot of these values (Figure 2.5) indicates that variability is lowest, SD ≈ 0.4°C, during January and February (weeks 1–8). Greatest variability, SD > 1.3°C, occurred during April through early June (weeks 13–23) and again from late September through early December (39–49). Peak variability, SD = 1.8°C, occurred in early June. Temperatures are moderately variable during the summer (weeks 24–38).

Spatial patterns. Although the PWW data set provides a relatively extensive temporal description of Hudson River water temperatures, it does so for only a single location along the river's length. The most complete data set for riverwide temperatures is the Hudson River Utilities' sampling programs conducted since 1974. The relationship between the PWW and the weekly average regional water temperature for the 12 regions of the Utilities' sampling program was examined through regression and correlation analysis as well as graphical analysis.

Regression and correlation analysis results indicate a high degree of similarity between the 12 regions and PWW. Correlation coefficients are all positive and highly significant (P ≤ 0.001), ranging from a high of 0.976 for Hyde Park to a low of 0.961 for Yonkers (Table 2.3). Similarity to the Hyde Park region would be expected to be greatest, based on the proximity of the PWW (km 122) to the Hyde Park region (km 124–137). The least similarity would be expected for the Yonkers region, based on the marine influence in the lower estuary. In fact, correlation analysis comparing all 12 regions among

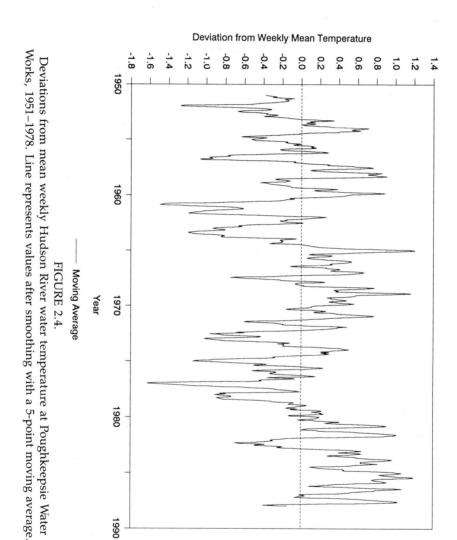

FIGURE 2.4.
Deviations from mean weekly Hudson River water temperature at Poughkeepsie Water Works, 1951–1978. Line represents values after smoothing with a 5-point moving average.

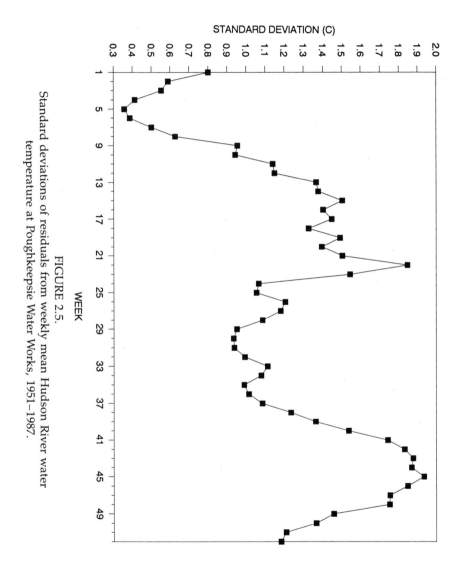

FIGURE 2.5.
Standard deviations of residuals from weekly mean Hudson River water temperature at Poughkeepsie Water Works, 1951–1987.

TABLE 2.3.
Correlation among regional weekly mean Hudson River water temperatures, 1974–1987.

	YK	TZ	CH	IP	WP	CW	PK	HP	KG	SG	CS
TZ	0.992										
CH	0.985	0.992									
IP	0.980	0.984	0.990								
WP	0.978	0.982	0.986	0.993							
CW	0.978	0.982	0.985	0.988	0.994						
PK	0.974	0.978	0.980	0.984	0.989	0.995					
HP	0.953	0.964	0.964	0.966	0.973	0.982	0.989				
KG	0.948	0.960	0.958	0.953	0.963	0.972	0.977	0.993			
SG	0.940	0.954	0.949	0.945	0.954	0.961	0.967	0.983	0.992		
CS	0.938	0.950	0.946	0.943	0.947	0.953	0.961	0.980	0.988	0.993	
AL	0.929	0.942	0.941	0.938	0.942	0.946	0.953	0.973	0.981	0.987	0.994

Note: See Frontispiece for region abbreviations.

themselves indicates a high degree of similarity among all regions, 0.9287 to 0.9946, but a greater degree of similarity among spatially proximal regions.

Regression results indicate a nearly regular decrease in intercepts and an increase in slopes of the regressions progressing upriver (Table 2.4). The slope of the relationship would be expected to be 1.0 and the intercept 0.0 if the regional mean temperature is the same as the PWW temperature. As with the correlation coefficients, the PWW temperatures most closely resemble those from the Hyde Park region. The Hyde Park slope and intercept values of 0.994 and −0.334, respectively, come closest to expected and are not statistically significantly different from 1.0 and 0.0 ($P > 0.05$).

The nearly regular trends in slope and intercept values suggest a systematic departure of temperature from the PWW temperatures. The nature of this departure is evident in plots of the average weekly PWW temperature over the period 1951–1987 compared with the average regional temperature over the period 1974–1987 (Figure 2.6). All regions appear to track the PWW temperatures closely from spring through July when freshwater inflow approaches its annual minimum. Beginning in about mid-August, however, temperatures in upriver regions begin to cool; regions farther downriver remain near the summer maximum temperature. This earlier cooling is due to the cooler temperatures in the Adirondack Mountain headwaters

TABLE 2.4.
Comparison between Poughkeepsie Water Works and regional weekly mean water temperature, 1974–1987.

Region	n	Intercept	Slope	SE Slope	RMSE	r^2	F-ratio	Probability
YK	304	2.343	0.874	0.015	1.630	0.923	3613.15	<0.001**
TZ	304	2.037	0.906	0.014	1.527	0.936	4427.33	<0.001**
CH	305	1.931	0.925	0.014	1.584	0.935	4368.99	<0.001**
IP	306	1.677	0.935	0.015	1.710	0.927	3851.05	<0.001**
WP	302	1.464	0.927	0.014	1.576	0.933	4198.86	<0.001**
CW	302	1.234	0.943	0.013	1.417	0.942	5371.34	<0.001**
PK	302	0.816	0.959	0.013	1.380	0.951	5797.00	<0.001**
HP	249	−0.334	0.994	0.014	1.097	0.953	4995.63	<0.001**
KG	251	−0.737	1.013	0.014	1.174	0.950	4727.37	<0.001**
SG	248	−0.721	1.010	0.016	1.260	0.943	4058.53	<0.001**
CS	248	−1.115	1.034	0.017	1.368	0.939	3826.49	<0.001**
AL	245	−1.805	1.068	0.019	1.494	0.927	3076.13	<0.001**

Note: See Frontispiece for explanation of region abbreviations.
n = sample size; RMSE = root mean square error; ** = highly significant, $P \leq 0.01$.

and to the smaller cross-sectional area of the northern river regions (Cooper et al. 1988) that results in a reduced residence time. Thus, high-flow and low-temperature events, which become more common in the fall, tend to rapidly drive warmer waters downstream out of the regions above Hyde Park (TI 1976). Regions downstream from Hyde Park tend to have higher temperatures than at PWW during the late summer and fall. Their larger cross-sectional areas cause a longer residence time, which makes the southern regions less influenced by short-duration high-flow events. Additionally, temperatures in lower regions are stabilized by the intrusion of marine waters and to some extent by the heat discharged by generating stations between km 68 and 107. The stabilizing influence of marine intrusion is also apparent in the relatively higher temperatures in the Yonkers region in early spring.

Regional variability was assessed from the deseasonalized data. The standard deviation of the residual yields a measure of variability without the influence of the seasonal cycle. The regional standard deviations (Figure 2.7) are consistent with the observations in the previous analysis; the more downriver regions, Yonkers through

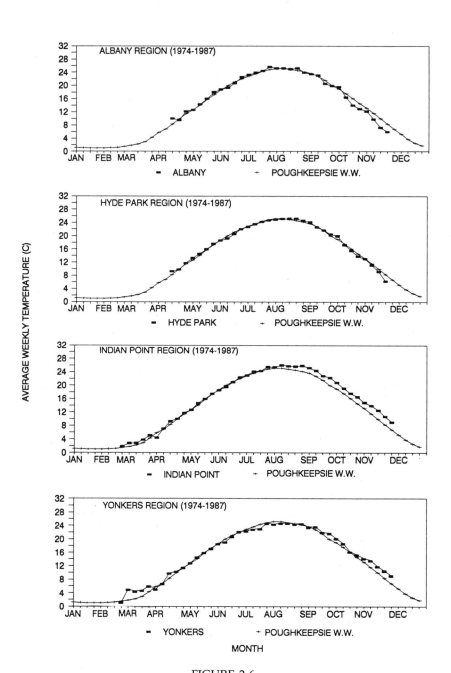

FIGURE 2.6.
Average weekly Hudson River water temperature in the Albany, Hyde Park, Indian Point, and Yonkers regions compared to Poughkeepsie Water Works temperature, 1974–1987.

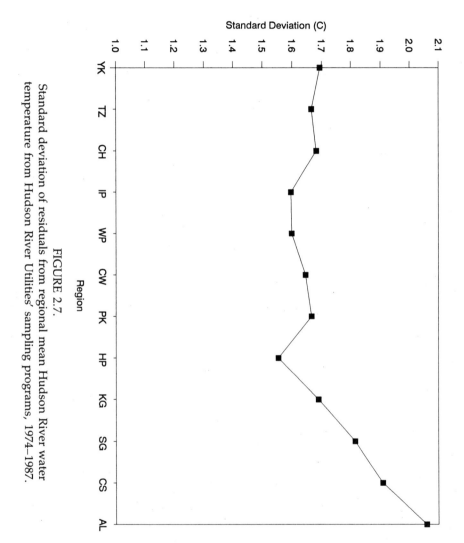

FIGURE 2.7.
Standard deviation of residuals from regional mean Hudson River water temperature from Hudson River Utilities' sampling programs, 1974–1987.

Kingston, tend to display less variability than do the upriver regions of Saugerties through Albany. The larger volume and influence of marine waters stabilizes the downriver variability.

Freshwater Discharge

Temporal patterns. Weekly average freshwater discharge is summarized in Figure 2.8. Over the period 1947–1987 the peak daily discharge rate measured at Green Island was 181,000 cfs on December 31, 1948. The minimum discharge was 882 cfs on September 2, 1968. Over the period of record the daily average discharge is approximately 13,800 cfs. The 5th, 50th, and 95th percentile daily flows are indicated in Figure 2.9. Typically, discharges peak from late April to early May, averaging approximately 30,000 cfs. Low flows, averaging approximately 6000 cfs, prevail from July through September. Flows increase in October and remain relatively constant at approximately 15,000 cfs until April.

As with the PWW water temperature data, weekly average Green Island flow data were analyzed using the ARMA model. The time-series modeling procedure indicated that the data series required deseasonalization, linear trend removal, and a first-order autoregressive component to reduce the data to white noise. The final model indicates that the discharge patterns are far less predictable than water temperature; total explained variance was 57.76% for the flow data as compared to 99.95% for the temperature data. As with water temperature, autocorrelation analysis indicated a high degree of correlation among observations separated by 52 weeks, indicating an annual cycle. The weekly coefficients describing this seasonal cycle, expressed as deviations from annual mean flow, are presented in Table 2.1.

The linear trend is described by the relationship $x_i = -377.6 + 0.354i$ where i is weeks since January 1, 1947. The positive slope suggests that flow has increased at an average rate of 18 cfs per year over the period of record.

After removal of the seasonal and linear trends, a significant amount of the remaining variation was explained by a first-order autoregressive (AR1) process:

$$x_t = 0.570 x_{t-1} + a_t$$

where

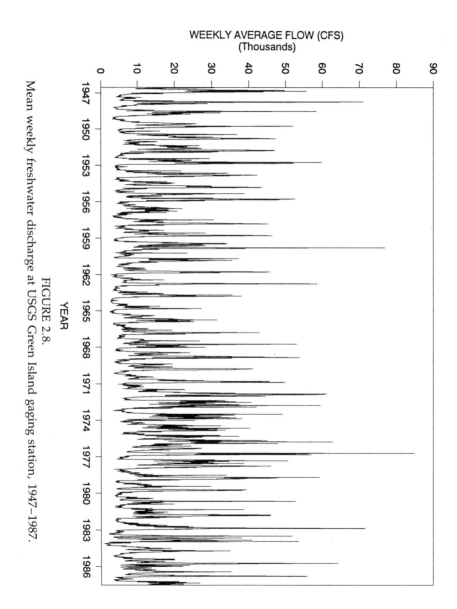

FIGURE 2.8.
Mean weekly freshwater discharge at USGS Green Island gaging station, 1947–1987.

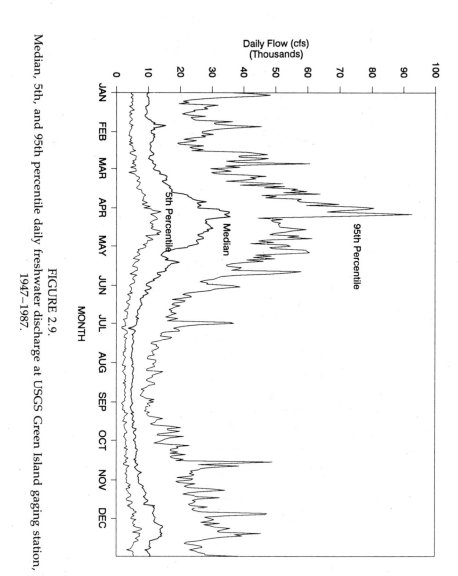

FIGURE 2.9.
Median, 5th, and 95th percentile daily freshwater discharge at USGS Green Island gaging station, 1947–1987.

x_{t-1} = detrended and deseasonalized flow at time t − 1
a_t = random shock

This AR1 model successfully reduced the remaining variation to white noise (Portmanteau Test X^2_{19} = 22.81, P > 0.05).

To determine periods of unusual discharge rates—i.e., periods of abnormally high or low flow rates—the residual flows, or deviations from weekly average flow, were computed. After smoothing with a 9-point moving average, several distinct periods of high and low flow became apparent (Figure 2.10). The most pronounced was during a period of severe drought, approximately 1960 through 1970. This was followed, from 1972 through 1980, by a period of above-average discharges. The period 1980–1987 has seen a return to drought conditions, but not of the same severity as the 1960–1970 period.

Seasonal patterns of variability were examined from the standard deviations of the weekly flow residuals. A plot of these values (Figure 2.11) indicates that the greatest variability in freshwater discharge occurs from late March through late June (weeks 12–25); the least, from mid-August through mid-October (weeks 33–42).

Salinity

Temporal patterns. Abood (1974, 1977) demonstrated a close relationship between salinity and flow in the lower Hudson River. The position of the salt front, defined as the 0.1 ppt isosal, may be estimated from the relationships:

$$L = 135 \, Q_f^{-0.38} \text{ for } Q_f \leq 27$$
$$L = 1948 \, Q_f^{-1.19} \text{ for } Q_f > 27$$

where

L = location of 0.1 ppt isosal in miles from the Battery, New York City
Q_f = freshwater flow in the lower Hudson River measured in 1000 cfs

The freshwater flow in the lower Hudson River includes the discharges from tributaries such as Kinderhook, Wallkill, Rondout, Fishkill, and Wappinger creeks as well as that from the upper Hudson River measured by the USGS gaging station at Green Island. Since most of these stations are ungaged, their contributions to total dis-

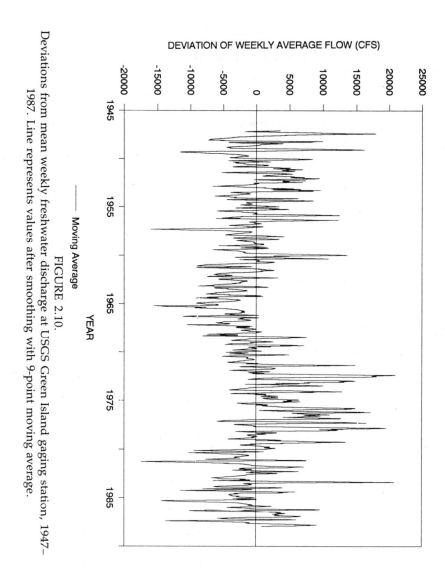

FIGURE 2.10. Deviations from mean weekly freshwater discharge at USGS Green Island gaging station, 1947–1987. Line represents values after smoothing with 9-point moving average.

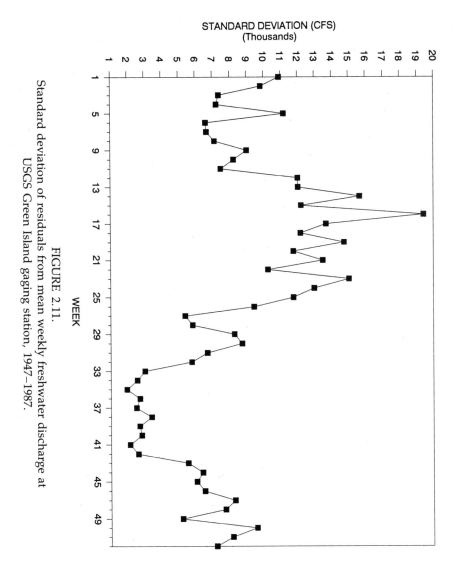

FIGURE 2.11.
Standard deviation of residuals from mean weekly freshwater discharge at USGS Green Island gaging station, 1947–1987.

charge must be estimated. Abood et al. (this volume) estimated these contributions to be:

$Q_f = 1.477\ Q_{GI}$ for January
$Q_f = 1.600\ Q_{GI}$ for February
$Q_f = 1.319\ Q_{GI}$ for March
$Q_f = 1.311\ Q_{GI}$ for April
$Q_f = 1.356\ Q_{GI}$ for May
$Q_f = 1.231\ Q_{GI}$ for June
$Q_f = 1.228\ Q_{GI}$ for July
$Q_f = 1.358\ Q_{GI}$ for August
$Q_f = 1.237\ Q_{GI}$ for September
$Q_f = 1.569\ Q_{GI}$ for October
$Q_f = 1.516\ Q_{GI}$ for November
$Q_f = 1.421\ Q_{GI}$ for December

where

Q_{GI} = Green Island flow in cfs

Abood (1977) noted that a lag period of roughly 5 to 10 days is required before changes in flow are reflected as changes in salt front position. More precisely, the lag period (t) can be described by the relationship:

$$t = (256.14/Q_f)^{0.4}$$

Applying the above relationships to the average Green Island flow during 1947–1987, the mean salt front position typically resides within the Tappan Zee to Poughkeepsie regions (Figure 2.12). During the spring high-flow period the salt front is typically near km 42; during the summer low-flow period it typically moves upriver to a position near km 105.

Spatial patterns. Empirical measures of regional and seasonal changes in salinity were determined from the Hudson River Utilities' Long River, Fall Shoals, and Beach Seine physical-chemical parameter sampling programs. During the period 1974–1987 average salinity was highest in the most downriver region, Yonkers ranging from a low of near 0 ppt to over 18 ppt. Average salinity decreased regularly in an upriver direction (Figure 2.13) until, by the Poughkeepsie region, values greater than 0 ppt were rarely recorded. Over the season, regional salinity values reflect the diminished flows of the sum-

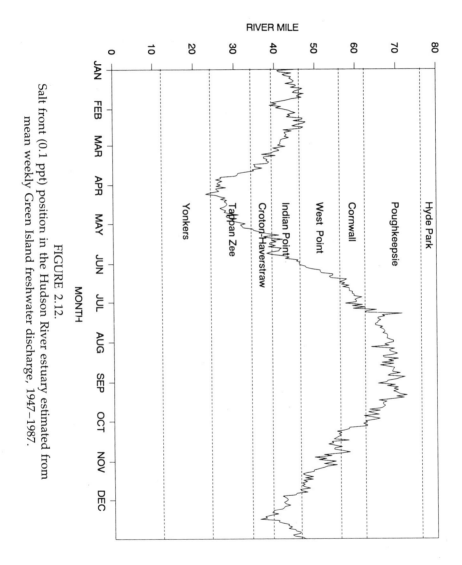

FIGURE 2.12. Salt front (0.1 ppt) position in the Hudson River estuary estimated from mean weekly Green Island freshwater discharge, 1947–1987.

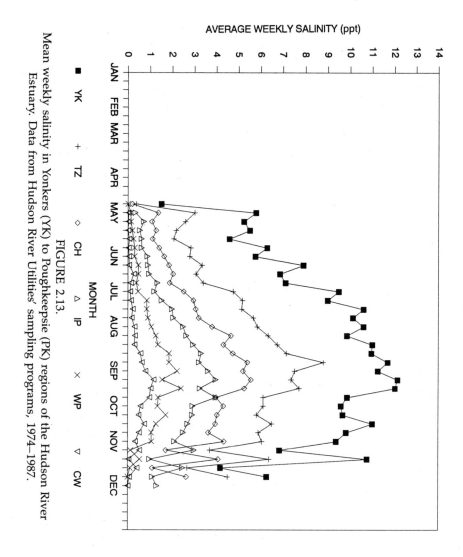

FIGURE 2.13. Mean weekly salinity in Yonkers (YK) to Poughkeepsie (PK) regions of the Hudson River Estuary. Data from Hudson River Utilities' sampling programs, 1974–1987.

mer months. In the Yonkers region salinity averaged approximately 6 ppt in May and gradually increased to approximately 12 ppt in August and September before decreasing to about 6 ppt in late November through December. The Tappan Zee region displayed a similar pattern, but at somewhat lower salinity values: spring salinity is near 3 ppt, peaks to approximately 7 ppt in the summer, then decreases to about 4 ppt in the fall. The same pattern is repeated in all the upriver regions as far as Hyde Park, but at decreasing average salinity.

The longitudinal relationship between freshwater inflow (average for preceding week) and salinity, as measured by the Hudson River Utilities' program, is displayed in Figure 2.14. At flows near 28,000 cfs, near the median spring flow, salinities in the Yonkers region averaged approximately 2 ppt and decreased to less than approximately 0.1 ppt by the Croton-Haverstraw region. At low summer flows of 4600 cfs, salinities at Yonkers averaged approximately 11 ppt and decreased to less than approximately 0.1 ppt by the Poughkeepsie region.

Variability, as measured by the standard deviations of the residual salinity (the difference between the weekly salinity and the 1974–1987 average salinity for that week), decreases in an upriver direction (Figure 2.15). In the Yonkers region, the region of greatest variability, 95% of the observations fell within 7.4 ppt of the 1974–1987 weekly average; in the Poughkeepsie region 95% of the observations fell within 0.4 ppt of this average.

DISCUSSION AND CONCLUSIONS

The patterns of variability and predictability in temperature and freshwater inflow/salinity certainly influence the distribution and success of fish spawning and use of the estuary as a nursery area. The exact nature of this influence is yet to be determined, but some general trends are apparent. We illustrate these trends using two species with very different life histories, striped bass and Atlantic tomcod.

The Hudson River striped bass life history characteristics of delayed maturity, long reproductive life, high fecundity, broadcast spawning, and rapid development of early life stages (Hoff et al. 1988b) are consistent with unpredictability of spawning success (Murphy 1968; Schaffer 1974). Spawning occurs in May and early June, generally in the middle portion of the estuary (Boreman and Klauda 1988). The trend is for temperature to increase rapidly and for fresh-

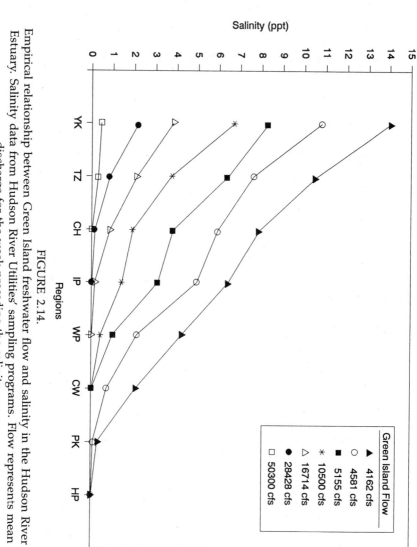

FIGURE 2.14.
Empirical relationship between Green Island freshwater flow and salinity in the Hudson River Estuary. Salinity data from Hudson River Utilities' sampling programs. Flow represents mean discharge for the week preceding the salinity survey.

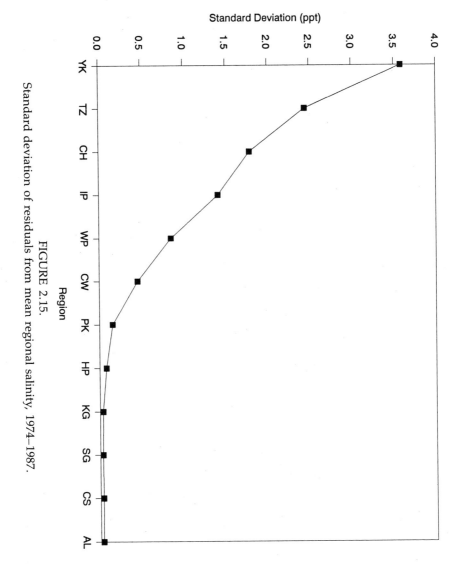

FIGURE 2.15. Standard deviation of residuals from mean regional salinity, 1974–1987.

water inflow to decrease, although both factors are relatively unpredictable at this time in comparison to other seasons. Use of a broad region of the middle of the estuary for spawning results in placement of the eggs and early larvae in a region of relatively low, but variable, salinity.

The temperature and flow environment in which the eggs and larvae will develop is not very predictable, at least from values of these factors over several prior weeks, cues that are available to the spawning adults. While the chance that conditions will be directly lethal for the early life stages appears small, flow and temperature may influence the food supply, feeding success, or growth rates, thereby reducing survival of larvae (Logan 1985).

In contrast, Atlantic tomcod spawn in midwinter (Klauda et al. 1988b; McLaren et al. 1988a) when temperature and flow are both highly predictable; temperatures will be low and freshwater flow moderate. Like striped bass, tomcod spawn in the middle estuary where salinity is consistently low during the spawning season. Although conditions for early life stages may seem harsh, their predictable nature makes it possible for a species to evolve a successful set of traits to survive them. The early maturity (at age 1), short life span, large egg and larval size, and slow development rate for early life stages (McLaren et al. 1988a) are all appropriate for a species that places offspring in predictable environments (Wilbur et al. 1974).

Variability and predictability of environmental factors are important but often overlooked considerations in understanding population dynamics of estuarine populations. Patterns in variability and predictability may give insight to the population characteristics and potential biological mechanisms controlling survival that are not likely to be found through analysis of mean environmental conditions. Other techniques for examining environmental predictability are available (Colwell 1974; Stearns 1981) and could be even more useful than those we have used. Predictability also can be used to explain patterns in species diversity (Slobodkin and Sanders 1969).

Acknowledgments

This project was developed in cooperation with the Hudson River utilities: Central Hudson Gas & Electric Corporation, Consolidated Edison Company of New York, Inc., the New York Power Authority, Niagara Mohawk Power Corporation, and Orange and Rockland Utilities, Inc. We thank Drs. K. A. Abood, T. L. Englert, and S. G. O'Connor for reviewing the manuscript.

WAYNE J. MANCRONI
MARTIN W. DALEY
WILLIAM DEY

3

Recent Trends and Patterns in Selected Water Quality Parameters in the Mid-Hudson River Estuary

ABSTRACT

Water quality variables affect the type, abundance, and spatial and temporal distribution of all forms of aquatic life. Since 1975, water quality has been routinely monitored in the Hudson River Estuary at river mile 66, just north of the Newburgh-Beacon Bridge. Five selected parameters (temperature, dissolved oxygen, conductivity, pH, and turbidity) were recorded weekly at the surface, mid-depth, and bottom at a mid-channel station over a 13-year period, 1975–1987. Throughout the study these variables have shown no significant long-term changes.

INTRODUCTION

Along with an enhanced recognition as a valuable natural resource, the Hudson River has experienced an increased demand for a myriad of uses. Recreational uses such as fishing, boating, sailing, and swimming are making a strong resurgence since environmental controls in the 1970s brought about improvements in water quality. As the population of the Hudson valley has grown, the river, once tapped for water supplies by only a few municipalities is now being considered for much greater withdrawals. Management of the Hudson, in terms of allocating its resources, and the maintenance and improvement of water quality will remain essential tasks if its full potential is to be realized.

This paper concerns recent (1975–1987) trends and patterns in water quality at one location in the middle estuary. Turbidity, pH, dissolved oxygen, conductivity, and temperature were recorded weekly from a reference station located at river mile 66. Freshwater flow at the Green Island Dam is used as an indicator of the amount of freshwater entering the estuary.

STUDY AREA

The Mohawk-Hudson watershed is one of five major drainage systems within New York state and the only one that includes a major estuary. The Mohawk-Hudson includes portions of four mountain systems: the Adirondacks, the Taconics, the Highlands, and the Catskills. For convenience, the Mohawk-Hudson watershed can be divided into three major sections: the upper Hudson drainage from Mt Marcy to Albany, the Mohawk drainage from Rome to Albany, and the lower Hudson drainage from the confluence of the upper Hudson and Mohawk drainages to Manhattan.

The estuarine, or tidally influenced, section of the Hudson River extends north from the southern tip of Manhattan Island (Battery Park—RM 0; KM 0) to the Federal Dam near Troy (Troy—RM 153; KM 246). The estuary is a relatively deep and straight channel; along the 153 miles of the estuary, there are only a limited number of wetland areas. The associated watershed extends from 19 to 56 miles (30–90 km) into the Catskill, Highland, and Taconic ranges. The most extensive tributary emptying into the estuary is the Wallkill-Rondout system, which has headwaters in northern New Jersey.

The water quality sampling station from which the long-term historical perspective has been developed is located on the north end of Newburgh Bay approximately 66 miles (106 km) upstream from the mouth of the river (Figure 3.1). This station is easily located since it is at mid-channel, directly aligned with the Roseton Generating Station oil dock catwalk, at a depth of 55 ft at low water.

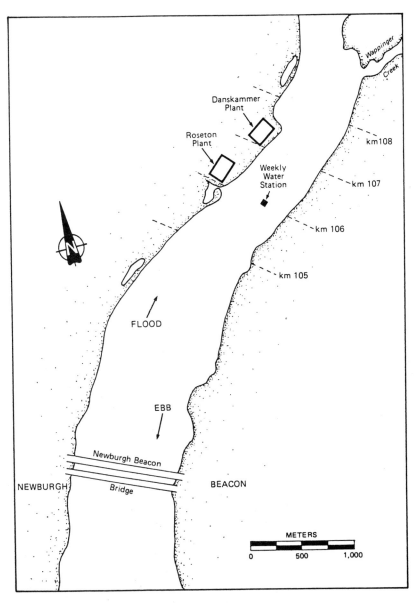

FIGURE 3.1.
Roseton and Danskammer Point Vicinity showing location of sampling station at river mile 66 (km 106).

Two aquatic ecosystems exist in the middle reaches of the lower Hudson, and water quality data from our reference site reflect the influence of both. The first ecosystem is a tidal freshwater river and the other a "typical" mid-Atlantic estuarine system. No fixed physical characteristics separate those ecosystems, and the transient boundary between freshwater and estuarine systems moves up and down stream throughout the year.

METHODS AND MATERIALS

Weather and river conditions (e.g., ice) permitting, water quality samples were collected from three depths at the reference station each week from 1975 through 1987. Temperature, flow, and conductivity were recorded for all years; dissolved oxygen, pH, and turbidity were recorded for all years except 1976, 1979, and 1980. Sampling procedures were begun at or close to low slack tide. Van Dorn or Nisken water samplers were used to obtain water samples from surface, mid-depth, and bottom. Where possible, calibrated instruments were used in situ to measure temperature, conductivity, and dissolved oxygen concentrations. The following meters or instruments were used: YSI-SCT, model 33 field thermometer for temperature, or Hydrolab 4001 for temperature and conductivity; YSI-DOA, model 57 or Martek IV for dissolved oxygen. All instruments were calibrated at appropriate intervals in accordance with the manufacturers' recommendations.

For pH, turbidity, or wet chemistry samples, samples were placed in BOD, turbidity, or polyethylene bottles, packed in ice, and taken to the laboratory for immediate analysis. Turbidity was determined by the Nephelometric method (APHA 1985) using an Ecologic Instrument Corporation Nephelometric turbidimeter model 104. Measurements of pH were recorded in the laboratory using Analytic Measurements, Inc. model 707B or a Beckman Expandometric model 3S-2 meters. When instruments were inoperative, dissolved oxygen was measured using the Winkler titration procedure. Conductivity was measured in accordance with procedures set forth in "Standard Methods of the Examination of Water and Wastewater" (American Public Health Association, 1985) and corrected to 25°C.

DATA SUMMARY

To describe the seasonal patterns for each water quality parameter and to provide a consistent temporal basis for comparison across years, the available water quality data were subjected to a 3-step summarization process. First, for each date the mean value across depths was calculated. Second, the data were apportioned into 52 weekly intervals starting with January 1. For example, week 1 would include any data entries for the time frame January 1–7; week 2, January 8–14, etc., ending with week 52 and December 31 (the last interval was normally an eight-day period). Occasionally, there would be weeks when no data were collected due to weather conditions, and other weeks when more than one sample series was taken. However, for the vast majority of the periods one sample was taken each week. If more than one sample was taken, the data were averaged. Finally the overall mean and standard deviation were calculated for each 52 weeks of the 13-year study period.

RESULTS

Freshwater Flow

Freshwater flow into the lower Hudson River demonstrates a historically consistent pattern of a "wet" spring followed by a "dry" summer/early fall period (Figure 3.2). The most variability can be found in months with the greatest freshwater flow (normally February, March, and April) and, conversely, the smallest variability is characteristic of the June through September period. The recent (1975–1987) pattern of daily mean freshwater flow (based upon annual values calculated from all monthly means and weighted by the number of days/month) is approximately 14,300 cfs and ranged from less than 9,800 cfs in 1980 to more than 21,300 cfs in 1976.

In the warmer months of the year (June–October), changes in freshwater flow can have the greatest effects upon other water quality characteristics within the estuary. During this period, freshwater flow into the estuary averaged 9,261 cfs (daily), but showed considerable variability across the 1975–1987 period, ranging from a low of approximately 5,400 cfs in 1980 to a high of approximately 17,600 cfs in 1976 (Figure 3.2). In general, the years 1975, 1976, 1977, and 1986 provided higher freshwater flow inputs, whereas 1980 and 1985 had relatively lower flows.

Water Temperature

The seasonal trend of water temperature for the mid-Hudson River Estuary displayed a typical spring warming trend, reaching a maximum river temperature in late July through mid-August (Figure 3.3).

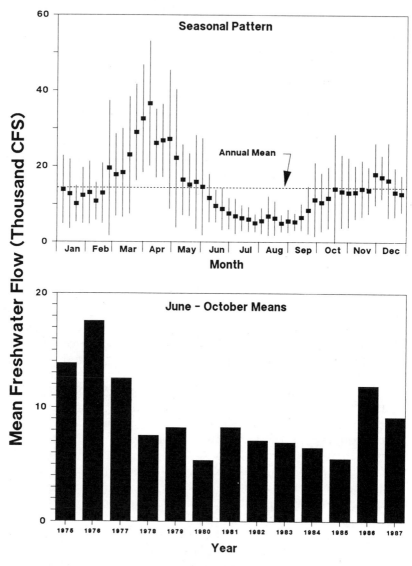

FIGURE 3.2.
Mean freshwater flow (CFS) at Green Island Dam, 1975–1987.

The highest river temperature recorded over the 1975–1987 period was approximately 28.5°C on August 1, 1975. From this summer high water temperatures decreased for the remainder of the year. The January through February seasonal temperature profile is incomplete in that river data were obtainable only when there was no river ice in

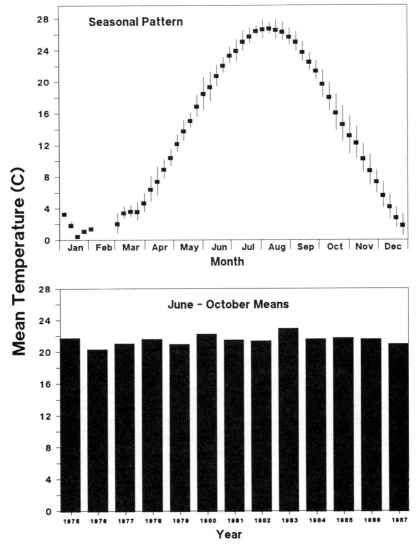

FIGURE 3.3.
Mean water temperature (°C) at river mile 66, 1975–1987.

the vicinity of the reference station. Milder conditions, when there was access to the reference station, are depicted with the fluctuating temperature profile exhibited in January and February. However, it is probably safe to surmise temperatures in the river during January and February average 1 to 2°C.

From June through October, corresponding to the lowest freshwater flow into the mid-estuary, annual mean temperature varied little over the 13 years of data (Figure 3.3). All mean temperatures were between 20 and 23°C.

The long-term temperature depth profile comparing the seasonal trends of surface and bottom temperatures reflects the consistency of water temperature across depths within the mid-estuary region (Figure 3.4). The Hudson River in the area can be characterized as a thoroughly mixed water body.

Turbidity

Temporal changes in turbidity appear to be directly related to fluctuations in the freshwater flow. This is evident from Figure 3.5, depicting turbidity concentration over the 13-year sampling period, compared with Figure 3.2. Peak turbidity values (averaging 60–80 NTUs, with peak concentrations approximately 170 NTU) occurred simultaneously with the peak freshwater flow into the mid-Hudson region (March–April). The lowest turbidity values in the region occur during the mid-summer season, which corresponds to the lowest freshwater flow. The increase in freshwater flow in the fall is reflected by the increased turbidity over a similar time frame.

pH

The pH values (Figure 3.6) exhibited a range characteristic of the majority of freshwater streams in New York state. In general, some of the highest reported values for pH have occurred in the winter/early spring period (January–March). However, mean seasonal pH values from mid-March through the end of the year have remained very consistent (mean pH values ranging from approximately 7.2 to 7.6).

Annual pH values show no evidence of any trend across the years (Figure 3.6). Despite the occurrence of precipitation, which tends to be naturally acidic (pH 4–5) in the mid-Hudson valley region (Becker and Boyle 1986), the consistency across years of pH values at the reference station suggests a strong buffering capability of Hudson River water. Across the ten years of data (no data reported for 1976, 1979, or 1980), none of the recorded values fell below pH 6, which is considered by NYSDEC as satisfactory for fish populations (Becker and Boyle 1986).

Dissolved Oxygen

Dissolved oxygen values clearly reflect an inverse relationship to water temperature. Peak dissolved oxygen concentration (approx-

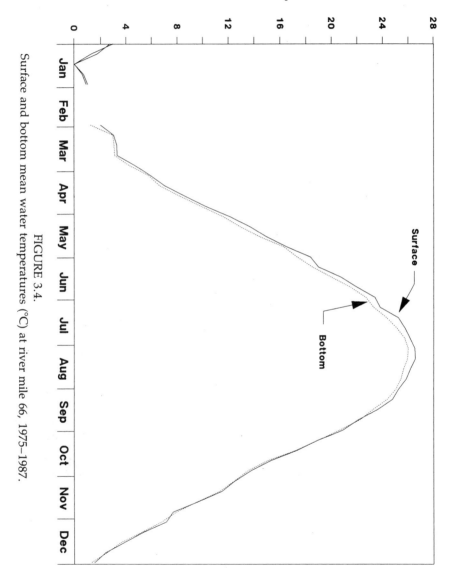

FIGURE 3.4. Surface and bottom mean water temperatures (°C) at river mile 66, 1975–1987.

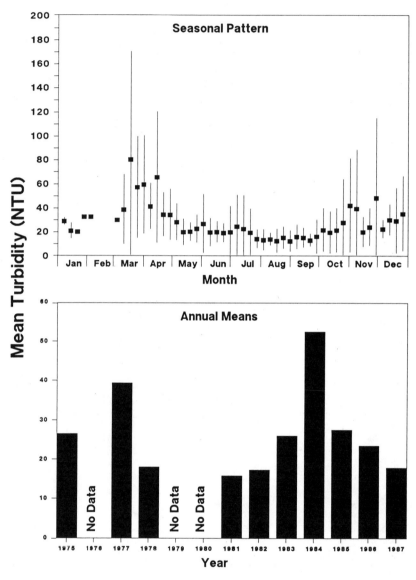

FIGURE 3.5.
Mean turbidity (NTU) at river mile 66, 1975–1987.

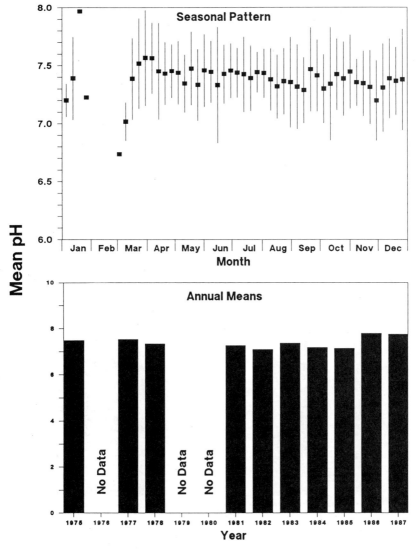

FIGURE 3.6.
Mean pH at river mile 66, 1975–1987.

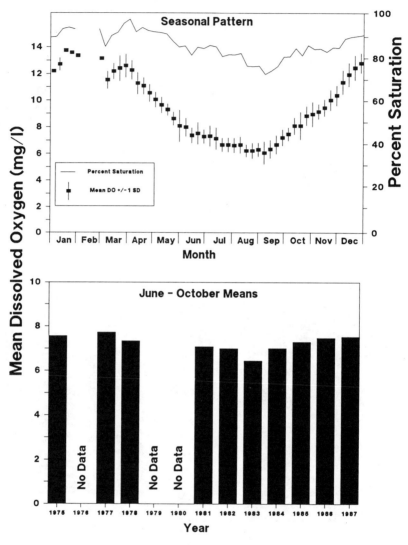

FIGURE 3.7.
Mean dissolved oxygen (Mg/L) at river mile 66, 1975–1987.

imately 14 mg/L) occurred in late January/early February (Figure 3.7). This corresponds to the lowest seasonal water temperatures (Figure 3.8).

During March, the mean dissolved oxygen concentration increased, most likely a result of an increase in primary productivity

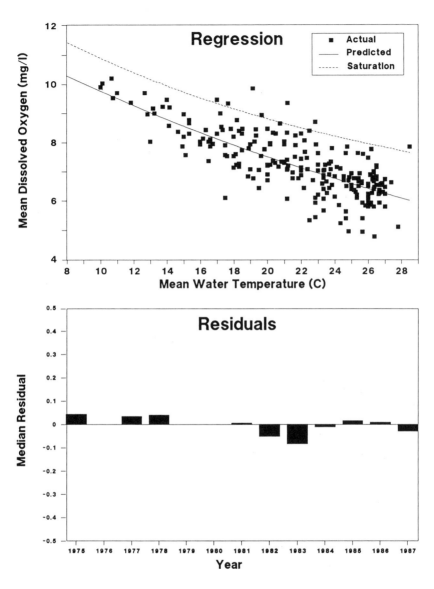

FIGURE 3.8.
Temperature versus dissolved oxygen regression analysis (top figure) and annual mean residuals (bottom figure), June–October 1975–1987.

(increased photosynthesis) within the river. Thereafter, mean dissolved oxygen concentration declined to a minimum of 6 mg/L during late summer.

Dissolved oxygen during the warmer months (June–October) averaged 6.5–7.5 mg/L with no evidence of either an increasing or decreasing trend across the historical period. Over these same months, individual mean dissolved oxygen values (surface, middle, and bottom combined) typically ranged from 60 to 90% saturation and exhibited a decreasing trend with temperature (Figure 3.8). Regression analysis produced the following linear model:

$$\text{Ln (D.O.)} = -0.026232 \times \text{Temp.} + 2.541588$$

where:

Ln (D.O.) = natural logarithm of dissolved oxygen (mg/L)
Temp. = water temperature (°C)

This model was highly significant ($P < 0.001$) and accounted for more than 56% of the variation in observed oxygen values. Median residuals about this regression line were less than 0.1 mg/L for each year and exhibited no apparent increasing or decreasing trend across years. These results document the consistency in dissolved oxygen concentrations in the mid-Hudson estuary during the study period. For a diversified warm-water biota, dissolved oxygen concentrations should remain at levels above 5 mg/L.

The 1975–1987 dissolved oxygen depth profile (surface vs. bottom) reflects similar values across depths (Figure 3.9). The data further support the temperature depth profile observations indicating thorough mixing within the mid-estuary region.

Conductivity

Seasonal patterns in mean conductivity are not evident until the end of August or early September when conductivity values above 300 micromhos indicate salt water intrusion (Figure 3.10). The intrusion of the salt front at this time is preceded by a period of lower freshwater flow into the mid-estuary region (Figure 3.2). Subsequent to the increase in conductivity recorded in late August, the mean conductivity fluctuated at or above 300 micromhos until early November and during this early fall period standard deviations of reported mean conductivities were highest. The highest conductivity values oc-

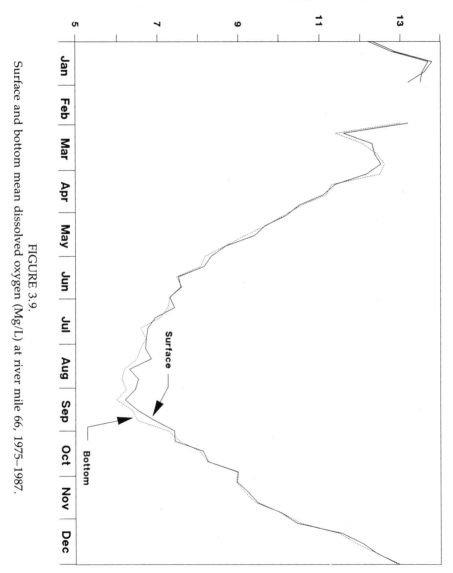

FIGURE 3.9.
Surface and bottom mean dissolved oxygen (Mg/L) at river mile 66, 1975–1987.

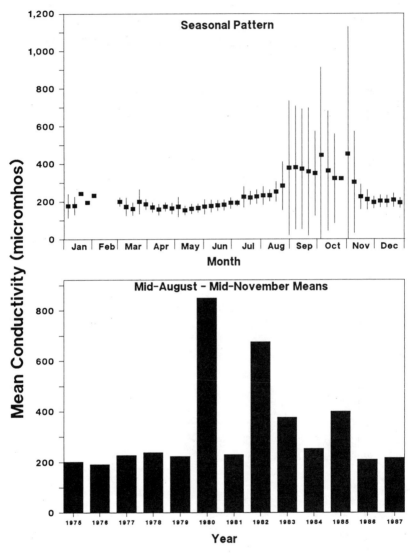

FIGURE 3.10.
Mean conductivity (micromhos) at river mile 66, 1975–1987.

curred in early November, averaging approximately 1,100 micromhos over the 1975–1987 period.

A comparison of surface to bottom conductivities over the 13-year study period reveals a higher conductivity value associated with the bottom stratum of the river (Figure 3.11). Differences in mean

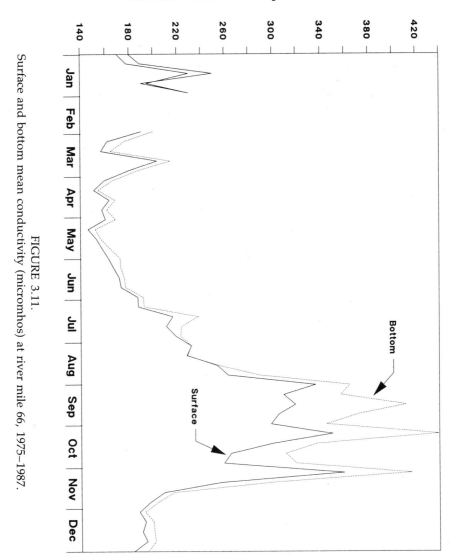

FIGURE 3.11. Surface and bottom mean conductivity (micromhos) at river mile 66, 1975–1987.

conductivity between depths were relatively small until late August/early September when bottom values became significantly higher than the surface values and remained so until early November. This corresponds to the seasonal occurrence of the salt front in the mid-estuary region and provides a further indication of the location of the leading edge of the heavier mass of intruding sea water.

Conductivity levels in the mid-August through November period from 1975 to 1987 have, for the most part, been at, or slightly above, 200 micromhos (Figure 3.10). Thus, for the majority of the 13 years, there was little or no intrusion of the salt front northward beyond the reference station. However, the four highest annual mean conductivities were reported during the six years from 1980 to 1985. Mean conductivity during the summer/fall periods of these four years ranged between 400 and 850 micromhos. Provided below are the summaries for each year from 1980 to 1985 with mean conductivity correlated with daily freshwater flow during the period from June to September. (Note the lines on Figures 3.12 through 3.14 showing mean conductivity and daily flow. The 300 micromho reference line is considered the lower bound to the initial salt water influence (TI. 1976). The average daily flow for June through October is 9,261 cfs.)

The highest sustained conductivity values for June through October were reported during *1980*. Corresponding to these high conductivity values were lower than average flow conditions (Figure 3.12). Freshwater flows averaged 4,000 cfs from July into late October. This is less than half the average flow normally reported during this period.

During June through October *1981*, the salt water intrusion had little impact on the mid-estuary region. The salt front did appear briefly in the vicinity of the reference station during September (Figure 3.12). The September through October daily freshwater flows were higher than average for this period. The result was an immediate decreasing conductivity to values approximating 200 micromhos, closer to background levels.

The interactions of the salt front and freshwater flows was observed again in *1982* (Figure 3.13). Whereas freshwater flows were higher than the long-term average in June and July, they decreased noticeably and averaged approximately 4,000 cfs for August through October. In late September, conductivity levels slowly began to rise, indicating a strong salt water intrusion, then gradually declined again in October.

In *1983* average freshwater flows decreased steadily during June and remained well below average for the period from late June

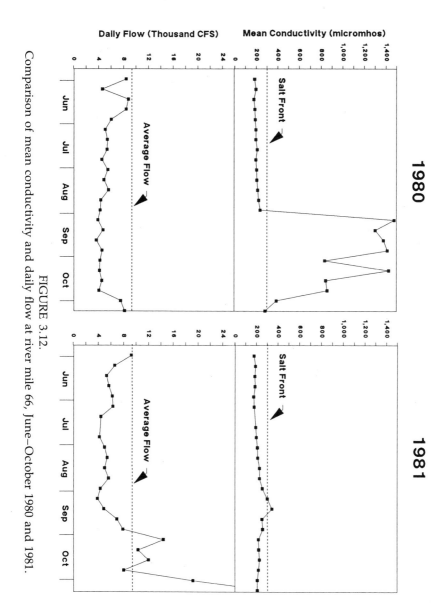

FIGURE 3.12. Comparison of mean conductivity and daily flow at river mile 66, June–October 1980 and 1981.

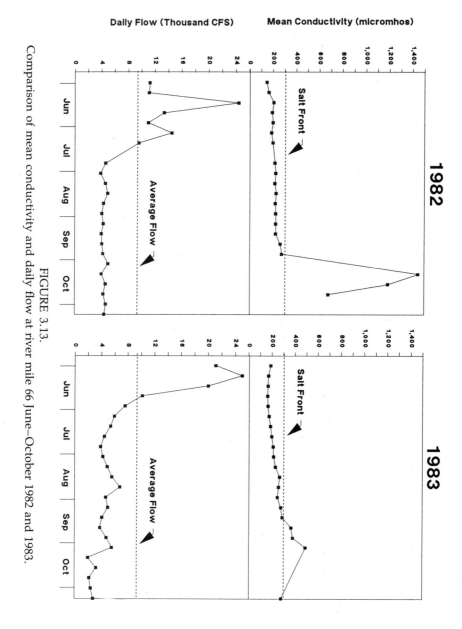

FIGURE 3.13. Comparison of mean conductivity and daily flow at river mile 66 June–October 1982 and 1983.

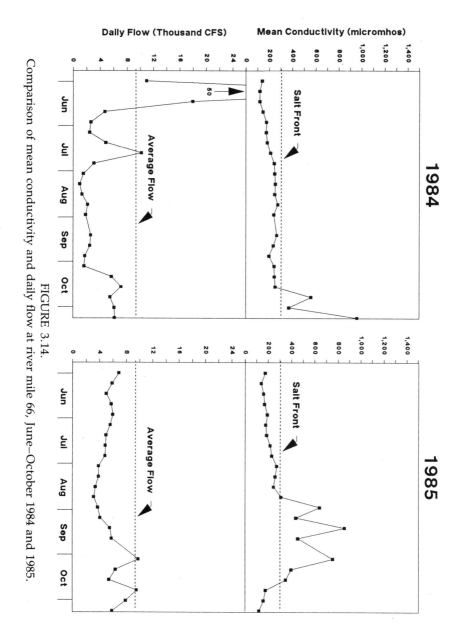

FIGURE 3.14. Comparison of mean conductivity and daily flow at river mile 66, June–October 1984 and 1985.

through October. Mean conductivity during this same time slowly increased, climbing above 300 micromhos during September. Conductivity was approximately three times lower during September and October of 1982 than in the comparable period of 1982, although the freshwater flow was similar.

Similarities between the 1983 plots of conductivity and daily flow and the 1982 data (Figure 3.13) include the occurrence of higher than average freshwater flows in the early summer period and the rapid decline of daily freshwater flows throughout the summer with the conductivities increasing to above 300 micromhos.

In *1984* a wet spring and early summer period kept the salt front below RM 66 (Figure 3.14). However, beginning in early August, daily freshwater flows were some of the lowest reported for this time, resulting in a slow but steady increase in mean conductivity levels. The influence of the salt front appeared in October as conductivity rose above 800 micromhos. Daily freshwater flow did rise above the extremely low values seen earlier in the summer, but these values never approached the average flow that historically has been reported during this period.

During *1985,* the salt front extended above the reference station beginning in late August (Figure 3.14). Freshwater flow remained, with few exceptions, below the daily average flow for this 5-month period. Increases in freshwater flows during October may have helped to decrease the conductivity of levels below the threshold of the salt front.

CONCLUSIONS

All water bodies can be drastically affected and influenced by parameters such as temperature, turbidity, pH, and dissolved oxygen. Certainly the Hudson River and its biota are affected by these water quality variables. In the Hudson these factors are in turn affected by freshwater flows from the diversified Mohawk-Hudson watershed as well as by other tributaries and interactions with the saltwater intrusion.

Freshwater flow causes a net movement of water into the estuary from its northerly confluence to the mouth of the river at Battery Park in New York City. Concomitantly, the leading edge of the heavier mass of intruding sea water (the salt front) moves northward and mixes with fresh water, which in turn lowers conductivity. These two forces constantly interact within the bounds of the estuary. At RM 66 the Hudson River is generally fresh water, except during periods of low freshwater flow (approximately 7,100 cfs) in the drier summer months, when salt water intrusion occurs (EA 1985). Ambient water temperatures vary both temporally (daily and seasonally) and spatially (length, width and depth). However, the estuary has maintained a predictable and stable temperature profile from 1975 to 1987. For dissolved oxygen and pH, the reported values are fairly consistent and well within acceptable limits for the successful growth and development of the species that frequently inhabit the mid-estuary. Seasonal changes in turbidity appear to be related to fluctuations in the freshwater input into the estuary; higher turbidity values were most prevalent during the rainy periods.

LEONARD J. HOUSTON
MARK W. LaSALLE
JOHN D. LUNZ

4

Impacts of Channel Dredging on Dissolved Oxygen and Other Physical Parameters in Haverstraw Bay

ABSTRACT

In an effort to assess the effects of channel dredging on the striped bass nursery in adjacent shallows, we monitored dissolved oxygen, turbidity, water temperature, and conductivity daily during dredging. Readings were taken at sunrise, and again during the first slack tide. Four stations around the dredge were sampled at the surface, mid-level and near-bottom depths. Weekly transects across the upper, central, and lower parts of the bay measured far-field effects and provided pre-dredging baseline data. The configuration of the dredge plume was examined under different tidal stages. Adverse dredging effects were minimal and mostly restricted to the near-bottom layer. Dissolved oxygen levels at the dredge site were within the normal variation at sites not affected by the dredging and exceeded those of the control station as often as they were lower. The maximum difference was never greater than 1.0 mg/l and usually less than 0.2 mg/l. The turbidity levels at the dredge site were consistently higher, but lower than those resulting from storm effects, and quickly returned to normal levels after dredging ceased. The plume from the clamshell dredge and barge overflow was very limited, with no effect on the adjacent shallows. The measure of readily oxidizable compounds (i.e., ferrous iron and free sulfides) provided a more reliable predictor of impacts on dissolved oxygen than measurements of total organic compounds.

INTRODUCTION

A 32-foot deep-draft federal navigation channel extends the length of the Hudson River from New York City to the port of Albany. Approximately 25 river miles from New York City the Hudson widens considerably, forming two broad expanses of water that are characterized by extensive shallows of less than 10 ft depth (mean low tide, MLW). The northernmost of these expanses, called Haverstraw Bay, was the site of proposed maintenance dredging during the late summer of 1986. Haverstraw Bay varies in width from just over two miles to nearly four miles across, and is roughly four miles in length (Figure 4.1). The bay, especially its extensive shallows, is an important nursery for several species of juvenile anadromous fish, including striped bass. Fisheries biologists from the New York State Department of Environmental Conservation (NYSDEC) were concerned that the project might adversely affect these fish by causing a decrease in dissolved oxygen (DO) levels in the shallows. Consequently NYSDEC, as part of its water quality certification under section 401 of the Clean Water Act, required the U.S. Army Corps of Engineers (the Corps) to monitor DO levels during the dredging to ensure that they did not fall below 4.0 mg/L.

Previous studies had indicated that dredge plumes are limited to the immediate vicinity of the dredge (Barnard 1978; Bohlen et al. 1979; Hayes et al. in press). Consequently the Corps believed it was unlikely for a plume generated in the channel to effect organisms in shallows. However, a number of factors contributed to making this particular proposed dredging a potential worst case with respect to effects on DO. The dredged material was relatively fine grained (72/16% silt/clay content), with a high total organic carbon content (6900–17000ug/g). Such material is likely to remain in suspension

84 Physical and Chemical Ecology

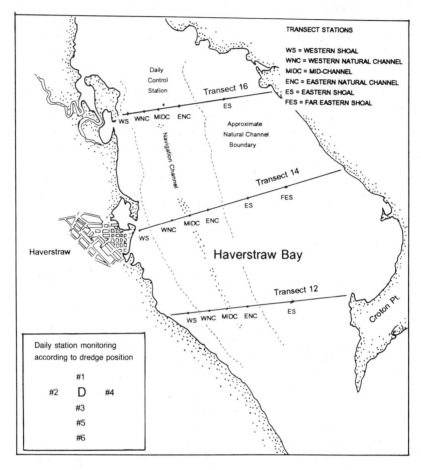

FIGURE 4.1.
Water quality monitoring stations in Haverstraw Bay
and around the dredge.

longest, and to provide a substantial source of biologically oxidizable compounds. The use of a bucket dredge, which physically digs sediment from the bottom and carries it through the water column to a waiting barge, also tends to resuspend more sediment than a hydraulic ledge (LaSalle et al. in press), which sucks sediment from the bottom through a pipeline or similar enclosure. To examine the question of DO impact, the Corps' Waterways Experiment Station (WES) developed a predictive model that used existing TOC levels in the sediment to predict worst-case DO reduction, based on biological action. WES also proposed a second model (COD) based on chemical oxidation of compounds frequently encountered in sediments. In order to evaluate these models and to look at overall Bay-wide impacts, the Corps expanded the monitoring program to cover the whole bay, not just the immediate dredging vicinity.

MATERIALS AND METHODS

Water quality was monitored along transects across the northern, middle, and southern ends of the bay (Figure 4.1). Stations were located in the navigational channel (32 ft. MLW), on both sides of the undredged part of the natural channel (21–28 ft MLW), and in both the eastern and the western shallows (10 ft or less MLW). These stations were sampled once a week at bottom, mid-depth, and surface (shallow stations had no mid-depth samples). Sampling began August 20, 1987, three weeks before the actual dredging, continued throughout the 5-week dredging operation, and concluded October 23, 1987, two weeks after dredging was finished. In situ DO was measured in mg/L with a YSI DO meter model 57. In situ temperature (°C) and conductivity (μhos/cm) were measured with a YSI salinity-conductivity-temperature meter model 33. Turbidity was measured in NTU in the lab from water samples taken with a 1-liter Wildco Kemmerer-style bottle sampler deployed at the same time the other parameters were measured. A Hatch turbidimeter model 2100A was used to analyze each water sample for turbidity within 24 hours of collection.

To assess near-field impacts from dredging, daily monitoring of the above parameters was undertaken throughout the dredging period (September 10–October 9, 1987). Station locations changed as the dredge moved, but were always located 300 ft from all four sides of the dredging plant. Two additional stations were located 600 and 1200 ft downstream of the dredge. A control station was located upstream, just above the northernmost extent of dredging. At each station the samples were taken at surface, mid-depth, and bottom. A full set of samples was collected at sunrise, and again at the first slack tide after sunrise, two periods during which natural DO levels are likely to be lowest for the day. If the first slack tide was less than one hour after sunrise, then no second set was collected that day. Crew changes, mechanical problems, and weather would often interrupt dredging, which was on a 24 hours/day, 7 days/week schedule. When one of these interruptions coincided with a sampling period, the data were still collected, but the period was designated as a non-dredging period, even though the interruption was brief and the dredge had operated throughout most of the night preceding the stoppage.

An attempt was made to determine the shape and extent of the dredge plume at two different tidal stages. Stations were located at 250 ft intervals from the working dredge for a distance of 2000 feet in each direction. The same parameters were measured, but only at the surface and bottom. Each water sample was also analyzed for suspended sediment (ss) in mg/L, according to standard methods. Because of time constraints, only the east/west stations were sampled during slack tide to see if the plume spreads out significantly during the periods of least current influence. During ebb tide only the north/south directions were sampled, to determine the effect of maximum downstream flow on the plume size and shape.

Sediment samples were collected from the transport barge to analyze Biological Oxygen Demand (BOD) and chemical oxidation of the sediment in order to test the model assumptions. Twelve samples (approximately 3 a week) were stored independently at 4°C and sent in four batches for laboratory analysis of ferrous iron and free sulfide content (the most readily oxidizable compounds). Four additional samples (approximately one a week) were similarly stored at 4°C and sent singularly for laboratory analysis of BOD. A daily sediment sample of the dredged material was collected from the transport barge, frozen, and sent in batches for laboratory analyses of TOC.

The two models developed to predict DO concentrations during dredging are described in Lunz et al. (1988). Basically, the biological demand model assumes that all organic material (measured as TOC) is volatile. Estimates of its oxygen demand are based on extrapolation from previous studies that determined the oxygen demand of sediments with various levels of volatile solids (Isaac 1965). Superimposed on this is a consideration of the residence time (based on cross sections and currents/tides in the bay) in which an individual particle of water would be exposed to the biological activity (4 days). By assuming all organics are subject to oxidation (not all are) and that they remain exposed for the full residence time (unlikely), the model should overestimate DO reduction.

The second model assumes that the bulk of the oxygen demand comes from rapid (seconds or minutes) chemical oxidation of readily oxidized compounds in the sediment (namely, the frequently encountered free sulfides and ferrous iron compounds). By using stochiometric equivalents for the oxidative reaction of these compounds, an estimate of the quantity of these compounds present in the sediment and resuspended by the dredge, and assuming complete oxidation of these compounds, this estimate of oxygen demand should also be an overestimate.

RESULTS

Figures 4.2 and 4.3 depict dissolved oxygen (DO) and turbidity levels within Haverstraw Bay before the dredging began. Turbidity is generally higher and DO slightly lower at the bottom of the water column. Figures 4.4 and 4.5 depict these same bay-wide parameters during the 5-week dredging operation and show a similar pattern. Baywide average DO levels (Table 4.1) in the shallows consistently exceed the DO levels of the deeper water habitats regardless of whether the dredge was operating within the navigation channel. The differences in DO between the shallows and deeper water hab-

TABLE 4.1.
Comparison of DO levels baywide and in the vicinity of an operating bucket dredge in Haverstraw Bay.

| | Bay-Wide Ag DO Levels* | | | DO Levels at Dredge Site | | | |
| | | | | Downstream | | Upstream | |
Date	NVC	NTC	SH	SR	SW	SR	SW
8/20	6.80	6.20	8.03	Pre Dredging			
8/27	6.50	6.60	6.87				
9/3	7.03	7.12	7.47				
9/11	6.13	6.16	6.21	6.30	6.00	6.30	5.60
9/17	6.53	6.43	6.84	6.50	6.70	6.40	6.20
9/22	5.63	5.79	6.19	5.60	—	5.60	—
9/30	6.37	6.21	6.54	7.40	—	7.30	—
10/8	7.83	7.96	8.10	7.90	—	8.20	—
10/13	7.97	7.89	8.29	Post Dredging			
10/23	8.37	8.40	8.76				

*Values based on average from 3 baywide transects
NVC = Navigation channel (32 ft MLW)
NTC = Natural river channel (23–28 ft MLW)
 SH = Shallows (under 10 ft MLW)
 SR = Sunrise sample
 SW = Slack water sample (not taken if within 1 hour of sunrise sample)

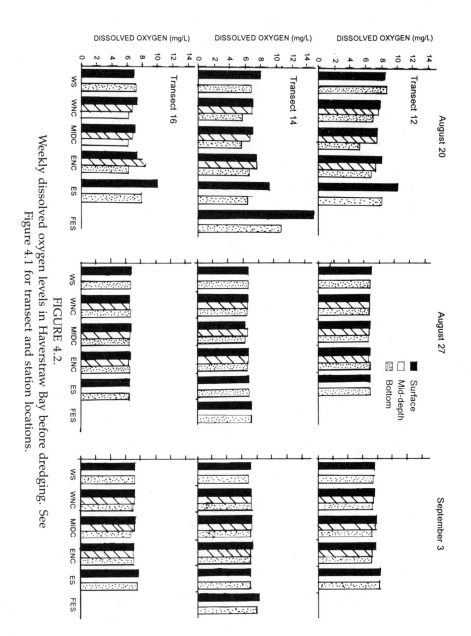

FIGURE 4.2.
Weekly dissolved oxygen levels in Haverstraw Bay before dredging. See Figure 4.1 for transect and station locations.

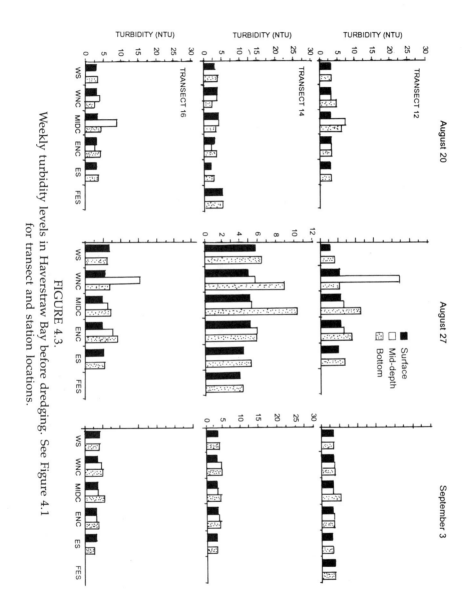

FIGURE 4.3.
Weekly turbidity levels in Haverstraw Bay before dredging. See Figure 4.1 for transect and station locations.

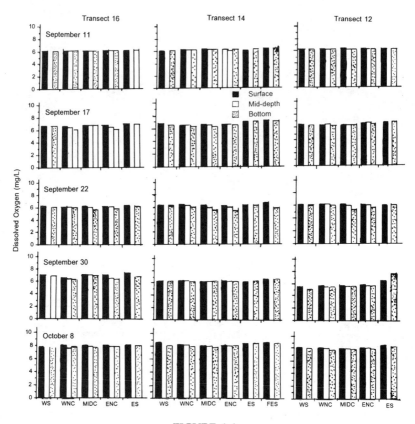

FIGURE 4.4.
Weekly dissolved oxygen levels in Haverstraw Bay during dredging. See Figure 4.1 for transect and station locations.

itats were somewhat less during the dredging period, but when the channel DO was lowest (September 22, 1987), the DO in the shallows was proportionately highest. Table 4.2 compares percent oxygen saturation calculated from the weekly transect data. The percentages tended to be highest in the shallows, and was generally lowest during the dredging, although the difference was significant at only 4 of the 16 transect stations. Table 4.3 compares turbidity levels from the weekly transects. Turbidity tended to decrease toward the channels, and was greatest during the dredging, the difference being significant at 7 of the stations.

Study of the orientation of the plume revealed the details of the near field impacts. Figure 4.6 shows levels of DO, turbidity, and

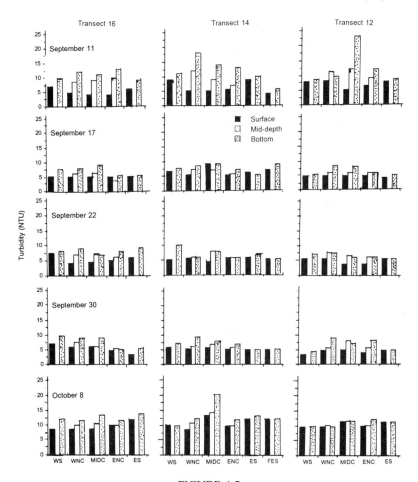

FIGURE 4.5.
Weekly turbidity levels in Haverstraw Bay during dredging. See Figure 4.1 for transect and station locations.

suspended solids (ss) within a 2000 ft radius of a dredge operating at flood tide. The greatest elevation of ss and turbidity occurred within a 500-ft radius of the dredge, with the oval shaped plume oriented upstream. A return to near ambient levels was observed between 1250 and 1500 ft of the dredge, although a second increase was found at the limit of sampling (2000).

Figure 4.7 represents data collected during the slack and ebb tides following the flood tide samples. During the ebb tide the plume has a slight downstream orientation but during the slack tide there

TABLE 4.2.
Average oxygen saturation levels for the 3 weekly transects sampled before, during, and after dredging of Haverstraw Bay (see Figure 4.1 for transect station locations).

		Mean (std dev) % Oxygen Saturation			
Transect	Station	Before	During	After	Significance*
16	WS	86.0 (4.8)	76.1 (4.1)	85.9 (0.4)	D:B&A
	WNC	80.2 (1.3)	74.1 (4.6)	83.7 (3.3)	D:A
	MIDC	77.9 (1.5)	74.2 (7.3)	85.2 (5.3)	none
	ENC	79.9 (1.3)	73.8 (5.9)	85.2 (2.6)	D:A
	ES	87.8 (9.9)	77.3 (5.7)	83.3 (6.6)	none
14	WS	82.8 (2.0)	74.8 (5.8)	82.9 (2.3)	none
	WNC	78.6 (7.8)	74.2 (4.8)	81.6 (1.1)	none
	MIDC	76.0 (6.9)	73.5 (6.7)	81.1 (0.4)	none
	ENC	82.7 (2.8)	73.3 (7.6)	81.2 (1.7)	none
	ES	82.3 (1.1)	77.7 (7.2)	86.9 (0.3)	none
	FES	104.9 (28.9)	78.4 (8.3)	86.1 (2.2)	none
12	WS	93.4 (13.6)	72.8 (10.1)	83.8 (0.8)	D:B
	WNC	84.3 (4.2)	72.1 (7.8)	80.6 (2.5)	none
	MIDC	75.9 (9.8)	73.3 (8.5)	76.8 (8.1)	none
	ENC	84.0 (1.6)	72.6 (7.3)	71.8 (16.6)	none
	ES	92.5 (9.7)	81.3 (6.1)	73.2 (14.8)	none

*Significant Kruskal-Wallis test, H(0.05, 5, 3, 2) = 5.25
Note: Based on nonparametric Tukey test where Q(0.05,3) = 2.394:
    D:B&A = Mean oxygen saturation levels during dredging are significantly different from mean levels before and after dredging.
    D:A = Mean oxygen saturation level during dredging is significantly different from mean level after dredging.
    D:B = Mean oxygen saturation level during dredging is significantly different from mean level before dredging.

was no apparent lateral spreading of the plume. The ebb tide samples showed lower ss and turbidity levels than at the flood, but generally repeated the pattern of heaviest impacts restricted to within 500 ft of the dredge, with some secondary elevation at the extreme limit of sampling. During slack tide the impacts on ss and turbidity lateral to the source appeared to have increased in magnitude although the

TABLE 4.3.
Average optical turbidity for the 3 transects sampled before, during, and after dredging of Haverstraw Bay (see Figure 4.1 for transect station locations).

		Mean (std dev) Optical Turbidity (in NTU)			
Transect	Station	Before	During	After	Significance*
16	WS	4.5 (4.5)	9.5 (9.5)	12.5 (0.7)	B:A
	WNC	4.7 (2.4)	9.8 (1.8)	15.3 (0.4)	B:A
	MIDC	5.8 (1.6)	9.9 (2.5)	14.0 (7.1)	B:A&D
	ENC	5.6 (2.9)	8.6 (8.6)	16.5 (10.7)	none
	ES	3.8 (1.5)	8.7 (3.5)	8.3 (0.4)	none
14	WS	4.5 (1.6)	9.0 (1.7)	9.9 (1.6)	B:A&D
	WNC	4.8 (3.4)	10.6 (4.7)	17.2 (12.4)	none
	MIDC	6.2 (3.6)	11.6 (5.4)	14.5 (4.9)	none
	ENC	4.2 (1.3)	8.7 (3.3)	13.1 (6.9)	B:A
	ES	3.6 (1.3)	7.8 (3.6)	10.5 (3.5)	none
	FES	4.4 (0.7)	7.2 (3.0)	8.3 (1.0)	none
12	WS	3.8 (0.5)	7.0 (2.3)	9.4 (0.9)	B:A
	WNC	4.6 (0.5)	8.6 (1.0)	18.1 (12.6)	B:A
	MIDC	7.0 (3.6)	10.9 (7.1)	19.0 (12.7)	none
	ENC	5.1 (3.0)	8.7 (3.1)	14.5 (4.9)	none
	ES	4.1 (2.2)	7.0 (2.7)	10.0 (1.4)	none

*Significant Kruskal-Wallis Test, H(0.05,5,3,2) = 5.25
Note: Based on nonparametric Tukey test where Q(0.05,3) = 2.394:
B:A = Before dredging mean turbidity significantly different than after dredging turbidity level.
B:A&D = Before dredging mean turbidity significantly different than both dredging and after dredging turbidity levels.

plume itself had not spread. During all tidal stages it was the bottom ss and turbidity that reflected the dredging activity. Surface levels remained relatively unaffected and the bottom DO showed little variation, remaining relatively consistent with the surface DO.

Based on the plume study, the 300 ft upstream and downstream bottom sampling stations were representative of the greatest dredging impacts. The weekly average monitoring results for these two

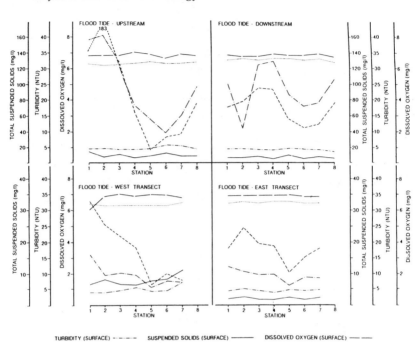

FIGURE 4.6.
Water quality around an operating dredge at flood tide.

stations are summarized in Table 4.4 together with a comparison of the values computed for the days when the samples were taken while the dredge was actually working. In nearly all cases the lowest average DO levels were recorded during slack tide both at the dredge site and at the control station. Difference between average DO levels and the control station ranged from +0.13 mg/L (dredge site higher than control) to −0.45 mg/L (dredge site lower than control). Mostly the dredge site DO levels were lower than those at the control stations, but more than 40% of the downstream values, and more than 20% of the upstream averages, equaled or exceeded the control station DO values. In addition the average DO values samples on the days when the dredge was working were equal to or greater than the average weekly DO values from all stations regardless of whether the dredge was working.

Table 4.5 depicts the daily differences between the dredge site and the control stations. The most commonly observed impacts oc-

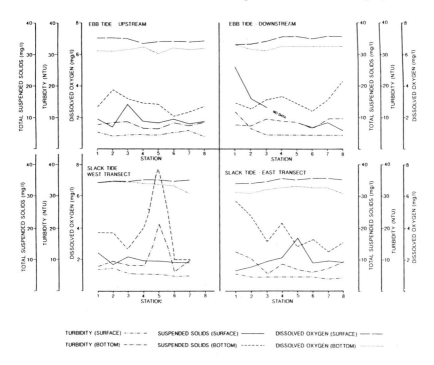

FIGURE 4.7.
Water quality around an operating dredge at slack and ebb tides.

curred at the upstream station during sunrise sampling, when the dredge site was lower than the control for 19 of 20 samples, the greatest difference being −0.4 mg/L on October 6. Nearly one-third of the sunrise samples (8 of 27) had the same or higher DO at the dredge site, though DO was never higher on those days that a dredge was actually working during the sampling period. This is in sharp contrast to upstream samples taken during slack tide, when half the samples (9 of 18) had dredge site DO values equal to or greater than those of the control sites and DO was often higher when the dredge was working. The greatest upstream difference between the dredge site and the control was measured during slack tide (−0.6 mg/L). DO at the downstream station was less frequently lower than the control, although the greatest differences of the whole study was at the downstream sunrise sample on October 6 (−0.7 mg/L).

Daily DO differences between the dredge site and the control varied from +0.5 to −0.7 mg/L, and averaged −0.09 mg/L over the

TABLE 4.4.
Average weekly sunrise (SR) and slack water (SL) bottom DO levels 300 ft upstream and downstream of a bucket dredge operation in Haverstraw Bay.

Week	Downstream Station				Upstream Station				Control Station			
	All Days		Dredging Days		All Days		Dredging Days		All Days		Dredging Days	
	SR	SL	SR	SL	SR	SL	SR	SL	SR	SL	SR	SL
1	6.53	6.40	6.80	6.60	6.60	6.13	6.60	6.20	6.65	6.40	6.60	6.50
(N)	(4)	(3)	(1)	(1)	(4)	(3)	(1)	(1)	(4)	(3)	(1)	(1)
2	6.24	6.02	—	6.40	6.13	6.05	—	6.30	6.43	6.16	—	6.40
(N)	(7)	(5)	(0)	(1)	(7)	(5)	(0)	(1)	(7)	(5)	(0)	(1)
3	6.13	6.10	6.40	6.10	6.22	6.05	6.65	6.05	6.19	6.23	6.85	6.23
(N)	(6)	(4)	(2)	(4)	(6)	(4)	(2)	(4)	(6)	(4)	(2)	(4)
4	7.31	7.33	7.40	7.43	7.37	7.35	7.41	7.43	7.37	7.20	7.50	7.37
(N)	(6)	(4)	(1)	(3)	(6)	(4)	(1)	(3)	(6)	(4)	(1)	(3)
5	8.38	8.15	8.57	8.15	8.40	8.10	8.60	8.10	8.73	8.15	9.00	8.15
(N)	(4)	(2)	(3)	(2)	(4)	(2)	(3)	(2)	(4)	(2)	(3)	(2)

N = number of daily samples

Note: If slack water was within 1 hour of sunrise, only 1 set of samples was taken that day. Dredging began on a Thursday (9/10/87) and ended on a Friday (10/9/87).

TABLE 4.5.
Daily difference in DO (mg/L) between the dredge site and control stations.

	Downstream Station		Upstream Station	
Date	SR (Dredging)*	SL (Dredging)	SR (Dredging)	SL (Dredging)
9/10	+0.3 (yes)	+0.1 (no)	0 (yes)	−0.3 (no)
9/11	−0.1 (no)	0 (no)	−0.1 (no)	−0.4 (no)
9/12	0 (no)		+0.1 (no)	
9/13	−0.6 (no)	−0.1 (no)	−0.2 (no)	−0.1 (no)
9/14	+0.1 (no)	0 (yes)	+0.2 (no)	−0.1 (yes)
9/15	−0.2 (no)		−0.2 (no)	
9/16	−0.1 (no)	−0.1 (no)	−0.1 (no)	0 (no)
9/17	0 (no)	−0.1 (no)	−0.1 (no)	−0.6 (no)
9/18	−0.2 (no)		−0.1 (no)	
9/19	−0.5 (no)	−0.6 (no)	−0.3 (no)	+0.3 (no)
9/20	−0.4 (no)	+0.1 (no)	−0.2 (no)	−0.1 (no)
9/21	0 (no)		+0.1 (no)	
9/22	−0.2 (no)		−0.2 (no)	
9/23	+0.3 (no)	+0.1 (yes)	+0.3 (no)	0 (yes)
9/24		−0.6 (yes)		−0.3 (yes)
9/25	0 (no)		−0.1 (no)	
9/26	−0.5 (yes)	0 (yes)	−0.1 (yes)	−0.6 (yes)
9/27	−0.4 (yes)	0 (yes)	−0.3 (yes)	+0.2 (yes)
9/28	−0.6 (no)	+0.1 (yes)	−0.3 (no)	+0.1 (yes)
9/29	+0.3 (no)	0 (no)	−0.1 (no)	+0.1 (no)
9/30	+0.2 (no)		+0.1 (no)	
10/1	+0.3 (no)		+0.3 (no)	
10/2	−0.1 (yes)	+0.1 (yes)	−0.1 (yes)	0 (yes)
10/3	+0.1 (no)	+0.3 (yes)	+0.1 (no)	+0.4 (yes)
10/5	−0.1 (no)	+0.5 (yes)	−0.1 (no)	+0.4 (yes)
10/6	−0.7 (yes)		−0.4 (yes)	
10/8	−0.5 (yes)		−0.2 (yes)	
10/9	−0.2 (yes)	−0.3 (yes)	−0.2 (yes)	−0.3 (yes)

*Indicates whether or not the dredge was operating during the sampling.
SR = sunrise sampling
SL = slack tide sampling

course of the dredging (−0.1 mg/L when the dredging was actually occurring). The average sunrise differences between downstream and upstream stations and the control were somewhat greater when the samples were collecting while the dredge was operating (−0.17 and −0.19 mg/L, respectively). However, this was not true during the slack tide sampling when differences among samples collected when the dredge was in operation (+0.02 and −0.02 mg/L, respectively) were less than those collected when the dredge was not working (−0.09 and −0.18 mg/L, respectively). At no time did the daily DO level ever drop below the 4.0 mg/L limit set by NYSDEC. In fact, the DO was never lower than 4.9 mg/L, and this only at one station for one tidal stage; most of the DO measurements exceeded 6.9 mg/L.

None of these differences between the dredge and control sites exceeded the natural variation among similar weekly transect stations sampled before dredging. Bottom DO levels in the navigation channel (station MIDC) sampled on the same date and tidal stage varied among those 3 transects by as much as 1.0 mg/L.

Both DO models were computed as described by Lunz et al. (1988), using actual TOC (9,000–17,000 ug/g), ferrous iron (176–483.1 mg/g) and free sulfide (1023.1–2621.6 mg/g) levels from samples taken during the monitoring. The biological model predicted maximum DO reductions of less than 0.1 mg/L, which is essentially the same as the average DO difference observed between the dredge site and the control, but does not account for the not infrequent greater DO differences (0.2–0.4 mg/L). The chemical demand model predicted oxygen reductions of 0.31, 0.63, and 1.60 mg/L, for suspended sediment concentrations of 100, 200, and 400 mg/L. The 200 mg/L level was most appropriated with respect to actual maximum measured field conditions (183 mg/L), and included the entire range of observed differences.

CONCLUSIONS AND DISCUSSION

Maximum daily DO differences between the dredge and control stations were under 1.0 mg/L, and averaged only 0.1 mg/L. Part of this can be attributed to natural variability within the bay, which was as great as 1.0 mg/L among stations in the navigation channel samples on the same day before dredging. The actual dredging impact on DO was probably less than the observed differences during dredging. Even under a worst-case scenario, as long as the baseline bay-wide DO levels are above 5.0 mg/L, there will be no danger of a dredging operation in the navigation channel depressing the DO levels to anywhere near the 4.0 minimum set by the NYSDEC. Actually, given the natural variation of DO levels, it is very likely that there would be no adverse effects even if baseline levels were below 5 mg/L. Consequently, since DO in Haverstraw Bay is nearly always at or above 5.0, channel maintenance will not have any indirect adverse impact on the shallow water nursery, nor on the juvenile striped bass and other species that inhabit it.

LaSalle et al. (in press) reviewed existing literature on dredging impacts and summarized the findings for different types of dredges. Table 4.6 is taken from their summary for bucket dredging, and the results presented are consistent with those of this study. Dredging impacts are primarily a bottom orient, near field phenomenon, with rapid reductions in ss levels away from the immediate vicinity of the dredge. Plume lengths reported by previous investigators varied from 1500 to 3250 ft but for those operations with ss levels similar to those measured in Haverstraw Bay (under 200 mg/L) the plume length was very similar to that observed here, 1250 to 1500 feet. With maximum impacts close to the dredge, the use of bottom samples at 300 ft upstream and downstream would provide an appropriate measure of the impact of the dredging. Findings from previous bucket dredge operations are also consistent with the use of these stations (LaSalle et al. in press).

Examinations of the actual measurements from the daily Haverstraw Bay monitoring program (Normandeau 1987) show only 6 occasions (out of 196 sampling events) when either of the lateral stations (2 and 4 in Figure 4.1) has a greater difference in DO than was observed between the upstream and downstream stations and the control, and even then the difference was no more that 0.1 mg/L greater. Similarly, on only three occasions was there a greater DO difference between the more distant 600 and 1200 ft stations (5 and 6 in Figure 4.1) and the control, and this difference did not exceed 0.2 mg/L.

The results of the monitoring study clearly demonstrate a very minimal impact on DO in the channel, with no adverse effect on DO in levels in the adjacent shallow water nursery areas. Bay-wide DO levels can vary so much on a given tide that it is difficult to attribute any of the observed differences between stations to the effects of dredging. The failure to demonstrate any consistent trend between the dredge site and control stations further supports the contention that the observed differences are due at least in part to natural variation. This would mean that the DO impacts listed in Table 4.6 are

TABLE 4.6.
Suspended solids levels reported from bucket dredging operations
(taken from LaSalle et al. in press).

Location	[SS] Field Characteristics
San Francisco Bay, CA	Nearfield concentrations of total suspended sediments were 21–282 mg/l. Suspended sediment concentrations in the water column 50 m downstream from the dredge were generally less than 200 mg/l and averaged 30–90 mg/l relative to background concentrations outside the plume of approximately 40 mg/l. The visible plume was about 300 m long at the surface and approximately 450 m long at a bottom depth of 10 m.
Lower Thames River Estuary, CT	Maximum suspended sediment concentrations of 68, 110, and 168 mg/l at the surface, mid-depth (3 m) and near bottom (10 m), respectively, were noted within 100 m downstream. These maximum concentrations decreased very rapidly to the background levels of 5 mg/l within 300 m at the surface and 500 m near the bottom. Suspended sediment concentrations adjacent to the dredge were 200–400 mg/l and approached background within approximately 700 m. Major perturbations were confined within 300 m of the dredge.
New Haven Harbor, CT	Suspended sediment plume (defined by transmissometer readings) was a well-defined small-scale feature extending over a distance of approximately 1000 m downstream.
Patapsco River, MD	Suspended sediment concentrations 22 m downstream from the dredging operation were 30 mg/l at near bottom depths of 10 m relative to background water column concentrations of approximately 10 mg/l or less.

(continued)

TABLE 4.6. (*Continued*)

Location	[SS] Field Characteristics
Japan	Maximum suspended sediment concentrations 7 m downstream from the dredging operation ranged 150–300 mg/l (defined using turbidity measurements) relative to background levels of less than 30 mg/l. These levels decreased by 50% at a distance of 23 m. Turbidity near the surface was generally lower than levels at mid-depth or near the bottom.
St. Johns River, FL	Sediment resuspension caused by bucket dredges showed that the plume downstream of a typical bucket operation may extend approximately 1000 ft (300 m) at the surface and 1500 ft (450 m) near the bottom. The average suspended sediment concentrations of all samples collected within 800 ft (240 m) of the dredge along upper water column and near bottom transects were approximately 106 and 134 mg/l, respectively. A comparison of suspended sediment concentrations from open and enclosed bucket dredge operations showed considerable reductions in suspended sediment concentrations in the upper water column (>50%) but increases in concentrations in the lower water column (>50%) due to "shock" waves created by the closed bucket.
Thames River Estuary, CT	The composition of material suspended by the dredge indicates that variations are similar to those produced by local storm events. Storm events affect a significantly larger area and display a higher frequency of occurrence than that characterizing typical dredging schedules. Both storm events and dredges increase particulate organic carbon concentrations and bias the material composition in favor of the inorganic components.

probably overestimates. Only one previous study looked at DO levels around a bucket dredge. Two sets of samples collected in the Arthur Kill (NY Harbor) showed DO levels 16 to 83% lower than minimum DO levels taken when no dredging was taking place (Brown and Clark 1968). In contrast, the Haverstraw Bay study never detected a reduction of more than 10% between the dredge site and the control station, and often found higher DO levels during dredging. This inconsistency between the findings of the two studies may be due in large part to differences in the sediments and residence time between the two operations. Sediments in the Arthur Kill were described as "black, soft, oily silt," with an "appreciable" oxygen demand (10 mg/L) and a prolonged residence time of 7 days. The Haverstraw Bay sediments had not been exposed to extensive industrial pollution, and had much lower BOD (1.22 mg/L), with residents about half as long. An additional difference may reflect the length of sampling effort: the Arthur Kill results are based on only 2 days worth of dredging data, as opposed to the 30-day Haverstraw effort.

Baywide oxygen saturation levels were lowest during the first 4 weeks of dredging, increasing to predredging levels during the last week of dredging and the 2-week postdredging period. Only 4 stations along 2 of the transects showed statistically significant lower percent of oxygen saturation during dredging (Table 4.2). Three of these stations were in the western, narrower part of the bay.

Within the channel there was no significant difference among the pre-, during-, and post-dredging periods. The reasons for such impacts are unclear, especially in view of the small DO impacts around the dredge, where maximum suspended sediment occurs. It is possible that the samples around the dredge are measuring rapid chemical oxidation of suspended sulfides and ferrous compounds, as in the COD model. The possible bay-wide impacts may be the result of longer biological oxidation acting on fine-grained particles that remain in suspension until they reach outside the channel, exemplified in the BOD model. The data are insufficient to answer this specific question, but the lowering of oxygen levels in the shallow clearly posed no threat to juvenile fishes.

In order to simulate channel conditions as much as possible, the control station had to be close to the navigation channel and still within Haverstraw Bay. In view of the upstream extent of the plume during flood tide (Figure 4.4) and the potential bay-wide impacts on oxygen saturation levels (Table 4.2), there might be some concern that the selected control station was actually under the influence of the dredge. This is probably not the case, because little dredging took place in the extreme northern limits of the channel, and the extent of the plume itself was generally less than 500 ft, well short of the control station. The dredge continued to move throughout the course of this study and yet the differences between the upstream and control stations remained fairly consistent. If the control station was influenced by it, it would have been during flood tide when the upstream arm of the plume was longest and differences would have been lowest at that time. Instead the average DO differences between the upstream and control stations were virtually identical with those measured during other tidal stages (−0.91 mg/L and −0.94 mg/L, respectively).

The fact that there seems to be a somewhat greater DO impact while the dredge was working, at least in the sunrise samples (Table 4.3), seems to lend support to the rapid (chemical) oxidation model, since it suggests a lessened effect after only a few hours interruption of the dredging. This might also cast some doubt on the validity of samples taken when the dredge was not working. Could the effects be greater than indicated by averages that include samples taken when the dredge was not operating? This is unlikely as the average daily DO differences between the dredge site and the control was −0.1 mg/L for the samples taken when the dredge was working and −0.084 for the days when the dredge was inoperative. It there is a difference, it is very slight. Even if only the data for the days when the dredge was working are considered, it would not significantly change the range or magnitude of the results, nor alter the conclusion that in neither the channel nor the shallows were DO levels affected.

The attempt to predict DO impacts by looking at the role of biological and chemical oxidation was inconclusive. Based on the observed DO levels, the COD model was less likely to underestimate the DO reduction. The difference between the models is primarily a matter of oxidation rates. The biological model assumes oxidation of the volatile component of the organic part of the sediments over a course of days. The chemical model assumes that the iron and sulfide compounds react in a matter of seconds or minutes, thereby producing an immediate oxygen demand. The latter seems to reflect more accurately the short time the solids remain in suspension and are subject to oxidation. This is supported by the rapid fall of ss levels within the plume (Figure 4.6 and 4.7). The chemical demand model predicted a DO reduction of 0.63 mg/L for ss level of 200 mg/L, which is close to the actual field conditions (183 mg/L). The predicted value is greater than the average observed reduction of 0.1 mg/L, but this may be the result of the fact that the model did not take into account mixing and partial oxidation. Though the COD model appears more reliable for predicting the full range of impacts, the potential bay-wide impacts on oxygen saturation warrant further consideration of longer term BOD impacts as well. Perhaps a combined model might be more appropriate, but at present the natural variation appears to account for the observed differences among stations.

In many ways this operation was a worst-case example for the Hudson River Federal Channel. The mechanical dredge that was used is the most disruptive of bottom sediments (LaSalle in press) and therefore is likely to produce the most extensive plume and the highest ss levels. The section of channel through Haverstraw Bay also has some of the greatest concentrations of fine grained sediments and the least current influence in the entire Hudson channel. Upstream areas tend to have coarser grained sediments (USACE-NYD 1985, 1988) and more pronounced river flow. Consequently dredging in these areas would suspend less material and it would settle out faster. Further, with stronger currents to offset the influence of flood tides (Figure 4.2), the plume should have less lateral spread. Finally, upstream dredging has historically used upland disposal, and hydraulic dredging is the standard method of operation. Together, a similar maintenance effort in the upriver reaches would have less adverse effect on the shallow water and wetland habitat outside the navigation channel.

KARIM A. ABOOD
E. A. MAIKISH
T. B. VANDERBEEK
M. U. McGOWAN

5

Evaluation of Induced Sedimentation in New York Harbor

ABSTRACT

Obstructions to flow, such as piles supporting platforms, can induce sedimentation in areas protected from prevailing river currents. The cause for this is primarily the flow resistance provided by these structures, which creates quiescent conditions that cause riverborne sediments to be deposited. Many factors influence induced-sedimentation rates: waterbody characteristics (hydrodynamics and water quality), site-specific conditions (circulation patterns, sediment sources, flow-impeding structures, adjacent structures), and platform design details (size, shape, and number of piles; spacing and distribution of piles and other flow-restricting structures). The magnitude of and interactions among these factors determine the extent of project-induced sedimentation.

The range of deposition rates observed in New York harbor is wide, from negligible (harbor areas at equilibrium) to moderate (2 to

12 in./year in Westway interpier basins) to substantial (more than 3 ft/year in the passenger ship terminal). These and other Hudson River and East River data (amassed from information on the River Walk and Waterside projects) are used to describe harbor nearshore sedimentation patterns. An empirical approach for evaluating project-induced sedimentation is presented along with examples of mitigating measures that can be incorporated into the design of pile-supported projects to minimize deposition.

NEW YORK HARBOR SEDIMENTATION

An overview of estuarine sedimentation processes is given below, followed by a brief description of lower Hudson nearshore sedimentation findings, the main topic of this paper. Because of its complexity, only a brief summary of sedimentation is given here. Further details and a more complete description of sedimentation in New York harbor, emphasizing the Hudson River reach between the Battery and the George Washington Bridge, and areas sheltered from prevailing river currents, have been reported by a number of investigators. Key references include Panuzio 1965; LMS 1972, 1983, 1988; Gross 1974, 1976; Abood, 1977; and Abood and Vanderbeek 1985; MPI 1983; PBQD 1984.

A major source of sediments in New York harbor is the watershed of the Hudson River and its tributaries, particularly from erosion of land in the drainage basin. The Hudson River sediment load is estimated at approximately 800,000 tons per year, or about 60 tons per square mile per year or about 0.5 pound per acre per year (about 67% of the total Hudson River/Upper Bay/Newark Bay waterborne solids) (Gross 1976). Another major source is the solids discharged via sanitary and storm sewers (about 270,000 tons/year). Secondary sources include direct solid waste disposal, dredging materials, industrial wastes, shore sediments, and bank erosion. Sewers and CSO outfalls terminating at or near the bulkhead line and direct solid waste dumping represent major sources of nearshore sedimentation.

In general, the sediments supplied by the watershed, which consist mainly of fine-grained lightweight particles, remain in suspension in freshwater reaches of the river. Very weak currents in such reaches are capable of transporting these sediments. Freshwater reaches experience a unidirectional net flow in the seaward direction throughout the water column. Therefore, only a small portion of suspended sediments settles in these reaches. As the sediments approach the location of the ocean-derived salt intrusion front, the transition from a one-layer to a two-layer system (a seaward-moving upper layer and a landward-moving lower layer) begins to substantially influence sedimentation patterns. This transition results in a very weak net velocity near the bottom, characterized by a change in direction from downstream to upstream. This location has been termed "null" point. Heavy shoaling usually occurs in the vicinity of the null point or near the ends of the salt-intruded reach, with heavier particles depositing just upstream from the salinity intrusion front and the lighter particles just downstream.

The presence of ocean-derived salt in the salt-intruded reach enhances a flocculation process among the remaining suspended sediments. This process continues as the sediments move downstream, mainly in the seaward-moving upper layer. After flocculation the sediments from aggregates that settle to the landward-moving lower layer. The rate of settling is controlled primarily by salinity and other environmental factors such as temperature, pH, physicochemical properties, concentration of sediments, river geometry, flow/circulation patterns, and turbulence.

In general, low pH, high temperature, low organic matter, and high suspended sediment concentrations enhance settling rates. Resuspended sediments settle faster than sediments that have never settled, probably because resuspended sediments already have flocs. Turbulence may increase the probability of particle contacts, but intense turbulence may disrupt the floc. In addition, turbulence plays an important role in transporting sediments from the seaward-moving upper layer to the landward-moving lower layer.

Hudson River sediments in the landward-moving lower layer are deposited in places where the bottom net velocities are too low to carry them in suspension. Therefore, the existence of density-induced lower-layer flows (net upstream velocity) prevents movement to sea of river sediments and causes the bottom to be shoaled and unstable. The magnitude of Hudson River density-induced circulating currents, salinity, and other factors (such as excessive cross-sectional area, eddies and crosscurrents, and sudden changes in river geometry) seems to move the region of heaviest shoaling to the mouth of the estuary.

More specifically, the shoaling material in the Hudson River is moved upstream along the navigation channels from the Battery to about 59th Street. North of 59th Street the New York side of the river has a deeper natural channel. The shoaling material continues its upstream movement, but stays mainly on the New York side until it reaches the vicinity of the George Washington Bridge, where the river cross-sectional area decreases rapidly.[1] Owing to the abrupt change in cross-sectional area, the predominantly upstream bottom current is partially interrupted, thereby causing turbulence in this area. The sediments carried in the bottom layer then reenter the upper layer because of the turbulence. Some portions of the material are then carried back toward the Battery by the net current moving downstream. The remainder of the sediments are carried upstream of the George Washington Bridge by the net landward-moving lower-layer flow and move along the main channel until they are deposited in the shallow areas in Haverstraw Bay where the current velocity is low.

Shoaling in the interpier basins and sheltered areas between the bulkhead line and the pierhead line below the George Washington Bridge is affected by the filling and emptying of the basins during each tidal cycle. When flooding, the river water enters the basins principally from the bottom of the main channel where the concentration of suspended material is greater. Conversely, water moving out from the basins during ebb tide empties over the entire water column, causing reduced ebb velocities (not sufficient to carry the sediments back to the main channel) and limiting scouring to the area near the pierhead line. The result is a net flow of sediment into these areas.

Piles, caissons, and other flow obstructions induce sedimentation in protected areas, primarily because of wake formation behind these structures—that is, reduction of ambient velocities,[2] resulting in the creation of quiescent conditions that cause riverborne sediments to be deposited. In addition, turbulence may increase the probability of particle contact, but intense turbulence may disrupt flocculation.

An example illustrating the influence of the presence of multiple circular pilings on flow velocity taken from Abood and Vanderbeek (1985) is given in Figures 5.1 and 5.2. Figure 5.1 is a time-averaged picture of the turbulent flow in the wake of a circular cylinder. Figure 5.2 presents the centerline velocity for a special case, approaching

---

[1]Between 1940 and 1945 some 13 million cubic yards of waste solids (40% believed to be rocks) were dumped under the bridge, substantially altering the channel cross section and river current and salinity patterns. The required amount of annual dredging of the lower Hudson since 1945 is nearly double the pre-1945 rate (Gross 1974).

[2]For example, the prevailing current in the main channel of the Hudson River near the Battery reaches approximately 2 to 3 knots; the north/south current in the interpier basins is typically 0.1 to 0.4 knots; the east/west current is about 0.05 to 0.1 knot.

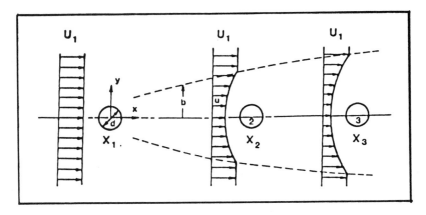

FIGURE 5.1.
Time average wake velocity (circular cylinder).

velocity = 1 fps, pile diameter = 1 ft, drag coefficient = 1, and a piling spacing of 30 ft. Several observations can be made from these results. First, the lowest velocity always occurs directly behind a piling, making it a likely place for sediment deposition. Second, as a result of the assumed reentrainment of undisturbed ambient flow, the velocities

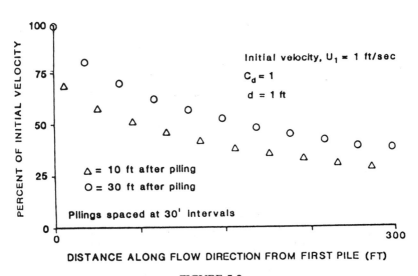

FIGURE 5.2.
Centerline velocity profile, wakes.

always attempt to return to their original level. Third, given an infinite series of pilings, the centerline velocity approaches zero unless the spacing between pilings is enough to allow the centerline velocity to recover fully.

Sedimentation rates decrease as basins become shallower until an equilibrium is reached between settling and scouring. Typical equilibrium depths range from −6 to −12 ft.[3] As basin or sheltered area depth is reduced by sedimentation, velocity increases and prevents further deposition. After the basin bottom reaches equilibrium, tidal and wave action erodes sediment accumulation above that elevation.

Equations relating deposition rates and scouring velocity to sediment characteristics similar to the ones described below have been reported. These are useful for obtaining gross estimates, but should be used with caution since they do not take into account prevailing river conditions.

The rate of deposition (S) of fine suspended sediment is related to suspended sediment concentration (c) as follows:

$$S = v\ c\ p/w \qquad (1)$$

where

v = settling velocity
p = deposition probability
w = unit weight of dry sediments

New York harbor v values ranging from 8 to 230 ft/day have been reported,[4] while w and c values range from about 20 to 50 lb/ft^3 and from 3 to 267 ppm, respectively, in the lower reaches of the Hudson River. Using an average c value of 30 ppm and assuming 100% deposition probability, these c and w ranges yield a wide sedimentation range from a minimum of 1.3 to a maximum of 94 in./year.

---

[3] These are basin averages; actual depths range from a minimum near the bulkhead line to a maximum near the pierhead line. Within the Westway interpier basins, for example, the predominant ultimate bottom slope between the two is about 1:100 (PBQD 1984).
[4] For clay particles, Johnson et al. (1986) reported v values ranging from 147 ft/day (for c < 25 ppm) to 4060 ft/day (for c > 300 ppm).

On the other hand, scouring velocity (v_s) may be approximated using the following formulation (Fair and Geyer 1961);

$$v_s = \sqrt{8k/f\ g\ (sg-1)d} \qquad (2)$$

where

k = -0.04 for ungranular sand and 0.06 or more for nonuniform (interlocking) sticky materials
f = Darcy-Weisback friction factor ($115.52\ n^2/R_h^{1/6}$ where n is Manning's coefficient and R_h is hydraulic radius)
sg = specific gravity
d = particle size, mm

Using a New York harbor average sg of 2.67, f of 0.03, k of 0.05, and d of 0.008 to 0.066 mm yields a wide range of v_s from a minimum of 0.17 to a maximum of 0.48 fps.

From the above analysis it is clear that the major factors influencing sediment transport are:

- *Hydrodynamic characteristics*, e.g., current velocity, water depth, basin geometry, flow, density-induced circulation, turbulence, mixing intensity
- *Sediment characteristics*, e.g., size, density, organic content, type
- *Water quality*, e.g., salinity, suspended solids, temperature, pH

Obviously, activities influencing these factors can affect sedimentation patterns. In addition, nature imposes its own perturbations. Extreme events, such as hurricanes, floods, droughts, and adverse meteorological conditions, can cause substantial disruptions in estuaries and variations in their parameters. If these factors were changed by either natural or artificial means, the sedimentation processes would also be affected accordingly.

Methods for Evaluating Sedimentation Rates

Mathematical models, physical models, dredging records, field measurements, and bathymetric data have been used to estimate sedimentation rates. The first four methods are outside the scope of this paper. Results obtained using, in particular, the third and fourth methods are given below. It should be noted that because both waterbody and site-specific factors influence sedimentation rates and the interactions among these factors are very complex, sedimentation modeling is an extremely difficult task.

The fifth method, the primary subject of this paper, consists of using a series of historical bathymetric data sets taken at the same location over a period of several years. A brief description of this approach is given below. Details are provided in Appendix A.

Figure 5.3 serves to define the fundamental parameters. Figure 5.3(1) depicts a typical interpier basin plan view. New York harbor depth data suggest the approximate relationships depicted in Figures 5.3(2) and 5.3(3). Figure 5.3(2) shows a typical water equilibrium depth profile extending from the bulkhead line, where the depth is zero, to D_b a short distance away, to the river channel depth (D_c) channelward of the pierhead line. The average basin equilibrium depth is D_e. (Basin depth, as used here, means weighted average [water volume/basin area] river bottom elevation referenced to the Borough President of Manhattan Datum [BPMD], which is equivalent to mean high water and is 2.75 ft above the national geodetic vertical datum of 1929.)

Figure 5.3(3) depicts the decrease in average basin depth from D_o at time = 0, through D_1, t_1 years later, to D_e ultimately (t = ∞). Hudson River bathymetric data (PBQD 1984) indicate an exponential rate of decrease in average depth with time.[5] For practical applications an effective equilibrium depth ($D_3 + rd_e$) may be used ($r = d_e/D_e$ typically around 0.1 or 0.2).

Available Hudson River data (PBQD 1984) yield the following representative values:

$S_1 \simeq$ 1:100 (range from 1:1000 to 1:100, with most points 1:100, 200, or 300)
$S_2 \simeq$ 1:5 (range from 1:4 to 1:8, with most points 1:4, 5, or 6)
nL $\simeq$ 50 ft (or, using a basin length, L, of 500 ft, n $\simeq$ 0.1)
D $\simeq$ 10 ft (BPMD)
$D_b \simeq$ 6 ft (BPMD)

D_b may be viewed as representing tidal and wave action, or:

$$D_b = TR + W \qquad (3)$$

---

[5]For example, the interpier basin between piers 56 and 57 decreased in mean depth from 28.86 ft in 1967, to 25.00 ft in 1972, to 17.76 ft in 1980, with an estimated D_e of 10 ft. These and similar data presented in PBQD (1984) suggest an exponential decay function.

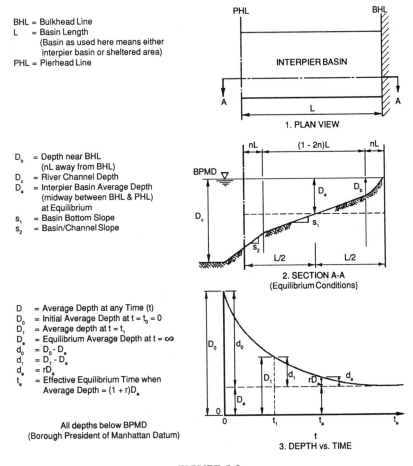

FIGURE 5.3.
New York harbor sedimentation definition sketches.

where

TR = tidal range (4 to 5 ft in New York harbor)
W = wave action (a foot seems reasonable)

Based on the above, the following ultimate depth relationship may be developed:

$$D_e = TR + W + (0.5 - n) LS_1 \tag{4}$$

Using representative values (TR = 5 ft, W = 1 ft, n = 0.1, and S_1 = 1:100) yields D_e = 8 ft (500 ft basin) and D_e = 10 ft (1000 ft basin)—that is, within observed values.

It should be noted that this equation only approximates basin sedimentation processes and should be used accordingly. It does, however, provide a convenient method of relating average equilibrium depths to basin profiles using local characteristics.

Sedimentation rates may be equated to the rate of change in average depth (D) with time (t). As shown in Appendix A, the exponential depth-time function depicted in Figure 5.3 yields the following rate of sedimentation (S) equation:

$$S = - k(D - D_e) \qquad (5)$$

The parameter k(D − t slope) may be obtained from two depth observations (D_o and D_1) taken t_1 years apart—that is:

$$k = \frac{1}{t_1} \ln (D_o - D_e)/(D_1 - D_e) \qquad (6)$$

where

$$D_e = \text{equilibrium depth}$$

Equation 5 yields point values: S_o for the year corresponding to the initial depth D_o, S_1 for the year corresponding to the depth observed t_1 years later, and so on. An average sedimentation rate (S) representative of the period between the two observations may be obtained by averaging S_o and S_1.[6] Of course, S_o is higher than $\bar{S}$ and S_1 is lower than $\bar{S}$, consistent with the observations presented above, as basin or sheltered area depth is reduced by sedimentation, velocity increases and acts against further deposition.

The ability of this method to yield results relatively quickly makes it attractive from a practical standpoint since it provides quick estimates of the relative influence of basin geometry. These estimates are particularly useful for comparing different waterbody segments of varying depths. It should be noted, however, that these relationships

---

[6]An approximate sedimentation rate indicative of average conditions during the period between two surveys may also be obtained assuming a linear rate of depth change, i.e., $\bar{S} = (D_o - D_1)/t_1$.

Induced Sedimentation   115

simplify sedimentation processes substantially and lump the details of circulation and sedimentation into empirical coefficients, for example k' and D_e, that are difficult to quantify.

New York Harbor Observations—Nearshore Sedimentation

A number of empirical approaches have been used to estimate New York harbor nearshore sedimentation rates, including:

- Annual dredging records
- Field observations using, e.g., staff gauges
- Bathymetric observations

Case study results obtained using these approaches are briefly described in this section. Major study locations are listed in Figure 5.4. Representative New York harbor sedimentation rates are given in Table 5.1.

Dredging Records

Panuzio (1965) used the annual quantities of material dredged from the Hudson River between 1948 and 1964 to estimate annual shoaling at piers in the Hudson River. Table 5.2 lists the annual shoaling estimates provided by the U.S. Army Corps of Engineers in 1965. It is clear from this table that the New Jersey side of the Hudson River accumulates substantially more sediments than the New York side, with the main contributor to this imbalance being the Weehawken-Edgewater segment. (Of course, the distribution of sediments may have shifted since 1964 since some piers are no longer in use or have been demolished.)

In terms of annual sedimentation rates, the values in Table 5.3 (based on information for slips 84 to 92 provided in Panuzio [1965]) may be obtained. Information provided by the Port Authority (J. Monaco, personal communication 1989) was used to calculate the sedimentation rates in Table 5.4.

Field Observations

Using sediment traps and staff gauges, direct field observations conducted in the vicinity of the proposed Hudson River Center (piers 76 to 81, including interpier [depth 6 to 12 ft below MLW] and underpier measurements [EEA 1988]) yielded the rates shown in Table 5.5. These accretion rates provide useful information, but they are not, of

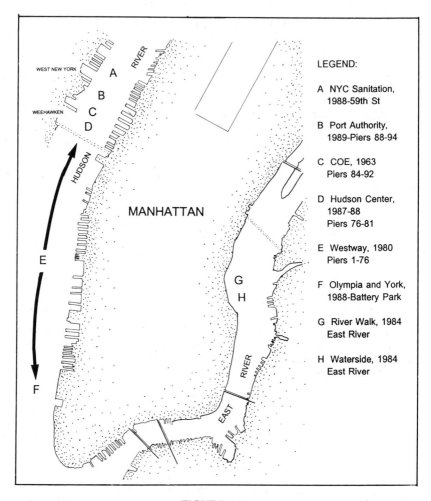

FIGURE 5.4.
Sedimentation observation sources.

course, sedimentation rates, since they do not reflect the influence of prevailing circulation patterns.

Another direct observation of rates under quiescient flow conditions may be obtained from the experience of Olympia & York Development Companies' (U.S.A.) intake at the World Financial Center. Water is pumped from the river into an intake basin, where it flows through traveling screens, is used for heat exchange, and is then discharged back to the Hudson. The intake is located under a pier

TABLE 5.1.
Sediment deposition rates in greater New York harbor.

Location	Sedimentation Rate (in./yr)	Source
1. Hudson River—south of George Washington Bridge	4–8	MPI 1983, Hudson River federal channel
2. Interpier areas—adjacent to Hudson River—NY side from Battery to W. 42nd St.	7 (Average) 2–9 (Range)	LMS 1983a, Water quality memo summarizing conditions within Westway project area from 1977 to 1983
3. Dredged areas, e.g., New York harbor	4–8	Bopp et al. 1981, Polychlorinated biphenyls in sediments of the tidal Hudson River, New York
4. Interpier areas—adjacent to East River—E. 18th to 24th St.	3 (Average) 4–6 (Range)	LMS 1984 (unpublished data)
5. Claremont Terminal Channel	~12	COE dredging permit applications by Claremont Terminal Corp. (1970) and Polarized Schiabo-Neu Company (1979)

slightly behind the pierhead line, at centerline elevation -25 ft MLW. It abuts the riprap, which slopes to about -40 ft MLW at the pierhead line. The intake basin is rectangular in shape, about 26 ft wide and 42 ft long. The intake pipe enters the basin at about 8 ft off the bottom, which is also the approximate elevation of the base of the traveling screen guides. Hence, there is a quiescent flow condition in the bottom 8 ft of the basin that creates a conducive environment for settling.

Over the long term, O&Y has removed about 1 ft of silt/sediment from the basin every two months, or about 6 ft/yr. This is done by taking the basin out of service, draining it, and manually cleaning out the muck. One of the reasons there is such a problem with silt in the basin is the location of the intake. On flood tide, deeper water (silt-laden) circulates under the pier, following the bottom profile. This brings the currents up along the riprap, right to the intake.

TABLE 5.2.
Summary of estimated annual shoaling at piers in Hudson River channel.

	Active Piers									Total Piers	
	Medium to Heavy Shoaling		Minor Shoaling (Less than 1,000 cu yd Per Slip)		Piers Changed in Use Since 1957			Piers not Used	Piers Demolished		
Locality	No.	Shoaling (cu yd)	No.	Shoaling (cu yd)	No.	Shoaling (cu yd)				No.	Shoaling (cu yd)
New York Side											
Battery to W. 40 St. (40–45 ft channel)	20	211,000	16	10,300	2	10,000		31	10	79	231,300
W. 40 St. to W. 59 St. (48 ft channel)	12	335,800	0	0	1	11,000		2	2	17	346,800
North of W. 59 St. (natural channel)	1	6,500	6	4,700	0	0		4	4	15	11,200
Total, N.Y. side	33	553,300	22	15,000	3	21,000		37	16	111	589,300
New Jersey Side											
Jersey City (40–45 ft channel)	13	138,200	15	0	2	0		12	0	42	138,200

Morris Canal Basin Jersey City (off 40–45 ft channel)	9	23,300	7	6,300	0	5	1	22	29,600
Hoboken (40–45 ft channel)	20	329,700	5	5,100	3	4	0	32	398,500
Weehawken (40–48 ft channel)	10	211,100	2	500	3	8	0	23	215,000
West New York (30 ft channel)	5	89,300	0	0	4	4	0	13	99,300
Guttenburg (30 ft channel)	2	6,000	0	0	0	0	0	2	6,000
North Bergen (30 ft channel)	5	16,000	0	0	0	2	0	7	16,000
Edgewater (30 ft channel)	5	186,100	7	0	1	19	0	32	216,100
Total, N.J. side	69	999,700	36	11,900	13	54	1	173	1,118,700
Grand Total N.Y. & N.J. SIDES	102	1,553,000	58	26,900	16	91	17	284	1,708,000

Source: Adapted from Hudson River Channel New York and New Jersey—Review of Reports. U.S. Army Corps of Engineers, New York District, August 1965.

TABLE 5.3.
Hudson River sedimentation rates obtained using 1965 COE shoaling estimates (piers 84 through 92).

Slip No.	Surface Area (sf)	Shoaling (cu yd)	Sedimentation Rate (ft/yr)
90–92	440,000	149,301	9.16
88–90	440,000	80,518	4.94
86–88	440,000	50,474	3.10
84–86	412,400	67,488	4.14
Total	1,732,400	347,781	5.42

Average depth ≃ 35–45 ft (MLW)

Random collections of total suspended solids (TSS) data over depth show an almost twofold difference between surface and bottom values, further adding to the problem.

Bathymetric Observations

Two sets of historical bathymetric data taken at the same location over a period of several years have been used to estimate sedimentation rates. The first and most comprehensive is the observations of the Hudson River Westway interpier basin from pier 21 to pier 76. The second set consists of historical East River depth observations representative of the interpier conditions that existed in the vicinity of River Walk.

TABLE 5.4.
Hudson River sedimentation rates obtained using annual dredging records (Passenger Ship Terminal and 59th Street).

Slip No.	Annual Dredging (cu yd)	Depth (ft MLW)	Sedimentation Rate (ft/yr)
88 to 94 (7 berths) Pass. Ship Terminal	335,000 (1989)	38	5.87
NYC Sanitation Transfer Sta. 59th St.	34,000 (1988)	20	3.20

TABLE 5.5.
Hudson River sedimentation and accretion rates (Hudson River Center).

Sedimentation Rate Using Staff Gauges (ft/yr)	Accretion Rate Using Traps (ft/yr)
Interpier −0.24 to 0.64, averaging 0.11	1.9
Underpier 0.16 to 0.88, averaging 0.57	2.7

The Westway observations included soundings conducted in 1972 and 1980, supplemented by information obtained in 1979 and 1981 and the New York City ports and terminals bathymetric data of 1965 and 1967 (PBQD 1984). PBQD measured the volume of sediment deposited in each interpier basin between 1972 and 1980, using the "average end area" method. These volumes were converted to average sedimentation rates ($\bar{S}$) and are plotted in Figure 5.5 against initial depth observations—that is, the 1972 values.

Three lines indicative of high, intermediate, and low sedimentation rates are shown in Figure 5.5. The straight lines, of course, represent the previously presented relationship between sedimentation rates and depth (Equation 5).

The intermediate line given in Figure 5 yields k = 0.041/yr and D_e = 10 ft. The range seen in Figure 5.5 is a measure of the time left until equilibrium depth is reached, with the low sedimentation line corresponding to longer periods and vice versa. The variability is probably due to the differences in the basin and sediment characteristics mentioned earlier, particularly the basin velocity, basin geometry, salinity gradients, suspended solids concentration, sediment type, and location of sediment sources.

The East River data (average sedimentation rate $\bar{S}$ vs initial depth) are given in Figure 5.6. These represent historical observations from the interpier basins formerly present in the River Walk project area. (Data indicating scouring [negative values] or questionable points are not plotted.)

Figure 5.7 compares the East River data with their Westway counterparts. As shown, the East River experiences somewhat lower rates than the Hudson River, primarily because of its stronger current velocities (as high as 4 or 5 knots) and lower suspended solids concentrations (4 to 8 ppm vs 10 to 130 ppm). The lower East River suspended solids concentration is probably a result of the much lower amounts of sediments supplied by the much smaller East River water-

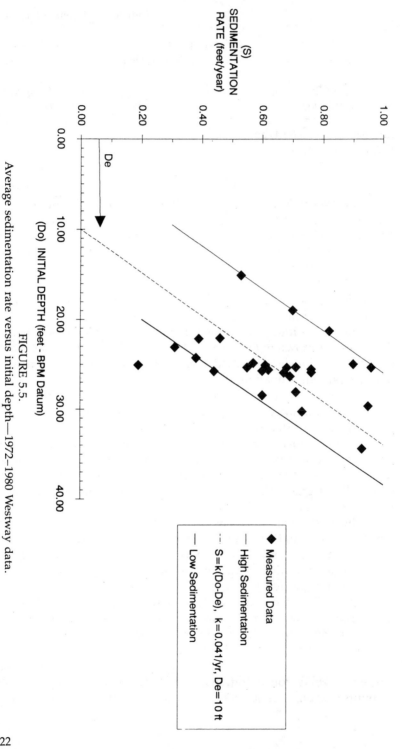

FIGURE 5.5.
Average sedimentation rate versus initial depth—1972–1980 Westway data.

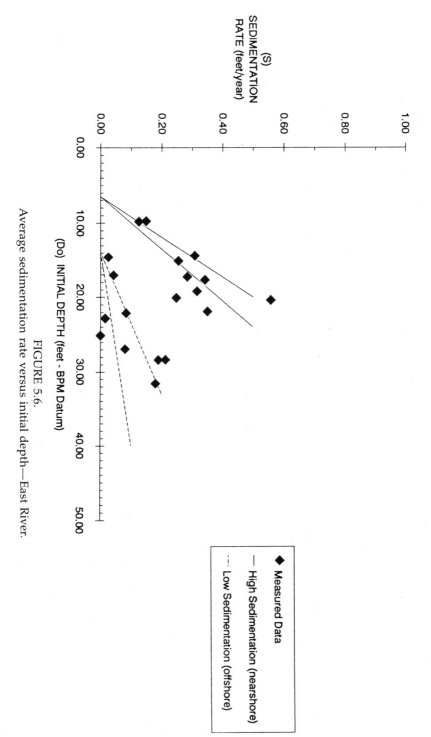

FIGURE 5.6.
Average sedimentation rate versus initial depth—East River.

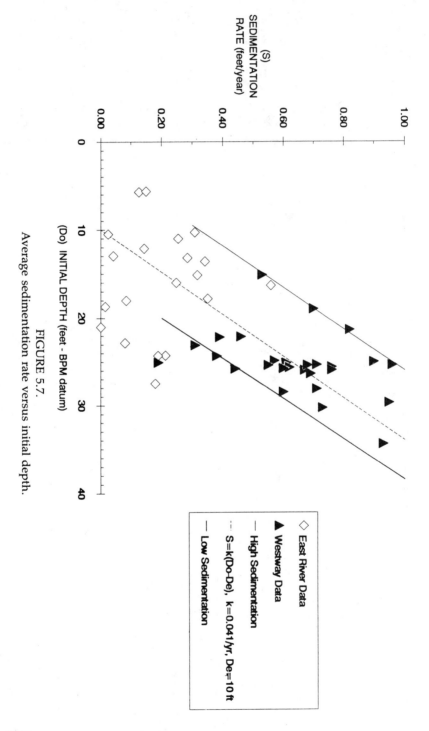

FIGURE 5.7.
Average sedimentation rate versus initial depth.

shed and fewer point sources on a waterbody basis. The Westway data were also used to calculate instantaneous sedimentation rates (using the exponential decay model [Appendix A]) and relate them to their corresponding depths (see Figure 5.8). The straight lines seen in Figure 5.5 are also shown in Figure 5.8, indicating that the exponential decay model yields values similar to the average sedimentation results.

Another East River case study is the under-platform observations conducted by Lawler, Matusky and Skelly Engineers (LMS) in 1984 under the Waterside deck (see Figure 5.9 for location). Waterside is a high-rise residential development built on a pile-supported platform north of the River Walk project site and extending from the north end of the United Nations School to approximately 29th Street. The development, built in the mid-1970s, provided a good opportunity to determine the equilibrium water depths under a platform structure in the East River. It should be noted that the Waterside piling arrangement was designed/spaced solely for structural support, apparently without any attempt to optimize tidal water flow; the site is completely platformed, without any open water; and the sewer outfalls discharge at the bulkhead and not at the pierhead line.

Seven transects were run, 6 approximately perpendicular to the shoreline, starting at the bulkhead, and 1 parallel to the shoreline. The transects were positioned on the basis of construction drawings showing the pilings' location and on the ability of the boat to pass between pilings. The transect locations are illustrated on Figure 5.9, along with the approximate bottom contour before construction at Waterside.

The bottom profiles of the 7 transects are illustrated on Figure 5.10. Under the Waterside development the water depths are almost uniformly 5–7 ft below MLW and slope sharply near the pierhead line. A comparison of the 1984 depth with the before-construction bottom contours indicates that significant sedimentation has occurred under Waterside, perhaps reducing the depth as much as 10–15 ft. It appears that the sedimentation has leveled off to an equilibrium depth of 5–7 ft. This observation cannot be confirmed, however, without a second survey of the site—undertaken after sufficient time has elapsed for addition sediment deposition to occur.

The cited data are quite variable, probably due to the previously mentioned man-made and natural perturbations. Nevertheless, it is clear from these results that the rate of sedimentation in sheltered (low-velocity) areas depends heavily on water depth (the deeper the basin, the greater the sedimentation rate). Properly used, Equation 5

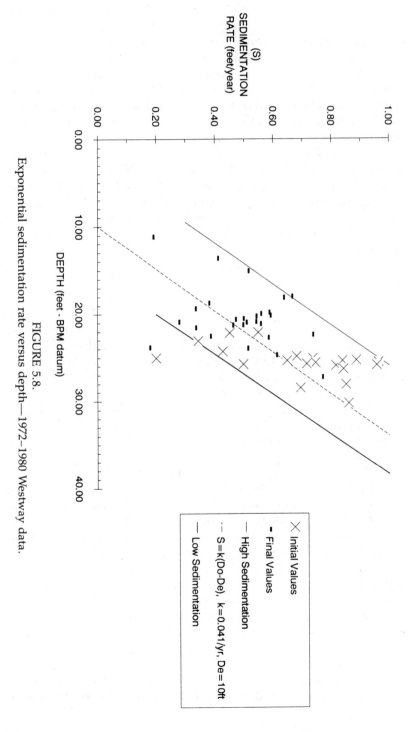

FIGURE 5.8.
Exponential sedimentation rate versus depth—1972-1980 Westway data.

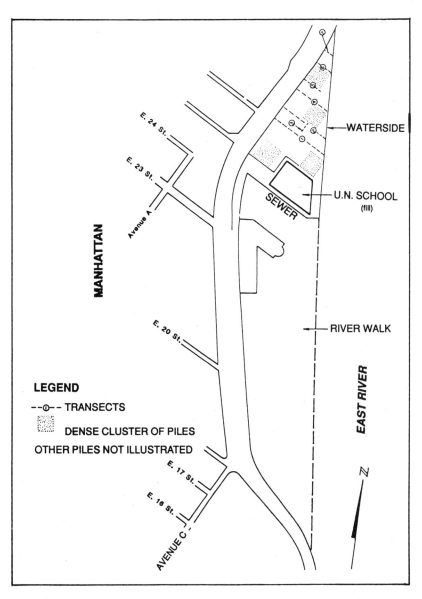

FIGURE 5.9.
Location of transects, Waterside fathometric survey, October 28, 1984.

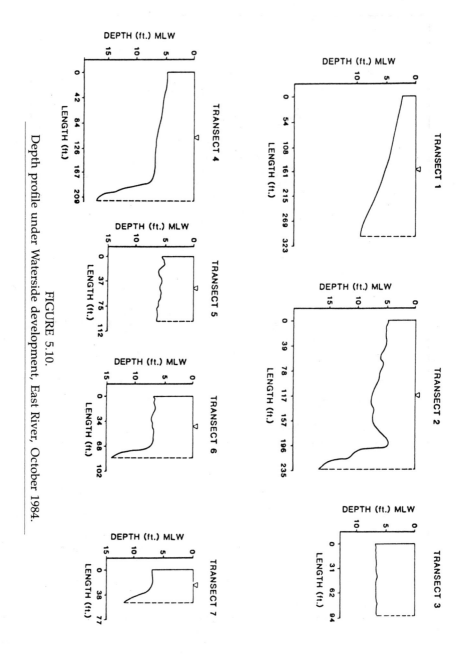

FIGURE 5.10.
Depth profile under Waterside development, East River, October 1984.

provides a convenient frame of reference and permits comparisons among relative sedimentation rates, taking into account initial water depths.

Mitigation Measures

Generally speaking, the primary consequence of induced-sedimentation is to reduce water depths in areas where there is moderate to deep water. This may result in a net loss of moderate depths preferred by some fish species and may cause localized water quality and stagnation problems. These impacts can be minimized or mitigated by incorporating into the design of pile-supported projects a number of environmental protection features, such as:

- Special/wide spacings between piles to minimize flow restriction
- Positioning of supported structures to allow portions of the platform to be supported by more widely spaced piles and other portions by denser piling clusters to provide habitat diversity
- Provision of open-water areas and flow channelization within the project site to maintain circulation and flushing
- Provision of access to areas so that deep water can be maintained via future maintenance dredging
- Extension of sewer outfalls to the pierhead line to prevent discharges of sediments and pollution beneath any platform structure
- Removal of existing areas of pollution and stagnation
- Provision of habitat features preferred by key species, wherever attainable.

These measures have been incorporated into the River Walk design depicted in Figure 5.11. Key River Walk features are summarized below:

- Piling cluster patterns with spacing up to 55 ft
- Multistory buildings repositioned to allow the outer portion of the platform to be supported by more widely spaced piles
- 30% of the project area to remain as open-water habitat
- Periodic maintenance dredging to be provided along a channel passing between the offshore and nearshore platforms, which will ensure adequate flow circulation and flushing
- Seven combined sewers now discharging at 5 locations along the bulkhead to be combined and extended to the pierhead line, closer

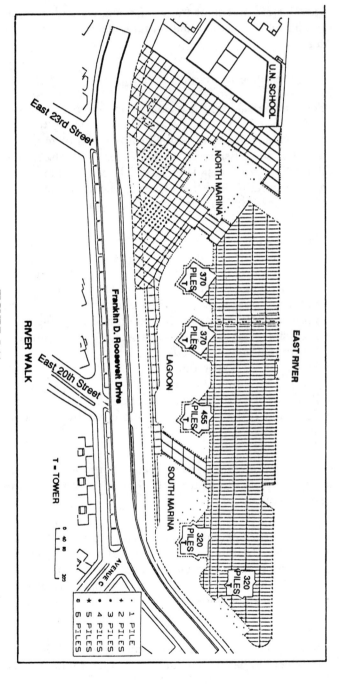

FIGURE 5.11.
River Walk project site plan.

to main channel flows where mixing and dispersion will be more efficient
- Existing stagnation and dead zone areas to be dredged
- Habitat diversity to be provided by maintaining deep (near the channel), intermediate (open-water segment), and shallow (near the shore areas) areas.

It is recommended that many of these and perhaps other mitigative and compensatory measures should be incorporated into pile-supported structures, whenever attainable, for the specific purpose of minimizing induced sedimentation and environmental disturbances.

APPENDIX A

Exponential Decay Model

The decrease in average depth with time depicted in Figure 5.3 may be expressed as follows:

$$(D - D_e) = (D_o - D_e) e^{-kt} \tag{A-1}$$

or

$$d = d_o e^{-kt} \tag{A-2}$$

where k = slope

An equation defining sedimentation rates (S) may be derived from Equation A-1:

$$\frac{dD}{dt} = S = -k e^{-kt} d_o = -kd$$

or

$$|S| = kd = k d_o e^{-kt} \tag{A-3}$$

or

$$|S| = k(D - D_e) \tag{A-4}$$

The parameter (k) may be obtained from two depth observations taken t_1 apart:

$$k = \frac{1}{t_1} \ln \frac{d_o}{d_1} \qquad (A\text{-}5)$$

or

$$k = \frac{1}{t_1} \ln \frac{D_o - D_e}{D_1 - D_e} \qquad (A\text{-}6)$$

Equations A-3 and A-5 provide:

$$|S| = \frac{d}{d_1} \ln \frac{d_o}{d_1} \qquad (A\text{-}7)$$

Equations A-3 and A-5 yield:

$$|S_o| = kd_o = \frac{d_o}{t_1} \ln \frac{d_o}{d_1} \text{ or } k = |S_o|/d_o \qquad (A\text{-}8)$$

and

$$|S_1| = kd_1 = \frac{d_1}{t_1} \ln \frac{d_o}{d_1} \qquad (A\text{-}9)$$

or

$$|S| = |S_o| \frac{d}{d_o} \qquad (A\text{-}10)$$

$$|S_1| = |S_o| \frac{d_1}{d_o} \qquad (A\text{-}11)$$

and

$$|S_o| = \frac{d_o}{t_1} \ln \frac{d_o}{d_1} \qquad (A\text{-}12)$$

An equation defining t'_e may be obtained from Equation A-2, above, as shown below:

$$d_e = r D_e = d_o e^{-kt'_e}$$

or

Induced Sedimentation   133

$$\ln d_e/d_o = -kt'_e \text{ or } t'_e = \frac{1}{k} \ln \frac{d_o}{d_e} \qquad (A\text{-}13)$$

Using equations A-5, A-8, and A-13 yields:

$$t'_e = \frac{d_o}{|S_o|} \ln \frac{d_o}{d_e} = \frac{d_o}{|S_o|} \ln \frac{d_o}{rD_e} \qquad (A\text{-}14)$$

or

$$t'_e = t_1 \frac{\ln d_o/d_e}{\ln d_o/d_1} \qquad (A\text{-}15)$$

The time interval (t_{12}) between two consecutive basin depths (D_1 and D_2) may be calculated using equation A-2:

$$t_{12} = t_2 - t_1 = \frac{1}{k} (\ln d_2/d_o - \ln d_1/d_o)$$

or, using equation A-5,

$$t_{12} = t_1 \left(\frac{\ln d_2/d_o}{\ln d_1/d_o} - 1 \right) \qquad (A\text{-}16)$$

Another expression may be derived from equation A-3 using an average sedimentation rate (S_{12}) or ($S_1 + S_2$)/2 as an approximate rate representative of the interval ($t_2 - t_1$). This approximation is reasonable as long as t_{12} is not too long and we are not nearing equilibrium. Employment of equations A-3 and A-5 yields:

or $\qquad t_{12} = (d_1 - d_2)/S_{12} = (d_1 - d_2) \div (kd_1 + kd_2)/2$

$$t_{12} = 2 t_1 (d_1 - d_2)/(d_1 - d_2) \cdot \ln d_o/d_1 \qquad (A\text{-}17)$$

6

Impact of Withdrawals on Hudson Salinity

ABSTRACT

   Withdrawals of freshwater for consumptive use have been evaluated in terms of the impacts these withdrawals would have on the salinity distribution. The time period, May through September 1988, has been used as a low-flow scenario for impact evaluation.
   As salinity concentrations are dynamic in nature, a transient, one-dimensional model of the tidal hydraulics and salinity transport was applied from the Battery in New York Harbor, to the head of tide at Troy. The governing equations of motion and salt conservation are coupled through the density term. This model, the MIT Transient Salinity Intrusion Model (TSIM), has been applied previously to the Hudson and to other estuaries, notably to the Delaware where it is used by the Delaware River Basin Commission to evaluate impacts of consumptive use and upstream flow regulation on positions of the salt front over long periods of time.
   Calculations were made of the time-varying velocities, water surface elevations, and salinity concentrations. The calculations were

made for a base scenario, and a withdrawal scenario consisting of a 100 mgd withdrawal at mile 65.5. Comparisons of the salinity concentrations are made at different locations, and a statistical comparison is presented in terms of the percent of time that a specified isochlor is exceeded.

INTRODUCTION

For the Hudson Estuary, the summer of 1988 was a period of relatively low freshwater inflow. As shown by the provisional flows of Figure 6.1, flows at Green Island have remained below 5,000 cfs for approximately four months with only two storm events during the entire period. There were many flows less than 4,000 cfs.

This study is an academic study—that is to say, it has not been commissioned either directly or indirectly by any federal, state, or city agency. Its purpose is to illustrate the possible effects (impacts) of withdrawal for consumptive use on the salinity (chlorides) in the Hudson Estuary. Obviously this impact will be the most severe under conditions of low flow, thus the summer 1988 data will form the basis

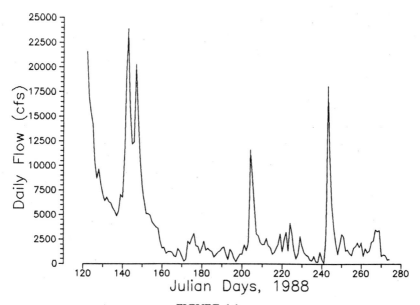

FIGURE 6.1.
Daily flows of Hudson River at Green Island (USGS Provisional Data, 1988).

for analysis. The application of an intratidal transient salinity intrusion model for this purpose yields dynamic chloride concentrations throughout the study period and permits the user to simulate the impact of a consumptive withdrawal at any location within the estuary. This approach has been used elsewhere: extensively on the Delaware Estuary (Thatcher and Harleman 1978, 1981; Thatcher et al. 1981) in order to provide a basis for regulatory action, and also on the Eastmain River Estuary in Canada (Lepage and Ingram 1986) to evaluate the impact of a major reduction in freshwater input. On the Hudson, this approach has been used by Harleman et al. 1972, and more recently by MPI 1986.

The summer of 1988 is thus of special interest to Hudson River planners and managers as it represents a recent low-flow scenario. Its value stems from the fact that recent (since the 1960s) changes in hydrography, hydrology, and water use are reflected in these more recent data.

MODEL SELECTION

The model selected for this study is a revised version of the MIT Transient Salinity Intrusion Model (Thatcher and Harleman 1972a,b, 1978). It consists of three partial differential equations plus the equation of state relating salinity and density. Functionally, it is composed of two submodels: the tidal dynamics model and the salt balance model. The continuity and longitudinal momentum equations constitute the tidal dynamics model; while the conservation equation for salt represents the salt balance model. The tidal dynamics model and the salt balance model are linked together by the water surface elevation, the time-varying discharge, and the dependency of density upon salinity as expressed in the equation of state.

The differential equations have been integrated in the lateral and vertical directions. As it is assumed that all quantities vary only along the longitudinal axis of the estuary, the model is one-dimensional. It is also a real-time, transient model, the time scale having been chosen so as to be small compared to a tidal period, but large compared to the time scale of turbulent fluctuations.

Governing Equations

The governing equations are:
Continuity Equations:

$$\frac{b\partial h}{\partial t} + \frac{\partial Q}{\partial x} - q = 0 \tag{1}$$

where

$b(x,t)$ = total width of the channel
$h(x,t)$ = depth from the water surface to the model datum
     = $z_o + d + \eta$
$z_o(x)$ = elevation of channel bottom above model datum
$d(x)$ = core channel depth at mean water + A_{core}/b_{core}
$A_{core}(x) = A_c(x)$ = cross-sectional area of primary flow channel at mean water
$b_{core}(x)$ = the channel width at mean water corresponding to the primary axial flow channel
$\eta(x,t)$ = water surface elevation relative to local mean water level
$Q(x,t)$ = cross-sectional tidal discharge
$q(x,t)$ = lateral freshwater inflow per unit length

Longitudinal Momentum Equation:

$$\frac{\partial Q}{\partial t} + u\frac{\partial Q}{\partial x} + Q\frac{\partial u}{\partial x} + gA_c\frac{\partial h}{\partial x} + \frac{gA_c d_c \partial \rho}{\rho\,\partial x} + 0.45\frac{gn^2 Q|Q|}{A_c R_h^{4/3}} = 0 \tag{2}$$
(ft sec units)

where

$u(x,t)$ = cross-sectional average longitudinal fluid velocity of the primary axial flow channel, including tidal and freshwater components
g = acceleration of gravity
$d_c(x,t)$ = distance from the water surface to the centroid of the cross section
$\rho(x,t)$ = fluid density
$n(x)$ = Manning's roughness coefficient
$R_h(x,t)$ = hydraulic radius

Conservation of Salt Equation:

$$\frac{\partial(A_T S)}{\partial t} + \frac{\partial(Qs)}{\partial x} = \frac{\partial}{\partial x}\left(EA_T\frac{\partial s}{\partial x}\right) \tag{3}$$

where

$s(x,t)$ = cross-sectional average salinity, ppt
$E(x,t)$ = longitudinal dispersion coefficient
$A_T(x,t)$ = total cross-sectional area, including conveyance and storage cross-sectional areas

Equation of State:

The equation relating density to salinity (or chlorides) has been based on a linear formulation developed by Thatcher and Harleman 1978, which includes temperature dependence. This relationship is:

$$\rho = A + B_s \tag{4}$$

where:

A and B are temperature-dependent coefficients based on the equation of Fofonoff and Tabata 1958.

SOLUTION OF EQUATIONS

The solution of these partial differential equations is accomplished by converting them to finite difference form for numerical solution by digital computers. The tidal dynamics model is represented according to an explicit finite difference scheme, and the solution to the salt balance model is made by a second order accurate, implicit finite difference scheme (Stone and Brian 1963).

The constraints imposed by the explicit finite difference scheme used in the tidal dynamics model are more demanding than those of the salt balance equation; the criterion for choosing the values of Δx and Δt is derived from the Courant criterion for explicit schemes. This criterion is

$$\Delta t \leq \frac{\Delta x}{u + c} \tag{5}$$

where:

$u(x,t)$ = cross-sectional average, longitudinal fluid velocity,
$c(x,t)$ = tidal wave speed = $\sqrt{gd}$

Input-Output Requirements

Given the time varying water surface elevations, maximum flood tide salinities at the downstream boundary, and time varying freshwater

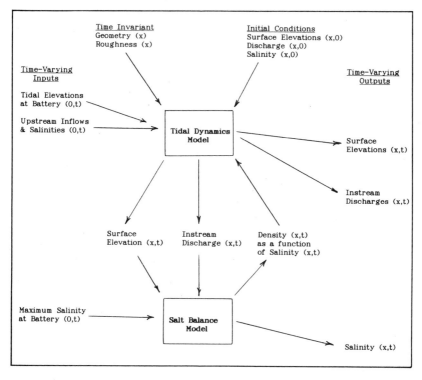

FIGURE 6.2.
Structure of transient salinity model.

inflows along the estuary, as well as geometry and roughness data, the model can predict transient conditions of water surface elevation, discharge, and salinity along the estuary. Figure 6.2 diagrams the interaction between the tidal dynamics model and the salt balance model in terms of input-output relationships. In general, the tidal dynamics model, running on specified initial and boundary condition data, generates the hydraulic input to the salt balance model, which in turn feeds back a predicted transient salinity distribution to the tidal dynamics model through the density gradient term in the momentum equation.

The geometry of the estuary and the longitudinal distributions of water surface elevation, freshwater inflow, tidal discharge, and salinity must be specified as initial conditions. The boundary conditions are treated as follows:

At the downstream boundary the water surface elevation must be specified as a function of time throughout each tidal cycle. This may be in the form of tables of water surface elevations at discrete time intervals or of an assumed cosine curve with specified high and low water tidal amplitudes, which generates the water surface elevations during each tidal cycle. The intratidal cycle downstream salinity boundary condition is treated in two parts depending upon whether the tidal flow is in the ebb or flood phase. During the ebb flow a gradient condition is specified, whereas during the flood flow the boundary salinity is linearly increased from its value at low water slack to a user-specified value.

Salt Balance Model

In the saline portion of an estuary the longitudinal dispersion coefficient, $E(x,t)$, is strongly dependent on the magnitude of the time-dependent longitudinal salinity gradient, which is a measure of the intensity of density-induced circulation. In well-mixed or nonsaline portions of the estuary, the Taylor dispersion coefficient, E_T, expresses the amount of mixing attributable to nonuniformities in the cross-sectional velocity and concentration distributions, which are neglected in the spatial averaging process. The longitudinal dispersion coefficient is formulated as follows:

$$E(x,t) = K \left| \frac{\partial \overset{\circ}{s}}{\partial \overset{\circ}{x}} \right| + 3E_T \qquad (6)$$

where:

K = dispersion parameter (ft²/sec)
$\overset{\circ}{s}(x,t)$ = normalized salinity = $s(x,t)/s_o(t)$
$s_o(t)$ = maximum salinity at the downstream boundary during flood tide
$\overset{\circ}{x}$ = normalized distance = x/L
L = length of estuary, and
E_t = 77 n U $R_h^{5/6}$ (ft-sec units)

K is a constant of proportionality, and its value is related to the degree of stratification of the saline portion of the estuary through the correlation:

$$\frac{K}{u_o L} = IE_D^{-1/4} \qquad (7)$$

where:

I = intercept of correlation: a calibration parameter
u_o = maximum velocity at the entrance
$E_D = \dfrac{P_T F_D^2}{Q_f T}$, a stratification parameter
P_T = the tidal prism, the volume of water entering on the flood tide
F_D = densimetric Froude number, $\dfrac{u_o}{(gd\,\dfrac{\Delta\rho}{\rho})^{1/2}}$
Q_f = fresh water inflow, and
T = the tidal period.

APPLICATION TO THE HUDSON ESTUARY

Schematization of Cross-Sectional Geometry

Detailed schematization of the Hudson Estuary was made by Harleman et al. 1972. Cross-section geometry was numerically described, and the estuary geometry was divided into 76 sections, based on NOS charts from the Battery to Troy. Sensitivity analysis was performed in order to arrive at a double, rectangular schematization consisting of a central conveyance area and an adjoining storage area in order to account for embayments and shallow areas that contribute little to longitudinal flow. The variations in conveyance width, total width and depths are shown in Figure 6.3.

Calibration of Tidal Hydrodynamics

Calibration of the tidal dynamics model under repeating mean tidal conditions was performed. The transient model was executed with the ocean boundary water surface elevations repeated cyclically over a fixed range. Manning's "n" was varied until model and prototype values for mean high and mean low tidal stages and phase lags were matched.

The study of Harleman et al. 1972 reported a verification of the tidal dynamics based on a single value of the Manning's "n" parameter of 0.015 throughout the entire estuary. For the present study a slightly better agreement was obtained using a variation of Manning's "n" shown in Figure 6.4. Figure 6.5 shows the new predictions versus observed high and low water planes.

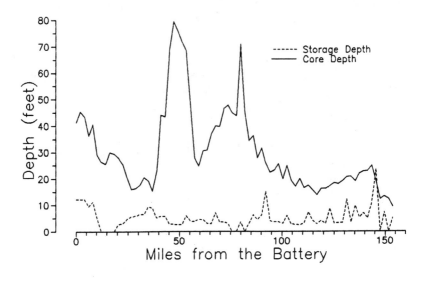
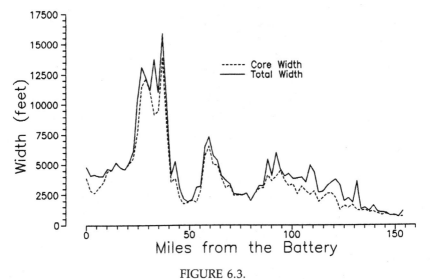

FIGURE 6.3.
Variations in conveyance widths, total widths, and depths. *Upper figure:* Schematized depths. *Lower Figure:* Schematized widths.

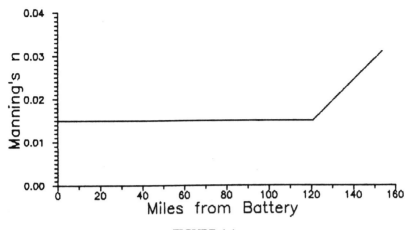

FIGURE 6.4.
Longitudinal variation in Manning's "n."

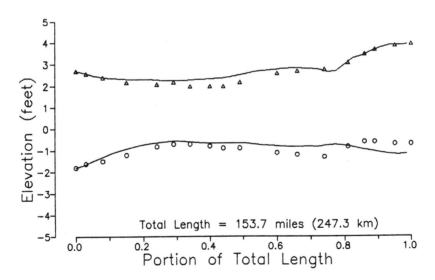

FIGURE 6.5.
Calibration of mean high and low water planes using values of Manning'"n" shown in figure 6.4. *Triangles:* High water values from National Ocean Services. *Circles:* low water values. Lines indicate calculated values.

Boundary Conditions

Upstream and tributary inflow boundary conditions are specified as pairs of daily discharge and corresponding chlorinity. The total flow from upland sources, both gaged and ungaged, was derived from the Green Island hydrograph (Figure 6.1) by multiplying the daily value by 1.26. This factor is based on the long-term analyses for summer conditions presented by Abood et al. (this volume).

In order to provide a background chloride concentration, all the observations from May 1988 through September 1988 from the Hudson River Estuary Monitoring Program (Hamilton personal communication) upstream of mile 80 were averaged. Figure 6.6 shows the distribution of these values. The mean chloride concentration is 0.020 ppt, about 0.1% of the value at the downstream boundary.

At the seaward end of the estuary the hydraulic specification is that of observed tidal elevations. The chlorinity and the temperature are also specified at the ocean boundary. Figure 6.7 shows the temperature and chlorinity data for the study period. The tidal elevation data and the temperature and salinity data are from the National

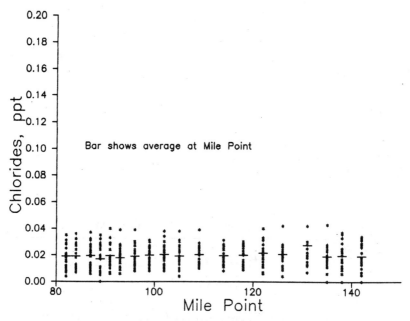

FIGURE 6.6.
Background chlorides above the salt front.

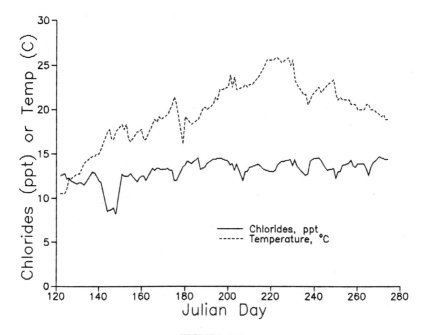

FIGURE 6.7.
Chlorides and temperature at the Battery, summer 1988 from NOAA/NOS data.

Ocean Service, NOAA 1988a,b. The temperature is specified, not calculated. The specified chloride concentration at this downstream boundary is that of the maximum chloride concentration on the flood, thus the calculation proceeds with a specified value only during inflow. A dispersive flux condition is used during outflow.

Validation of Calculated Salinity with Observed Data

Data gathered as part of the Hudson River Estuary Monitoring Program (Hamilton 1989, pers. commun), in its preliminary form, has been used for model validations. These data are "boat run" data, thus observations are at different stations at different times. Nonetheless, even after depth averaging there are 1371 observations: a considerable database. Figure 6.8 gives a visualization of these data. In order to calibrate the model to these data, "I", the intercept of the dispersion correlation, was varied. This was the *only* parameter varied. A value of 12.5×10^{-4} gave the calibrations shown in Figure 6.9.

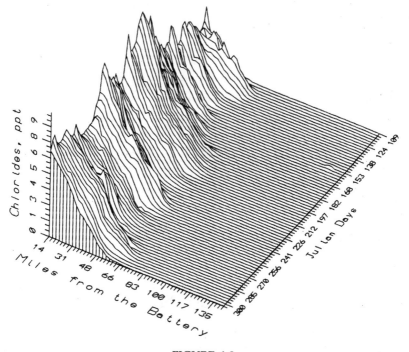

FIGURE 6.8.
Visualization of chloride observations May-September 1988
(provisional data).

IMPACT OF WITHDRAWALS ON THE CHLORINITY DISTRIBUTION

Withdrawal of Hudson water can be simulated by using the model's existing facility for specifying lateral inflows and their concentrations. By specifying a negative value, the model will correctly account for the withdrawal, at the specified concentration. This procedure works well for cases where the withdrawal concentration is known. Such a calculation is appropriate for evaporative losses such as those caused by power plants, as the salt remains in the river, implying that the loss is at zero concentration (UEC 1974a,b). However, the calculation would be inaccurate when the instream concentration at the point of withdrawal is not known, but is part of the solution. For this study is was necessary to reformulate the model so that the implicit finite-difference representation of equation (3) included terms for the withdrawal at the unknown concentration.

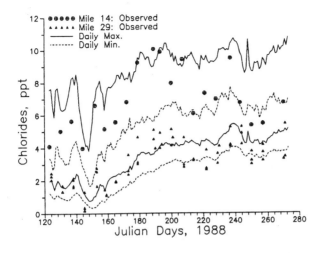
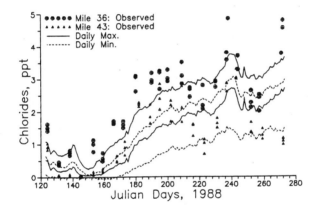
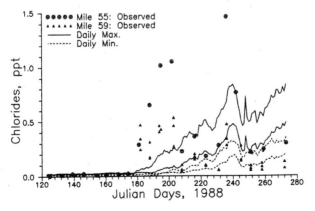

FIGURE 6.9.
Calibration of model to observed chlorides.

148   Physical and Chemical Ecology

The model calculates the chloride concentration every five minutes throughout the simulation period. Such voluminous data can be processed in a variety of ways in order to illustrate the impact of withdrawal for consumptive use. Two approaches have been taken to illustrate this impact; however, they are by no means the only ones possible.

Percent of Time that a Specified Concentration is Exceeded

The study period encompasses a low flow period of approximately four months, June through September. This length of time means that about 235 tidal exchanges will contribute to maximum and minimum chlorides for each tidal cycle. Thus, at each mile point or location, it is possible to tabulate the number of times that a particular concentration has been exceeded. Such a tabulation can be normalized over the entire period by means of a percentage of the total number of times possible. In other words, a simple frequency tabulation is made at locations within the study area. Figure 6.10 presents this tabulation in graphic form for 250 and 50 ppm chlorides. The solid line shows the impact for a withdrawal of 100 mgd located at mile point 65.5.

Increase in Chlorides due to Withdrawal

The model calculates chloride concentrations at each station of the finite difference network at 5-minute intervals. Every fourth value was stored for plotting. A direct comparison of the calculated chloride concentrations at stations of interest is a means of evaluating the impact of withdrawal on the chloride intrusion. Figure 6.11 shows this increase for stations at mile 43 and 59.

DISCUSSION

This study illustrates the ability to predict the impact of a withdrawal for consumptive use on the salinity distribution within the Hudson Estuary. Like all modeling studies, this study should be subject to scrutiny in terms of its accuracy and reliability. A simple mass balance can show that a withdrawal of fresh water upstream will lead to an increase in chlorinity. The question is: How much is the increase that corresponds to a specified withdrawal, and under what conditions?

This particular modeling approach is applied to answer the above question. Its accuracy is based on the calculation of the time

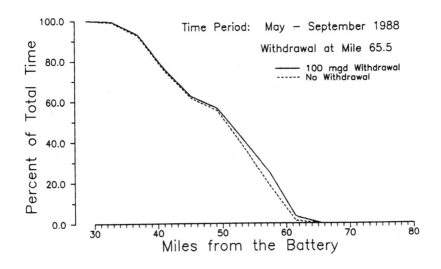

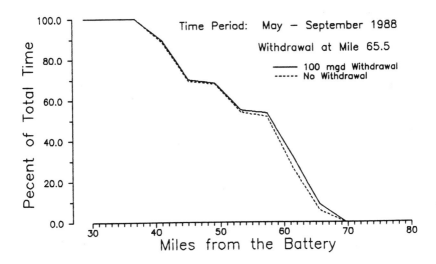

FIGURE 6.10.
Percent of time a particular isoclhor is exceeded.

150   Physical and Chemical Ecology

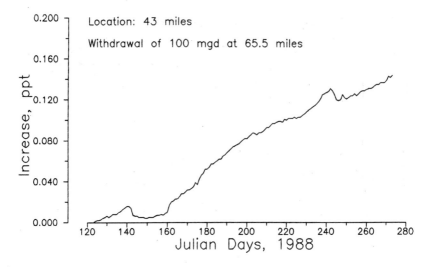

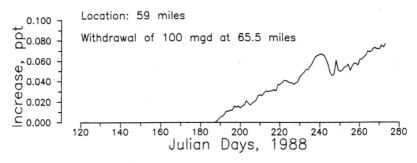

FIGURE 6.11.
Predicted increase in chloride concentration at 43 and 59 miles from the Battery due to withdrawal of 100 mgd at river mile 65.5.

varying hydraulics of the estuary subject to daily variations in freshwater inflow and intratidal variations of surface elevation at the downstream boundary. To further increase the accuracy of the calculation, the momentum equation includes a density term that is related to the salinity distribution through an equation of state.

The solution to the salt balance equation is developed at a time scale of minutes, thus avoiding the approximations resulting from time averaging over one or more tidal cycles. The finite difference

Impact of Withdrawals 151

scheme (Stone and Brian 1963) is one that does not introduce significant numerical dispersion. Nonetheless, the form of the dispersion relationship can lead to inaccuracies in the predicted salinity distribution. The particular dynamic calculation of the dispersion coefficient specified by equation 6 is the result of studies on several estuaries and flumes, and has been notably successful in the Delaware Estuary. Figure 6.9 shows that the model predicts Hudson salinities in good agreement with those observed over the period of 150 days, the agreement extending over several orders of magnitude. This calibration leads to confidence in the model as a tool for evaluating the impact of changes in fresh water inflows or withdrawals such as those forming the subject of this study.

The author would like to point out, however, that alternative formulations for the dispersion relationship have been proposed and may be equally valid or better. A general review of these relationships can be found in Fischer et al. 1979. Of direct interest for the Hudson Estuary is the work by Posmentier and Raymont 1979. The evaluation of alternative formulations for the dispersion coefficient require additional data and additional study.

A second source of inaccuracy is the data base itself. It should be noted that in order to prepare this paper on a timely basis, both the fresh water inflow data at Green Island and the long-term monitoring data are considered to be "provisional" data. This means that for any decisions to be taken using these data their accuracy should be further verified. A particular problem exists in defining the chlorinity at the downstream boundary in that the observed density data are not representative of the entire cross section, but are based on observations at the Battery tide station, at one side of the entrance to the estuary. Future studies would benefit from a more complete definition of the chlorinity at the downstream boundary.

CONCLUSIONS

Withdrawal for consumptive use in the Hudson Estuary can be evaluated through the application of a cross-sectionally averaged, longitudinal, transient salinity model such as the one documented in this study. The impact of withdrawals can be quantified using scenarios based on observed conditions thus giving those who make management decisions a tool for the evaluation of alternatives. The summer of 1988 may well provide a new low-flow scenario for studies of water quality in the Hudson Estuary.

PAUL LINSALATA
NORMAN COHEN

7

Hudson River Radionuclide Research Revisited: Watershed Removal of Fallout Radionuclides and Long-Term Trends in the Estuary

ABSTRACT

For more than 20 years the New York University Institute of Environmental Medicine has monitored certain radionuclides in the water, sediments, fish, and rooted vegetation of the Hudson River Estuary and its drainage basin. One goal of this study has been to verify models relating power reactor nuclide discharges at Indian Point to dosimetric consequences of persons using the Hudson's resources.

Radionuclides reach the Hudson from reactor discharges, fallout inputs, and erosion of sediments in the upper basin. Since 1966 the input of ^{239}Plutonium to the river estuary has been dominated by erosion of fallout-contaminated soils in the watershed. Particulate erosion is the major source of watershed input for both ^{239}Pu and

^{137}Cs. Reactors at Indian Point contributed about 34% of the decay-corrected ^{137}Cs from all sources.

Mean concentrations of ^{137}Cs have shown sharp declines since the relatively large reactor discharges in 1971. Since the mid-1970s concentrations in whole fish and water of reactor-based nuclides such as ^{134}Cs, ^{60}Co, ^{58}Co, and ^{54}Mn have generally been below detectable limits.

Fifty-year effective dose equivalents through both swimming and water consumption are currently negligible. Compared with cosmic and external terrestrial radiation, additional contributions from reactor effluents are vanishingly small.

INTRODUCTION

The New York University Institute of Environmental Medicine (NYUIEM) has maintained a radioecological studies program on the Hudson River Estuary and its watershed over the past 25 years as a result of the enhancement in the radiation background environment caused primarily by fallout from nuclear weapons testing in the 1950s and 1960s, and beginning in the mid-1960s, effluents from commercial nuclear power reactors. Many individual projects were undertaken during this period to further our understanding of the principal mechanisms controlling the inputs, environmental distribution, and fate of various natural and anthropogenic radionuclides within the Hudson Estuary (Hairr 1974; Lentsch 1974; Mauro 1974; Jinks 1975; Paschoa et al. 1979; Olsen 1979; Linsalata 1984). But the overall emphasis of the program has been on assessing the radiological impact on humans from man-made sources. We do not attempt to summarize earlier findings and conclusions but rather provide up-to-date results, on both research and routine surveillance aspects of radionuclides—sources, sinks, distributions, and dosimetric consequences based primarily on data obtained in the 1980s.

This paper focuses on two aspects of the program. (1) Estimating the long-term contributions to the lower river (that portion below the federal lock at Troy, New York) of weapons fallout of ^{239}Plutonium (an alpha-particle emitter with radiological half-life of 24,000 y) and ^{137}Cesium (a beta-gamma emitter with half-life of 30.2 y) from erosion and runoff within the watershed. We believe that the methods developed here concerning radionuclides provide a useful framework for considering the impact to the lower river from other soil-bound contaminants. (2) Summarizing the results of the long-term monitoring and dose assessment program as conducted in the region surrounding the Indian Point pressurized water reactors at RM 42.

METHODS

During the period 1969–1981 a routine monitoring program for ^{137}Cs, ^{134}Cs, ^{60}Co, ^{54}Mn released from reactors and ^{137}Cs from fallout was conducted at sampling locations shown in Figure 7.1. Water was collected continuously from submerged pumps about one m off bottom in mid-channel at Chelsea (RM 65, NYC Auxiliary Pumping Station) and composited (40 liters) biweekly. This site serves as a control location for comparison with a near shore location one mile south of the reactors at Verplank, N.Y. (RM 41, samples taken about 1–2 m below mean low water). All water was passed through 45 μm filters and dissolved and particulate phases were assayed separately following chemical concentration of filtrates (Chelex-100 used for transition metals and copper ferrocyanide for Cesium). Nonmigratory resident fish were obtained by beach seine, approximately once per month, May to October, at Esopus, N.Y. (a control location at RM 87) and at Tompkins Cove directly opposite the reactors. Fish were sorted and analyzed by species (predominantly white perch, bluegill and pumpkinseed sunfish, white catfish, brown bullheads, shiner, young striped bass, American eel, killifish, and carp). Between 15 and 30 fish samples were analyzed per year per location. For simplicity in presenting results, unweighted annual average values were computed from all samples of resident fish. Adult shad and striped bass (5–10 each year) were obtained during the spring run from commercial fishermen in Haverstraw Bay and filleted prior to analysis. Samples of the top 2–4 inches of bottom sediments were obtained by Emery dredge once per month, May through October from each of the locations shown in Figure 7.1. Although data exists from many gravity core samples, which were taken simultaneously, discussion here is limited to dredge samples from the surface of the substratum. All gamma-emitting radionuclide measurements made during this period were by NaI(Tl) spectrometry incorporating a linear, weighted least squares regression program developed specifically for this project.

Since 1983, a reduced monitoring effort has been in effect. Water (100 liters) was collected by grab sampling (mid-channel, mid-depth) three times per year (June, August, October) adjacent to Chelsea and

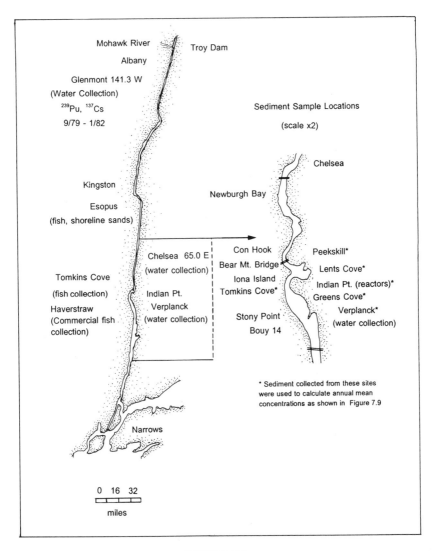

FIGURE 7.1.
Hudson River sampling locations.

Verplanck; surface sediment collection was limited to these same time periods with all Figure 7.1 stations maintained; fish (resident species only) were obtained by trawling three to four times per year at both control (north of Newburgh) and Indian Point (±4 miles) locations. All gamma-emitting radionuclide determinations since 1983 have been by Ge spectrometry using commercially available data reduction software.

A separate, but related, program was begun in 1978 to determine the sources and fate of plutonium and ^{137}Cs in the Hudson River estuary. Plutonium isotopes were analyzed in soil cores collected in 1982 from various locations in the watershed (Figure 7.1). Plutonium $^{239+240}$ and ^{238}Pu were measured; by convention we refer to the former as ^{239}Pu. Monthly composites of continuously sampled water were taken between September 1979 and January 1982 from a then newly created station at Glenmont (RM 141), near the head of tidal waters, and many cores and dredge samples taken over the length of the river, mostly during 1980. Plutonium isotopes were measured by alpha spectrometry following chemical separation and purification. Although we refer to Plutonium measurements obtained in sediments and water, these data have been published elsewhere (Linsalata et al. 1980, 1985; Simpson et al. 1987). We report here only results related to the soil cores as these data are germane to the erosional input model discussed in the first half of this paper.

SOURCES OF RADIONUCLIDES TO THE RIVER ESTUARY

Reactor Inputs

A continuous function of the NYUIEM has been to evaluate radionuclide inputs to the river estuary from major sources. Reported annual discharges occurring since the onset of nuclear power generation at Indian Point are summarized in Table 7.1. Peak discharges occurred in 1971 as a result of an undetected leak in the primary heat exchange loop of Unit 1, which was taken out of service in 1974. Since power generation began in 1962, totals of 50 Ci of ^{137}Cs, 36 Ci of ^{134}Cs, 32 Ci of ^{60}Co, 21 Ci of ^{58}Co, and 44 Ci of ^{54}Mn have been discharged to liquid effluent. Accounting for physical decay to 1987, these quantities are reduced to 37 Ci of ^{137}Cs, 1 Ci of ^{134}Cs, 6 Ci of ^{60}Co, <0.7 Ci of ^{58}Co, and <0.1 of ^{54}Mn (Table 7.1).

Earlier work has demonstrated that no plutonium of reactor origin has been discharged to the river estuary (Linsalata 1979; Linsalata et al. 1980, Linsalata 1984). As for other transuranic elements, from very limited data reported earlier for surface sediment samples collected in the vicinity of Indian Point (NYUMC, 1985), we have not observed any ^{241}Am or ^{243,244}Cm above the levels expected from global fallout deposition.

TABLE 7.1.
Annual reactor discharges of ^{137}Cs, ^{134}Cs, ^{60}Co and ^{54}Mn to the river estuary.[a]

Year	(Ci)				
	^{137}Cs	^{134}Cs	^{60}Co	^{53}Co	^{54}Mn
1966	0.10	~0.10[b]	1.68	—	3.80
1967	1.30	~1.30[b]	5.27	—	14.40
1968	2.30	~2.30[b]	3.82	—	5.90
1969	5.80	~5.80[b]	3.88	5.82	5.30
1970	1.26	1.10	2.56	2.23	0.80
1971	22.55	16.44	4.80	2.04	10.08
1972	6.48	4.32	1.20	0.24	2.40
1973	0.60	0.36	0.24	2.40	0.12
1974	0.70	0.25	0.30	1.47	0.10
1975	1.44	0.68	2.49	0.71	0.35
1976	1.54	0.76	0.39	0.41	0.06
1977	0.68	0.38	0.25	0.61	0.08
1978	0.60	0.27	0.29	0.35	0.05
1979	0.80	0.29	0.18	0.36	0.04
1980	0.72	0.23	0.28	0.61	0.04
1981	0.39	0.22	1.32	1.59	0.13
1982	0.59	0.25	0.19	0.09	0.02
1983	0.17	0.05	0.42	0.24	0.04
1984	0.43	0.25	0.49	0.39	0.03
1985	0.44	0.23	0.28	0.18	0.01
1986	0.38	0.21	0.57	0.72	0.02
1987	0.75	0.24	0.74	0.67	0.01
Totals	50.1	36.0	31.6	21.2	43.8
Totals (decay-corrected to 1987)[c]	36.6	0.92	5.95	—	0.03

[a] Discharge data obtained courtesy of the Consolidated Edison Co. of New York, Inc., and the New York Power Authority. Although Indian Point Unit I went critical in 1963, power generation was maintained at a low level until 1966 and no releases are assumed to have occurred prior to 1966.

[b] Cesium-134 was not measured isotopically prior to 1969. Isotopic measurements conducted by Lentsch (1974) during 1969 and 1970 indicated a ^{134}Cs/^{137}Cs ratio of unity. This ratio was assumed to exist for discharges occurring prior to 1969.

[c] Total input, corrected for decay = $T_i^c = (T_i + T_{i-1}^c\, e^{->t})$.

Fallout Inputs

Fallout deposition from past and to a much smaller extent more contemporary detonations of nuclear weapons in the atmosphere has contributed still measurable quantities of ^{137}Cs, ^{239,240}Pu, ^{238}Pu, and ^{241}Am among others, to the Hudson. Fallout from weapons testing has not contributed measureable quantities of ^{134}Cs, ^{60}Co, ^{58}Co, or ^{54}Mn. Thus the presence of these isotopes in river estuary sediments can be reasonably attributed to reactor discharges.

The fallout deposition of ^{137}Cs in New York City since 1954 is shown in Figure 7.2. The annual deposition of ^{137}Cs and ^{239,240}Pu over the same time period (the deposition rate of ^{239,240}Pu is about 2% that of ^{137}Cs) from weapons fallout is calculated from the measured deposition of fallout-produced ^{90}Sr and the ratio of the annual mean NYC surface-air concentrations of ^{137}Cs to ^{90}Sr (EML 1982). Based on measurements of fallout ^{137}Cs and ^{239,240}Pu in soil cores taken at various locations within the watershed in 1982 (Table 7.2), the integrated soil accumulation of these radionuclides is in reasonable agreement with the estimated, decay-corrected values obtained from the NYC deposition data of 112 mCi/km^2 for ^{137}Cs and 2.19 mCi/km^2 for ^{239,240}Pu. Accordingly, the time history and magnitudes of fallout deposition estimated from the NYC data are appropriate for estimating radionuclide depositions to the entire 293 km^2 watershed. Peak inputs from fallout are shown to have occurred between 1962 and 1964 (Figure 7.2), corresponding to the maximum atmospheric testing prior to the Nuclear Test Ban Treaty of 1963.

Minimal deposition occurring after 1981 ($\approx$ mCi/km^2 of ^{137}Cs per year) is the result of the absence of any significant atmospheric testing since October 1980 (Linsalata and Cohen 1982). Estimates of the cumulative deposition of ^{137}Cs and ^{134}Cs in the New York metropolitan area from Chernobyl fallout in 1986 are 0.26 and 0.14 mCi/km^2, respectively (EML, 1986). Chernobyl fallout contributed about 75 mCi of ^{137}Cs and 40 mCi ^{134}Cs during approximately 30 days in May 1986. The impact of Chernobyl fallout on ^{137}Cs and ^{134}Cs concentrations in the Hudson River samples was shown to be negligible (NYUMC 1988).

THE DRAINAGE BASIN AS A CONTINUOUS SOURCE OF FALLOUT NUCLIDES

Erosion Estimates and Sediment Input to the Lower River

The removal of surface-deposited fallout radionuclides from soils via erosional processes constitutes a major and continuous pathway for

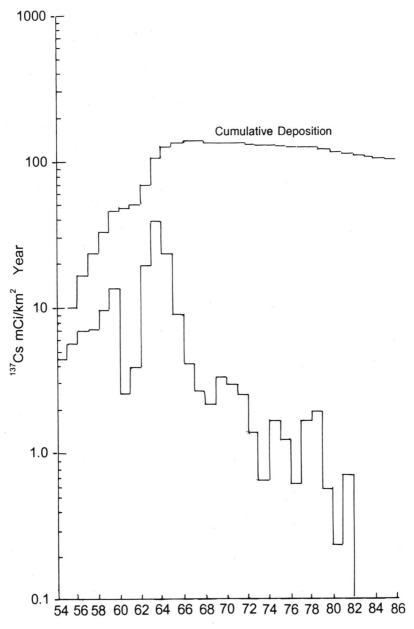

FIGURE 7.2.
Annual and cumulative deposition of fallout ^{137}Cs
in the New York City area.

TABLE 7.2.
Summary of natural radionuclide concentrations and cumulative activity of man-made radionuclides in soil cores collected from the watershed.

Map No. (2)	Site	Cumulative Activity (mCi/km² ± 1 SD)		$^{239}Pu/^{137}Cs$	Mean Concentration (pCi/g ± 1 SD)				Comments on Land Usage
		^{239}Pu	^{137}Cs		^{40}K	^{228}Th	^{226}Ra		
1	Warensburg, N.Y.	N.A.[1]	182 ± 4	—	19.2 ± 1.5	0.7 ± 0.1	0.6 ± 0.1		Undisturbed-owner verified
3	New Baltimore, N.Y.	1.80 ± 0.06	121 ± 6	.015 ± .001	18.7 ± 3.4	1.6 ± 0.1	1.4 ± 0.2		Undisturbed-owner verified
2	Glen, N.Y.	1.60 ± 0.07	108 ± 5	.015 ± .001	18.6 ± 1.1	1.1 ± 0.1	1.0 ± 0.1		Tilled-owner verified
4	Selkirk, N.Y.	1.70 ± 0.10	75 ± 4	.023 ± .002	15.1 ± 0.5	0.6 ± 0.1	0.7 ± 0.1		Uncertain; possibly tilled to a depth of 10 to 15 cm within past 25 years
5	Newburgh, N.Y.	N.A.	77 ± 4	—	8.3 ± 0.8	1.0 ± 0.1	0.9 ± 0.1		Uncertain; possibly tilled to a depth of 13 cm within past 25 years

[1] N.A. = not analyzed.
[2] See Figure 7.1.

their entry into rivers and estuaries (Lentsch 1974; Linsalata 1984; Olsen et al. 1981; Simpson et al. 1987; Foster and Hakonson 1987). Due to strong binding tendencies of both radionuclides to soil and freshwater sediments ($K_{d's} \approx 10^5$, Linsalata et al. 1985), the delivery of ^{137}Cs and ^{239,240}Pu to the Hudson River from the watershed occurs predominantly in association with eroded soils and to a lesser extent as soluable components entering the river via runoff.

We have used USDA (1974) estimates of soil erosion from both disturbed (tilled) and nondisturbed land within the 3 distinct subbasins of the watershed (the upper Hudson, the Mohawk, and the lower Hudson), together with estimates of the fractional delivery of eroded soils to their respective riverine endpoints as the basis for calculating fallout ^{137}Cs and ^{239,240}Pu inputs to the lower Hudson from erosion.

For the entire watershed, the total soil loss rate is estimated to be 1.03×10^{10} kg y^{-1} (Table 7.3). The average soil loss rate is estimated to be 0.29 kg/m^2 y^{-1}, a value virtually identical with that calculated for the entire New York state area (0.3 kg/m^2 y^{-1} [USDA 1974]).

The estimation of soil loss occurring in each subbasin can be used to determine the fractional delivery of eroded soils (and sorbed contaminants) from land surfaces into a receiving water body, provided that data on the transport of suspended soils (sediments) is obtainable. Sediment rating curves for the two major tributaries of the lower Hudson were constructed from available data (USGS 1977, 1978, 1979, 1980, 1981) on sediment load and mean discharge for the upper Hudson River at Waterford and for the Mohawk River at Cohoes, N.Y.

The equations resulting from the least squares regression of the data for each river system are:

Upper Hudson River: $Y = 0.0059 (x)^{1.98}$ $r^2 = 0.82$ (1)
Mohawk River: $Y = 0.0071 (x)^{2.12}$ $r^2 = 0.89$ (2)

where:

Y = suspended sediment load (mtons/day = 10^3 kg/day)

and

X = monthly mean discharge (m^3/s) for each river.

The exponents or slopes of the best fit lines fall within the range of 2.0 to 3.0 reported by Leopold et al. (1964) as typical of most river systems.

TABLE 7.3.
Subbasin soil loss estimates.

Sub-basin	Total Area (km²)[1]	Total Soil Loss (kg/yr) × 10⁻⁸ [1]	Avg. Soil Loss (kg/m²-yr)	Delivery Ratio[3]	% Area Disturb.[2]	Avg. Soil Loss (kg/m²-yr)		
						Disturbed	(Tilled)[4]	Non-disturbed
Upper Hudson	11598	15.9	0.137	~0.08	9.3	0.745	(0.62)	0.1
Mohawk	9365	46.9	0.501	~0.05	22.6	1.65	(1.1)	0.1
Lower Hudson	14071	39.9	0.284	?	21.6	0.962	(0.83)	0.1
Entire watershed	35034	102.7	0.293	—	—	—	—	—

[1] Calculated from data reported by U.S.D.A., 1974. Total soil loss includes losses from all cropland, pastureland, woodland, urban land, construction sites, "other land," stream and road banks.
[2] Disturbed land area includes that land currently cropped, formerly cropped, urban land, and construction sites.
[3] The delivery ratio (DR) is defined as the ratio of the amount of sediment reaching the outlet of a watershed to the amount of sediment produced by erosion (i.e., the gross erosion). To estimate the DR for the Mohawk and upper Hudson River basins under typical flow conditions, monthly mean discharge rates for those rivers during WY1969 (mean Green Island discharge = 388 m³/s compared to a 55-year mean of 376 m³/s) were used in power function relationships describing sediment flux as a function of mean discharge.
[4] Values in parentheses for tilled land represent the average soil loss estimates for disturbed land minus those losses occurring from stream banks. This estimate is more representative of soil losses occurring over truly tilled land as opposed to those calculated for disturbed land, which include stream bank erosion.

The rating equations indicate that, for equal discharge, the particulate load (Y) of the Mohawk will exceed that for the upper Hudson, which is not surprising considering that total estimated soil loss in the Mohawk subbasin was shown (Table 7.3) to be three times greater that that estimated for the upper Hudson subbasin.

Mean monthly discharge rates for the upper Hudson and Mohawk rivers were available for WY1969, a year in which river discharge as measured at the Green Island gaging station was very similar to the long-term average (388 m^3/s vs 376 m^3/s). Since sediment load measurements for WY1969 were not made by USGS, equations 1 and 2 were used to estimate the loads for typical flow rates. Annual suspended loads for typical discharges were calculated to be 250,713 mtons and 124,983 mtons for the Mohawk and upper Hudson Rivers, respectively. For typical discharges, the Mohawk River and its subbasin may thus account for two-thirds of the particulate load coming over the Troy Dam.

From Table 7.3, the total soil loss in the upper Hudson subbasin was estimated to be 15.9×10^8 kg/y, while 46.9×10^8 kg/y was the estimated loss for the Mohawk subbasin. Thus, the best estimates for the delivery ratio (DR) (see footnote, 3, Table 7.3) for each subbasin are:

$$\text{upper Hudson subbasin: DR} = \frac{1.24 \times 10^8 \text{ kg/y}}{15.9 \times 10^8 \text{ kg/y}} = 0.079$$

$$\text{Mohawk subbasin: DR} = \frac{2.51 \times 10^8 \text{ kg/y}}{46.9 \times 10^8 \text{ ky/y}} = 0.054$$

These values of the DR appear reasonable when compared to a mean DR of 0.042 ± 0.061 ($\pm$ 1 SDM) determined by Wade and Heady (1978) for 105 major United States rivers.

In addition to eroded soil entering the lower Hudson River from the Mohawk and upper Hudson, the many smaller tributaries south of the Troy Dam all contribute eroded soil in unknown quantities. Some of these streams are gaged for flow determination, although concentrations of suspended particulates are not measured. In the absence of these data we assume arbitrarily that the DR for the lower subbasin is intermediate (≈ 0.165) between that estimated for the upper Hudson and Mohawk subbasins. A DR of 0.65 for the tributaries south of the Troy Dam would correspond to an annual sediment delivery of $(39.9 \times 10^8 \text{ kg/y} \times 0.065) = 2.6 \times 10^8$ kg/y, and a total delivery to the lower river, for average discharges, of $(2.6 + 1.25 + 2.51) \times 10^8 = 6.4 \times 10^8$ kg/y.

Panuzio (1965) has estimated an annual suspended sediment load of 7.5×10^8 kg/y from twice daily samples collected at Poughkeepsie, N.Y. (RM 72) from September 1959 to August 1960. This estimated load is 17% greater than the load estimated here. The annual mean discharge at Green Island during WY1960 was 487 m³/s, 25.5% greater than the annual mean discharge for WY1969. It is not surprising that the sediment load estimated during WY1960 exceeds that estimated for WY1969, given the difference in mean discharge rates. It would appear that a DR of 0.065 for the lower subbasin results in a total estimate river suspended load that is consistent with Panuzio's findings.

A MODEL OF PLUTONIUM AND CESIUM MIGRATION IN WATERSHED SOILS

For Pu and Cs, as well as for other contaminants introduced to the surface, soil usage and composition will have a marked effect on the concentration/depth profiles established in soils over time. Tilling the soil dilutes the surface concentration of a surface deposited, tightly soil-bound contaminant. The degree of dilution is dependent mainly on the depth of tilling. For undisturbed soil, the concentration/depth profiles of the radionuclides can be represented as negatively sloped exponentials (Figure 7.3), with the magnitude of the slopes dependent on a multitude of processes including soil porosity and permeability, particle size distribution, pH, Eh, precipitation and evapotranspiration rates, organic composition, biological reworking of the soil, the temporal history of pollutant introduction, and the elemental solubility in soil solutions.

For the purpose of reconstructing Pu and Cs input to the lower river, estimating the rate at which these elements are being deleted from the surface soils is most important. As the nuclides penetrate the soil, they become less susceptible to erosive forces and a continual reduction in the magnitude of particulate-bound and soluable radionuclide that reaches the river is expected. Since the average rate of soil loss for tilled and undisturbed soils has already been determined, the focus is shifted to a determination of how the soil concentration of ^{239}Pu and ^{137}Cs have changed over time.

A schematic of the soil model is shown in Figure 7.4. The rectangular boxes labeled 1st (or A), 2nd (or B) 3rd (or C) . . . N, represent the soil compartments. Each of the 12 compartments is 2.54 cm thick (corresponding to the depth of sample sectioning) with the exception of N, the residual compartment, which represents all

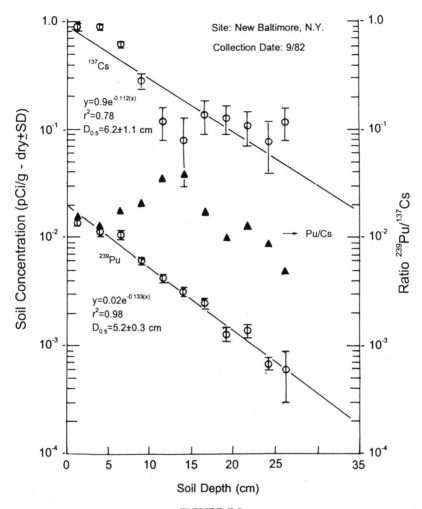

FIGURE 7.3.
^{137}Cs and ^{239}Pu in composite undisturbed soil cores collected from the lower Hudson River subbasin.

depths greater than 26.7 cm (i.e., the greatest depth sampled). The transfer rate constants, labeled $C_{1,2}$, $C_{2,3}$, $C_{3,4}$, etc., represent the downward fractional transfer rates of radionuclides between soil compartments one and two, two and three, etc. The rate constant CH represents the horizontal transfer rate constant resulting from the erosional removal of soil and radionuclide from the first (surface) compartment.

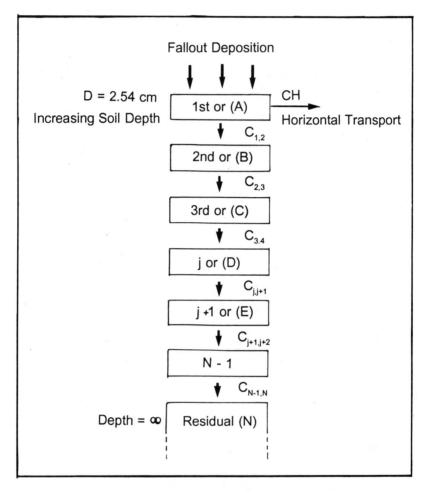

FIGURE 7.4.
Model schematic for predicting radionuclide migration in undisturbed soil.

Compartmental transfer rate constants were introduced one at a time, their magnitude allowed to vary, and the resulting radionuclide depth profile for each iteration compared with that measured at the New Baltimore, N.Y. site (Figure 7.3). The goodness of fit of the model distribution was determined after each iteration by comparing the magnitude of the sum of the squared deviations of the (observed-expected) radionuclide accumulations (i.e., the residual sum of squares) from each soil compartment. The "best fit" to the observed data was taken to be that combination of rate constants yielding a minimum value for the residual sum of squares.

The model contains the following assumptions:

a) The annual fallout deposition to the Hudson watershed is identical to that reported in Figure 7.2;
b) The deposition occurring each year is uniformly and instantaneously mixed within the surface soil compartment (0-2.54 cm); and
c) with the exception of horizontal transfer, all radionuclide transfer from one compartment to the adjacent deeper compartment occurs in one direction only and is instantaneous, resulting in complete mixing within the receiving compartment.

The model was designed to output, in increments of one year (beginning in 1954), the accumulated soil activity (i.e., mCi/km^2) and the fractional accumulation, normalized to the actual measured accumulations per cm, within each soil compartment resulting from the integrated fallout delivery of ^{137}Cs and ^{239}Pu through the year for which the depth profile is calculated. The equations determining the accumulations of each radionuclide within each compartment, expressed as functions of the annual fallout deposition, the decay constants, and the transfer rate constants have been given elsewhere (Linsalata 1984).

Many iterations of the program were run before a suitable minimum number of different rate constants (and their magnitudes) were found. The normalized (i.e., fractional accumulation/cm/compartment) ^{239}Pu accumulation expected within each soil compartment for the year in which the sample was taken, together with the measured value (±1 SD), is shown as a function of depth in Figure 7.5 left. For the normalized data, the model produced three overpredictions, three underpredictions, and five values within ±1 SD of the measured results. From the observed and predicted ^{137}Cs compartment accumulations (Figure 7.5 right), it is apparent that the model performs adequately down to a depth of 15 to 17 cm, below which depth continous underpredictions result. The uniformity of the measured ^{137}Cs profile beneath 10 cm is difficult to reconcile. Additional measurements of undisturbed soil should be carried out to determine the reproducibility of the observed profile and to adjust the model transfer constants as necessary.

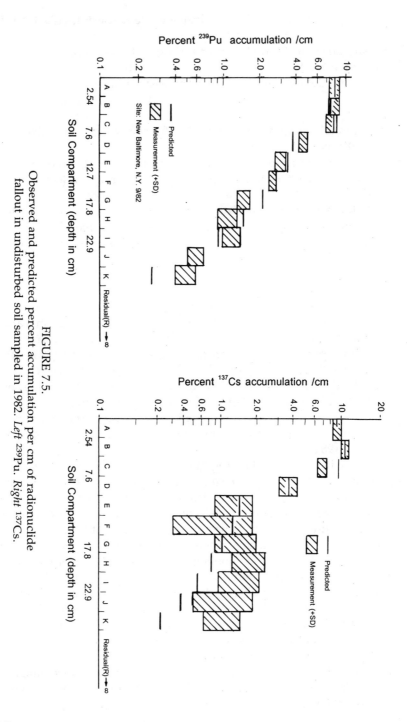

FIGURE 7.5. Observed and predicted percent accumulation per cm of radionuclide fallout in undisturbed soil sampled in 1982. *Left* ^{239}Pu. *Right* ^{137}Cs.

RECONSTRUCTION OF FALLOUT ^{239}Pu AND ^{137}Cs INPUT TO THE LOWER HUDSON FROM THE WATERSHED

Estimates of the annual, subbasin delivery of fallout-deposited ^{137}Cs and ^{239}Pu to the river from particulate erosion of undisturbed soil were obtained from the following equation:

$$I_i = P_{i,1} \times CH \times A \times Dr \times ER \qquad (4)$$

where:

I_i = annual particulate-bound radionuclide input to river in the ith year (mCi/y);
$P_{i,1}$ = the expected radionuclide accumulation for the ith year in the surface soil compartment (mCi/km^2)
CH = horizontal loss rate constant from the surface compartment resulting from particulate erosion (per year);
A = surface area of undisturbed land in each subbasin (km^2);
DR = the delivery ratio as determined for each subbasin (unitless); and
ER = the enrichment ratio (unitless).

The enrichment ratio is calculated as the concentration of radionuclide measured in suspended solids in the river (pCi/kg), divided by the concentration in the surface or erosion compartment. The term enrichment refers to the fact that the size distribution of eroded particles that ultimately reach the river will be skewed toward the smaller diameter particles as larger ones are depleted by earlier deposition on the landscape. The enrichment expected in "fines," together with increasing ^{239}Pu and ^{137}Cs soil concentrations, which we have observed with decreasing particle sizes (Linsalata 1984), will result in enhanced ^{239}Pu and ^{137}Cs concentrations on suspended sediment relative to bulk soil. Using the mean ^{239}Pu and ^{137}Cs concentrations previously determined (Linsalata et al. 1985) in suspended solids collected at RM 141 between 1979 and 1981 (18.9 and 2267 pCi/kg, respectively) and in the surface 2.54 cm of the New Baltimore soil core (14.0 and 900 pCi/kg, respectively), the enrichment ratios for ^{239}Pu and ^{137}Cs are 1.4 and 2.5, respectively. Larger ERs were used for tilled soils due to lower concentrations measured within the tilled layer of the Glen soil core (Table 7.2). The horizontal or erosion rate constant CH, for undisturbed land, was derived from the USDA soil loss estimate of 0.1 kg/m^2/y. For a compartment thickness of 2.54 cm, and a soil bulk density of 1.4 g/cm³, the loss rate constant, CH, is equal to 0.0028 per year.

The annual loss of particulate-bound radionuclides from disturbed or tilled soils was calculated in a slightly different fashion from that shown by equation 3. Since soil compartment accumulations are controlled by gross physical mixing, there is no difference in compartment accumulations and, thus, no need to compartmentalize the annual tilled-soil accumulations. Since the average soil loss rates are considerably higher for disturbed vs undisturbed soil (Table 7.3), the depths to which the radionuclides are mixed from tilling were continually readjusted in order to predict the proper radionuclide concentration as a function of time.

The annual runoff delivery of fallout ^{239}Pu of ^{137}Cs to the lower river was calculated as:

$$I^D_i = C^D_i \times F_i \tag{5}$$

where:

I^D_i = Annual input to river of dissolved ^{239}Pu or ^{137}Cs for the ith year (fCi/y);
C^D_i = equilibrium concentration expected in runoff (dissolved phase) for the ith year (fCi/L); and
F_1 = annual fresh water discharge for the ith year (calculated as 1.4 × annual mean discharge at Green Island [L/y]).

Equilibrium concentrations in runoff were approximated by:

$$C^D_i = C^s_i / K_{d(a)} \tag{6}$$

where:

C^D_i = expected equilibrium concentration in the dissolved phase for the ith year (FCi/L);
C^s_i = expected equilibrium concentration in the solid phase for the ith year (fCi/kg); and
$K_{d(a)}$ = apparent distribution coefficient (L/kg) (= 1 × 10^5 for ^{137}Cs and 1.8 × 10^5 for ^{239}Pu (Linsalata et al. 1985).

To solve for C^D_i on an annual basis, the assumption is made that equilibrium conditions exist between the radionuclide concentrations in the surface layer of soil (top 2.54 cm) and in runoff. Equilibrium condition may truly exist during low and moderate runoff conditions, although this assumption will not be valid during heavy runoff conditions when the upper soil layer becomes saturated (or armored), causing additional precipitation to skirt off the surface. Under these conditions, concentration in runoff calculated using equation 5 would underestimate the true concentrations. The expected surface soil concentrations used in these calculations were those determined using the soil model. Since undisturbed soil is representative of 82% of the total watershed area, the equilibrium runoff concentrations were calculated assuming all soils were undisturbed.

Deposition directly to the surface of the river estuary has certainly contributed significant amounts of ^{137}Cs and ^{239}Pu. Given that solid-solution equilibrium partitioning is established quickly in the river the dissolved concentrations in freshwater reaches of the river, assuming a constant deposition rate, can be expressed by:

$$C^D_i = R_i/[F_i(1+K_{d(a)} M)] \qquad (7)$$

where:

C^D_i = equilibrium concentration (dissolved) expected for the ith year as a result of direct deposition (fCi/L);
R_i = annual fallout deposition rate for the ith year to the freshwater surface area (mCI/y);
F_i = annual freshwater discharge for the ith year (L/y);
$K_{d(a)}$ = ^{239}Pu or ^{137}Cs apparent distribution coefficient for fresh water (L/kg); and
M = average concentration of suspended solids (kg/L).

Annual mean dissolved concentrations of fallout ^{137}Cs and ^{239}Pu in freshwater reaches of the Hudson would then be approximated as [$C^D_i + C^{D'}_i$]. Concentrations of dissolved phase ^{137}Cs expected in river freshwater are reported in Table 7.4, along with the annual average dissolved phase concentrations computed from long-term measurements at Chelsea, excluding the sample means for 1964 and 1965[1], the expected annual averages are generally well within a factor of two of the annual averages computed from the samples

---

[1]Drought conditions during these years resulted in maximum salt water intrusion. As a result, the $K_{d(a)}$ used for ^{137}Cs is expected to be much less than the value of 1×10^5 used for fresh waters (Linsalata et al. (1985). Use of a lower $K_{d(a)}$ would result in higher estimates of dissolved phase concentrations.

TABLE 7.4.
Estimated equilibrium concentrations of ^{137}Cs (dissolved) in runoff and Hudson River fresh water.

Year	Estimated Equilibrium Conc. (fCi/L)			Annual Mean Conc. Calculated from Chelsea[3] Data (fCi/L±SEM)	(N)
	In Runoff[1]	From Surface Deposition[1]	Total[2]		
1954	1	7	8	NA[4]	
1955	3	9	12	"	
1956	4	9	13	"	
1957	6	15	21	"	
1958	8	15	23	"	
1959	11	23	34	"	
1960	11	3	14	"	
1961	11	7	18	"	
1962	15	39	54	"	
1963	25	83	108	"	
1964	29	52	81	~300	
1965	28	23	51	200±10	(24)
1966	27	8	35	100±9	(11)
1967	25	5	30	30±3	(15)
1968	23	3	26	NA	(0)
1969	22	5	27	25±3	(6)
1970	20	5	25	24±2	(18)
1971	19	3	22	~11	(9)
1972	18	1	19	~13	(13)
1973	16	1	17	13±6	(13)
1974	15	2	17	13±4	(16)
1975	14	1	15	21±4	(14)
1976	13	1	14	10±11	(15)
1977	12	2	14	10±4	(15)
1978	11	3	14	17±4	(23)
1979	10	1	11	28±11	(17)
1980	9	1	10	22±7	(14)
1981	9	2	11	16±3	(12)
1982	8	1	9	NA	(0)

[1] Estimated dissolved concentrations in runoff and those resulting from fallout deposition directly to the surface of the river estuary were calculated from eqs. 5 and 6, respectively. A constant $K_{d(a)}$ of 1×10^5 L.kg^{-1} has been assumed.

[2] Total concentrations expected in river freshwater were calculated as the sum of the concentrations resulting from runoff and from surface deposition.

[3] (N) represents the number of biweekly composite samples analyzed each year from the Chelsea location for the period 1969–1981. Prior to this, grab samples were taken. SEM represents the standard error of the mean = $SDM/\sqrt{n}$.

[4] NA = Not analyzed.

collected at Chelsea. Although much fewer measurements are available, ^{239}Pu monthly composits collected continuously at RM 141 (Glenmont) yielded annual mean dissolved concentrations of 0.11 ± 0.02 fCi/L (±SEM, N = 11) for 1980 and 0.17 ± 0.02 fCi/L (N = 12) for 1981. Predicted results for these years are 0.09 and 0.08 fCi/L.

The estimated annual inputs of fallout ^{239}Pu to the river estuary from surface deposition, runoff, and erosion of disturbed and undisturbed land surfaces are shown in Figure 7.6 left. Estimated annual inputs from runoff and particulate erosion have also been summed and are shown in Figure 7.6 as "total watershed input." Barring contributions from the marine environment, it is clear from Figure 7.6 left that the input of fallout ^{239}Pu to the river estuary has, since 1966, been dominated by inputs arising from the erosion of fallout contaminated watershed soils. A similar conclusion was reached by Olsen et al. (1981) in their attempt to formulate an input model that would reflect the observed depth distribution of ^{239}Pu and ^{137}Cs in a Hudson River sediment core removed from an area characterized by a moderately rapid sediment deposition rate (1cm/y).

The estimated annual delivery of fallout ^{137}Cs to the Hudson

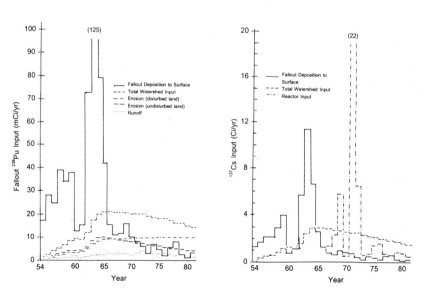

FIGURE 7.6.
Estimated delivery of radionuclides to the Hudson River estuary. *Left* ^{239}Pu. *Right* Fallout and reactor released ^{137}Cs.

River Estuary resulting from surface deposition (to the entire surface area) and particulate erosion plus runoff (combined and reported as "total watershed input") is shown in Figure 7.6 right. Included in 7.6 right are the annual quantities released from the Indian Point reactors. Excluding reactor inputs during 1969, 1971, and 1972, annual inputs of ^{137}Cs to the river estuary have, since 1965–1966, been dominated by removal processes occurring in the watershed. Based on reactor ^{137}Cs discharges occurring after 1982 (Table 7.1), this conclusion remains valid.

From Hudson River samples collected from freshwater reaches in 1969 and 1970, Lentsch (1974) also concluded that inputs from the watershed were more significant than fallout directly to the surface of the river during those years. The reconstructed history of ^{137}Cs input from the watershed is very similar to that developed for ^{239}Pu, as would be expected based on their similar large distribution coefficients, the similar depth profiles in soils, and the identical time period of fallout from the atmosphere. It is clear from Figures 7.6a and 7.6b that particulate erosion is, and has been, the major source of watershed input for both ^{239}Pu and ^{137}Cs.

Inputs of ^{239}Pu and ^{137}Cs to the river from the watershed have declined since about 1970 (Figure 7.6). The declining inputs are mainly attributed to both the migration of these nuclides to deeper soil and to the greatly reduced rates of fallout deposition. The effective half-times for decline (which include the processes of radiological decay, penetration into the soil, and erosional removal) are estimated (by regression of the predicted "total" watershed inputs reported in Figures 7.6 for 1972–1983) to be 20 years for ^{239}Pu and 13 years for ^{137}Cs. The difference in effective half-times is mainly attributable to the much shorter radiological decay half-life of 30.2 y for ^{137}Cs than 24,000 years for ^{239}Pu.

A summary of the estimated input budgets (excluding marine contributions) for both nuclides is reported in Table 7.5. Summing the input quantities expected from each source, totals of 1.0 Ci of ^{239}Pu (or greater depending on the probable contribution from the marine environment) and 111 Ci of ^{137}Cs are estimated as having been delivered to the river estuary as of 1980. Based on the input estimates in Table 7.5, the reactors at Indian Point have contributed $\approx$ 34% of the decay-corrected total ^{137}Cs derived from all sources. The total input estimates for Pu and Cs developed here are in excellent agreement with those given in an earlier publication (Simpson et al. 1987), although certain differences exist with respect to the magnitudes of ^{137}Cs input from erosion (19 Ci vs 34 Ci) and runoff (20 Ci vs 5.2 Ci).

TABLE 7.5.
Cumulative inputs of ^{239}Pu and ^{137}Cs to the Hudson River Estuary: total mCi as of 1980.

	Watershed		Direct Dep. to Surface[2]	Ind. Pt. Reactor Effluent	Marine Sources	Total
	Runoff (Dissolved)	Partic. Erosion				
^{239}Pu	52	343	639	0	?(+)[3]	>1,034
^{137}Cs[1]	5,170	33,932	34,000	38,000	?(−)[4]	111,102
Pu/Cs	0.01	0.01	0.019	0	—	—

[1] Decay corrected.
[2] River-estuary surface area of 293 km² used.
[3] Marine sources have probably contributed significant quantities of ^{239}Pu to the estuary. Accordingly, the total input quantity shown is a low estimate (Simpson et al., 1987).
[4] Salinity-related desorption has probably removed ^{137}Cs from the estuary sediments.

LONG-TERM MONITORING RESULTS FOR RADIOCESIUM

Control Locations

Annual mean concentration of ^{137}Cs in surface sediments from Newburgh Bay, whole resident fish from Esopus Meadows, and water filtrates from Chelsea (our control locations) are plotted in Figure 7.7 for the period 1964–1987. The most striking aspect of the long-term trends observed in the freshwater reaches of the river estuary is the persistence of fallout-derived radiocesium in these major components of the aquatic ecosystem.

Beginning in the late 1960s (i.e., well after the period of peak input from fresh fallout (deposition), a gradual decline in ^{137}Cs mean concentrations is evident for surface sediments of Newburgh Bay, in mixed species of nonmigratory fish, and dissolved in fresh water. Assuming, for simplicity, that the rate of decline in these sediments is governed by first-order kinetics and that inputs of fallout ^{137}Cs occurring after 1967 were negligible compared to those that occurred earlier, the decline of ^{137}Cs concentrations in Newburgh Bay surface sediments 1971–1987 is occurring with an effective half-time of 11.5 years ($r = -0.81$). This effective half-time must be considered a max-

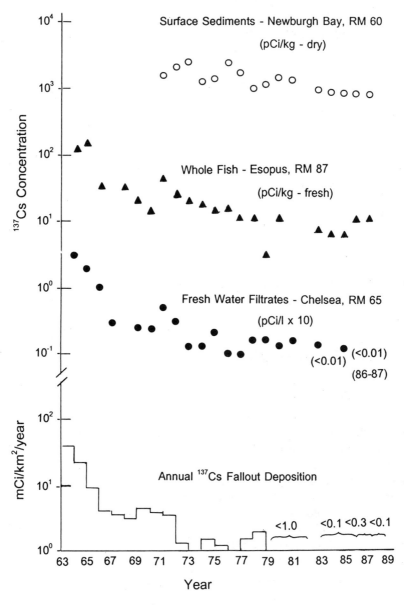

FIGURE 7.7.
Annual mean ^{137}Cs concentrations in water, fish, and sediments sampled at least 17 miles upstream from Indian Point.

imum value since additional inputs from both watershed erosion and "fresh" fallout deposition were occurring after 1967 (Figure 7.6).

A gradual decline in the mean ^{137}Cs concentrations in resident fish collected from upstream regions since the peak ^{137}Cs inputs from fallout deposition in 1967 is also evident from the Figure 7.7 data. Again, using a simple, single exponential model, the slope of the least squares regression fit to the concentration vs time data (1968–1987) can be used to calculate a maximum effective reduction half-time for fallout ^{137}Cs in resident freshwater fish of 8.7 years (r=−0.75). This half-time, which should not be confused with the biological half-time of radiocesium in estuarine fish (100–300 days; Jinks 1975), as measured following acute uptake, is actually an estimate of the rate of change (λ_e = ln 2/8.7 y = 0.08 /y) of available fallout ^{137}Cs to freshwater fish. That measurements of dissolved ^{137}Cs in freshwater regions can be used as a gross predictor of ^{137}Cs levels in various species of whole fish is indicated by regressing the long-term data (1964–1987) of mean ^{137}Cs concentrations in fish and freshwater filtrates (<0.45 μm) from Chelsea. The resulting equation:

$$Y(\text{conc. in fish pCi/kg}) = 501 \, (\text{pCi/L})_{diss} + 6.7$$

is obtained with r^2 = 0.85 and standard error of ± 16.7 (pCi/kg). We note that the magnitude of the uncertainty associated with the above expression is such that uncertainty in predicting average concentrations in mixed, freshwater fish species from mean dissolved levels of ^{137}Cs of <0.02 pCi/L exceeds 100%.

The long-term data for ^{137}Cs (fallout and reactor inputs) in various types of samples collected from the Indian Point vicinity are shown in Figures 7.8 and 7.9. Mean concentrations in resident fish and vegetation are seen to closely parallel concentrations in the water column (Figure 7.8) with sharp declines evident in all media following the relatively large discharges recorded during 1971 (Table 7.1). Concentrations in fish and water observed since 1983 have been among the lowest recorded since routine surveillance began in 1970, reflecting the low annual discharges of ^{137}Cs that have been sustained (Table 7.1). Beginning in the mid-1970s, and continuing to the present, concentrations in whole fish and water (dissolved) of other reactor-released radionuclides, such as ^{134}Cs, ^{60}Co, ^{58}Co, and ^{54}Mn, have generally been below detection limits, i.e., 10–14 pCi/kg (fish) and <0.02–0.04 pCi/L (water) for samples collected in the Indian Point vicinity. Cesium-137 concentrations in flesh of adult, anadromous species, such as shad and striped bass (Figure 7.8) are consistently

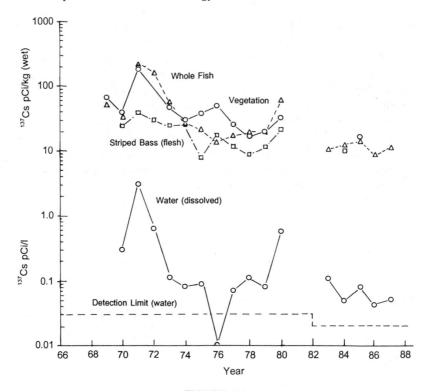

FIGURE 7.8
Annual mean ^{137}Cs concentrations in whole fish, rooted vegetation, and water (dissolved) collected from the Indian Point area.

lower than those recorded in resident species (Linsalata et al. 1986). This may result from migratory tendencies as well as from different feeding habits (e.g., shad do not feed actively during their spring spawning period in the estuary).

The annual average concentrations of ^{137}Cs in fish and water (dissolved) collected in the reactor vicinity were used to determine bioaccumulation factors (BF = pCi/kg / pCi /L) for ^{137}Cs, the nuclide of greatest dosimetric significance with respect to fish ingestion. The overall mean values (±SEM) for the ^{137}Cs (and ^{134}Cs) BF for fish collected in the typically brackish waters near Indian Point are as follows:

resident species:	225 ± 30
striped bass (flesh):	135 ± 31

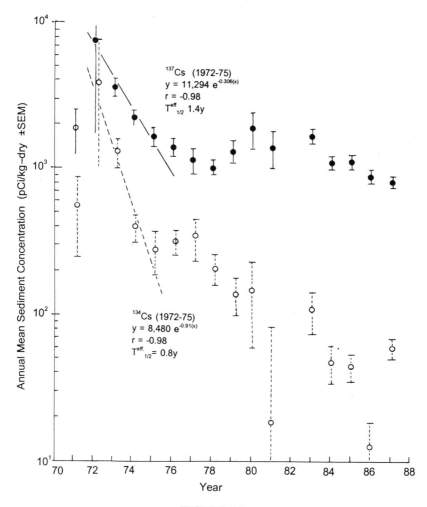

FIGURE 7.9.
Annual mean ¹³⁷Cs and ¹³⁴Cs concentrations in surface sediments collected in the vicinity of the Indian Point reactors.

shad (flesh):	64 ± 22
blue claw crab (flesh):	86 ± 45

As recently discussed (Linsalata et al. 1986), the use of these values in dosimetric models results in dose estimates from fish ingestion that are at least nine times lower than model estimates that rely on the "generic" (non site-specific) BF of 2,000 developed for freshwater environments (NRC, 1977).

The long-term (1970–1987) annual average concentrations of ^{137}Cs and ^{134}Cs (radiological half-life = 2.06 y) in surface sediments collected in the vicinity of Indian Point[2] are shown in Figure 7.9. The abrupt increase noted in 1972 resulted from the highest discharges ever recorded from this site (16 Ci ^{137}Cs and 11 Ci ^{134}Cs released between October 1971 and February 1982). Reactor releases of both ^{137}Cs and ^{134}Cs were very low for the remainder of the 1972 calendar year (0.52 Ci ^{137}Cs and 0.41 Ci ^{134}Cs) as well as during 1973, 1974, and 1975 (Table 7.1) compared to the quantities released between October 1971 and February 1972. Assuming a negligible contribution was made to the sediment radiocesium concentration from inputs (reactor and fallout) occurring after 1972, the rate of decline of ^{137}Cs and ^{134}Cs in surface sediments of the Indian Point vicinity can be determined from single exponential fits of the annual mean sediment concentrations for 1972 through 1975 as shown in Figure 7.9. The effective removal rates (λ_E), which include losses from both radiological decay (λ_{rad}) and physicochemical processes (λ_{pc}), are calculated to be 0.51/y and 0.91/y for ^{137}Cs and ^{134}Cs, respectively.

Since $\lambda_E = \lambda_{pc} + \lambda_{rad}$, the physicochemical removal rate constant (λpc) is calculated to be 0.49/y based on ^{137}Cs data and 0.57/y based on ^{134}Cs data ($\bar{x} = 0.53/y$). Although the processes (e.g., ion exchange and flushing during salinity intrusion, particle scouring, bed load transport, and burial/diffusion to deeper layers in the sediment) responsible for the removal of reactor radiocesium from the Indian Point vicinity surface sediments are expected to be identical in magnitude for the different isotopes, the apparently slower (by 15%) λ_{pc} value calculated from the ^{137}Cs data is attributed to ^{137}Cs input to the areas sediment from fallout and to relatively higher ^{137}Cs/^{134}Cs ratios in liquid effluent following peak inputs. These effective loss rate constants correspond to effective clearance half-times for reactor-re-

---

[2]The same locations (Lents Cove, Peekskill Bay, Indian Point mid-channel, Tomkins Cove, Verplanck, and Greens Cove) were sampled each season (approximately one sample per month per location May-October 1970–1980) with the exception of data reported for 1971 and 1972 (only the Indian Point mid-channel station sampled), 1981 (one sample point for each location on 6/16/81), 1982 (no data), and 1983–1987 (approximately three samples from each of these locations per year). The annual mean concentrations for all station samples in the Indian Point vicinity (Figure 7.9) were calculated by computing the grand average of the individual station averages.

leased radiocesium in surface sediments of the Indian Point vicinity of 1.36 y for ^{137}Cs and 0.76 y for ^{134}Cs. This rate of decline in the brackish sediments of the Indian Point vicinity is about eightfold faster than that calculated for the predominantly freshwater sediments of Newburgh Bay. This difference can be attributed primarily to salinity-related desorption of freshly deposited reactor radiocesium during period of saline intrusion (Lentsch 1974; Jinks and Wrenn 1976; Linsalata et al. 1985).

Based on the sediment ^{137}Cs data obtained 1975–1987, it would appear from Figure 7.9 that steady state concentrations exist in surface sediments with respect to source inputs (i.e., erosional input of fallout and ^{137}Cs and reactor discharges) and removal terms. Since reactor discharges) and removal terms. Since reactor discharges have been fairly constant over the more recent 5-year period at ≈ 0.4 Ci/y, the surface sediments should, under steady state conditions, contain a reactor-produced ^{137}Cs inventory equal to:

$$\frac{0.4 \text{ Ci y}^{-1}}{0.51 \text{ y}^{-1}} \approx 0.8 \text{ Ci}$$

Performing a similar calculation for ^{134}Cs, the surface sediments should contain a reactor-produced ^{134}Cs inventory equal to:

$$\frac{0.21 \text{ Ci y}^{-1}}{0.91 \text{ y}^{-1}} \approx 0.2 \text{ Ci.}$$

Thus, if there were no fallout-produced ^{137}Cs in sediments of the IP vicinity, we might expect to see under equilibrium conditions, ^{134}Cs/^{137}Cs ratios in surface sediments of $0.2/0.8 = 0.25$. The fact that we observe ratios on the order of 0.06 for sediments collected in 1986 and 1987 implies a continued, strong ^{137}Cs contribution in surface sediments from fallout.

Environmental Dosimetry

Fifty-year committed effective dose equivalents (to adults) from measured anthropogenic nuclides along aquatic pathways at control and reactor-vicinity locations have been calculated using ICRP-30 (ICRP 1979) ingestion dose factors, annual mean concentrations in aquatic media, and estimated intake rates or utilization times. The methods used for doses accrued via ingestion of fish and freshwater, externally

TABLE 7.6.
Summary of dose estimates resulting from ^{137}Cs + ^{134}Cs measurements in environmental samples.*

Dose Pathway	Usage Factor	Committed Effective Dose Equivalents ($nSv \pm 1$ SD)		
		Upstream Background Dose	Downstream Dose	(Downstream-Upstream)
Fish consumption (indigenous sp.)	3.9 kg y$^{-1\,a}$	50±50 (1971–80)^b	640±80 (1971)	590±90
"	"	"	70±40 (1974–80)^c	20±60
Water consumption	803 ℓ y$^{-1\,d}$	20±30 (1971–80)^e	not applicable	—
Shoreline recreation	140 h y$^{-1\,h}$	110±40 (1976–79)^f	460±110 (1977–78)^g	350±120
	12 h y$^{-1\,h}$	10±4 (1976–79)^f	40±10 (1977–78)^g	30±10
Swimming	50 h y$^{-1\,i}$	<<10 (1971–80)	10±4 (1971)	10±4
			0.1±0.1 (1979)	<1

*The sampling years for which the dose estimates are based are shown in parentheses.
^{a} Based on data in NMFS (1980).
^{b} Based on data from Figure 7.7.
^{c} Based on the average dose from ^{137}Cs + ^{134}Cs determined between 1974 and 1980 (Fig. 7.8 data).
^{d} Based on ICRP-30 fluids intake of 2.2 ℓ d^{-1}.
^{e} Based on long-term (1971–1980) average concentrations of dissolved ^{137}Cs and ^{134}Cs as measured at Chelsea, NY
^{f} From shoreline core data obtained at Esopus, N.Y.
^{g} Based on the mean exposure rate of 0.33 ± 0.08 μR/h^{-1} for ^{137}Cs + ^{134}Cs in Verplanck shoreline cores.
^{h} Twelve hours per year usage factor based on recommendations in Regulatory Guide 1.109 (NRC77). The 140 h y^{-1} usage factor is used for the purposes of this study and is based on an 8 h per week usage for a 17-week "summer session."
^{i} Fifty hours per year swimming usage factor is currently employed by the utilities for environmental dose assessment.

via swimming, and from external exposure along the estuary's banks have been previously described in detail (Linsalata et al., 1986).

Since, among all discharged radionuclides, radiocesium isotopes have been shown to be accountable for more than 75% of the radiation dose potentially received by people using the Hudson's resources (Jinks et al. 1973; Lentsch 1974; Wrenn et al. 1974; NYUMC 1988). We show a summary of the ^{137}Cs + ^{134}Cs doses calculated from environmental samples collected at upstream control and Indian Point vicinity locations during the year of maximum discharge (1971) and for subsequent time periods, which are reflective of routine discharges (Table 7.6).

From Table 7.6 it is clear that doses accrued through both swimming at Verplanck and consumption of water from Chelsea have been, and are currently, negligible. The two exposure pathways of relevance to human beings are fish consumption of resident species of fish (70±40 nSv/y, which is equivalent to 0.007 mrem/y, as averaged over the period 1974–1980) and external exposure resulting from shoreline recreation as calculated from core data obtained at Verplanck Beach. Maximum dose rates range from 40–460 nSv/y or from 0.004 to 0.046 mrem/y depending on utilization time and the exposure geometry assumed in calculation. Given the decline in radionuclide discharges that occurred in the 1980s (Table 7.1), the potential human exposures are correspondingly lower than those summarized in Table 7.6. When compared with cosmic and external terrestrial radiation doses measured at this locality from the natural radiation environment (0.4–1.25 mSv/y or 40–125 mrem/y; Jinks et al., 1973), the additional contributions from reactor effluents can be considered as vanishingly small.

Acknowledgments

This work has been supported by research contracts with the Consolidated Edison Co., Inc., of N.Y. (1969–1984) and the New York Power Authority (1978–1989), to whom the authors are indebted. Partial support was also provided by Center Grant no. ES00260, from the National Institute of Environmental Health Sciences, Center Grant no. 13343, from the National Cancer Institute, and Special Institutional Grant no. 00009, from the American Cancer Society.

II. FISHERY BIOLOGY

WILLIAM L. DOVEL
ANTHONY W. PEKOVITCH
THOMAS J. BERGGREN

8

Biology of the Shortnose Sturgeon (*Acipenser brevirostrum* Lesueur, 1818) in the Hudson River Estuary, New York

ABSTRACT

A knowledge of the life history of the shortnose sturgeon in the Hudson River provides a basis for management and conservation of this endangered species. Between 1975 and 1980, 2,750 shortnose sturgeon were tagged. In 1979 and 1980 the peak spawning period occurred between April 28 and May 11 in the reach between Coeymans and Troy (km 200 to 246). After spawning they move south to feed during the summer, some as far as the Tappan Zee. In the winter they concentrate near Esopus Meadows (km 140). Recapture data indicate that some individuals repeat this pattern of migration in successive years. The spawning population is estimated to be about 13,000 fish.

Pollution and impingement at power plants are potential threats to the shortnose sturgeon. Commercial fishing, however, appears to

188 Fishery Biology

have little effect. Channel dredging in the spawning and nursery areas could affect both adults and early life history stages and it is recommended that channel dredging north of Haverstraw Bay be done after June 15.

INTRODUCTION

The shortnose sturgeon and the Atlantic sturgeon (*Acipenser oxyrhynchus* Mitchill) were present in the Hudson when Dutch settlers first explored the River (Mitchell 1811), but it was not until the mid-1930s that an effort was made to gain an understanding of the life history of the shortnose sturgeon. The work of the New York State Department of Conservation (Greeley 1937) produced valuable information but did not define the spawning area or other important aspects of the life history of the species.

In the 1960s and 70s, data on the occurrence of the shortnose sturgeon in the Hudson was gathered through the extensive efforts of electric power industry consultants working for Consolidated Edison Company of New York, Niagara Mohawk Power Corporation, Central Hudson Gas and Electric Corporation, and Orange-Rockland Utility Company. However, these efforts did not appreciably increase our knowledge of the species in the Hudson Estuary. At that time, the early life stages of the shortnose sturgeon and the Atlantic sturgeon were difficult to differentiate. Similarities in morphology and overlapping distribution patterns led to most of the confusion.

The paucity of information on the shortnose sturgeon prior to the 1970s can be attributed to a lack of interest in the species. The occurrence of the "roundnoser" was well known to commercial fishermen (personal communication, C. White, commercial fisherman) but was never recorded in the scientific literature. The purpose of this study was to determine the basic life history characteristics of the shortnose sturgeon, with special emphasis on location of the spawning ground.

AREA OF INVESTIGATION

This investigation took place throughout the estuarine portion of the Hudson from New York City (km 19) to the Federal Dam at Troy, N.Y. (km 246, Figure 8.1). The authors apply the term "estuary" to the Hudson upstream to the Federal Dam at Troy, N.Y., in keeping with the definition of Pritchard (1967). The waters south from

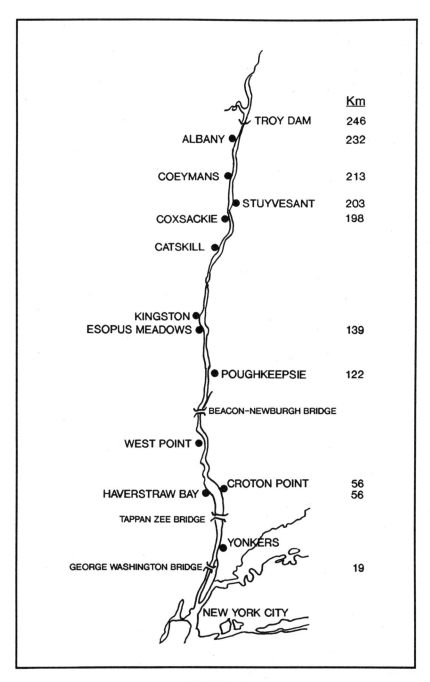

FIGURE 8.1.
The Hudson Estuary.

Haverstraw Bay (km 54–64) are brackish for most of the year, whereas waters of the upper Hudson above Newburgh (km 98) are almost always fresh. The salt-freshwater interface normally occurs near Yonkers, N.Y., during late winter and early spring, and then moves upstream to about Newburgh by late summer.

Much of the bottom of the Hudson Estuary is composed of silt, sand and clay. The channel is periodically dredged to a depth of about 11.8 m to maintain a navigational route for ocean-going ships to Albany-Troy, N.Y. (km 232–246). Some bottom areas of the upper estuary are characterized by rock, primarily shale, slate, and granite (Johnsen 1966). The Federal Dam at Troy, just south of the confluence of the Hudson and Mohawk rivers, restricts the free movement of fishes and ship traffic upstream of the dam.

MATERIALS AND METHODS

Field Methods

The endangered classification of the shortnose sturgeon restricted the types of sampling gear used for collecting specimens. Techniques that required sacrificing specimens were excluded. In addition, the extensive area of investigation, a 246 km reach of the Hudson, placed further constraints on the sampling effort. Accordingly, two basic sampling schemes were employed; one, a rigid sampling design appropriate for a 42 km reach of the upper Hudson (km 204 to 246), in the vicinity of a proposed power plant site near Stuyvesant, N.Y. (Pekovitch 1979), and second, an exploratory approach that permitted the flexibility to alter sampling efforts according to success in locating sturgeon.

The sampling gear used and brief descriptions of procedures are given in Table 8.1. Additional details of the techniques and sampling design are given in Dovel (1979), Pekovitch (1979), and Dovel (1981, Appendices).

Substrate composition was determined by Ponar and Van Veen benthic grab samples in an effort to investigate any correlation between substrate type and spawning areas. Water temperature, salinity (when appropriate), and oxygen level were measured with a Yellow Springs Instrument oxygen meter (YSI Model 57).

An epibenthic sled (Dovel, 1964) fitted with a 1.0 m plankton net of number 0 Nitex mesh, a General Oceanics flowmeter, and a retractable fabric scoop were used to collect the early life stages (eggs and larvae on and immediately above the river bottom). The sled was towed into the current for three minutes at a speed of one to two knots.

Drift and anchor gill nets were used to collect juveniles and adults. Anchor nets, with bar mesh comparable to that of drift nets (Table 8.1), were 30.5 m long and weighted on each end with approximately 44 kg of large chain. Drift and anchor nets were deployed both parallel and perpendicular to current flow, and immediately above (but in contact with) the riverbed. Drift nets were set for a few minutes to about 1 hr, as appropriate, at slack water and as permitted

TABLE 8.1.
Sampling gear used for shortnose sturgeon research in the Hudson Estuary (1975–1980).

Life Stage and Data Collected	Gear Type
I. Environmental Parameters	Temperature—RS-5 Beckman, Salinometer
	Substrate Type—Ponar Grab, Van Veen Bottom Grab
	Depth—Ross Straight-line Fathometer
	Oxygen—YSI (Yellow Springs), model 57 Serial Number 5875
II. Eggs and Larvae	1.0 Meter Henson Net with #0 Nitex Mesh on an Epibenthic Sled (Dovel 1964) with General Oceanics Flowmeter. Sled equipped with scooping device (see text).
III. Larvae, Juveniles, and Adults	Semiballoon Otter Trawl (6.4 meter head rope).
	Wing mesh—3.8 centimeter
	Throat mesh—3.2 centimeter
	Cod-end mesh—1.3 centimeter
	Semiballoon Otter Trawl (10.7 meter head rope).
	Wing mesh—3.8 centimeter
	Throat mesh—2.5 centimeter
	Cod-end mesh—6.5 centimeter
	Tow speeds—approximately 2.5 mph
IV. Juveniles and Adults	Drift Gill Nets (137 m long and 2.4 m deep, 5.1 to 7.6 cm bar mesh).
	Anchor Gill Net (30.5 m long and 1.8 m deep, 5.1 to 8.9 cm bar mesh).

by ship traffic. Anchor nets were normally set for about 24 hr. Sampling time was reduced if sturgeon exhibited signs of stress due to increased water temperature. Gill net efforts were concentrated between km 208 and 246. A limited (spot check) effort was made downstream of km 64, in an attempt to monitor initial spawning migration.

Otter trawls were used to collect larvae, juveniles, and adults (Table 8.1). Trawls with fine mesh liners were towed along the bottom for up to 50 min, both into or with the current depending on the suitability of the substrate. A 6.4 m trawl was used between km 202 and 246. A 10.7 m trawl, rigged according to Bagenal (1964), was used between km 19 and 246.

A scanning approach was used in an attempt to track the movements of adult shortnose sturgeon migrating upriver to the spawning ground. Three field crews sampled back and forth over three adjacent 35 km reaches between km 139 and 246.

Shortnose sturgeon were tagged with Carlin-Ritchie tags (Dovel and Berggren 1983) placed under the anterior portion of the dorsal fin. Sturgeon were tagged at numerous locations throughout the Hudson, but mostly on the overwintering and spawning grounds.

Age determinations were made from pectoral bone sections prepared by two modifications of the Cuerrier (1951) technique (Dovel and Berggren 1983), and as described in Stone et al. (1982). The first pectoral fin ray, and occasionally the second and third, were surgically removed immediately above the basal joint from live fish. The rays were dried for several weeks to several months prior to preparation. Wounds caused by removal of fin rays healed in less than a year.

Large rays (greater than 1.0 cm diameter) were embedded, with a strip of paper carrying specimen data, in hard clear Epon or Epoxy mounting fixative poured into a stoppered section of plastic tubing. The epoxy formed a cylinder from which transverse sections (0.2 to 0.4 mm thick) were cut with a coping saw. Roughcut sections were polished or filed smooth and glued, polished side down, to a glass slide with 5-mn clear Epoxy. The rough sawed upper face of the ray was then smoothed by filing, or by scraping a scalpel blade backward over the bone. Small rays, embedded in the same way, were sectioned (0.02 cm thick) with an American-Edsel miniature lathe with a circular saw blade (7.6 cm diameter) and did not require polishing.

Age was determined by immersing bone sections in xylene for examination under low-power magnification (less than 70X) illuminated by transmitted light. Manipulation of the light source was necessary to produce the best viewing image.

Estimates of the size of the 1979 and 1980 spawning populations of shortnose sturgeon were calculated using a modified Petersen mark-recapture model (Seber 1973). Several population estimates were developed in this study but estimates are presented only for adult sturgeon caught on the spawning ground.

RESULTS AND DISCUSSION

Between October 1975 and October 1978 a total of 360 adult shortnose sturgeon was tagged in the Hudson between km 19 and 213 (Dovel 1978) but only three fish were recaptured. During 1979–80, an additional 2,390 sturgeon were tagged and 359 were recovered. Adult sturgeon were taken regularly in low numbers in commercial gill nets in Haverstraw Bay between 1975 and 1978, but efforts to recapture marked fish or collect juvenile stages from the lower Hudson were unsuccessful. The capture of a few larvae and young-of-the-year sturgeon between km 104 and 246 in 1977 (New York Electric and Gas, 1978) indicated that sturgeon spawning and early feeding activities probably occurred in the upper Hudson.

Concurrent with field efforts, correspondence with many commercial fishermen along the Hudson, particularly Everett Nack (Claverack, N.Y.) and George Clark, Jr. (Port Ewen, N.Y.), revealed that large numbers of mature shortnose sturgeon could be found, in winter, in the vicinity of Kingston, N.Y. (km 140). On the basis of these findings, we chose to attempt to mark sturgeon on this wintering ground and monitor their movement to the spawning ground. Clark and Nack were subsequently employed to capture sturgeon for tagging.

Prespawning and Spawning Activities

In the spring of 1979, ice on the river and inclement weather precluded tagging on the wintering ground until March 17. From that date until April 30, 602 shortnose sturgeon were tagged at km 140 between Vanderburgh Cove and Esopus Meadows. Nine sturgeon, tagged downstream prior to 1979, were recaptured during that period. Concurrent trawling efforts in the lower Hudson (km 38 to 67) produced 56 yearling and older sturgeon but no ripe females.

By mid-April 1979, when water temperature was 8.0–9.0°C, shortnose sturgeon were not found in the vicinity of km 140 where they were abundant only a few days previously. Therefore, sampling was moved upstream, with a limited effort continuing in Haverstraw

Bay. Efforts to tag and recapture sturgeon were concentrated on the spawning ground (km 200 to 246).

In 1979, the peak spawning period for the shortnose sturgeon occurred between April 28 and May 11 in the 33 km reach of the Hudson between the Federal Dam at Troy, N.Y., and Coeymans, N.Y. (Pekovitch 1979; Dovel 1981b). Recapture data indicate that the primary upstream migration of sturgeon from a wintering ground in the channel off Esopus Meadows (km 140) took place during the latter part of March, April, and May. No sampling was conducted above the dam where spawning could occur, depending on lock operation.

In the early spring of 1980 mark-and-recapture efforts were continued at the overwintering site and on the spawning ground. A total of 795 sturgeon were tagged and 239 previously marked fish were recovered.

Collecting efforts on the spawning ground prior to April 19, 1980, produced no shortnose sturgeon. On April 19 and 20 many sturgeon, three carrying tags, were captured at km 211 (Coeymans, N.Y.). During the rest of April and May several hundred adult sturgeon, including 137 marked fish were collected between km 214 and 238.

On May 1, 1980, a concentration of adult shortnose sturgeon was located off the Albany Steam Station (km 232), but no sturgeon were collected in gill nets set for 24 hours slightly upstream (km 235). On May 9 and 10, 92 adult sturgeon were caught between km 234 and 242. By mid-May, adult sturgeon were present immediately below the dam at Troy, N.Y. (km 246), one month after adult sturgeon no longer appeared in samples in the Esopus Meadows area. Therefore, in the spring of 1980 the concentration of sturgeon moved approximately 106 km in 30 days, from the Esopus Meadows area to the dam at Troy. The results of the 1980 efforts verified the pattern of overwintering, spawning migration, and spawning activities observed in 1979.

Many of the tagged shortnose sturgeon were recaptured several times (Table 8.2). Two adult sturgeon (EO91 and E550) occurred in sequence on the overwintering, spawning, and overwintering grounds and one adult sturgeon (F113) occurred on the spawning, overwintering, and spawning grounds. These observations, along with the high recovery rate of marked sturgeon on the spawning ground in 1980 (Table 8.3), suggest a tendency for sturgeon to move as a group. This was also observed by Dadswell et al. (1984).

Most spawning in 1979 and 1980 occurred when water temperature was 10.0 to 18.0°C. This coincides with spawning temperature reported for a landlocked population of shortnose sturgeon

TABLE 8.2.
Multiple recaptures of tagged shortnose from the upper Hudson Estuary (1979–1980).

Tag Area	Winter 1979	Spawn 1979	Winter 1979–80	Spawn 1980	Total Captures
Tag Number					
D075[a]		R		R	3
D748[b]		R	R		3
D879[c]		R,R			3
E039	T		R,R		3
E071	T		R	R	3
E091	T	R	R		3
E092	T		R,R		3
E151	T	R		R	3
E550	T	R	R		3
E537	T	R,R			3
S472	T	R		R	3
S476	T		R,R		3
S930	T	R	R		3
D937		T		R,R	3
D966		T,R,R			3
D971		T		R,R	3
D984		T,R	R	R	4
E102		T	R	R,R	4
E194		T		R,R	3
F113		T	R,R	R	4
E736			T	R,R	3
F072			T	R,R	3
G564			T	R,R	3

[a] Tagged Dec 1977.
[b] Tagged Apr 1978.
[c] Tagged Jun 1978.

in the Connecticut River (Taubert and Reed 1978). Sturgeon of the Delaware River were reported to be ripe and running-ripe by mid-to-late April (Meehan 1910; Hoff 1965), whereas sturgeon of the St. John River, New Brunswick, Canada, are reported to spawn between mid-May and mid-June (Dadswell 1979).

Female shortnose sturgeon with nearly ripe eggs have been collected in Haverstraw Bay, 160 km downstream from the spawning ground, in November (C. White, commercial fisherman). Female sturgeon, with nearly ripe eggs, have also been observed in the lower

TABLE 8.3.
Daily record of shortnose sturgeons caught, tagged, and recaptured in the upper Hudson from April 15 to May 14, 1980.

Date	Water Temperature (C)	Number Caught	Number Tagged	Number Recaptured	Recaptures as % of Number Caught
Apr 15	—	1	1	0	—
19	—	7	7	2	28.6
20	—	4	4	1	25.0
23	9.7	4	4	1	25.0
24	9.7	19	18	4	21.0
25	10.6	56	54	21	37.5
26	11.2	19	19	3	15.8
27	11.2	60	34	15	25.0
28	11.5	14	14	3	21.4
29	11.2	20	19	3	15.0
30	12.1	8	8	2	25.0
May 1	11.3	17	17	6	35.3
2	13.0	17	15	7	41.2
3	13.0	60	35	12	20.0
4	13.6	64	2	16	25.0
5	14.1	38	35	6	15.8
6	14.8	60	42	17	28.3
7	14.8	19	18	5	26.3
8	15.3	34	33	8	23.5
9	15.2	33	31	8	24.2
13	16.9	18	6	4	22.2
14	16.8	11	10	1	9.1
Totals		583	426	145	24.9

Hudson in March to May. Therefore, an observation of females carrying eggs that appear to be mature can be misleading with respect to determining spawning ground location.

Two conclusions can be derived with respect to the occurrence of shortnose sturgeon on the overwintering and spawning grounds. First, at least some adult sturgeon occur on the wintering ground in consecutive years. Second, at least some adult sturgeon will occur on the spawning ground in consecutive years.

Recapture data indicate the presence of adult shortnose sturgeon in the spawning area as early as March 30 (Table 8.4). Recaptures on April 3 and 4 corroborate arrival by the first week of April.

TABLE 8.4.
Earliest dates on which adult shortnose sturgeon were observed
on the spawning ground.

Tag Number	Date of First Capture on Spawning Ground
D945	March 30, 1979
D905	April 3, 1979
F113	April 3, 1980
E936	April 4, 1980

The duration of stay on the spawning ground based on recapture data is up to 30 days (Table 8.5).

Early Development-Nursery Area

Field efforts in May, June, and July 1977 through 1979 concentrated on collection of eggs, larvae, and juveniles of the shortnose sturgeon. No eggs, and only 54 larvae and postlarvae (Figure 8.2) were collected.

Small shortnose sturgeon were collected near the river bottom in channel areas approximately 10 m deep among semibuoyant debris (primarily soft wood worn smooth). The few larvae and juveniles collected from the upper Hudson (km 104 to 246) were collected by extensive sampling with the epibenthic plankton sled. Only three

TABLE 8.5.
Duration of time spent by adult shortnose sturgeon on the spawning ground, based on repeat recaptures.

Tag Number	Number of Days between Recaptures	Year
D989	15	1979
G122	16	1980
D927	17	1979
D962	19	1979
D923	20	1979
D966	20	1979
D917	21	1979
E988	21	1979
D879	30	1979
F072	30	1980

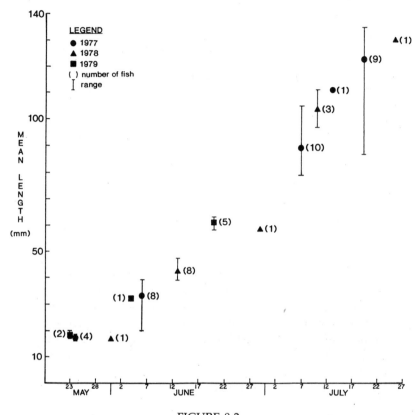

FIGURE 8.2.
Length distribution of larval and young-of-the-year shortnose sturgeons collected in the Hudson River Estuary. (Hazelton Environmental Sciences and the Oceanic Society 1977–1979).

immature sturgeon (17.5, 20.5, and 32.0 mm) were found in 13,400 m³ of water strained from samples in the spring of 1979.

Impingement data at the Albany Steam Station (km 232), located adjacent to the spawning area, provided information on density of young-of-the-year and yearling shortnose sturgeon in that area and the early growth rate for the 1983 year class (LMS, 1984b, 1985b). A total of 86 young-of-the-year and one yearling was impinged between October 1982 and September 1983 (LMS 1984b). Only two young-of-the-year and nine yearlings were impinged from April 1984 to April 1985.

It appears that the 1982 and possibly the 1983 year-classes of shortnose sturgeon may have been unusually large. This assumption is based on the observed ratio of the number of shortnose sturgeon to the number of Atlantic sturgeon collected in the lower Hudson (km 0 to 64) in the winter and early spring of 1984 (Malcolm Pirnie 1984 a, b, and c). In January through April 1984, juvenile shortnose sturgeon, generally less than 45.0 centimeters long, and juvenile Atlantic sturgeon were about equally abundant. This ratio was not observed by intense sampling in the same area from 1975 to 1980 (Dovel and Berggren 1983). During that period the ratio observed was approximately 10 to 1, Atlantic to shortnose.

The precise size of the nursery area for shortnose sturgeon is difficult to determine because of the small number of young collected in the lower Hudson, and the fact that early life stages were not differentiated from the Atlantic sturgeon in past studies by power industry consultants (Hoff et al. 1977). However, the occurrence of a few young-of-the-year shortnose sturgeon in Haverstraw Bay in the winter of 1983–84 suggests that the 180 km freshwater portion of the Hudson, from Haverstraw Bay to the Federal Dam at Troy, is the nursery area for the first year of life (Dovel 1978). Pottle and Dadswell (1979) record a similar freshwater distribution of juvenile shortnose sturgeon in the Saint John River, Canada.

Growth

An indication of the growth of shortnose sturgeon in the upper Hudson (km 104 to 246) during the first few weeks of life is given in Table 8.6 and Figure 8.1. Impingement data from the Albany Steam Station at km 232 (LMS, 1984 and 1985) corroborate this growth pattern.

TABLE 8.6.
Mean length of age 0 shortnose sturgeon collected form the Hudson Estuary 1979–1980.

Month Date	May 23–31	June 1–15	June 16–30	July 1–15	July 16–24
Year					
1977	17.5(4)	33.8(8)	—	91.2(11)	123(9)
1978	17.0(1)	42.2(8)	58.0(1)	103.7(3)	130(1)
1979	18.8(2)	32.0(1)	61.2(5)	—	—
Weighted Mean	17.8(7)	37.6(17)	60.7(6)	93.9(14)	123.7(10)

TABLE 8.7.
Comparison of calculated average growth (cm) of Atlantic and shortnose sturgeons.

Age[a]		J	F	M	A	M	J	J	A	S	O	N	D
						Growing Season							
0	Shortnose					[b]							
	Atlantic						[b]						
1	Shortnose[c]					29.2							(14)
	Atlantic[d]						32.5						(4)
2	Shortnose[c]					40.6							(19)
	Atlantic[d]						53.7						(5)
3	Shortnose[c]					43.7							(2)
	Atlantic[d]						63.1						(8)

[a] Age as of 1 January.
[b] Approximate date of hatching.
[c] Mean size (no. of specimens) from Table 8.3.
[d] From Dovel and Berggren (1983, Table 4).

Yearling shortnose sturgeon in the Saint John River, Canada, are estimated to reach lengths of 15 to 19 cm in July of their second summer (Dadswell et al. 1984). Data from the Hudson (Tables 8.7 and 8.8, and LMS, 1985) indicate that yearlings may exceed 30 cm in length by their second summer. Shortnose sturgeon and Atlantic sturgeon of the Hudson Estuary grow at approximately the same rate in their first year (Table 8.7). By comparison, the lake sturgeon (*A. fulvescens*) attains a length of 23 cm at the end of the first year (Priegel and Wirth 1971). Length frequency distribution of shortnose sturgeon collected from the Hudson Estuary in this study is given in Figure 8.3. The lengths represented are primarily for adult sturgeon collected on the overwintering and spawning grounds.

Dadswell et al. (1984) compared the growth of the shortnose sturgeon throughout its range. Sturgeon grow at a faster rate in southern estuaries but attain maximum size in northern ecosystems. The largest sturgeon caught in the Saint John River was a 143 cm long (total length, TL), 23.6 kg specimen. The largest from the Hudson was 107 cm TL and weighed 10.7 kg.

TABLE 8.8.
Age determinations for 61 shortnose sturgeons 55 centimeters or less in total length.

Line No.	Length	Weight (Grams)	Age[a] (Yr/Mo)	Line No.	Length	Weight (Grams)	Age[a] (Yr/Mo)
1	27.0	85.0	0/11	32	43.0	396.9	1/11
2	27.2	85.0	1/11	33	43.0	396.9	1/11
3	27.2	85.0	0/11	34	43.0	396.9	1/11
4	27.5	85.0	0/11	35	44.0[b]	481.9	4/11
5	28.5	113.4	0/11	36	44.0	498.8	1/11
6	28.5	113.4	0/11	37	44.5	453.6	1/11
7	28.5	113.4	0/11	38	44.5	368.5	3/11
8	28.5	113.4	0/11	39	45.0	481.9	4/11
9	28.5	113.4	0/11	40	45.5	481.9	5/11
10	29.0	113.4	0/11	41	45.5	453.6	2/11
11	29.5	113.4	0/11	42	46.0	510.3	4/11
12	30.0	113.4	0/11	43	46.0	425.2	4/11
13	30.5	113.4	0/11	44	46.0	510.3	5/0
14	32.0	141.7	0/11	45	47.0	453.6	6/11
15	34.0	198.4	0/11	46	48.0	510.3	5/11
16	34.5	311.8	1/11	47	48.0	538.6	5/11
17	34.5	311.8	1/11	48	49.0[b]	878.8	7/11
18	37.0	255.1	1/11	49	49.5	680.4	4/11
19	37.0	255.1	1/11	50	50.5	822.1	5/8
20	39.5	311.8	1/11	51	51.0	708.7	4/11
21	40.5	340.2	1/11	52	52.5	935.5	6/11
22	40.5	311.8	1/11	53	54.5	907.2	5/11
23	40.5	311.8	1/11	54	55.0	737.1	4/11
24	41.0	311.8	1/11	55	55.0	680.4	4/11
25	41.0	340.2	1/11	56	55.0	963.9	6/11
26	41.5	340.2	1/11	57	55.0	992.2	9/11
27	42.0[b]	396.9	4/11	58	55.0	822.1	5/11
28	42.0	283.5	1/11	59	55.0	822.1	7/11
29	42.0	340.2	2/11	60	55.0	1135.1	15/11
30	42.5	283.5	1/11	61	55.0	935.5	7/11
31	43.0	396.9	1/11				

[a] Age using May 1 as date of birth.
[b] U-snout

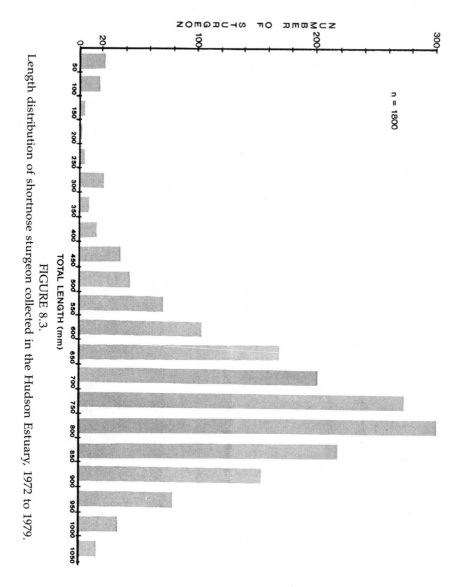

FIGURE 8.3. Length distribution of shortnose sturgeon collected in the Hudson Estuary, 1972 to 1979.

Age Determinations

Ages of sturgeon are extremely difficult to interpret (Kohlhorst et al. 1980). Variations in the metabolic characteristics of individual fish may produce false annuli. Sokolov and Akimova (1976) and Kas'yanov and Zlokazov (1974) discuss the formation of these false annuli. A similar annuli pattern was observed for Atlantic sturgeon (Dovel and Berggren 1983) collected from the Hudson Estuary; however, the false annuli for the Atlantic sturgeon were usually much less prominent than those assumed to be true annular rings. Sokolov and Akimova (1976) suggest the possibility that the annulus is formed in autumn (October-November) for some sturgeon, as was found by Hogman (1968) for whitefish (*Coregonus* sp.). Sokolov and Akimova (1976) explain the formation of spring and autumn rings as "connected with" the onset of a period of intensified growth in spring-summer, and an abrupt decrease in feeding in autumn-winter, respectively.

Age determinations for shortnose sturgeon of the Hudson are complicated by bone deterioration apparently caused by a fungus. Age determinations for 61 sturgeon from 50 to 55 cm TL are presented in Table 8.8. No attempt was made to age sturgeon longer than 55 cm TL. The prohibition of sacrificing sturgeon because of their endangered status made it imprudent to attempt calculations of age by sex for sturgeon captured on the spawning ground.

Summer and Fall Migrations

Adult shortnose sturgeon, after overwintering near Esopus Meadows (km 140), migrate upstream in the spring to spawn, then migrate south in the Hudson (some as far as the Tappan Zee) to feed during summer. Several adults tagged on the spawning ground from late March to early May 1979 and 1980 were recaptured in the Haverstraw Bay area (km 56 to 64) in June. These sturgeon most likely migrated from the overwintering ground upstream to the spawning ground, then moved downstream to Haverstraw Bay. Shortnose sturgeon of the Saint John River, Canada (Dadswell 1979), Kennebec River, Maine (Squiers and Smith 1978), the Connecticut River (Buckley 1982) and the Pee Dee-Wingah system, South Carolina (Marchette and Smiley 1982), have a similar migration pattern to downstream feeding areas (Dadswell et al. 1984).

Adult shortnose sturgeon occurred infrequently in samples collected from the upper Hudson Estuary (km 200 to 246) after late May in 1977 (New York Electric and Gas 1978). Adult and immature sturgeon are, however, found throughout freshwaters of the Hudson in summer. This suggests random movement away from the spawning ground. Hoff et al. (1977) reported the capture of 125 sturgeon in 1976 and about the same number in 1977 in shallow areas of the lower Hudson. Wilk and Silverman (1976) caught 6 sturgeon in Sandy Hook Bay, N.J., off the mouth of the Hudson, between mid-July and mid-September 1976. We presume that shortnose sturgeon found in New Jersey waters are indigenous to the Hudson.

In the fall, as water temperature declines, adult shortnose sturgeon that participate in the next spring spawning migration move toward the main overwintering ground off Esopus Meadows. By December, sturgeon are abundant in this area. At the same time, some sturgeon move into deeper, warmer channel locations in Haverstraw Bay and the Tappan Zee, apparently for the winter. It is not known if these sturgeon migrate substantial distances downstream as winter approaches, or if they have spent the latter part of the summer in the Haverstraw Bay-Tappan Zee area. No evidence exists for other areas of concentrations of sturgeon in winter. However, some channel areas of the lower Hudson have not been adequately sampled, especially in the reach from Charles Point (km 69) to Cornwall-On-The-Hudson (km 91) where the bottom configuration is very irregular.

Shortnose sturgeon of the Hudson Estuary apparently do not exhibit as pronounced anadromous migration characteristics as the Atlantic sturgeon. The two species differ primarily in size and in location of spawning grounds (Figure 8.4). However, juveniles of both species may occur together in winter. A few juvenile Atlantic sturgeon were found, along with shortnose sturgeon, at the upstream overwintering area for the shortnose. The larger Atlantic sturgeon is apparently more dependent on coastal areas (Dovel and Berggren 1983) than the shortnose sturgeon, but can probably tolerate the inshore estuarine habitat during most of the year.

The shortnose sturgeon migrates as far upstream to spawn as accessible habitat permits. Because of its preference for freshwater habitat, it is found primarily in the upper Hudson. However, individuals do disperse far downstream into brackish water, perhaps further downstream in years of greater abundance. Three pieces of evidence support such a concept. First, the 1982 and 1983 year-classes appear to have been unusually large (pers. observ.). Second, Normandeau Associates, Inc. (Geoghegan, et al., this volume) collected a greater number of shortnose sturgeon from the Croton Point area (km 56) in the 1980s than was taken by intensive sampling from 1975 to 1980 (Dovel 1981). And third, the length-frequency distribution of the

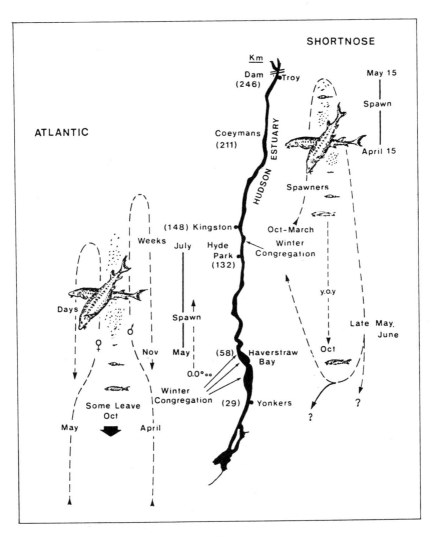

FIGURE 8.4.
Schematic representation of the basic temporal and spatial movements of Atlantic and shortnose sturgeons in the Hudson Estuary. The Atlantic sturgeon is anadromous, while the shortnose sturgeon spends most of its life in fresh and brackish water. (From Dovel 1981b, Table 3).

sturgeon collected by Normandeau Associates (Geoghegan et al., this volume) was bimodal; more specimens were in the 45 to 65 cm range from 1983 to 1988 than observed by Dovel (1981). Mean size of adults in the vicinity of Croton Point appeared to have declined commensurate with increased abundance. The trend, if real, could indicate that the benthic community of the middle and lower Hudson may not be able to support large numbers of young of the Atlantic and shortnose species. Further, this reach of the Hudson is predominantly a nursery for the Atlantic species, which prefers more saline waters than the shortnose. This pattern of potential interaction between two closely related species and the environment supports a concept of specific ichthyoniches but adds the dimension of flexibility of niche in response to changes in year class strength.

Rationale for Basic Migrations

Most shortnose sturgeon research has documented migrations—in fall, winter, and spring to spawn; in spring and summer to feeding areas; in fall and winter to overwintering areas. Dadswell et al. (1984) summarize the complex migrations by specific activity. Buckley and Kynard (1985) believe that reproductive condition is probably the principal factor that determines the use of a specific location and that age of fish may influence the choice of an area. A review of the scientific literature clearly indicates a lack of specific habitat requirements by sturgeon (Dadswell et al. 1984). For example, shortnose feed over mud, sand, sandy-mud, gravel, off emergent plants, in fresh water, salt water, and at all depths. We can only presume that the shortnose sturgeon adapts to its native estuary and that movement of individual sturgeon represent its life history pattern.

The authors propose a basic rationale for the composite movements of shortnose sturgeon in the Hudson Estuary and address these movements as they apply to other estuarine ecosystems. First, we conclude that the shortnose sturgeon is tolerant of a wide range of conditions found in the estuarine habitat. We believe that the utilization of specific habitats, exclusive of spawning and perhaps overwintering areas, is a random response to the environmental conditions of the ecosystem, which is influenced by the state of gonad development. The repetitious occurrence of the same life stages of different year-classes in specific locations is the only long-term consistent movement pattern (e.g., spawning always occurs in the same general area). Fluctuations of environmental factors (light, water temperature, turbidity, current patterns, water salinity, and invertebrate prey fauna) influence sturgeon movement for only short periods of time.

The environmental tolerance of the shortnose sturgeon and the ability of the species to adapt to nonestuarine conditions is demonstrated by the presence of sturgeon in the partially landlocked Holyoke Pool on the Connecticut River (Taubert 1980) and Lake Marion-Moultrie, S.C. (Marchette and Smiley 1982), both closed ecosystems. The dam at Troy, N.Y., on the Hudson, may have altered the original spawning habitat in the Hudson Estuary. Sturgeon, probably shortnose, were observed by early settlers to congregate upstream from the dam near the Cohoes Falls in spring (Mitchill 1811).

With the assumption that the shortnose sturgeon tolerates a variety of habitats, its occurrence in specific habitats takes on new meaning. We believe that most movement is strongly influenced by the reproductive process. As the reproductive organs mature and water temperature approaches the optimum spawning range, perhaps either ascending or descending, sturgeon experience a greater stimulus to move toward the spawning ground. This would explain the progressive movements of ripening sturgeon upstream toward the spawning area in fall (Dadswell 1979; Buckley 1982; Buckley and Kynard 1985), in winter (Heidt and Gilbert 1978; Greeley 1935), and spring (all sturgeon literature). This could also explain concurrent downstream movements of immature and resting-stage adults. If maturation is an increasing stimulus to migrate to the spawning area, then the reverse should also be true; immature sturgeon and mature individuals in a resting reproductive stage are inclined to respond primarily to other physiologic needs, and probably move away from upstream areas of relatively colder water, during winter. Such downstream movements are documented by Dadswell (1979) and Buckley (1982). Thus, the movements of sturgeon during a long maturation period and prolonged durations between spawning activities could be very confusing if correlated to and considered restrictive to specific habitats. If, on the other hand, habitat requirements are considered secondary to spawning needs, then it is easy to perceive movements of sturgeon as changing from random feeding activities to spawning-induced migrations that gain momentum as the sturgeon's reproductive organs mature. The specific habitat occurrence of shortnose sturgeon in various stages of readiness to spawn is probably determined by chance, with some congregation in more suitable locations, the characteristics of which remain much the same from year to year.

Our hypothesis for the characteristics and impetus of sturgeon migrations could provide insight with respect to other species of sturgeon that exhibit both fall and spring migrations toward the spawning ground. Such populations occur in river systems where the spawning grounds are located some distance from summer feeding areas—Volga, Danube, Dnieper, Rhine, of Eurasia (Berg 1948). The requirement to travel long distances to the spawning ground may produce a prespawning migration in the fall, perhaps stimulated by water temperature. Nikolsky (1961) states that individual sturgeon reach sexual maturity at varying times in different reservoirs. Thus, it is logical to assume that the stimulus to migrate toward the spawning ground varies with individual sturgeon, but may be strongest in spring and fall as water temperature approaches optimal spawning range, otherwise prespawning migrations would not be restricted to only fall and spring.

Morphological Abnormality

A small percentage (less than 2%) of shortnose sturgeon collected in the Hudson Estuary between 1975 and 1980 exhibited a physical deformity best described as a "U-snout." This deformity (Figure 8.5) was observed in sturgeon over a wide size range. Deformed fish appear normal in all other aspects. The deformity does not appear to be associated with an active pathogenic condition.

POPULATION ESTIMATE

The spawning population of shortnose sturgeon in the Hudson Estuary was estimated to be about 13,000 fish (Table 8.9). Age determinations indicated that most sturgeon were five years and older (Table 8.8). The estimate was calculated from the recapture of marked sturgeon on the spawning ground. Calculations of the size of the spawning populations in 1979 and 1980 were 12,669 and 13,844 fish, respectively, using a modified Petersen model (Seber 1973). This model assumes a "closed" population with essentially no change in the size of the population between the period when the sturgeon were marked (on the overwintering ground) and recaptured (on the spawning ground), a few weeks later. In both years the population experienced the transition from relative dormancy in the wintering area to active spawning at a location at least 70 km upstream. This transition occurred over a period of two months, which assured adequate mixing of the marked fish in the general spawning population.

Recapture data provide some insight into the relationship be-

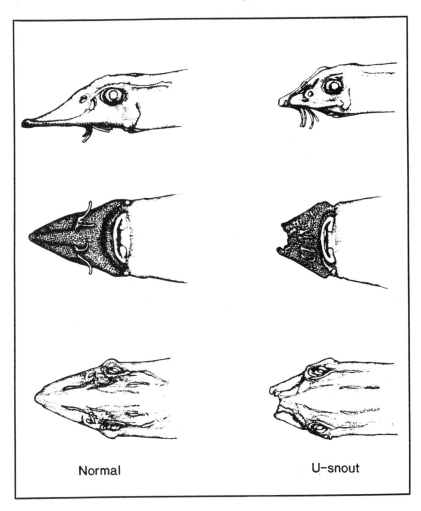

FIGURE 8.5.
Deformed (U-snout), right, and normal young-of-the-year shortnose sturgeon, left, from the Hudson Estuary.

tween the size of the spawning population and the size of the total population of adult shortnose sturgeon in the Hudson Estuary. If most adult sturgeon routinely move between the overwintering and spawning areas in sequences compatible with the concept of an annual spawning migration, then the population estimate of 13,000 fish

TABLE 8.9.
Peterson estimate of population size for selected pairs of sampling periods for the spawning population of shortnose sturgeon.

Period	Location	Initial Marks (M)	Catch (C)	Recaptures (R)	Population Size[a]	95% Confidence Interval[b]	
						Lower Limit	Upper Limit
1	EM	548					
2	SG '79		899	38	12,669	9,080	17,735
3	EM	811					
4	SG '80		698	40	13,844	10,014	19,224

Period
1 = March 19, 1979 to Arpil 20, 1979—Esopus Meadows
2 = April 20, 1979 to May 31, 1979—Spawning Ground
3 = October 2, 1979 to April 10, 1980—Esopus Meadows
4 = April 10, 1980 to May 17, 1980—Spawning Ground

[a] Population size estimate by: $N^* = \dfrac{(M+1)(C+1)}{(R+1)}$

[b] Confidence interval estimate by multiplying the 95% confidence interval for N/ (Chapman 1948, table shown in Appendix A of Seber 1973) by MC. The distribution of recaptures R is approximated by the Poisson distribution with M = /N, which is appropriate since $p = R/C < 0.1$.

would represent almost the entire adult population. This possibility is supported by the record of the percentage of marked sturgeon found in collections made on the spawning ground in the spring of 1980. A surprisingly high and consistent occurrence of marked sturgeon in samples was observed despite movement of fish to and from the spawning ground. Over 80% of the sturgeon recaptured met conditions that assure random mixing of marked fish throughout the population. In a 30-day period, daily calculations of the percentage recovery of marked shortnose ranged from 9.1 to 41.2%, with a mean of 24.9% (Table 8.3). Obviously, a substantial percentage of the population of adult shortnose sturgeon carried marks in the spring of 1980, perhaps close to one-quarter of the population. If 2,750 tagged sturgeon actually represent one quarter of the population, the total estimate would be 11,000 fish, 85% of the estimate developed.

IMPACTS OF HUMAN ACTIVITIES ON THE SHORTNOSE STURGEON OF THE HUDSON

Commercial Fishing

Normal operations of commercial fisheries in the Hudson do not subject the species to excessive exploitation. The relatively small area off the navigation channel between Vanderburgh Cove and Esopus Meadows, where shortnose sturgeon congregate in winter, is not a major commercial fishing area.

In the late 1800s and early 1900s some ice fishing was conducted, but this no longer occurs due to the instability of surface ice, which is continually broken up by Coast Guard ice breakers maintaining a navigational route to Albany. Therefore, shortnose sturgeon first become vulnerable to commercial fishing after the ice breaks, about mid-March, and at the time when the population begins to migrate upstream to the spawning ground. Only drift gill nets are suitable for use in the upper estuary at this time due to detritus in spring runoff. More importantly, in late winter and early spring most commercial fishermen are traditionally preoccupied with preparations to fish for the American shad (and the striped bass until the early 1980s) farther downstream. By the time sturgeon congregate on the spawning ground the shad fisheries are in full swing. Even if commercial fishermen were not involved in other fisheries, it would not be practical for them to travel appreciable distances from home to harvest a resource that does not presently provide a reasonable profit. Therefore, until the sturgeon is more abundant or the roe (caviar) and flesh command a higher price, it is not likely that the species will be exposed to more fishing pressure than is presently exerted by a few fishermen seeking an occasional meal.

Commercial fishermen downstream occasionally catch shortnose sturgeon while fishing for other species. Many of the sturgeon caught are apparently moving at random. Thus, any data that might be obtained from this incidental catch would not reveal population movement or migration.

Shortnose sturgeon are protected from commercial fishing pressure by the prohibition of fishing in channel areas through which most migration of sturgeon takes place. Therefore, there is no obvious reason to anticipate that the shortnose sturgeon population of the Hudson, were the fish not classified as endangered, would be substantially harmed by commercial fishing activities if fishing pressure does not change appreciably from the current level.

Channel Maintenance Dredging

Documentation of the basic life history activities of the shortnose sturgeon makes it possible to propose a maintenance dredging schedule for the Hudson, synchronized to the biology of the species. Dredging of channel areas between Coxsackie and the dam at Troy (km 198 to 246) from April 15 to June 15 has potential for adverse impact on adult and recently hatched sturgeon. Dredging would have progressively less impact as summer approaches and sturgeon spread downstream. Accordingly, it is recommended that channel dredging from Haverstraw Bay and northward be done in summer—that is, after June 15.

Fungal Disease—Fin Rot

More than 75% of the adult shortnose sturgeon examined in this investigation had severe incidence of fin rot caused by a fungus (Table 8.10). This disease may have lethal and sublethal impacts. The high incidence of fin rot could be caused by reduced immunity, possibly a result of deterioration of the epithelial mucus coating. This has been documented for the channel catfish (*Ictalurus punctatus* LeSueur) exposed to toxaphene (Grant 1979). Dr. Ira Salkin, New York Department of Health, stated that the fungus *(Leptolegnia caudata)*, identified by Dr. Roland Seymour, department of botany, University of Ohio, is somehow involved with the fin rot of sturgeon, either as a primary pathogen that overcomes the fish's immune system or as a secondary pathogen that has invaded after disease resistance has been reduced by the presence of a foreign substance. Mr. Ward Stone, pathologist for New York State Department of Environmental Conservation stated, "It is not beyond the realm of possibility that PCBs are causing pathophysiological changes that lower the sturgeon's resistance to fin rot."

Association between fungal infection and shortnose sturgeon populations is not recent. Ryder (1890) stated that fungi and probably mold are "seriously destructive to the life of the ova of the [shortnose] sturgeon in moderately quiet waters." In April 1909 shortnose sturgeon eggs from the Delaware River were fertilized at the Torresdale Hatchery. Most of these eggs "fungussed" (Meehan, 1910). Fin rot is, for the most part, a sublethal condition. However, fungal infestation of eggs could contribute to low egg survival, and thus be a contributing factor to the shortnose sturgeon's current classification as endangered.

In the spring of 1979 the senior author conducted an impromptu

TABLE 8.10.
Incidence of fin rot on 585 shortnose sturgeons, 1980.

Day	Number of Specimens	Number with Fin Rot	Percentage with Fin Rot	Temp. C
1	28	22	78.6	9.5–10.3
2	29	19	65.5	
3	29	18	62.1	
4	29	15	51.7	
5	29	13	44.8	11.0–11.5
6	29	14	48.3	
7	28	8	28.6	
8	29	21	72.4	
9	27	26	96.3	12.7–13.2
10	29	22	75.9	
11	28	24	85.7	
12	35	33	94.3	
13	33	29	87.9	
14	34	30	88.2	13.3–14.1
15	35	31	88.6	
16	35	29	82.9	
17	35	33	94.3	
18	35	33	94.3	
19	30	27	90.0	16.3–17.2
Totals	586	447	76.3	

sturgeon egg survival examination. Eggs and sperm, stripped from sturgeon, were mixed and the fertilized eggs incubated separately in water from the Hudson and commercial spring water. A few of the eggs incubated in spring water hatched with some fungus present (Dovel 1981). All eggs incubated in water from the Hudson became infected by fungus and died in less than 48 hours. It seems reasonable to conclude that water in the spawning area of the upper Hudson in spring has a substantial potential for fungal infestation of newly deposited eggs. It seems logical to assume that the fungi associated with the observed fin rot and poor egg survival could be the same. However, the fungus that attacked the eggs was not identified.

Dissolved Oxygen

We have no evidence that dissolved oxygen (DO) level in waters of the upper Hudson affected reproduction and early development of shortnose sturgeon in the period of this investigation. In spring 1979 oxygen levels were consistantly high, often near 10 ppm. If spawning would occur a short time later (perhaps two weeks), declining DO and an increase in water temperature could place the spawning sturgeon under stress. Sturgeon collected in gill nets before and during the spawning period, when water temperature was generally less than 15°C, showed no signs of stress when held in nets up to 24 hours. As water temperature increased above 15°C, sturgeon showed some signs of stress when held in nets for periods less than 12 hours. Sturgeon under stress were characterized by reduced activity and accelerated opercular action.

The discharge effluent from the Rensselaer-Troy Municipal Sewage Treatment Plant (km 237) could potentially decrease dissolved oxygen in the shortnose sturgeon spawning ground, especially during unusually warm, quiet (windless) periods in late May. These conditions could be conducive to the growth of fungus and to the observed mortality of incubating eggs (Dovel 1981).

Water Quality and Toxic Chemicals

The bio-accumulation of toxic chemicals in the upper Hudson, especially but not limited to PCBs, merits special consideration with respect to potential impacts on shortnose sturgeon. The sturgeon is vulnerable because it spawns, feeds, grows, and overwinters in the reach of the estuary between Esopus Meadows (km 140) and the Federal Dam at Troy (km 246), an area where PCBs have been concentrated for years (Sloan and Armstrong 1988). The potential pathological effects of PCBs and other chemicals need to be investigated with respect to sturgeon health and reproductive success, especially since high concentrations of PCBs have been found in shortnose. Pathologist Ward Stone found concentrations of 22.1 to 997.0 ppm in the flesh of four sturgeon collected on the spawning ground (Dovel 1981).

Electric Power Generating Plants

Cooling-water withdrawal at the Albany Steam Station (km 232), located near the spawning and nursery areas of the shortnose sturgeon, presents a potential risk to the species (Dovel 1979; LMS, 1984, 1985). Impingement, and possible entrainment, could be a significant problem because the entire spawning population passes within a few meters of the steam station intake. Mature fish, eggs, and newly hatched larvae are vulnerable.

Hoff and Klauda (1979) report the impingement of 39 shortnose sturgeon at power plants along the Hudson 1969–1979. In the past impingement of sturgeon was of significant concern (Barnthouse 1979). However, available data should not be used to assess impact until impingement (and entrainment) are correlated with plant operation (volume of water withdrawal), and an assessment is made of the characteristics of the sturgeon population that was present. The necessity to "scale up" the number of sturgeon impinged on power plant intake screens has been recognized (Barnthouse 1979; Marcellus 1979) in order to provide a more accurate assessment of adverse impact associated with electric power generation on the Hudson Estuary.

A data compilation by Hoff and Klauda (1979) indicates that young-of-the-year shortnose sturgeon, as young as two months of age, move rapidly downstream and thus are vulnerable to impingement and entrainment at any of the power plants located between Troy and Haverstraw Bay (Indian Point, Bowline, Roseton, Lovett, Danskammer, and the Albany Steam Station). The operation of power plants along the upper Hudson has the greatest potential for causing losses to sturgeon during its prespawning migration, spawning activities, and the initial downstream movements of larvae. Plant operations in the lower Hudson have a greater potential impact for impingement of sturgeon as they migrate to and from the upstream spawning ground through channel areas.

Future Shortnose Sturgeon Research

Several aspects of the life history of the shortnose sturgeon deserve further study. Movements of sturgeon between the Hudson Estuary and the Atlantic Ocean should be investigated. It is possible that some sturgeon leave the estuary and go to sea for undetermined periods of time. To date, the only evidence that sturgeon from the Hudson approach coastal areas is the documentation of a few sturgeon in Sandy Hook Bay, N.J. (Wilk and Silverman 1976). These specimens were assumed to have been native to the Hudson. None of 2,750 sturgeon tagged in the Hudson were recovered seaward of New York City.

There are two logical times when the shortnose sturgeon could leave the Hudson; first, as a continuation of the postspawning, downstream migration, and second, as water temperature declines in fall. Declining water temperature stimulates emigration of the Atlantic sturgeon (Dovel and Berggren 1983) and could do the same for the shortnose sturgeon.

Another aspect of the shortnose sturgeon life history that remains unknown is the whereabouts of most juvenile sturgeon in the estuary, especially two-year-old fish. Juveniles may be dispersed over an extensive portion of the estuary, in low densities. They would be difficult to monitor with conventional sampling methods; sampling effort expended throughout the 246 km estuary has simply been inadequate. More extensive sampling may require a special effort to perfect more efficient techniques.

The consideration that two-year-old shortnose sturgeon are especially elusive could also be the result of a misinterpretation of the ages of young sturgeon. Accordingly, new effort should be devoted to find an efficient technique for determination of age. Recent improvement in preparing sturgeon pectoral fin bones for age determination (Stone et al. 1982) should facilitate a much needed evaluation of the characteristics of annuli formation.

The occurrence of fin rot on adult shortnose sturgeon and the apparent susceptability of eggs to fungal infection should be the subject of a special study. The possibility that fungal infections may cause low egg survival of sturgeon in the upper Hudson and lead to conditions contributing to its endangered status should be investigated. In addition, definitive identification of the fungi associated with fin rot and egg infections should be made.

Finally, we believe that the carrying capacity of the Hudson and competition with the co-generic species *A. oxyrhynchus* may be primary factors influencing movement and specific habitat use by each year class of shortnose sturgeon. This possibility should be considered in the planning stages for further estuarine fisheries research on the Hudson.

PAUL GEOGHEGAN
MARK T. MATTSON
ROGER G. KEPPEL

9

Distribution of the Shortnose Sturgeon in the Hudson River Estuary, 1984–1988

ABSTRACT

From April through December 1983–1988, 136 shortnose sturgeon, *Acipenser brevirostrum*, were captured in the Hudson River Estuary by otter trawls, 1.0 m epibenthic sleds, and 3 m beam trawls as a by-catch to 3 utility sponsored monitoring programs. All shortnose sturgeon were returned to the river alive after being weighed and measured for total length in mm (TL). Shortnose sturgeon ranged from 104 to 1200 mm TL, with a mean total length of 671 mm. Weights ranged from 0.4 to 7.1 kg with a mean weight of 2.0 kg. Shortnose sturgeon were captured between km 42–220, but were most common between km 140–149 in the vicinity of Kingston, N.Y., and at km 55 in the Croton Point area. Pooled catch data from our studies supported the life history model of Dovel et al. Our data also indicated a concentration of shortnose sturgeon in the Croton Point area (km 55) in the fall, although this may be an artifact of a fixed station study design. The Croton Point area and the Kingston region (km 140–149) appeared to be important locations for shortnose sturgeons in the fall because more of them were captured from these areas than any others.

INTRODUCTION

The shortnose sturgeon (*Acipenser brevirostrum*) is an important fish in the Hudson River Estuary because of its classification as a federally endangered species. However, little work since 1980 has been devoted solely to monitoring the distribution and population dynamics of this species. Recent reports (Hoff et al. 1988a; Dovel 1981b; TI 1981) presented life history data collected up to 1980 for the Hudson River shortnose sturgeon. The shortnose sturgeon is a regular by-catch of routine monitoring programs funded by the Hudson River utilities. We summarize the shortnose sturgeon catch data from recent years of three Hudson River monitoring programs: the 1983–1988 White Perch Stock Assessment Study (White Perch Study), the 1984–1988 Ichthyoplankton Survey, and the 1984–1988 Fall Juvenile Survey, and relate this distribution to a current life history model of the shortnose sturgeon in the Hudson River (Dovel et al. this volume).

METHODS

An otter trawl (Table 9.1) was used in the White Perch Study to sample 20 fixed stations in the Hudson River (Table 9.2) from September through mid-December in the fall of 1983–1988 and from mid-April through June in the spring of 1984. One tow at each station was collected biweekly for 8 weeks during the fall of 1983 through 1987, and for 7 weeks during the fall of 1988. During the spring of 1984 sampling was conducted for 10 consecutive weeks. Fixed location sampling stations were distributed between km 42 and km 174 (Table 9.2). Trawling was conducted during the daylight and against the current for a duration of ten minutes.

A 1 m epibenthic sled (Table 9.1) was used in the 1984–1988 Ichthyoplankton Survey to sample for 8–12 consecutive weeks from April through mid-July of each year (Table 9.3). A 1 m epibenthic sled (1984) or 3 m beam trawl (1985–1988) was used in the 1984–1988 Fall Juvenile Survey to sample biweekly from mid-July into or through November of each year (Table 9.3). These surveys used a stratified random sampling design to allocate 74–85 (Ichthyoplankton Survey)

Distribution of Shortnose Sturgeon

TABLE 9.1.
Specifications of gear used in this study.

Program	Gear	Gear Dimensions	Mesh Size
White Perch Study	White Perch Trawl	8.5 m (footrope)	Body 5.1 cm (stretch) Cod end linear 1.3 cm (stretch)
Ichthyoplankton Survey	Epibenthic Sled	1.0 m	500 microns
Fall Juvenile Survey (1984 only)	Epibenthic Sled	1.0 m	3000 microns
Fall Juvenile Survey (1985–1988)	3 m Beam Trawl	2.7 m	Body 3.8 cm (stretch) Cod end 3.2 cm (stretch) Cod end liner 1.3 cm (stretch)

or 143 (Fall Juvenile Survey) samples per week among the 12 standard regions of the Hudson River between km 0 and 246. The 1 m epibenthic sled and the 3 m beam trawl were towed against the current primarily at night, for a duration of 5 minutes.

Shortnose sturgeon from these programs were collected as part

TABLE 9.2.
Fixed sampling site locations and number of samples.

River Region (km)	Fixed Station Location (km)	Number of Samples per Week
Tappan Zee (38–53)	42, 50	4
Croton-Haverstraw (54–61)	55, 60	4
West Point (74–88)	87	2
Cornwall (89–98)	92	2
Poughkeepsie (99–122)	109	2
Kingston (137–149)	148	2
Saugerties (150–170)	153	2
Catskill (171–198)	174	2

TABLE 9.3.
Frequency and location for epibenthic sled and beam trawl samples.

Survey	Year	Gear	Sampling Dates	River Km	Average Number of Samples/Week
Ichthyoplankton	1984	Epibenthic Sled	4/30–7/13/84	19–224	85
Fall Juvenile	1984	Epibenthic Sled	7/16–10/25/84	19–224	143
Ichthyoplankton	1985	Epibenthic Sled	4/29–7/11/85	19–224	85
Fall Juvenile	1985	3 m Beam Trawl	7/22–11/14/85	19–224	143
Ichthyoplankton	1986	Epibenthic Sled	4/26–7/14/86	19–246	82
Fall Juvenile	1986	3 m Beam Trawl	7/21–12/1/87	19–246	143
Ichthyoplankton	1987	Epibenthic Sled	4/13–7/13/87	19–246	78
Fall Juvenile	1987	3 m Beam Trawl	7/13–11/16/87	19–246	143
Ichthyoplankton	1988	Epibenthic Sled	4/17–9/9/88	0–246	74
Fall Juvenile	1988	3 m Beam Trawl	7/17–10/28/88	19–246	143

of the by-catch. All shortnose sturgeon were counted and most were measured for total length in mm (TL) and weighed to the nearest 10 g. All shortnose sturgeon were returned to the river as quickly as possible after capture and no mortality was recorded in these programs.

RESULTS

Seasonal Distribution

Shortnose sturgeon (136) were captured in the Hudson River during 1983–1988 from April through December at km 42 through 220. The only shortnose sturgeon captured in April during the White Perch Study occurred in the upriver Saugerties region (Table 9.4). However, in May 2 shortnose sturgeon were captured in the Tappan Zee region and 4 were captured in the Croton-Haverstraw region. In April

TABLE 9.4.
Monthly distribution of 74 shortnose sturgeon captured in the Hudson River during the 1983–1988 white perch stock assessment program.[a,b]

River Region (km)	Number of Samples	Number of Shortnose Sturgeon Captured								
		Apr	May	Jun	Jul	Aug	Sep	Oct	Nov	Dec
Tappan Zee (38–53)	228		2							
Croton-Haverstraw (54–61)	228		4				3	19	8	7
Indian Point (62–74)	0									
West Point (75–88)	114							1		
Cornwall (89–98)	114								1	
Poughkeepsie (99–122)	114							1		
Hyde Park (123–136)	0									
Kingston (137–149)	114			4				12	3	2
Saugerties (150–170)	114	1	1					3	1	1
Catskill (171–198)	114									

[a] April, May, and June were only sampled in 1984.
[b] July and August were not sampled in 1983–1988.

through June, 3 shortnose sturgeon were captured during the Ichthyoplankton Survey in the upper regions of the Hudson River Estuary, 1 in the Catskill region in April (745 mm TL), 1 in the Albany region in May (875 mm TL), and 1 in the Saugerties region in June (620 mm TL). These three fish were the only shortnose sturgeon captured during the Ichthyoplankton Survey from 1984 to 1988. During the White Perch Study, 4 shortnose sturgeon were captured in the Kingston region in June (Table 9.5).

During July and August, the distribution of the shortnose sturgeon was centered downriver of the Saugerties region (km 159) as shown by the by-catch from the Fall Juvenile Survey (Table 9.5). Short-

TABLE 9.5.
Monthly distribution of 60 shortnose sturgeon captured in the Hudson River during the 1984–1988 fall juvenile white perch survey.

River Region (km)	Number of Samples	Numbers of shortnose sturgeon captured				
		Jul	Aug	Sep	Oct	Nov
Tappan Zee (38–53)	1,710	4	1		1	
Croton-Haverstraw (54–61)	1,080		1		1	
Indian Point (62–74)	495					
West Point (75–88)	225	2	2	1	1	
Cornwall (89–98)	450		7	1		
Poughkeepsie (99–122)	225	3	1	1		
Hyde Park (123–136)	270	4	3		2	
Kingston (137–149)	405		1	13	4	
Saugerties (150–170)	540		1		2	1
Catskill (171–198)	675			2		
Albany (199–243)	540					

nose sturgeon were captured between km 47 and 159, and more fish were captured in the Cornwall and Hyde Park regions than any other regions. By September, catch data from the White Perch Study and the Fall Juvenile Survey indicated a possible center of distribution in the Kingston region (Tables 9.4 and 9.5).

During October, November, and December catch data from the White Perch Study indicate a second possible center of distribution in the Croton-Haverstraw region; 37 fish were captured in this region (Table 9.4). Shortnose sturgeon were also captured in the Tappan Zee and Croton-Haverstraw regions during the Fall Juvenile Survey, but the majority of the captures occurred upriver, in the Hyde Park, Kingston, and Saugerties regions (Table 9.5). In early December, 7 fish were captured in the Croton-Haverstraw region during the White Perch Study (Table 9.4).

Length Frequency Distribution

Length of shortnose sturgeon captured in the Hudson River between 1983 and 1988 ranged from 104 to 1200 mm TL. The length frequency distribution of shortnose sturgeon pooled among sampling programs and years (Figure 9.1) indicated a model length of between 700 and 750 mm TL. Assuming a length at maturity of 45 to 55 cm fork length (Dadswell et al. 1984), most (approximately 90%) of the shortnose sturgeon captured were mature. The smallest shortnose sturgeon (104 mm TL) was captured at km 55 on September 24, 1987, and based on data presented in Dovel et al. (this volume) was a young-of-the-year fish. The largest shortnose sturgeon (1,200 mm TL) was captured at km 55 on October 4, 1988. This fish was slightly less than the maximum known size for shortnose sturgeon throughout its range (Dadswell et al. 1984: 122 cm) and is greater than those reported for shortnose sturgeon from the Hudson River by Hoff et al. (1988a: 1,100 mm TL), Koski et al. (1971: 932 mm TL) and Dovel et al. (this volume: 1070 mm TL). The length-weight regression for (121) shortnose sturgeon captured was:

$$\log_{10} W = (2.91)\log_{10} L - 5.01 \quad r^2 = 0.79$$

where

$$W = \text{weight in g and}$$
$$L = \text{total length in mm}$$

This length-weight regression is similar to those reported in Hoff et al. (1988) and Dovel et al. (1984) for shortnose sturgeon from the Hudson River.

DISCUSSION

According to the generalized life history model of the shortnose sturgeon of Dovel et al. (this volume), spawning occurs during April and May in the upper Hudson River between km 200 and 246. After spawning the adult fish disperse downstream throughout the river, and during the summer some individuals may leave the Hudson River. As fall and winter approaches, the adults move upstream and

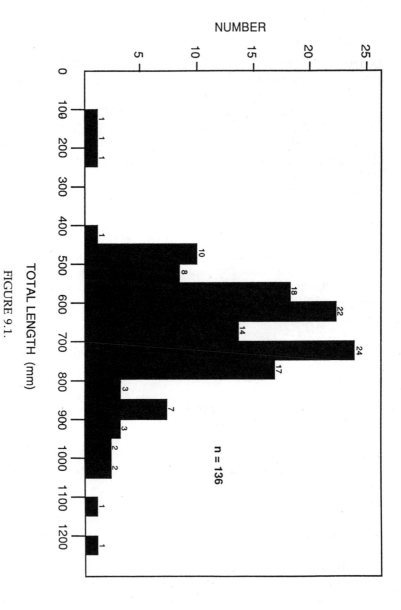

FIGURE 9.1. Length frequency distribution of Shortnose Sturgeon collected in the Hudson River during the 1983–1988 White Perch Stock Assessment Study and the 1984–1988 Hudson River Ichthyoplankton and Fall Juvenile Surveys.

congregate in the Kingston region between km 137 and 149. Dovel et al. (this volume) specifically identified the Esopus Meadows area at km 140 as an overwintering area for shortnose sturgeon.

Our catch data from the White Perch Study were in agreement with this life history model (Table 9.4). During the month of April, the only shortnose sturgeon captured was found at km 153. In May another shortnose sturgeon was captured at km 153 and 6 shortnose sturgeon greater than 600 mm TL were captured between km 26 and km 37. The presence of 6 shortnose sturgeon of a size that indicates sexual maturity downstream of km 37 during May appeared to differ from the life history model of Dovel et al. (this volume). These fish were captured on May 7, 14, and 30 and assuming a peak spawning season of April 15 to May 15 (Dovel et al. this volume), it was possible that these fish had already spawned and were dispersing downriver. Using a movement rate of 16.5 km/day for shortnose sturgeon from the Connecticut River (Buckley and Kynard 1985) these Hudson River fish could have moved from the spawning grounds between km 200 and 246 to the downriver site of capture (km 26-37) in 11 days. Alternatively, evidence that the shortnose sturgeon is a nonannual spawner (Dadswell et al. 1984) would suggest that the 6 fish captured between km 26 and km 37 may not have participated in the spawning migration. Distribution of shortnose sturgeon during April, May, and June come from the White Perch Study. The White Perch Study was conducted during these months only in 1984 and it is unknown if the shortnose sturgeon distribution observed in 1984 was representative of other years.

As water temperatures decreased in September through December, the distribution of shortnose sturgeon appeared to center around the Kingston (km 137-149) and Croton-Haverstraw regions (km 54-61; Table 9.4). Specifically, the fixed sampling stations at km 148 and km 55 in the White Perch Study consistently yielded the most shortnose sturgeon during the period 1983-1988. Our data from the Kingston region was in agreement with the model of Dovel et al. (this volume), which identified the area between km 137 and km 149 as an important overwintering area for shortnose sturgeon. The Croton-Haverstraw region has not been previously identified as a major overwintering area for shortnose sturgeon. Dovel (1979) observed that some shortnose sturgeon may be found with more numerous Atlantic sturgeon in the Tappan Zee and Haverstraw Bay (km 38-61) during the fall and winter. TI (1981) reported that adult shortnose sturgeon in "resting" condition appeared to overwinter in Haverstraw Bay (km 54-61) but no sexual condition data were presented. The Croton-

Haverstraw region generally received twice the sampling effort in the White Perch Study when compared with upriver regions because 4 fixed sampling stations were located in this region (Table 9.2). However, most ($31/42 = 83\%$) of the shortnose sturgeon captured in the Croton-Haverstraw region were from only 2 sampling stations located off Croton Point at km 55 in 6 m of water. Therefore, the increased sampling effort does not solely account for the increased numbers of shortnose sturgeon caught in the Croton-Haverstraw region.

Catch data from the Fall Juvenile Survey also was in agreement with the life history model (Figure 8.4 of Dovel et al. this volume). During the months of July and August, all shortnose sturgeon were captured downstream of km 159, in agreement with a dispersal downstream after spawning. During the months of September, October, and November, the distribution of shortnose sturgeon was centered in the Kingston region, specifically at km 140–149. This was in agreement with both the White Perch Study catch data and the identification of the Esopus Meadow area as an overwintering area (Dovel et al. this volume). In contrast with the White Perch Study, only 2 shortnose sturgeon were captured in the Croton-Haverstraw region in the Fall Juvenile Survey (Table 9.5).

Sampling locations are randomly allocated to river regions in the Fall Juvenile Survey, compared to the White Perch Study where sampling stations are fixed. A random allocation of sampling effort is more likely to provide an accurate description of the distribution of shortnose sturgeon in the Croton-Haverstraw region because sampling effort will be distributed throughout the region and not concentrated at a few fixed stations. The abundance of shortnose sturgeon in the Croton-Haverstraw region observed in the White Perch Study during the fall may be an artifact of the fixed station sampling design. Two sampling stations located off Croton Point accounted for 83% of the sturgeon captured in the White Perch Study in the Croton-Haverstraw region. The Croton Point area may be a location of high local abundance, and shortnose sturgeon catch data from this area probably were not representative of the entire Croton-Haverstraw region. Shortnose sturgeon have occurred repeatedly in confined areas (Dadswell 1979). In the St. John River, New Brunswick, Canada, multiple recaptures of tagged shortnose sturgeon during July through September within confined areas suggested that some shortnose sturgeon become resident within certain localities (Dadswell 1984). The area off Croton Point may be a location where some shortnose sturgeon become resident during the winter.

Other areas of high local abundance of shortnose sturgeon may exist in the Hudson River, possibly in locations not routinely sampled. Further monitoring of shortnose sturgeon by-catch from existing monitoring programs, and investigation of catch data from past programs may identify these areas and provide valuable data on the distribution of the shortnose sturgeon in the Hudson River.

Acknowledgments

Funding for the programs was provided by Central Hudson Gas and Electric Corporation, Consolidated Edison Company of New York, Inc., the New York Power Authority, Niagara Mohawk Power Corporation, and Orange and Rockland Utilities. The field work for the 1983–1988 Hudson River Ichthyoplankton and Fall Juvenile Surveys, and the 1983–1984 White Perch Stock Assessment Studies was conducted by Normandeau Associates, Inc., under the direction of Mr. Michael J. Ricci. Lawler, Matusky, and Skelly, Engineers, Inc. (LMS) conducted the 1984–1988 White Perch Stock Assessment Study. Mr. John Matousek of LMS provided access to these data.

ROBERT E. SCHMIDT

10

Temporal and Spatial Distribution of Bay Anchovy Eggs through Adults in the Hudson River Estuary

ABSTRACT

The bay anchovy (*Anchoa mitchilli*) may well be the most abundant estuarine fish on the Atlantic coast. Bay anchovies serve as an important forage fish for valuable commercial species. They are pelagic macrozooplankton feeders and may compete for those resources with *Alosa* spp. and larval and juvenile Moronidae.

The data presented in this paper are derived from surveys done by Texas Instruments during 1976–79. The study area is defined as the Hudson River Estuary from the George Washington Bridge (km 19) to the dam at Troy (km 243). Distribution of various life stages was described by an ichthyoplankton survey (tucker trawl and epibenthic sled), a beach seine survey, and a trawl survey.

Adult anchovies first appeared in the Hudson Estuary in May when water temperatures were 17–19°C. They remained in near shore areas until early June when they moved offshore and spawned. The distribution of adults during spawning is directly related to salinity.

Peak egg abundance occurred in the lower 40 km of the estuary during June and July. Eggs were collected as far north as Albany and were present through the end of August when ichthyoplankton sampling ceased. The distribution of the postlarvae mirrored the egg distribution, but postlarvae were collected further upstream as the summer progressed. The distances involved precluded migration or passive transport as unequivocal explanations for this pattern and therefore the pattern is probably due to late season spawning in the upper estuary.

Adults left the estuary after spawning and recruitment of the juveniles occurred simultaneously. The majority of juveniles were collected in the lower estuary, but, reflecting postlarval distribution, juveniles were taken as far north as Albany. Consistent catches of juveniles <25 mm TL through the beginning of November indicated that spawning occurred through the fall. Late fall spawning could be due to a few adults that did not migrate from the estuary or to sexually mature young-of-the-year anchovies.

Downstream emigration from the study area of juveniles began with declining temperatures at the end of August. Most juvenile anchovies had left the estuary by the middle of November.

INTRODUCTION

McHugh (1967) considered the bay anchovy (*Anchoa mitchilli*) as probably the most abundant western Atlantic coastal fish. It is often the most common species in estuaries (Massman 1954; Derickson and Price 1973; Dahlberg 1972). Dovel (1981a) reported that bay anchovies comprised 94.6% of all ichthyoplankton collected in the lower Hudson estuary and 89% of the ichthyoplankton in the Patuxent River (Dovel 1971). Maximum densities in Dovel's (1981) study were 237 anchovies per m^3.

Larval and juvenile bay anchovies are primarily pelagic macrozooplankton feeders (Carr and Adams 1973; Stevenson 1958; Odum 1971). Due to their abundance and density, they probably significantly alter the composition and distribution of zooplankton communities. Presumably anchovies would compete with other syntopic ichthyoplankters for food items when resources are limited. Anchovies are food for predators that are economically important in the Hudson

River such as striped bass (*Morone saxatilis*), and Atlantic tomcod (*Microgadus tomcod*) (Hollis 1952; Grabe 1980).

Despite their abundance and wide distribution, few papers have been written summarizing anchovy biology (Stevenson 1958; Vouglitois et al. 1987). The purpose of this paper is to discuss the distribution and movements of bay anchovies within the Hudson River Estuary and to define some problems that may warrant further investigation.

MATERIALS AND METHODS

Study Area

The Hudson River Estuary is tidal for 243 km from the Federal Locks and Dam at Troy, New York, south to the Battery at the southern tip of Manhattan. Salinity intrusions commonly reach km 100 during summer months. Abood (1974, 1977), Darmer (1969), Leslie et al. (1988), and Limburg et al. (1986) provided descriptions of the physical and chemical aspects of the estuary.

For this study, the estuary was divided into 12 sampling regions (Frontispiece) from the George Washington Bridge (km 19) to the Troy Dam (km 243). The boundaries of these regions are arbitrary and do not divide the estuary evenly. Samples were evenly allocated to these regions, however.

Eggs and Larvae

There are two engraulids in the Hudson River (Smith 1985), both of which may spawn in the study area. These two species cannot be distinguished in the egg through early post–yolk-sac stages. Therefore, it is possible that both species are represented in the samples. The striped anchovy (*A. hepsetus*) is uncommon (Smith 1985) and it probably does not contribute substantial numbers of eggs or larvae to the Hudson River. Thus, all engraulid larvae are classified as *A. mitchilli* in this paper.

The analyses in this paper are primarily based on surveys conducted by Texas Instruments from 1976–1979 designed to collect early life stages of fishes. These surveys were not designed specifically to collect anchovies.

Survey methods, gear, and sampling allocations were consistent within and among years from 1976 to 1979 (Klauda et al. 1988a). Surveys began in mid-April. A survey consisted of 200 samples collected weekly during the day until June, and at night thereafter through early August. Samples were allocated to the 12 regions based on a stratified random design keyed to the distribution of striped bass eggs and larvae in prior years. Relevant water quality data (e.g., temperature and salinity) were collected during each type of sampling.

Bottom samples were collected with a 1.0 m^2 epibenthic sled (505 μm mesh) in water >2 m deep, and midwater and surface samples were collected with a 1.0 m^2 Tucker trawl (505 μm mesh). Tow speeds for the sled and trawl were 1.0 and 0.9 m/sec, respectively. Tow duration for both gears was 5 minutes. The mouth openings, net areas, net porosities, tow speeds, and tow durations were designed for sustained filtration efficiencies greater than 85% (Trantor and Smith 1968). Calibrated digital flow meters were suspended within the nets to record volume sampled. Calibrated electronic flow meters were mounted on the towing cable just above the gear to record towing speed. Double trip release mechanisms permitted opening and closing the nets at specific depths.

Weekly estimates of densities were calculated (Klauda et al. 1988b) for three developmental stages: eggs, yolk-sac larvae, and post–yolk-sac larvae. The latter stage is designated as postlarvae in the rest of this paper. Larvae were considered to be in the yolk-sac stage until the digestive system was fully developed regardless of the degree of yolk retention. The postlarval stage included those specimens with a complete digestive system but without a full complement of fin rays. Once the fin rays were fully developed, the young were defined as juveniles.

The mean weekly densities of each life stage in each of the 12 sampling regions were plotted as isopleths. Data for 1976–1979 were averaged, because the variation among years was negligible. The values plotted as isopleths were arbitrarily selected to represent the range of densities (in orders of magnitude) and to emphasize the spatial and temporal distributions of the highest densities.

Juveniles and Adults

The distribution of the older stages was monitored with two surveys conducted throughout the study area. One survey used a 30 m seine (0.48 cm mesh in the bunt) and sampled 100 beaches biweekly during the day from April through mid-December 1976–1979. A stratified random design, keyed to juvenile striped bass distributions in previous years, was used to allocate samples from 1976 to 1978. In 1979 the samples were randomly allocated to each of the 12 regions on the basis of relative shore area (0–3 m deep). Seine hauls were standardized as described by Young et al. (1988). Distributions were calculated on the basis of mean biweekly catch per haul in each region.

The second survey used a 3.6 m (headrope) otter trawl with 0.6 cm mesh in the cod end liner. This survey, known as the "try trawl" survey, sampled offshore areas 1.5–6.0 m deep. Approximately 100 randomly selected sites were sampled biweekly during the day from April through mid-December in 1979 only. Samples were allocated to each of the 12 regions in proportion to the shoal volume, areas less than 6 m deep. Tows were made at 1.5 m/sec against the prevailing current for approximately 10 minutes. Distributions were calculated as in the seine survey.

A subsample of juvenile anchovies collected during each seine and bottom trawl survey was preserved in 10% formalin and returned to the laboratory for length measurements. Total lengths were taken after the fish had been in formalin for at least 2 days. Laboratory studies showed that no significant shrinkage occurred after this period.

RESULTS AND DISCUSSION

Adult bay anchovies appeared in the study area beginning in late April–early May usually when water temperatures reached 17–19°C. Catch per unit effort (CPUE) in beach seines was highest in late May and early June (Figure 10.1) in the three southernmost sampling regions (km 19–61).

When trawl catches were compared in these areas during the spring, CPUE increased to its maximum about a month later than in the beach seines (Figure 10.1). This can be interpreted as an offshore movement possibly related to spawning since ichthyoplankton gear began to catch bay anchovy eggs in late May or the first week in June. Distribution of adults in the Hudson River is positively correlated with salinity (Figure 10.2) as reported by Wang (1974) in the Delaware River, yet adults are consistently collected at the Troy Dam (km 243). Adults are uncommon in the Hudson after the end of August because they either die after spawning or leave the estuary.

Densities of bay anchovy eggs were greatest in the southernmost 40 km of the study area and fell off sharply after the beginning of August (Figure 10.3). Egg distribution north of this area was patchy, but eggs, like the adults discussed above, were collected consistently from year to year up to the Troy Dam.

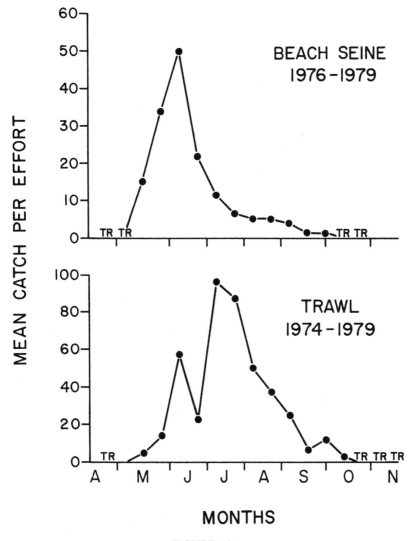

FIGURE 10.1.
Catch per effort of bay anchovy adults in the 3 southern sampling regions of the Hudson River Estuary. Points plotted are average catch per effort in all years sampled from biweekly beach seine and trawl surveys. TR = <1 anchovy per unit effort.

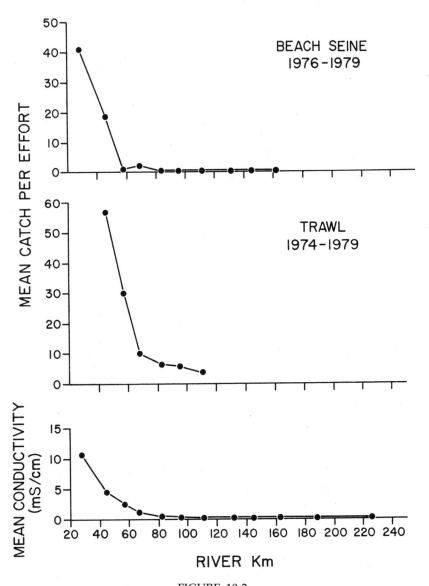

FIGURE 10.2.
Catch per effort of bay anchovy adults in the Hudson River Estuary. Points plotted are average catch per effort in each sampling region over all years sampled. Conductivity data are averages from all surveys.

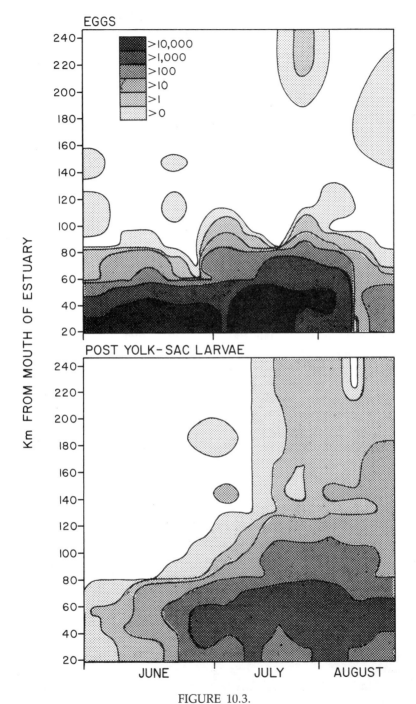

FIGURE 10.3.
Density isopleths (no./100 m³) of bay anchovy eggs and postlarvae in the Hudson River Estuary 1976–1979. Data are averages for weekly Tucker trawl and epibenthic sled samples for all sampling regions over all years.

Eggs of the bay anchovy hatch in about 24 h at 28° C (Jones et al. 1978). The yolk–sac larva has little yolk and this stage was rare in Hudson River ichthyoplankton collections. I saw very few specimens in the American Museum of Natural History Hudson River larval fish collection out of many thousands of anchovy larvae. Wang and Kernehan (1979) stated that anchovy yolk-sac larvae are epibenthic. Jones et al. (1978) reported that yolk-sac larvae transform in 15–25 h, which, combined with a benthic habitat, could explain why yolk-sac larvae are poorly sampled in the Texas Instruments surveys. Because catches of yolk-sac larvae were erratic, data for this life stage are not presented.

The Texas Instruments program, Bourne and Govoni (1988), Dovel (1971, 1981), and Olney (1983) collected weekly or biweekly samples. Given that eggs can hatch in 24 h and that the yolk-sac stage lasts for only 15–25 h (Jones et al. 1978; Fives et al. 1986), each sample of these life stages in all these studies could well be different cohorts although spawning of the population persists over a long period of time. Colby (1988) made a clear case that sampling designs need to be adjusted to the appropriate scale of the phenomenon to be measured. The temporal scale used in all these studies was inadequate to determine the distribution of anchovy eggs and yolk-sac larvae because the period between samples was much larger than the developmental time for those life stages. Judging by the disparity in egg distribution vs postlarval distribution in the Hudson (Figure 10.3), I suspect that the spatial scale used in this study was too large as well.

A one- or two-week sampling interval may be reasonable when discussing postlarval distribution, since this stage lasts approximately 45 days (Fives et al. 1986). Thus the pattern of postlarval distribution in Figure 10.3 may be a reasonable picture of this life stage in the Hudson River. Care must be taken, however, in inferring the process behind distributional changes since several processes may be occurring simultaneously that cannot be distinguished at this point. Distributional patterns are being altered by passive transport in water masses, increasingly more active movement of the larvae as they grow, mortality (which might be quite different in different areas of the river), and recruitment from newly hatched eggs whose distribution has thus far not been precisely determined. Therefore hypotheses explaining changes in anchovy distribution must be viewed as tentative unless they include all possible causes of distributional change.

The planktonic postlarvae were commonly collected in ichthyoplankton gear. Densities of postlarvae were highest in the southernmost 60 km of the study area and from late June through the end of August (Figure 10.3). This distribution correlates well with highest egg densities but was delayed by 3–4 weeks, a phenomenon also observed by Olney (1983). Olney suggested that daytime gear avoidance by older larvae could explain this delay. We sampled with different gear at night and still observed a delay between the two stages. It may be that postlarvae are not recruited to the gear until they are about two weeks old, but we have no length frequency data to support this hypothesis.

Postlarvae were found farther north in the Hudson Estuary as the season progressed and were collected in low densities but consistently throughout the entire study area from mid-July until sampling ceased at the end of August. Similar observations of late season upstream distributions of bay anchovy larvae were made in the Potomac (Lippson et al. 1980), Chesapeake Bay (Dovel 1971), and the Delaware estuary (Wang and Kernehan, 1979). Lippson et al. suggested that passive upstream transport of larvae caused this observed pattern. Rapid upstream transport is feasible in the Hudson only as far upstream as the salt front penetrates (roughly km 80 [Cooper et al. 1988]). If the larvae migrate vertically on a tidal cycle, are in the salt wedge as it moves upstream, and leave the salt wedge when it moves downstream, they may be transported northward in the Hudson. Some larval fishes (Boehlert and Mundy 1988) and invertebrates (Epifanio 1988) do this, but there is no indication in the literature that bay anchovies behave in this fashion. Bourne and Govoni (1988) demonstrated diel vertical migration of *Anchoa* spp. larvae in Narragansett Bay and suggested that this behavior coupled with the long residence time of water in the bay may explain larval retention for these species. However, diel vertical migrations would not necessarily cause upstream transport of larvae in the Hudson, since the tidal cycle is not diel. Therefore, I do not think that daily or seasonal movement of the salt front can explain the distribution of bay anchovy larvae in the Hudson River.

Dovel (1971), and Wang and Kernehan (1979) suggested that the anchovy larvae actively migrated upstream. I think this is unlikely in the Hudson due to the distance necessary to travel from the salt front to Albany (160 km), the small size and presumed poor swimming ability of the larvae, and the fact that net transport is south (downstream) in the upper Hudson Estuary (Abood 1977). High mortality in the areas of the river where larvae are dense could give the impression of a movement upstream, but this could not explain the presence of the larvae in Albany. For the Hudson estuary, it makes more sense to suggest that postlarvae in the northern estuary were spawned there by adults penetrating into the freshwater section of the river.

One striking pattern in postlarval anchovy distribution appears when the anchovy data are compared to postlarval *Alosa* spp. (Schmidt et al. 1988). The latter distributions were derived from the same data set in the same manner as the anchovy postlarval distribution reported here. Highest densities of both taxa exceeded $10^4/1000$ m^3 and highest postlarval densities were allopatric in the Hudson River. River herring were concentrated from km 80–243 from mid-May through early July, whereas bay anchovies were concentrated south of km 80 from mid-June through the end of August (Figure 10.3). The upriver distribution of anchovies occurred in mid-July and increased in density through August (Figure 10.3) when river herring larval density in the northern estuary was sharply declining.

There might be a long-term coevolutionary explanation for this pattern. Perhaps competition is decreased since it is likely that both taxa feed on similar zooplankters (both are very similar morphologically). Perhaps the larger river herring postlarvae (spawned earlier) are predators on the smaller bay anchovies and the observed patterns are a result of a predator-prey interaction. Much more observation needs to be made on these questions.

Since the Texas Instruments ichthyoplankton sampling ceased at the end of August, I do not know how long postlarvae persist in the Hudson River. Postlarvae were reported in New York harbor in December (TI 1976). Dovel (1981) found 7 mm larvae (which would be 13–14 days old [Fives et al. 1986]) in Haverstraw Bay (km 55) in late September. Anchovy eggs were taken as late as November in Barnegat Bay, New Jersey (Vouglitois et al. 1987).

Juveniles were recruited to the population (or the gear) beginning in early July (Figure 10.4). Highest catches in trawls and beach seines were in the southernmost 75 km of the estuary, but juveniles were collected as far north as Albany (km 243) as the postlarval distribution would predict.

Catch per effort of juvenile bay anchovies declined abruptly after the end of September in trawls and beach seines. This decline may be the result of migration out of the study area into the New York Bight, the south shore of Long Island, and northern New Jersey (Vouglitois et al. 1987) and perhaps Long Island Sound. Length frequencies of juvenile anchovies during this migratory period indicate an extended spawning period in the Hudson River (Figure 10.5).

Maximum size of bay anchovies is 100 mm TL, although they are more usually around 70–80 mm (Hildebrand 1963). Thus anchovies

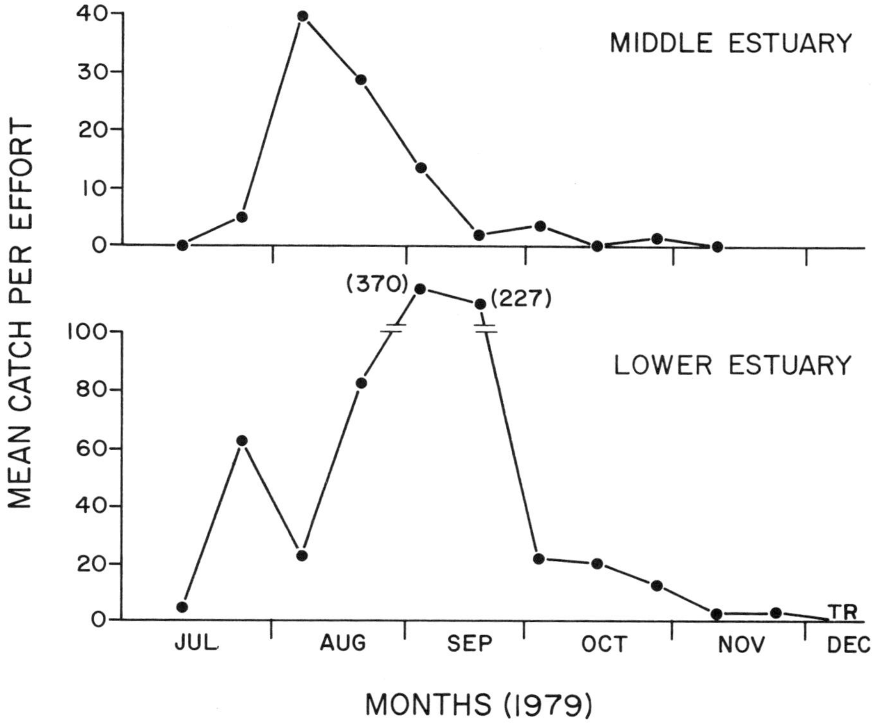

FIGURE 10.4.
Catch per effort of juvenile bay anchovies in trawls in the Hudson River Estuary, 1979. The middle estuary is defined as km 75–98 and the lower is km 19–75.

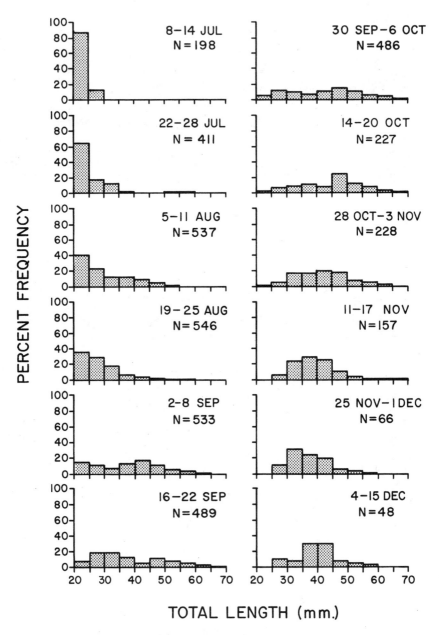

FIGURE 10.5.
Length frequency of bay anchovies collected in 1979 in the Hudson River Estuary.

attain at least 75% of their maximum size by late fall in North Carolina (Fives et al. 1986) and in the Hudson River (Figure 10.5). Fives et al. (1986) therefore suggested that bay anchovies do not exceed 1.5–2 years old. To my knowledge, no one has aged anchovies in the Hudson River, but the data suggest that they would not exceed 1.5 years old.

Hildebrand and Cable (1930) observed bay anchovies at 45–60 mm with developed eggs in late July and early August in Beaufort, North Carolina. Stevenson (1958) found that anchovies became sexually mature at 35–40 mm. Fives et al. (1986) stated that anchovies spawned early in the summer could easily attain those sizes by the late summer or early fall of the same year.

The persistent collection of eggs up to the end of August and through an unknown period afterward in the Hudson River makes spawning by anchovies less than a year old a viable explanation for the extended spawning period of this species. No observations have been recorded suggesting that late summer young-of-the-year anchovies are sexually mature in the Hudson. A short-lived species like this one could increase its fecundity by spawning more than once (iteroparous) and juvenile anchovies should be examined to determine their sexual maturity.

RECOMMENDATIONS

Despite their abundance in the Hudson and other East Coast estuaries, some aspects of bay anchovy biology are poorly known. The age structure of the population should be determined. The distributions of eggs and yolk-sac larvae is still poorly understood and the lack of yolk-sac larvae in collections needs an explanation. The trophic dynamics of this species may be significant to zooplankton populations in the lower Hudson and should be documented.

Acknowledgments

Thanks to all the TI personnel, now scattered, who gathered the data I used in this paper. I appreciate the support of Consolidated Edison, Inc., and thank them for allowing me to use their data files. Collection of these data was funded by Central Hudson Gas and Electric Corp., Consolidated Edison Company of New York, Inc., the New York Power Authority, Niagara Mohawk Power Corp., and Orange and Rockland Utilities. The figures were drafted by Kathleen A. Schmidt. This is Bard College Field Station-Hudsonia Contribution #54.

ALAN W. WELLS
JOHN A. MATOUSEK
JAY B. HUTCHISON

11

Abundance Trends in Hudson River White Perch

ABSTRACT

White perch is one of the most abundant fish in the Hudson River Estuary. Because of its abundance, distribution, and trophic position, it was selected for study as a potential indicator of environmental changes related to power plant operation. After 15 years of study, trends in white perch abundance may permit evaluation of anthropogenic impact on this estuary.

Twenty separate indices of annual abundance were examined via regression analysis and cluster analysis. The results indicate that the numbers of white perch eggs, yolk-sac, and post–yolk-sac larvae have increased in recent years. The number of young-of-year was high in the early and mid-1970s with a peak in 1978 and 1979, then followed by a rapid decline through the 1980s. Adult numbers, especially as measured by fully recruited age classes, have been increasing over time. The paradoxical result of increasing egg, larval, and adult abundance coupled with decreasing young-of-year abundance suggests that the catchability of young-of-year fish has decreased in recent years.

One possible explanation for a decrease in juvenile catchability may be an increase in unsampleable habitats, such as weedy backbays, nearshore shallows, and water chestnut beds. Water chestnut beds have been expanding since the cessation of an eradication program in 1975.

INTRODUCTION

Intensive investigations of the Hudson River ecosystem arose from environmental issues initially raised over the proposed construction of the Cornwall pumped storage facility. The dispute began in 1963, and by the late 1960s had grown to include not only the effects of the pumped storage facility, but also the effects of fossil and nuclear power plant operation on local fish populations. In an effort to determine the operational impact of these facilities on the Hudson River ecosystem, the Hudson River Utilities (Central Hudson Gas and Electric Corporation, Consolidated Edison Company of New York, Inc., New York Power Authority, Niagara Mohawk Power Corporation, and Orange and Rockland Utilities, Inc.) undertook a series of ecological sampling programs beginning in the late 1960s.

One species of primary interest was the white perch (*Morone americana*). This species was especially well suited as an indicator of the potential effects of sustained power plant operation on fish populations because (1) it is a resident species throughout most of the estuary, (2) it is one of the most abundantly collected species in the region, (3) it plays a major role in the Hudson River ecosystem, and (4) it supports only a limited commercial and recreational fishery, thereby lessening confounding sources of mortality.

After a lengthy period of legal proceedings and hearings, the procedural issues surrounding the case were resolved by a negotiated settlement agreement in 1980. However, the biological issues concerning the effects of power plants on fish populations remained unresolved (see Talbot 1983 and Barnthouse et al. 1984 for additional details). During the court hearings scientists estimated the power plant removal of young-of-year (YOY) white perch to be between 10 and 20% annually. Whether or not this removal rate was detrimental to the population was a major point of disagreement. Regulatory agency scientists argued that such removal rates would cause the population to decline; the utilities and their consultants argued that biological compensatory mechanisms would be sufficient to maintain the population. It was generally acknowledged by both sides, however, that the year-to-year variation in white perch year-class strength would mask the ability to detect any short-term changes in stock abundance. Van Winkle et al. (1981) and Vaughan and Van Winkle (1982) estimated that it would require approximately 20 years of impingement data to be 50% certain of detecting a 50% reduction in mean year-class strength.

After 15 years of monitoring, sufficient data may now be available to detect changes in stock abundance. If annual power plant removal rates were between 10 and 20% and the white perch population was unable to compensate for these losses, then the current population should be reduced by an average of 52 to 79% from the 1980 level. Studies such as Bath and O'Connor (1982) and Klauda et al. (1988a), as well as numerous annual reports issued by the Hudson River Utilities, have summarized much of the biological information on white perch. The purpose of this paper is to synthesize this information and to assess the status of the stock. Analyses are presented to determine whether the stock has declined in recent years.

MATERIALS AND METHODS

A wide variety of studies, using various methods, has been conducted over the years, but not all are suitable for assessing year-class strength and abundance trends. The strengths and weaknesses of most of these studies are summarized in Klauda et al. (1988b). Studies reviewed for potential use in our assessment include the Hudson River Utilities' Longitudinal River Survey (LRS), Fall Shoals Survey (FSS), Beach Seine Survey (BSS), White Perch Stock Assessment Program (WPSAP), and the New York State Department of Environmental Conservation (NYSDEC) beach seine program. Entrainment and impingement studies from Roseton and Danskammer Point were also examined. Detailed descriptions of field and laboratory methods can be found in annual reports from those studies (Table 11.1) and in Klauda et al. (1988b).

Longitudinal River Survey

The Hudson River Utilities' LRS program, begun in 1973, was not standardized until the following year. The program was designed to obtain information on ichthyoplankton temporal and spatial abun-

TABLE 11.1.
Data sources for assessment of Hudson River white perch stock.

	Impingement		Entrainment		River Programs	
Year	Danskammer Point	Roseton	Danskammer Point	Roseton	Year Class Rept.	Stock Assessment
1972						LMS 86b
1973						LMS 86b
1974	LMS 78a	LMS 78a			TI 75	LMS 86b
1975	LMS 78b	LMS 78b			TI 78a	LMS 86b
1976	LMS 79a	LMS 79a	LMS 79a	LMS 79a	TI 78b	LMS 86b
1977	LMS 79b	LMS 79b	LMS 79b	LMS 79b	TI 80a	LMS 86b
1978	LMS 80a	LMS 80a	LMS 80a	LMS 80a	TI 80a,b	LMS 86b
1979	LMS 80b	LMS 80b	LMS 80b	LMS 80b	TI 81	LMS 86b
1980	LMS 81a	LMS 81a	LMS 81a	LMS 81a	BAT 83	LMS 86b
1981	LMS 82	LMS 82		EA 82	BAT 83	LMS 86b
1982	LMS 83	LMS 83	EA 83	EA 83	NAI 85a	LMS 86b
1983	LMS 84	LMS 84	EA 84	EA 84	NAI 85b	NAI 85c
1984	EA 85	EA 85	LMS 85	LMS 85	MM 86	NAI 85c
1985	EA 86	EA 86	LMS 86	LMS 86a	V 87	LMS 86b
1986	LMS 87b	LMS 87b	EA 87	EA 87	LMS 89	LMS 87a
1987					LMS 89	LMS 88

TI   = Texas Instruments, Inc.
NAI = Normandeau Associates, Inc.
MM   = Martin Marietta Environmental Systems
LMS = Lawler, Matusky & Skelly Engineers
EA   = Ecological Analysts, Inc.
V   = Versar, Inc.
BAT = Battelle

dance. Sampling was conducted with a 1-m² net on an epibenthic sled and a 1-m² Tucker trawl, each with 505 μm mesh in each of 12 regions (Frontispiece). Approximately 175 to 210 samples per survey (usually four to five days in duration), with 9 to 15 surveys per season, were collected. Sampling effort was allocated to regions and strata using a procedure optimized for the distribution of larval striped bass. From 1974 through 1979, sampling was conducted from mid-April through mid-August; in 1980 from mid-March through early July; post-1980 from April through early July. Early season samples were generally collected during daylight hours; beginning in May or

June, sampling was conducted at night to maximize catches of older striped bass life stages.

An index of annual abundance was conducted for egg, yolk-sac larvae (YSL), and post–yolk-sac larvae (PYSL) life stages from the geometric mean standing crop. The standing crop was obtained by multiplying the regional mean catch per cubic meter by the volume of the region. Because the start and end of the sampling period varied from year to year, the index was restricted to data from the period common to all years, May 14 through July 7.

Fall Shoals Survey

Although the FSS began in 1973, standardized depth strata were not established until 1974. The program has focused primarily on striped bass, white perch, and Atlantic tomcod. Typically, biweekly trawl samples were taken from August through December; in some years, however, sampling started as early as July and ended as early as mid-October. Three depth strata—a shoal region (≤ 6 m), a bottom region (>6 m but within 3 m from the river bottom), and a channel region (>6 m but above 3 m from bottom)—were generally sampled. Prior to 1979 no samples from near surface, mid-depth, or upriver from km 122 were taken. The channel stratum was sampled with a 1-m^2 Tucker trawl; the bottom and shoal strata, until 1985, with a 1-m^2 epibenthic sled. Beginning in 1985 the two bottom strata were sampled with a 3-m beam trawl.

In constructing abundance indices from the FSS, only data from mid-August through early October were used to ensure comparability among years. Also, the indices included only the shoal stratum from the Yonkers through Indian Point regions and the bottom stratum from the Tappan Zee through Poughkeepsie regions. Remaining strata and regions were not sampled consistently over the study period. Data from 1985 through 1987 were adjusted for relative gear efficiency (NAI 1986) since the beam trawl replaced the epibenthic sled for bottom and shoal habitat sampling in those years.

Beach Seine Survey

The BSS was initiated in 1973, although a regular sampling schedule did not begin until 1974. The program has relied on a 30.5 m beach seine to collect samples weekly or biweekly. The wings of the net have 2.0 cm stretch mesh; the bag, 9.5 mm stretch mesh. The net sampled an area of approximately 450 m^2, taking approximately 100 samples per survey from river km 19 to 245. Samples were taken during daylight hours except for 1973–1974, when some night sampling was done. During 1973–1980, sampling was conducted from April through December. In 1981 the program dates were reduced to August through October. In 1984 the program was expanded to include July and in 1985 further expanded to include November. This program was directed primarily toward YOY and yearling striped bass and white perch.

The BSS standing crop index was based only on the mid-August through early October data to ensure comparability. All 12 regions were included in these indices because all regions were sampled in all years. The standing crop was obtained by multiplying the regional mean catch per square meter by the area of the stratum.

The Hudson River Utilities have developed three indices derived from the combined FSS and BSS standing crop estimates: the geometric mean method index, the summer regression index, and the fall regression index. The standing crop estimates were obtained by multiplying the average strata fish concentration times the strata area (BSS) or volume (FSS), then adding the estimates together to obtain the combined standing crop. The geometric mean method index estimate was based on combined standing crop values from July to early September. The index value was obtained by extrapolating the geometric mean value to August 1 using the daily instantaneous mortality rate of 0.00379. The summer regression index was calculated by regression of weekly combined standing crop data from August through mid-October to estimate the standing crop on August 1. When the regression slope was not statistically significant, the index was calculated as a geometric mean. The fall regression index was calculated by regression of weekly combined standing crop data from the first week of September to the first week of October to estimate the standing crop on September 15. Again, when the regression was not significant, the index was calculated as a geometric mean.

White Perch Stock Assessment Program

Since 1971 the Hudson River Utilities have sponsored a comprehensive sampling program, the results of which have been used in the assessment of the white perch stock. The program has undergone several changes in emphasis and scope since its inception, especially in sampling stations (Table 11.2) and sampling periods. Generally, the program has consisted of biweekly trawl samples collected from September through mid-December. Throughout the program a 9.1 m flat

TABLE 11.2. White perch stock assessment program—sampling stations, 1971–1987.

	Upper Estuary (River miles 78 to 107)						Middle Estuary (River miles 39 to 77)						Lower Estuary (River miles 26 to 38)								
	CSD	CSS	SGD	SGS	KGD	KGS	PKD	PKS	CWD	CWS	WPD	WPS	CD	CS	ND	NS	PD	PS	BB	BID	BC
1971																		X	X	X	X
1972																		X	X	X	X
1973																		X	X	X	X
1974																		X	X	X	X
1975																	X	X	X	X	X
1976																	X	X	X	X	X
1977																X	X	X	X	X	X
1978															X	X	X	X	X	X	X
1979												X	X	X	X	X	X	X	X	X	X
1980											X	X	X	X	X	X	X	X	X	X	X
1981										X	X	X	X	X	X	X	X	X	X	X	X
1982									X	X	X	X	X	X	X	X	X	X	X	X	X
1983	X	X	X	X	X	X	X	X	X	X	X	X	X	X	X	X	X	X	X	X	X
1984	X	X	X	X	X	X	X	X	X	X	X	X	X	X	X	X	X	X	X	X	X
1985	X	X	X	X	X	X	X	X	X	X	X	X	X	X	X	X	X	X	X	X	X
1986	X	X	X	X	X	X	X	X	X	X	X	X	X	X	X	X	X	X	X	X	X
1987	X	X	X	X	X	X	X	X	X	X	X	X	X	X	X	X	X	X	X	X	X

CSD = Catskill Deep, CSS = Catskill Shallow, SGD = Saugerties Deep, SGS = Saugerties Shallow
KGD = Kingston Deep, KGS = Kingston Shallow, PKD = Poughkeepsie Deep, PKS = Poughkeepsie Shallow
CWD = Cornwall Deep, CWS = Cornwall Shallow, WPD = West Point Deep, WPS = West Point Shallow
CD = Croton Deep, CS = Croton Shallow, ND = Nyack Deep, NS = Nyack Shallow
PD = Piermont Deep, PS = Piermont Shallow, BB = Bowline Bay, BID = Bowline Inlet Discharge, BC = Bowline Channel

otter trawl was used. The wings and body have 5.1 cm stretch mesh; the cod end, 3.8 cm stretch mesh with a 1.3 cm stretch mesh liner.

During 1974 some additional specimens were collected with trap nets and gill nets. These fish were not identifiable within the data set. Although inclusion of these fish could potentially bias all indices involving this year class, we believe that the loss of data continuity would more seriously hamper interpretation than any bias introduced by the additional specimens.

During the period 1971 through 1977 sampling was conducted only in the Haverstraw Bay region of the lower estuary. Beginning in the fall of 1978 additional trawl stations were added in the Tappan Zee region, extending the downriver limit of the study area to Piermont (km 42). From 1983 through 1987 the field program consisted of samples conducted at 20 fixed stations extending from Piermont (km 42) to Catskill (km 172). The stations were paired—shallow shoal (3 to 5 m) and deep channel (6 to 18 m)—at 10 locations over three regions: lower estuary (km 42–61), middle estuary (km 62–124), and upper estuary (km 125–172). The Tappan Zee and Haverstraw Bay stations were the only ones sampled consistently from 1978 through 1987, with the exception of 1980. During field sampling all white perch caught were enumerated. A random subsample of 100 from each region and sampling period were returned to the laboratory for further analysis. Results from scale analysis were used to construct an age-length key that was used in turn to estimate the age structure of the entire field sample from the measured subsample.

Four indices were derived from the white perch stock assessment data, two based on YOY catches and two on age 3+ and older fish. The first index is based on the average catch per unit effort (CPUE) and YOY from all lower estuary stations, the second on the average CPUE for YOY only from the two continuously sampled Haverstraw Bay stations, Bowline Channel (BC) and Bowline Inlet Discharge (BID). This second index can be used to assess the influence of station changes over the study period. The deletion of the Bowline Bay (BB) station, a shallow water location, after 1982 could have biased the lower estuary station index. LMS (1982) reported that in the years 1971–1981, catches were higher in station BB than in BID and BC in 9 of 11 years, and stated that the shallow, baylike location may offer a preferred habitat to white perch, especially YOY.

The third and fourth indices were based on summing all age 3+ and older individuals from a given year class. The 3+ and older criterion was used because, as LMS (1988) noted, catches of the same year class increase in years subsequent to their birth—that is, full recruitment to the sampling gear does not occur until approximately age 3. For example, the average CPUE for the 1982 year class in 1982 was 9.1/10 min tow. The catch of this year class increased in subsequent years, peaking in 1985 at 27.8/10 min tow. The fourth index, based on stations BID and BC, was constructed from 3+ and older individuals for the same reasons as discussed for YOY.

NYSDEC Beach Seine Survey

NYSDEC has conducted a beach seine survey since 1981. Although the program is directed toward YOY striped bass, records for other important species, such as white perch, have also been kept. The program relies on a 61 by 3 m beach seine to collect samples on a biweekly schedule. The net has a stretch mesh size of 13 mm. Before 1985 the program consisted of six biweekly runs from late August through early November. Since 1985 nine biweekly runs of 25 seine hauls have been taken from mid-July through early November. Beaches sampled were from the lower Hudson River between km 40 and 64.

The NYSDEC beach seine program maintains catch data for both YOY and adult (yearling and older) white perch. Because sampling effort is relatively constant from year to year, the number caught can be used directly as an index of abundance.

Hudson River Utilities Entrainment and Impingement Programs

Entrainment and impingement values for the years 1974 through 1987 were available for Danskammer Point and Rosèton Generating Stations, both located in the middle estuary at km 107 and 105, respectively. Because the indices are based on data from a fixed location, they may be biased by year-to-year differences in distribution. Because white perch appear to prefer fresh and low salinity waters, their distribution may be influenced by changes in freshwater inflow and the corresponding changes in the position of the salt front (Wells and Young, this volume).

Entrainment samples were typically collected from May through July, although only through June in some years. Roseton samples were collected from the main discharge flow, Danskammer Point samples from the intake canal (1.0 m from the canal bottom). Twenty-four 1-hr samples per day were collected, with sampling intensity ranging from every other day during periods of peak abundance to every seventh day during nonpeak periods. Samples were pumped through a 10.2 cm pipe into plankton nets suspended in water-filled holding containers. An index of relative annual entrainment abundance was derived from the May 1 through June 15 geometric mean average abundance for egg, YSL, and PYSL stages. The May through June 15 period represented the sampling period common to all years.

Impingement collections are typically 24 hrs long at least one day a week. In early years, or when especially high impingement rates were encountered, several additional days per week were sometimes sampled. The average impingement rate was estimated for each month by dividing the total number of white perch caught by the volume sampled. An index of relative annual impingement abundance was derived from the January–December monthly arithmetic average number impinged per million cubic meters of intake water. Prior to 1981 only total white perch impingement catch was available. Beginning in 1980 the catch was categorized by age group—YOY, yearling, and older.

Statistical Methods

Ordinary least squares regression analysis (SAS 1985) was used to test for trends in the abundance indices over time. The sampling year was taken as the independent variable and the natural log of the abundance index as the dependent variable. The average rate of change, expressed as an annual percentage, was calculated as percent change = $100(e^b - 1)$ where b is the regression coefficient, i.e., slope. Associations among the indices were determined using a weighted pair-group average clustering algorithm (Davis 1973), with Pearson's correlation coefficient as a similarity measure.

RESULTS

Longitudinal River Survey, Eggs

The geometric mean standing crop estimates for white perch eggs indicated a slight increase, averaging 7.1% per year, over the period 1975 through 1987. However, this increase was not statistically significant (Table 11.3). The lowest mean standing crop, 1,705 million, occurred in 1977; the highest, 152,096 million, in 1984. This index was significantly correlated with the LRS yolk-sac–larvae index, $r = 0.734$ ($P \leq 0.01$) (Table 11.4).

Longitudinal River Survey, Yolk-Sac Larvae

Over the period 1975 through 1985 the geometric mean standing crop estimates for YSL suggested a slight, but nonsignificant, downward trend averaging 4.2% per year. The lowest standing crop, 2,585 mil-

TABLE 11.3.
Abundance index and trend analysis for selected Hudson River white perch studies, 1968–1987.

Program/Index Life Stage	LRS Egg	LRS YSL	LRS PYSL	BSS YOY	FSS YOY	CSC/GM YOY	CSC/SR YOY	CSC/FR YOY	WPSAP YOY	WPSAP/2 YOY
Units	×10⁶	×10⁶	×10⁶	×10⁶	#/1000m³	×10⁶	×10⁶	×10⁶	#/10min	#/10min
Year										
1968										
1979										
1970										
1971									53.4	
1972									52.1	
1973									33.1	27.5
1974	27,515	12,099	60,127	8	1.32				28.2	13.3
1975	35,886	23,341	302,741	18	5.90	43	38	38	40.7	12.4
1976	1,705	6,393	250,083	23	3.92	24	32	18	30.1	18.1
1977	22,233	8,924	249,058	18	0.59	7	6	5	23.6	8.0
1978	12,255	9,213	937,019	23	1.09	26	43	15	87.1	13.1
1979	47,857	36,398	536,238	33	5.38	47	71	24	77.7	28.2
1980	9,303	2,585	875,895	24	2.52	42	59	19	38.5	4.3
1981	120,412	83,385	1,338,238	23	1.81	31	38	18	20.7	20.4
1982	64,189	3,748	694,875	25	0.82	32	37	22	9.1	3.0
1983	152,096	34,842	417,408	22	0.82	25	19	18	7.4	9.8
1984	30,854	6,732	1,336,806	10	0.37	11	9	10	0.3	1.3
1985	23,548	7,147	997,001	12	0.09	10	12	9	12.2	34.5
1986	8,690	5,023	839,056	15	0.17	17	13	13	6.1	13.4
1987				14	0.09	10	12	12	12.5	23.3

Program/Index Life Stage	WPSAP >3+	WPSAP/2 >3+	WYSDEC YOY	WYSDEC ADULT	Dansk. Imping.	Roseton Imping.	Dansk. Egg	Dansk. Larvae	Roseton Egg	Roseton Larvae
Units	#/10min	#/10min	×10³	×10³	#/mg	#/mg	#/MCM	#/MCM	#/MCM	#/MCM
Year										
1968	2.6									
1969	3.7									
1970	12.5	43.2								
1971	8.7	3.2								
1972	7.9	6.2								
1973	9.1	9.7								
1974	28.2	16.2			0.7105	0.3733				
1975	32.0	14.1			0.8054	0.6123				
1976	24.2	10.3			1.2230	0.5290			65	16
1977	24.1	17.1			1.3002	0.5988			24	16
1978	34.2	28.5			0.5456	0.2135	257	15	25	16
1979	27.5	37.2			0.8349	0.3443	99	39	21	25
1980	22.4	29.6			1.8991	0.5259	241	61	75	28
1981	25.9	22.9	7.5	2.8	1.3767	0.4689			105	42
1982	40.7	41.1	9.0	10.0	1.9937	0.2195	57	64	129	38
1983	57.4	69.3	5.9	7.0	2.3047	0.4876	50	77	180	75
1984	37.2	58.9	4.1	5.5	2.1701	0.1614			85	36
1985			1.6	1.6	1.2503	0.1727	676	318	167	261
1986			5.8	1.9	1.6122	0.1525	1406	169	197	77
1987			1.9	1.3	2.6613	0.3367	719	69	174	86
Slope	0.1485	0.1366	−0.2251	−0.2535	0.0837	−0.0730	0.2106	0.2079	0.1849	0.1988
SE of slope	0.0224	0.0376	0.0953	0.1189	0.0229	0.0280	0.1245	0.0722	0.0432	0.0338
Annual Change (%)	16.0	14.6	−20.2	−22.4	8.7	−7.0	23.4	23.1	20.3	22.0
Probability	<0.0001	0.0030	0.0646	0.0861	0.0032	0.0229	0.1417	0.0282	0.0016	0.0004
Significance	**	**	NS	NS	**	*	NS	*	**	**

TABLE 11.4.
Pearson's correlation coefficients among selected Hudson River white perch studies.

	LRS Egg	LRS YSL	LRS PYSL	BSS YOY	FSS YOY	CSC/GM YOY	CSC/SR YOY	CSC/FR YOY	WPSAP YOY	WPSAP/2 YOY
	1	2	3	4	5	6	7	8	9	10
1		**	NS	NS	NS	NS	NS	NS	NS	*
2	0.734		NS	NS	NS	NS	NS	NS	NS	*
3	0.223	0.340		NS	NS	NS	NS	NS	NS	NS
4	−0.209	0.170	−0.036		*	**	**	NS	*	NS
5	−0.239	−0.048	−0.362	0.537		**	**	**	*	NS
6	−0.065	0.214	−0.143	0.777	0.792		**	**	*	NS
7	−0.147	0.192	−0.089	0.855	0.706	0.920		*	**	NS
8	−0.010	0.175	−0.196	0.467	0.813	0.847	0.623		NS	NS
9	−0.425	−0.201	−0.289	0.562	0.565	0.563	0.738	0.347		NS
10	−0.612	−0.561	0.280	0.060	0.154	−0.050	0.078	−0.048	0.222	
11	0.496	0.109	0.389	−0.041	−0.356	−0.142	−0.341	0.058	−0.389	−0.509
12	0.650	0.169	0.508	0.050	−0.417	−0.160	−0.216	−0.205	−0.403	−0.449
13	0.282	0.531	−0.157	0.838	0.709	0.931	0.826	0.891	0.108	−0.615
14	0.763	0.797	0.149	0.586	0.300	0.611	0.476	0.706	−0.349	−0.770
15	0.453	0.273	0.332	−0.143	−0.498	−0.372	−0.439	−0.319	−0.698	−0.284
16	−0.392	−0.218	−0.622	0.273	0.535	0.341	0.209	0.375	0.131	−0.126
17	−0.459	−0.386	0.218	−0.733	−0.493	−0.643	−0.608	−0.699	−0.399	0.267
18	−0.108	−0.224	0.622	−0.698	−0.448	−0.604	−0.588	−0.676	−0.517	0.537
19	0.122	−0.046	0.556	−0.496	−0.584	−0.346	−0.510	−0.113	−0.723	0.140
20	−0.088	−0.237	0.606	−0.511	−0.424	−0.409	−0.400	−0.356	−0.363	0.598

	WPSAP >3+	WPSAP >3+	NYSDEC YOY	NYSDEC Adult	Dansk. Imping.	Roseton Imping.	Dansk. Egg	Dansk. Larvae	Roseton Egg	Roseton Larvae
	11	12	13	14	15	16	17	18	19	20
1	NS	*	NS	*	NS	NS	NS	NS	NS	NS
2	NS	NS	NS	*	NS	NS	NS	NS	NS	NS
3	NS	NS	NS	NS	NS	*	NS	NS	NS	*
4	NS	NS	*	NS	NS	NS	*	NS	*	NS
5	NS	NS	NS	NS	NS	*	NS	NS	NS	NS
6	NS	NS	**	NS	NS	NS	NS	NS	NS	NS
7	NS	NS	*	NS	NS	NS	NS	NS	NS	NS
8	NS	NS	**	NS	**	NS	NS	NS	**	NS
9	NS	NS	NS	*	NS	NS	NS	NS	*	*
10	NS	NS	NS	NS	*	NS	NS	NS	NS	*
11		**	NS	NS	NS	NS	NS	NS	NS	NS
12	0.736		NS	NS	NS	NS	NS	NS	NS	NS
13	−0.197	−0.630		NS	NS	NS	NS	NS	NS	NS
14	0.565	0.372	0.676		NS	NS	NS	NS	*	NS
15	0.516	0.722	−0.141	0.283		NS	NS	NS	NS	NS
16	−0.299	−0.476	0.252	0.075	−0.125		NS	NS	NS	NS
17	−0.649	−0.750	−0.382	−0.800	0.081	−0.531		NS	**	**
18	0.488	0.689	−0.536	−0.550	−0.029	−0.458	0.544		NS	*
19	0.743	0.630	−0.293	−0.335	0.635	−0.343	0.569	0.572		
20	0.816	0.790	−0.665	−0.477	0.092	−0.406	0.382	0.943	0.611	

* = $p < 0.05$
** = $p < 0.01$
NS = not significant, $p > 0.05$

lion, occurred in 1981, followed immediately by the highest, 83,385 million, in 1982.

Longitudinal River Survey, Post–Yolk-Sac Larvae

The annual geometric mean standing crop of this life stage indicated a significant increase over the period 1975 through 1987, averaging 18.1% per year. The lowest standing crop, 60,127 million, occurred in 1975. The highest, 1,338,238 million, coincided with the peak YSL standing crop in 1982. However, the 1985 standing crop, 1,336,806 million, almost equaled that observed in 1982. This index displayed the highest degree of correlation to the Danskammer Point larval entrainment index, $r = 0.621$, although the correlation is not significant, probably due to the small number of comparisons, 8.

Hudson River Utilities Beach Seine Survey, Young-of-Year

YOY standing crops for the period 1974–1987 peaked in 1979 at 33 million. Although the lowest standing crop, 8 million, occurred in 1974, estimates for 1984–1988 were also relatively low, ranging from 10 to 15 million. The overall, slightly downward, trend in abundance, averaging 1.3% per year, is not statistically significant. This index was significantly correlated to the combined standing crop indices, which are partially derived from the BSS, and to the FSS index, $r = 0.537$ ($P \leq 0.05$).

Hudson River Utilities Fall Shoal Survey, Young-of-Year

The CPUE in the FSS program has shown a significant decrease over the period 1974–1987, averaging 22.9% per year. The highest CPUE, $5.90/1000$ m^3, occurred in 1976. Catches fell to $0.09/1000$ m^3 in 1985 and 1987. Catches during 1986 were the next lowest on record, $0.17/1000$ m^3.

Geometric Mean (GM) Combined Standing Crop, Young-of-Year

The GM combined standing crop index values peaked in 1979 at 47 million and subsequently declined to a low of 10 million in 1985 and 1987. Only a single year, 1977 at 7 million, was lower. Overall, the index has been decreasing at an average rate of 7.0% per year. However, this decrease is not statistically significant.

Summer Regression (SR) Combined Standing Crop, Young-of-Year

The SR index results indicated an average downward, but nonsignificant, trend of 8.6% per year. This index indicated a standing crop of 38 million in 1975, declining to 6 million in 1977. This was followed by an increase to the highest index on record, 71 million, in 1979. Thereafter, there was a general decline, at least to 1984. Standing crops since 1983 have been low, ranging from 9 to 13 million.

Fall Regression (FR) Combined Standing Crop, Young-of-Year

The FR index indicated a general downward trend of 4.2% per year. However, this decrease is not statistically significant. The standing crop peaked at 38 million during the first year, 1975. The lowest standing crop, 5 million, was recorded in 1977. Standing crops since 1983 have been low, ranging from 9 to 13 million.

White Perch Stock Assessment Program (All Stations), Young-of-Year

CPUE data for all lower estuary stations were moderately high from 1971 through 1977, ranging from 23.6 to 53.4/10 min tow. Catches peaked in 1978 and 1979 at 87.1 and 77.7/10 min, respectively. Thereafter, catches decreased continuously to a low of 0.3/10 min in 1984. Catches during 1985–1987 recovered slightly, ranging from 6.1 to 12.5/10 min. Over the entire time period, catches decreased significantly at an average rate of 15.1% per year.

White Perch Stock Assessment Program (BID and BC), Young-of-Year

While the average CPUE index for the Bowline Inlet Discharge and Bowline Channel stations has decreased slightly, 3.2% annually, over the period 1973–1987, this decrease is not statistically significant. CPUE values were moderately high during 1973–1978, ranging from 8 to 27.5/10 min, then reached a peak at 28.2/10 min in 1979. Catches generally decreased, reaching a low of 1.3/10 min, in 1984. Thereafter, catches increased, with a high of 34.5 in 1985. This index was only weakly correlated with the WPSAP YOY index based on all stations, $r = 0.222$ ($P > 0.05$).

White Perch Stock Assessment Program (All Stations), Adult

The average CPUE index based on the age 3+ and older individuals from a given cohort has significantly increased over the period 1968–

1984, the last year for which the index could be computed. The average rate of increase was 16.0% per year. The lowest index, 2.6/10 min, occurred in 1968; the highest, 57.4/10 min, in 1983.

White Perch Stock Assessment Program (BID and BC), Adult

The average CPUE index based on the Bowline Inlet Discharge and Bowline Channel stations increased significantly, at an average rate of 14.6% per year, over the period 1970–1984. The index increased more or less continuously from a low of 3.2/10 min in 1971 to a high of 69.3 and 58.9 during 1983 and 1984, respectively. This index was significantly correlated to the WPSAP 3+ and older index based on all stations, $r = 0.736$ ($P \leq 0.01$). The index value of 43.2/10 min observed in 1970 was included in the above analyses, but is somewhat suspect owing to the small number of specimens in the age-length key used to derive this number. Deletion of this value would increase the slope coefficient—that is, increase the rate of population increase, and increase the similarity between this index and the WPSAP 3+ and older index based on all lower estuary stations.

NYSDEC Beach Seine Survey, Young-of-Year

Over the period 1981 through 1987 this index has decreased at an average rate of 20.2% per year. However, due to the small number of years, only 7, the decrease cannot be considered statistically significant. The highest catch, 9000 individuals, occurred in 1982; the lowest, 1600 individuals, in 1985.

NYSDEC Beach Seine Survey, Adult

The NYSDEC index, based on yearling and older fish, has decreased at an average rate of 22.4% per year. As with the YOY index, this decrease is not statistically significant because of the shortness of the time series. The highest catch, 10,000 individuals, occurred in 1981; the lowest, 1300 individuals, in 1987. This index was moderately correlated with the NYSDEC YOY index, $r = 0.676$, but not significantly, because of the small sample size.

Danskammer Point Generating Station, Impingement

The impingement rate (number of fish per unit volume) at Danskammer Point increased significantly over the period 1974–1987, averaging 8.7% per year. The lowest impingement index, 0.5456/million gallons, occurred in 1978; the highest, 2.6613/million gallons, in 1987.

Impingement catches consist of all age groups—YOY, yearling, and older. YOY fish constituted an average of 19.2% (SD = 9.0%) of the catch at Danskammer Point, at least for the period 1981–1987 when age composition data were available.

Roseton Generating Station, Impingement

The impingement rate (number of fish per unit volume) at Roseton has decreased significantly over the period 1974–1987, averaging 7.0% per year. The highest impingement index, 0.6123/million gallons, occurred in 1975; the lowest, 0.1525/million gallons, in 1986. YOY fish constituted an average of 60.0% (SD = 19.0%) of the catch at Roseton for the period 1981–1987, when age composition data were available. Despite the fact that the Roseton plant is located next to the Danskammer Point plant, the catch composition between the two plants is significantly different (paired t-test, t = 5.46, P ≤ 0.01).

Danskammer Point Generating Station, Entrainment, Egg

Over the period 1978–1987 (excluding 1981 and 1984 because of missing data) the concentration of eggs in entrainment samples at Danskammer Point increased at an average rate of 23.4% per year. Although this rate of increase is not statistically significant, there is a relatively low probability of its occurring by chance alone (P = 0.1417). The lowest concentration, 50/million m^3, occurred in 1983; the highest, 1406/million m^3, in 1986.

Danskammer Point Generating Station, Entrainment, Larvae (Yolk-Sac and Post–Yolk-Sac Larvae

Over the period 1978–1987 (excluding 1981 and 1984 because of missing data) the concentration of larvae in Danskammer Point entrainment samples increased significantly, at an average rate of 23.1% per year. The lowest concentration, 15/million m^3, occurred in 1978; the highest, 318/million m^3, in 1985.

Roseton Generating Station, Entrainment, Egg

Between 1976 and 1987, concentrations of white perch eggs in Roseton entrainment samples increased significantly. The average rate of increase was 20.3% per year. The lowest concentration, 21/million m^3, occurred in 1979; the highest, 197/million m^3, in 1986. Pre-1980 years ranged from 21 to 75/million m^3, all post-1980 years except 1984 exceeded 100/million m^3.

260   Fishery Biology

Roseton Generating Station, Entrainment, Larvae (Yolk-Sac and Post–Yolk-Sac Larvae)

Over the period 1976–1986 the concentration of larvae in Roseton entrainment samples increased significantly, averaging 22.0% per year. Concentrations increased from 16/million m^3 during 1976–1978 to a peak of 261/million m^3 in 1985. Concentrations decreased to 77 and 86/million m^3 in 1986 and 1987, respectively.

Cluster Analysis

Clustering of the 20 by 20 matrix of correlation coefficients revealed two major patterns of similarity within the abundance indices (Figure 11.1). The first cluster, referred to as the non-YOY cluster, consisted of the Longitudinal River Survey egg, YSL, and PYSL indices, the Roseton egg and larval indices, the Danskammer Point larval index, and adult indices such as the WPSAP 3+ and older, NYSDEC yearling and older, and Danskammer Point impingement (60% yearling and older). The second cluster, referred to as the YOY cluster, was composed almost entirely of YOY-based indices. The only non-YOY index in this cluster is the Roseton impingement index. However, as discussed previously, the Roseton impingement catch averaged approximately 80% YOY. Two indices, the Danskammer Point egg entrainment index and the WPSAP YOY (BID and BC) index were clustered. For reasons that will become apparent in subsequent discussions, these two indices are likely allied with the non-YOY and YOY clusters, respectively. Both clusters displayed positive correlations within each cluster, but were negatively correlated to each other.

The non-YOY cluster indices generally displayed an increasing, or positive, trend in abundance over time. Of the three egg stage indices, all displayed an increasing trend. The Roseton egg entrainment regression was significant, with an average annual increase of 20.3%; the LRS egg index increased at 7.1% annually. Although the Danskammer Point index did not cluster with this group, it displayed an increase of nearly identical magnitude to that calculated from the Roseton data, 23.4%. Three of the four larvae (including YSL and PYSL) regressions were significant, with positive annual increases of a magnitude similar to that calculated for egg indices: 18.1, 23.1, and 22.0%. Three of four indices for older fish also displayed a significant increasing abundance trend: 16.0, 14.6, and 8.7%. The only downward trend, based on NYSDEC data, was not significant and was based on only seven observations.

The nine indices forming the YOY group all displayed a down-

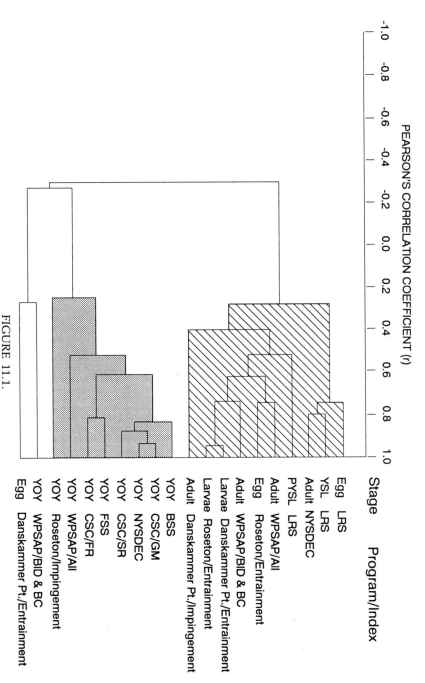

FIGURE 11.1. Similarity, as measured by Pearson's correlation coefficient (r), among white perch stock indices.

ward abundance trend over time: −1.3, −22.9, −7.0, −8.6, −4.2, −15.1, −3.2, −20.2, and −7.0%. Three of the decreases were statistically significant. There appears to be a tendency for the nearshore indices such as the BSS and Roseton impingement decreases, −1.3 and −7.0%, respectively, to be less than offshore indices such as the FSS, WPSAP, and NYSDEC trawl indices, −22.9, −15.1, and −20.2, respectively, suggesting YOY are disappearing from offshore regions at a faster rate than from nearshore regions.

DISCUSSION

The indices described above are intended to provide a measure of white perch abundance trends in the Hudson River Estuary. A declining population should produce fewer eggs, larvae, YOY, and, subsequently, fewer adults over time while an expanding population should produce the converse. Our review suggests that there have been significant increases in egg and larval abundance over time, a marked decrease in YOY, especially since about 1979, and a significant increase in the number of older adults since the early 1970s. The rate of population increase of older individuals closely parallels the rate of increase in the egg and larval stages. This result suggests that YOY white perch are present in the river but are not being sampled in proportion to their abundance.

The underrepresentation of young white perch in samples can be supported from several additional studies. Annual catch curves, derived from the white perch stock assessment program (LMS 1986b, 1987a, 1988a), display a nearly level left-hand limb indicative of incomplete recruitment. Using the method described by Robson and Chapman (1961), LMS found that statistically significant underrepresentation occurred until approximately age 3. Although this incomplete recruitment has been demonstrated only for the white perch stock assessment trawl program, it likely occurs in other programs as well. For example, the average CPUE for yearling and older fish is higher than that for YOY in 4 of 7 years of the NYSDEC program.

What is the reason behind this underrepresentation? Given the wide variety of sampling gears and the extensive river mile coverage, the most reasonable explanation appears to be that there are habitats preferred by YOY white perch that are not representatively sampled. The habitats are, most likely, tributary streams, weedy backwater areas, and nearshore shallows. Support for this is available from several sources. A special study conducted in 1984 indicated high concentrations of white perch in Hudson River tributary streams (NAI 1985c). Yearling white perch were most abundant in tributaries of the lower river region (Peekskill Bay and Fishkill Creek), while older white perch were abundant in the upriver tributaries (Esopus, Catskill, and Stockport creeks). Carlson (1986), in a study of fish habitat usage in the upper Hudson River, reported that white perch catches were higher in tributaries, vegetated backwaters, and shore than in offshore areas. Schmidt (1986) noted that YOY white perch were especially abundant in the marsh areas of Tivoli North Bay. The higher catches of YOY white perch at the BB station reported by LMS (1982) also support this hypothesis.

Further support is offered from a special study conducted in 1986 and 1987 that compared previously unsampled shoal regions (1.8–2.7 m deep) of the Hudson River Utilities surveys to adjacent sampled regions (Metzger et al. this volume). These shoal regions were historically unsampled due to difficult accessibility and sampling hazards. Average concentrations of white perch in these areas were found to be significantly greater than in the sampled regions.

The decreasing YOY catch since about 1979, despite an apparently expanding population, suggests that the catchability of white perch has been decreasing over time. This implies that conditions that result in the underrepresentation of young white perch have changed. One habitat that may be increasing over time are the beds of aquatic vegetation. During 1986 and 1987, LMS (1989) determined that peak white perch egg distribution was from km 76 through 211, and noted that spawning appeared associated with shallow, vegetated areas. Consistently large catches of eggs were made between Cold Spring and Danskammer Point (km 89–106), Hyde Park and Kingston (km 124–150), Esopus Creek and Catskill Creek (km 166–182), and km 198–209. All of these areas were shallow with extensive mats of floating vegetation, primarily of the exotic water chestnut (*Trapa natans*). A study conducted in Tivoli bays (Schmidt and Kiviat 1988) indicated that water chestnut beds were excellent habitat for small fish. Compared to water celery (*Vallisneria*) and water milfoil (*Myriophyllum*) beds, water chestnut beds supported the greatest abundance and diversity of young fish.

If water chestnut beds are an important reservoir of young white perch, then the observed post-1979 decline in YOY might be attributable to an expansion of these beds. Water chestnut was introduced into the upper Hudson River drainage in 1884 (Hook 1985). It quickly spread and was considered a pest by the 1930s. An eradication program using hand-pulling and the herbicide 2,4-D was largely successful in controlling the species, but because of tightened federal standards on the use of 2,4-D the program was stopped in 1975. Water chestnut rapidly regained dominance in sheltered coves and shallows as far south as Constitution Island (km 86), with isolated patches as far south as Iona Island (Schmidt and Kiviat 1988). Increasing beds of aquatic vegetation could increase the proportion of the population inaccessible to standard sampling techniques. Dense beds of aquatic weeds could also enhance survival probability of YOY and account for an overall increase in white perch population.

KIM A. McKOWN
BYRON H. YOUNG

12

Effects of Year Class Strength on Size of Young-of-the-Year Striped Bass

ABSTRACT

Surveys of the abundance of young-of-the-year have produced indices that are good measures of recruitment success in striped bass. Biweekly samples were taken by the New York State Department of Environmental Conservation from 1976 through 1988 at 25 stations in nursery areas of the Tappan Zee-Haverstraw Bay region. Indices of relative abundance showed large variations from a low of 3.9 in 1985 to a high of 60.7 in 1987.

Abundance indices were low in 1985 and 1986 and high in 1987 and 1988. Regressions of biweekly mean lengths from 1985 through 1988 reveal that the 1985 and 1986 bass had greater mean lengths than 1987 and 1988 fish. These variations suggest that mean size is inversely related to year class strength, possibly because of reduced competition or increased survival of larger young during poor years.

Growth rates, however, do not appear to be influenced by year class strength.

INTRODUCTION

Striped bass (*Morone saxatilis*) are an important commercial and recreational fish. There has been a decrease in the abundance of striped bass along the Atlantic Coast for the last 10 to 15 years. Due to this decline, the Atlantic States Marine Fishery Commission in conjunction with the coastal states, has been monitoring striped bass populations along the coast. One method of monitoring the population is by sampling young-of-the-year (YOY) in their nursery areas. Goodyear (1985) found a good relationship between Maryland's striped bass landings and corresponding indices of YOY abundance. He felt the YOY index was a good measure of recruitment.

Indices of annual young-of-the-year abundance for striped bass are available for all the major spawning areas. The various indices were summarized by Borman and Austin (1985). The Maryland index, which has the longest duration, started in 1954. The indices of the Virginia portion of the Chesapeake Bay and the Roanoke River-Albermarle Sound complex of North Carolina follow closely behind, starting in 1955. The Hudson River has index data from a variety of sources since 1969. The New York State Department of Environmental Conservation (NYS DEC) commenced the current investigation of striped bass spawning success in 1976.

Young-of-the-year (YOY) striped bass have been sampled in the nursery area from 1976 through 1988. The survey produces yearly indices of relative abundance (mean number of fish caught per seine haul) and total length.

METHODS AND MATERIALS

Collections for this project were made using a 200 × 10 ft × ½ inch stretched mesh beach seine (61 m × 3m × 13 mm stretched mesh) set by boat at standard stations in the Tappan Zee-Haverstraw Bay region of the Hudson River (Figure 12.1). Nine biweekly sample runs of 25 seine hauls each were scheduled. Prior to 1985 only six biweekly sample runs were scheduled. Presently the survey commences approximately mid-July and ends in early November. In all years prior to 1985, sampling commenced in late August and termi-

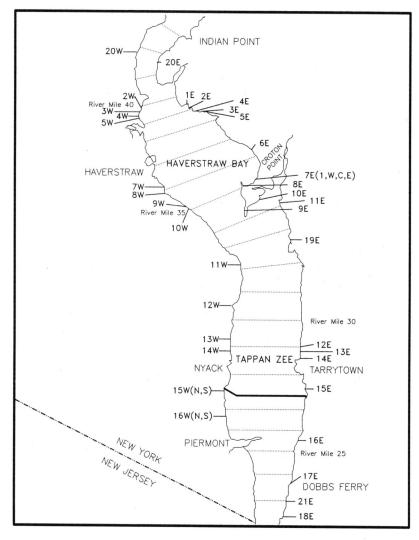

FIGURE 12.1.
NYSDEC young-of-year striped bass seine stations.

nated in early November. The expanded catch data are identified by dates.

Fish captured were sorted by species, counted, and returned to the water. All striped bass and selected other species were retained in 5 gallon buckets (20 liters) for length determination. Each striped bass was checked for a magnetically coded wire tag using a portable tag detector. In addition to the fisheries data, the following parameters were recorded at each station: date, time, gear handling, air temperature, water temperature, salinity, dissolved oxygen, tide stage, cloud cover, wind velocity, and wave height. Salinity and dissolved oxygen were determined by titration using LaMotte test kits. Air and water temperatures were taken using a hand-held thermometer.

Striped bass were measured to the nearest millimeter for fork length and total length. Scales were removed from larger striped bass (>115 mm) to determine their age. Scale samples were removed from the area between the dorsal fins and above the lateral line.

RESULTS

An index of relative abundance for young-of-the-year (YOY) striped bass was calculated each year from the catch data (Figure 12.2 and Table 12.1). The indices from 1976 through 1988 have large variations, though there were no distinct trends. The indices for the last 4 years have displayed the largest fluctuations over the 13 years of this study. The 1987 and 1988 indices were the two highest, while the 1985 and 1986 were the first and third lowest. The 1987 index, 60.7, was 15.6 times higher than the 1985 index, 3.9. The 1988 index, 52.3, was the second highest recorded during this study. The catch in 1988 was more evenly distributed spatially (Figure 12.3) and temporally (Figure 12.4) compared with the 1987 catch.

Mean total length (TL) by week was determined for the 1985 through 1988 data, and a least squares linear regression was calculated for each year (Figure 12.5). The regressions for 1985 through 1988 were compared (Figure 12.6). There was a significant increase in length over the 9 weeks for every year (alpha = 0.001). The slopes were tested, and there was no significant difference in the slopes between years. This suggests that the growth of young striped bass was similar over the 4 years. The means were tested using Tukey's studentized range test (SAS 1985). The 1985 and 1986 striped bass had significantly larger biweekly mean size compared to the 1987 and 1988 bass (alpha = 0.05).

DISCUSSION AND CONCLUSIONS

The Atlantic Coast YOY striped bass indices show large annual variations, but the Chesapeake Bay (Maryland and Virginia) and

FIGURE 12.2.
Hudson River young-of-year striped bass abundance indices, 1976–1988.

TABLE 12.1
Hudson River Index of relative abundance for YOY striped bass from 1976 to 1988.

Year	Number Hauls	Number Y-O-Y Captured	C/f	Std. Dev.	Std. Error	Number Zeros	Median	Mode	Range
1976	86	1404	16.3	—	—	6	10	1	0–108
1977	88	3495	39.7	72.7	7.8	4	9	4	0–386
1978	70	2928	41.8	81.3	9.7	9	10	1	0–382
1979	117	584	5.0	8.0	0.7	39	2	0	0–43
1980	149	3594	24.1	57.8	4.7	34	6	0	0–548
1981	131	2822	21.6	42.6	3.7	11	9	1	0–346
1982	143	4364	30.5	48.0	4.0	8	14	10	0–285
1983	148	7112	48.1	110.7	9.1	8	18	12	0–1178
1984	146	5425	37.2	89.9	7.4	6	15	7	0–906
6 Weeks									
1985	146	574	3.9	5.8	0.5	51	1	0	0–31
1986	147	904	6.1	9.0	0.7	34	2	0	0–55
1987	150	9100	60.7	157.8	12.9	13	18	1	0–1333
1988	145	7584	52.3	45.1	3.7	2	39	28	0–205
9 Weeks									
1985	216	993	4.6	6.6	0.4	71	2	0	0–32
1986	222	1942	8.7	11.3	0.8	38	4	0	0–57
1987	225	18649	82.9	184.6	12.3	13	34	1	0–1432
1988	220	15488	70.4	85.4	5.8	2	47	28	0–869

Effort and Distribution of Haul Seines Increased after 1978

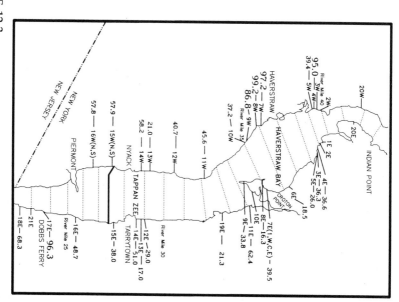

FIGURE 12.3. Catch per effort by station for 1987 and 1988.

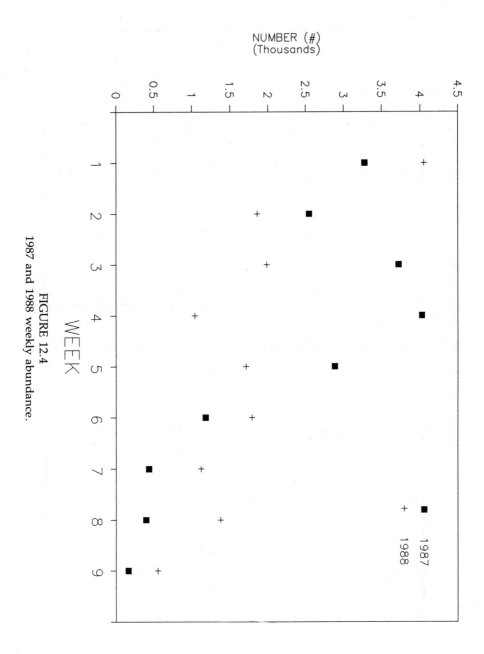

FIGURE 12.4 1987 and 1988 weekly abundance.

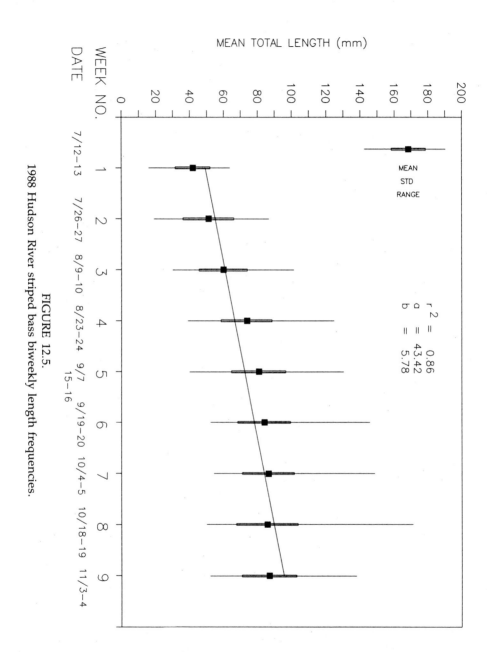

FIGURE 12.5.
1988 Hudson River striped bass biweekly length frequencies.

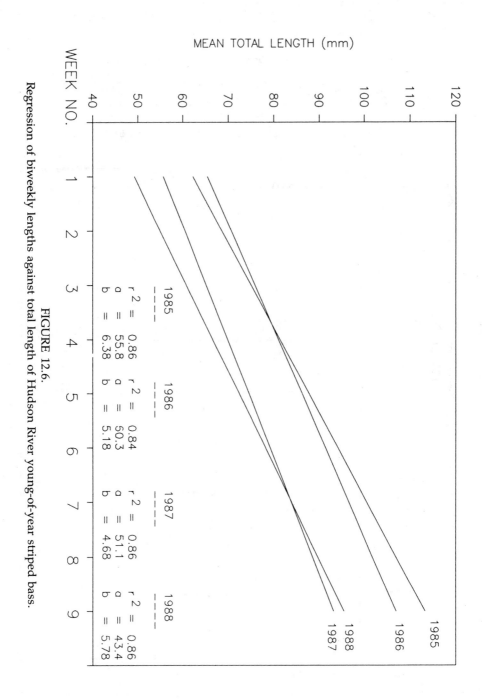

FIGURE 12.6. Regression of biweekly lengths against total length of Hudson River young-of-year striped bass.

Roanoke River indices have declined since the 1970s (Boreman and Austin 1985). The Hudson River index has shown no decline; furthermore, recent evaluations of post–yolk-sac larva indices show an increasing trend in abundance (Heimbuch et al. this volume). Crecco (1989) found a positive correlation between the Hudson River Utilities YOY striped bass indices from 1974 through 1988, versus May and June water temperatures ($r^2 = 0.68$, $P < 0.002$). The parameters for two stock recruitment models were statistically significant only after the environmental factors were subtracted. This suggests that the annual variability in year class strength of Hudson River striped bass is affected mainly by hydrographic events during and shortly after spawning. On the other hand, the YOY indices from the 1950s through 1979 for the Chesapeake Bay and Roanoke River were correlated with several environmental parameters, but when the 1980–1988 data were added no correlation was found. This suggests that environmental variability was not responsible for recent declines, and that at low stock levels stock-dependent effects appear to be increasingly important.

Our studies suggest that variations in year class strength may have an effect on the mean TL of the year class. Small year classes have a larger mean TL than do large year classes, possibly due to decreased competition or increased survivorship of larger YOY during poor years. Growth rate, however, does not appear to be influenced by year class strength.

WILLIAM L. DOVEL

13

Movements of Immature Striped Bass in the Hudson Estuary

ABSTRACT

This paper provides an interpretive summary of the seasonal movements of immature striped bass in the Hudson River based on a review of the existing literature.

The patterns of distribution of immature striped bass are consistent from year to year. Hatching begins in May and by mid-summer the young-of-the-year begin to move downstream. Some leave the estuary, others congregate in low current eddy areas immediately downstream from the salt front. From early January to mid-February there are no mass movements, but some evidence suggests that individual fish continue to emigrate. In late February movements become more pronounced. Some juveniles begin to move upstream while others continue to emigrate. During March and April yearling bass tend to move upstream while most age II fish move out of the Hudson. Some age II fish, however, move upstream and there is evidence suggesting that some striped bass may never leave the estuary.

Striped bass occur in a variety of habitats and do not appear to orient to any particular bottom type. As the bass grow, their movements evolve from largely passive to actively discriminatory. Major estuarywide seasonal movements are to a large degree determined by a combination of estuarine water circulation, water temperature and the changing feeding habits of young bass. The emigration of immature bass is influenced by their vertical position in the water column; those that occur in surface waters encounter a net seaward flow. Declining water temperatures stimulate the bass to drop down in the water column to an area where they encounter intruding salt water. Rising water temperatures stimulate the bass to ascend the water column where some continue to feed in the estuary while others emigrate to the sea.

These movements serve to assure that the young fish find optimal habitats within the estuary.

INTRODUCTION

The purpose of this paper is to offer an interpretation of the complex observed movements of the early developmental stages of striped bass in the Hudson River Estuary. It is recognized that some elements of the relationships postulated here have not been tested and cannot yet be documented specifically; however, none of the elements presented are refuted by the available data.

For two decades (1964–1984) the Hudson River striped bass fishery has been the subject of intensive research to determine the vulnerability of the resource to human activities. Most of this research has been sponsored by the Consolidated Edison Company of the New York and was designed to assess the impact of power-generating facilities on the striped bass and other natural resources of the Hudson. The studies were concentrated chiefly in the middle reach of the estuary between Yonkers (km 29) and Poughkeepsie (km 121). The major thrust of most of this research was a quantitative estimation of the potential net loss of striped bass from the Hudson population. Virtually no effort was made to define the behavior of immature striped bass or to determine interactions between the bass and other components of the ecosystem. Moreover, a review of results of that research reveals a lack of uniformity in field and analytical tech-

PROCEDURES

Using compatible elements of various data arrays, I compiled a graphic summary to provide a perspective of the basic sequence of occurrence of various life history stages of striped bass in the Hudson Estuary. Median numbers of bass collected were plotted horizontally to represent distribution on a particular date, and vertically over time, to provide a two-dimensional overview of spatial and temporal distribution for a particular year class (Figure 13.2). A plot of the total catch for each sampling date was used to portray an estuarywide trend in the distribution of each life stage. Patterns of movement of marked and recaptured young bass (older than yearlings but still immature) were superimposed over the plots of the abundance of young-of-the-year and yearling bass to confirm the changing distributional pattern of immature bass in the estuary. Records of young bass impinged at power plants were also used to determine periods when such bass were absent from areas with operating power plants. This information was particularly valuable for winter periods when sampling was limited by inclement weather.

My interpretation of the basic distribution and movements of immature bass (eggs, yolk-sac larvae, post–yolk-sac larvae, juveniles, and yearlings) in the estuary upstream from Yonkers during the spring, summer, and fall comes from fisheries data collected prior to December 1983, primarily from the following reports: for 1974—McFadden et al. 1977; for 1975—McFadden et al. 1977, 1978; for 1976—McFadden et al. 1978, TI 1979a; for 1977—TI 1980; for 1978—TI 1980; and for 1979—TI 1981. The field collecting by power-industry consultants that produced the distribution data for juvenile bass was not continuous through the winter, but sampling was continued in the fall until no specimens were collected (late December) and commenced in the spring prior to the return of young bass to shore areas (late March). This sampling pattern should not affect interpretations of bass behavior, but should be recognized.

The behavior of young striped bass in the lower Hudson during winter is based on data from the 1979 to 1984 efforts to determine the potential impacts of the proposed construction of a section of interstate highway on the west side of Manhattan (Westway). The original analysis of the Westway data by Martin Marietta Environmental Systems (1984) was directed toward a mathematical modeling effort. Samples collected for discrete 10-day periods during winter and early spring (January through April 1984) were analyzed independently by habitat zones (shallow, interpier, and deep) in order to develop population estimates for particular geographic areas along the Hudson below Peekskill, N.Y. This approach was also used to investigate the possibility that the young bass seek specific types of habitat.

The same relative density data for young bass were used here to define seasonal bass movements, especially downstream movements. Declining densities were interpreted as the departure of bass from an area whereas increasing densities indicated arrival.

While the sampling effort for the Westway study (as described by the New Jersey Marine Science Consortium [1984] and observed by the author) provides important data for analysis of winter distribution and movements of young bass, it has several aspects that might allow short-term movements to go undetected and possibly lead to erroneous conclusions about movement during the winter period. These include: (1) sampling design, (2) field sampling schedule, and (3) data pooling.

The stratified random sampling design is appropriate for monitoring a homogeneous distribution of organisms, but it reduced the opportunity to adequately monitor the concentrations of bass in discrete areas. In reality, the bass distribution was patchy and constantly changing. Also, my analysis of the distribution of young bass indicates a strong affinity with features of the environment other than substratum—that is, channels and shoals, which are often pathways of movement, depending on water temperature.

Field sampling for the Westway study was conducted by 10-day periods. However, I have often observed dramatic changes in the occurrence of young bass in the lower estuary over relatively short periods of time. Therefore, sampling at 10-day intervals may have allowed significant changes in the patterns of movement into and out of areas along the estuary to go undetected. Furthermore, while field crews were encouraged to complete the sampling as early as possible, weather and other circumstances sometimes shifted the sampling schedule so that the data may not be representative of the entire period. In addition, pooling samples for 10-day periods undoubtedly obscured recognition of fish activity that took place over shorter periods of time.

MODEL

The movements of immature striped bass in the Hudson Estuary are complex and undoubtedly associated with stimuli that change with time. While the existing fisheries techniques allow the calculation of estimates of fish abundance in specific geographic areas, without a knowledge of the patterns of fish movements such data are difficult to use in resolving the overall population dynamics of the species throughout its range of occurrence. The interpretation presented here addresses the movements of striped bass through the estuary from the federal dam at Troy, N.Y., to coastal areas adjacent to the New York metropolitan area (Newark Bay, the Arthur Kill, the upper New York Harbor, Jamaica Bay, the East River, and the western end of Long Island Sound (Figure 13.1). The Hudson, from the Battery at Manhattan and upstream 246 km to the Troy Dam is a typical Atlantic coastal estuary (Pritchard 1967) and analogies with other estuarine ecosystems are drawn where appropriate.

DISTRIBUTION AND MOVEMENTS

The distribution of various life history stages of young bass throughout the lower Hudson, from egg deposition to about age 2 and in relation to the salt front, is illustrated in Figure 13.3. Changes in fish abundance are discussed below by season.

Summer (Young-of-the-Year)

Spawning commences in May in the region between Indian Point and West Point (Raney 1952; Rathjen and Miller 1957; TI 1979a, 1980) and extends progressively upstream (McFadden et al. 1977; TI 1979a, 1980). Polgar et al. (1976) were of the opinion that striped bass in the Potomac River also spawned farther upstream as the spawning season progressed.

Eggs are found upstream to the vicinity of Albany (TI 1980) but occur in greatest concentrations between Catskill and Indian Point. Striped bass hatch in fresh water usually north of Haverstraw Bay (Figure 13.3), and the early stages (yolk-sac larvae, post–yolk-sac larvae and juveniles) are soon found throughout the estuary. Undoubtedly some of the larvae found upstream are hatched there, but others may be transported upstream by tidal currents (TI 1980a). Active feeding begins after about a week and during the summer the young bass change from plankton feeders to predators and feed primarily in shoal areas (Raney 1952; TI 1976b).

Emigration commences by mid-summer and is reputed to accelerate as water temperature declines in the fall (Raney 1952; TI 1977; McFadden et al. 1978; Young 1981). A few young-of-the-year bass have been found outside the Hudson in Long Island Sound by the

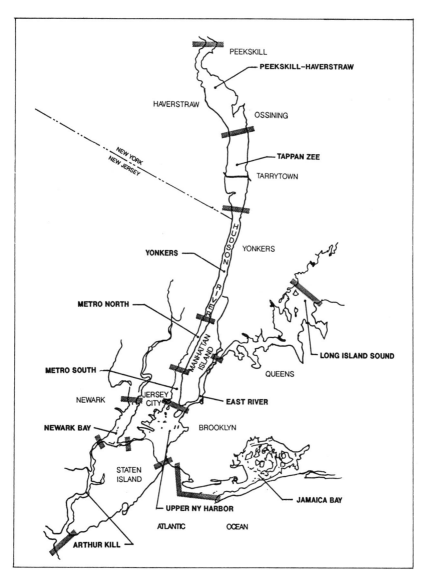

FIGURE 13.1.
The Hudson estuary: Westway Fisheries Study sampling zone locations.

first of August (Young 1979). Similar downstream movements of early developmental stages of bass have also been documented for the Patuxent River (Ritchie and Koo 1968; Mihursky et al. 1976), the Potomac River (Polgar et al. 1975; Boynton et al. 1981), the Sacramento-San Joaquin Delta area (Calhoun 1953; Chadwick et al. 1977; Sasaki 1966), Virginia rivers (Markle and Grant 1970), the Delaware Estuary (Bason 1971), and the Chesapeake and Delaware Canal (Kernehan et al. 1981).

Fall (Young-of-the-Year)

Evidence that young-of-the-year bass move out of the upper Hudson Estuary (vicinity of Albany) by late fall is found in the pattern of seasonal impingement of young bass at power plants between km 59 (Bowline) and km 233 (Albany Steam Station) shown in Figure 13.3. Impingement occurred throughout the year at Bowline, Lovett, Indian Point, Roseton, and Danskammer, but only from May through October at the Albany Steam Station (McFadden et al. 1978; Figure 13.3). Congregation of bass at power generating facilities in the lower Hudson, in winter, is possibly influenced by the presence of heated discharges.

The rate at which young bass move through the estuarine nursery is determined by several natural phenomena, but primarily by tidal current. Downstream transport is slow because bass feed in shoal areas rather than in mid-channel waters. Downstream movement is further reduced by the behavior of bass in relation to tidal changes. As low, slack water approaches (at the time at which the young bass occur farthest downstream in the tidal cycle) the shoal areas where bass feed (Raney 1952; Merriman 1937) are exposed. Thus, the small bass are away from shore where they are carried upstream with the initial thrust of the flood tide (McFadden 1978). This feeding pattern, associated with tidal action, tends to keep the small bass in the estuary and is responsible for a slow net movement downstream through the nursery.

The fish that leave the river in late July may be the first ones hatched, those that encounter an optimal food supply, or those that make optimal use of downstream transport. The mean size of the bass in the lower part of the estuary during fall is larger than that of individuals of the same year class occurring farther upstream (TI 1977). There are, however, additional factors that could hasten the emigration of bass toward coastal areas as they grow. For example, adult striped bass are voracious predators that depend on good eye-

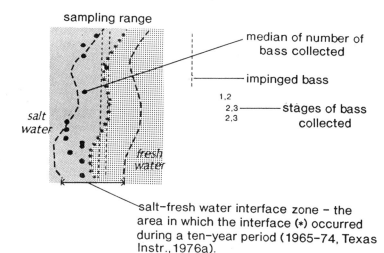

Sampling Regions
AL = Albany
CS = Catskill
SG = Saugerties
KG = Kingston
HP = Hyde Park
PK = Poughkeepsie
CW = Cornwall
WP = West Point
IP = Indian Point
CH = Croton-Haverstraw
TZ = Tappan Zee
YK = Yonkers
NY-M = New York Metro Area
UH = Upper Harbor
ER = East River
NB = Newark Bay

Life Stage Designation
(1) Eggs, 1978, Texas Instr., 1980, Table B-39
(2) Yolk Sac Larvae, 1978, Texas Instr., 1980, Table B-42
(3) Post Yolk Sac Larvae, 1978, Texas Instr., 1980, Table B-45
(4) Juveniles, 1978, Texas Instr., 1980, Table B-51
(5) Yearlings, 1984, Malcolm Pirnie, 1984, Vols. 1, 2 & 3
(6) Yearlings, 1977, Texas Instr., 1980, Table B-58
(7) Age II, 1984, Malcolm Pirnie, 1984 Vols. 1, 2 & 3

FIGURE 13.2.
Explanation of symbols used in Figure 13.3.

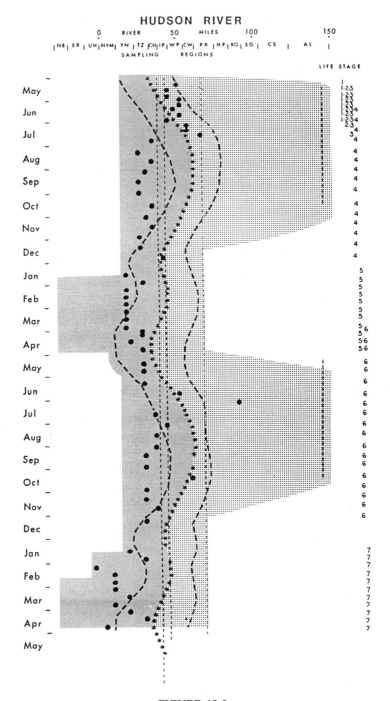

FIGURE 13.3.
Sequential occurrence of early developmental stages of striped bass collected from the Hudson Estuary, New York-New Jersey.

sight and thrive best in waters of high clarity. Thus, developing bass probably would be progressively stimulated to move out of relatively turbid estuarine areas and to marine waters of greater clarity, possibly following the clearer saline waters in the salt wedge. In addition, the downstream movement in late summer could be hastened by a declining food source in the mid-estuary as water temperature decreases. Thus, some of the movement of immature striped bass in the Hudson during warm periods and as water temperatures begin to decline in the fall is undoubtedly discriminatory, but with appreciable assistance from downstream surface flow.

Movements away from the upper harbor presently occur by three principal routes: via the East River to western Long Island Sound (McFadden et al. 1977; TI 1977); via the Kill Van Kull into Newark Bay (Anselmini 1974; McFadden et al. 1978); and through the Verrazano Narrows. The relative importance of the three routes is difficult to assess, primarily because the bass distribution in Long Island Sound, Newark Bay-Hackensack River, and Atlantic habitats has not been determined. The occurrence of some yearlings in Jamaica Bay (MPI 1984a, 1984b) and in Great South Bay, South Oyster Bay, and Hempstead Bay (Byron Young, personal communication) suggests some movement through the Narrows. The low numbers of juvenile bass found below Liberty Park on the New Jersey side of the Hudson (Himchak 1982) and off Brooklyn and Staten Island (MPI 1984a, 1984b, 1984c) suggest that the Narrows may be the least important emigration route for bass less than a year old.

Winter (Young-of-the-Year)

The concentration and movements of the young bass in waters of the lower estuary during winter are revealed by data collected during the Westway study (USACE 1984; MPI 1984a, b, and c). Variations in densities for the different areas sampled from December 1983 to April 1984 are used to interpret bass movement (Figure 13.4, vertical bars).

With the first substantial decline in water temperature, bass begin to move to the lower Hudson (TI 1977, 1979, 1980; McFadden et al. 1977, 1978). Temperature, food, light, and other factors assuredly interact to determine distribution and movements. Rathjen and Miller (1957) stated that young-of-the-year striped bass move into brackish waters of the Hudson as they grow. Similar movements have been noted in other estuaries. Calhoun (1953) found that young bass in the Sacramento-San Joaquin Delta exhibited a comparable pattern of movement into salt waters. In the Hudson, an unknown proportion

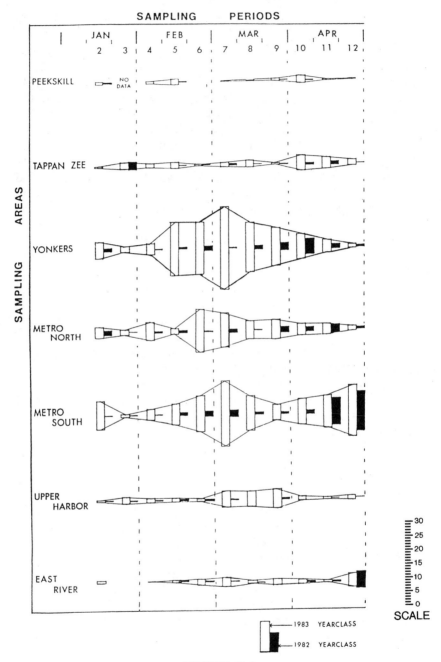

FIGURE 13.4.
Catch-per-unit effort of young striped bass from the lower Hudson by 10-day sampling periods.

of the new year class remains in the river, with most of them moving into saline waters of the lower estuary (McFadden et al. 1978).

As water temperatures continue to decline, the small bass become less active, feeding slows, and the fish begin to descend the water column (LMS 1984; MPI 1984a, b, and c). It is not known to what degree this descent is active or passive; nevertheless, the small bass begin to accumulate in low-current eddy areas in the lower part of the Hudson estuary (USACE 1984). Most of the young bass found above the Battery in winter are concentrated between the Tappan Zee Bridge and the Upper Bay (LMS 1984; MPI 1984a, 1984b, 1984c; USACE 1984).

Prior to mid-January there is a pronounced emigration of young bass (McFadden et al. 1977; Raney 1952; TI 1977, 1979). From early January through mid-February no pronounced trend is evident. Increasing mean catches at Yonkers, Metro North, and Metro South in mid-January apparently represent congregation and the final stage of the seaward movement begun in the fall and early winter. By late January, water temperature in the Hudson is usually approaching winter minimum.

The movements of young bass during the winter, although not pronounced, are continuous. Bass are found in numerous low-current areas of the lower estuary where water temperature is slightly higher than in shallower areas upstream (MPI 1984a, b, and c). Possibly this higher temperature stimulates continued emigration and this could explain why there were no recaptures from more than 8,500 small bass tagged in the Hudson adjacent to Manhattan from late February to late April in 1984 (C. Watola, New Jersey Marine Science Consortium, personal communication).

Small bass that are slow to move down the estuary in winter descend the water column before reaching salt water. Water temperatures decline while these small fish are still upstream, their activity is much reduced, and they are more subject to transport downstream by the flow of fresh water (Figure 13.5). When these bass reach the vicinity of the salt front, the resistance at the interface between the incoming salt water along the bottom of the estuary and the fresh water moving toward the sea reduces the capacity of the freshwater flow to suspend and transport the small bass downstream. Thus the small bass "fall out" and accumulate immediately downstream of the salt front (McFadden 1978; Clark and Smith 1969) where net water movement is minimal. The blocking action is in effect a trapping action equivalent to a "sediment trap" where particulate matter is retained in brackish water of estuaries (Postma 1967).

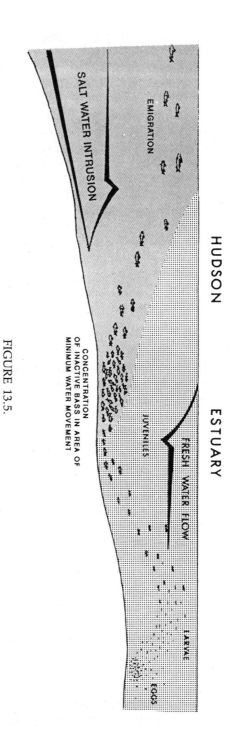

FIGURE 13.5. A generalized diagram of the downstream movements of developing striped bass.

The concentration of immature bass in the vicinity of the salt front will usually occur downstream from the salt/freshwater interface because the momentum of a stronger freshwater flow carries the fish past the interface before their vertical descent (Figure 13.5 and 13.6). This is like the "settling lag" described by Postma (1967) for particulate matter. McFadden et al. (1977) and LMS (1984) document a gradual accumulation of small bass in deeper waters of the lower estuary off the metropolitan area in the winter as water temperature declines. TI (1979b) and McFadden et al. (1978) found that young bass tend to associate with the salt front during winter.

A clear pattern of occurrence of small bass in the lower Hudson is recognizable by late February (Figure 13.4). Bass that occur in the lower estuary at that time were distributed in a gradient of abundance between Yonkers and the Upper Harbor; relatively few are found north of Yonkers and the highest concentration is in the vicinity of the salt front (MPI 1984a, 1984b). During this period 99.5% of all yearling bass collected (579) in the estuary north of the Battery were found in waters of less than 15.0 ppt salinity. Almost 50.0% are found in water of less than 2.0 ppt but less than 0.01% are found in fresh water.

Although bass movements are continual, late February to early March represents the transition from fall and winter to spring movements. This transition between growing seasons also provides the best opportunity to interpret the stimuli for changes in the direction of movement of young bass. If movements are discriminatory, they should be stimulated by some predominant environmental factor, but I have been unable to identify any such factors other than salinity. If, on the other hand, the movements are involuntary there should be a direct correlation with physical movement of water masses and this appears to be true for small bass in the estuary.

The most important winter concentration areas are in water more than 4.6 m deep in the vicinity of the salt front (usually off Yonkers-Metro North). In late February channel waters off Yonkers yielded the highest mean catch of striped bass in deep areas north of the Battery (USACE 1984). Only the adjacent shallow area of Metro North, still in the vicinity of the salt front, produced a greater number of small bass at that time. Winter concentration lasts only for a brief period (a matter of days) when the bass are least active in the later winter just before water temperature begins to increase. It is not a period of no movement and therefore the concept of "overwintering" in the sense of residence is erroneous.

The pattern of winter movements of immature striped bass between the George Washington Bridge and the Morris Canal (24 to 32

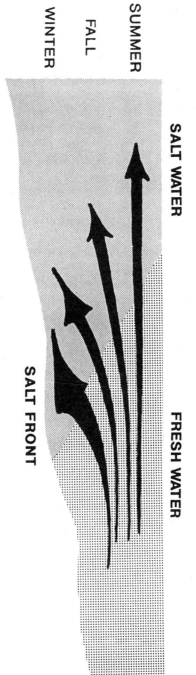

FIGURE 13.6.
A generalized diagram of the seaward movements of young striped bass and other species.

km downstream from the salt front) is suggested by an investigation conducted in 1982–83 (LMS 1984). Abundance was high in early winter, low in mid-winter, peaked again in late winter, decreased in early spring, and then increased again until the termination of the study in late April. Based on these data, the following interpretation is offered to explain the movements of immature striped bass in the metropolitan area during the winter of 1982–83. In December large numbers of immature bass move through the waters surrounding Manhattan (Figure 13.7–1). As the water temperature approached the winter minimum (Figure 13.7–2) the abundance off Manhattan declined to a mid-winter low (Figure 13.7–3) suggesting that emigration had slowed as the bass congregated upstream near the salt front. A subsequent increase in abundance (Figure 13.7–4) confirms that major movement through the metropolitan area had been suppressed for a short period in mid-winter.

A consistent pattern of fluctuating abundance and movements of yearling bass in the lower Hudson is apparent (Figure 13.8) when trends of relative abundance of young bass off Manhattan during the winters of 1982–83 and 1983–84 are compared (LMS 1984 and USACE 1984). At a comparable age, juvenile bass of the 1982 year-class were slightly more abundant that bass of the 1983 year-class one year later. The timing of increases and decreases in relative abundance (interpreted here to imply movement) for the young bass collected during the two winters varied by only a few days. This difference can be attributed to differences in water temperature (a stimulus for movement), year-class size (density dependent spread), differences in the estuarine circulation pattern (as influenced by precipitation), sampling error, or a combination of factors. Regardless, the general similarity between the two years suggests a common response to winter environmental conditions.

The movements of immature striped bass in the lower estuary provide insight with respect to whether or not small bass are dependent on specific physical areas for survival during the winter. The influence of the trapping action that concentrates the small bass near the salt front and the sequence of bass movement through the metropolitan area imply that immature bass orient to the water mass and not to the substrate. Characteristics of the water mass at a particular location change; those of the substratum do not. The actual association between fish and the water mass could involve water salinity or other factors. Because the concentrations of small bass did not appear correlated with waters of specific salinities at any other time (Martin Marietta Environmental Systems 1984) and because the fish are least

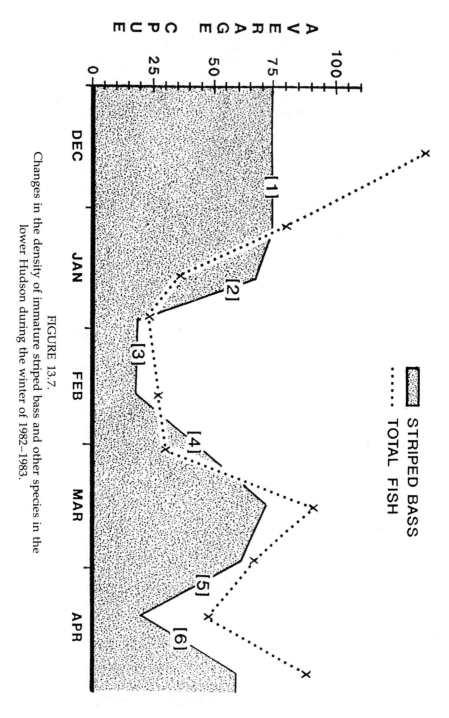

FIGURE 13.7. Changes in the density of immature striped bass and other species in the lower Hudson during the winter of 1982–1983.

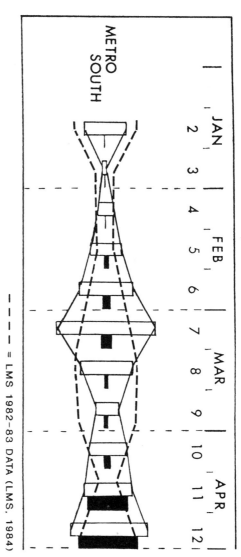

FIGURE 13.8.
Catch-per-unit effort of immature striped bass in the lower Hudson in the winter of 1982–1983.

active in the cold period, I postulate that much of the movement that results in the accumulation of bass near the salt front is passive, associated primarily with the pattern of water movement (i.e., the meeting of opposing water masses) and secondarily with water temperature. The conclusion that movements of immature striped bass in mid-winter is passive is supported by the fact that the highest concentrations of bass near the salt front occur about a month after water temperatures reached their winter minimum.

Orientation to water mass rather than to bottom type is also indicated by the variety of habitats in which the fish occur—namely, open areas off Yonkers, enclosed interpier areas and semienclosed basins from western Long Island Sound to Newark Bay. All these habitats seem to provide suitable space for young bass, which must conserve energy in winter, but they have dissimilar bottom types and differing water quality. Apparently, the only common characteristic of these dissimilar habitats is the general pattern of water movement. Figure 13.9 is a schematic representation of my interpretation of the activities of immature striped bass in the vicinity of the salt front from fall to spring.

Movements of small bass in January and February from areas adjacent to Yonkers down the Hudson and around the Battery into the East River and toward Long Island Sound can be accomplished by simply moving with the tidal currents. Some support for this hypothesis comes from Bowermaster (1986) who describes how swimmers circumnavigating the island of Manhattan during the summer use the ebb tide to move from Spuyten Duyvil to the Battery, then, with a change of tide, ride the flood water northeasterly into the East River. Similarly, the movements of small bass east into Long Island Sound and west into Newark Bay certainly can be aided by tides.

Spring (Yearling and Age II Bass)

As water temperatures increase in early spring, immature bass ascend the water column (LMS 1984; MPI 1984b and c). Some continue emigration while others begin to move upstream. The upstream component of this movement is indicated by the position of the median numbers of juveniles collected during July of each year (Figure 13.2). Ritchie and Koo (1973) have also observed juvenile bass moving upstream in the Putuxent River in spring. The larger juveniles, however, tend to move toward the sea at this time, as indicated by Rathjen and Miller (1957), TI (1977), and Figure 13.2 and 13.3. McFadden et al.

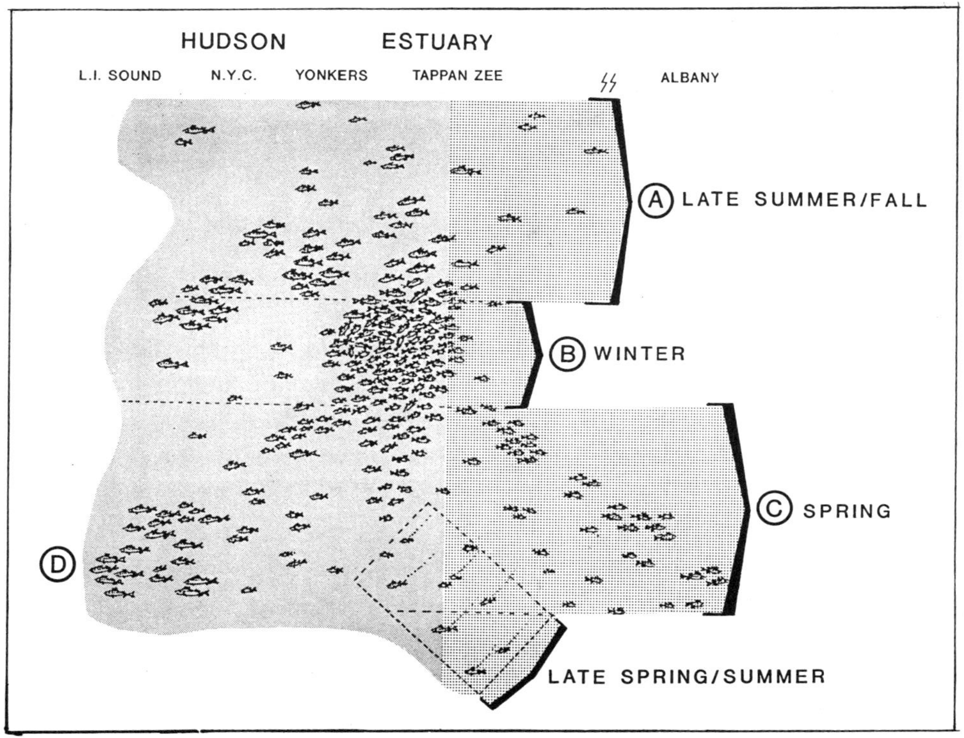

FIGURE 13.9.
Generalized Diagram of the downstream movements of immature striped bass.

(1977) recognized such divergent movements in Hudson River bass. These movements are summarized in Figure 13.9.

The most important shift in density of striped bass in the lower Hudson begins in early March. From late February to early March the density of bass increases at Yonkers and Metro South while concurrently decreasing at Metro North, thus suggesting movement away from the Yonkers-Metro North area, both upstream and toward the ocean. From early March to late April a relatively consistent decline of yearling bass in the Yonkers and Metro North areas coincides with a pattern of erratic increase in density in other areas, especially Metro South. This indicates that the area in the vicinity of the salt front is the primary source for young bass, which disperse throughout the Hudson and adjacent areas in spring.

The pattern of changing densities in the Metro South area (Figure 13.3), downstream from the main winter concentration area, indicates that the Metro South region is both an avenue of transport and an area of accumulation, perhaps peripheral to the main area of concentration slightly upstream. The decline in abundance of small bass in the Metro South area in mid-to-late March followed by an increase through April seems attributable to the departure of bass from this area followed by the movement of additional bass into the area from immediately upstream (Yonkers-Metro North). It is also possible that some young bass move into the lower Hudson from adjacent areas as increasing water temperatures stimulate renewed fish activity in April. These data indicate that the occurrence of young bass in the Metro South area is characterized by continual, although sporadic, movements.

The trend in abundance of yearling and age II bass collected during the Westway study (New Jersey Marine Science Consortium 1984) indicates that those two groups, as well as some larger and smaller bass, participate in two basic movement patterns in early spring (March through April). Yearling bass tend to move upstream (Figures 13.4 and 13.10), while age II bass (fish not approaching maturity) move out of the Hudson as indicated by the progressive occurrence of this age group down the estuary and into the East River in April 1984 (Figure 13.4). A similar downstream movement of age II bass was evident in 1982–83 data (LMS 1984) as shown in Figures 3.1–9A to 3.1–9I of the report by the USACE (1984). The simultaneous movements upstream and downstream did not, however, appear to be strictly age-dependent and would indicate the possibility that some movements of both age groups were random. A spring increase in the number of 2-year-old bass in the reach from the Tappan Zee to

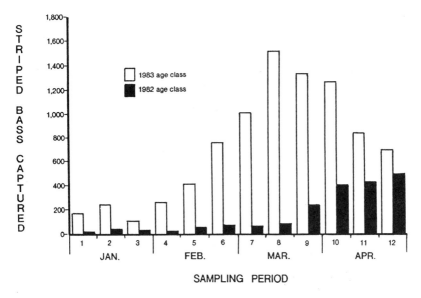

FIGURE 13.10.
Total numbers of striped bass of the 1982 and 1983 year classes collected December 1983 to April 1984.

the East River suggests a possible upstream movement of some 2-year-old bass, which is in contrast to the general pattern whereby bass of that age leave the Hudson. These may be precocious males participating in a prespawning migration (TI 1980; McFadden et al. 1978).

Yearling bass are able to feed in turbid estuarine waters and probably continue the feeding pattern of the previous summer, which can delay their departure from the estuary and may, in fact, be reflected in upstream dispersal. Upstream movement can also result as yearling bass are carried along with intruding salt waters. Thus, transport upstream can be either active (associated with feeding and inshore-offshore synchronization with tidal movements) or passive. I believe that most of the smaller bass that return upstream in spring probably do not move farther downstream in winter than the immediate vicinity of the salt front. It is conceivable, however, that some young bass move past the Battery in the fall or winter and then return to participate in the upstream spring movement.

With reduced freshwater flows the low salinity region of brackish water expands to increase the volume of habitat where inver-

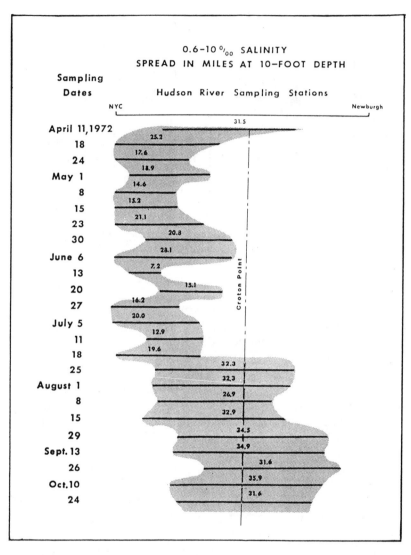

FIGURE 13.11.
Profile of the critical low salinity nursery zone for striped bass in the Hudson Estuary, spring and summer, 1972.

tebrates occur in great abundance—a habitat regarded as an excellent nursery for larval and juvenile fishes. This same habitat contracts during the winter when the fish feed less and do not grow (Figure 13.11).

By age II most striped bass have left the estuary and moved to the coastal areas. There are, however, exceptions to this. Mark and recapture studies demonstrate that some yearling and older bass are still found in the Hudson at a time when most (90.0% of a year class) have migrated to coastal waters (TI 1979a). Yearling bass tagged between kilometers 68 and 96 were recaptured both upstream and off Manhattan 10 to 20 months later (TI 1979a).

Some bass may never leave the Hudson. Local fishermen recognize individual fish that do not possess the sharp, contrasting colors of bass returning from the ocean to spawn as "strawberry bass" (Charles White, commercial fisherman, personal communication). These probably are individuals that have been in the river for an appreciable period. They may be fish that have never left the river or they may simply be individuals that entered the lower reaches of the river before the main run.

DISCUSSION

The Role of Salinity

Tagatz (1961) showed that young bass were tolerant of sharp changes in salinity and temperature. Nevertheless, the finding that immature striped bass accumulate in waters of low salinity immediately downstream from the salt front in winter (MPI 1984a, 1984b, 1984c; USACE 1984) demonstrates the importance of the low-salinity region of the estuary.

The distribution of bass in the growing season coincides primarily with, but is not restricted to, low-salinity waters, which extend over the greatest distance during that season (Dovel 1973, 1981). Similar distribution patterns relating to the salt gradient have been recorded for other estuarine ecosystems. Turner and Chadwick (1972) reported an abundance of young striped bass in the mixing zone between fresh and salt waters of the Sacramento-San Joaquin Estuary. Smith (1970) reported that the nursery grounds for striped bass are typically in waters with salinities of less than 3.2 ppt. Bason (1971) found that 1- to 3-year old bass were most abundant in salinities between 2 and 12 ppt, and Dovel (1971) stated that juveniles prefer salinities of 0.1 to 11.0 ppt. The low-salinity waters immediately downstream from the salt front, where juvenile fishes of many species congregated in several Virginia rivers, has been termed the critical zone (Massman 1963).

During the winter the estuarine salinity gradient is contracted downstream and the presence of immature fish in those waters, whether by discriminatory or involuntary activities, occurs as a concentration immediately downstream from the salt front. Thus, young striped bass in the Hudson inhabit the same general water mass (brackish waters) year round despite the fact that the geographic distribution changes substantially. The continual presence of immature bass in brackish waters assures their presence in estuarine shallows in the summer and places them in a deeper and more stable habitat in the winter (Figure 13.3).

III. FISHERIES METHODS

JOHN R. YOUNG
ROGER G. KEPPEL
RONALD J. KLAUDA

14

Quality Assurance and Quality Control Aspects of the Hudson River Utilities Environmental Studies

ABSTRACT

During the utility-funded ecological studies on the Hudson River in the 1970s, Texas Instruments developed a comprehensive quality assurance (QA) program to ensure that the study results would form an adequate basis for testimony in adversarial regulatory hearings. An independent QA/QC group was responsible for implementing the QA program, but all major functional components of the organization were important in its success. The QA program covered all aspects of the studies; sample collection and analysis, data management, data analysis and interpretation, and report production. For many activities, especially laboratory analyses, statistical quality control inspection plans were developed and implemented.

The QA program was effective in producing a high-quality data set that stood the test of intensive scrutiny in adversarial hearings. Most aspects of the QA program have been continued in the ongoing monitoring studies of the 1980s.

INTRODUCTION

Quality is a common subject in the media today. Every week newspaper and magazine articles appear that discuss the "quality" of our manufactured products and services. In trade journals, the "Deming philosophy" or "Taguchi methods" are common topics. Organizations such as the American Society for Testing and Materials and the American Society for Quality Control promote programs, education, and standardization of methods to improve quality. Seminars are given to instruct organizations how to implement programs to increase the quality of their output.

This flood of interest in quality in the popular press and business world has some parallel in the field of chemical measurements (Taylor and Stanley 1985; Taylor 1987; Coffey et al. 1988). But, with a few exceptions (Chang 1982; Ellis 1985a, 1985b, 1986, 1988), it has not yet become a common theme in fisheries, ecology, and environmental impact assessment literature. Although researchers in biological fields certainly are concerned with the quality of their results, and routinely take measures to ensure high quality, they seldom include descriptions of quality assurance (QA) aspects of their studies in technical reports, books, or journal articles. We question these omissions. Perhaps the QA aspects are viewed simply as steps that any prudent scientist would take when conducting research, therefore no overt descriptions are needed. Page limitations imposed by journal editors may also discourage inclusion of QA methodolgies in manuscripts submitted for publication.

We contend that neither explanation is adequate. We assert that there are no generally accepted standards for QA in ecological and fisheries research. Many, if not most, research activities appear to be done with little thought to the inherent sources of error associated with the process. A nonexhaustive survey of 25 references on the methodology of fisheries surveys, impact assessment, and environmental monitoring published between 1966 and 1985 provided little or no guidance in QA (Table 14.1). In fact, only 2 of the references even mentioned QA, data quality, or quality control (QC) in the index.

There are recent indications that formal QA programs are be-

TABLE 14.1.
Fisheries, ecology, and impact assessment literature reviewed for guidance in establishing QA programs.

Source	Treatment of Quality Issues
Bagenal 1974	Contains several papers on effects of errors in aging fish
Bagenal 1978	Brief discussions of errors in aging fish and fecundity determination
Battelle 1975	None
Cairns and Dickson 1973	Brief mention of QC in EPA water quality monitoring program in paper by C. I. Weber
Cairns, Patil, and Waters 1979	None
Calhoun 1966	Brief discussion of errors in aging fish
Canter 1979	None
Canter and Hill 1979	None
Cormack, Patil, and Robson 1979	None
Dickson, Cairns, and Livingston 1977	None
Edmondson and Winberg 1971	Thorough discussion of potential bias in sampling and analysis methods
EIFAC 1975	Efficiency and variability of various fish sampling techniques
Gulland 1966	None
Gulland 1969	None
Hartman 1975	None
Hocutt and Stauffer 1980	Includes chapter by E. J. Crossman on value of maintaining a reference collection of identified specimens
LMS 1978d	None
Seber 1973	None
Southwood 1978	Thorough discussion of collection and extraction efficiency of various sampling methods
Tranter 1968	Thorough treatment of field sampling techniques for zooplankton
University of Washington 1985	None
Van Winkle 1977	Chapter by M. A. Kjelson

(continued)

TABLE 14.1.
(Continued)

Source	Treatment of Quality Issues
	discusses collection efficiency in juvenile fish sampling
Ward 1978	None
Weber 1973	Mentions need for reference collections to verify identification of organisms. No specific discussion of QA programs
Worf 1980	Brief description of QA aspects of federal biomonitoring programs in paper by C. I. Weber

coming more prevalent in ecological research, particularly in research sponsored by EPA. Although examples of QA programs in the refereed literature are still sparse, they are available in EPA project reports. An excellent example is the QA Plan for the EPA's Episodic Response Project (Peck et al. 1988).

Our goals in this paper are (1) describe the QA/QC aspects of the Hudson River Ecological Study conducted for the Hudson River Utilities by Texas Instruments Ecological Services Group (TI) in the 1970s, (2) stimulate thought about the process of ecological data collection and analysis so that more effective methods of maintaining data quality may be developed in the future, and (3) encourage other researchers to describe QA activities and report their results.

For this presentation, we define QA activities as those actions that were undertaken to ensure that data and analyses would be adequate for their intended purpose—to serve as the basis for expert testimony on the effects of actual and planned power plant operations on Hudson River fish populations. QC activities are defined as activities that ensure that accuracy and precision of measurements and processes are known and within specified numerical limits. Thus QC data are collected within the program of QA activities.

ORIGINS OF THE QA PROGRAM

Three separate imperatives provided the impetus to establish a QA program in the early years of the Hudson River Ecological Study, circa 1972–1973. Perhaps the most compelling factor was the virtual certainty that the data would ultimately be used as the basis for expert testimony in a highly adversarial courtroom proceeding. Managers and technical personnel recognized that a "trail of evidence" would be extremely valuable once the study results were taken into the courtroom. This concept was a guide in designing the original QA activities. Each unit of information was to be traceable from the collection of the sample in the field, through laboratory analyses and entry of values onto data sheets, the conversion of raw data to an electronic format, and the numerical and statistical data analysis, and finally as legally defensible data in reports or testimony.

Secondly, it was desirable that the QA program conformed with the requirements of Title 10, Code of Federal Regulations, Part 50, Appendix B, which specifies QA criteria for nuclear power plants and fuel processing facilities. Although 10 CFR 50 does not directly set requirements for nonradiological impact assessment and monitoring studies, the concepts outlined in this section were seen as also desirable for environmental work. Much of the environmental work conducted in the early 1970s was done under contract with engineering firms constructing nuclear power plants. These firms were required to follow 10 CFR 50 in their efforts, and TI viewed similar compliance as a good marketing strategy in developing a QA program for biological work.

The third imperative in developing a QA program resulted from the prior familiarity the TI Science Services Division had with QA. Many of Science Services Division's top managers had come from the TI Equipment Group, which derived a major share of its business from government contracts for electronic equipment. Government contracts generally require strict QA programs to assess and control the level of defective merchandise delivered to military and government agencies. TI managers were already familiar with the benefits of these QA programs, and knew how to implement QA policies in a manufacturing environment. However, when the TI managers began to design a QA program for the Hudson River Ecological Study, they quickly learned that state-of-the-art QA in biological sampling consisted of little more than detailed descriptions of methodology. Statistical QC methods, although commonplace in manufacturing, had not yet been applied to the field of environmental sampling. The QA program that TI developed for their Hudson River studies was a pioneering effort that stimulated similar programs by other research groups working on other impact assessment studies.

HUDSON RIVER ECOLOGICAL STUDY ORGANIZATION

TI involvement with the Hudson River Ecological Study expanded rapidly from 1972 to 1974. Expansion required a program organization that could successfully plan, implement, and coordinate a major impact assessment study. The multifaceted study included a long series of discrete tasks that began with definition of study objectives, continued to sample collections in the river, and ended with the preparation of technical reports and legal testimony. The study was conducted in a litigious milieu with a high degree of visibility to the scientific community and the general public. Therefore, the program organization also required critical review and evaluation of each study task, and detailed documentation of task procedures, products, and performance review results.

The program organization developed and implemented by TI included five major functional components (Figure 14.1). Three of these components were coordinated directly by the on-site Program Manager.

(a) The operations component encompassed those study tasks that collected samples in the river and at the Indian Point power plant, and processed these samples in the laboratory. The core tasks assigned to the operations component were ichthyoplankton (early life stages), fisheries (older life stages), biocharacteristics of fish and ichthyoplankton (length, weight, fecundity, etc.), impingement (Indian Point), and water quality measurements. Operations tasks also included development of an experimental striped bass hatchery, and several special studies.

(b) The technical component encompassed those study tasks that involved analytical interactions with operations tasks, data analyses, preparation of project reports, and participation in adjudicatory hearings. To maximize continuity between the technical and operations components of the program, regular interactions were an essential task of the technical staff. Seminars on various analytical topics such as sample allocation strategies, dynamics of fish populations, and mark-recapture techniques were presented to the operations staff. Technical staff members were also periodically assigned to operations staff field crews and required to participate in sample collection and processing of the laboratory data that would later be analyzed and interpreted by the technical staff.

(c) The administration and control component supported the entire

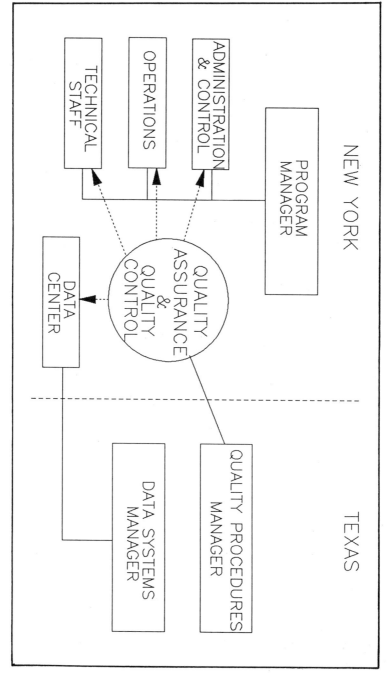

FIGURE 14.1.
The Texas Instruments project organization for the Hudson River Ecological Study.

program. Major tasks included budgetary evaluation, facilities and equipment maintenance, personnel records, and clerical support.

The other two major components reported to management in TI's Dallas headquarters.

(d) A data center was coordinated by the Data Processing Systems Manager. Data center functions included maintenance of data files, computer programing, and statistical analysis. The data center staff worked closely with the operations component in sample allocation tasks, with the technical component in data analyses, and with a QA/QC component in project documentation.

(e) The fifth major component was QA/QC, an indirect function coordinated by the TI Quality Procedures Manager. The QA/QC component was separate from the rest of the project organization to ensure independent evaluations of quality within the TI Hudson River program. The QA/QC component was divided into two subcomponents, data documentation and control (DD&C) and analytical quality control (AQC). The DD&C group interacted substantially with all other components, while AQC interacted primarily with the technical component and the data center. Activities carried out by QA/QC included standard operating procedure (SOP) conformance inspections of field and laboratory tasks carried out by the operations component, and review of the analytical tasks performed by the technical component.

FIELD AND LABORATORY OPERATIONS

Field Crew Organization and Responsibilities

Field crews were organized around the requirements of the task and usually consisted of 3 or 4 people. The crew leader was responsible for ensuring that all functions were performed according to approved SOPs and was accountable for verifying data accuracy. Each crew member had specific functions. The crew leader, in addition to operating the vessel and locating sampling sites, was able to check on the sample analysis or the data recording. On small boats the crew leader recorded all data in addition to selecting sample sites and operating the boat.

Training of Field Crews and Lab Technicians

Field technicians had to serve as crew members for relatively long periods (at least 1–2 years) before they were given the responsibility of crew leaders. Due to the diversity of field tasks performed, crew leaders were either assigned to small boat operations (e.g., beach seines, gill nets) or to the large boat operations (e.g., ichthyoplankton or bottom trawl surveys). The skills required to operate the large vessels (up to 45 feet), during night sampling and the navigational hazards of the Hudson River allowed for only a few (3–4) individuals to qualify as large boat crew leaders. Many more individuals (at least 10–15) were qualified as small boat crew leaders.

Crew member training consisted almost entirely of on-the-job training; however, many of the operations staff had received formal training in fisheries sampling and laboratory techniques at colleges or technical schools. New crew members were assigned to crews in such a way that there was no more than one inexperienced member per crew. Although lab technician training was also essentially on-the-job, more difficult tasks (larval fish taxonomy) usually required extensive instruction by qualified taxonomists before that individual was able to independently analyze samples.

Standard Operating Procedures

Standard operating procedures were developed for nearly every aspect of the study program, including sample collection, sample analysis, data center functions, and administration. By 1977 the SOPs filled two large three-ring notebooks. SOPs were invaluable in maintaining comparability of methods over all 18 years of the study, from 1972 to the present.

Even the smallest revisions to these procedures required review and approval by the staff involved in the affected activity, the TI Program Manager, and the Con Edison Program Manager. DD&C shepherded suggested changes through meetings to discuss their potential effects and obtained all necessary approvals. Once a change had been approved, DD&C circulated copies of the modified sections to all owners of the SOP and retrieved the superceded pages. Thus everyone had the same set of procedures. Since SOPs were controlled documents, each copy of an SOP was assigned to a particular individual who was responsible for inserting revisions and returning old pages to DD&C.

DD&C also conducted audits of all operations to ensure that

SOPs were being followed. Prior to an audit, the auditor would review the SOP for the activity to be audited, and the DD&C supervisor would contact the operations group leader to inform him that an audit would be conducted. During the audit, the DD&C auditor would observe activities and subsequently file a report of the findings. Departures from approved procedures were reported to the DD&C supervisor and to the operations supervisor for corrective action.

Instrument Calibration

All water quality monitoring instruments were calibrated according to manufacturer's recommended procedures prior to use each day (Table 14.2) by technicians assigned to a laboratory water chemistry section. These technicians were qualified to prepare the standards used for calibration and to make adjustments or repairs to the instruments. For tasks that required crews to remain away from the lab overnight, the crew leader was responsible for the daily calibration, but the reference standards were prepared by the water chemistry section.

Flowmeter Calibration

At the initiation of the ichthyoplankton and juvenile studies in the early 1970s, TI selected a single flowmeter, the General Oceanics model 2030 for all volumetric sampling efforts. This mechanical flowmeter was suspended in the mouth opening of the sampling gear to record distance traveled through the water. Tow speed was measured with a similar electronic meter, model 2031, which recorded speed in m/sec on an on-deck readout unit.

TABLE 14.2.
Calibration procedures for water quality instruments used in the Hudson River Ecological Study.

Parameter	Instrument	Frequency	Standards	Tolerance[a]
Temperature	YSI model 33	Daily	ASTM thermometer	±0.5°C
Dissolved Oxygen	YSI model 57	2 Daily	Saturated air	±0.1 ppm
Conductivity	YSI model 33	Daily	10 g/l NaCl solution	±5%
Turbidity	Hach 2100	Daily	100 FTU solution	±5%
pH	Sargent-Welch	Daily	4, 7, 10 buffers	±0.3 units

[a] During calibration, meter reading must be adjusted to within the tolerance value of the standard.

Although the manufacturer provided a standard conversion factor for these meters that gave an estimate of the distance traveled through the water (and consequently allowed for sample volume calculation), it was decided to calibrate each meter prior to each weekly survey. Moreover, in order to avoid overuse of any particular meter, at least three meters rotated as samples were taken. Flowmeter calibration therefore became a costly undertaking with an inventory of several dozen meters being continually calibrated.

Calibration was conducted at the Johns Hopkins University High Turbulence Flume. Meters were run through the flume at six velocities ranging from 40 to 90 cm/sec and regression equations were calculated for distance traveled as a function of meter revolutions. If the accuracy of volume calculations from these regression equations resulted in a 95% prediction interval wider than 30 m^3 for the standard 300 m^3 sample (i.e., ± 5%), the flowmeters were removed from service and returned to the manufacturer for repair or replacement. Electronic flowmeters were similarly treated if velocity readings differed from the flume velocity by more than 10%.

Although the calibration procedures were effective in identifying faulty flowmeters and establishing individual volume conversions, meters could still fail during use. To ensure that defective meters were immediately removed from service, the field crew checked the reading for each sample against acceptable ranges listed in the SOP. Samples for which readings did not fall within the acceptable range were voided and retaken immediately.

Quality Control Inspection

In addition to audits for SOP compliance, laboratory tasks such as length and weight determinations, ichthyoplankton sample sorting, ichthyoplankton and older fish identification, fecundity analyses, and aging were also subjected to QC inspection plans. These inspection plans were based on commonly used plans from manufacturing environments (Hansen 1963; Duncan 1974).

For most operations, an inspection plan was implemented for each individual technician performing the operation. This approach was more costly than conducting the inspection on the laboratory as a whole where all individuals' work was pooled for QC inspection. The major advantage of the individual-based plan was that individual performance could be accurately monitored, which assisted in either retraining or replacing technicians who were not meeting an adequate performance level. However, certain tasks (e.g., checking of marked fish in impingement samples) required many technicians and made the individual-based system unfeasible.

Continuous sampling plans (CSP) for attributes were used where the process being examined was conducted on a more or less continuous basis, and where characteristics being measured could be defined as acceptable or defective. For some operations a defect could be defined for an individual fish or measurement, while for other operations the entire sample became the inspected item.

Single-stage plans (CSP-1) required a complete inspection of all items until a predetermined number (i) of consecutive items was found to be free of defects. A defect was defined as a measurement outside of the tolerance limit. Once i consecutive items were found acceptable, sampling was reduced to only a randomly chosen fraction (f) of additional items. If any item was found to be defective, 100% inspection was reinstituted until i consecutive items were again found acceptable. Plans were designed to ensure that, as a worst case, the fraction of all items that were defective did not exceed the predetermined average outgoing quality limit (AOQL).

A variation of the single-stage plan, CSP-3, was also used for some tasks. In CSP-3, if a defect was found while sampling at f intensity, the next 4 samples were also inspected. If none were defective, sampling continued at f; if any defects were found, sampling reverted to 100%.

Lot-by-lot inspection plans, based on MIL-STD 105 (Hansen 1963) were also used, primarily where the process was discontinuous in nature or the items to be inspected differed greatly in character. In lot-by-lot plans, items to be inspected were grouped into lots. The number of items inspected in each lot and the number of defective items allowed were determined by the acceptable quality level (AQL), tolerable fraction of items that could be defective, and by the number of items in a lot. Lots in which the number of defective items exceeded the acceptance value were inspected completely. Multiple-level plans, in which the number to be inspected varied with past performance, were also used for lot-by-lot inspection.

Fish and ichthyoplankton identification and enumeration, and fecundity analyses, were all monitored using individual-based CSP-1 inspection plans (Table 14.3). Initial consecutive nondefective items required to leave 100% inspection mode were $i = 10$ for fisheries tasks and $i = 14$ for ichthyoplankton. Sampling intensity levels were $f = 10^{-1}$ for fisheries and $f = 14^{-1}$ for ichthyoplankton. Tolerances for these analyses were generally ±10%. In the case of larval fish identification, the tolerance was very stringent, because error rates were

TABLE 14.3.
Quality control inspection plans used for laboratory procedures
in the Hudson River Ecological Study.

Task	Type	AOQL	i	f¹	Defect Tolerance	QC Item
Fisheries						
Counts of fish	CSP-1	10%	10	10	±10% of total count	Taxon
Identification	CSP-1	10%	10	10	±10% of total count	Taxon
Length	CSP-3	10%	18	20	±3% of total length	Fish
Weight	CSP-3	10%	18	20	±3% of total weight	Fish
Aging	Lot	11%[a]			±0 years	Lot
Finclips	CSP-1	11%	4	3	0 missed finclips	Lot
Fecundity	CSP-1	10%	10	10	±10% of total egg count	Fish
Ichthyoplankton						
Sorting	CSP-1	10%	14	20	10% of total count	Sample
Identification	CSP-1	10%	14	20	±10% of total count	Taxon/stage

[a] Lot-by-lot inspection plan was designed to 10% AQL, which produced an AOQL of 10.7%.

calculated for each species and life stage in the sample and then summed; the sample failed if the total error rate of all species and life stages exceeded 10%.

CSP-3 plans were used for checking length and weight measurements. These parameters were not difficult to determine and seldom fell outside the tolerance level of ±3%. CSP-3 plans were used instead of CSP-1 because a single error did not cause immediate return to 100% inspection mode.

Examination of juvenile and yearling fish in impingement samples for finclips was checked with a laboratory-based CSP-1 sampling plan. After initial checking for finclips as impingement samples were processed, striped bass, white perch, and Atlantic tomcod were retained and pooled into 2000 fish lots. For this task, only 4 consecutive error-free lots were needed before sampling, at $f = 3^{-1}$, could begin. There was no tolerance level set because even a single missed finclip was considered a failure and caused the sampling to revert to 100% inspection.

Age determination was sampled with an individual-based lot-by-lot plan. Samples, defined as all scales or otoliths for an individual fish, were grouped by species, length group, and biweekly period into lots of up to 60 samples. A subset of samples from each lot was randomly selected and examined by a second reader. The number to be examined varied from 5 to 25, depending on the lot size and whether the plan was in a normal or tightened inspection mode. If the second age determination did not agree with the first, the sample was considered defective. If the number of defects in a lot exceeded the acceptance number, the entire lot was reexamined and inspection shifted into the tightened mode.

DATA MANAGEMENT

Data management for the project was a crucial activity that became progressively more difficult each year. Since the initial studies were not viewed to be a long-term effort, data management decisions were made to optimize short-term efficiency. By 1978 the task of managing the data base and producing timely analyses had become very difficult. Due to numerous, but relatively small, changes made in the program objectives each year, the data files were never totally compatable from one year to the next. These differences made multiyear analyses very difficult and required continual modification of existing software.

In 1979 TI began a data standardization project designed to streamline the data analysis task. In this effort TI converted nearly all project data to hierarchical SAS (SAS Institute 1982) data sets. The format-free nature of SAS data sets permitted minor changes in sampling programs without requiring major changes in analytical software or data base design. In the process of converting to SAS data sets, all codes and variables were reviewed for consistent meanings and units of measurement. Variables whose meaning or coding had changed throughout the program were carefully recoded and standardized. The SAS conversion and standardization was accomplished by a team from all of the operational groups, led by the data processing group and the data documentation and control group.

The DD&C group had the primary responsibility for QA activities pertaining directly to data management. Key activities in this area were: (1) cataloging and control of all data-related documents, (2) review of completed raw data sheets prior to data entry, (3) control and documentation of data revisions.

The project generated a tremendous volume of paperwork that DD&C cataloged and maintained. Preservation of this paperwork was necessary to maintain the "trail of evidence" that might be necessary in legal proceedings. Thus the field notebooks filled out by the crew leaders, data sheets, instrument calibration logs, QC inspection logs, computer data listings, computer programs, copies of hand calculations, and other forms of documentation were all cataloged and controlled. Anyone needing documentation from the files was required to sign it out and return it.

The direct management of the data was also the DD&C group's responsibility. DD&C personnel would review each data sheet for legibility and completeness prior to sending them out for data entry. Data were converted to electronic format by a double keypunch process in which every record was entered twice. If the two entries were not identical, the keypunch operator would resolve the differences. This process was very effective in eliminating nearly all data entry errors.

After data files were returned from keypunching, the data processing group ran data verification software on the files. These programs consisted of univariate checks for values out of predetermined ranges, and bivariate and multivariate tests in which several data values would be checked for compliance with expected relationships. Values that were outside the expected ranges were flagged for further examination.

The DD&C group would take the error check reports and try to resolve suspicious data values. Results of these checks were recorded and saved. Any changes to the data sets were documented. If changes were made to a data set that had already been used for analyses, the appropriate analytical personnel were advised of the change so that analyses could be rerun or revised as appropriate.

DATA ANALYSIS AND REPORTS

QA activities associated with data analysis and report production were conducted jointly by the data center, technical staff, and AQC. These activities were meant to ensure that data analyses and statistics presented in reports or testimony would be without errors. The entire process, from collection of raw data to report production, was considered in the design of the QA program.

Methods used to analyze study data for annual project reports or hearings testimony generally conformed with standard analytical procedures (SAP). However, these procedures were more flexible than the SOPs used by the operations group because they were intended to serve as guidelines, not as requirements. Other analytical approaches were also used when they proved to be more appropriate.

The structure and content of each project report were developed by a senior member of the technical staff who was designated the Report Coordinator of that report by the Technical Director. Each Report Coordinator worked closely with and integrated the contributions of a team of scientists who prepared the various sections of the report. Large TI project reports such as the Year Class series were subdivided into discrete modules and written as stand-alone draft documents that could be circulated as separate elements for review, but later bound together under a single cover in the final version.

The array of analyses proposed for each project report was carefully reviewed for appropriateness by several members of the technical staff, including the Technical Director, and statisticians from the data center. After each proposed analysis was reviewed and approved, a data center Work Request form was completed by the report section author and forwarded to the data center for processing. The Work Request form became a part of the analytical documentation package that was later reviewed by AQC.

The data center Work Request specified the data sets to be used, and any appropriate subsets by species, life stages, sampling gear, locations, or time periods. The methods to use in calculation were written down and referenced to any prior programs or previous reports. The analyst also specified how the program could be checked for correctness. After review, work orders were sent to the data processing group for assignment to specific programmers.

Upon beginning work on a work order, the programmer would review the analysis with the requestor to resolve any questions or ambiguities. For complex analyses, many lengthy conversations were sometimes needed to discuss details of the algorithms. The programmer developed a program to conduct the analysis and sent a test run of the program using a reduced data set to the analyst, who checked the calculations for errors. Only after resolution of errors was the analysis run on the entire data set. The programmer included comments within the program to help in debugging or modifying the program, and completed a documentation file for the analysis. This documentation of the software was extremely valuable since experienced programmers were very much in demand and seldom remained with the project longer than two years.

Analytical staff members would take the final output and make further calculations or draft tables and figures directly from the output. These tables and figures formed the basis for interpretation of study results in the reports.

From first draft to final version, TI project reports and written direct testimony were reviewed and revised at several steps along an analytical QC sequence. The draft report sections authored by members of the report team were first reviewed by the Report Coordinator, who also integrated the separate sections into the complete document. During this initial review, tables, figures, and calculations were concurrently reviewed by AQC.

AQC reviewed all analyses that pertained to key study tasks such as entrainment estimates. Other analyses were reviewed in part based on a subsampling plan. Unless another plan was requested by the Report Coordinator and approved by the Technical Director, the subsampling plan had an AOQL of 0.1. Defective values were defined as those that differed from the correct value by more than the rounding precision. Subsampling was done in accordance with the Lot Tolerant Percent Defective plan (Schilling 1978). Discrepancies between the original and QC values encountered during AQC review were first resolved with the authors and then corrected prior to preparation of the final version report. AQC results for project reports were documented and stored.

When a draft report passed the AQC review, it went to the Technical Editor for nontechnical editing, and formatting to enhance visual quality. Each draft report was reviewed by the Technical Editor and occasionally by the Program Manager before it was submitted to the utility clients.

The nature of TI contractor-client relationship with the Hudson River Utilities precluded a "peer review" of project reports in the traditional sense of that process. Therefore, the project reports are appropriately classified as "grey literature." Inclusion of a traditional peer review step in TI report review process would presumably have further enhanced the quality of the final versions. However, we are confident that the intensity of the TI internal QC effort was sufficient to correct major calculation errors. When study data and analyses found their way into hearings testimony, critique reached an intensity far beyond the traditional peer review process of even the most prestigious journals.

HEARINGS PREPARATION

Involvement in adjudicatory hearings was a major part of the TI Hudson River study activities, especially during the late 1970s. Direct participation in hearings was handled by a small group of senior technical staff members supported by other individuals with expertise in specific technical disciplines. The hearings group also worked closely with the operations and QA/QC components of the program to describe clear trails of evidence for key data sets or analyses that were thoroughly dissected during months of rigorous cross-examination in the courtroom and repeatedly challenged in written interrogatories prepared by consultants and attorneys for the regulatory agencies and intervenor groups (Christensen and Klauda 1988).

DISCUSSION

The QA/QC activities conducted as part of the Hudson River Ecological Study had several effects on the program. First, and most obviously, the quality of the existing data is higher than it would have been without these functions. Many sources of errors were eliminated entirely, while other sources were identified and corrected before they were incorporated into the data base. The standardization of methods and field audits helped ensure that, no matter who was in the field handling the nets or in the laboratory analyzing the samples, the data would be comparable to other data collected within or among years of the study.

A second benefit was that, by its mere existence, the QA program kept the concept of quality in everyone's consciousness. The entire organization, both the client and consultant, was squarely behind the philosophy of the program, and therefore poor work or shortcuts in sampling or analysis were not tolerated. In our opinion, this support from upper management was essential for the effectiveness of the QA program.

Most aspects of the QA program have been continued in sampling programs conducted for the utilities in the 1980s by other environmental consultants. QC inspection plans, SOP conformance audits, and data error checking have been maintained, and in some cases enhanced. In recent years, the utilities have attempted to make QC data more accessible and to use the data to further improve the sampling program. Utility contractors now include results of the QA activities in project reports and provide the QC data to the utilities. Geoghegan et al. (in press) provide an example of how QC data have been used to reduce data recording errors in a mark-recapture study.

One could rightfully ask whether the benefits of an extensive QA program were worth the expense. For example, from 1974 through 1980, TI allocated about 15% of its several million dollar annual study budget to QA/QC activities. This expenditure level for QA may seem excessive, but when one considers the intense scrutiny to which the TI study data were subjected, the money spent on QA seems realistic. However, for a researcher designing a new study today, would the time and money spent on QA/QC be better allocated to collecting and analyzing more samples, rather than reanalyzing a significant fraction of the samples to determine data quality?

To answer this question, it is necessary to go back to our definition of QA and explicitly consider the intended purpose of the data to be collected. We feel that some type of QA program should certainly be a part of every ecological study; however, the intensity of the program can vary widely. Data that are likely to be used as part of a litigation process probably demand the highest degree of quality that can reasonably be achieved. On the other hand, data that are being collected to measure gross trends in some environmental measure probably have a lesser need for a stringent QA program.

In most instances, the type of answers to be determined from the data should also be considered. If hypotheses about the mean level of a variable are to be tested, random unbiased errors in measurements will make differences among mean values harder to detect. However, increasing the sample size may be more effective in raising the statistical power of the analysis than decreasing the measurement error through a stringent QA program. In contrast, if hypotheses about the size of the sample variance are to be tested (for example, use of the variance to mean ratio to infer whether organisms are randomly distributed throughout the habitat) then measurement errors will inherently bias the statistical test. For this type of question, the QA program should be relatively intense to reduce the bias to a minimum.

We hope that this presentation will stimulate thought about the need for QA activities in ecological research. Other researchers can see what was, and is, done in the utilities' Hudson River studies, and may use this information to design better QA programs for their own studies. Finally, we recommend that all researchers include at least brief descriptions of QA/QC activities in their reports, books, and journal articles. In many instances, analyses and summary of the QC data will help others in estimating what level of QA activities to build into their own studies.

Acknowledgments

The authors thank Howard Baker, Larry Bowles, Dave Kimble, Kathy Klauda, Don Strickert, Ray Toole, and Paul Zweiacker for their help in recalling the history of the QA program for this manuscript. The task would certainly have been much easier 10 years ago; today, it would have been impossible without their recollections and insight. We also acknowledge the contributions of many unnamed individuals in designing and implementing the QA program.

MARK T. MATTSON
PAUL GEOGHEGAN
DENNIS J. DUNNING

15

Accuracy of Catch per Unit Effort Indices of Atlantic Tomcod Abundance in the Hudson River

ABSTRACT

Average catch per unit effort (CPUE) is a relative index of population abundance that generally requires less sampling effort than absolute estimates. However its accuracy can be determined only by comparison with some other valid estimate of absolute population size. We compared CPUE indices with Peterson mark-recapture estimates of the spawning population of the Atlantic tomcod in the Hudson River for the winters of 1982–83, 1983–84, 1985–86, 1987–88, and 1988–89. Spawning tomcod were caught in boxtraps between km 28 and km 123, fin clipped, and released during December to February of each year. Subsequently they were recaptured by bottom trawling between km 0 and km 18.

The spawning population estimates were 12.5 million fish in 1982–83, 6.7 million in 1983–84, 2.1 million in 1985–86, 3.5 million in

1987–88, and 5.9 million in 1988–89. Boxtrap CPUE indices were highest in 1988–89 and lowest in 1978–88, whereas Trawl CPUE indices were highest in 1982–1983 and lowest in 1987–88. Logarithmic transformation did not improve the accuracy of these CPUE indices. The CPUE indices measured order of magnitude changes in Atlantic tomcod population size.

INTRODUCTION

Average catch per unit of effort (CPUE) is commonly used as an index of population abundance for fish (Ricker 1975) and other animals (Seber 1982). CPUE, which is a relative index, generally requires less sampling effort than absolute estimates of population size, because it requires only a random sample of similar-effort units from a common region and time interval. However, the accuracy of a CPUE index of abundance can be determined only by comparison with valid estimates of absolute population size. If there is a good correlation between a CPUE index and the corresponding population estimates, it may be possible to convert the CPUE index of relative abundance into reasonably accurate estimates of absolute population size (Seber 1982).

The Atlantic tomcod population in the Hudson River has been studied since 1974 as part of a utilities biological monitoring program. Valid Petersen mark-recapture estimates of adult Atlantic tomcod population size are available for the winters of 1982–1983, 1983–1984, 1985–1986, 1987–1988, and 1988–1989 (NAI 1989). This study was undertaken to identify the best (most accurate and precise) CPUE index of the Hudson River Atlantic tomcod winter spawning population size for these years based on both boxtrap and trawling surveys. If an accurate and precise CPUE index could be calculated using the by-catch of Atlantic tomcod in a winter striped bass (*Morone saxatilis*) trawling survey (Dunning et al. this volume), the scope and cost of the current Atlantic tomcod mark-recapture program could be reduced.

METHODS

Field Procedures

Boxtraps were set at 17 sites along the east and west banks of the Hudson River from Yonkers (km 28) north to Poughkeepsie (km 123).

The 1 × 1 × 2 m traps with 1 cm (stretch) mesh netting were fished without leads in 1 to 12 m of water. Traps were lowered into the water by wire cable and firmly attached to a shore structure (e.g., dock, pier, bulkhead). All traps were checked and repositioned daily, Monday through Friday, during the December through February spawning seasons of 1982–1983, 1983–1984, 1985–1986, 1987–1988, and 1988–1989. These were the same boxtrap sampling sites and procedures reported in annual surveys from 1974–1975 through 1979–1980 (Klauda et al. 1988b; McLaren et al. 1988a).

The Hudson River between Battery Park (km 0) and the George Washington Bridge (km 18) was sampled by bottom trawls. The channel of this region, collectively referred to as the Battery, was fished at a depth of 5–15 m using bottom trawls equipped with rock-hopper roller gear. This roller gear permitted deployment of the trawls over the relatively rough bottom conditions found at the edge of the navigational channel. From January through March of 1983 and 1984, and from November through April of 1985–1986, 1987–1988, and 1988–1989, 9 or 12 m high-rise trawls were deployed on Monday through Friday of each week. The 9 m (foot-rope) trawl with a 3.8 cm (stretch) mesh cod end and a vertical height of about 3.6 m was fished in each of the five sampling seasons. The 12 m trawl with about 4.9 m vertical lift was fished during 1985–1986 (7.5 cm stretch mesh cod end) and 1987–1988 (3.8 cm stretch mesh cod end). Approximately 15 and 5 tows per day were made with the 9 m trawl and 12 m trawl, respectively. Randomly selected sampling days were balanced during the two seasons when both trawls were fished so that at the end of a two week period, each trawl would be deployed on 5 days. Each trawl tow was ten minutes, and the trawl was towed against the current at a boat speed (through water) of between 1.2 and 1.7 m-per-second. The towing wire was set with a length-to-depth ratio of between 2:1 and 4:1.

All Atlantic tomcod caught in boxtraps or trawls were checked for evidence of prior marking. Unmarked fish were fin-clipped, using coded combinations of fins (one or two fins, not caudal) indicating the gear and weekly or biweekly period of collection, and released. Atlantic tomcod that appeared to be recaptured from the other release gear were preserved in 10% buffered formalin and taken to the laboratory for fin-clip verification. Fin-clip recaptures from the same gear were released again as quickly as possible after fin-clip code and length were recorded. Fin-clipped fish were released away from the capture site but within 400 m to reduce the possibility of immediate recapture.

Atlantic tomcod fin-clip recaptures were verified by microscopic examination. A verified fin-clip exhibited a straight cut perpendicular to the long axis of most or all of the adjacent rays. Irregular or rounded cuts across adjacent rays suggested damage other than cutting, or fin rot that resembled a fin-clip. Fish with these anomalous fin-clips represented 2–11% of the initial recaptures, and were not considered valid recaptures.

Fin regeneration was recognized for both verified and anomalous fin-clips, particularly for Atlantic tomcod at large more than two months. Verified and anomalous fin-clips on regenerated fins were differentiated by the same criteria used for nonregenerated fins. The age of recaptured fish and the amount of fin regeneration were both used to identify fin-clip recaptures from previous seasons. Only age 2+ fish with extensive fin regeneration were considered recaptures from the previous season.

Analytical Methods

CPUE. Atlantic tomcod CPUE was calculated for boxtrap sets or trawl tows from which valid data were collected and no sampling problems were encountered. Sets or tows that caught Atlantic tomcod but encountered problems were used only for mark-recapture estimates. Sampling problems were generally related to gear deployment, which would affect CPUE—that is, a tear in the boxtrap netting or termination of a trawl tow before the ten-minute duration.

Boxtrap sampling durations approximated 24 hours during Tuesday through Friday (weekdays) and 72 hours on Monday (weekend), with occasional longer durations due to weather (ice) conditions. Boxtrap CPUE was calculated as Atlantic tomcod catch per hour (C/H) for each sampling week (Monday–Friday). Trawl catch statistics were expressed as Atlantic tomcod catch per ten-minute tow (CPUE10). Mean CPUE10 was only calculated for the 9 m trawl, because this trawl was fished consistently in each of the five sampling seasons. Atlantic tomcod caught in the 12 m trawl were enumerated, examined for fin-clips, and used in the mark-recapture estimator.

Mark-recapture estimates. Valid Petersen estimates of Hudson River Atlantic tomcod population size were required to determine the best CPUE index. Although Petersen population estimates were calculated for 1975–1976 through 1979–1980 (McLaren et al. 1988a), we did not consider these estimates valid because marked fish were probably not randomly mixed with unmarked fish in the recapture samples (NAI 1989). Valid Petersen estimates that satisfied the assumptions of the estimator were available only for the 1982–1983, 1983–1984, 1985–1986, 1987–1988, and 1988–1989 spawning seasons (NAI 1989).

Chapman's modification of the Petersen mark-recapture estimator (Ricker 1975) was the single-census method used to calculate the size of the Atlantic tomcod spawning population in the Hudson River. This modified Petersen statistic satisfied the 7 basic assumptions of a single-census, closed-population, mark-recapture estimator and was considered the best estimate of the Atlantic tomcod population size (NAI 1989). A known number of fish were caught in boxtraps, fin-clipped, and released between Yonkers and Poughkeepsie during the December through February spawning period. The total catch and number of fish marked in boxtraps and recaptured by trawls between January and April were used to estimate the spawning population size.

The formula for the adjusted Petersen estimator (Ricker 1975) is:

$$N = [(M + 1)(C + 1)] / (R + 1)$$

where

N = estimated population size,
M = number of marked fish, adjusted for handling mortality,
C = number of fish examined for marks, and
R = number of marked fish recaptured.

Confidence intervals around the estimates were calculated by considering the number of recaptures as a Poisson variable (Ricker 1975).

CPUE indices of abundance. We defined the best CPUE index as the statistic that exhibited the smallest deviation from Petersen mark-recapture estimates of the Atlantic tomcod population size. The best index of abundance should be both accurate and precise enough to resolve (meaningful) differences among annual population estimates. At high population levels, order of magnitude resolution of abundance differences may be acceptable. However, for relatively low population levels, more precise resolution of abundance than order of magnitude changes may be required. For management or monitoring studies, a coefficient of variation (CV) of 25–50% may be most appropriate (Robson and Regier 1964).

Boxtrap and trawl CPUE indices of abundance were evaluated to determine if they provided reasonably accurate and precise measures of annual changes in Atlantic tomcod population size. In each of the five winters, CPUE indices were calculated for the box trap C/H during the Petersen estimate release period and for the mean 9 m trawl CPUE10 during the recapture period. Within these periods, three combinations of space and time were used to select CPUE indices based on peak abundance: (1) the week of peak abundance, (2) river mile of peak abundance, and (3) week and river mile of peak abundance (note: river mile designations were used by field crews to identify sampling sites and were not converted to km). In addition, the geometric mean for each of the 9 m trawl CPUE indices was calculated to transform the data and minimize the effects of extreme high or low catch samples on the variance of each statistic. Geometric mean boxtrap C/H was not calculated. All data analysis was performed using the SAS statistical software package (SAS 1985).

RESULTS AND DISCUSSION

CPUE Patterns

Atlantic tomcod weekly C/H in boxtrap sets from piers and bulkheads in the Hudson River between Yonkers and Poughkeepsie peaked during mid-December through January in each of the five winters (Figure 15.1). The Tappan Zee (km 40–47) and West Point (km 82–84) boxtraps typically contributed most to the peak, except in 1987–1988 and 1988–1989 when relatively few fish were caught in Tappan Zee (Table 15.1). Atlantic tomcod CPUE in the 9 m trawl exhibited several peaks in weekly mean CPUE10 in the Battery region of the Hudson River in each of the five sampling seasons (Figure 15.1). In 1985–1986, 1987–1988, and 1988–1989, when trawling was conducted in November, a CPUE10 peak was observed in that month (Figure 15.1). In all five winters, at least 2 peaks in CPUE10 were observed from later January through March (Figure 15.1).

The timing of peaks in boxtraps and trawls is consistent with the Atlantic tomcod spawning migration described previously (Klauda et al. 1988b; McLaren et al. 1988a), and interannual variation may be related to water temperature influences on gonadal maturation. The first (late November) peak in trawl CPUE10 represents the movement of prespawning fish into and through the Battery. The boxtrap peak C/H in early January represents the movement of spawning Atlantic tomcod into and through near shore and shoal areas of the middle estuary (Figure 15.2). Multiple peaks in trawl CPUE10 during January

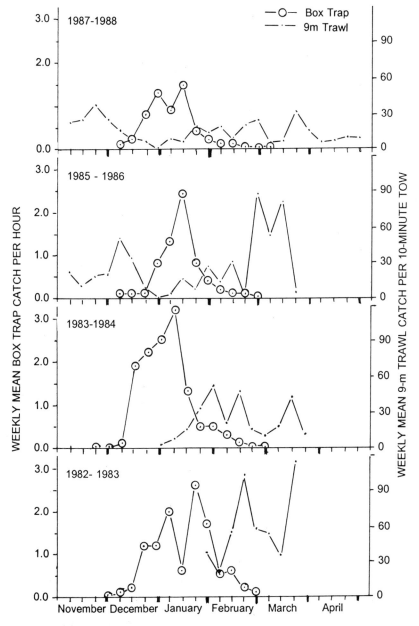

FIGURE 15.1.
Weekly mean catches of Hudson River Atlantic tomcod in box traps and 9-m trawl tows.

TABLE 15.1.
Seasons and Weeks of peak boxtrap catch per hour (C/H)
of Atlantic tomcod.

				Box trap C/H in Region		
Year	Parameter[a]	Sampling Period		All[b]	Tappan Zee[c]	West Point[d]
1982–1983	Season	29 Nov–26 Feb		1.0	1.3	1.6
	Peak	17 Jan–23 Jan		2.6	4.0	4.3
1983–1984	Season	28 Nov–06 Mar		0.9	0.7	2.1
	Peak	02 Jan–08 Jan		3.2	4.8	5.8
	Peak	09 Jan–15 Jan		2.5	0.5	6.2
1984–1985	NS					
1985–1986	Season	02 Dec–31 Jan		0.6	0.8	1.1
	Peak	06 Jan–12 Jan		2.4	4.5	4.2
1986–1987	NS					
1987–1988	Season	30 Nov–26 Feb		0.4	0.2	0.9
	Peak	04 Jan–10 Jan		1.5	0.8	3.3
1988–1989	Season	28 Nov–26 Feb		1.7	0.5	4.1
	Peak	19 Dec–25 Dec		5.2	1.1	14.7
	Peak	26 Dec–01 Jan		4.6	1.6	11.1

[a] Season = entire boxtrap sampling period.
 Peak = week of peak boxtrap C/H in region. In all years except 1983–1984 and 1988/1989, peak C/H occurred in the same week in all regions.
 NS = not sampled.
[b] All = Yonkers (km 29) through Poughkeepsie (km 122).
[c] Tappan Zee (km 40–47).
[d] West Point (km 82–84).

through March represent the movement of fish back into and through the Battery after spawning.

Population Size

The best Petersen mark-recapture estimates of Atlantic tomcod spawning population size were based on spawning fish caught, fin-clipped, and released from boxtraps set between Yonkers and Poughkeepsie and recaptured by trawling in the Battery during the postspawning down river migration (NAI 1989). These estimates—available for 1982–1983, 1983–1984, 1985–1986, 1987–1988 and 1988–

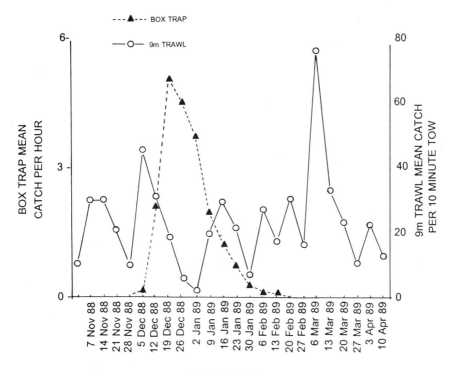

FIGURE 15.2.
Weekly changes in Atlantic tomcod catch per unit of effort for box trap and 9 m trawl samples in the lower Hudson River, winter 1988–1989.

1989—were 12.5, 6.7, 2.1, 3.5, and 5.9 million fish in each year, respectively (Table 15.2). The winter survey was not conducted in 1984–1985 and 1986–1987.

CPUE Indices of Abundance

Boxtrap and trawl CPUE were examined as indices of Atlantic tomcod abundance in the lower Hudson River. Box trap C/H is a measure of M (the number of fish marked and released) in the Petersen mark-recapture estimator. Trawl CPUE10 is a measure of C (catch) in the Petersen mark-recapture estimator. If M or C varies in constant pro-

TABLE 15.2.
Peterson mark-recapture statistics for the Atlantic tomcod population size in the Hudson River.

Box Trap Marking Period	Trawl Recapture Period	M	C	R	Petersen Statistics[a] Population Estimate (Millions with 95% Confidence Limits)		
					Lower	Estimate	Upper
29 Nov 82–26 Feb 83	02 Jan 83–18 Mar 83	17,522	14,053	18	8.1	12.5	20.3
28 Nov 83–06 Mar 84	02 Jan 84–25 Mar 84	25,004	6,655	24	4.6	6.7	10.2
02 Dec 85–31 Jan 86	30 Dec 85–21 Mar 86	13,953	21,755	144	1.8	2.1	2.5
14 Dec 87–29 Jan 88	04 Jan 88–22 Apr 88	12,458	10,473	36	2.6	3.5	5.0
12 Dec 88–29 Jan 89	09 Jan 89–15 Apr 89	43,589	16,776	123	5.0	5.9	7.0

[a] M = Number of fish marked and released in boxtraps, adjusted for handling mortality of 10% prior to January 1 and 2.5% on and after January 1.
C = Number of fish caught and examined for fin-clips from trawls.
R = number of Atlantic tomcod fin-clip recaptures released from boxtraps and recaptured by trawls.

portion with total population size, then CPUE can be used as a reliable index of population abundance. M or C should also be directly proportional to population abundance when fishing effort is randomly distributed over a closed population or when the population is randomly distributed with respect to a geographically fixed sampling effort. A closed population can be defined for a Petersen estimate of abundance as a period of relatively constant values of R/M and R/C (Cormack 1968; NAI 1989; Young et al. 1988). If these statistics are relatively constant for the same time period among several years, then mean CPUE from this time period should be a reliable index of absolute abundance.

Selecting a period of stable R/M or R/C for one year does not assure stability of these statistics for all years. However, the boxtrap release period (December–January) and the trawl recapture period (January–March) have consistently been the periods of stable, within-year R/M and R/C statistics for the Atlantic tomcod spawning population Petersen estimate of abundance during the winters of 1982–1983, 1983–1984, 1985–1986, 1987–1988, and 1988–1989 (NAI 1989). Boxtrap C/H and mean 9 m trawl CPUE10 for the 5 winters during these time periods were selected as the best indices of Atlantic tomcod abundance for comparison with Petersen population estimates.

These CPUE indices did not accurately track changes in the 5 population estimates calculated by the Petersen estimator (Table 15.3). Boxtrap C/H, mean 9 m trawl CPUE10, geometric mean 9 m trawl CPUE10, and the Petersen estimate were highest in the winter of 1982–1983, and decreased for the winter of 1983–1984. The Petersen population estimate was lower in 1985–1986 than in 1987–1988. However, mean CPUE10 and geometric mean CPUE10 for the 9 m trawl were approximately two times higher in 1985–1986 than in 1987–1988. Boxtrap C/H did not change between 1985–1986 and 1987–1988. Between 1987–1988 and 1988–1989, the Petersen estimate nearly doubled and both mean 9 m trawl CPUE10 and geometric mean 9 m trawl CPUE10 increased proportionally. However, boxtrap C/H increased 4 times between these periods and was the highest among the 5 winters in 1988–1989. In 1988–1989, the trawl CPUE10 indices were comparable to 1983–1984 and 1985–1986, but the population estimate was only similar to 1983–1984. Both the boxtrap C/H and 9 m trawl CPUE10 indices exhibited the least accuracy and precision when Petersen population estimates were low.

Boxtrap C/H calculated for the week, region, or the week and region of peak abundance (Table 15.4) did not improve the description of year-to-year changes in Atlantic tomcod population size as

TABLE 15.3.
Boxtrap and 9 m trawl catches as indices of Hudson River Atlantic tomcod abundance.

Year	Petersen Population Estimate in Millions	Box Trap CPUE During the Release Period		9 m Trawl CPUE during the Recapture Period				
		Hours Fished	C/H	Number of Tows	Mean CPUE10	SE	Geometric Mean CPUE10	SE
1982–1983	12.5	34,635	1.0	157	64.4	4.9	35.6	0.1
1983–1984	6.7	37,812	0.9	242	24.2	2.0	12.6	0.1
1985–1986	2.1	29,252	0.7	619	30.4	1.6	12.5	0.1
1987–1988	3.5	33,794	0.7	624	13.1	0.7	7.3	0.1
1988–1989	5.9	19,226	2.8	730	23.0	1.1	12.5	0.1

TABLE 15.4.
Indices of Hudson River Atlantic tomcod abundance by week, river mile, and week and river mile of peak catch.

CPUE Index	Box Trap C/H or Mean 9 m Trawl CPUE10 in Year					
	1982–1983	1983–1984	1985–1986	1987–1988	1988–1989	
Petersen estimate in millions	12.5	6.7	2.1	3.5	5.9	
Box Trap Release Period						
Week[a]	2.6	3.2	2.4	1.5	5.2	
River mile[a]	1.6	2.1	1.1	0.9	6.7	
Week and river mile[a]	4.5	6.2	4.5	3.3	14.7	
9 m Trawl Recapture Period						
Week[a]	115.3	52.6	88.1	31.8	78.0	
River mile[a]	68.6	24.0	34.0	21.1	36.4	
Week and river mile[a]	116.8	49.1	80.6	37.1	50.2	

[a] For periods and locations of the maximum observed mean catch per unit of effort.

estimated by C/H for the entire release period (Table 15.3). Boxtrap C/H was highest in 1988–1989, however the Petersen estimate of absolute population size was highest in 1982–1983 (Table 15.4). Mean 9 m trawl CPUE10 for the week, river mile, and for the week and river mile of peak abundance (Table 15.4) also did not improve the description of year-to-year changes in abundance provided by mean CPUE10 or geometric mean CPUE10 for the recapture period (Table 15.3). Mean 9 m trawl CPUE10 indices were highest in 1982–1983 in agreement with the Petersen estimate. However, in 1985–1986 mean 9 m trawl CPUE10 indices were higher than the same CPUE10 indices calculated for 1983–1984, 1987–1988, and 1988–1989 (except for river mile of peak abundance in 1988–1989). However, the Petersen population estimate showed the opposite trend and was lower in 1985–1986 than in 1983–1984, 1987–1988, or 1988–1989 (Table 15.4).

The CPUE indices of Atlantic tomcod population size were not greatly affected by the incidence of zero catch samples. Weeks and regions in which no Atlantic tomcod were caught constituted only 5.0%, 12.7%, 24.0%, 18.6%, and 21.3% of the total hours fished by boxtraps in 1982–1983, 1983–1984, 1985–1986, 1987–1988, and 1988–1989, respectively. Trawl samples where no Atlantic tomcod were caught were only 5.1% ($8/157$), 3.7% ($9/242$), 8.7% ($21/889$), 9.5% ($78/895$), and 4.1% ($48/1183$) of the total number of valid 9 m trawl tows in 1982–1983, 1983–1984, 1985–1986, 1987–1988, and 1988–1989, respectively. Furthermore, calculation of geometric mean CPUE10 for the 9 m trawl, which would reduce the effects of extremely high or low values, did not greatly improve the accuracy of the index.

A CPUE abundance index that was highest in 1982–1983, decreased in 1983–1984, was lowest in 1985–1986, next to lowest in 1987–1988 and similar to 1983–1984 in 1988–1989 would most accurately reflect changes in the Petersen population estimate. All CPUE indices examined for both boxtraps and trawls failed to track either the direction or pattern of percent change from year-to-year exhibited by the absolute population estimates (Table 15.5). Boxtrap C/H indices typically increased in 1983–1984, remained high in 1985–1986 while the Petersen estimates decreased, and peaked in 1988–1989 when the Petersen estimate was similar to 1983–1984. Box trap C/H increased by 23–38% from 1982–1983 to 1983–1984 (except C/H for the entire release period, which decreased by 10%), while the Petersen estimate of absolute population size decreased by 46%. Boxtrap C/H increased 247–644% between 1987–1988 and 1988–1989, while the Petersen estimate increased by 69%. Trawl CPUE10 indices tracked changes in the Petersen estimates from 1982–1983 to 1983–1984 and from 1987–1988 to 1988–1989, but increased while the Pe-

TABLE 15.5.
Percent change in CPUE index as a measure of accuracy of CPUE indices.

	Percent Change[a]			
CPUE Index	1982–1983 to 1983–1984	1983–1984 to 1985–1986	1985–1986 to 1987–1988	1987–1988 to 1988–1989
Petersen Estimate	−46%	−69%	+67%	+69%
Box Trap C/H for				
Release period	−10%	−22%	0%	+300%
Peak week	+23%	−25%	−38%	+247%
Peak river mile	+31%	−48%	−18%	+644%
Peak week and river mile	+38%	−27%	−27%	+345%
9 m Trawl CPUE10 for				
Recapture period	−62%	+26%	−57%	+76%
Peak week	−54%	+67%	−64%	+145%
Peak river mile	−65%	+42%	−38%	+73%
Peak week and river mile	−58%	+64%	−54%	+35%

[a] Percent change = [CPUE index for second year − CPUE index for first year]/CPUE index for first year × 100.

tersen estimate decreased between 1983–1984 and 1985–1986 (Table 15.5). Thus CPUE indices were only capable of distinguishing differences in population abundance that were at least an order of magnitude for the range of population size and CPUE observed, particularly at low population levels. According to the standards for other population studies (Robson and Regier 1964), these CPUE indices may not provide the precision and accuracy needed for management decisions based on the changes in Hudson River Atlantic tomcod population abundance.

It may be possible to develop a better CPUE index of Atlantic tomcod population size if gear deployment was directed toward maximizing the catch of Atlantic tomcod, and if the sampling effort was randomized. However, the sampling effort for the 9 m trawl was allocated to maximize the catch of striped bass greater than 150–200 mm total length (Dunning et al. this volume); Atlantic tomcod were a by-catch of this trawl effort in 1985–1986, 1987–1988, and 1988–1989. A better CPUE index of Atlantic tomcod population size may be developed based on a "standard station" concept, where CPUE is calculated from a standard trawl station or stations for a standard time period, assuming that the Atlantic tomcod population distributions was randomized with respect to this location and that the probability of capture remained constant from year to year.

Acknowledgments

Funding for this project was provided by Central Hudson Gas and Electric Corporation, Consolidated Edison Company of New York, Inc., New York Power Authority, Niagara Mohawk Power Corporation, and Orange and Rockland Utilities under terms of the Hudson River Cooling Tower Settlement Agreement. This project was developed in cooperation with the New York State Department of Environmental Conservation. Field work was conducted by Normandeau Associates, Inc., under the direction of Mr. Michael J. Ricci, Field Supervisor. Special thanks to the field, laboratory, and data processing staff at Normandeau Associates, Inc., for their contributions to this ongoing study. The authors also respectfully acknowledge the insight and constructive comments of two anonymous reviewers.

DENNIS J. DUNNING
QUENTIN E. ROSS
WILLIAM L. KIRK
JOHN R. WALDMAN
DOUGLAS G. HEIMBUCH
MARK T. MATTSON

16

Postjuvenile Striped Bass Studies after the Settlement Agreement

ABSTRACT

Prior to the Hudson River Cooling Tower Settlement Agreement in December 1980, studies of juvenile striped bass conducted by the electric utility industry focused on the movements of subadult and adult striped bass, estimates of age structure and size of spawning run, and population parameters that include fishing mortality rates, maturity, growth rates, fecundity, and egg diameter. The emphasis of subsequent programs has been to recapture hatchery striped bass age 1+ and 2+ and to determine their contribution to the river's stock. Hatchery fish were marked with coded magnetic wire tags and can also be recognized on the basis of growth patterns on their scales. Naturally reproduced striped bass, captured during the hatchery evaluation were tagged and released as part of a stock assessment. Refined capture and tagging techniques minimize handling mortality and maximize recapture data. The direction of postjuvenile striped studies after the Settlement Agreement expires in 1991 will depend on whether stocking of hatchery striped bass will be continued.

INTRODUCTION

The Hudson River Cooling Tower Settlement Agreement (Sandler and Schoenbrod, 1981) represented a compromise among electric utilities, government agencies, and environmental groups concerning the utilities' responsibility to protect the fisheries of the Hudson Estuary versus the cost of such measures for 10 years (beginning on May 14, 1981). The Settlement Agreement required that the utilities conduct a biological monitoring program at a cost of $2 million annually, escalated for inflation, in addition to adopting measures to reduce and offset fish entrainment and impingement mortality. The monitoring program was to include an evaluation of mitigation adopted by the utilities and an assessment of adult fish stocks.

Among the mitigation provided was the installation of variable speed pumps at Indian Point Units 2 and 3 to help minimize the cooling water flows required for efficient operation during the spring and fall, outages at Bowline Point, Indian Point Units 2 and 3, and Roseton between May 10 and August 10, a barrier net in front of the cooling water intakes at Bowline, a modification to the intakes at Indian Point Units 2 and 3, and the construction and operation of a striped bass *Morone saxatilis* hatchery. Prior to the Settlement Agreement, it was demonstrated that Hudson River striped bass could be artificially propagated from local brood stock using a combination of intensive and extensive culture methods, and that stocked juveniles appeared to survive as well as wild juveniles (McLaren et al. 1988b). Based in part on this information, the utilities agreed to construct and operate a hatchery to produce 600,000 young-of-the-year striped bass, averaging 76 mm long, for stocking the Hudson River each year from 1983 through 1990. The 600,000 production goal exceeds the number of striped bass annually impinged at Bowline, Indian Point Units 2 and 3, and Roseton—that is, generally less than 100,000.

The major postjuvenile striped bass studies funded by the electric utilities prior to the Settlement Agreement were conducted from 1976 through 1979. Basic life history information was collected, including age composition, maturity, fecundity, length, weight, and population size (Young and Hoff 1981; Hoff et al., 1988b; Dew 1988), as well as movements (McLaren et al. 1981), and the relative contribution of the Hudson River stock to the Atlantic coast fishery (Berggren and Lieberman 1978; Grove et al. 1976). The primary purpose for collecting this information was to estimate the impact of power plant operation on striped bass in the Hudson River using population models (Savidge et al. 1988), although it was also used to evaluate the feasibility of supplementary stocking of juvenile striped bass into the Hudson River (McLaren et al. 1988b).

Subsequent to the Settlement Agreement, studies of postjuvenile striped bass were designed primarily to evaluate the stocking of hatchery striped bass into the Hudson River. The collection of data for the postjuvenile stock assessment was designed to complement the evaluation of stocking.

This paper: (1) describes the primary objectives of monitoring studies designed to evaluate stocking of striped bass into the Hudson River and to collect data useful for an assessment of the Hudson River striped bass stock, (2) summarizes the results of those studies, and (3) provides recommendations for postjuvenile striped bass studies after the Settlement Agreement expires.

EVALUATION OF STOCKING

Marking

To permit identification of hatchery fish upon recapture, a coded magnetic wire tag is inserted in the cheek of each fish before it is released into the Hudson River. Accurate estimates of the hatchery proportion require information on the rate of tag loss and tagging mortality and on the detection efficiency of the method used for determining the presence of hatchery tags. The loss rate 8–10 weeks after tagging, for tags placed vertically in the cheek muscle of hatchery fish, ranged from 86% to 94% and occurred primarily during the first 2 weeks after tagging (Dunning et al. in press). The mortality rate during this period ranged from <1% to 3%.

Routine examination of striped bass on the Hudson River is conducted with a V-shaped field detector, which is compact and portable. A larger, nonportable, tube-shaped detector has been used to determine efficiency of the field detectors. During the comparison of detectors, fish captured in the Hudson River were passed through both devices. The efficiency of the tube detector was considered to be 100% based on tests conducted by the manufacturer, Northwest Marine Technologies. Based on the paired comparisons, the efficiency of the field detector was estimated to be 99% (Mattson et al. in press).

Subsequent to the decision to use magnetic tags, another approach for distinguishing hatchery and wild fish was examined using growth patterns on the scales of striped bass. Most scales from hatchery fish had thick, widely spaced circuli near the focus corresponding to rapid growth, followed by an abrupt growth check, possibly resulting from handling, tagging, and adaptation to natural food sources after release into the Hudson River. About 90% of the young-of-the-year and 95% of the yearling fish could be correctly identified as hatchery or wild based solely on differences in scale patterns (Humphreys et al. in press). Because the Atlantic States Marine Fisheries Commission (ASMFC) recommends that all striped bass stocked into coastal waters be marked if one million or less are stocked (ASMFC 1989), the use of scales will not replace the use of coded wire tags.

Sampling Program

Valid estimates of the proportion of hatchery fish in the population require that hatchery and wild fish be randomly mixed at the time of sampling or that sampling be random among all habitats occupied by hatchery and wild striped bass. At the time the sampling program was designed, there was evidence to suggest that these assumptions might not be met for juvenile fish. A subsequent study of the distribution of hatchery and wild striped bass from 1985 through 1987 appears to confirm the fact that hatchery and wild fish are not randomly distributed as juveniles (Wells et al. submitted for publication). It also appears that the routine annual sampling of juvenile striped bass for the electric utilities and for the New York State Department of Environmental Conservation (NYSDEC) is not strictly random because some habitats are excluded (Metzger et al. this volume).

Although it has not been tested, the assumption of random mixing of hatchery and wild striped bass appears more reasonable for postjuveniles because they will be moving within the estuary for at least a year longer than juveniles. Therefore, sampling was focused on these older fish. Sampling for postjuvenile striped bass generally occurs between November and May in the lower Hudson River Estuary.

The expected cost of tagging hatchery fish and recapturing striped bass in the Hudson River was high, $0.50 and $42 per fish respectively (Dunning and Ross 1986). Thus, development of a cost effective mark-recapture program required calculating the number of fish that would have to be tagged and the number of striped bass that would have to be examined for recaptures. Assuming that all hatchery fish are tagged and that the proportion of hatchery fish to wild striped bass in the Hudson River was 1%, then 6,100 striped bass would have to be examined at each age to be 95% certain that the estimate of the proportion is within ±25% of the true proportion (Heimbuch et al. in press). Because striped bass in the Hudson River decrease in abundance with age, both the cost and difficulty of recapturing sufficient numbers of hatchery striped bass increase with age at which the proportion is to be estimated. The ages of striped bass where the required sample size is most likely to be met are 1+ and 2+. Striped bass of these ages can be efficiently sampled during the winter and spring in the lower Hudson River.

Preliminary estimates of the proportion of hatchery fish in a cohort, which is a function of the number of fish stocked and the abundance of wild fish in a given year, has varied across years from 1984 through 1986. The observed range in the proportion has been from about 0.1% in the 1984 cohort to 3% in the 1985 cohort (Normandeau Associates, Inc. 1988).

STUDIES IN SUPPORT OF A STRIPED BASS STOCK ASSESSMENT

Tagging

The number of postjuvenile fish that must be captured for the hatchery evaluation appeared to be large enough to permit reliable mark-recapture estimates of the annual survival rate from age 1+ to 2+ and the abundance of age 2+ striped bass in the Hudson River to be calculated (MMES 1986). Therefore, at the same time that striped bass caught in the field were examined for hatchery tags, they were tagged externally and released.

Considerable attention was given to the choice of tag type. From 1976 through 1979 an anchor tag had been inserted below the second dorsal fin to mark striped bass in the Hudson River. However, based on the number of fish over 40 cm long that were tagged and the actual recovery rates, Ricker (1979) determined that the return rate of this tag type was lower than expected, a fact he attributed to tag shedding and mortality during the tagging process. To address these possibilities, tag retention and tagging mortality associated with 3 tag types were studied as part of the monitoring program prior to the initiation of the hatchery evaluation program. The tags used were an anchor tag, an internal anchor-external streamer tag (inserted in the abdomen), and a dart tag (inserted below the second dorsal fin). The tags were evaluated by holding tagged and untagged striped bass in cages in the Hudson River for up to 24 h and by holding striped bass in outdoor pools for up to 180 d. In addition, fish released into the Hudson River and recaptured up to 2 years later were examined. Based on the superior retention rate of internal anchor tags, the low mortality of tagged fish relative to untagged controls (Dunning et al. 1987) and a review of the tagging literature, the internal anchor tag was selected for the Hudson River studies beginning in 1985. Subsequent recaptures of striped bass tagged with internal anchor tags indicated that the legend on 35% of the tags was physically abraded and the anchor on 11% of the tags was protruding through the abdominal wall near the tag insertion site (Mattson et al. in press). To correct these problems, both the tag design and material used in manufacturing the tags were changed in 1987. The effectiveness of these changes will be evaluated in the remaining years of the monitoring program.

Handling Techniques

Reportedly, striped bass become stressed easily and lengthy handling periods can result in high mortality (Wydoski and Emery 1983). Moreover, mortality appears to be directly related to higher water temperatures (Dunning et al. 1987). Killing large numbers of striped bass by capture and handling for a stocking evaluation and mark-recapture studies of postjuveniles could negatively impact a stock that has represented a significant part of the coastal population of striped bass in recent years (Fabrizio 1987) and produce large biases in mark-recapture estimates of abundance and mortality (Arnason and Mills 1987). Therefore, a study was conducted to develop capture and handling techniques that prevent or minimize injury to fish. Immediate mortality of striped bass captured in 9 m and 12 m trawls could be kept to an average of 2% and 1% respectively at river temperatures $\leq 14°C$ (Dunning et al. 1989) by not removing the cod end of the gear from the water until all fish were removed. With this procedure, there was no increase in delayed mortality with increasing river temperature up to 14°C.

Aging

Correct assignment of age to striped bass that are marked and recaptured is critical for accurate abundance and survival estimates. The results from the mark-recapture study and the hatchery evaluations have permitted validation of the criteria used to designate annuli and to differentiate true annuli from false annuli (Park et al. in preparation). Using the best criteria for identifying true annuli, the age of 1+ through 5+ Hudson River striped bass could be determined with 93% accuracy.

Migration

Quantitative, stock specific information on coastal movements of striped bass is needed to develop a comprehensive model of the Atlantic migratory striped bass stock and to better manage the fishery (Goodyear 1978). The migration of striped bass tagged and released in the Hudson River from 1984 through 1988 was analyzed using tags returned by fishermen. Each tag had a reward value, a tag number, and a return address. Tag returns were coordinated by the Hudson River Foundation for the utilities.

In contrast to the results obtained from tagging striped bass in the Hudson River during 1976 and 1977 (McLaren et al. 1981), the proportion of total recaptures from outside the river increased significantly with length and by season from spring through autumn (Waldman et al. in press). The geographic range of recoveries extended from the Bay of Fundy, Nova Scotia, to Cape Hattaras, North Carolina. Comparisons with previous studies suggest that the coastal range of Hudson River striped bass has expanded since mid-century. This result cannot be explained by a higher tag shedding rate for larger fish in earlier studies (Waldman et al. in press).

Abundance and Survival

The results from the mark-recapture studies of striped bass in the Hudson River are being used to estimate survival and abundance of age 1+ and 2+ fish and validate early life stage indices (Heimbuch et al. this volume). A new index, based on post–yolk-sac larval (PYSL) abundance, may be better for estimating relative year class strength because it avoids some of the shortcomings of the historically computed juvenile indices (e.g., limited geographical sampling of the river, sampling a fixed and very small portion of the river, and a change in sampling gear [Heimbuch et al. this volume]). The mark-recapture estimates of abundance for the 1984 and 1985 year classes are consistent with the corresponding PYSL index values. Because two data points are insufficient to convincingly demonstrate a relationship, further work is underway to confirm that PYSL abundance reliably reflects year class strength.

Quality Assurance and Quality Control

From 1984 through January 1989, over 53,000 striped bass have been tagged and released into the Hudson River as part of the monitoring program. To provide a mark-recapture data base of known quality, to provide program managers feedback on how to reduce data recording errors and to provide documentation for future investigators, formal Quality Assurance (QA) and Quality Control (QC) procedures have been expanded and implemented (Geoghegan et al. in press). These include a training program for technicians, improved data acquisition procedures, audits to verify adherence to written field procedures, double keypunching data, and computer error checking. The procedures were designed to cost effectively ensure that no more than 1 data point in 100 will contain an error.

FUTURE STUDIES

Complex and politically sensitive decisions regarding alternative actions to mitigate power plant impacts on the Hudson River striped bass population must be made when the Settlement Agreement expires on May 13, 1991. These decisions must consider: (1) multiple, conflicting objectives (e.g., conserving fish stocks, meeting demands of electric power consumers, and maintaining high quality commercial and recreational fisheries), (2) a dynamic and complex natural system, an understanding of which is needed to project the consequences of alternative actions, and (3) interacting management actions (e.g., regulation of commercial and sport fisheries, mitigation of power plant effects and collection of fisheries data). Methods exist for systematically considering these factors and arriving at reasonable and justifiable decisions (Keeney and Raiffa 1976). These methods begin by partitioning the overall decision process into tractable units, with the scientific considerations initially treated independently of the economic considerations of benefits, costs, and value trade-offs (Walters 1986). Subsequent to the detailed analysis of the component parts, all the relevant information is synthesized to produce a ranking of alternatives that reflects the best scientific judgment of the involved experts and the values and preferences of the public being served. Alternative actions may include combinations of monitoring, regulation of power plant operation, stocking of fish into the Hudson River, and regulation of fishing effort.

Uncertainty will accompany almost every facet of the decision process, from assessing the current status of the stocks and estimating the effectiveness of current mitigation required by the Settlement Agreement to determining the economic costs of alternative actions. Therefore continued monitoring of postjuvenile striped bass is likely to be very important. Development of a decision analysis model during the remaining years of the Settlement Agreement may help identify additional data requirements, assist in the selection of regulatory actions, improve our understanding of the dynamics of the striped bass population of the Hudson River, and reduce the risk of making decisions.

One of the key pieces of information that will be needed to evaluate the effect of power plant operation on the Hudson River striped bass population and to manage that fishery will be a valid index of year class strength. Additional years of abundance and survival data for age 1+ and 2+ striped bass are needed to validate the recently developed post–yolk-sac index and other juvenile indices. At present, estimates from only two years of relative abundance (1984 and 1985) are available.

Two key assumptions are required for valid mark-recapture estimates of abundance and survival of striped bass in the Hudson River: (1) unmarked age 2+ striped base that are captured originate from the Hudson River and (2) the ratio of tagged to unmarked age 2+ striped bass in the river at the time of sampling is the same as it is in all other areas inhabited by striped bass. Methods for testing these assumptions are being examined by the utilities and the DEC (B. Young, personal communication).

SUSAN G. METZGER
ROGER G. KEPPEL
PAUL GEOGHEGAN
ALAN W. WELLS

17

Abundance of Selected Hudson River Fish Species in Previously Unsampled Regions: Effect on Standing Crop Estimates

ABSTRACT

Since the early 1970s, year-class strength and standing crops of selected species of larval and juvenile fish have been monitored by the Hudson River Utilities to evaluate the impact of power plant operation on fish populations. Historically, upriver shoal areas, which account for 34.4% of the total shoal stratum ($\leq$20 ft depth) and about 5% of the river volume, have not been sampled. Relative abundance in these shoals is assumed to be equal to that in the bottom stratum.

In 1986 and 1987 ichthyoplankton and fish were collected from previously unsampled shoals. Data from proximal geographic regions, sampled with equivalent gear, were analyzed for statistical differences in abundance from previously unsampled shoals and previously sampled bottom strata.

Abundance of white perch juveniles in both years was greater in previously unsampled shoals than in adjacent bottom strata. When adequately sampled, striped bass and bay anchovy juveniles were also more abundant in shoal strata.

Similar analyses applied to larval data showed statistical differences in abundances for some species, although most of the differences were specific to sampling regions and time periods. These results indicate that historic standing crop estimates for some target species may be low. Observed differences can be related to life history and river characteristics.

INTRODUCTION

Since 1973 the abundance and distribution of Hudson River fish and ichthyoplankton have been studied for the Hudson River Utilities. The data in these reports are used to estimate the year-class strength and standing crop of selected species. In 1980 a Settlement Agreement resulted from a long legal battle over the need for cooling towers at three generating stations. The agreement limited water use for power generation on the Hudson River and acted to protect Hudson River fish communities. The agreement stipulated outages and reduced flows for selected plants. An assessment program was developed to determine whether the outages and reduced flows actually produced the intended beneficial effects to fish populations (Sandler and Schoenbrod, 1981). Several of the approaches used to evaluate the efficacy of outages require accurate estimates of relative abundance and standing crop for selected species by life stage (Martin Marietta 1986).

A key assumption underlying the estimates of abundance and standing crop is that target organisms are representatively sampled. Doubt has been cast on this assumption because, historically, not all essential habitats have been sampled. Obstructions, dense aquatic plant growth, or limitations in gear have restricted sampling in some locations and prevented a few areas from being sampled at all. For the purpose of estimating fish and ichthyoplankton abundance in year class reports, the density in unsampled areas has been assumed to be equivalent to that of adjacent areas. Initially, this assumption was acceptable for several reasons. The life history patterns of most key species suggest that abundance is greater in shallow waters and shoals than in bottom areas; thus, estimates based on bottom samples are likely to be conservative—that is, underestimate the actual abundance. In any event, given that no major habitat changes occur in either stratum, the populations of unsampled regions are likely to be consistent through time, thus permitting valid comparisons of stock abundance among years. Since the Settlement Agreement there has been speculation that these historically unsampled areas may provide excellent habitat and harbor greater numbers of fish than historically sampled areas.

Routine, annual sampling for fish and ichthyoplankton takes place from river mile (RM) 12 to RM 152 (Figure Frontispiece). This portion of the Hudson River is divided into 12 longitudinal regions; each is then further divided into 4 strata: beaches and shores (water depth less than 10 ft), shoals (water depth 10–20 ft), bottom (the lower 10 ft of the water column in areas with a depth of 20 ft or more), and channel (all other areas) (Figure 17.1). Samples are collected from all areas where it is practical to deploy standard gear. Routine programs for both fish and larvae are summarized by Wells et al. in this volume.

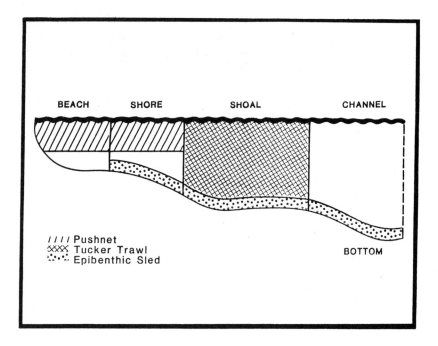

FIGURE 17.1.
Schematic of river strata and sampling gear used in the special ichthyoplankton study to evaluate abundance in previously unsampled regions.

Klauda et al. (1988a) identified the strengths and weaknesses associated with the data generated by each program. The unsampled areas fall into two general categories:

Unsampled upriver shoals include areas in the West Point, Poughkeepsie, Hyde Park, Kingston, Saugerties, Catskill, and Albany regions that are not sampled for either juvenile fish or ichthyoplankton. Taken together, these unsampled shoals account for 34.4% of the total shoal volume and about 5% of the entire river volume (Table 17.1). For each of the unsampled shoal areas the density of juveniles, eggs, and larvae is assumed to be equal to that of the bottom stratum.

Unsampled shore zones include the shoreline along most of the Hudson River estuary that is not accessible with the 100-ft beach seine for the collection of juveniles or with standard ichthyoplankton gear. Only limited areas of the shoreline have the proper bottom contour, freedom from submerged obstructions, and open beach area to retrieve a seine. The density of juveniles in these unsampled areas is assumed to be equal to that on adjacent sampled beaches.

Historically, shore zones have not been sampled for ichthyoplankton because of the difficulty in operating large boats and deploying the standard gear (1.0-m^2 epibenthic sleds and Tucker trawls) in shallow water. The density of ichthyoplankton in the shore zone is assumed to be equal to that of the shoal in the corresponding region. Thus, for ichthyoplankton, the bottom densities for unsampled upriver shoals regions have been used to calculate standing crops in both shore and shoal strata.

In 1986 Normandeau Associates, Inc. (NAI), evaluated the possibility of sampling previously unsampled areas with modified sampling gear and identified areas so choked with aquatic vegetation in the summer or other obstructions as to make sampling impossible with any gear. Although a considerable portion of the shore areas above mile point (MP) 50 cannot be sampled because of the vegetation, sampleable shoals in previously unsampled regions were identified (NAI 1987). In 1986 and 1987 special studies estimated the abundance of selected fish and ichthyoplankton species in previously unsampled areas and compared the estimates with those from adjacent areas. The purpose of these studies was to evaluate the adequacy of the assumption that densities in adjacent areas reasonably represent densities in historically unsampled areas. This question is partic-

TABLE 17.1.
Stratum and region volumes (m³) and surface areas (m²) used in analysis of the 1986 and 1987 Hudson River data.

Geographic Region	Channel Volume	Bottom Volume	Shoal Volume	Region Volume	Shore Zone Surface Area
Yonkers	143,452,543	59,312,978	26,654,767	229,420,288	3,389,000
Tappan Zee	138,000,768	62,125,705	121,684,992	321,811,465	20,446,000
Croton-Haverstraw	61,309,016	32,517,633	53,910,105	147,736,754	12,101,000
Indian Point	162,269,471	33,418,632	12,648,163	208,336,266	4,147,000
West Point	178,830,022	25,977,862	2,647,885[a]	207,455,769	1,186,000
Cornwall	94,882,267	36,768,629	8,140,123[a]	139,791,019	4,793,000
Poughkeepsie	228,975,052	63,168,132	5,990,260[a]	298,133,444	3,193,000
Hyde Park	131,165,041	32,012,000	2,307,625[a]	165,484,666	558,000
Kingston	93,657,021	35,479,990	12,332,868[a]	141,469,879	3,874,000
Saugerties	113,143,296	42,845,077	20,307,338[a]	176,295,711	7,900,000
Catskill	83,924,081	42,281,206	34,526,456[a]	160,731,743	8,854,000
Albany	32,025,080	13,517,183	25,606,842[a]	71,149,105	6,114,000
Total	1,461,633,658	479,425,027	326,757,424	2,267,816,109	76,555,000

[a] Historically unsampled shoals. Volume added to bottom stratum for analytical purposes.

352

ularly important as the Settlement Agreement approaches its end and efforts are made to identify and characterize changes in stock abundance and standing crop.

METHODS AND MATERIALS

Juvenile Fish

In 1986 the juvenile fish program focused on five species: bay anchovy, Atlantic tomcod, and striped bass from the West Point region; white perch from the Kingston region; and American shad from the Catskill region (Table 17.2). In 1987 fish were collected from the Kingston and Saugerties river regions. In both years previously unsampled upriver shoal areas (10 to 20 ft) and the previously sampled bottom stratum adjacent to the unsampled shoals were sampled with 2.0 m beam trawls.

The 2.0 m beam trawl and its deployment have been previously described (LMS 1989). Tow duration was approximately 5 min at a velocity through the water of 150 cm/sec. Tow velocity was established by an electronic flowmeter mounted alongside the research vessel with on-deck readout. A calibrated digital flowmeter (General Oceanics model 2030) mounted in the center of each net mouth was used to calculate the volume of water filtered for each sample. The sample volume was estimated to be approximately 850 m^3. All sampling was done at night.

In 1986, 36 samples were collected from shoals and 40 from

TABLE 17.2.
Sample design for juvenile fish beam trawl collections.

Sample Dates	Region	Depth (ft)	Number of Samples	Target Species and Life Stage
Sep 8–11 1986	Catskill	10–20	10	American shad
		>20	10	
Sep 22–25 1986	Kingston	10–20	10	White perch
		>20	10	
Sep 9–16 1986	West Point	10–20	16	Atlantic tomcod
		>20	20	Bay anchovy
				Striped bass
1987	Kingston/	10–20	34	White perch
	Saugerties	>20	33	

bottom strata; in 1987, 34 samples were collected from shoals and 33 from the bottom strata of the Kingston/Saugerties region. All young-of-year fish were preserved in 10% formalin and returned to the laboratory for identification. All yearling and older fish were sorted by species and counted by length class. Following field analysis, all yearling and adult fish were released.

Ichthyoplankton

Ichthyoplankton special studies were conducted in three regions: Catskill, Poughkeepsie, and Tappan Zee, each selected to yield the maximum number of target species and life stages (Table 17.3). To evaluate very shallow shore regions, the shore zone was subdivided into two strata: beaches 1–5 ft deep and shores 6–9 ft deep (Figure 17.1). Samples from the Catskill and Poughkeepsie regions were used to evaluate abundance in both upriver unsampled shoals and beach areas. Samples from the Tappan Zee region were used only to evaluate the effect of unsampled shore zones. Most samples were collected in the Catskill region (Table 17.3).

Three types of sampling gear were employed in previously unsampled regions: a 1.0-m² Tucker trawl, a 1.0-m² epibenthic sled, and a 1.0-m² pushnet. All nets were equipped with 505 μm mesh. The epibenthic sled used in previously unsampled areas had a smaller frame than the gear used historically in order to deploy the rig in shallow, confined areas. The bottom water stratum (>20 ft) was sampled with the epibenthic sled; the shoal strata (10 to 20 ft) were sampled with the epibenthic sled and the previously described 1.0-m² Tucker trawl gear (LMS 1989). The beach strata (1 to 5 ft) were sampled with the 1.0-m² pushnet, the shore strata (5 to 10 ft) with both the pushnet and the epibenthic sled. All sampling was conducted at night. Sample duration for all gear was 5 min at a tow speed of 90 cm/sec for the Tucker trawl and 100 cm/sec for the epibenthic sled-mounted net. The pushnet was operated at 90 cm/sec. Tow velocity was established and maintained by an electronic flowmeter with on-deck readout.

A calibrated digital flowmeter (General Oceanics model 2030) mounted in the center of the net mouth was used to calculate the volume of water filtered for each sample. Two velocity meters were used for the pushnet: one mounted inside the net mouth and a second outside the net mouth. The difference in meter readings was used to determine net filtration efficiency.

Laboratory analysis of the 1987 ichthyoplankton special study

TABLE 17.3.
Sample design for 1987 ichthyoplankton collections.

Region	Sample Dates 1987	Gear	Depth (ft)	Number of Samples	Target Species and Life Stage
Catskill	May 18–22	Pushnet	1–5	50	American shad eggs and yolk-sac larvae
		Epibenthic sled	5–10	25	
		Pushnet	5–10	25	
		Epibenthic sled	10–20	33	
		Tucker trawl	10–20	67	
		Epibenthic sled	>20	40	
Poughkeepsie	June 8–11	Pushnet	1–5	18	Striped bass and white perch post-yolk-sac larvae
		Epibenthic sled	5–10	9	
		Pushnet	5–10	9	
		Epibenthic sled	10–20	19	
		Tucker trawl	10–20	18	
		Epibenthic sled	>20	10	
Tappan Zee	Jun 23–26	Pushnet	1–5	15	Bay anchovy post-yolk-sac larvae
		Epibenthic sled	6–9	8	
		Pushnet	6–9	9	
		Epibenthic sled	10–20	16	
		Tucker trawl	10–20	16	

samples included identification of all specimens, determination of life stages for selected species, and total length measurements. For both juveniles and ichthyoplankton catch per unit effort (CPUE) was used as an index of abundance. Analysis of variance (ANOVA) was used to investigate the sources of variation and differences in CPUE by year, gear, and life stage for previously sampled and unsampled strata. The dependent variable was ln (CPUE + 1) where CPUE is catch per 1000 m^3. For a preliminary statistical evaluation of 1986 juvenile data, a factorial ANOVA using the SAS GLM (SAS 1985) procedure with Type III sum of squares was used to compare data from different strata. This procedure is unaffected by the order in which independent variables are entered into the analysis. Results indicated significant effects associated with gear and life stage. To clearly identify significant differences between previously sampled and unsampled regions, data were divided into gear, regions, and life stages, then subjected to individual ANOVA (SAS GLM, Type I sum of squares). Where statistical differences were identified, the relationship among means was explored using Student-Newman-Keuls groupings (SAS 1985).

RESULTS

Juvenile Fish

CPUE of species by year class for previously sampled bottom strata was compared with abundance in previously unsampled shoal strata in the West Point, Kingston, and Catskill regions (Table 17.4). Statistical analysis of the catches from unsampled shoals and adjacent bottom strata indicates that white perch are more abundant in previously unsampled shoals than in adjacent bottom areas in the Kingston and West Point regions (Table 17.5, Figure 17.2). Catches of yearlings and older fish were also higher in the Catskill shoals, but the differences were not statistically significant. Bay anchovy young-of-year and yearlings were more abundant in the West Point shoals than in the bottom stratum; only the differences for yearlings were statistically significant, however. Statistically larger catches of young-of-year American shad were collected in Catskill from the bottom stratum compared to the shoal stratum. The shad may have been collected from the channel stratum (midwater areas) as the open-mouthed beam trawl moved through the water column. The numbers were low in both strata, however. CPUE of striped bass and Atlantic tomcod were not significantly different between shoals and bottom in the West Point region. During 1987, when all sampling was conducted in

TABLE 17.4.
CPUE (No./1000 m³) in previously unsampled shoals and adjacent bottom strata.

	Previously Sampled Bottom							Previously Unsampled Shoals						
	YOY		Yearling		Older		YOY		Yearling		Older	
	Mean	Std. Dev.	Mean	Std. Dev.	Mean	Std. Dev.	Mean	Std. Dev.	Mean	Std. Dev.	Mean	Std. Dev.
Catskill 1986												
American shad	1.97	2.18	0.00	0.00	0.00	0.00	0.71	1.42	0.00	0.00	0.00	0.00
White perch	1.31	3.39	3.94	5.33	7.72	7.43	0.15	0.58	13.03	29.62	16.86	21.38
Kingston 1986												
White perch	5.08	7.05	5.81	5.09	25.62	19.06	7.29	7.72	21.37	19.43	70.01	35.72
West Point 1986												
Bay anchovy	0.63	0.56	0.18	0.37	0.00	0.00	3.73	4.53	4.32	3.15	0.00	0.00
Striped bass	0.09	0.29	0.00	0.00	0.10	0.31	1.40	2.05	0.00	0.00	0.00	0.00
Atlantic tomcod	16.69	29.08	0.00	0.00	0.00	0.00	10.63	14.20	0.00	0.00	0.00	0.00
White perch	1.11	1.91	0.59	1.30	0.93	3.06	31.80	44.08	21.61	34.60	44.03	74.10
Kingston/Saugerties 1987												
Bay anchovy	2.24	3.29	0.00	0.00	0.00	0.00	2.78	4.23	0.00	0.00	0.00	0.00
Striped bass	2.25	5.41	0.00	0.00	0.00	0.00	5.03	7.16	0.00	0.30	0.05	0.30
Atlantic tomcod	0.43	0.99	0.00	0.00	0.00	0.00	0.00	0.00	0.00	0.00	0.00	0.00
White perch	5.21	5.18	7.01	7.19	26.15	33.70	14.04	17.89	41.66	41.30	68.52	76.22

TABLE 17.5.
Results of ANOVA (GLM) on the effect of previously unsampled shoals vs previously sampled bottom strata.

			Error Probability[a]		
Year	Region	Species	YOY	Yearling	Older
1986	West Point	Bay anchovy	0.06	0.0001 U > B	—
		Striped bass	0.06	—	0.33
		Atlantic tomcod	0.64	—	—
		White perch	0.002 U > B	0.05 U > B	0.06 U > B
	Kingston	White perch	0.45	0.009 U > B	0.003 U > B
	Catskill	American shad	0.05 B > U	—	—
		White perch	0.18	0.33	0.14
1987	Kingston/ Saugerties	White perch	0.005 U > B	0.01 U > B	0.18
		Striped bass	0.03 U > B	—	—
		Bay anchovy	0.62	—	—
		American shad	0.11	—	—

[a] Error probabilities of 0.05 or less indicate a statistically significant effect. Where significant effects are identified, the relationship between means from unsampled (U) vs previously sampled (B) strata as demonstrated by Student-Newman-Keuls, appears below the probability.

the Kingston/Saugerties region, statistically significant differences in CPUE between strata were identified for striped bass and white perch (Table 17.5). For both of the *Morone* species, abundance in the previously unsampled shoals was greater than that in the bottom stratum. Only white perch abundance showed a consistent pattern between 1986 and 1987 (Table 17.6). Abundance in shoals exceeded that in bottom strata for both years in all regions sampled. These differences were statistically significant for the Kingston and West Point regions.

Abundance of young-of-year striped bass in previously unsampled shoals was significantly greater than that in the bottom stratum during 1987. No statistical difference was noted in 1986 when few bass were collected. In 1986 bay anchovy young-of-year and yearlings

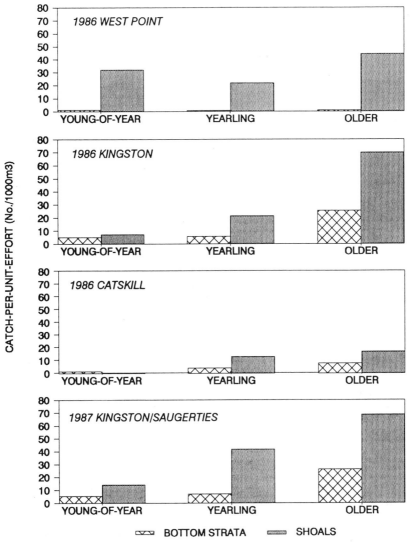

FIGURE 17.2.
Comparison of white perch in previously unsampled shoals and previously sampled bottom stratum.

TABLE 17.6.
Summary of differences in abundance between previously unsampled shoals and adjacent bottom strata.

	1986	1987
White perch	shoals > bottom	shoals > bottom
Striped bass	NSD	shoals > bottom
Bay anchovy	shoals > bottom	NSD
American shad	bottom > shoals[b]	NSD
Atlantic tomcod	NSD	insufficient data

[a] ANOVA at = 0.001 using SAS GLM, SAS 1985.
[b] For Catskill region only. Riverwide comparison shows nonsignificant difference.
NSD—Not significantly different for total fish.

were more abundant in the West Point shoal samples than in the bottom samples; the difference in yearlings was statistically significant. No differences were apparent for bay anchovy or American shad young-of-year fish.

Ichthyoplankton

American Shad

American shad ichthyoplankton in the Catskill region were distributed so that eggs were most abundant in shoals, yolk-sac larvae (YSL) were generally dispersed throughout the strata, and post–yolk-sac larvae (PYSL) were most abundant in shallow areas (Figure 17.3). Statistical analysis of catch data for American shad eggs in the shoal region indicated that the epibenthic sled and Tucker trawl collected similar numbers. Similarly, catches from epibenthic sled collections in the shore zone were no different from those collected by pushnet.

Comparison of egg catches by stratum demonstrated that abundance in the bottom stratum is significantly greater than abundance in shoals, shore, or beach strata ($P = 0.0001$). Therefore, estimates of total egg standing crop based on the assumption that bottom abundance adequately represents abundance in shoals, shore, and beach zones overestimate the real standing crop of shad eggs. This overestimate affects only the uppermost river regions, Albany, Catskill, and Saugerties, where eggs were in the greatest abundance. American

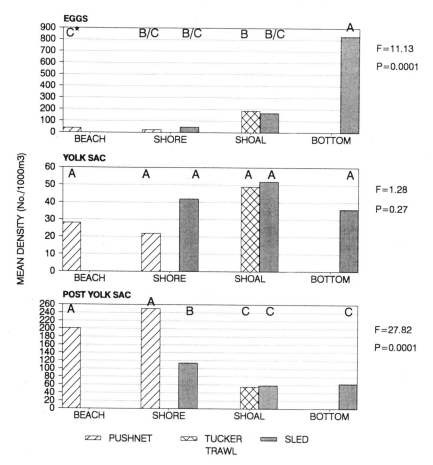

* Note: Letters denote Student-Newman-Kuels Groupings. Strata/gear with the same letter are not significantly different Alpha = 0.05.

FIGURE 17.3.
American shad ichthyoplankton from the Catskill region, 1987; comparison of mean density (no./100 m³) by stratum.

shad spawn in flat shallow areas or in river channels where water depths range from 3 to 30 ft and currents range from <1 to >3 fps (Walburg and Nichols 1967). The preponderance of eggs in the bottom stratum may reflect a preference in the location of deposition or a redistribution brought about by current patterns. Eggs are demersal and nonadhesive, thus subject to movement with currents. At the time of the special study (May 18–22, 1987) water temperatures in the Catskill region were less than 21°C. Hatching thus required several days, during which time eggs could be redistributed through the strata. In 1987 the period of peak egg abundance occurred in late April, earlier than reported for previous years. The collections taken for this special study thus reflect conditions toward the end of the period of peak abundance.

Abundances of shad YSL were not significantly different by gear or stratum. Peak YSL abundance in 1987 occurred during mid-May in the Albany region (LMS 1989).

The special study occurred shortly after peak PYSL abundance. Catches of PYSL American shad were statistically greater in shallow beach and shore strata than in the shoals and bottom stratum. Pushnets collected more PYSL in beach and shore strata than did epibenthic sleds in the shore strata. Results of river-long larval sampling in 1987 (LMS 1989) indicate that little longitudinal movement of early life stages took place. Downstream movement of PYSL was apparent in the river-long data, with densities consistently higher in downstream shoals than in channel-area bottom strata. Data from previously unsampled upriver shore strata suggest that these areas contain even greater densities than observed in downriver shoals.

Bay Anchovy

The abundance of bay anchovy eggs and PYSL in beach and shore zones was compared with the abundance in historically sampled shoals in the Tappan Zee region (Figure 17.4). Spawning typically occurs from May to September from the Tappan Zee south. Eggs were more abundant in shoals than in the shallow shore and beach strata. No statistically significant differences in CPUE of bay anchovy PYSL were identified among gear types or strata using ANOVA ($P = 0.66$). In the absence of demonstrable differences among beach, shore, and shoal strata, standing crop estimates based on shoal data adequately represent standing crop data for bay anchovy PYSL.

White Perch

The special study on white perch ichthyoplankton was conducted in the Poughkeepsie region (June 8, 1988); however, greater numbers were collected in the Catskill region during the shad special study (May 18, 1988). Although the study was not designed to evaluate the distribution of eggs among strata, analysis of egg data indicated that

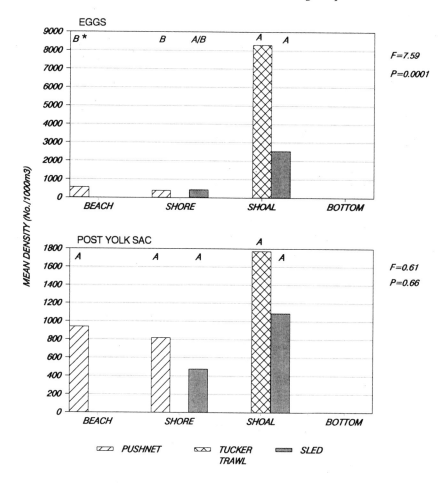

FIGURE 17.4.
Bay anchovy ichthyoplankton from the Tappan Zee region, 1987; comparison of mean density (No./1000 m³) by stratum.

significantly more eggs were collected from bottom and shoal strata for both the Poughkeepsie (Figure 17.5) and the Catskill (Figure 17.6) regions. Collections in shallow strata produced fewer eggs.

White perch deposit demersal adhesive eggs in upriver embayments and tributaries. The eggs are easily dislodged and collected

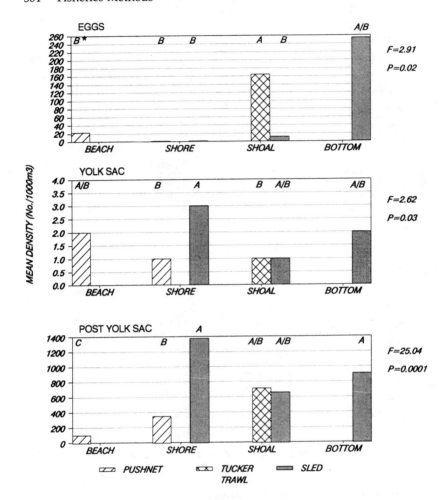

FIGURE 17.5.
White perch ichthyoplankton from the Poughkeepsie region, 1987; comparison of mean density (No./1000 m³) by stratum.

with ichthyoplankton sampling gear. Thus, egg distribution may not adequately reflect deposition locations or dominant strata. The distribution of eggs observed during the special study, especially those collected by Tucker trawl, may reflect locations of eggs dislodged by strong currents and freshwater runoff patterns.

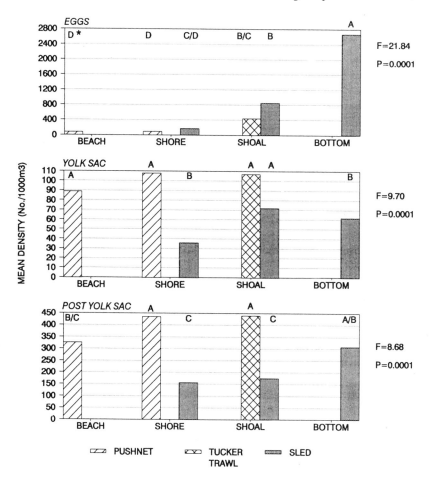

*Note: Letters denote Student-Newman-Kuels Groupings. Strata/gear with the same letter are not significantly different Alpha = 0.05.

FIGURE 17.6.
White perch ichthyoplankton from the Catskill region, 1987; comparison of mean density (No./1000 m^3) by stratum.

Few YSL were collected in the Poughkeepsie region. In the Catskill region, however, YSL were collected from all strata by all gear types. Although statistical differences in the abundance of YSL were apparent, the differences were not attributable solely to differences among strata. In general, epibenthic sleds in the Catskill region collected fewer white perch YSL than either pushnets or the Tucker trawl.

PYSL of white perch are more dispersed than eggs or YSL through sampling regions (Klauda et al. 1988b). Both the Poughkeepsie and Catskill regions showed statistically significant differences in CPUE, although the pattern was not consistent between regions. The upriver Catskill region sampled on May 18–22 produced catches that were relatively similar among strata; catches by epibenthic sled, however, were lower than those from other gear deployed in the same strata. In Poughkeepsie, catches of PYSL from shore, shoal, and bottom strata were also similar, but, in contrast to the Catskill region, catches from epibenthic sleds were similar or higher than those from other gears.

To summarize: in the Catskill region more white perch PYSL were collected by pushnets than sleds, but in the Poughkeepsie region sleds collected more than pushnets. Assuming that these statistically significant differences are real, they must be attributable to some regional difference that affects gear deployment. The most obvious difference is the presence of aquatic vegetation, primarily water chestnut, in the upriver Catskill region.

Striped Bass

The distribution of striped bass PYSL among strata was evaluated from samples collected in the white perch study conducted in the Poughkeepsie region. Previously unsampled shores and shoals produced large numbers of larvae (Figure 17.7). Within these unsampled regions significantly larger catches were made from the shores than from the shoals. No differences were apparent between the catches of pushnets or epibenthic sleds deployed in the shore strata. Collections made by Tucker trawls and epibenthic sleds in the shoals produced similar catches, suggesting that PYSL were relatively evenly distributed through the water column during the special study. These results indicate that historic estimates of striped bass standing crop based on abundance in bottom regions underestimate actual abundance and standing crop of PYSL because shore strata may support greater larval densities.

DISCUSSION

The data indicate that, for most species, abundance in the bottom strata adequately represents or is less than abundance in pre-

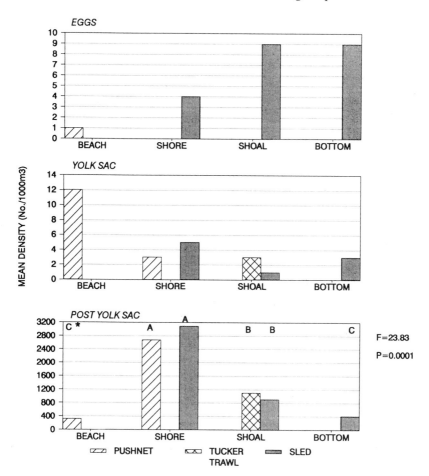

FIGURE 17.7
Striped bass ichthyoplankton from the Poughkeepsie region, 1987; comparison of mean density (No./1000 m³) by stratum.

viously unsampled shoals; therefore, historic values for abundance and standing crop are a reasonable estimate of real values. For those species whose abundance in the shoals statistically exceeds that in the bottom stratum, historic estimates, although reasonable approximations, tend to underestimate standing crops.

Two life stages of American shad—eggs and young-of-year—were more abundant in bottom strata than in adjacent shoals. For young-of-year this relationship was apparent in 1986 but not in 1987. It is possible that during 1986 young-of-year were captured in the upper water column as gear was retrieved.

Underestimation of densities in unsampled shoals is likely to have a greater impact on the estimates of white perch standing crops than of other target species. White perch is a resident species that is more abundant than the other species in upriver shoals. In addition, only white perch showed consistent, statistical differences through years, regions, and year classes. Data for this species have been used to explore the impact of consistent underestimation of abundance in unsampled upriver shoals. A differential factor representing the ratio of abundance in shoals to that in the bottom stratum indicates the degree to which abundance has been adequately estimated (Table 17.7). Factors near 1 indicate that abundances in the two strata are similar and adequately represent each other. Factors range from 0.1 for young-of-year in the Catskill region in 1986 to 30 for older fish in the West Point region in 1986. The range is large because of variations in distribution between strata over the length of the river; CPUE varies both among strata and from region to region. Because the distribution of fish among shoals and other strata is variable by region, data from the specific regions sampled during the special study cannot readily be applied to *all* unsampled upriver shoals. However, most differential factors fall within 2 to 4—that is, the CPUE in shoal samples is two to four times higher than the CPUE of the bottom.

The differential factor at West Point (30) is extraordinarily skewed to the shoals. The CPUE data suggest that abundance in the shoals is similar to that in the upriver Kingston region, but that abundance in the bottom is lower than elsewhere in the river. The West Point region is the deepest portion of the river and may be habitat that is not used by white perch. Nonetheless, the West Point data highlight variability in habitat usage.

Wells et al. (this volume) note an apparent decline in the abundance and standing crop of young-of-year white perch from 1979 to the present, and suggest that this age class is not sampled in consistent proportion to its abundance. Certainly, young-of-year are more abundant in unsampled shoals than in regularly sampled areas (Figure 17.2), suggesting that abundance estimates have been low. The question of whether this underestimation has been consistent from year to year is more difficult to answer on the basis of existing information. Van Winkle et al. (1981) noted the year-to-year variation in year-class strength. This variability, combined with the regional

TABLE 17.7.
Relationship between shoals and bottom abundance (CPUE) of white perch.

Abundance	All Regions	West Point	Kingston	Catskill
1986				
YOY				
Shoals	10.9	31.8	7.3	0.15
Bottom	2.2	1.1	5.1	1.3
Factor	5.0	29.0	1.5	0.1
Older				
Shoals	56.9	65.4	91.4	29.9
Bottom	14.3	1.5	34.4	11.7
Factor	4.0	44.0	2.5	2.5
Total				
Shoals	67.8	97.2	138.2	42.9
Bottom	16.5	2.6	39.5	13.0
Factor	4.0	37.0	3.5	3.0
1987				
YOY				
Shoals			14.0	
Bottom			5.2	
Factor			2.7	
Older				
Shoals			110.2	
Bottom			33.2	
Factor			3.3	
Total				
Shoals			124.2	
Bottom			38.4	
Factor			3.2	

variations in distribution between shoal and bottom strata, suggests that habitat usage may not be consistent through time. The impact of such inconsistency is difficult to gauge, but, regardless of the magnitude of its variation, the effect would be consistent underestimation, a negative bias.

To evaluate the effect of the negative bias on abundance estimates of white perch, estimates based on CPUE from previously unsampled upriver areas were compared to estimates based on CPUE in adjacent strata, the historic method. Data from fall shoals and beach seine collections during the week of sampling in upriver areas were used for historic standing crop estimates (Table 17.8) (LMS 1989).

TABLE 17.8.
1987 fall shoals and beach seine surveys standing crop data (in thousands) for young-of-year and yearling and older white perch from 14 September 1987 to 24 September 1987—standard errors (in thousands) are printed below each standing crop. "NS" indicates that the stratum was not sampled.

Region	Young-of-Year				Yearling and Older			
	Fall Shoals			Beach Seine	Fall Shoals			Beach Seine
	Channel	Bottom	Shoal	Shore	Channel	Bottom	Shoal	Shore
Yonkers	0	0	0	0	0	0	36	6
	0	0	0	0	0	0	21	4
Tappan Zee	0	0	0	61	0	187	1221	337
	0	0	0	30	0	77	273	178
Croton-Haverstraw	0	0	8	221	0	142	1228	213
	0	0	4	66	0	30	216	136
Indian Point	0	24	0	63	0	206	290	52
	0	24	0	39	0	50	89	36
West Point	141	37	NS	67	0	43	NS	23

Cornwall	141	9	15	38	0	23	186	18
	0	5	8	98	0	188	19	25
Poughkeepsie	0	5	NS	33	0	109	NS	19
	0	53	NS	0	0	880	NS	6
Hyde Park	0	27	NS	0	0	702	NS	4
	93	66	NS	4	282	373	NS	1
	93	21	NS	4	181	102	NS	<0.5
Kingston	0	64	NS	74	0	490	NS	21
	0	32	NS	33	0	72	NS	17
Saugerties	82	10	NS	68	327	542	NS	140
	82	6	NS	31	327	121	NS	99
Catskill	0	0	NS	116	168	224	NS	155
	0	0	NS	66	87	44	NS	62
Albany	0	4	NS	2	0	66	NS	8
	0	4	NS	2	0	19	NS	8
Total standing crop	316	261	24	774	776	3342	2961	987
	188	54	9	125	383	739	360	257

Using these data, 234,000 young-of-year white perch are estimated for upriver bottom regions adjacent to previously unsampled shoals. Assuming similar densities in adjacent shoals, 49,000 young-of-year white perch are attributed to unsampled shoals in the historic method. Given that data from previously unsampled shoals indicate that abundance is underestimated by a factor of 2, the actual abundance in unsampled shoals would be 98,000 young-of-year white perch. The resulting difference between the two estimates is 8% of the total weekly standing crop attributed to bottom, channel, and shoal strata, and 3.6% of the weekly total, including shore strata. If abundance in unsampled shoals is underestimated by a factor of 4, actual unsampled shoal abundance is 196,000 young-of-year white perch, 24% of the total bottom standing crop and 10% of total standing crop. If abundance in unsampled shoals is underestimated by a factor of 4, the number of additional fish is less than the standard error attributable to weekly channel estimates.

The standing crop comparison described above for young-of-year white perch was also made for similar estimates of juvenile and older fish (Table 17.9). The effect of underestimating actual abundance in shoals is greater for these age classes than for young-of-year. If shoal abundance estimates from bottom strata are underestimates of actual shoal abundance by a factor of 4, then weekly total standing crop of white perch may be low by 12 to 35%.

Underestimating weekly standing crops in unsampled shoals is likely to have a greater impact on white perch standing crops than on

TABLE 17.9.
Comparison of standing crop estimates (in thousands) for juvenile white perch.

	White Perch	
	Young of Year	Yearling and Older
Adjacent bottom abundance	234	2618
Shoals based on bottom abundance (historic method, i.e., factor 1)	49	840
Shoals based on underestimation factor 2	98	1680
Shoals based on underestimation factor 4	196	3360
Total weekly standing crop	601	7079
Total weekly standing crop with beaches	1375	8066

those of other target species. White perch is a resident species found primarily in shoal strata. Those species that migrate downriver as juveniles (striped bass, American shad, Atlantic tomcod, and bay anchovy) would progressively vacate regions with unsampled upriver shoals.

Historically, weekly standing crops for selected larval species and life stages have been estimated from CPUE data collected during the river-long sampling survey in a manner similar to the estimation of juvenile standing crops (LMS 1989). Riverwide, total standing crop estimates are based on weekly estimates. Where CPUE data are unavailable—that is, shore and beach strata plus upriver shoals—the abundance in adjacent strata is used to estimate standing crop in unsampled strata. Results of sampling PYSL striped bass in previously unsampled upriver areas indicate that abundance in the Poughkeepsie shore strata is seven times that in the adjacent bottom stratum (Table 17.10). Abundance in unsampled shoals is approximately two and one-half times that in the adjacent bottom. Using these distributional ratios, standing crop estimates based on the actual data from previously unsampled areas were compared with estimates based on the assumption of equivalent abundance in adjacent sampled and unsampled data. Estimates are calculated on a region-

TABLE 17.10.
Post–yolk-sac larvae of striped bass CPUE (no./1000 m^3) in the Poughkeepsie region.

Strata Gear	Mean	Median	SNK	Ratio to Bottom Mean Abundance
Beach				
Pushnet	321	275	C	
Shore				
Pushnet	2684	2484	A	6.5
Epibenthic sled	3093	2079	A	7.5
Shoals				
Epibenthic sled	910	828	B	2.2
Tucker trawl	1103	930	B	2.7
Bottom				
Epibenthic sled	410	302	C	
F Value		23.83		
Probability		0.0001		

by-region basis to reflect the actual distribution of striped bass PYSL among river regions. The Albany region, which is the largest unsampled shoal area, did not include any striped bass larvae (Table 17.11). The peak of striped bass PYSL occurred in the Poughkeepsie vicinity.

In order to calculate standing crops based on the abundance

TABLE 17.11.
1987 longitudinal river survey standing crop data (in thousands) for striped bass post-yolk-sac larvae and young-of-year from 8 June 1987 to 12 June 1987. Standard errors (in thousands) are printed below each standing crop. "NS" indicates that the stratum was not sampled.

	Post–Yolk-Sac Larvae		
	Channel	Bottom	Shoal
Yonkers	0	0	0
	0	0	
Tappan Zee	365	129	405
	134	129	269
Croton-Haverstraw	654	1236	1491
	249	516	275
Indian Point	23483	3742	2280
	7599	2271	790
West Point	209919	28655	NS
	30763	7042	
Cornwall	91787	28214	2408
	15251	7087	771
Poughkeepsie	138869	36181	NS
	20058	9590	
Hyde Park	52667	7813	NS
	6783	2135	
Kingston	7211	6666	NS
	2839	3784	
Saugerties	2926	1678	NS
	2114	632	
Catskill	385	392	NS
	249	192	
Albany	77	0	NS
	77	0	
Total standing crop	528343	114704	6584
	41204	14715	1169

TABLE 17.12.
Comparison of standing crop estimates (in thousands)
for post–yolk-sac striped bass.

	Striped Bass Post–Yolk-Sac
Bottom abundance adjacent to unsampled shoals	81,385
Shoals based on bottom abundance (historic method)	7,529
Shoals based on underestimation factors of 7 for shores and 2.5 for shoals	19,680
Total standing crop	649,631

distribution ratios, the shore and beach strata were estimated to represent one-quarter of the total shoal volume. The beach and shore volumes were not separated, even though data suggest that their abundances may differ. The standing crop in bottom strata adjacent to unsampled shoals was 81 million PYSL. Using the assumption that bottom abundance represents shoal abundance, the standing crop in adjacent shoals was estimated at 7.5 million striped bass PYSL (Table 17.12). Revised estimates based on distributional ratios attribute 19.7 million larvae to unsampled shoals, which is higher than historic estimates by 12 million larvae. In comparison to the total standing crop estimate of 649.6 million larvae, the underestimate is only 1.8%, less than the standard error associated with the weekly standing crop estimate for bottom samples (14.7 million larvae). Since the underestimate is small in comparison to both the total weekly standing crop and the standard errors associated with standing crop data, historic standing crops do not appear to be substantially biased as a result of substituting bottom density values for the shoals.

Acknowledgments

Thanks to Gerri Scheinin, Rosalia Uy, and Micah O'Connor for their skills with computers and to M'lou Pinkham and Donna Randall for their comments and review of the text. This work was funded by Consolidated Edison Company of New York, Inc.

DOUGLAS G. HEIMBUCH
DENNIS J. DUNNING
JOHN R. YOUNG

18

Post-Yolk-Sac Larvae Abundance as an Index of Year Class Strength of Striped Bass in the Hudson River

ABSTRACT

Catch per unit effort data of Hudson River young-of-year striped bass have been collected annually (using standardized sampling procedures) since 1974 by the utilities operating power plants on the Hudson River, and since 1981 by the New York State Department of Environmental Conservation. Among other applications, these data have been used to compute numerous different indices of annual young-of-year abundance, which have been the basis for assessments of trends in abundance of the Hudson River striped bass stock. This paper reviews the sampling programs and data used for the historically computed indices of abundance and recommends an index that is best suited to detecting trends in young-of-year abundance. The recommended index is based on post–yolk-sac larvae data collected by the utilities-sponsored longitudinal river ichthyoplankton sampling program. This index avoids many of the shortcomings of historically computed indices when used for the purpose of detecting long-term trends in abundance.

BACKGROUND

Six relatively large-scale field sampling programs conducted on the Hudson River during the past decade have collected young-of-year striped bass. The Hudson River utilities (utilities) have sponsored beach seine and fixed-frame trawl (Tucker trawl, epibenthic sled, and beam trawl) sampling programs for juvenile fish, and an ichthyoplankton sampling program that collected eggs, yolk-sac larvae, and post–yolk-sac larvae (PYSL) (Versar, Inc. 1987). The New York State Department of Environmental Conservation (NYSDEC) has conducted two beach seine sampling programs, one targeted to striped bass and one targeted to American shad, and a bottom trawl program (Versar, Inc. 1988).

Each of these programs has produced catch-per-unit-effort (CPUE) data for young-of-year striped bass (juveniles or PYSL). Among other applications, the data have been used to compute various indices of young-of-year abundance. These indices have been the basis for assessments of trends in abundance of the Hudson River striped bass stock.

OVERVIEW OF PROGRAMS

The three utilities-sponsored programs (beach seine, fixed-frame trawl—referred to as the fall shoals program—and ichthyoplankton—referred to as the longitudinal river program) have been conducted since 1974. With the exception of the fall shoals program, each of these programs has used the same gear types in all years of the program. For bottom sampling, the fall shoals program deployed epibenthic sleds from 1974–1984 and beam trawls since 1985. Each of the three NYSDEC programs have been conducted using standardized sampling procedures since 1981 (Figure 18.1).

Each of the six sampling programs can be characterized in terms of the locations subject to sampling by the program. Because the three utilities-sponsored programs employ stratified random sampling designs, it is convenient to describe the geographic extent of sampling

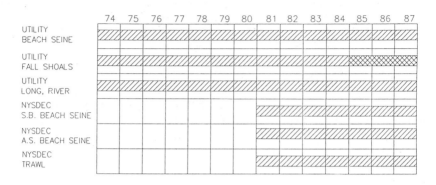

FIGURE 18.1.
Years in which the 6 field sampling programs were conducted, 1974–1987.

in terms of these sampling strata. The sampling strata are defined by 12 longitudinal river regions from Albany south to Yonkers (Frontispiece) and 5 habitat strata—channel, bottom, shoal bottom, shoal midwater, and shore (TI 1977).

The utilities-sponsored longitudinal river (Long River) program sampled the channel stratum from the Catskill region through the Yonkers region in all years of the program. The Long River program also sampled the shoal stratum (bottom and midwater) from the Indian Point through Yonkers regions, and sampled the bottom stratum from the Albany through Tappan Zee regions (Figure 18.2). The utilities-sponsored beach seine program sampled only the shore stratum. Beach seine sampling was conducted from the Yonkers through Albany regions in all years of the program (Figure 18.3). The utilities-sponsored fall shoals program sampled the bottom stratum from the Hyde Park through Tappan Zee regions in all years of the program. The shoal bottom stratum was sampled from the Indian Point through Yonkers regions (Figure 18.4). The channel and shoal midwater strata also were sampled during the fall shoals program from 1979 to 1987; however, the catches for juvenile striped bass were extremely low—a total of only 21 were collected from 1979–1985 (Versar 1987).

The NYSDEC striped bass beach seine program sampled the shore stratum from the Indian Point through Yonkers regions in all

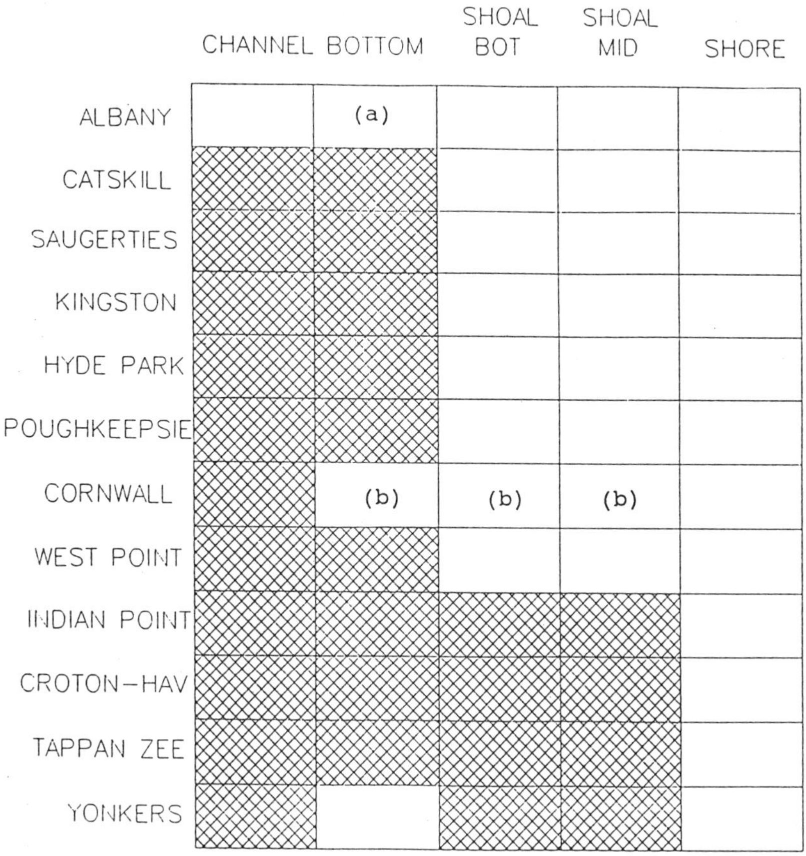

Striped Bass Year Class Index 379

	CHANNEL	BOTTOM	SHOAL BOT	SHOAL MID	SHORE
ALBANY		(a)			
CATSKILL	▨	▨			
SAUGERTIES	▨	▨			
KINGSTON	▨	▨			
HYDE PARK	▨	▨			
POUGHKEEPSIE	▨	▨			
CORNWALL	▨	(b)	(b)	(b)	
WEST POINT	▨	▨			
INDIAN POINT	▨	▨	▨	▨	
CROTON-HAV	▨	▨	▨	▨	
TAPPAN ZEE	▨	▨	▨	▨	
YONKERS	▨		▨	▨	

FIGURE 18.2.
River regions (rows) and habitat strata (columns) sampled during the utilities' Long River sampling program. (a) Epibenthic sled sampling was conducted in all years but 1975 and 1976. (b) Standard sampling was conducted in all years but 1975.

years of the program (Figure 18.5). The NYSDEC American shad beach seine program sampled the shore stratum in the Cornwall, Poughkeepsie, Catskill, and Albany regions (Figure 18.6). The NYSDEC bottom trawl program sampled the bottom, and the deepest waters of the shoal bottom, strata in the Tappan Zee through Cornwall regions (Figure 18.7).

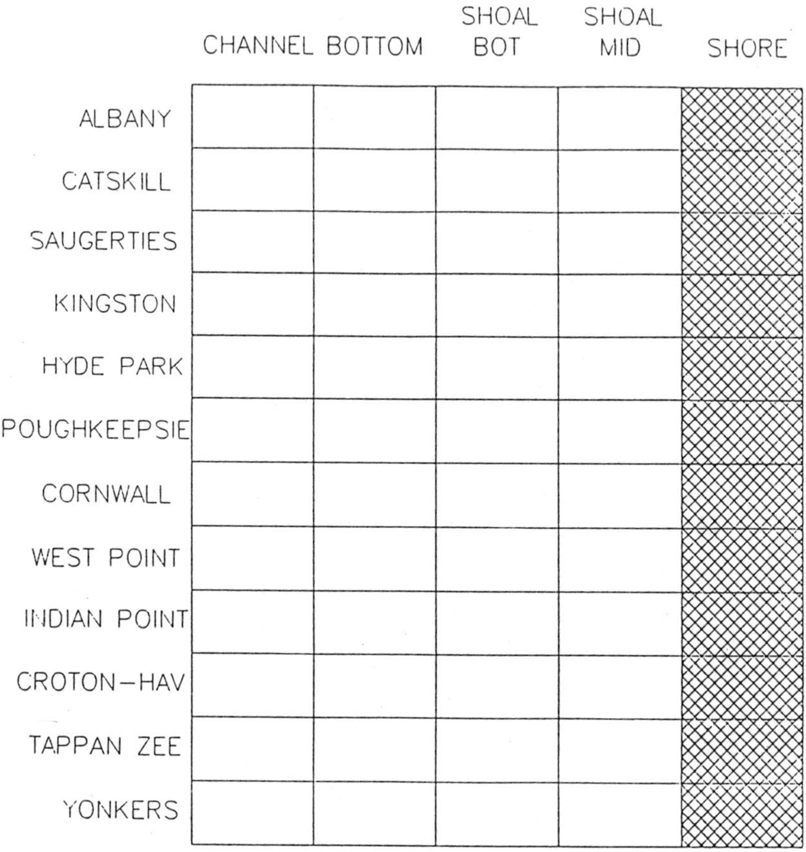

	CHANNEL BOTTOM	SHOAL BOT	SHOAL MID	SHORE
ALBANY				▓
CATSKILL				▓
SAUGERTIES				▓
KINGSTON				▓
HYDE PARK				▓
POUGHKEEPSIE				▓
CORNWALL				▓
WEST POINT				▓
INDIAN POINT				▓
CROTON–HAV				▓
TAPPAN ZEE				▓
YONKERS				▓

FIGURE 18.3.
River regions and habitat strata sampled during the beach seine sampling program.

EVALUATION OF PROGRAMS

The Long River, beach seine, and fall shoals programs sponsored by the utilities provide the longest time series of fish abundance data collected on the Hudson River. The utilities' Long River and beach seine programs are preferred for assessing trends because they have produced the longest time series of data using the same gear. Although the fall shoals program has been conducted for as many years, a gear change in 1985 makes the assessment of long-term trends difficult. Replacement of the epibenthic sled with the beam

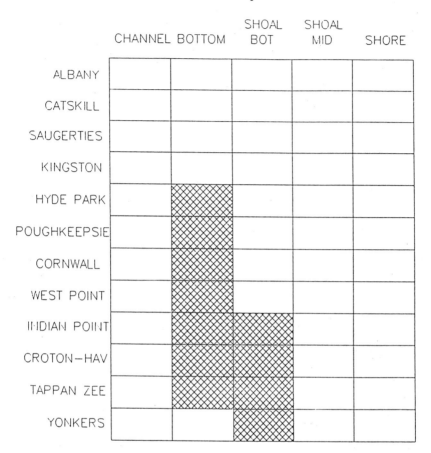

FIGURE 18.4.
River regions and habitat strata sampled during the fall shoals sampling program.

trawl was motivated by the high proportion of zero catches of young-of-year striped bass by the epibenthic sled (Normandeau Associates, Inc. 1986).

Among the utility programs the Long River program has provided the most extensive geographic coverage of sampling. All other things being equal, greater geographic coverage should produce a more reliable index of abundance because a greater proportion of the young-of-year habitat would be subject to sampling. Sampling programs that fail to survey the entire young-of-year habitat can be se-

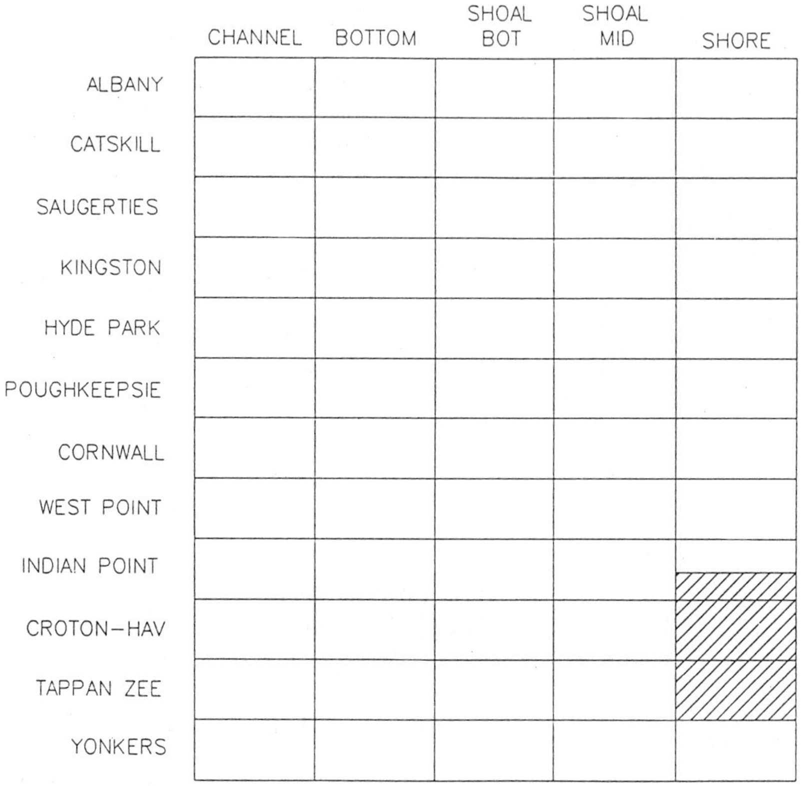

	CHANNEL	BOTTOM	SHOAL BOT	SHOAL MID	SHORE
ALBANY					
CATSKILL					
SAUGERTIES					
KINGSTON					
HYDE PARK					
POUGHKEEPSIE					
CORNWALL					
WEST POINT					
INDIAN POINT					////
CROTON–HAV					////
TAPPAN ZEE					////
YONKERS					

FIGURE 18.5.
River regions and habitat strata sampled during the NYSDEC striped bass beach seine sampling program.

riously biased by among-year differences in the proportion of the young-of-year population inhabiting the areas subject to sampling. As a result, it may be impossible to distinguish changes in population abundance from changes in availability. Whether this requirement, of an equal fraction inhabiting the areas subject to sampling in all years, is satisfied can be addressed by examining the annual average CPUE from programs sampling different areas concurrently.

The number caught per haul in beach seine sampling can be described as a random variable that is related to the actual number of

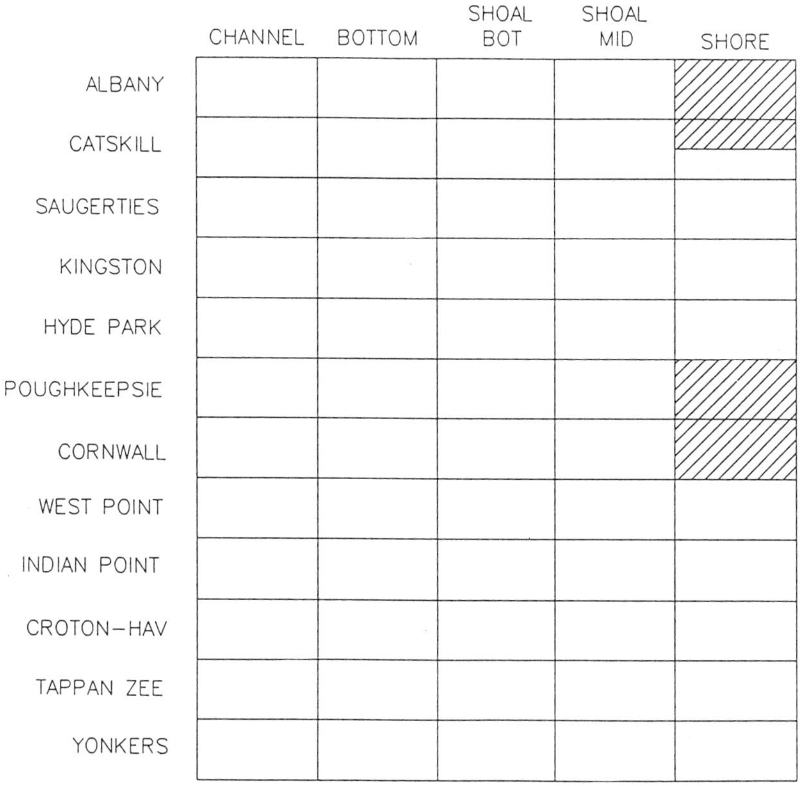

	CHANNEL	BOTTOM	SHOAL BOT	SHOAL MID	SHORE
ALBANY					/////
CATSKILL					/////
SAUGERTIES					
KINGSTON					
HYDE PARK					
POUGHKEEPSIE					/////
CORNWALL					/////
WEST POINT					
INDIAN POINT					
CROTON-HAV					
TAPPAN ZEE					
YONKERS					

FIGURE 18.6.
River regions and habitat strata sampled during the NYSDEC American shad beach seine sampling program.

juveniles present at the location and time the sample was collected as follows:

$$E_r(Y_{Bity}) = q_{Bity} N_{Bity}$$

where

Y_{Bity} = the number caught at beach (B) location i at time t in year y
$E_r(Y_{Bity})$ = expectation of Y_{Bity} under identical conditions (replicates, r) at location i at time t in year y

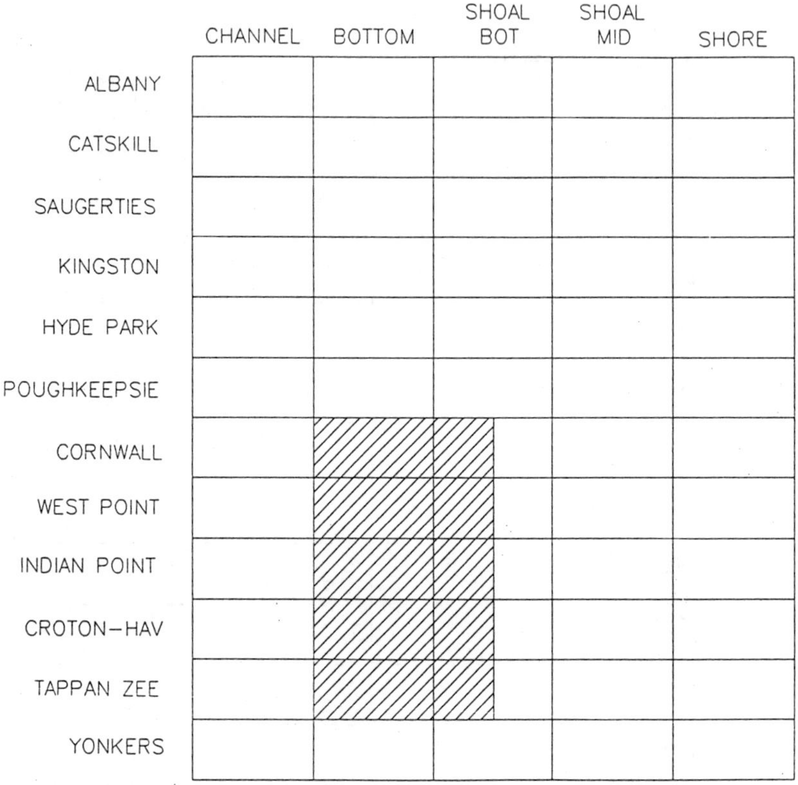

384   Fisheries Methods

	CHANNEL	BOTTOM	SHOAL BOT	SHOAL MID	SHORE
ALBANY					
CATSKILL					
SAUGERTIES					
KINGSTON					
HYDE PARK					
POUGHKEEPSIE					
CORNWALL		//////	//////		
WEST POINT		//////	//////		
INDIAN POINT		//////	//////		
CROTON–HAV		//////	//////		
TAPPAN ZEE		//////	//////		
YONKERS					

FIGURE 18.7.
River regions and habitat strata sampled during the NYSDEC bottom trawl sampling program.

N_{Bity} = the number of juveniles actually present at beach location i at time ti in year y

q_{Bity} = gear efficiency of the seine fished at location i at time t in year y.

The expected catch per unit effort (averaged over all locations and times subject to sampling) can be expressed as,

$$E_t[E_i[E_r(Y_{Bity})]] = K_{By}N_y$$

where

E_t = the expectation over all times t
E_i = the expectation over all locations (beaches) i
K_{By} = proportionality coefficient
N_y = the riverwide abundance of juveniles in year y.

The coefficient K_{By} can be interpreted assuming that the gear efficiency (q_{Bity}) and abundance (N_{Bity}) are independent and assuming the gear efficiency is constant among years. The coefficient K_{By} is proportional to the average fraction of the riverwide population inhabiting the beaches subject to sampling:

$$E_t[E_i[E_r(Y_{Bity})]] = q_{By} b_y N_y f_{By}$$

where

$q_{By} = E_t[E_i(q_{Bity})]$
$f_{By} b_y N_y = E_t[E_i(N_{Bity})]$
b_y = average proportion of the riverwide juvenile population inhabiting the area subject to beach seine sampling in year y

and

f_{By} = the fraction of the area subject to sampling by beach seine that is sampled with a single seine haul in year y

Similarly, for a concurrent offshore sampling program:

$$E_t[E_i[E_r(Y_{Aity})]] = q_{Ay} a_y N_y f_{Ay}$$

where

Y_{Aity} = the number caught at offshore (A) location i at time t in year y
$q_{Ay} = E_t[E_i(q_{Aity})]$
$f_{Ay} a_y N_y = E_t[E_i(N_{Aity})]$
a_y = average proportion of the riverwide juvenile population inhabiting the area subject to offshore sampling in year y
f_{Ay} = the fraction of the area subject to offshore sampling that is sampled with a single haul

and

$$a_y + b_y \leq 1$$

Therefore, the ratio of mean CPUEs is proportional to the ratio of the fractions inhabiting the two areas subject to sampling by the two programs:

$$\frac{E_t[E_i[E_r(Y_{Bity})]]}{E_t[E_i[E_r(Y_{Aity})]]} = K \cdot \frac{b_y}{a_y}$$

where

$$K = \frac{q_{By}}{q_{iy}}$$

assuming that the average gear efficiencies do not vary among years—that is, for all y:

$$q_{By} = q_B$$

and

$$q_{Ay} = q_A.$$

Data from 1974 to 1985 (Versar 1988) indicate that this ratio (k) has varied considerably (Figure 18.8) for the utilities' beach seine and fall shoals sampling programs. The observed variability is greater than would be expected due to sampling variances only (Versar 1988). Thus the fraction of the young-of-year striped bass population that inhabited the shore stratum or the fraction that inhabited the bottom strata appears to have varied considerably among years.

This result indicates that CPUE estimates from either a beach seine or offshore sampling program alone will not consistently represent young-of-year abundance. Attempts have been made to combine data from beach seine and offshore sampling programs (Versar 1987). However, valid estimates of the relative probability of capture for the beach seine and the offshore trawl gear are required for such an approach to produce meaningful results. Although estimates have been generated (TI 1978, 1979), the representativeness and precision of these estimates are questionable (Versar 1987, Young et al. 1988).

For the foregoing reasons, the utilities' beach seine and fall shoals programs, and the NYSDEC beach seine and trawl programs may not be well suited for assessing trends in abundance of young-of-year striped bass. However, the Long River program has produced as

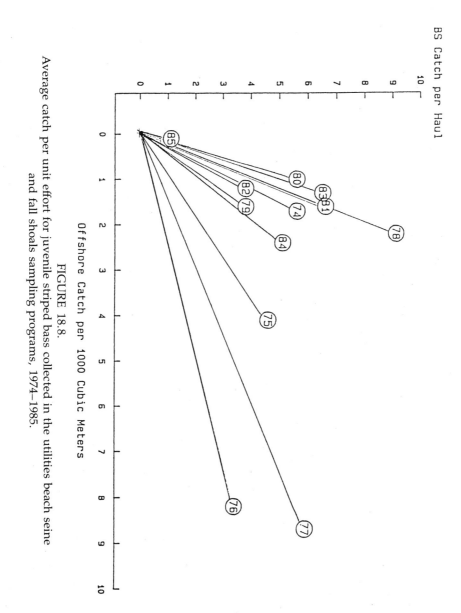

FIGURE 18.8.
Average catch per unit effort for juvenile striped bass collected in the utilities beach seine and fall shoals sampling programs, 1974–1985.

many years of data as the utilities' beach seine and fall shoals programs, and has sampled a much greater geographic extent than either of these two programs. Accordingly, the Long River program is less likely to be affected by the problem of among-year variability in the fraction of the young-of-year population subject to sampling. The PYSL life stage is the oldest, and therefore would be the most indicative of year class strength, of the life stages sampled effectively by the Long River program. For these reasons an index of young-of-year abundance based on PYSL CPUE data from the utilities' Long River program has been developed.

PYSL INDEX OF ABUNDANCE

The PYSL index represents the average relative abundance of a weekly cohort from the time it enters the PYSL life stage to the time it leaves the PYSL life stage. The PYSL index (I) was computed as:

$$I_y = \sum_{t=tmin}^{tmin+7} Z_{t,y}$$

where

I_y = index value in year y
$Z_{t,y}$ = estimated riverwide average CPUE for PYSL in week t of year y
tmin = first week of PYSL presence in year y.

The expected value of this index can be shown to be proportional to the average abundance of a weekly cohort as follows:

$$E(I_y) = \sum_{t=tmin}^{tmin+7} E(Z_{t,y})$$

$$= \sum_{t=tmin}^{tmin+7} \left(k_1 \sum_{i=1}^{4} N_{t,y,i} \right)$$

$$= k_1 \sum_{i=1}^{4} \sum_{j=1}^{4} N_{(tmin+j+i-2),y,i}$$

$$= k_2 \frac{1}{4}\sum_{i=1}^{4}\left(\frac{1}{4}\sum_{j=1}^{4} N_{(tmin+j+i-2),y,i}\right)$$

where,

$i = 1 + m$ for the weekly cohort that recruits to the PYSL life stage in week tmin + m

$N_{t,y,i}$ = riverwide abundance of weekly cohort i in week t of year y

k_1, k_2 = proportionality constants

and

$\left(\frac{1}{4}\sum_{j=1}^{4} N_{(tmin+j+i-2),y,i}\right)$ = weekly average PYSL abundance of cohort i in year j

This method of computation is based on the assumptions that 1) four weekly cohorts comprise the vast majority of PYSL during each year (Pearson 1938; Polgar 1977; Rogers, Westin, Saila 1977). These assumptions require that the period of PYSL presence in the river is 7 weeks. Data summaries of PYSL CPUE from the Long River program for the 14 years of interest indicate that this condition did exist in all years.

The PYSL index values were compared to mark-recapture estimates of abundance of the 1984 and 1985 year classes of striped bass (Coastal Environmental Services, Inc. 1989). These mark-recapture estimates are based on striped bass tagged at age 1+ and recaptured at age 2+. The mark recapture estimates of abundance for the 1984 and 1985 year classes are consistent with the corresponding PYSL index values (Figure 18.9). However, two data points (even though falling roughly on a line with zero intercept as is required) are insufficient to convincingly demonstrate a relationship. Additional years of data are needed before this can be viewed as strong evidence that the PYSL index is a reliable measure of year class strength.

To assess whether a trend over years in relative abundance of PYSL striped bass was present, the index values were fitted to the following regression model using weighted (by the inverse of the sampling variance) least squares:

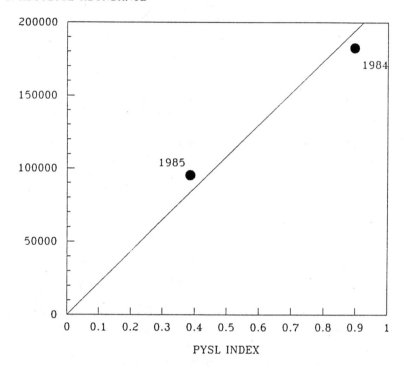

FIGURE 18.9.
Approximately proportional relationship between PYSL index values and mark-recapture estimates at age 2+ for the 1984 and 1985 year classes of Hudson River striped bass. (line through points and origin fit by eye)

$$I_y = ac^t$$
$$n(I_y) = n(a) + t(n(c))$$

where,

$t = y - 1973$
$c = 1 - b$
b = average annual (fractional) rate of change.

The regression was found to be significant at the 0.05 level with a significantly nonzero positive slope. This result indicates that, on

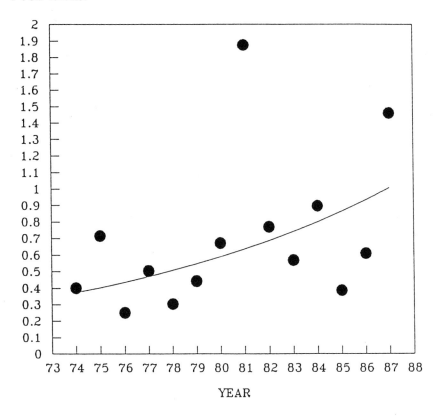

FIGURE 18.10.
Post–yolk-sac larvae index values for Hudson River striped bass, 1974–1987.

the average, the abundance of PYSL striped bass has increased from 1974 to 1987 (Figure 18.10). The estimated average rate of increase is 7.9% per year.

LEV R. GINZBURG
SCOTT FERSON

19

Assessing the Effect of Compensation on the Risk of Population Decline and Extinction

ABSTRACT

Since the probabilistic models used to estimate risks are in general difficult to validate, because doing so requires extremely large data sets, it is especially important to evaluate the assumptions used in these models. The risk of a population's declining or becoming extinct depends sensitively on the presence and character of compensatory mechanisms that control responses to mortality. We quantified this dependence for Hudson River *Morone saxatilis* (striped bass) using two standard models of compensation, the Beverton-Holt and Ricker functions. A null model that includes no compensation shows a relatively high risk of population decline at all levels, because there is no equilibrating force drawing the population to its carrying capacity and away from low levels. This forms a standard against which to compare the effects of compensation of different intensities. Increasing the strength of compensation in the Beverton-Holt function results in decreasing the risks of population decline. This is true as well with the Ricker function for small or moderate levels of compensation. However, for very strong Ricker-type compensation, cycling or even "deterministic chaos" is induced and the risks of population declines actually increase.

INTRODUCTION

When the public and technical communities first became aware of the need to monitor and regulate anthropogenic damage to the natural environment, impacts were measured in terms of total change in the natural system, as though the consequences of human activities could be condensed into a single number. In recognizing spatial, temporal, and circumstantial variation in natural systems, researchers have come to modify the way they express impacts. Probabilistic estimates, such as the chances or "risk" that a biological population will decline in abundance or go extinct, are becoming more common in environmental impact assessments. This is the result of a growing recognition among researchers that our impact estimates cannot be insulated from the fact that the abundances of real organisms naturally fluctuate in a randomly and sometimes radically changing environment. It may be true that probabilistic estimates are the only estimates that are useful in such circumstances. What does it mean to say that a power plant will increase fish mortality by 5% if normal yearly variation in mortality is 25% for the species?

The egg survival of *Morone saxatilis* (striped bass) in the Hudson River depends on, among other things, the water temperature in a critical period during spawning. Very small differences in environmental conditions can result in a many-fold change in survival (see Westin and Rogers 1978; Dey 1981). Because we cannot predict the weather and a host of incidental factors that affect a population's abundance, it is foolhardy to believe we can say precisely how the abundance will change in the coming years. The best we can do is exploit our knowledge of the statistical characteristics of the weather and other factors to predict the likely ranges for a population's mortality and fecundity rates. From these we can derive the chances that the population will decrease (or increase) to a certain level. With this approach, an environmental impact that changes the population size, a vital rate, its variability, or some other aspect of the biology can be expressed as the additional risk of the population reaching the given level. This can be accomplished by using analytical methods or, if convenience or tractability dictate, computer simulations. Thus, a measurement of, say, a power plant's impact could be made in terms of the extra risk of a population decline attributable to the presence of the facility.

Politically minded scientists and managers appreciate one other feature of the probabilistic estimates of impact: they explicitly avoid concrete predictions. This is both the good thing about these kinds of estimates, and it is also the bad thing about them. It is good because it admits the native stochasticity that is inherent in ecological processes. It is bad because it is hard to falsify a probabilistic prediction. Shrugging with the immunity of a weather forecast, we can always claim we never said the population would not go extinct; we just said it had low probability to go extinct. In fact, validating probabilistic models requires extremely large data sets that include information not only on means but the statistical distributions of the phenomena modeled. For most systems with any level of complexity, this virtually assures that no relevant and complete data set will soon be collected. A practical response to the two-edged sword of probabilistic prediction is, of course, to scrupulously evaluate the assumptions of the models used to make the estimations. Another is to assure that where uncertainty persists in the modeling process, we make conservative assumptions. That is, when we are concerned with the risk of an undesirable event such as a population's reduction or extinction, we evaluate upper bounds on the probability that it will occur. This uncertainty ranges from imprecision in the value of a vital rate that is hard to measure, to tentativeness in decisions about the model's structure itself.

The methods of ecological risk analysis are used to estimate the probability that a population will suffer extinction or fall below some specified level of abundance, a fate that can be termed "quasiextinction" (Ginzburg et al. 1982). We use this term inclusively for population declines and extinctions. Two related demographic characteristics are typically associated with a great deal of measurement uncertainty and play an important role in computation of quasiextinction risks: recruitment into the population and survivorship of the recruits. Theoretical considerations and our experience (Saila et al. 1989; Ferson et al. 1989b) with computer simulations in estimating quasiextinction risks suggested that they can be quite sensitive to the form and strength of compensation in the population model. This paper explores the sensitivity of quasiextinction risk to the strength of compensation using standard models of the phenomenon.

COMPENSATION

Biological populations typically produce more offspring than can survive to reproduce themselves. The causes of their death include a variety of natural phenomena such as predation, competition, and disease. But because populations overproduce in this way, we often observe that they have a certain elasticity to human-induced mortality. The mechanisms that allow populations to absorb anthropogenic impacts without appreciable effect on the population totals are called compensation (see Chen 1987 for a review).

Compensation works through a mechanism that ties the effective value of a vital rate such as survivorship or fecundity per individual to the absolute density of the population. In such a circumstance, the chance that an individual dies or the average fecundity or reproductive success experienced by an individual is not constant or even statistically stationary, but rather changes as a function of the density of the population. As such, compensation is one aspect of the general phenomenon of density dependence, the significance of which for natural populations has been debated in ecology for decades (see Hassell 1986; Strong 1986). Compensation is often viewed as a mechanism regulating natural population size toward its equilibrium (known as the carrying capacity). For example, when a population is overcrowded, production of offspring or their survival is often depressed, due to competition among the offspring for finite resources or perhaps to changes in parental behavior. When the population is undercrowded relative to the equilibrium population size, these effects are lessened so that production and survivorship are comparatively accelerated. Thus it is a "restoring force" that tends to draw the population size over time to the carrying capacity.

McFadden (1977) argued for the importance of compensation in fish populations that suffer anthropogenic mortality. And certainly, the very fact that many species are able to survive coexistence with humans, as tumultuous as it can be, is evidence that there are mechanisms that permit populations to recover from serious insults of many kinds. But inferences or assumptions in many discussions on this topic suggest that populations have untold, unmeasured capacity to absorb impacts. Often this amounts to little more than wishful thinking, and when there are no field measurements to justify it, it may have a darker character. So what level of security is plausible from compensatory mechanisms at work in natural populations? To answer this question, we conducted a sensitivity study to see how our estimates for the risks of quasiextinction change as the strength of compensation is varied in the model of population dynamics.

THE MODELS AND PARAMETERS

M. saxatilis in the Hudson has been the subject of numerous studies (see Merriman 1941; Saila and Lorda 1977; Westin and Rogers 1978; Texas Instruments 1981). It is an iteroparous fish that can live up to 20 or more years. In this species, compensation effects are mostly seen in early life stages. Assuming this, we used two standard stock-recruitment models to relate total reproductive effort to reproductive success: the Beverton-Holt function (Beverton and Holt 1957; Ricker 1975, page 291) and the Ricker function (Ricker 1954, 1975, page 282). Both of these nonlinearities were expressed as relationships between the number of eggs produced each year and number of zero-year-old recruits actually entering the population. The Beverton-Holt function is

$$N_0 = \frac{1}{\left(\rho + \frac{k}{eggs}\right)}$$

where N_0 is the number of zero-year olds, eggs is the potential reproduction from a single year, and ρ and k are parameters for this model of compensation. The Ricker function is

$$N_0 = \alpha \, eggs \, \exp(-\beta \, eggs)$$

where α and β are parameters for the Ricker model.

These functions are included in RAMAS (Ferson et al. 1988), an age-structured population model that incorporates environmental stochasticity and estimates the risk of quasiextinction. In RAMAS, the next year's age distribution is computed from the current one under the rules

$$eggs = \sum f_i N_i r$$

$$N_{i+1}(t + 1) = p_i N_i(t) \quad \text{for } i \geq 0$$

where t represents time and i indexes age; N_i, f_i, and p_i are age-structured vectors of abundance, fecundity, and survivorship; r is sex ratio as the fraction females; and N_0 is computed from either the

Beverton-Holt or Ricker function above. The fecundity and survivorships are random variates drawn from a distribution described statistically by a mean, coefficient of variation, correlation structure, and the form of the distribution (i.e., whether it is constant, normal, or lognormal).

Ferson et al. (in press) derive parameters for a simulation of *M. saxatilis* using RAMAS. The values are expressed in terms of numbers of individuals rather than in biomass or other units. The rates p_i for $i > 0$ are normally distributed; p_o and all the f_i are lognormally distributed. The age-structured means are listed in Table 19.1. The coefficients of variation are 0.45 for the survival of zero-year olds, 0.056 for survival in all other classes, and 0.34 for all fecundities. Since little is known about how they covary, the vital rates were simulated without cross correlations. Sex ratio is approximately 50:50, so r is 0.5. These parameters yielded a growing population, which we brought to equilibrium (i.e., less than 5% net average chance over 25 years) by introducing 40% reduction in fecundity. We set the abundances in N to an arbitrary vector and generated 250 replicate trajectories over an initial equilibration period. We used the mean vector after 50 years as the starting distribution of abundances.

TABLE 19.1.
Estimated vital rates for *M. saxatilis* in the Hudson River.

Age i	Survival $\bar{p}_i$	Fecundity $\bar{f}_i$
0	1.93E-6	0
1	0.785	0
2	0.785	0
3	0.785	0
4	0.785	11190
5	0.785	111100
6	0.785	411700
7	0.785	747200
8	0.785	1084000
9	0.785	1451000
10	0.785	1676000
11	0.785	2022000
12	0.785	2301000
13	0.785	2285000
14	0.785	2342000
15	0.785	2591000
16	0.785	2591000
17	0.785	3019000

We ran separate simulations for the Beverton-Holt and Ricker models of compensation. For each, we varied the strength of compensation over a wide range from zero to extremely strong compensation. To do this, we first chose a value for κ (or β) and then found the value of ρ (α) that yielded the same mean total adult population size at equilibrium that we observed when no compensation was used in the model. "Adult" means all age classes greater than zero years old; we used adults rather than the total of all classes because RAMAS uses adult abundance as the variable with which to express quasiextinction risks. This is reasonable when, as in this case, the stochastic variation in abundance of zero-year olds often obscures the more significant variation in the older age classes. Figures 19.1 and 19.2 show the resulting functions used in the simulations as well as the actual parameter values they represent. The functions do not all intersect at one point because we calibrated with adults rather than eggs.

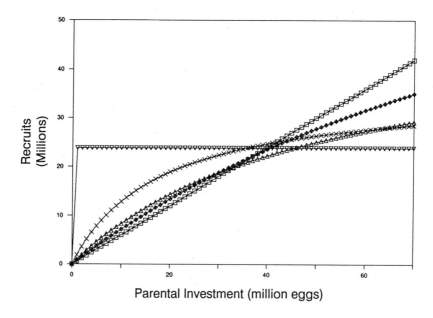

FIGURE 19.1.
Beverton-Holt functions that yield the same total mean adult population size. The straight line (boxes) represents the reproductive success that yields an equilibrial population size without compensation effects. For the other functions, the steeper the curve at the origin, the stronger the compensation. Boxes — $\alpha = 0.6$, $\beta = 0.0$; Pluses — $\alpha = 0.6$, $\beta = 1.0E-10$; Diamonds — $\alpha = 1.0$, $\beta = 1.3E-8$; Triangles — $\alpha = 1.97$, $\beta = 3.0E-8$; Crosses — $\alpha = 20.0$, $\beta = 1.0E-7$; Inverted triangles — $\alpha = 80.0$, $\beta = 3.0E-7$

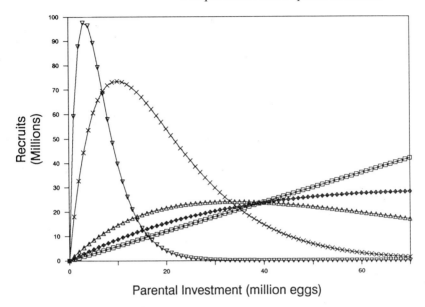

FIGURE 19.2.
Ricker functions that yield the same total mean adult populations size. The more pronounced the dome of the curve, the stronger the compensation.

These pairs of parameters define different population models that all have the same carrying capacity and the same mortality and fecundity schedules, and thus differ only in the character and strength of the compensation in the zeroth age class (and, necessarily, the equilibrial age structure comprising the carrying capacity). For every model, we made 250 replicate simulations of the population trajectory over 25 years. The output from these simulations were the quasiextinction risks as functions of several threshold values.

RESULTS

Figures 19.3 and 19.4 summarize the effect of compensation of the Beverton-Holt kind on quasiextinction risk of *M. saxatilis*. They show superimposed quasiextinction curves for the six different strengths of compensation. We used a wide range of compensation strengths, not especially because there is evidence that populations experience them, but to explore the relationship between compensation and risk. Each quasiextinction curve gives the probability that the population's total size will fall below a given threshold abundance (x-

400   Fisheries Methods

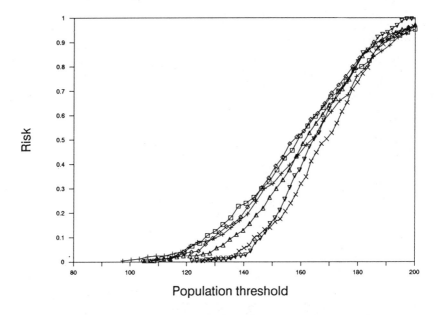

FIGURE 19.3.
Quasiextinction risk curves corresponding to the six different strengths of compensation as modeled by the Beverton-Holt function. Each curve gives the probability that a population experiencing that level of compensation will fall as low as or lower than a population threshold at some time during the next 25 years.

axis) at least once during the 25 years of the simulation. Therefore a curve above or to the left of another experiences greater risks of population declines. The additional risk is the vertical difference between two curves, which in several cases in the figures can be substantial.

Using the Beverton-Holt formulation, the null model that includes no compensation shows a relatively high risk of population decline at most low population levels. This occurs because there is no equilibrating force drawing the population trajectories to the carrying capacity and thus, under stochasticity, they can wander to low levels. Increasing the strength of compensation decreases the risks that a population declines just because compensation tethers the population to its carrying capacity. This is true as well with the Ricker function for small or moderate levels of compensation. However, with the Ricker function, strong compensation dramatically increases the risks of

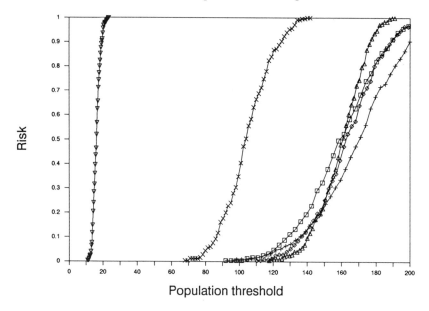

FIGURE 19.4.
Quasiextinction risk curves corresponding to the six different strengths of compensation as modeled by the Ricker function. Symbols correspond to the legend in Figure 19.2.

population declines. The strong nonlinearity induces cycling or even "deterministic chaos" (May and Oster 1976; Schaffer and Kot 1986) in the population trajectories and causes them to explore more widely the possible space of variation. Thus the quasiextinction risks at all abundance levels are higher.

The empirical evidence that addresses whether populations can display limit cycles and chaos in natural circumstances has only recently received much attention and opinions are divided. But a somewhat simpler cousin to these phenomena is well known. Over vigorous reproduction can produce a superabundant population that devastates the local environment and results in the crash of the population. This has been called the "indirect route to extinction" (Andrewartha and Birch 1984, page 193) and mediates a boom-and-bust population cycle sometimes called a J-curve. In this case, compensation is a restoring force, but it overshoots the equilibrium so much that new mechanisms come into play, which precipitate the population crash. Deer herds are a classic example of this but several species, including some fish, probably experience it regularly or occasionally. The possibility that natural populations suffer greater risks of declines on account of their compensatory mechanisms should temper our hope (McFadden 1977; Chen 1987) that compensation mollifies anthropogenic impacts to the population.

It is of course wrong to think that the Beverton-Holt and Ricker functions as we have modeled them here exhaust the possible forms of compensation in natural populations. We could have modeled compensation in other vital rates in addition to survival, on other age classes in addition to zero-year olds, and with other functions in addition to the particular equations we have used. For instance, there are several models of density dependence that can be expressed in a variety of ways by making vital rates for a particular age class depend on abundance of the same or another class or sum of classes. These may be especially useful in modeling the demographic complexities of social organisms. Even if they are not exhaustive, however, the Beverton-Holt and Ricker functions are reasonably representative of two distinct kinds of compensation. One results in an asymptotically constant output of recruits and the other reduces output with growing abundance of competing individuals.

CONCLUSIONS

Quasiextinction risk is not a monotonic function of the strength of compensation. Increasing compensation does not always lower the risk. Even so, for low thresholds, simulations without compensation seem to give conservative estimates of risk, except in cases of very strong Ricker compensation. Error in the estimation of compensation could translate into a considerable error in estimation of extinction risk.

Acknowledgments

We thank Reşit Akçakaya from the State University of New York at Stony Brook, Abe Silvers from the Electric Power Research Institute, Dennis Dunning and Quentin Ross from Consolidated Edison, and John Young from the New York Power Authority for their consultations on the *M. saxatilis* data. The simulations were done using RAMAS. The RAMAS methodology has been implemented in two programs for the IBM PC family of computers and compatibles. RAMAS/a was developed for academic users and is available from Exeter Publishing, Ltd. (516-689-7838). RAMAS 3 was developed under contract with the Electric Power Research Institute. EPRI members can obtain RAMAS 3 free of charge from the Electric Power Software Center (214-655-8709). Individual license agreements for nonmembers can be negotiated through the EPRI Commercial Development Department (P.O. Box 10412; Palo Alto, CA 94303). This is contribution 723 in Ecology and Evolution at the State University of New York at Stony Brook.

IV. ESTUARINE ECOLOGY

ROY R. STOECKER
JANET COLLURA
PHILLIP J. FALLON, JR.

20

Aquatic Studies at the Hudson River Center Site

ABSTRACT

Interpier and underpier areas along the west shore of Manhattan provide important habitats for fishes and invertebrates. A 26-month environmental survey of a site in the Hudson River under and around Pier 76, conducted between February 1986 and March 1988 was designed to provide comparative data on conditions and organism communities under and between the piers. The site is shallow and reasonably flat with no apparent contour differences between the underpier and interpier zones, but the current velocities were slightly higher under the pier than in the interpier areas. There was no significant difference in water quality or sedimentation between the two zones although sedimentation rates were highly variable. Light penetration was one meter or less in the open, not measurable under the pier.

Thirty-six species of finfish and 80 taxa of benthic invertebrates were collected. There were no detectable differences in the benthic invertebrate fauna under and between the piers, but some species of fishes were more abundant under the pier and others show a preference for the interpier area. Gill nets caught more fish in the interpier region but small trawls yielded more fish in the underpier zone. It is apparent that fish populations use both habitats.

INTRODUCTION

The New York City Public Development Corporation is cooperating with Hudson River Center Associates in the planned development of mixed-used project on the Hudson River Center site. The site is located between West 35th and West 40th Streets, Manhattan, on land under water from 12th Avenue to the pierhead line. The total size of the site is approximately one million square feet. The purpose of this study was to describe the ecology and selected physical aspects of the site.

The overall program consisted of two separate but complementary studies, a 26-month (baseline) study of the entire site, and a 20-month comparison (UP/IP) of the ecological and physical conditions under the pier with those of the interpier environment.

A preliminary survey revealed that the site had relatively uniform depth, substratum type, and water quality. The only major feature was Pier 76. The relatively small size of the site and its uniformity guided the choice of a standard fixed point sampling scheme. On the basis of the preliminary survey, benthic stations were located in areas considered representative and fisheries trawl stations (transects) were located so as to cover the entire site. (Figures 20.1 and 20.2).

Pier 76 is approximately 227 m (750 ft) long and 76 m (250 ft) wide. It has a surface area of 17,252 square meters (187,500 square ft or 4.30 acres). The deck is reinforced concrete with the underside 2.4 m above mean low water (MLW) and 1.1 m above mean high water. Pilings supporting the platform are wood, approximately 35 cm in diameter. From MLW to the underside of the platform the pilings are enclosed in concrete; their total diameter is 60 cm.

The pilings are set in straight north-south rows running across the platform. The distance between the rows is 240 cm. These openings are called "slots" and there are 61 slots between the east base of the main platform and the offshore edge. Approximately one-third of the slots have "batter" pilings in addition to the main pilings. These batter pilings occupy the center portion of the slot and thereby prevent access. The pilings also form 68 longitudinal rows separated by approximately 75 cm. The entire platform is surrounded with a timber

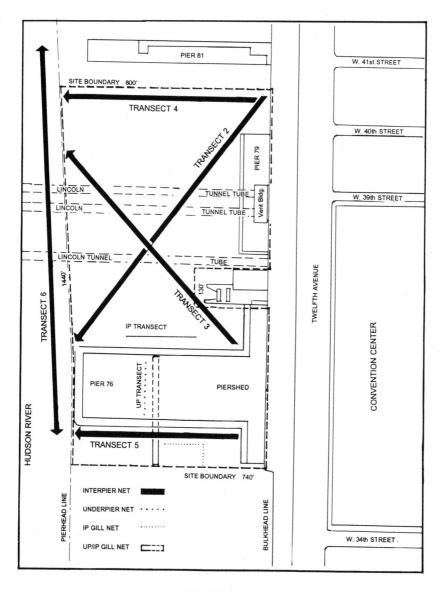

FIGURE 20.1.
Fisheries station locations, Hudson River Center, Manhattan.

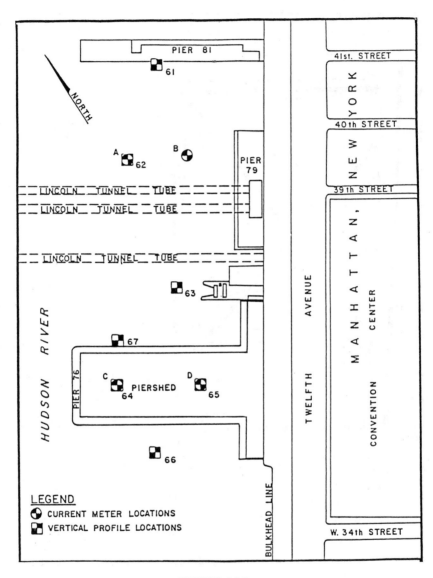

FIGURE 20.2.
On-site hydrology stations.

fendering system consisting of timber pilings with 20 by 20 cm timbers set parallel to the water surface at mid-tide range. The fendering system is in poor condition.

Because of the difficulty of sampling under the pier, the study design could not be developed fully until new types of gear had been selected and successfully tested. Gear that did not work was tried repeatedly over twelve months in order to be certain that seasonal phenomena were not the reason for its failure.

This paper is a condensed version of a longer and more detailed report prepared in September 1988 for the New York City Public Development Corporation (EEA 1988). In addition to the longer version, two technical supplements are available; the first contains the details of the hydrology study (Ocean Surveys, Inc. 1987) and the second, the report on the statistical analyses (Rohlf 1988).

METHODS

Fisheries

Interpier trawl samples. Interpier trawling was conducted with a 30-ft semiballoon otter trawl with large rubber rollers. The trawl was deployed against the bulkhead by lowering the net over the stern. The boat was then run ahead as the trawl doors went over. Trawls were run from the bulkhead out to the pierhead line at a speed of 150 cm/sec. When the net reached the pierhead line (at which point the water depth abruptly increased from 15 to 60 ft), it was winched back on board.

After the net was retrieved, the entire catch was removed and all fish were identified to species, counted, and measured to the nearest centimeter. Every attempt was made to return the fish to the river alive. Any unusual catches, other than fish, were also recorded.

Six transects (Figure 20.1) were sampled twice each month: four (T-2, T-3, T-4, and T-5) were on the project site, one (T-6) was along the pierhead line, and one (T-7, not illustrated), was an interpier comparison station north of the site. Interpier trawling started in February 1986 and was completed in March 1988. Collections were made in 25 out of 26 months (no samples in February 1987), a total of 312 samples.

All otter trawl data are presented as catch-per-unit-effort (CPUE), calculated as the number of fish caught per 800 ft of tow.

Underpier/Interpier comparison trawl samples. The fish community under Pier 76 was sampled with an experimental trawl net, hereafter called the UP trawl. This trawl was similar to the one used by Cantelmo et al. (1985) during the Westside Highway Programs. The mesh size was identical to that of the large interpier net, but the net was scaled down to a 6 ft wide by 2 ft deep mouth opening, with a chain foot rope (no rubber rollers). The doors were constructed of marine plywood, 10 by 16 in. The net was deployed from an inflatable dinghy powered by a 2.2 horsepower engine at the end of slot 33 and towed upcurrent under the pier. Towing speed was the same as for the larger otter trawl, 150 cm/sec.

The underpier (UP) station and interpier (IP) area north of and adjacent to Pier 76 (Figure 20.1) were trawled 5 times during each sampling effort. All fish were identified to species, counted, and measured. Samples were taken at least once a month from August 1986 to January 1987. From February 1987 to March 1988, the effort was quadrupled, a total of 20 UP and 20 IP tows each month (grand total—618 samples).

Interpier gill nets. Two 200-foot gill nets (2 in. stretch mesh) were set perpendicular to each other once a month on the southern side of Pier 76 (Figure 20.1). Nets were set in the afternoon and retrieved at dawn the following day. Gill nets were set and retrieved on the same days as the interpier trawls. The nets were set from May 1986 to January 1987 and March 1987 to March 1988 for a total of 44 samples.

UP/IP comparison gill nets. A new type of UP/IP comparison program was initiated during November 1987. Prior to this time, attempts to sample under the pier with gill nets had failed due to snagging on various underpier structures. A quarter-inch steel cable was suspended underneath the platform from one side to the other and from this a 100 ft by 8 ft gill net was hung by suspender cables under the center of the platform. The footrope had an extra heavy leadline and rested on the bottom. Heavy mushroom anchors held the ends of the net in place. The net had two 50-ft panels, one of 1¼ in. and the other 2 in. stretch mesh. The net was deployed in slot 30, adjacent to the site of the UP trawls (Figure 20.1). An identical net was deployed at the same time in the adjacent interpier area south of the pier and the same distance offshore. The comparison gill nets were deployed twice monthly from November 1987 to March 1988 for a total of 20 sets.

Benthic Invertebrates

Benthic grab survey, baseline study April 1986 to March 1988. Grab stations were located in seven interpier locations, 5 (B-2 through B-6) on-site and two (B-7 and B-8) off-site. A single underpier station (UP-1) was set up at the beginning of the program and midway through the program; after 4 quarters of baseline samples, a second underpier station (UP-9) was established. Samples were collected with a 0.05 square meter Ponar bottom grab, except during the first two sampling periods when a smaller (0.025 square meter) petite Ponar sampler was used for the underpier samples. Although the petite Ponar was easier to manage in the small craft and tight quarters, concern over the comparability of the data from the two kinds of samplers caused us to switch to the larger sampler for all collections.

Individual samples (the entire contents of the Ponar grab) were washed on a 0.5 mm mesh sieve (except the April samples when a 1.0 mm sieve was used) to remove fine particles, then transferred to a jar, labeled, and preserved with 10% buffered formalin. Rose bengal stain was added to the formalin to aid in later sorting of the organisms. In the laboratory the organisms were identified to species level whenever possible although the oligochaetes, chironomids, nemertineans, anthozoans, and hydrozoans were left as higher taxa because of the difficulty of identification or small size and scarcity of specimens.

Benthic stations were sampled quarterly from April 1986 to March 1988. A total of 324 samples was collected.

Colonization. Artificial substrata consisting of solid concrete blocks were suspended below the low water mark about 2 feet above the bottom in three locations (C-1, C-2, C-3). The blocks were set at C-2 and C-3 on March 31 and April 1, 1986. Station C-1 under Pier 76 was added in June 1986. Samples were collected in June, October, and December 1986 (total 15 samples). Upon retrieval of the blocks, all attached organisms were scraped off a 10 cm by 10 cm area and preserved in 10% formalin. Samples were processed as described for the benthic samples.

Water quality. Water quality parameters were recorded with each sample. Salinity (o/oo), dissolved oxygen (ppm DO), and water temperature were measured with YSI meters, and water transparency was determined with a Secchi disk. All measurements (except Secchi) were taken at mid-depth. More than 1000 water quality samples were processed during the study.

Bathymetry. Continuous soundings were recorded along 15 tracklines spaced at 50-ft intervals and oriented perpendicular to Pier 81. Measurements were made with a Raytheon DE-719 survey grade echo-sounder, which incorporated adjustments for sound speed calibration, tide, and draft. The survey vessel was positioned through use of a hip chain and pairs of range poles along a baseline established on Pier 81. Continuous soundings were also recorded along two tracklines parallel to and immediately south of Pier 76. In addition, spot soundings were taken at selected locations under Pier 76.

Hydrology. A hydrology survey of the site was conducted March 23–27, 1989 (Ocean Surveys 1987). On the first day of the field program four Endeco Type 105 in situ recording current meters were placed as shown in Figure 20.2. Water depths at MLW were: Station A—2.1 m, B—2.1 m, C—3.3 m, and D—2.0 m. The meters were set approximately at mid-depth. Additional current readings near surface and near bottom were taken with a direct reading Endeco Type 119 current meter, lowered to selected depths.

Sedimentation. Sedimentation was studied by three methods—sediment traps, staff gauges, and grain size analysis, each of which provided a different piece of information on sediment rates.

Sediment traps were constructed by placing a ten-pound layer of concrete in a heavy gauge plastic bucket (30 cm high and 26 cm in diameter). Eight traps, four under Pier 76 and four in the interpier area, were set on May 28, 1987, and examined for the first time on August 27, 1987. The sediment traps measured the gross accretion of sediment particles falling out of the water column.

Staff gauges were built of 1-in. PVC pipe. The lower 1 m of each pipe was painted with antifouling paint and 1-cm graduations were marked, also with antifouling paint. The gauges (4 underpier, 4 interpier) were pushed into the bottom and their upper ends were secured to prevent movement. The initial reading of the mudline was taken with a remotely operated vehicle (ROV), the MiniRover Mark II. Use of the ROV allowed the readings to be taken in real time and simultaneously taped for later analysis and confirmation. Initial readings were made February 18, 1987, and follow-up readings on July 21 and November 18, 1987.

Sediment chemistry. Sediment samples were taken twice during the 26-month study at each of the 8 Ponar grab stations. Samples were collected from the upper layers of the substratum (0–15 cm) with a Ponar grab sampler. The first set of samples (April 1986) was analyzed in a New York State approved laboratory for heavy metals, petroleum derived hydrocarbons, PCBs, and DDT. The analyses were performed on an EP Extract according to USEPA EP Toxicity procedure (40 CFR Part 261—Appen. II), except oil and grease and petroleum hydrocarbon tests, which were performed on total samples. The second set of samples (September 1986) was also analyzed by the EP Toxicity procedure. A complete pesticide scan was included in the analysis.

Light transmission. Light transmission was measured four times during the program with a Li-Cor meter at interpier locations and near the center of the underpier area. Measurements were taken above the water surface and at 10 cm intervals below the surface. Readings were made on April 29 and November 13, 1986, September 10 and November 17, 1987.

RESULTS

Interpier Trawls

Results of the interpier trawls are presented in Table 20.1. The most abundant species was the Atlantic silverside although its small size and tendency to school (Bigelow and Schroeder 1953) disproportionately influences the counts. The dominant species was the striped bass, which occurred in 55% of the trawl samples and represented 18% of the catch. Other major species were the summer flounder with a frequency of 42% and a winter flounder with a frequency of 39%. American eel, alewife, American shad, Atlantic tomcod, white perch, and hogchokers all occurred in more than 10% of the samples. Of the 36 species taken, 14 can be considered as minor or incidental species, each representing numerically less than one % of the catch.

Average CPUE ranged from a low of 25.0 fish per trawl at T-7 to a high of 38.4 fish per trawl at T-4. Some species appeared to prefer certain locations—for example, white perch were most abundant at T-4 and least abundant at T-2. Striped bass were encountered most often at T-3, T-4, and T-7, and least often at T-2, T-5, and T-6. Winter flounder showed a strong preference for T-6, which is located along the channel edge. Overall the transects had similar numbers of species.

The number of species taken at the on-site transects (T-2 to T-6) ranged from 3 in January 1988 to 17 in August 1986, with an average of 9. Striped bass were found in 96% of the 25 months sampled. Winter flounder occurred in 92% and summer flounder and tomcod

TABLE 20.1.
Summary of 30-ft otter trawl catch data.

Taxa	Occurrence* (Percent of Samples)	Total Caught	Percent of Total
American eel	16.2	227	2.03
Blueback herring	0.3	1	0.01
Alewife	18.6	1,284	11.47
American shad	10.5	193	1.72
Atlantic menhaden	3.0	18	0.16
Atlantic herring	9.5	75	0.67
Rainbow smelt	4.7	30	0.27
Oyster toadfish	0.3	1	0.01
Goosefish	0.3	1	0.01
Atlantic tomcod	26.4	1,111	9.93
White hake	0.3	3	0.93
Spotted hake	1.4	25	0.22
Silver hake	1.4	5	0.04
Red Hake	0.3	2	0.02
Atlantic silverside	33.1	3,516	31.41
Northern pipefish	3.4	11	0.10
Lined seahorse	0.3	1	0.01
White perch	32.1	972	8.68
Striped bass	55.1	2,005	17.91
Bluefish	7.8	50	0.45
Atlantic moonfish	0.7	2	0.02
Weakfish	0.7	14	0.13
Northern kingfish	0.3	1	0.01
Atlantic croaker	2.0	15	0.13
Scup	0.3	1	0.01
Striped mullet	0.7	2	0.02
Atlantic mackerel	0.3	1	0.01
Butterfish	5.1	40	0.36
Northern searobin	2.4	15	0.13
Striped searobin	1.0	3	0.03
Searobin spp.	1.0	3	0.03
Grubby	1.7	6	0.05
Summer flounder	41.6	563	5.03
Windowpane	2.0	6	0.05
Winter flounder	38.5	435	3.89
Hogchoker	13.9	507	4.53
Unidentified Ictalurid	0.3	1	0.01
Unidentified species	2.7	47	0.42
Total number, all taxa:		11,193	

*Percent of trawls, out of 312, in which the species was recorded occurred in 72% of the sampling months. Monthly CPUE data for off-site and on-site areas are compared in Figure 20.3.

Comparison Trawls

The final method of underpier trawling was developed in July 1986. The data presented here are from August 1986 through March 1988, during which time 309 tows were made under the pier and 309 concurrent tows were made in the interpier area.

A total of 249 fish was caught, 166 under the pier and 83 in the interpier area. Species caught included summer flounder, winter flounder, white perch, American eel, alewife, striped bass, Atlantic tomcod, and Atlantic silverside, all of which were also caught in the large otter trawl.

White perch was the most abundant species in the underpier samples with 99 specimens representing 60% of the underpier catch. The next most abundant species was the winter flounder (23 fish, 14% of the total). The most abundant species in the interpier collections was the striped bass (33 fish, 39% of the catch), followed by the white perch with 15 fish representing 18% of the total. Figure 20.4 provides a monthly summary of CPUE in the UP/IP samples.

Interpier Gill Nets

The number of fish caught in the gill nets in the interpier zone ranged from 58 in May 1986 to none in several months. Species caught included striped bass, summer flounder, Atlantic menhaden, bluefish, hogchoker, winter flounder, and American eel, all of which were also taken in the interpier trawls.

Gill net sets consisted of two nets set at right angles to each other. Over the 22 months sampled, a total of 249 fish was collected. The east-west net, which was perpendicular to the current, accounted for 94 fish while the north-south net caught 155 fish.

UP/IP Comparison Gill Nets

The 20 gill net sets yielded a total of 101 fish, 12 in the underpier nets and 89 in the interpier sets. White perch accounted for 66% of the catch; the next most abundant species were striped bass (14%) and Atlantic herring (13%). The majority of the fish (77%) was collected in November 1987.

Benthic Grab Survey Baseline Study

Approximately 80 taxa were found in the 324 grab samples. The mean quarterly number of taxa and density of macroinvertebrates is given

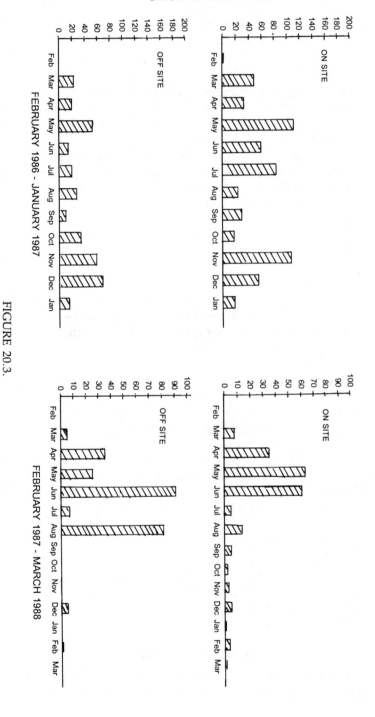

FIGURE 20.3.
Monthly summary of otter trawl catches. a. February 1986–January 1987; b. February 1987–March 1988.

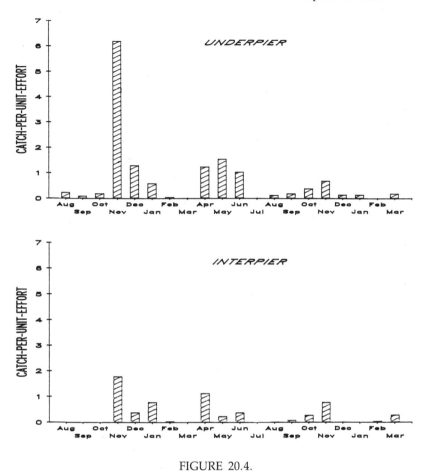

FIGURE 20.4.
Interpier/underpier summary August 1986–March 1988.

in Table 20.2. The relatively low number of taxa in the April samples may be the result of using a 1 mm mesh sieve (rather than 0.5 mm mesh) for these samples. The highest number of taxa in April 1986 was found at B-4. In June 1986 it was at UP-1, in September 1986 it was at B-5, and in December 1986 it was at UP-1 again. In April 1986 the densities ranged from 232 to 5,090/m^2 but these may also have been biased downward by the use of the 1.0 mm sieve.

Also in April 1986, the lowest density was at UP-1, but this may be due to the lower sampling efficiency of the petite Ponar. Densities in the June 1986 samples ranged from 1,700/m^2 at station B-3 to

TABLE 20.2.
Benthic invertebrate summary analysis: baseline survey April 1986–March 1988.

Sta	Apr	Jun	Sep	Dec	Mar	Jun	Sep	Dec	Mar	Mean
						Number of Taxa				
UP1	7	17	21	28	29	19	24	20	20	21
B-2	10	11	22	26	30	10	20	20	33	20
B-3	10	12	16	19	22	19	18	16	31	18
B-4	14	11	20	23	—	19	22	25	27	20
B-5	9	14	22	19	25	23	27	26	29	22
B-6	10	13	16	20	22	19	24	25	29	20
B-7	10	8	18	22	25	20	20	23	22	19
B-8	11	15	15	18	19	16	26	22	31	19
UP9	—	—	—	—	23	20	26	26	27	24

Sta	Apr	Jun	Sep	Dec	Mar	Jun	Sep	Dec	Mar	Mean
					Estimated Abundance (Number/square meter)					
UP1	232	60,352	42,733	41,460	21,040	8,447	30,473	22,347	13,587	26,741
B-2	2,030	5,147	31,740	30,153	9,907	187	5,253	12,047	6,600	11,452
B-3	780	1,700	5,553	6,673	3,407	3,040	5,113	8,000	7,820	4,676
B-4	3,765	8,100	27,880	14,593	—	10,347	7,533	6,660	4,907	10,473
B-5	1,510	48,627	53,247	34,660	33,940	19,067	13,853	14,260	11,460	25,625
B-6	1,353	14,960	39,787	21,640	18,500	23,873	19,633	17,313	14,413	19,052
B-7	1,647	5,800	18,707	13,747	13,213	8,320	3,860	6,560	5,687	8,616
B-8	5,090	35,927	76,140	36,507	27,893	21,967	9,380	11,933	15,333	26,686
UP9	—	—	—	—	18,700	18,960	18,373	12,660	5,307	14,800

Number of Taxa

Sta	Apr	Jun	Sep	Dec	Mar	Jun	Sep	Dec	Mar	Mean
UP1	2.20	1.92	2.08	2.28	2.71	1.86	2.79	1.84	1.62	2.14
B-2	2.32	1.35	1.27	1.99	3.21	2.61	1.18	2.30	2.91	2.13
B-3	2.35	1.72	1.55	2.33	2.44	2.02	2.09	2.01	2.73	2.14
B-4	1.51	0.65	1.20	1.92	—	1.50	2.81	2.63	3.33	1.94
B-5	1.86	1.75	2.18	1.98	1.18	1.15	2.83	2.85	3.03	2.09
B-6	2.46	0.63	0.52	1.22	1.22	0.85	1.57	1.99	2.16	1.40
B-7	1.99	0.90	1.11	1.86	1.88	1.70	2.55	2.76	3.11	1.98
B-8	1.48	1.02	1.03	1.39	1.51	1.10	2.65	2.87	2.70	1.75
UP9	—	—	—	—	2.00	1.91	2.56	2.99	2.94	2.48

Species diversity: Shannon-Weaver Index, log to the base 2 version.

Dominance

Sta	Apr	Jun	Sep	Dec	Mar	Jun	Sep	Dec	Mar	Mean
UP1	66	76	77	72	56	76	44	80	84	70.1
B-2	65	88	94	83	43	61	92	62	63	72.3
B-3	66	79	89	67	72	82	81	77	62	75.0
B-4	83	94	98	84	—	93	56	68	47	77.9
B-5	80	76	70	79	91	94	61	61	55	74.1
B-6	61	95	98	92	94	95	92	81	78	87.3
B-7	73	94	99	86	86	90	68	51	46	77.0
B-8	84	94	97	93	90	94	70	49	62	81.4
UP9	—	—	—	—	76	78	61	52	54	64.2

Dominance: Percent composition of the two most numerous species found in the station's samples.

60,352/m² at UP-1. In September 1986 densities ranged from 5,553 at B-3 to 76,140 at B-8. Finally, December 1986 samples ranged from 6,673/m² at B-3 to 41,460/m² at UP-1. During 1986 the highest total macroinvertebrate densities were at stations UP-1, B-5, and B-8. Station B-3 had consistently low densities.

Densities during 1987 and March 1988 were variable at each station and over time. During March 1987 station B-3 had the lowest density (3,040) and B-5 the highest (33,940). In June B-2 had only 187 organisms/m² while B-6 had 23,873. In September the lowest density (3,860) was at B-7 and the highest (30,473) was at UP-1. December samples ranged from a low of 6,560 at B-7 to a high of 22,347 at UP-1. Finally, in March 1988, B-4 had a low of 4,907 and B-8 had the highest numbers with 15,333 per square meter.

Over the nine-quarter study period, stations UP-1 and B-8 had the greatest density of macroinvertebrates and stations B-3 and B-7 had the lowest.

Of the 80 taxa collected from the nine stations during the nine sampling periods, 55 were found in the underpier samples and 76 in the interpier samples. Overall the mean number of taxa was 44.5 at the underpier stations and 48.7 at the interpier stations. It should be noted that UP-1 was initiated in March 1987, hence covers only part of the study period.

Mean density for the underpier stations was 20,805 organisms/m² and for the interpier stations it was 15,481. The numbers at the interpier station ranged from 4,669 to 27,513 organisms/m².

Colonization Samples

Colonization samples were recovered from locations C-2 and C-3 after 12, 29, and 37 weeks of exposure. Samples were collected from C-1 after 17 and 25 weeks. The eight samples yielded 25 taxa and the number of taxa in a sample ranged from 9 to 17. The highest number was found in June; the lowest in December. Total density estimates also followed this pattern, ranging from a high of 236,656/m² at C-2 in June to a low of 19,300/m² at C-3 in December. The differences in total number of taxa and density among stations were not consistent, although C-2 consistently had the highest density of organisms.

Water Quality

The average monthly temperature (all transects combined) ranged from 1.3°C in February 1986 to 24.6°C in July 1987. The average salinity ranged from 3.8 o/oo in October 1987 to 18.7 o/oo in September

1986. Dissolved oxygen ranged from 13.0 ppm in February 1988 to 3.5 ppm in August 1986. The Secchi depth averaged 0.77 m.

Bathymetry

Depths within the study area ranged from 3.0 to 27.0 ft MLW. Most of the interpier area was fairly uniform in depth and ranged from 6 to 12 ft. Depths increased rapidly at the pierhead line. Channel depths are 60 to 70 ft. The underpier area appeared to have the same water depths as the interpier area although fewer soundings were taken. The mean tidal range of the site is 4.3 ft.

Hydrology

Currents at the Hudson River Center site are tidally dominated and generally parallel to shore with primary flows to the northeast during flood tide and to the southwest during ebb tide. The site lies outside the main flow of the river and within the shelter of pierhead line. As a result current speeds are considerably lower than typically reported for the central sections of the lower Hudson River.

The outer stations (A and C on Figure 20.2) are farthest from shore and nearest the main Hudson flow. Consequently they had the strongest currents with speeds exceeding 10 cm/sec during 57–60% of the record. In contrast the stations nearest the shore (B and D) had speeds in excess of 10 cm/sec only 45 to 48% of the time.

Currents were strongest at station C, where speeds exceeded 20 cm/sec during 13% of the record. Currents at A, B, and D, exceeded 20 cm/sec only 6, 5, and 1% of the time, respectively. This is due to the greater exposure of station C to ebb tidal currents, while station A is partially sheltered from ebb currents by vessels secured to Pier 81 to the north.

Peak ebb and peak flood current speeds are of equal magnitude at stations A and C. At B maximum current speeds occur during flood tide, whereas Pier 81 shelters station B during ebb tide. Currents at station D were somewhat higher on the ebb than during the flood tide, as a result of its exposure to the north.

Directional changes due to tidal reversal occur very abruptly at all stations. Current speeds decrease briefly to less than 5 cm/sec, then increase quickly as the current direction reverses.

Vertical profiles indicate that current speeds and directions are fairly uniform throughout the water column except during tidal reversals when directions are in transition and speeds drop.

Velocity readings from underpier stations (C and D) were compared to corresponding interpier stations (A and B) for the period 0700 to 1830, March 25, 1987. This time period was selected as being representative of the entire data set. Mean values of 24 half-hour velocity readings were as follows:

		Underpier			Interpier
	Station	velocity cm/sec		Station	velocity cm/sec
Offshore	C	14.8		A	13.6
Inshore	D	10.8		B	9.8

During this tidal cycle, the data indicate that the current flows under the pier are marginally greater than those in the interpier zone.

The width of Pier 76 is approximately 76 m. Assuming an average velocity of 14.8 and 10.8 cm/sec, we calculate the transit time for the underpier area to be 8.6 minutes at station C and 11.7 minutes at station D.

Sedimentation

Of the eight traps set, one underpier and 4 interpier traps were recovered. The other three were lost when ice cut the tether lines. The underpier trap had a sediment load of 20 cm. This trap was the one set nearest the bulkhead. An accumulation of 20 cm over a 90-day period indicated a gross accretion rate of 0.222 cm/day or 81 cm per year. The interpier traps (from near bulkhead to pierhead) showed accretions of 13, 13, 15, and 16 cm, a mean rate of 0.158 cm/day or 58 cm/year.

Staff gauges were examined on July 21, 1987, 153 days after placement. Eight staff gauges were originally placed. Two (one underpier, one interpier) were lost. Both underpier and interpier results were highly variable. Interpier rates ranged from very low net scouring to very high net sedimentation. Staff gauges from underpier revealed low to very high net sedimentation rates.

Sediment Chemistry

Sediment samples were taken on April 3 and September 17, 1986. Most of the parameters tested were at or below detection limits.

Light Transmission

Light transmission readings were taken four times: April 4 and November 13, 1986, September 10 and November 17, 1987. The readings were highly variable with interpier air (0 cm) readings 175 to

1,300 microeinsteins (μe), depending on sky conditions. Light transmission under the pier was essentially zero. Light transmission in the interpier zone ranged from 12 μe or less at 150 cm depth on three occasions to 220 μe on September 10, 1987, when the water was exceptionally clear.

DISCUSSION

The large otter trawl was much more successful for collecting fishes than stationary gear such as gill nets. Other survey programs in New York harbor have also found this to be true (Cantelmo et al. 1985) although the same gill nets fished in Long Island Sound usually captured large numbers of resident and transient fishes. It may be that trash and detritus in the harbor foul the nets, allowing the fish to avoid entanglement.

We believe that the otter trawl is highly efficient for collecting in the interpier areas. The heavy footrope scrapes the upper sediment layers and even collects surface macroinvertebrates. The headrope, buoyed by floats, stays approximately 8 ft above the bottom, and since the trawl was usually towed in 8 to 12 feet of water, it sampled a large fraction of the water column.

As with many multiyear fisheries studies, the results varied from year to year. The most striking variation was the difference in fish collected between September 1986 and March 1987, and the corresponding period, September 1987 through March 1988.

Seasonal differences in density and species composition of benthic invertebrates in grab samples were pronounced. The increase in number of taxa from April to December possibly reflects the recruitment of species throughout the warmer months, with the highest number of species occurring in the fall. Species density was highest at most stations in September 1986, then declined somewhat in December. June densities, however, were almost as high, even slightly higher at stations UP-1, B-5, and B-8. The results of the 1987 benthic sampling program indicate that the overall species density declined from the 1986 values and then remained at an approximately constant level. Other investigators noted peak microinvertebrate densities (200,000 organisms/m^2) in late spring (COE 1984). While densities at UP-1 did peak at 60,352/m^2 in late spring, most peaks were observed in September 1986 (up to 76,140 individuals/m^2 at station B-8). The magnitude of density is not directly comparable to the COE study because of the inclusion of nematodes in their figures. These meiofaunal forms were not sampled in the present study. Samples collected during the cooler months of April and December had the highest diversity (and the lowest dominance). Possibly because of low oxygen levels during the summer months fewer species are able to survive. The preponderance of only a few species that are tolerant of low oxygen levels would depress the species diversity measure.

We found no differences in density, number of taxa, species diversity, or dominance between the benthic fauna of the underpier and interpier zones. Slight trends are present but they do not seem to be statistically significant. The soft clam (*Mya arenaria*) was almost always most abundant in the underpier samples. One species of isopod was also more prevalent underpier but not strikingly so. The densities of other species were similar at the interpier and underpier stations. Overall, the results obtained from the present study show that the site area exhibits species composition and seasonal trends similar to other lower Hudson River study areas (COE 1984).

The most abundant finfish obtained in the present study was the Atlantic silverside. Bay anchovy (which has a similar appearance) is also a dominant forage fish (Bigelow and Schroeder 1953). Both typically occur in schools. For large collections, identifications are made on subsets rather than the entire collection and it is possible that some bay anchovies were collected and included in the silverside count, although our preserved collections do not show this to be the case. Bigelow and Schroeder (1953) state that schools of silversides are made up of similar sized individuals, and are found in shallow water, which agrees with the findings of the present study.

There is a great amount of data on striped bass in the Hudson, both from the Westside Highway project and from steam electric generating station studies. It is obvious from the present study that striped bass inhabit the interpier and underpier zones. The other fish species found were typical for the area and indicate that the site is utilized on a transient basis by most species and probably on a semipermanent basis by winter flounder and American eel.

Presented below are the results of the Hudson River Center collections for the same months (although for different years) as the Westway Upper Metro collections. The Hudson River Center data are for December 1986 to March 1987; the Westway data are for December 1982 to March 1983.

Hudson River Center		Westway (Upper Metro)	
Species	% Composition	Species	% Composition
Striped bass	52.5	White perch	37.6

White perch	17.6	Tomcod	22.9
Winter flounder	11.4	Striped bass	19.0
Tomcod	10.3	Winter flounder	8.8
All others	9.6	All others	11.7

Comparison of the two data sets reveals that the same four species made up 90.4 and 88.3% of the total respective collections. Given the high degree of variability in finfish collections, this is a good correlation. It indicates that the Hudson River Center finfish populations are similar to populations encountered at the locations studied during the Westway program.

The UP/IP trawl collections show that American eel, white perch, and winter flounder were collected more often in the underpier environment areas, whereas alewife and striped bass were collected more often in the interpier zone.

In contrast to the UP/IP trawl samples, the UP/IP comparison gill net survey yielded more fish from the interpier zone than under the pier but because of small sample sizes it is not possible the assess the statistical significance of this difference or to judge whether the difference is due to small sample size or greater efficiency of the trawl.

ROBERT WILL
LEONARD J. HOUSTON

21

Fish Distribution Survey of Newark Bay, New Jersey, May 1987–April 1988

ABSTRACT

A fish distribution survey was conducted in Newark Bay, New Jersey, from May 1987 to April 1988 to establish a baseline data base prior to deepening of the federal navigation channel in Newark Bay and Kill Van Kull, both of which are part of the Hudson Raritan estuary system. Samples were taken monthly for the entire sampling period. Newark Bay supports substantial fish populations. Fishes, especially tomcod and winter flounder, the most common species in the area, were more abundant in the navigation channel than in the shallows. Abundance seems to be more closely correlated with depth than with oxygen, salinity, or temperature. Newark bay is a significant nursery area for the young of several species and Port Newark channel is an overwintering area for striped bass and white perch.

INTRODUCTION

In response to a congressional resolution, the New York District of the U.S. Army Corps of Engineers (the Corps) was charged with studying the feasibility of deepening the Newark Bay and Kill van Kull navigation channels (Figure 21.1). As part of the feasibility study, the impact of the deepening project on fish and other marine organisms has to be evaluated. There has been little recent work on the fisheries of Newark Bay although in 1983-84 the area was sampled as part of a larger wintertime study of fish distribution in the New York harbor/Lower Bay area (USACE-NYD and USDOT 1984) and additional sampling was conducted in 1984-85 as part of a year-long New York harbor survey (USFWS 1985; Woodhead and McAfferty 1986). Both surveys indicated that a viable fish population existed in Newark Bay at that time, but because of differences in gear and time of sampling, it was not possible to differentiate between relative use of shallow and channel habitats in Newark Bay. This, in part, led to concerns expressed by the U.S. Fish and Wildlife Service that the deepening project might lead to loss of shallow water habitat used by fish. The present study was designed to document fish distribution patterns before the deepening of the Newark Bay/Kill van Kull navigation channel, and also to provide a comparison of channel versus shallow habitat. It is the intention of the Corps to survey the same area again after dredging, in order to determine what effects, if any, the deepening project has on fish in the area.

MATERIALS AND METHODS

Otter trawl and gill net samples were taken each month from May 1987 to April 1988 from the New Jersey turnpike bridge to the abandoned railroad bridge at the mouth of Newark Bay (Figure 21.1). Otter trawl samples were taken in the main navigation channel (samples TA and NB3), in the Port Newark deep water spur channel (NB2) and on the adjacent shallows on both sides of the main channel (samples T2-T5). Gill net stations were located only on the shallow flats, some close to the shallow water otter trawl sites (GN6, GN9, GN11, GNA, and GNB). Because of heavy ship traffic it was not possible to set gill nets in the navigation channels. A total of 7 otter trawl stations (3 channel and 4 shallow) and 5 gill net stations were sampled monthly for one year.

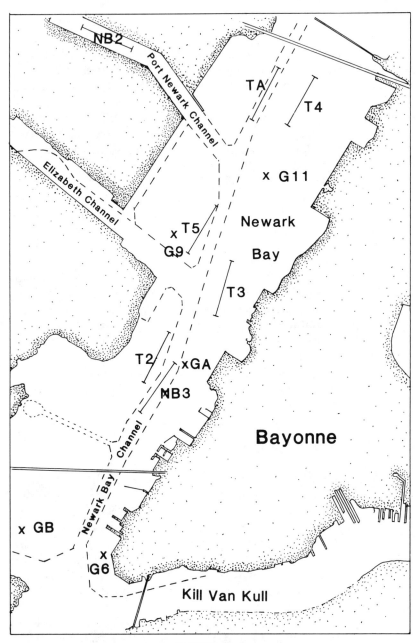

FIGURE 21.1.
Newark Bay study area.

The otter trawls had 30 ft mouth openings with 32 by 16 in. steel reinforced wooden doors. Five-minute tows were made against the tide. Mesh size was one in. in the main body with a ¼ in. liner in the cod end. Fishes collected ranged in size from a 33 mm bay anchovy to a 1003 mm striped bass.

The gill nets were polypropylene "experimental" nets 60 ft long and 8 ft high with three equal sections of 1¼, 1¾, and 2¼ in. mesh. Nets were set just off the bottom with 15 pound anchors and left to fish overnight (approximately 24 hours). All fish were identified, measured (total length), and anomalous features were recorded. Blueclaw crabs were also counted, measured, and sexed. A hydrolab Surveyor II system calibrated before each day's use was used to determine dissolved oxygen (mg/L), pH, salinity (measured directly as ppt), and temperature just before each otter trawl and immediately before retrieval of each gill net. The depth at which the parameters were taken was recorded and correlated with the depth of the fish sample.

RESULTS

Total Catch and Seasonal Abundance

The species caught are listed by gear in Table 21.1. A total of 8100 fish representing 38 species was caught during the survey. Monthly abundances of fishes caught in trawls (Figure 21.2) show a peak in late June, with a steady decline, to a winter low in January and February. The number of species caught follows the same general trend (Figure 21.3). Both figures, however, show a decrease in July that is contradictory to the overall trend.

Only 12 species and 5.5% of the combined catch were taken in gill nets. The Atlantic menhaden was clearly the most abundant species in the gill nets, making up more than 91% of the catch. Striped bass (3.0%) and Atlantic tomcod (2.3%) were the only other species taken in any numbers (Table 21.2). Three species, Atlantic tomcod, bay anchovy, and winter flounder, together made up nearly 88% of the total trawl catch. The next most abundant species was the spotted hake (3.8%). Eight other species each accounted for ½ to 1% of the catch and the remaining 23 species together made up only about 3% of the total trawl catch. Table 21.3 lists the monthly trawl catches for the twelve most abundant species.

All species caught in the gill nets except the Atlantic herring were also caught in trawls. The predominant species in gill nets, the

TABLE 21.1.
List of species caught in Newark Bay by all gear.

Species	Otter Trawl	Gill Net
Alewife *(Alosa pseudoharengus)*	X	X
American eel *(Anguilla rostrata)*	X	X
American shad *(Alosa sapidissima)*	X	X
Atlantic herring *(Clupea harengus)*		X
Atlantic menhaden *(Brevoortia tyrannus)*	X	X
Atlantic silverside *(Menidia menidia)*	X	
Atlantic tomcod *(Microgadus tomcod)*	X	X
Bay anchovy *(Anchoa mitchilli)*	X	
Blueback herring *(Alosa aestivalis)*	X	
Blueclaw crab *(Callinectes sapidus)*	X	X
Bluefish *(Pomatomus saltatrix)*	X	X
Butterfish *(Peprilus triacanthus)*	X	
Grubby *(Myoxocephalus aenaeus)*	X	
Hogchoker *(Trinectes maculatus)*	X	
Northern pipefish *(Syngnathus fuscus)*	X	
Northern puffer *(Sphoeroides maculatus)*	X	
Northern sea robin *(Prionotus carolinus)*	X	
Pinfish *(Lagodon rhomboides)*	X	
Pumpkinseed *(Lepomis gibbosus)*	X	
Red hake *(Urophycis)*	X	
Scup *(Stenotomus chrysops)*	X	
Seahorse *(Hippocampus sp.)*	X	
Silver hake *(Merluccius bilinearis)*	X	
Smallmouth flounder *(Etropus microstomus)*	X	
Smooth flounder *(Liopsetta putnami)*	X	
Spotted hake *(Urophycis regius)*	X	
Striped anchovy *(Anchoa hepsetus)*	X	
Striped bass *(Morone saxatilis)*	X	X
Striped killifish *(Fundulus majalis)*	X	
Striped sea robin *(Prionotus evolans)*	X	
Summer flounder *(Paralichthys dentatus)*	X	
Unidentified flatfish *(Order Pleuronectiformes)*	X	
Unidentified sculpin *(Family Cottidae)*	X	
Unidentified stickleback *(Family Gasterosteidae)*	X	
Weakfish *(Cynoscion regalis)*	X	
White hake *(Urophycis tenuis)*	X	
White perch *(Morone americana)*	X	X
Windowpane *(Scophthalmus aquosus)*	X	
Winter flounder *(Pseudopleuronectes americanus)*	X	X

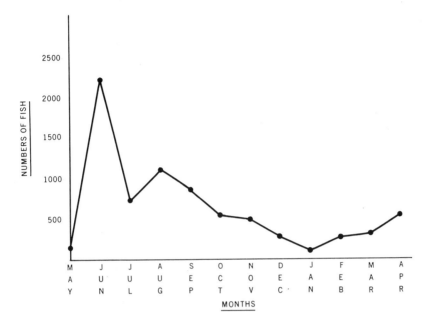

FIGURE 21.2.
Total monthly abundances of all fish caught by trawl.

Atlantic menhaden, made up only 1% of the trawl catch, while the two most abundant trawl species (tomcod and winter flounder) accounted for only 3% of the gill net catch.

Size and Age Distribution

Tomcod were first captured in large numbers in June. These fish averaged 82 mm total length (range 30 to 245 mm). Only 2.5% were longer than 160 mm and therefore most of them were young-of-the-year from the 1987 winter spawning (Hardy 1978; Smith 1986). Young-of-the-year fish continued to dominate the catch through the summer and fall, with the average size increasing to 161 mm by December. Assuming a minimum size at maturity of 170 mm (Hardy 1978), most of the fish in the December catch were at or near maturity, and field notes indicate that many were gravid. However, catches during the height of the tomcod spawning season in the Hudson (January–February; Smith 1986) were near zero in Newark Bay. During March the tomcod reappeared in trawl catches with an average size of 185

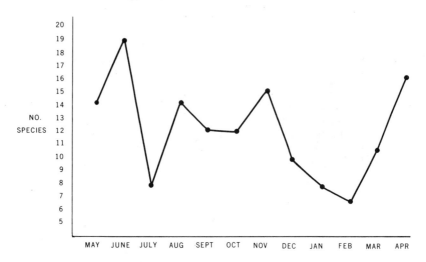

FIGURE 21.3.
Total number of species caught in trawls, by month.

mm (110–265 mm). Therefore, these were second-year fish from the 1987 spawning.

Winter flounder also appear first in the June trawls, ranging in size from 40 to 259 mm, with an average total length of 153 mm. Nearly all (93%) were 70–230 mm, suggesting that they were second-year juveniles spawned in 1986 (Bigelow and Schroeder 1953; Martin 1978); no mature adults were caught in June. By October the trawl catches could be divided into two distinct size groups. Approximately one-third were under 100 mm, and therefore probably YOY from the 1987 spawning. The proportion of this size class increased during the ensuing month becoming the major component by January, when their size ranged from 55 to 99 mm. By April this group had grown to 80–159 mm and the larger second-year fish were essentially absent from the catches.

The bay anchovy was the third most abundant fish, also becoming numerous in the June trawl catches. The June fish ranged in total length from 50 to 89 (average 70) mm and were probably adults from an early 1987 spawning (Jones et al. 1978). Late summer and fall catches contained smaller fish, with 93% of the August catch ranging in size from 40 to 59 mm. More than 80% of the September and October catches were in the 40–60 mm range and were probably from

TABLE 21.2.
Monthly gill net catches of the three most abundant species caught in Newark Bay.

Species	May	Jun	Jul	Aug	Sep	Oct	Nov	Dec	Jan	Feb	Mar	Apr
Atlantic menhaden	39	46	53	71	83	0	1	1	0	0	0	26
Striped bass	1	4	1	0	1	0	3	2	0	0	0	0
Atlantic tomcod	1	0	0	0	0	0	3	2	0	0	0	2

a second spawning in 1987. There may also be a third spawning, as the October catch has a sizable number (11.5%) of fish less than 40 mm long.

Striped bass were rarely caught before October, when 13 YOY (from the 1987 spawning) ranging in length from 100 to 180 mm were caught in trawls. Catches in November (7 fish) and December (4 fish) were small, and included YOY from trawls and larger fish (more than 220 mm) from gill nets. The latter were probably yearlings from the 1986 season. The largest catches of striped bass (up to 37 fish) occurred in the winter trawls. These were mostly YOY 60 to 190 mm long; only three yearlings were included. Only one possibly mature fish, 1003 mm, was caught during the entire survey.

White perch were common only in the January and March trawls. They ranged in total length from 80 to 220 mm. Most (93.5%) were 100 to 200 mm long and were probably immature second-year fish (Hardy 1978; MPI 1982; Smith 1986) from the 1986 spawning.

The menhaden was the only species taken in large numbers by gill nets. They ranged from 210 to 340 mm (average 262). Gill net catches were consistent throughout the summer (44 to 68 fish per month), with trawl catches becoming higher in July (45 fish) and August (15 fish). Fish caught by both types of gear were similar in size with total lengths from 150 to 339 (ave. 240) mm. Eighty-eight percent of the catch was between 220 and 279 mm total length and all were probably mature 3-year-old fish from the 1985 spawning (Bigelow and Schroeder 1953; Jones et al. 1978). Menhaden were absent from fall and winter catches, reappearing in the April 1988 samples, when they averaged 297 mm (range 220–359 mm).

Alewife and blueback herring were captured in lesser numbers and over a shorter time span than the menhaden. The alewife was common (19 fish) in the May trawl catches, when it averaged 131 mm

TABLE 21.3.
Monthly abundances of the twelve most common species of fish caught by trawl in Newark Bay.

Species	May	Jun	Jul	Aug	Sep	Oct	Nov	Dec	Jan	Feb	Mar	Apr
Atlantic tomcod	5	1441	183	248	62	128	375	93	1	0	45	82
Bay anchovy	17	490	372	750	678	242	1	9	0	0	0	0
Winter flounder	15	250	106	59	38	131	128	180	25	262	160	165
Spotted hake	0	3	0	0	0	0	0	0	0	0	33	256
Striped bass	1	5	1	1	5	13	7	4	37	9	19	1
White perch	0	0	0	0	5	0	1	1	26	0	50	0
Atlantic menhaden	32	54	99	87	84	0	1	1	0	0	0	26
Blueback herring	14	0	0	0	0	56	15	0	0	0	0	6
Grubby	4	3	0	0	0	0	0	11	5	10	15	4
Alewife	19	2	5	0	0	5	10	3	0	0	1	0
Red hake	0	0	0	0	0	0	1	1	1	1	4	32
Bluefish	0	0	7	15	31	0	0	0	0	0	0	0

in total length (range 100–209 mm). By the next month the numbers were sharply reduced (2 fish) and none were taken during the rest of the summer. The fall trawl catches included a few alewife (3–10 fish) with zero catches from January to the end of the survey. Most of the small spring and fall catches were probably two- and three-year-old juveniles though a few might have been small mature fish (Jones et al. 1978; Smith 1986). The blueback has a similar pattern of spring and fall presence in the bay, but they were more abundant. The May catch (15 fish) averaged 112 mm (90–219). October (56) and November (15) fish were smaller, averaging 79 mm (60–99 mm). These smaller fish from the fall trawl samples were YOY from that year's upstream spawning, whereas the larger fish were most likely juveniles 2 or 3 years old (1986 or 1985 spawning) (Jones et al. 1978).

Spotted and red hake were caught in substantial numbers only in the spring 1988 trawls; they were both absent in the May 1987 catches. The spotted hake was the most abundant, with 33 fish in March and 256 in April. These fish averaged 137 mm TL (range 70–201). This is too small for maturity, thus they are probably in their second year (1987 spawning) (Hardy et al. 1978). Red hake catch was highest in April (32 fish), when they averaged 141 mm, with a range of 90 to 229 mm. This would suggest that they were also in their second year (Hardy et al. 1978).

Grubby were mostly caught in the winter (5–15 fish from December to March). They ranged in size from 30 to 110 mm in December (ave. 82 mm). The average in April (4 fish) was only 76 mm.

Bluefish were caught only in summer trawls. They ranged from 45 to 196 mm. The average total length was 105 mm in July and 110 mm in September. These were probably juveniles in their second year from the 1976 spawning (Hardy 1978).

Depth Distribution

Table 21.4 is a comparison of the average trawl catches from the undredged shallows (generally less than 10 ft deep) and the dredged navigation channel, in which depth is maintained at 35 ft. A comparison is also made between the main channel (Stations TA and NB3) that runs north and south through the length of the bay and a spur channel (NB2). This distinction was made because the spur channel is perpendicular to the main tidal and current direction. It passes almost entirely through a major cargo facility (Port Newark) and dead ends after one and a half miles. Circulation and currents might be expected to be lower than in the main channel. The com-

TABLE 21.4.
Total catch, percent composition, and average catch by habitat of the twelve most abundant fish species captured by trawl in Newark Bay.

Species	Number Caught	Percent Catch	Channel (Average)	Interpier (Average)	Shallow (Average)
Atlantic tomcod	2634	34.4	80.0	60.2	4.4
Bay anchovy	2519	32.9	0.6	11.4	49.6
Winter flounder	1578	20.6	60.0	1.0	4.9
Spotted hake	293	3.8	11.3	1.1	0
Striped bass	90	1.2	1.2	2.6	0.8
White perch	77	1.0	0.2	6.6	0
Atlantic menhaden	73	1.0	2.8	0.9	0
Blueback herring	50	0.7	0	0	1.0
Grubby	43	0.6	1.4	0.1	0.2
Alewife	41	0.5	0.4	0.4	0.6
Red hake	40	0.5	1.7	0.2	0
Bluefish	38	0.5	0.6	0	0.5

Channel = stations TA, NB3
Interpier = stations NB2
Shallow = stations T2, T3, T4, T5

parison in Table 21.4 is based on average trawl catches since the numbers of samples were different in the three habitats.

Table 21.4 reveals that 8 of the 12 most abundant species were more abundant in the navigation channels than in the shallows. Twice as many striped bass and 30 times as many white perch were caught in the spur channel as in the main channel. Six species—winter flounder, spotted hake, red hake, grubby, Atlantic menhaden, and Atlantic tomcod—occurred more frequently in the main channel than in the spur. The differences ranged from 25% more Atlantic tomcod to 60 times as many winter flounder. Two species showed a higher average catch in the shallows; about four times as many bay anchovy were caught in the shallows as in the channels, and all the blueback herring were taken in the shallows. Two species, alewife and bluefish, showed no distinct difference in average trawl catches among the three habitats.

In general, the distribution was similar regardless of the age of the fish. However, nearly all YOY winter flounder were taken in the shallows whereas older juveniles (130 to 150 mm) dominated the channel catches. YOY striped bass are caught mostly in the shallows

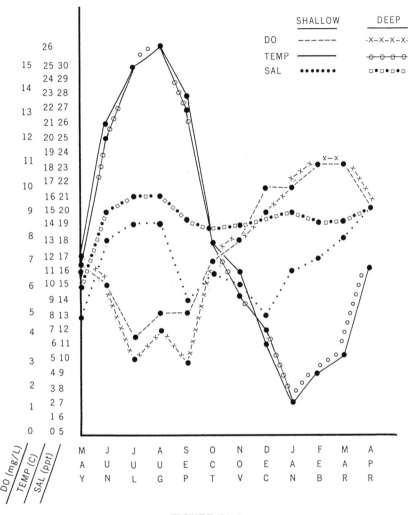

FIGURE 21.4.
Comparison of monthly mean temperature, dissolved oxygen, and salinity of shallow and deep water Newark Bay habitats.

during the fall and mostly in the channels, especially the spur channel, in the winter.

Figure 21.4 compares the physical parameters of the deep and shallow habitats over the course of the study. The spur channel is not separated since its DO and salinity patterns were virtually the same as the main channel. Temperatures were about one degree (C) warmer in the spur channel in the winter. The deeper channels had substantially more saline waters throughout the year. During the summer, the deeper channels had oxygen levels up to 1mg/L lower than the shallows.

Blueclaw Crabs

The monthly abundances of blueclaw crabs captured by all gear are given in Figure 21.5. The numbers of each sex were similar except during May through July when substantially more males were caught. Crab abundance peaked during the fall and dropped off precipitously at the start of winter.

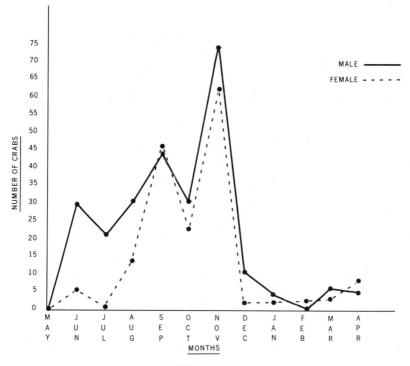

FIGURE 21.5.
Monthly abundances of male and female blueclaw crabs captured in Newark Bay by all gill nets and trawls.

DISCUSSION

The results of the present study are similar to those of the 1984–85 survey that was conducted as a part of a larger program sampling the fishery of New York harbor. Fishes caught in 1984–85 but not in 1987–88 were Atlantic cod, black sea bass, bluegill, carp, cusk eel, hickory shad, lookdown, northern kingfish, rainbow smelt, rock gunnel, spotfin butterflyfish, tautog, and threespine stickleback. Fishes caught in 1987–88 but not in 1984–85 were Atlantic silverside, northern puffer, northern searobin, pinfish, pumpkinseed, red hake, seahorse, smallmouth flounder, smooth flounder, striped anchovy, striped killifish, and white perch (Woodhead, personal communication; USFWS 1985). All the species listed, regardless of which study they were reported from, represent incidental catches of species that are either rare visitors to the bay or inhabit areas that were not sampled efficiently by the gear employed. The red hake might be an exception; 40 hake were caught by our deep channel trawls but none were taken in the high-rise trawl used in the 1984–85 survey. All the red hakes were juveniles, suggesting that the nursery area changed from year to year, possibly as a result of difference in year-class success.

It is also of interest to compare the catches in the main part of the harbor, upper New York Bay, from the previous harbor study with those in Newark Bay. Several species of fish that were caught in substantial numbers in the upper bay (tautog, cunner, Atlantic sturgeon, four-spot flounder, and northern kingfish) were absent from our Newark Bay catches. In view of the proximity of the harbor to the open ocean, and the essentially marine nature of many of these fish, this difference is not surprising. In contrast, we found only incidental catches of fish in Newark Bay that were not collected in the upper bay. This leads to the conclusion that the Newark Bay is an ancillary to the larger harbor fishery, and supports a similar population.

The average otter trawl catches clearly show that for the portion of the population sampled by our gear, fish are more abundant in the Newark Bay navigation channels than in its shallows (Table 21.4). A possible explanation for this lies in the relationship between fish occurrence and physical parameters. Fish abundance does not seem to be correlated with DO levels since these values are almost identical in deep and shallow stations throughout a significant part of the year. There is some variation from June to September when DO levels in the channel averaged between 3 and 4 mg/L and shallow stations averaged 4 to 6 mg/L. This reflects typical summertime estuarine stratification but the deeper channels still had higher catches in spite of the lower DO levels.

Temperature ranged from a high of 26°C in August to a low of 1 to 2°C in January and showed a clear inverse relationship to dissolved oxygen. Temperature readings in channel and shallow stations were very close, even in summertime when dissolved oxygen levels were lower in the channels. Thus the preference for channels cannot be related to temperature.

Salinity differences between deep and shallow stations, however, are quite striking. Although the monthly average salinities ranged from 15 to about 21 ppt in the channels and 13 to 20 in the shallows, deep water salinities were consistently greater. This was particularly apparent from September to February and is the result of estuarine circulation.

It is not possible, given the scope of this study, to assess the relative effects of depth and salinity on fish distribution in Newark Bay. However, since almost all estuarine fish have wide salinity tolerances, it appears that depth is the more important. Woodhead and McAfferty (1986) found more fish in the channels in lower New York bay but could not correlate differences in abundance statistically with salinity differences between the shallows and the channels. Currents may also influence fish distribution but neither our study nor that of Woodhead and McAfferty measured this.

Of the 12 most abundant fish species, eight occurred more frequently in deep channels than in the shallows. These were tomcod, winter flounder, spotted hake, striped bass, white perch, Atlantic menhaden, grubby, and red hake. All of these except the menhaden are benthic fishes to varying degrees. Only one menhaden was caught in the shallow water trawls, compared to 72 fish caught in deep water. This is despite the fact that menhaden were by far the most abundant fish in the gill nets.

Seventy-three of the 77 white perch caught were captured in the spur channel (NB2) and all were caught between December and March, the time of lowest water temperature. This suggests that Port Newark channel is an overwintering area for white perch. This species may be attracted by the relatively higher temperature of the spur channel, which remains about one degree C above that of the main channel or it may prefer the presumably slower currents in this dead-end channel. Both of these conditions would enable the fish to spend less energy to maintain themselves during the winter. Striped bass may also have used the channel for overwintering, moving into the channel from the shallow water stations where they were abundant during the fall. Both species were significantly more abundant in dead-end channels and interpier areas out of the main current flow during a previous winter survey of the harbor (USACE 1984). Neither species is known to spawn in either the Passaic or Hackensack rivers, which empty into the northern part of the bay, therefore it is likely that both groups of juveniles are coming from the Hudson since juveniles of these species are known to move down the Hudson and into the harbor with the onset of cooler water (USACE 1984).

Two of the 12 most common species, the bay anchovy and the alewife, occurred more frequently in the shallows (Table 21.4). Ninety-five percent of the bay anchovies were caught in shallow trawl stations. A possible explanation is that they feed on plankton, which may be concentrated in the upper part of the water column, since Newark Bay is turbid and light is attenuated rapidly. The blueback herring, which were not caught at all in deep trawls, apparently uses the shallows as a nursery area or while in transit from spawning grounds upstream. Both the alewife and blueback herring are schooling species and it is possible that they could have been missed by the trawls.

Red hake and bluefish were the only species that were as abundant in the shallows as in the deeper channels.

The overall pattern of seasonal abundance with its clear peak in late spring reflects the influx of juvenile fish (many YOY) in Newark Bay. Juvenile tomcod average 66 mm in June and increase in size throughout the summer and fall, then disappear as they reach maturity in December and return again in March when their average size is 185 mm. Previous studies summaried by MPI (1982) show that this species moves down the Hudson after spawning and it is possible that part of the population continues into Newark Bay followed by juveniles hatched during the winter that move into the bay later in the spring and use it as a nursery during the summer and fall.

Tomcod and winter flounder account for more than half the yearly catch and they also account for 73% of the fish caught in June. Seventy percent of these fish are juveniles, thus it is clear that a major ecological function of Newark Bay is as a nursery for these species. The preponderance of small fish in the catches of the other species suggests that the bay's role as a nursery is substantial but the relatively low numbers of many of these species may indicate that Newark Bay is a secondary nursery for those species and their primary nursery areas are the upper New York bay and the lower Hudson. A partial explanation for the gradual decline in fish numbers from August to January is recruitment of juveniles out of Newark Bay and into the oceanic population.

The number of species caught varies from a high of 19 in June to a low of 7 in February (Figure 21.3). Although there is an anomalous sharp decline in the number of species in July, there is still a general pattern of the greatest number of species in summer and fall, followed by low numbers in the winter and a subsequent increase in spring. This pattern is typical in northeastern estuaries. Dissolved oxygen levels as low as 3 mg/L were recorded during the August decline and these levels are low enough to cause an exodus of some species from Newark Bay and discourage the influx of others. Interestingly, however, DO levels were just as low in September when 12 species were found and overall abundance was greater. Part of the September increase could be the result of the anadromous species (alewife, blueback herring) and menhaden moving back into the bay from upstream areas. This would not explain the increase in winter flounders, which do not spawn upstream.

Three hundred forty-nine blueclaw crabs, ranging from a 21 mm juvenile to a 220 mm adult, were caught during the survey. The majority of these were juveniles. Figure 21.5 indicated that crab abundance peaks in the fall and declines dramatically during the winter for all ages and both sexes. This suggests that the crabs either leave the bay or burrow into the bottom beyond reach of the trawl during the winter. In general the crabs tend to move into deeper channels in the fall, possibly preliminary to moving out of the bay altogether.

CONCLUSIONS

The major finding of this study is that most of the 12 most common species of fishes are more abundant in the deep navigation channels, particularly the main channel. Only two of the most common species were more abundant in the undredged shallow flats and two showed no difference. This preference for the channels is not well correlated with any of the physical factors measured during this survey but it does have significant management implications. In the past, attention has been focused on shallow water estuarine areas as important fish habitats, and while this may be true of smaller fish such as killifish, anchovies, and Atlantic silversides caught in beach seines in Newark Bay (USFWS 1985), it is not generally true for the size of fish caught in the present study. Furthermore the greater frequency of occurrence of fish in deep areas within the estuary seems to be true for other parts of the New York-New Jersey harbor area and the lower New York bay as well (Woodhead and McAfferty 1986).

A second important finding of this study is that Newark Bay acts as a significant nursery for tomcod and winter flounder as well as a variety of anadromous species. In addition the spur channel through Port Newark seems to provide suitable conditions for striped bass and white perch to overwinter.

It is interesting that the tomcod, which is listed as endangered in New Jersey, was the most abundant fish in Newark Bay and also accounted for the largest share of the biomass (although this was not specifically measured). Its status as an endangered species in New Jersey should be reevaluated since the species reached its extreme southern limit in the state and its scarcity south of Newark Bay may be only the result of its intolerance of warmer water.

DAVID LINTS
STUART E. G. FINDLAY
MICHAEL L. PACE

22

Biomass and Energetics of Consumers in the Lower Food Web of the Hudson River

ABSTRACT

A simple carbon budget is developed for producers and consumers in the lower food web of the Hudson River. We summarize biomass and production data for phytoplankton, zooplankton, and planktonic bacteria based on a two-year field study at a station near Kingston, N.Y. Data for benthic bacteria, macrophytes, and benthic macroinvertebrates are derived from the literature. Using general assumptions about production to biomass ratios and growth efficiencies, estimates of carbon flow through phytoplankton, macrophytes, zooplankton, bacteria, and benthic macroinvertebrates are calculated.

Phytoplankton and macrophytes account for most of the biomass in the system, but planktonic bacteria are the most important in terms of production and respiration. Total consumer production is approximately 3 times higher than primary production, suggesting that the food web is supported by inputs of detritus from outside the system. Respiration is about 5 times higher than primary production, indicating that the Hudson River is a heterotrophic ecosystem. Total pelagic respiration and production are higher than similar processes in the benthos. On the other hand, biomass and production by benthic macroinvertebrates are higher than zooplankton, indicating that benthic organisms may be more important in supporting fish production.

INTRODUCTION

Carbon budgets present a useful summary of the major components and fluxes among ecosystem components. These budgets represent a first step in understanding ecosystem processes and interactions. Carbon budgets allow one to identify the relative importance of individual components and suggest what information is insufficient or lacking.

We have developed a simple conceptual model of the lower food web of the Hudson River Estuary (Figure 22.1). This model depicts the major allochthonous inputs of carbon into the estuarine portion of the Hudson River (below the Troy dam) from upstream, the watershed, and sewage. Primary production by phytoplankton and macrophytes are the major autochthonous carbon inputs. Carbon in the estuary has several fates, including export to the sea and permanent burial. The balance of the carbon is utilized by organisms. We depict the major components of the food web as trophic groups in Figure 22.1, including planktonic bacteria, planktonic grazers, benthic decomposers, benthic invertebrates, predatory invertebrates, and fish.

The food webs of tidal freshwater rivers are poorly described relative to other aquatic systems such as streams, lakes, saline estuaries, and coastal environments (Odum 1988). This shortcoming is especially striking given the twin concerns of recruitment of anadromous fish populations in tidal freshwater systems and the effects of anthropogenic impacts on these environments. Recruitment and year-class success of anadromous fish are partly a function of interannual variability in food web processes (Gladden et al. 1988). Furthermore, transfer of toxic chemicals to fish and shellfish and potentially to human beings are partly the result of food web interactions.

In the present paper we summarize available data on the biomass, productivity, respiration, and carbon demand of the lower portion of the Hudson River food web (excluding fish and predatory invertebrates). Our summary is based on data collected in a two-year study of the lower food web and literature data. We present evidence that the Hudson River is a heterotrophic ecosystem and that pelagic

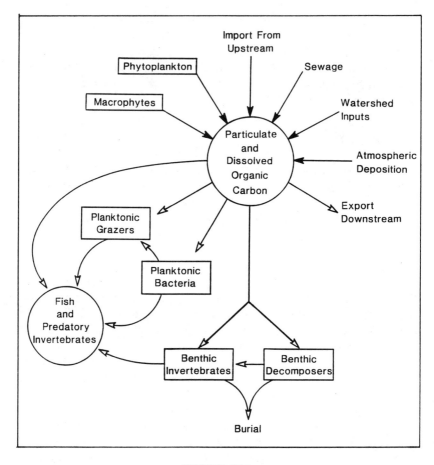

FIGURE 22.1.
Conceptual food web model. This model represents material fluxes in the Hudson River. External sources are represented by solid arrows, food web components are represented by boxes, and material fluxes are indicated by open arrows representing component interactions.

microorganisms including bacteria and algae dominate the metabolism of the system.

METHODS

Biomass and production estimates are based on samples collected biweekly at a station off of Kingston Point, river mile (RM) 91, from April 1987 to December 1988. Our analysis applies to the mid-

Hudson area near the Kingston station, as sampling at other sites has revealed substantial differences among stations. Seston concentrations and bacterial densities showed little or no significant variation in longitudinal transects, but chlorophyll concentrations and zooplankton densities showed significant variation among stations.

Phytoplankton biomass and pelagic primary production data were obtained for the Kingston area (Cole et al. in press). Water samples were collected from 3 depths (surface, 2.5m, and 5.0m) for bacteria. Bacterial abundance samples were fixed in the field with buffered formalin (final concentration 1%). Bacteria were stained and counted using the acridine orange direct count method (Hobbie et al. 1977). Bacterial biomass was estimated using a conversion factor of 2×10^{-14} g C cell^{-1} (Findlay et al. 1986; Lee and Fuhrman 1987).

Bacterial production was determined by the ^{3}H-thymidine (TdR) incubation method accounting for isotope dilution (Fuhrman and Azam 1980; 1982; Findlay et al. 1984). Ten ml water samples were incubated with 40 µCi of ^{3}H (methyl)-thymidine (80 Ci/mmole, NEN) at in situ temperatures for 30 min. Incubations were terminated by addition of 2 ml of 5% formalin. Zero time controls were fixed with formalin immediately after addition of labeled TdR. Bacteria were collected on 0.2 µm polycarbonate filters, washed 3× with cold 5% TCA and frozen for later DNA extraction. Isotope dilution was determined with a series of unlabeled TdR additions ranging from 6 to 24 times the concentration of labeled thymidine added (50 nM). There were four levels of cold TdR addition, and three replicates for each level. Isotope dilution was estimated for each set of samples collected at the Kingston station. The x-intercept of isotope dilution plots gives an estimate of the "effective pool size"—that is, the concentration of labeled and unlabeled TdR participating in DNA synthesis. DNA was extracted under alkaline conditions and precipitated with cold TCA and collected and washed with centrifugation (Findlay et al. 1984). DNA was hydrolyzed in hot TCA and subsamples of the final hydrolysate were radioassayed in a Beckman LS1800 scintillation counter. Quench was determined from the relationship between H# and counting efficiency (Horrocks 1977). Bacterial production was calculated knowing the DPM incorporated into DNA and the effective pool size of TdR: Prod = DPM/(1*h) × nmoles TdR/DPM added × 2×10^9 cells/nmole. The conversion factor for cells produced per nmole TdR incorporated may vary considerably. We have used 2×10^9 following the recommendation of Moriarty (1986).

Triplicate microzooplankton and macrozooplankton samples were collected using a pump and filtering the samples through a 35 µm and 73 µm mesh plankton net respectively. Carbonated water was added to the samples to narcotize the zooplankton and samples were then fixed with a 4% sucrose-formalin solution (60 g sucrose per liter) to a final concentration of 2%. The microzooplankton were enumerated at 100× with a minimum of 100 animals counted in each sample. The macrozooplankton were enumerated at 25×. In most cases the entire sample was counted. At very high densities subsamples were counted with at least 100 organisms from each major group counted. Macrozooplankton body lengths were measured using an image analysis system and mean lengths for each taxa were used to estimate biomass using length-weight regressions from the literature (Bottrell et al. 1976), following Bird and Prairie (1985). Microzooplankton biomass was estimated using an average of 0.065 μg dry wt. per individual (Makarewicz and Likens 1979). Zooplankton production was calculated separately for the three main groups of zooplankton: Rotifera, Cladocera, and Copepoda, due to large differences in production/biomass ratio (P/B) estimates. The P/B ratios used, 32 for Rotifera, 19 for Cladocera, and 4.3 for Copepoda, were obtained from data reported by Makarewicz and Likens (1979). An average net growth efficiency of 25% was used to determine carbon assimilation and respiration (Schroeder 1981). Biomass and production for the pelagic components were calculated by integrating over 8.0 m, the mean depth for the Kingston area based on surface area:volume data (Gladden et al. 1988).

Benthic bacterial data were obtained from Austin and Findlay (1989). These workers investigated the benthic bacterial communities of the Tivoli Bays, located a few km north of the Kingston sampling station. Data from a high organic sediment (11% AFDM) in Tivoli South Bay were used to estimate bacterial biomass and production in the high organic main channel sediments.

Benthic macroinvertebrate data were obtained from Simpson et al. (1984, 1986). They surveyed the benthic macroinvertebrate communities in the Hudson River main channel and we used data from their sampling station at Kingston (station #15, RM 94) to determine average benthic macroinvertebrate biomass. A P/B ratio of 5.8 was used to estimate production of macroinvertebrates (Bonomi 1979; Banse and Mosher 1980). An average net growth efficiency of 25% was assumed to calculate carbon assimilation and respiration (Schroeder 1981).

Macrophyte biomass data for the Kingston area were obtained from Schmidt and Kiviat (1988). We assumed that macrophytes cover all areas of the river less than 3 m in depth (Gladden et al. 1988). For the Kingston region, 22% of the river bottom is less than 3 m. Macrophyte biomass was converted to production using an average P/B ratio of 2.0 (Moeller 1985; Adams and McCracken 1974; Winberg et al. 1972; Sorokin 1972). Macrophyte respiration was calculated based on a production/respiration ratio (P/R) of 1.33 (Edwards and Owens 1962). This ratio is in the lower range of the literature values (0.2–10.0), but is used because the turbid nature of the Hudson River makes it likely that respiration is a large proportion of gross production (Ikusima 1965; Westlake 1966; McGahee and Davis 1971).

Respiration data in carbon units were converted to either mmoles O_2 m^{-2} d^{-1} or g O_2 m^{-2} d^{-1} to compare calculated respiration with direct measurements of oxygen consumption. To make this comparison, it was assumed that $CO_2 : O_2$ is 1:1 molar.

RESULTS

Values for standing stocks and associated fluxes for the components of the lower food web are presented in Table 22.1. These values represent growing season means (April to December) as noted in the methods. In most cases, we estimate fluxes such as assimilation and respiration from measurements of biomass or production, using conversion factors derived from the general literature.

Phytoplankton biomass is 6.0 g C m^{-2} (Cole et al. in press). Phytoplankton net production integrated to 0.75 m, the depth of the photic zone, averages 0.36 g C m^{-2} d^{-1} (Peierls et al. 1988). Respiration is 0.48 g C m^{-2} d^{-1} (Cole et al. unpubl. data). Phytoplankton gross production (assimilation: the sum of production and respiration) is 0.84 g C m^{-2} d^{-1}.

Macrophytes have an average biomass of 75 g C m^{-2} within the macrophyte beds (Schmidt and Kiviat 1988). According to Gladden et al. (1988), 22% of the Kingston area is < 3 m in depth. Assuming that macrophytes can occupy this entire area, their standing stock is 16.5 g C m^{-2} of river-bottom surface area. However, visual observation of the bottom suggests that they do not occupy the entire area < 3 m deep; therefore, our estimate probably represents the upper limit. Macrophyte production, assuming a growing season of 200 days, is approximately 0.165 g C m^{-2} d^{-1} and their respiration is about 0.124 g C m^{-2} d^{-1}.

Pelagic bacteria in the Hudson River have a biomass of 100 µg C l^{-1}, which represents 0.8 g C m^{-2} integrated over 8 m. The bacterial cells are small, < 1 µm, with a rapid turnover rate. Bacterial production (168 µg C l^{-1} d^{-1}) integrated over 8 m is 1.35 g C m^{-2} d^{-1}.

TABLE 22.1.
Hudson River lower food web data.

	Biomass [g C m^{-2}]	P/B	Production [g c m^{-2}d^{-1}]	NGE	Assimilation [g C m^{-2}d^{-1}]	P/R	Respiration [g C m^{-2}d^{-1}]
Pelagic							
Phytoplankton	6.0		0.36		0.84*		0.48*
Bacteria	0.8		1.348	@50%	2.696*		1.348*
Zooplankton Sum	0.175		0.02*		0.081*		0.061*
Rotifera	0.09	32	0.014*	@25%	0.058*		0.043*
Cladocera	0.056	19	0.005*	@25%	0.021*		0.016*
Copepoda	0.029	4.3	6.2 × 10^{-4}*	@25%	2.5 × 10^{-3}*		1.9 × 10^{-3}*
Pelagic Sum	6.975		1.728		3.617		1.889
Benthic							
Macrophytes	16.5*	2	0.165*		0.289*	1.33	0.124*
Bacteria	0.8		0.05	@50%	0.1*		0.05*
Macroinvertebrates	5*	5.8	0.14*	@25%	0.56*		0.42*
Benthic Sum	22.3		0.355		0.949		0.594
Total	29.275		2.083		4.566		2.483

*These estimates are based on literature or assumptions. All other estimates are based on direct measurement.

Assuming a growth efficiency of 50%, their carbon assimilation is 2.7 g C m^{-2} d^{-1}. Benthic bacterial biomass is approximately 0.8 g C m^{-2}, based on data from Tivoli South Bay, which has similar sediments (Austin and Findlay 1989). Production was also estimated using their data and is approximately 0.05 g C m^{-2} d^{-1}. Once again, assuming a growth efficiency of 50%, the carbon assimilation of benthic bacteria is 0.1 g C m^{-2} d^{-1}.

Average zooplankton biomass in the Kingston area is 0.175 g C m^{-2}. Zooplankton production, assuming a growing season of 200 days, is 0.02 g C m^{-2} d^{-1}, and their respiration is 0.061 g C m^2 d^{-1}.

Benthic macroinvertebrate populations are also variable in the river, but are a significant component of the lower food web, especially in the Kingston area. The average biomass of benthic macroinvertebrates is 5.0 g C m^{-2} (Simpson et al. 1986). Their production is 0.14 g C m^{-2} d^{-1} and, at 25% growth efficiency, their carbon assimilation is 0.56 g C m^{-2} d^{-1}.

DISCUSSION

Estimates of the carbon budgets for components of the lower food web of the Hudson River ecosystem allow us to make comparison of the significance of various groups in terms of their contribution to biomass, production, and respiration. Primary producer biomass in the Hudson River substantially exceeds consumer biomass (Figure 22.2), although our estimate of macrophyte biomass must be interpreted as an upper limit. Benthic macroinvertebrates account for about half of the total consumer biomass. Consumer production, however, is approximately three times higher than autochthonous primary production (Figure 22.3). High consumer production is due primarily to planktonic bacteria. Production by these organisms exceeds primary production, whereas in a variety of freshwater, estuarine, and marine environments, planktonic bacterial production is typically 30% of phytoplankton primary production on an areal basis (Cole et al. 1988). As is the case with production, consumers respire about three times as much carbon as the autochthonous producers (Figure 22.4). Again, planktonic bacteria account for the majority of the respiration in the system. All our estimates of respiration are derived from the biomass or production data. Independent measurements of benthic respiration conducted in a *Vallisneria* bed during July 1988 (McCarron and Findlay 1989) of 1.3 g O$_2$ m^{-2} d^{-1} agree well with our calculated value of total benthic respiration of 1.6 g O$_2$ m^{-2}

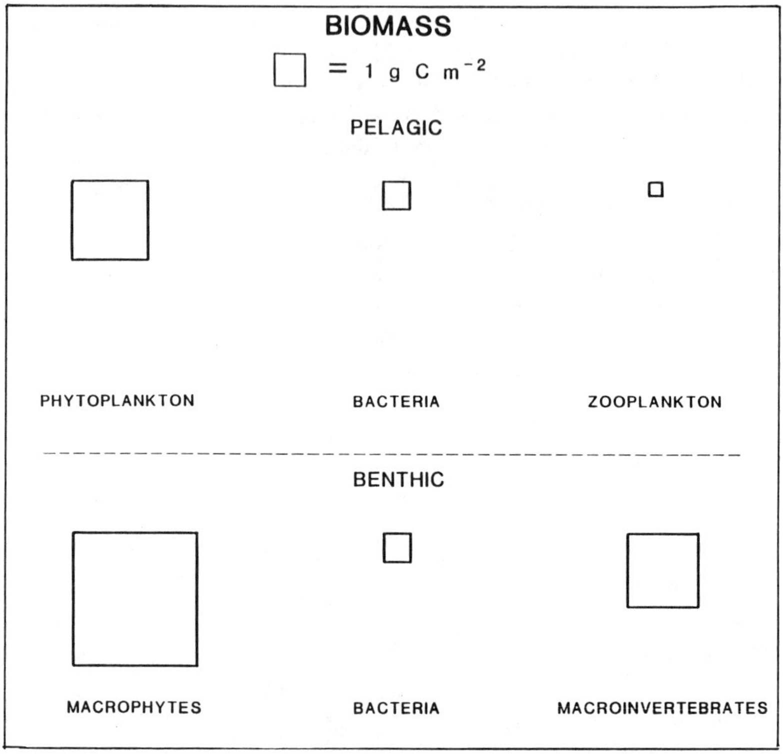

```
┌─────────────────────────────────────────────────────┐
│                    BIOMASS                          │
│              ☐ = 1 g C m⁻²                          │
│                    PELAGIC                          │
│                                                     │
│   ┌────┐                                            │
│   │    │            ☐                  ▫            │
│   │    │                                            │
│   └────┘                                            │
│                                                     │
│  PHYTOPLANKTON      BACTERIA        ZOOPLANKTON     │
│  - - - - - - - - - - - - - - - - - - - - - - - - - │
│                     BENTHIC                         │
│                                                     │
│  ┌─────┐                            ┌─────┐         │
│  │     │             ☐              │     │         │
│  │     │                            │     │         │
│  └─────┘                            └─────┘         │
│                                                     │
│  MACROPHYTES       BACTERIA     MACROINVERTEBRATES  │
└─────────────────────────────────────────────────────┘
```

FIGURE 22.2.
Biomass data for the lower food web in g C m⁻². The boxes are proportional to a scales of 1 unit = a g C.

d^{-1}. Furthermore, if we sum all our respiration values to obtain an average total system respiration of 6.6 g O_2 m^{-2} d^{-1}, this value agrees well with actual measurements of total system respiration made during 1988 (Garritt and Howarth 1989).

Our carbon model allows comparison of the relative contribution of benthic versus pelagic processes. For primary producers, macrophytes represent a larger standing stock than phytoplankton, but the more rapid turnover of phytoplankton results in a greater rate of production and respiration. Analogously, the biomass of benthic and pelagic bacteria is roughly equal, but again, the rapid doubling times (approximately 1 d^{-1}) of planktonic bacteria yield a much greater contribution to production and respiration. It should be noted that

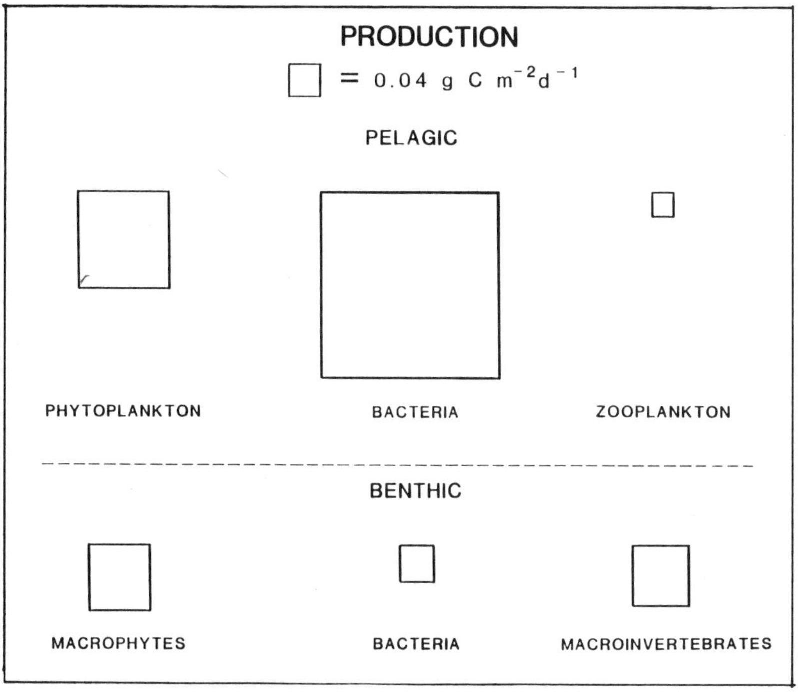

PRODUCTION

☐ = 0.04 g C m^{-2} d^{-1}

PELAGIC

PHYTOPLANKTON   BACTERIA   ZOOPLANKTON

BENTHIC

MACROPHYTES   BACTERIA   MACROINVERTEBRATES

FIGURE 22.3.
Production data form the lower food web in g C m^{-2} d^{-1}. The boxes are proportional to a scale of 1 unit = 0.04 g C m^{-2} d^{-1}.

our values for benthic bacteria include only the top 1 cm of sediment and it is likely that deeper layers contain actively growing bacteria. The TdR method for measuring bacterial production probably underestimates anaerobic production (McDonough et al. 1986; Fallon et al. 1983), so total benthic bacterial production may be significantly higher than we have estimated. Invertebrates are an important food for fishes in the Hudson (Gladden et al. 1988), and benthic invertebrates are clearly more abundant and more productive than zooplankton. We do not have detailed information on the trophic ecology of Hudson River fishes, but the inference is that benthic invertebrates are important in supporting fish production.

The data set for the lower food web of this section of the Hudson River is incomplete. Pelagic and benthic protozoans may be important in the Hudson River, but very little is known about their

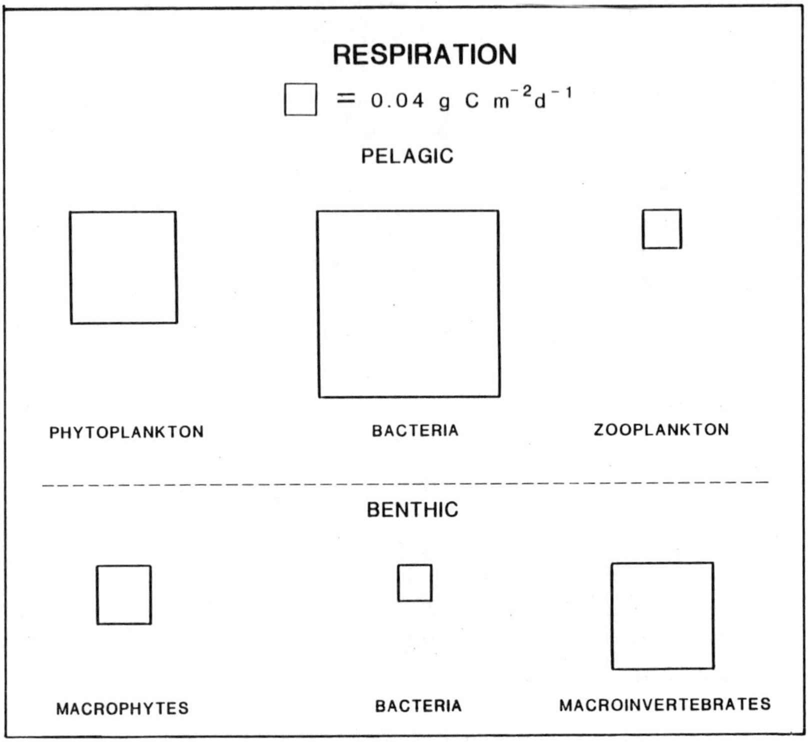

FIGURE 22.4.
Respiration data for the lower food web in g C m^{-2} d^{-1}. The boxes are proportional to a scale of 1 unit = 0.04 g C m^{-2} d^{-1}.

populations. In the Tappan Zee area, pelagic protozoan abundance varies between 10^3–10^4 l^{-1} (Capriulo unpubl. data). No data are available for benthic protozoa and meiofauna. Organisms living attached to macrophytes in the main stem of the Hudson may be significant, but density estimates do not exist. There is also evidence that there may be a benthic algal component in the Kingston area (Bianchi personal communication), but no data on biomass are available at present. All these groups are potentially important producers or consumers in the Hudson River.

The River Continuum Concept (Vannote et al. 1980) predicts that large rivers should be heterotrophic systems, due to light limitation of photosynthesis in these turbid systems (e.g., Cummins 1979). A corollary to this prediction is that allochthonous carbon sources should be as large or larger than autochthonous primary production. Hudson River data support this prediction because consumer carbon assimilation, especially by planktonic bacteria, far exceeds primary production. The system, therefore, depends on external carbon inputs from watershed run-off, upstream sources, and sewage loading. One consequence of the heterotrophic nature of the Hudson is that the river as a whole is more likely to regenerate inorganic nutrients that would be exported to the coastal sea. The heterotrophic nature of the Hudson also raises questions about how the food web operates. Do bacteria and detritus constitute the base resource for higher organisms in the food web? Alternatively, are the food web and higher trophic level production dependent on the limited primary production, with bacteria primarily a respiratory sink for carbon? These questions cannot be answered at present, but they are fundamental to understanding the food web in the Hudson and other riverine systems.

Acknowledgments

This research was made possible through two grants from the Hudson River Foundation (#016/86B/005 and #005/87B/011). We would also like to thank Jon Cole, Nina Caraco, and Ben Peierls for their helpful discussion in the preparation of this manuscript; Dave Strayer for his assistance; Erik Kiviat, Bob Schmidt, and Bob Howarth for their contributions to the data; and Tom Bianchi for critical review of the manuscript.

ROBERT E. SCHMIDT
A. BARTH ANDERSON
KARIM LIMBURG

23

Dynamics of Larval Fish Populations in a Hudson River Tidal Marsh

ABSTRACT

Freshwater tidal marshes are suspected to be important nursery areas for Hudson River fishes. Several recent studies on Tivoli South Bay, a tidal marsh dominated by water-chestnut (*Trapa natans*), provided an initial estimate of the role of this marsh as habitat for fish larvae.

Drift net samples of the inlet stream (Saw Kill) indicated that larvae of some species (alewife, white perch, white sucker) are imported into the marsh. Light trap surveys and dip netting of *Trapa* rosettes indicated that these species do not remain in the marsh after water-chestnut plants begin to cover the surface in June.

Trapa beds are important spawning areas for carp, golden shiner, spottail shiner, and banded killifish. Light trap studies indicated that *Trapa* beds contained more larvae than beds of water-celery (*Vallisneria*) or watermilfoil (*Myriophyllum*).

There is a complicated exchange of larvae between the mainstream Hudson River and the marsh through openings in the railroad bed that separates South Bay from the Hudson. More larvae are exchanged at night than in the daytime. Alewife and white perch larvae move in and out with the tide. Substantial numbers of carp and bluegill larvae are exported during the summer. Other species may leave the marsh later in the season or as juveniles.

INTRODUCTION

Tidal wetlands are a nursery area for food and game fishes (e.g., Odum et al. 1978). Freshwater wetlands have been shown to be exporters of larval fish biomass (e.g., Chubb and Liston 1986), implying that adults select these habitats for spawning and the larvae spend some of their life feeding in the wetland food web. During this part of their ontogeny, growth rates are very rapid and relatively large quantities of energy must be available. Little effort has been made in the Hudson Estuary to try to determine the magnitude of this nursery function for larval fishes, and consequently we know little about the role of tidal wetlands in supporting fish production in the estuary.

Recently, primarily through the Polgar Fellowship program, considerable effort has been directed at studying one tidal freshwater marsh, the Tivoli South Bay ecosystem. As a summary of these studies, Findlay et al. (1988) described a model of carbon flux in South Bay. Several components of this model were estimates taken from other marshes because data were lacking from South Bay. Secondary consumers (primarily fishes) were identified as one important component of the model that was poorly understood. In the last two years, several studies have been done that provide data on the larval fish communities in South Bay. This paper presents a synthesis of the temporal and spatial dynamics of the South Bay larval fish community.

MATERIALS AND METHODS

Study Area

The Tivoli Bays area (Figure 23.1) comprises >300 hectares of freshwater-tidal shallows and wetlands on the east shore of the Hudson River, 160 km north of the Battery, southern Manhattan. The Tivoli Bays are one of four geographic components of the Hudson River

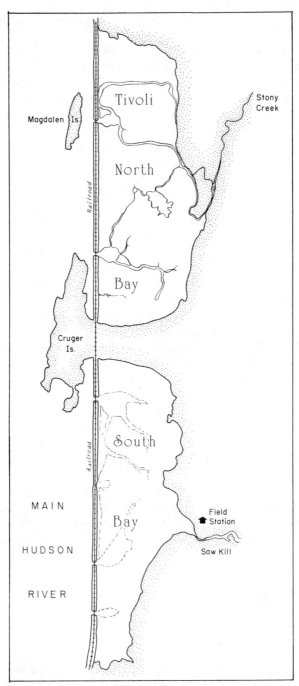

FIGURE 23.1.
Tivoli Bays, Hudson River, New York.

National Estuarine Research Reserve. Tivoli South Bay is separated from the main river by a railroad bed built on fill in 1850. Three small bridges allow the 1.2 meter tide to exchange through the causeway. South Bay is 1–2 m deep at high tide and extremely shallow with exposed mudflats at low tide. The Saw Kill, a nontidal perennial stream with a watershed of 68 km^2, is the main tributary to South Bay. At the north end is a 15 ha stand of wooded tidal swamp separating South and North Bays. Water-chestnut (*Trapa natans*) covers South Bay in the summer. Before water-chestnut and Eurasian watermilfoil (*Myriophyllum spicatum*) became abundant in the tidal Hudson, the widespread plant communities in sheltered shallows like South Bay were probably dominated by water-celery (*Vallisneria Americana*), pondweeds (*Potomogeton* spp.), and a variety of other, mostly native, "submerged" aquatic vascular plants (Muenscher 1937). Floating-leaved species were rare or absent. Tivoli North Bay (Figure 23.1) is slightly larger than South Bay, has two instead of three railroad bridges, and its major perennial tributary (Stony Creek) is smaller than the Saw Kill. North Bay is largely (ca 80%) intertidal marsh dominated by narrowleaf cattail (*Typha angustifolia*), purple loosestrife (*Lythrum salicaria*), spatterdock (*Nuphar advena*) and arrow arum (*Sagittaria* sp), but has small subtidal pool and creek habitats with beds of water-celery and watermilfoil, and smaller areas of water-chestnut, and mixed "submerged" aquatics. Outside (west of) the railroad, between Cruger Island and Magdalen Island, is an extensive subtidal shoal dominated by water-celery and watermilfoil.

Fishes

Larval fishes were sorted from samples by eye or with a low power stereo dissecting microscope and stored in 70% ethanol following a suggested protocol for fish larvae (Lavenberg et al. 1984). Fishes were identified by sight or with Auer (1982), Fuiman et al. (1983), and Lippson and Moran (1974). Specimens were classified into one of four categories: egg, yolk-sac larvae, postlarvae (no yolk sac visible), or juveniles (complete complement of fin rays), and counted.

Input: Larval Fish Transport in the Saw Kill

Downstream drift is a well-documented phenomenon for invertebrates (Waters 1962, 1965; Hynes 1970; Muller 1978), and fish larvae drift synchronously with invertebrates (Armstrong and Brown 1983; Elliott 1967; Clifford 1972; Reisen 1972; Griffith 1974; Mancini et al. 1979). These authors document a bigeminous pattern (Waters 1962,

1965) for larval fishes: a peak of drift approximately 2 hr after sunset and a smaller peak about 2–3 hr before sunrise, thus most larvae are transported in 6 hr at night.

Drift of fish larvae has been documented for many families (Manteifel et al. 1978). Although methods differ in detail, transport of fish larvae in a lotic system was usually estimated by sampling drift with static nets over a period of time and estimating the volume sampled by the nets and flow of the system (Clifford 1972; Mansfield 1984; Armstrong and Brown 1983).

The Saw Kill was sampled weekly from March 15 through the end of June 1988, for a total of 15 weeks. Sampling was done after sundown but within 3 hr of sundown to coincide with the presumed maximum drift of organisms.

Drift was sampled by staking rectangular standard drift nets with 303 μm mesh (Waters 1962) into the stream bed. Three drift nets were fished for each sample. Nets were to be deployed for about 20 min, a time that the literature suggested was reasonable for sampling fishes. However, the time nets were fished was reduced when water velocities were high or substantial debris was present. Times that nets were put in and taken out were recorded so we could calculate actual fishing time for each net. Drift nets were initially placed in the tidal mouth of the Saw Kill, but we were concerned that the very abundant *Gammarus* collected would consume or otherwise destroy the fish larvae. Subsequently we placed the nets above tidal influence.

While nets were fishing, estimates of flow were made in order to calculate volume of water sampled by each net. Water velocities were estimated by timing the drift of a neutrally bouyant object over a measured distance. Measurements were in triplicate and if velocities were obviously different at the different nets, velocities were measured near each net. If a net was not totally submerged, the distance from the water surface to the top center of the drift net opening was measured with a meter stick. The area of the net mouth actually fishing was calculated accordingly.

When nets were retrieved, contents (fishes, invertebrates, detritus) were emptied and backwashed into glass jars and formaldehyde was added to approximate a 10% solution in the field. Those preserved samples were returned to the laboratory.

In order to calculate instantaneous transport, we estimated total flow of the stream each time we sampled. Bank to bank depth transects were taken with a tape and a meter stick and cross-sectional area was calculated from these data. One data point was missing (May 20) due to high water. The cross-sectional area was estimated for this date from a geometric mean regression of all other average velocities vs cross-sectional area data.

Numbers were converted to densities (/m^3) for each sample, which were then averaged for each date from the triplicate samples. Instantaneous transport (#/sec) was estimated by multiplying densities by the estimated total river flow. Estimates of total export from the Saw Kill were made by assuming that our instantaneous transport values were average for the 6 hr that we could expect larval fish drift and that stream flow and larval drift would not vary significantly over the week following the sample. Thus instantaneous transport values were multiplied by 42 hr to derive an order of magnitude for transport in that week.

In Situ: Larval Fish Produced in South Tivoli Bay

In this part of the study we used six light traps modified from a design by Faber (1981). Each trap was a rectangular box constructed from 4 pieces of 6 mm Plexiglas (23.4 × 15.8 cm). Traps had a single recessed slot on each of the four vertical sides, two oriented vertically and the other two were horizontal. At the bottom of each trap was a hole with a #8 rubber stopper, which could be removed to empty the trap. This portion of the box was submerged and a styrofoam collar kept the traps at the surface. The light source, a waterproof flashlight, was secured to the top of each trap, illuminating the trap from above.

Traps were retrieved by placing a 505 μm plankton net around the bottom of the trap and then lifting the net and the trap from the water (thus catching fish that might be washed out of the slots). Next, the rubber stopper was removed from the bottom of the trap to flush the contents into the net. The contents of each trap were then emptied into jars and formaldehyde was added to bring the samples to approximately a 10% concentration.

The above methods were used to sample larval fish in two different studies. In 1987 the purpose of the larval fish collections was to compare densities and species composition among *Trapa*, *Myriophyllum*, and *Vallisneria* beds. The latter two submerged aquatic plants were displaced by *Trapa* in South Bay (Muenscher 1937). In 1988 the purpose of the collections was to document the larval fish communities in *Trapa* beds in more detail and to estimate the standing crop of larvae in South Bay.

Trapa is the predominant vegetation in South Bay and the beds of the other species extant in 1987 were not logistically accessible, therefore we sampled *Vallisneria* and *Myriophyllum* at sites in Tivoli

North Bay. Although extensive near-monocultures of the two submerged plants have been seen at Tivoli Bays in previous years (E. Kiviat, personal communication), it was difficult to locate homogeneous stands of any size in 1987, and they appeared highly variable in shoot density and shoot size. We selected two sites for each taxon from inside North Bay (near the northern railroad bridge) and outside the bay in the shallows of the main river, because stands inside North Bay and outside the bay were visibly different.

Sampling began on June 15, 1987, and was done approximately once per week through September 15. The *Trapa* bed in South Bay was sampled weekly approximately 250 m from the mouth of the Saw Kill. One *Myriophyllum* and one *Vallisneria* bed was sampled each week, alternating between North Bay and the main Hudson sites every other week. Sampling in North Bay was done at or near low tide to ensure that the light traps were actually fishing in the vegetation. Sampling the *Trapa* beds had to coincide with high water because it became impossible to move a canoe through the plants at low water. Therefore we sampled when a low tide occurred within 4 hr after sunset, as close to once a week as we could. All three vegetation beds that were sampled in a week were sampled on the same night. In North Bay, the traps were tied to each other and anchored at one end to keep them from drifting in the current. The cords tying the traps together had snap swivels on each end and were an average of 1.6 m (1.4–1.8) long. Thus the traps sampled a linear patch of vegetation about 8–9 m long. The dense surface growth of *Trapa* prevented any drifting, but the traps were placed about the same distance apart as in the other vegetation.

In the 1988 study, sampling began on June 1, when waterchestnut plants were visible at low tide, and concluded on July 29. Samples were collected in the same area as the previous year. By concentrating sampling during this period, we intended to describe early seasonal changes in the larval fish community that were not seen in the previous year.

Three principal sampling methods were employed to monitor larval populations in a diversity of habitats within the bay. These methods were nocturnal light trapping, diurnal dip netting in the *Trapa* beds, and both diurnal and nocturnal dip netting along the edge of the bed. We hypothesized that the species composition obtained would be similar between light traps and dip nets.

Sampling in 1988 was done every other night, weather permitting. The traps were deployed from a canoe between sunset and sunrise during slack high tide. Traps were consistently fished for between 0.5–0.6 hr.

Measurements of the decrease in light intensity with distance from the traps were taken with a LI-50 Data Logger light meter. Light intensity measurements were made in areas of high and low water-chestnut density.

A six-station transect was established adjacent to the light trap sampling area at a right angle to the edge of the *Trapa* bed. Dip net samples were taken at roughly 25 m intervals along the transect. Dip-netting began on June 27, 1988, when the water-chestnut had reached the water's surface at high tide. During the day, once a week, the transect was traversed and larvae were collected with a 505 μm plankton net. Sampling consisted of quickly sliding the plankton net under a *Trapa* rosette and then lifting, shaking, and washing the rosettes with approximately 4 l of water to dislodge any fish larvae that were in the plant. Samples were preserved as described above.

On June 27, 1988, we collected qualitative data on larval and juvenile fishes along the edge of the *Trapa* bed. Schools of larvae were taken with a fine mesh dip net, preserved, and returned to the laboratory. Specimens from this method were identified but we made no attempt to measure the area sampled by the dip nets.

The light trap and dip net methods were compared, based on ranking species by abundance and testing for differences using Kendall's tau. An estimate of total larvae in South Bay was derived by calculating the surface area that a light trap sampled from the light meter data and simply multiplying by the surface area of the bay (115 ha, Goldhammer and Findlay 1988). Our assumptions were that larval fish density is similar throughout the bay and that fishes responded to light up to 35 cm from the trap, the maximum distance from the trap that light was detectable.

Output: Larval Fish Exchange between South Bay and the Hudson

Samples of larval fishes were taken at each railroad bridge (Figure 23.1) at approximately weekly intervals beginning June 4, 1988, and extending through the beginning of August. Each weekly trip consisted of sampling at each bridge including one ebb and one flood tide in the day, and one ebb and flood at night. Since sampling for 24 hr is physically difficult, often day and night samples were taken a day apart rather than consecutively.

Larvae were collected with a 0.5 m conical plankton net (505 μm mesh) lowered over the edge of the bridge. Efforts were made to sample at mid-tide rather than near slack high or low. Duplicate samples were collected each time.

Volume of water sampled was estimated by multiplying the surface area of the net mouth by the velocity of the water and dividing by the time the net was fished. Nets were usually fished for 5 minutes. Velocity was measured by timing an object thrown in the water from one side of the bridge to the other (8–11 m). This gave us an average velocity for the bridge.

Samples were transferred from the net to plastic bags and formaldehyde was added to approximate a 10% concentration. Numbers of each species for each collection were converted to densities ($\#/m^3$).

Since too few data points were available to analyze for all variables, we chose to ignore differences among bridges and only consider dates, day/night, and ebb/flood tides as independent variables. We used a nested complete factorial ANOVA with tide nested within time of day nested within dates. A $\log_{10}$ transformation of density data was used in the analysis because of the large variation in observed densities (5 orders of magnitude). Only the first 5 sampling dates were analyzed, since no fishes were collected after July 10, 1988.

Tidal exchange between the Hudson and South Bay is approximately 10^6 m^3 of water per tidal cycle (Goldhammer and Findlay 1988). We therefore estimated larval fish flux on any given sampling date by multiplying our average densities by 10^6. Our assumptions are that our averages represent densities throughout the tidal cycle.

RESULTS

Input

Six species of fishes were exported from the nontidal area of the Saw Kill into South Bay: *Alosa pseudoharengus* (32.0% of the total exported), *Catostomus commersoni* (30.8%), *Etheostoma olmstedi* (27.2%), *Morone americana* (5.5%), unidentified eggs (2.4%), and *Notropis hudsonius* (2.1%). Total eggs and larvae exported was calculated to be 4.4×10^5 from April through June (Table 23.1). Of the species collected, only the tessellated darter (*E. olmstedi*) could be considered a resident of the nontidal Saw Kill (Schmidt 1987). The other species are either anadromous (alewife; *A. pseudoharengus*) or potadromous in the Saw Kill.

There were species specific seasonal differences in export (Table 23.1). White suckers (*C. commersoni*) were the only fish collected early in the season. Tessellated darters and alewives appeared in late May overlapping the white suckers by 2 weeks. White perch (*M. americana*) and spottail shiners (*N. hudsonius*) were taken only in June.

With the exception of a few white sucker postlarvae, only eggs

TABLE 23.1.
Larval fishes collected in drift nets in the nontidal Sawkill, 1988.

Date	Stage	Species	#/m^3	#/hr	#/week
Mar 31	e	Catostomus commersoni	0.264	922	4×10^4
Apr 7	e	Catostomus commersoni	0.240	1227	5×10^4
Apr 14	e	Catostomus commersoni	0.076	402	2×10^4
Apr 21	e	Catostomus commersoni	0.004	36	2×10^3
May 5	e&p	Catostomus commersoni	0.113	646	3×10^4
May 12	e	Catostomus commersoni	0.027	243	1×10^4
May 20	y	Etheostoma olmstedi	0.171	3305	2×10^5
	e&y	Alosa pseudoharengus	0.114	2204	9×10^4
May 26	p	Catostomus commersoni	0.043	596	3×10^4
	y	Etheostoma olmstedi	0.021	291	1×10^4
	e	Alosa pseudoharengus	0.107	1483	6×10^4
Jun 2	e&y	Alosa pseudoharengus	0.121	542	2×10^4
	e	Morone americana	0.027	121	5×10^3
Jun 9	y	Notropis hudsonius	0.036	273	1×10^4
Jun 16	e	Morone americana	0.089	601	3×10^4
Jun 24	e	Unidentified	0.093	323	1×10^4
Total				13,215	4.4×10^5

or yolk-sac larvae were collected in this part of the study. Thus the Saw Kill is exporting primarily the earliest developmental stages into South Bay, presumably maturation would occur in the bay.

In Situ

Light trap data from 1987 indicated that *Trapa* beds had a higher density (Figure 23.2) and a greater number of species than *Myriophyllum* or *Vallisneria* beds. A total of 81 specimens was collected in the *Trapa* beds (Table 23.2). A distinct seasonality was evident in that in June and early July the collections were dominated by cyprinid larvae (carp, goldfish, golden shiner, and spottail shiner). After mid-July, banded killifish were the only fish larvae consistently collected and, except for 3 unidentified specimens, were the only species taken.

Alosa pseudoharengus was only collected once on June 16 when *Trapa* density was still low. Of the other species drifting out of the Saw Kill, only spottail shiners were collected in light traps and they may have been spawned in the *Trapa* beds rather than in the Saw Kill.

In 1988, with more intensive sampling, 1364 individuals of 12

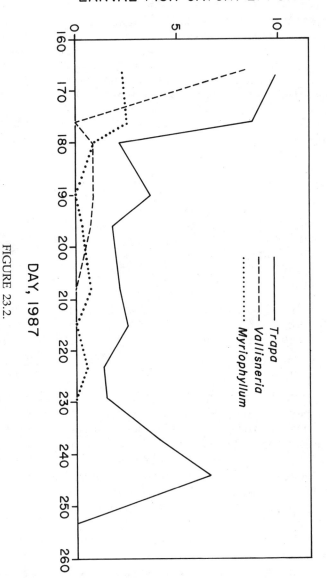

FIGURE 23.2. Catch per unit effort of larval fishes in light traps in *Trapa* compared to other plant communities, Tivoli Bays. One unit of effort is 100 minutes of trap fishing time.

TABLE 23.2.
Larval fishes collected in the *Trapa* beds in Tivoli South Bay, Hudson River, N.Y.

Species	1987	1988
Notemigonus crysoleucas (golden shiner)	4	777
Cyprinus carpio (carp)	22	315
Fundulus diaphanus (banded killifish)	36	204
Notropis hudsonius (spottail shiner)	8	34
Catostomus commersoni (white sucker)	0	13
Alosa pseudoharengus (alewife)	1	10
Carassius auratus (goldfish)	7	0
Other species	3	11
Total	81	1,364

taxa were collected. Species composition in light trap and dip net samples was similar, ranks (Table 23.3) were not significantly different (Kendall's tau = 0.6). Thus the light traps were not being any more selective than the dip nets.

As in 1987, alewives were collected early in the season, but once *Trapa* grew up to the surface at high tide, alewives were no longer taken in light traps. Dominant species in 1988 (together comprising over 95% of individuals collected) were golden shiner, carp, and banded killifish (Table 23.2). Again, banded killifish were collected later in the season than the other species (end of June) but we did not sample after July in 1988. White suckers were collected at the margins of the *Trapa* beds but were not seen in the dense *Trapa* stands.

Light meter measurements indicated that light from the traps was not detectable (same as background light) at about 35 cm in dense *Trapa* beds and 55 cm in sparse beds. We used the 35 cm value in our calculations since most of the bay is dense *Trapa*. Each trap, therefore, sampled 0.39 m^2. Given that the surface area of Tivoli South Bay is 115 ha and that our average larval catches ranged from 2 to 20 individuals per trap, our estimate of standing crop of larvae in South Bay ranges between 10^6–10^7 during June and July. In order to calculate total larval fish production of South Bay for the season, we needed to estimate turnover of the larval fish population. We cannot do this directly with the data at hand but, in order to alter the order of magnitude of our standing crop estimate, turnover would have to exceed 10 times per summer. We think that magnitude of turnover is unlikely, therefore our estimate for total larval production for the entire bay for the

TABLE 23.3.
Species collected in light traps and dip nets in *Trapa* beds, 1988, ranking based on total numbers.

Species	Rank	
	Light Traps	Dip Net
Carp	1	2
Golden shiner	2	1
Banded killifish	3	3
Spottail shiner	4	5
Fourspine stickleback	5	4
Alewife	+	—
Alosa spp.	+	—

summer season would be 10^6–10^7. This estimate is one or two orders of magnitude higher than export from the Saw Kill.

Output

A total of 6817 fishes was collected in this study. Ten species were identified, with alewives (*Alosa pseudoharengus*) being the most abundant (83% of the specimens collected; Table 23.4). In contrast, very few blueback herring (*A. aestivalis*) were identified. Early larval stages of these two species cannot be distinguished until dorsal fin rays develop, therefore a specimen was arbitrarily designated as an alewife unless it possessed obvious blueback characters. Therefore, the alewife numbers may be a slight overestimate.

Likewise, it is not possible to distinguish larvae of *Lepomis gibbosus* (common sunfish) and *L. macrochirus* (bluegill). Both are present in this area of the Hudson and we categorized all the larvae as bluegills. Both species were probably included in our samples.

Samples taken after July 10, 1988, contained no fishes. Fishes may still be moving in and out of the bay during this period but either densities were too low to be sampled with our methods or the fishes are large enough to avoid the nets, or both. The rest of our analyses are based on the five samples that contained larval fishes: June 4/5, June 11/13, June 19/21, June 28/29, and July 8/10.

The ANOVA indicated that larval fish densities significantly changed with date ($p < 0.001$) and that there were significantly higher densities at night compared to daytime ($0.05 < p < 0.01$). No other

TABLE 23.4.
List of larval fishes collected at the bridges in South Tivoli Bay,
June–July 1988.

Species	Number Collected	Percent of Total
Alosa pseudoharengus (alewife)	5674	83.2
Cyprinus carpio (carp)	519	7.6
Morone americana (white perch)	465	6.8
Lepomis macrochirus (bluegill)	84	1.2
Etheostoma olmstedi (tessellated darter)	28	0.4
Notemigonus crysoleucas (golden shiner)	17	0.2
Alosa aestivalis (blueback herring)	14	0.2
Notropis hudsonius (spottail shiner)	12	0.2
Fundulus diaphanus (banded killifish)	3	<0.1
Carassius auratus (goldfish)	1	<0.1
Total	6817	

main effects were significant and the only interaction term that approached significance was the date by day/night comparison (p = 0.059). Since tide (ebb/flood) was never a significant factor in the above analysis, the majority of fishes are probably being washed in and out of South Bay with the marsh being neither a source nor a sink of fish larvae.

Since we did not include species as a factor in the above analysis, it made sense to look at species composition (Table 23.5) by sampling date, time of day, and stage of tide. Alewives made up a higher percentage of the ichthyofauna on flood tides during the day although densities were lower under these conditions. White perch did not show a clear pattern. These two species were probably being passively transported in and out of the marsh with the tide.

All other species collected, except golden shiners, were clearly nocturnal. Carp and bluegills were concentrated on ebb tides, which makes it likely that these two species were exported from the marsh.

Actual numbers of fishes moving in or out of the bay were calculated from Table 23.5 for the three most abundant species (Table 23.6). From these data and Goldhammer and Findlay's (1988) estimate of 10^6 m^3 of water being exchanged on one tide, we can roughly estimate the numbers of organisms being transported. For alewives, 10^9 to 10^7 individuals are flushed in and out of the marsh on each tidal cycle from the beginning of June to the middle of June, respectively.

TABLE 23.5.
Larval fishes collected at Tivoli South Bay bridges in relation to time of day, tide, and date, 1988.

	Species									Average Density
	Ap	Ma	Cc	Eo	Nc	Nh	Lm	Fd	Aa	
4/5 Jun										
Day	93.6	6.4								2130
Night	77.8	3.2	16.5	1.2	0.9	0.5				8598
Ebb	81.5	2.2	15.2	<0.1	0.4	0.6				6507
Flow	83.2	6.7	7.1	2.0	1.0					4221
11/13 Jun										
Day	91.2	6.1	1.2				1.5			213
Night	43.1	28.7	25.2	0.9		1.7	0.4			1030
Ebb	37.0	20.2	40.1			1.5	1.1			638
Flow	67.2	29.5	0.4	1.6		1.3				605
19/21 Jun										
Day	73.5	24.7			1.7					128
Night	3.3	2.8	65.4		0.4		27.7	0.4		410
Ebb	18.2	7.5	47.3		0.6		26.1	0.4		425
Flow	35.4	12.5	50.8		1.3					113
28/29 Jun										
Day	78.3	21.7								49
Night	86.3	10.4							3.3	99
Ebb	81.7	15.9							2.4	92
Flow	88.7	9.2							2.2	46
8/10 Jul										
Day	93.6	6.4								12
Night	9.5		43.6				39.1	1.4	6.5	114
Ebb	9.4		46.5				38.8		5.3	104
Flow	62.7	4.0					16.0	8.0	9.3	22

Compared to alewives, an order of magnitude fewer white perch are flushed in and out of the marsh in the beginning of June (10^8) falling to 10^6 by July 10. This species persisted in high densities for a longer period than alewives.

Carp have a net export of 10^8 individuals per tidal cycle for the first 3 samples in June. This value is an order of magnitude higher than our estimates for total larval fish production for the entire bay from the light trap data. Either the light traps were fished in an area of low productivity or our assumptions about the densities of larvae

TABLE 23.6.
Numbers of alewives, white perch, and carp larvae moving in or out of Tivoli South Bay, 1988.

		Species		
Date	Direction	Ap	Ma	Cc
4/5 June	in	3512	283	299
	out	5303	143	989
11/13 June	in	406	178	2
	out	236	129	256
19/21 June	in	40	14	6
	out	77	32	201
28/29 June	in	41	4	0
	out	75	15	0
8/10 July	in	14	1	0
	out	10	0	48

moving under the bridges were wrong. Without further sampling, we cannot suggest which sampling method may be in error.

DISCUSSION

The four studies summarized above present a broad picture of the temporal and spatial changes in the South Bay larval fish community. Input from the Saw Kill is small compared to our estimates of production in the *Trapa* beds and tidal flux of larvae under the railroad bridges. However, a better assessment of the tidal portion of the Saw Kill is needed.

The alewives and white perch drifting from the Saw Kill apparently do not remain in the marsh once *Trapa* begins to grow in June. W. E. Odum (personal communication to KEL) said that clupeid larvae in general avoid vegetation. Some of the white suckers leaving the Saw Kill remain in the marsh but inhabit the edge of *Trapa* beds. Thus the ecotone community differs from that in the dense *Trapa*. Paller (1987) made a similar observation in a South Carolina freshwater marsh.

Some of the cyprinid larvae produced in the *Trapa* beds may move into the edge community as they grow. Faber (1980) observed this behavior in golden shiners. We need to look more closely at this aspect of larval fish biology in South Bay.

The significant role of submerged aquatic vegetation as a nursery for larval and juvenile fishes has been well documented (Chubb and Liston 1986; Gregory and Powles 1985; Rozas and Odum 1987; Weinstein 1979). Two possible reasons to explain this nursery function are presence of an abundance of small food organisms and protection from predators.

Trapa has a high density of epiphytic macroinvertebrates and, due to the large surface area of the plant, *Trapa* supports large numbers of macroinvertebrates (Schoeberl and Findlay 1988). The densities of these epiphytic organisms on *Trapa* in South Bay (Schoeberl and Findlay 1988) were an order of magnitude higher than densities reported for *Myriophyllum* and *Vallisneria* plants (Keast 1984). This higher density of food organisms compared to other Hudson River macrophytes may then explain the higher density of larval fish in *Trapa* beds that we observed.

It appears to us that *Trapa* would provide a better refuge for small fishes than other submerged aquatic vegetation in the Hudson Estuary. The morphology of the plant seems to be more structurally complex than other submersed macrophytes. Dense (Gotceitas and Colgan 1987) and complex (Werner et al. 1983; Savino and Stein 1982) refugia are more effective places to hide for small fishes. Whether the fishes perceive the vegetation in the same way that we do is unknown. However, the above observations would explain why we found more larvae in dense *Trapa* stands compared to areas where *Trapa* was sparse.

The dominant species of fish larvae inhabiting *Trapa* beds are poorly understood in the Hudson ecosystem. The biology of carp and golden shiners has not been studied in the Hudson or any other estuary and the role of these abundant and fairly large species in estuaries is unknown. Spottail shiners and banded killifish are also very abundant species in the Hudson, but little is known about their biology.

Therefore, it is difficult to discuss coupling of *Trapa* productivity (or epiphytic invertebrate productivity) to the fish resources of the Hudson without investigating biology of the species that dominate the *Trapa* larval fish communities. Also, we do not know if *Trapa* communities are similar throughout the Hudson estuary.

Carp and bluegills were the only species detected being exported from the marsh. Export of fish biomass may be occurring in other species. For instance, in a brief study of larval movement between the estuary and North and South Bays, Limburg (1987) found greatest larval fluxes on nighttime ebb tides, especially for *Alosa* spp. larvae. Larval fluxes dropped substantially after July 10 in that study as well. Fishes leaving the marsh as juveniles would not be sampled well using our methods. Also, it is likely that much of the fish biomass leaves the marsh in the fall when *Trapa* senesces, and we did not sample beyond mid-August.

In terms of numbers of larvae, the flux of fishes under the railroad bridges seems the most significant interaction between larval fishes and the marsh that we measured. The dominant species, alewives and white perch, were not associated with *Trapa* in our other samples. It appears that these larvae are forced into the *Trapa* beds on flood tides. The vegetation is quite thick close to the underpasses and, if we consider these larvae as having little mobility, many larvae must be carried in among the *Trapa* rosettes. We wonder if these larvae may be feeding in the vegetation.

Acknowledgments

These studies were supported by grants from the Hudson River Foundation to KEL and RES (#005/87R/012) and RES and Erik Kiviat, Hudsonia Limited (#022/86B/016), and by Polgar Fellowships awarded to ABA and CB. We thank Sean Smith, Loretta Stillman, John Echols, Kristi Inserra-Echols, Kate Braun, Andrea Cooper, Nancy Urban, and Daniel Bolin for their help in the field and laboratory. We especially appreciate the moral support of Betsy Blair, Hudson River National Estuarine Research Reserve, and John Waldman, Hudson River Foundation. Kathleen A. Schmidt drafted the figures. This is Bard College Field Station-Hudsonia contribution #55.

EDWARD H. BUCKLEY

24

A Case for the Restoration of the Estuarine Ecosystem of Croton Bay/Croton River and Associated Tidal Marshes

ABSTRACT

Croton Bay and the estuary of the Croton River form a "shallows" unit that was and could be the functional gem of the Hudson Estuary. It is only one square mile in area, yet it may be worth millions of dollars annually in reducing predation upon juvenile striped bass, and in providing us with a model to establish functionally similar areas in Haverstraw Bay. Prior to 1970, the functional beauty of the Croton Bay/Croton Estuary system was the existence of nearly 190 acres of dense submerged aquatic vegetation, with tidal flow through it carrying planktonic populations and organic detritus to and from the Croton Estuary and marshes. The author has observed that fish over a few centimeters in length rarely enter dense stands of water milfoils (the primary species), whereas the smaller juvenile fish frequently abound there during the summer. This may be the only type of environment in the estuary where food is abundant and predation significantly reduced for juvenile striped bass. The hypothesis is presented that the decline in submerged aquatic vegetation and marsh vegetation is the result of upwelling groundwater coming from the adjacent landfill, which is located on 65 acres of former marshland. A restoration with sanctuary classification is proposed for this area before it is developed into a marina like the Stony Point Bay/Minisceongo Creek estuary.

PRESENTATION

Because the impacts of man and technology on the natural resources of the Hudson are major concerns, I want to give you an update on the Croton Bay/Croton River estuarine system, which is a prime example of multiple impacts upon the estuary, and a place where major corrections can be made that will make a measurable difference at a cost-effective price.

The Croton Bay/Croton River estuary complex (Figure 24.1) is an extraordinary resource. It is the tarnished gem of the estuarine fisheries nursery in the Hudson River. This paper is a positive statement that several important ecological features can be restored there, and warrant our best efforts to do so. It is not a "quick fix" situation that politicians, agencies, and most of us prefer. Instead, it will require long-term management based on supportive research. The task will be cost-effective if it is done thoughtfully. Furthermore, what can be learned and can be done at Croton has applicability to the Peekskill Bay/Annsville Creek estuary, to the Stony Point Bay/Minisceongo Creek estuary, even with the marina there, and conceivably to other areas of the summertime estuarine fisheries nursery of the Hudson. I think of the estuarine fisheries nursery as centered in Haverstraw Bay, but including the reach from Hastings/Piermont to Beacon/Newburgh, although it does extend farther. The ideas to be discussed here will focus on the Croton Bay/Croton River area.

In his book, *The Natural and Unnatural History of the Hudson River*, Boyle (1969) vividly described "progress" that impacted upon the estuarine ecosystem at Croton. The Croton River was truncated by dams, first in 1842, and then in 1906. The latter dam essentially eliminated the Croton watershed (370 square miles) from the Hudson. The Croton watershed now provides an urban water supply and a small streamlike flow for the estuary. Only during the short periods when the Croton reservoir overflows the dam does the riverbed become

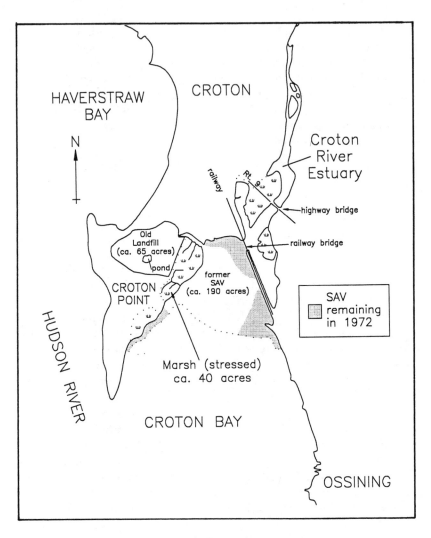

FIGURE 24.1.
Map of Croton Point, Croton Bay, and Croton River Estuary showing the old 65-acre landfill on tidal marshland with a pond on top created from recycled leachate, and the adjacent 40-acre tidal marsh stressed by upwelling ground water from the landfill. The dotted line in Croton Bay marks the outer limit of the former 190 acres of submerged aquatic vegetation, while the three shaded areas within it show where submerged aquatic vegetation survived in 1972.

filled. Around 1850, the railroad was built across the mouth of the Croton River, most of it on fill. That design both restricts and concentrates tidal flow in and out of the Croton River. Of course I recognize the advantages of energy-efficient commuter service by rail, but our environment pays part of the price. In his book, Boyle also describes the diverse bird life of the Croton Estuary, as well as the bountiful fisheries there at the turn of the century, and reports that at Croton Point in 1930 William Vogt inspired Roger Tory Peterson to write his now-famous bird guide. These events seemed long ago when I first saw the Croton Estuary in 1965.

What was so special about the Croton Bay/Croton River estuary in the late 1960s? When the breeze was in the right direction to waft the essence of landfill away, and the New York Central was not discharging oil into the river at the railroad bridge, it was a fascinating place, with patches of beauty and some unexpected treats on every visit, because nature was diverse and bountiful. Within the estuary, the main center of action was the shallow productive bay containing nearly 190 acres of dense submerged aquatic vegetation (SAV) that provided a protective fisheries nursery. What made it extraordinary, however, was the flow of more than 2000 acre-feet of the most productive waters through the SAV daily with the tides. The flood tides carried abundant plankton in from the deeper shallows of Croton Bay, while the ebb tides carried plankton along with additional algae and organic detritus freed from the marshes. Dissolved oxygen levels in the bay waters were high throughout the summer, usually exceeding 8 mg O_2/liter, and often were supersaturated with oxygen. Fortunately, this healthy state in the waters of Croton Bay has persisted. Another exceptional feature of Croton Bay was the extraordinary storm protection provided by Croton Point. The only storms that can produce destructive waves in Croton Bay are storms from the south, and in that case the tides are always elevated so that wave stress on SAV and benthic communities is reduced substantially.

During the late 1960s and early 70s, SAV in Croton Bay was very dense, and a small boat had to be poled through the area by its oars. The SAV was coated with epiphytic algae, which were scraped off and consumed by invertebrate periphyton that, in turn, were eaten by juvenile fish. Throughout June, July, and August, juvenile fish were usually present in abundance, wriggling through the dense vegetation in bursts of a few centimeters after every disturbance. Rarely did we see evidence of larger fish among the SAV, but visibility was extremely restricted. The larger mummichogs (*Fundulus heteroclitus*) and banded killifish (*Fundulus diaphanus*) were the largest fish regularly seen. Much larger fish were frequently seen near the edge of the SAV where the plants were clumped or sparse. In spite of the turbidity at ebb tide, large fish could sometimes be seen side by side facing the SAV, apparently feeding on organisms moving out with the tidal flow, and changing position only slightly to get all they wanted.

For decades, a putative function of SAV was to enhance the survival of juvenile fish by partially excluding large predators and by diminishing the foraging efficiency of the predators that did enter. Those concepts fit the field observations at Croton, but nothing approaching quantitative measurements could be made, although we tried to do so in 1970 and in 1971. Recently, the first data were published from field experiments, which showed that SAV does protect small fish from predation (Rozas and Odum 1988), and confirmed earlier laboratory experiments that showed less predatory success of piscivores in SAV (Mitchell and Hunter 1970; Glass 1971; Sullivan and Atchison 1978; Lascara 1981; Savino and Stein 1982).

Another putative role of SAV was that of an abundant food source for secondary producers (i.e., epiphytic algae for invertebrate epiphytes, and both of these as food sources for juvenile and small fish). Chironomids can be a large portion of the invertebrate epiphyte population in brackish SAV, and their impressive productivity has been documented in estuarine SAV of the Hudson River (Menzie 1980). Currently, *Palaeomonetes pugio* is being studied in the Croton River (I. Smith and J. S. Tashiro, Bard College), and a range of invertebrates in tidal freshwater SAV of the Hudson (M. Kelly and W. Perrote of Marist College). Standing crop densities of invertebrate fauna have been documented as being higher in SAV than in unvegetated shallows (Gerkin 1962; Menzie 1980; Crowder and Cooper 1982; Gilinsky 1984). During the 1980s progress was also made in documenting the large concentrations of fish in marine and estuarine SAV (Orth and Heck 1980; Kemp et al. 1984; Orth et al. 1984; Rozas and Odum 1988). SAV interferes with the collection of fish from those sites to the degree that conventional methods of fish collection become useless (Nielson and Johnson 1983; Kuslan 1984). Lack of quantitative fish sampling in SAV has led to underestimates of the importance of the SAV habitat as nursery/feeding refuges (Heck and Thoman 1984). Recently, portable "pop-nets" have demonstrated much greater numbers of small fish in SAV (Serafy et al. 1988). These increases are by two orders of magnitude for the smaller fish, and appear to be approaching real quantitation—an exciting and essential development for evaluating the functions of SAV. Now there are tools to document many of the functions of the Croton Bay/Croton River estuarine system as a protective and productive fisheries nursery, but there is a problem. The 190 acres of submerged aquatic vegetation are no longer there. The bay still supports abundant plankton production, and still attracts juvenile fish during the summer months, and presumably, juvenile fish still attract their predators. Therefore, the former SAV area of Croton Bay that appeared to be exceptionally protective is now an area where the survival of juvenile fish is probably no better than average and could be worse than average if their predators are attracted preferentially to Croton Bay by the abundance of juvenile fish.

This loss of SAV leaves us with two related, but different, problems. One is the loss of this particular 190-acre community of SAV. The second problem is to recognize that it is a loss. As a nation, we spend millions of dollars annually to eradicate SAV. Just as marshes have been filled in order to use "waste" land, SAV is eradicated to facilitate drainage and navigation, to provide safer and more aesthetic swimming and boating, and, occasionally, just to provide what some people consider a better view of the water. It is very important to the Hudson River ecosystem that researchers studying it begin their own evaluation of SAV and recognize that at Croton Bay there are probably more ecological reasons for SAV than anywhere else in the estuary. *Submerged aquatic vegetation belongs in Croton Bay.*

No direct cause and effect relationship has been established for the disappearance of the 190 acres of SAV in Croton Bay or for the disappearance of 25 acres of cattails (*Typha angustifolia*) and of hibiscus and saltmeadow grass (*Hibiscus palustris* and *Spartina patens*) in the main Croton Point marsh where vegetation in all 40 acres of that marsh is stressed. My hypothesis is that the loss of species and the environmental stress on remaining species is related to the ground water regime (Figure 24.2) produced by the old Westchester County landfill, which covers 65 acres of former estuarine marshland. The first evidence I found of severe environmental stress and of upwelling occurred in August 1968 in a community of cattails adjacent to the landfill. All cattails in a 15 m × 30 m zone of upwelling had died and only a few remnant parts remained in a pool of water that appeared motionless except for its constant drainage along the margin of the landfill. The weight of the landfill had depressed the marsh surface and created a tidal drainage channel there. Tides flooded the area twice daily, with normal spring tides covering that section of the marsh with 15 to 20 cm of water. There was no more than a fifty-foot transition zone between highly productive cattails and the dead cat-

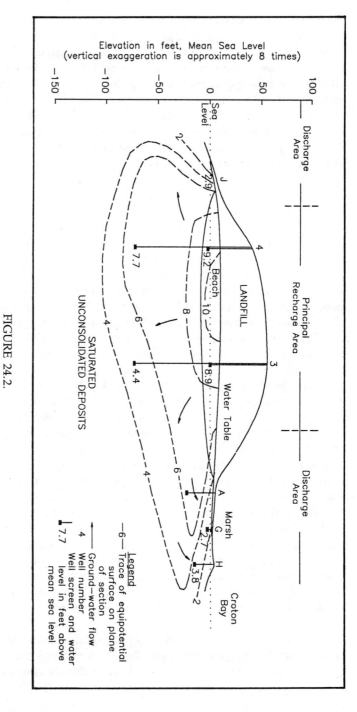

FIGURE 24.2. Generalized hydraulic profile through ground water reservoir across beach, old landfill, and marsh in 1972, as interpreted by Geraghty and Miller, Inc., 1973. Landfill is now twice as high with steeper slopes. Current ground water profile is unknown. (Reproduced with permission of Geraghly and Miller, Inc.)

tails in the upwelling area. The transition zone retained its dense growth in 1968. The growth, however, was somewhat stunted, and this was accentuated by a lack of flowering heads.

In September 1968, with the help of many volunteers, I measured the above-ground productivity of the major plant communities in the Croton Point marsh, and subsequently mapped them at a 1:1200 scale from aerial photographs. We found no other stressed areas that September. In 1969 the upwelling area in the marsh extended somewhat, possibly doubling in size, but growth elsewhere appeared normal in the spring and early summer. By August there was an obvious reduction in seed heads on cattails, and many hibiscus leaves began to yellow in early August, shortly after flowering. By mid-September, large areas of cattails turned the golden color of ripening wheat and the hibiscus dropped their yellowed leaves well before any frost.

During the winter of 1969/70, more than 20 acres of cattails collapsed and washed out with the tides. The bare marsh sediments remained exposed through much of the spring of 1970 until *Pluchea purpurascens* established itself from seed as the dominant species in 1970 over those 20 acres of former cattail marsh. The hibiscus and saltmeadow grass community continued to survive with depressed growth, but was unable to halt the intrusion of reed grass (*Phragmites communis*), which also had depressed growth. Meanwhile, SAV in Croton Bay appeared to be thriving. It was composed predominantly of *Myriophyllum* spp with patches of *Potamogeton perfoliatus* and scattered understory of *Vallisneria americana*. *Vallisneria americana* was present also as pure stands where tidal flows were strongest. In 1971 more cattails collapsed in the marsh, while SAV in Croton Bay appeared normal. In 1972 still more cattails collapsed, and a spatial correlation was made between the movement of ground water from the landfill and the rotting of roots of most of the marsh vegetation* (Boyce Thompson Institute 1972; Geraghty and Miller, Inc. 1973). In the latter two weeks of July 1972, approximately 150 acres of SAV (*Myriophyllum* and *Potamogeton*) floated away with the tide. By mid-September, the *Vallisneria* also disappeared from the same area. The

---

*Among the former dominant species, *Typha angustifolia* and *Hibiscus palustris* are most susceptible, while *Phragmites communis* and *Spartina alterniflora* are most resistant. *Lythrum salicaria*, *Spartina patens*, and *Distichlis spicata* are intermediate. Normal minor species like *Eleocharis parvula* and *E. calva*, *Echinochloa walteri*, *Agrostis alba*, *Polygonum pensylvanicum*, *P. punctatum* and *P. hydropiperoides*, *Rumex mexicanus*, *Chenopodium ambrosiodes*, and *Impatiens capensis* have become the dominant species in the higher stressed areas.

tops of the SAV looked normal, but the roots had rotted. SAV was left in only three areas (Figure 24.1).

At that time, the cooperating hydrologists (Geraghty and Miller, Inc.) did not believe that a correlation could be made between the flow of ground water from the landfill and the loss of SAV in Croton Bay. One possible cause for the decay of roots in the marsh vegetation and SAV was toxicity of heavy metals that were abundant in the ground water within the landfill. However, the concentration of heavy metals in the leaves of marsh plants at Croton was not different from that found elsewhere in the estuary. The levels of heavy metals in upwelling water at Croton were often less than the concentrations in the receiving waters of the Hudson River. Heavy metal toxicities could still be a causal factor, since we now realize that quantitative measurements, particularly by foliar analysis, cannot detect all metal toxicities, and sensitivities to heavy metals change when roots are under anaerobic conditions such as upwelling of anaerobic water from the landfill.

In 1974 the growth of plants in the Croton marsh indicated a slight decrease in the environmental stress (Boyce Thompson Institute 1975). That was correlated with a slight decrease in the hydrological head of ground water within the landfill (Geraghty & Miller, Inc. 1974). The apparent reason for this decrease was that the landfill was filling so rapidly with garbage, building debris, and additional cover fill that the new layers never became water-saturated, and thus acted like a cap. In my report to the Office of the U.S. Attorney and to Westchester County, the main theme was that water must be kept out of the landfill to reduce the environmental impact in the estuarine marsh. The loss of the SAV of Croton Bay could not be associated with the landfill at that time because the calculated groundwater heads from the landfill were only significant for several hundred feet out into the bay (Figure 24.2).

Throughout the latter 1970s the environmental stress decreased. This was indicated by the poor but improving growth of plants in the marsh, and the establishment of scattered plants of *Myriophyllum* and *Potamogeton perfoliatus* in Croton Bay. (*Vallisneria* may have returned, but it is much more difficult to detect.) However, along with the return of some SAV in Croton Bay, there was a loss of SAV within the three areas that survived in 1972. Mud flats formed in two of the areas, and erosion occurred at the third.

After 1970 there was a continuous problem of leachate flow from the sides of the landfill. Starting in the late 1970s, Westchester County dealt with the problem by pumping this leachate, which was diluted by much larger volumes of runoff, to the top of the landfill where a pond formed. Previous reports to the county (Boyce Thompson Institute 1972, 1975; Geraghty and Miller, Inc. 1973, 1974), made the county aware that adding water to the landfill would increase the environmental problems in the same marsh that they were committed by court order to restore. For several years there was no apparent increase in environmental stress in the marsh or elsewhere. Also, percolation of water from the pond into the landfill was surprisingly slow and the pond continued to grow.

Then in 1981, severe stress hit the marsh again. By 1982, all the gains of the late 1970s were lost and the entire 40 acres of the marsh were obviously stressed. In 1983 no SAV was found in Croton Bay. Possibly it was there in the spring, but certainly it was gone by August. Therefore, on both occasions the SAV community was affected approximately two years after the marsh community. Both the marsh plants and SAV lost their underground structures. The larger SAV area in Croton Bay was affected in 1983 after the larger marsh area was affected in 1982. The former consulting hydrologist, David Miller of Geraghty and Miller, Inc., stated recently that ground water from the landfill could extend across the bay, but that has not been investigated. This is particularly plausible because most of the soils of both Croton Point and of the underlying sediments of Croton Bay have a common origin and stratification. They are the remaining deposits of the Croton River delta that was formed during the recession of the last glaciation. In my opinion, the groundwater from the landfill is probably responsible for the loss of SAV in Croton Bay, as well as desirable plant species in the adjacent marsh.

It is now essential for the scientific community to determine the direct cause and effect relationships. David Bouldin and Barbara Bedford at Cornell University have initiated studies on some of the subtle balances among heavy metals when roots are under anaerobic conditions. Field and laboratory studies of anaerobic root metabolism in marsh plants and SAV are being planned that are applicable to conditions at Croton.

Another essential area of investigation is sedimentation in Croton Bay. The depth of Croton Bay is critical to survival of SAV, and that has changed recently in some areas. Re-creating a sediment contour that provides the correct depths for SAV communities and maintaining those depths, and possibly expanding the area suitable for SAV, are all challenges to be considered. The present situation provides an outstanding opportunity to learn not only how to restore a protective and productive fisheries nursery in Croton Bay, but also how to create and how to maintain similar nurseries in the estuary. Currently, we have no adequate measurement of what is required or what can be produced by a SAV-centered fisheries nursery, but we have a unique opportunity to quantitate processes and simultaneously restore estuarine functions to an area that is extraordinarily well-designed by nature.

If ground water from the landfill is the primary source of environmental stress upon roots of both SAV and marsh vegetation, then restoration of those estuarine communities will be long-term. The seven growing seasons, from 1974 to 1980 inclusive, demonstrated the slow rate of improvement (decrease in stress) that can be expected if the landfill is capped to stop the recharge of ground water within the landfill. The preceding statement assumes that maximum ground water levels in the center of the landfill received no additional recharge from 1973 to 1980, and that maximum ground water level continued to decrease after 1973 (Geraghty and Miller, Inc. 1974) until 1981. It is also assumed that the hydrologic center was recharged again, starting in 1981, by water percolating down from the pond(s) of diluted leachate that was created on top of the landfill directly above the hydrologic center (Geraghty and Miller, Inc. 1972, 1974). Boundaries both the observed intensity and the extent of upwelling was greater in 1983 and 1985 than in the early 1970s, I estimate that it will be at least 10 years before the environmental stress decreases to the levels that occurred in 1980, even if the landfill is capped next year. In 1980 the environmental stress was considerable. For example, it was too high for one of the worst (and most beautiful) marsh weeds, purple loosestrife (*Lythrum salicaria*), to invade the area. Excluding such species as purple loosestrife and reed grass (*Phragmites communis*) will require constant vigilance during some portions of the recovery, probably the mid portion. Troublesome species are not expected in Croton Bay as the SAV community returns there, but maintaining an appropriate depth of water for the SAV community in an efficient and environmentally sound manner will be a challenge. Once the SAV community is reestablished, it is unlikely that the sediments will shift significantly, since this did not happen when SAV thrived there previously.

The Croton Bay/Croton River estuarine system is the gem of the fisheries nursery of the Hudson River. Estuarine processes within Croton Bay are superbly protected by Croton Point, and are further enhanced by their connection to the estuary of the Croton River. These areas rate both protection and commitment to restoration. Therefore it is appropriate to establish them as an estuarine sanctuary. That objective is completely in keeping with the current negotiations between the Hudson River Fishermen's Association and the County of Westchester regarding plans for an estuarine environmental center at Croton Point.

Acknowledgments

Without the recent research and assistance of Professor William E. Odum (University of Virginia), Dr. William C. Dennison (Horn Point Laboratories, University of Maryland), and Professor David R. Bouldin (Cornell University), this presentation would not be possible.

V. SUMMARY

C. LAVETT SMITH

25

What Do We Really Know about the Hudson?

New York is a water state. Within its borders there are more than 70,000 miles of streams, some 4,000 lakes and ponds, and parts of two of the largest lakes in the world. There is also the Hudson River Estuary. Between 1927 and 1939, the New York State Conservation Department conducted one of the most thorough biological surveys ever attempted and during the course of this survey the upper Hudson was studied in 1932, the Mohawk Hudson in 1934, and the lower Hudson in 1936. Following these surveys, however, little attention was paid to the estuary until the 1960s when the public concern over plans to build additional power plants along the river forced the utility companies to sponsor research directed at assessing their potential effects on the river and its biota. These investigations, collectively known as the Hudson River Ecological Study (Klauda et al. 1988b), and subsequent inquiries, such as the one designed to predict the effects of the West Side Highway project, have made the Hudson River estuary one of the world's most intensively studied large ecosystems.

We frequently hear the criticism that all of this expensive research has failed to provide any real understanding of how this or any other estuarine ecosystem functions. Let us examine this critical assessment in the light of the present papers.

First of all, what do we really want to know about the estuary? What is our ultimate goal and what do we mean by "understanding" in the context of estuarine ecology?

Most of the research conducted during the Hudson Ecology Study has been designed to answer specific questions, often with great precision. The principal goal of this research was to enable us to predict the effect of specific changes in the ecosystem resulting from projects such as the construction and operation of the Cornwall Pumped Storage Facility or the installation of cooling towers at Indian Point. Today such limited goals must be expanded to the all-inclusive one of developing a general model that will permit us to predict the effects of all kinds of changes to the ecosystem, ranging from fishery regulations to global warming.

How close are we to truly useful predictive models? As the papers in Part One demonstrate, we have acquired a great deal of information on certain physical aspects of the river so that it is now possible to predict with reasonable accuracy the effect on the location of the salt front of exceptionally high or low rainfall (Abood et al.; Wells et al.), or the effect of removing large amounts of drinking water from the river (Thatcher). We have good historical data from which we can derive water quality trends (Mancroni et al.) and correlations with natural and man-made factors associated with the burgeoning human population, such as channel dredging (Houston et al.) and highway construction (Abood et al.), the construction of sewage treatment plants, and the operation of nuclear power plants (Linsalata and Cohen). To this extent our goals are nearing realization.

In the biological world of the estuary, however, the magnitude of our task is just being recognized, in spite of a considerable emphasis on the study of fisheries and fish population dynamics. The reasons for this slow progress are, it appears, mostly operational.

THE COMPLEXITY OF BIOLOGICAL SYSTEMS

Many organisms have complex life history patterns, and each life stage has a unique set of environmental requirements. We seldom have reasonably complete life history information for the most common species (Dovel et al.; Schmidt). Many species have seasonal movements within the estuary and we are just beginning to unravel these different behaviors (Dovel et al.; Dovel; Geoghegan et al.). The interactions between organisms and their environments are extremely complex, and it is rare for one factor to have a single, direct effect. Moreover, as populations sizes increase and decrease, they affect other species and often the physicochemical environment as well. It has proved time-consuming to sort out the interactions between organisms and their environment, which includes other organisms; progress has been disappointingly slow.

THE FOCUS ON A FEW TARGET SPECIES AND SPECIFIC SITES

This self-limiting approach has resulted mainly from economic constraints. Research on the large scale demanded by holistic estuarine studies is extremely expensive. The organizations paying for the studies simply cannot afford to subsidize any long-term work unless its results are immediately applicable to the problem at hand. Moreover, because environmental issues are frequently contested in the courts, data collecting is often extremely precise, narrowly channeled, and sometimes unnecessarily costly (Young et al.). Under such constraints, consultants cannot exercise the luxury of exploring side issues, no matter how promising they may be, unless there is an immediate need for the peripheral information. Consequently, much of the Hudson River ecological study has been site- and species-specific and aimed at answering particular questions, rather than unraveling underlying causes.

We indeed have studied effects, rather than causes. A common approach has been to determine what fraction of a given species occurs in a particular area and then to ask what would be the effect on the entire estuarine population if that fraction were lost. Such an approach avoids the more nebulous questions of underlying causes, but since we have not found out why the organisms were at that site in the first place, the studies have to be repeated for the next site without bringing us any closer to a predictive model. This approach generates large quantities of data but does little to further our understanding. The paper by Metzger et al. examines the consequences of limiting one's sampling to only a few parts of the river. Similarly, most research has been focused on a few species that were considered to be the most important because of their size, or their recreational or commercial value. As a result, much effort has been centered on the striped bass (McKown and Young) and white perch (Wells et al.) and almost none on the introduced carp and goldfish in spite of the fact that carp and goldfish are extremely abundant and make up a large fraction of the fish biomass in the river.

THE FAILURE TO MAKE DATA GENERALLY AVAILABLE

Another problem is that much of the information that has been accumulated has never become generally available. Thanks to summary papers by Klauda and his co-workers (1988), the most important studies can now be identified, but many are buried in the gray literature—reports with limited distribution—so they are still difficult to obtain and are certainly not as well-known or as well-utilized as they should be. Undoubtedly much more extremely valuable information remains sequestered in researchers' files, having never made it into either the published literature or proprietary reports.

THE LACK OF ANY UNIFYING THEORETICAL BASE

The most critical difficulty of all, it seems to me, is the lack of effort toward synthesizing the data already available. Individual investigators appear to be so closely involved with their particular research that they have neither the time nor inclination to make any attempt to construct an integrated picture. As a result, we have little in the way of an underlying theoretical basis with which to interpret our findings.

Most investigators concerned with a single aspect of the estuary find that they are so overwhelmed with the complexity of their specialty that they cannot conceive of mastering any other facets of the system; hence they are reluctant even to try to produce some sort of comprehensive synthesis. I believe that all investigators ought to be encouraged to present their work in terms of its significance to the estuary as a whole, and that such interpretations should be attempted even if most later prove to be erroneous. All branches of science progress by successive approximations and subsequent refinements; estuarine science is no exception. Speculation and discussion should certainly be encouraged as long as they arise from hard data and sound observations. Many scientists are loathe to try to make connections on the basis of limited observations. Certainly it should be our goal to have all observations replicated and to draw statistical inferences from adequate data. It should be borne in mind, however, that the first step is to generate hypotheses that can be subjected to rigorous testing. Hypotheses are the key to progress, for without them there can be no testing.

Since the 1981 Settlement Agreement, the character of research in the Hudson River has begun to change. For example, Dunning et al. have pointed out that the utilities research programs are now aimed at assessing the effectiveness of mitigation programs, especially the stocking of hatchery-raised striped bass. There also seems to be a greater tendency to review data that are already available in order to compare methods (Mattson et al.) and develop better indices (Heimbuch et al.) and additional models (Ginzburg and Ferson).

Today, a good many researchers are finding the Hudson Estuary a convenient laboratory for the study of phenomena that are of much wider significance and they hope that their results will be applicable to other ecosystems. Some even contend that the object of ecological research should be an understanding of the natural world, without any additional special goals. For them the question of how the information is to be used is a separate issue, of little concern to the investigator conducting the studies. Such "pure" research provides a welcome antidote to limited "practical" science. Nevertheless, the ability to make accurate forecasts is often the bottom-line test of our knowledge, and here the pragmatist and the idealist share a common goal.

Financial support for research in the Hudson River now comes from several and somewhat disparate (e.g., NYSDEC, McKown and Young; Hudson River Foundation, Schmidt; Institute for Ecosystems research, Lints et al.; USACE-NYD, Houston et al. Will et al.) and this too, makes a much more diversified approach to data gathering inevitable. For example, the surveys of Newark Bay included all of the fishes instead of selected species (Will et al.) and the habitat comparisons of Stoecker et al. were based on invertebrate communities as well as piscine ones. The paper by Schmidt et al. considers all the fishes that use tidal freshwater marshes as nursery areas and Lints et al. have constructed an energy budget for the entire estuary. Finally, the paper by Buckley makes a plea for the restoration of ecosystems in the Hudson as illustrated by the badly misused Croton Bay.

Inasmuch as this sampling of papers on Hudson River ecology reflects the current interests of the scientists working on the Hudson, it is encouraging to see that we are finally reaching the stage of examining how the system works rather than simply what it does.

Abbreviations

Con Ed	Consolidated Edison Company of New York
CHGE	Central Hudson Gas and Electric Corporation
EA	EA Science and Technology (Formerly Ecological Analysists, Inc.), a division of EA Engineering, Science, and Technology, Inc.
HRES	Hudson River Environmental Society
LMS	Lawler, Matusky, and Skelly, Engineers (formerly QLM)
MPI	Malcolm Pirnie, Inc.
NAI	Normandeau Associates, Inc.
NMFS	National Marine Fisheries Service
NMPC	Niagara Mohawk Power Company, Inc.
NYSDEC	New York State Department of Environmental Conservation
NYPA	New York Power Authority
ORU	Orange and Rockland Utilities
PASNY	Power Authority of the State of New York, presently New York Power Authority
QLM	Quirk, Lawler, and Matusky, Inc.
TI	Texas Instruments, Inc.
USACE-NY	U.S. Army Corps of Engineers—New York District

All common and scientific names of fishes follow the recommendations of the American Fisheries Society Committee on Names of Fishes (1980).

Literature Cited

Abood, K. A. 1974. Circulation in the Hudson Estuary. Ann. N.Y. Acad. Sci. 250: 39–111.

Abood, K. A. 1977. Evaluation of circulation in partially stratified estuaries as typified by the Hudson River. PhD dissertation, Rutgers University, New Brunswick, NJ.

Abood, K. A., G. A. Apicella, and Alan W. Wells. This volume. Evaluation of Hudson River freshwater flow trends.

Abood, K. A., and T. B. Vanderbeek. 1985. Microcomputer simulations of jets and wakes. Pp. 31–36 in Hydraulics and hydrology in the small computer age. Vol. 1. New York: Am. Soc. Civil Engineers.

Adams, M. S., and M. D. McCracken. 1974. Seasonal production of the *Myriophyllum* component of the littoral of Lake Wingra, Wisconsin. J. Ecol. 62(2): 457–67.

Aleveras, Ronald A. 1973. Occurrence of a lookdown in the Hudson River. N.Y. Fish Game J. 20(1): 76.

American Public Health Association. 1985. Standard methods for the examination of water and wastewater. 16th ed.

Andrewartha, H. G., and L. C. Birch. 1954. The distribution and abundance of animals. Chicago: University of Chicago Press.

Anselmini, L. D. 1974. An ecological study of the Hackensack River in the vicinity of the Hudson River generating station, Jersey City, N.J.: Ichthyol. Assoc.

Arnason, A. N., and K. H. Mills. 1987. Detection of handling mortality and its effects on Jolly-Seber estimates for mark-recapture experiments. Canadian J. Fish. Aquat. Sci. 44: 64–73.

Armstrong, M. L., and Arthur V. Brown. 1983. Diel drift and feeding of channel catfish alevins in the Illinois River, Arkansas. Trans. Am. Fish. Soc. 112(2B): 302–7.

ASMFC (Atlantic States Marine Fisheries Commission). 1989. Draft Revised ASMFC interstate striped bass management plan. Washington, D.C.

Auer, N. A. 1982. Identification of larval fishes of the Great Lakes basin with emphasis on the Lake Michigan drainage. Great Lakes Fishery Comm., Special Publ. 82–3, Ann Arbor, Michigan. 744 pp.

Austin, H. K., and S. Findlay. 1989. Benthic bacterial biomass and production in the Hudson River Estuary. Microb. Ecol.

Bagenal, T. B. 1964. An analysis of the variability associated with the Vigneron-Dahl modification of the otter trawl by day and by night and a discussion of its action. J. Cons., Cons. Perma. Int. Explor. Mer 24(1): 62–69.

Bagenal, T. (ed.). 1974. The ageing of fish. Surrey: Unwin Brothers Ltd. 234 pp.

Bagenal, T. (ed.). 1978. Methods for assessment of fish production in fresh waters. International Biological Pregramme Handbook No. 3. (3rd edition). Oxford: Blackwell Scientific Publications. 365 pp.

Bain, M. B., and J. L. Bain. 1982. Habitat suitability index model for coastal stocks of striped bass (*Morone saxatilis* Walbaum). U.S. Fish and Wildl. Serv. Office of Biol. Serv. (Prepared for National Coastal Ecosystems Team).

Banse, K., and S. Mosher. 1980. Adult biomass and annual production/biomass relationships of field populations. Ecol. Monogr. 50(3): 355–79.

Barnard, W. D. 1978. Prediction and control of dredge material dispersion around dredging and open-water pipeline disposal operations. Tech

Rept. DS-78-13. Vicksburg: U.S. Army Engineer Waterways Experiment Station.

Barnthouse, L. W. 1979. Letter to Eric Erdheim, Eng., U.S. National Oceanic and Atmospheric Administration. April 25.

Barnthouse, L. W., J. Boreman, S. W. Christensen, C. P. Goodyear, W. Van Winkle, and D. S. Vaughan. 1984. Population biology in the courtroom: the Hudson River controversy. BioScience 34(1): 14–19.

Bason, W. M. 1971. Ecology and early history of striped bass, Morone saxatilis, in the Delaware Estuary. Ichthyol. Assoc. Bull.

Bath, Dale W., C. Allen Beebe, C. Braxton Dew, Robert H. Reider, and Jack H. Hecht. 1977. A list of common and scientific names of fishes collected from the Hudson River, 1976. Proc. Fourth Symposium on Hudson River Ecology. HRES, 6 pp.

Bath, D. W., and J. M. O'Connor. 1982. The biology of the white perch, Morone americana, in the Hudson River Estuary. Fish. Bull. 80(3): 599–610.

Battelle. 1975. Environmental impact monitoring of nuclear power plants. Source book of monitoring methods. Vols. 1 and 2. Prepared for Atomic Industrial Forum. 918 pp.

Battelle. 1983. 1980 and 1981 year class report for the Hudson River monitoring program. Prepared for ConEd.

Becker, A., and R. H. Boyle. 1986. The vulnerability of lakes, ponds, and reservoirs in the Hudson Highlands to acidification. Prepared by Hudson River Fisherman's Association.

Beebe, A., and I. R. Savidge. 1988. Historical perspective on fish species composition and distribution in the Hudson River Estuary. Am. Fish. Soc. Monogr. 4: 25–36.

Berg, L. S. 1948. Freshwater fishes of the U.S.S.R. and adjacent countries. Vol. (translated from Russian for the National Science Foundation, Washington, D.C., by Israel Program Sci. Trans., Jerusalem, 1962).

Berggren, T. J., and J. T. Lieberman. 1978. Relative contribution of Hudson, Chesapeake, and Roanoke striped bass, Morone saxatilis, stocks to the Atlantic coast fishery. Fish. Bull. 76: 335–45.

Beverton, R. J. H., and S. J. Holt. 1957. On the dynamics of exploited fish populations. London: Fishery Investigation, Ministry of Agriculture, Fisheries, and Food.

Bigelow, H. B., and W. C. Schroeder. 1953. Fishes of the Gulf of Maine. Fish. Bull. 74, vol. 53. viii+577 pp.

Bird, D. F., and Y. T. Prairie. 1985. Practical guidelines for the use of zooplankton length-weight regression equations. J. Plank. Res. 7(6): 955–60.

Boehlert, G. W., and B. C. Mundy. 1988. Roles of behavioral and physical factors in larval and juvenile fish recruitment to estuarine nursery areas. Pp. 51–67 in Larval fish and shellfish transport through inlets (M. P. Weinstein, ed.). Am. Fish. Soc. Symp. 3.

Bohlen, W. F., D. F. Cundy, and J. M. Tramontano. 1979. Suspended material distributions in the wake of estuarine channel dredging operations. Estur. Coast. Mar. Sci. 9: 699–711.

Bonomi, G. 1979. Ponderal production of *Tubifex tubifex* Miller and *Limnodrilus hoffmeisteri* Claparede (Oligochaeta, Tubificidae), benthic cohabitants of an artificial lake. Boll. Zool. 46: 153–61.

Boreman, J., and H. M. Austin. 1985. Production and harvest of anadromous striped bass stocks along the Atlantic coast. Trans. Am. Fish. Soc. 114(1): 3–7.

Boreman, J., and R. J. Klauda. 1988. Distributions of early life stages of striped bass in the Hudson River Estuary, 1974–1979. Am. Fish. Soc. Monogr. 4: 53–58.

Bottrell, H. H., A. Duncan, A. Giliwicz, Z. M. Grygierek, E. Herzig, A. Hillbrecht-Ilkowska, H. Kurasawa, P. Larsson, and T. A. Weglenska. 1976. A review of some problems in zooplankton production studies. Norw. J. Zool. 24: 419–56.

Bourne, D. W., and J. J. Govoni. 1988. Distribution of fish eggs and larvae and patterns of circulation in Narragansett Bay—1973–1975. Pp. 132–48 in Larval Fish and Shellfish transport through inlets (M. P. Weinstein, ed.). Am. Fish. Soc. Symposium No. 3.

Bowermaster, J. 1986. Manhattan swim-around. It was a very dirty race. Outside. December.

Box, G. E. P., and G. M. Jenkins. 1976. Time series analysis: Forecasting and control. San Francisco: Holden-Day.

Boyce Thompson Institute. 1972. Croton Point Ecology. Exhibit A. Assessment of Environmental Impact of Waste Disposal Area. Report to Westchester Co. 74 pp.

Boyd, C. E. 1979. Water quality in warmwater fish ponds. Agricultural Experiment Station Auburn University. 359 pp.

Boyle, R. H. 1969. The Hudson River: a natural and unnatural history. New York: W. W. Norton and Co. 304 pp.

Boynton, W. R., T. T. Polgar, and H. H. Zion. 1981. Importance of juvenile striped bass food habits in the Potomac Estuary. Trans. Am. Fish. Soc. 110: 56–63.

Brockwell, P. J., and R. A. Davis. 1987. Time series: Theory and Methods. New York: Springer-Verlag.

Brown, C. L., and R. Clark. 1968. Observations on dredging and dissolved oxygen in a tidal waterway. Water Resources Research 4(6): 1381–84.

Buckley, J. L. 1982. Seasonal movement, reproduction, and artificial spawning of shortnose sturgeon (*Acipenser brevirostrum*) from the Connecticut River. MS thesis, Univ. Massachusetts, Amherst. 64 pp.

Buckley, J., and B. Kynard. 1985. Yearly movements of shortnose sturgeon in the Connecticut River. Trans. Am. Fish. Soc. 114(6): 813–20.

Burgman, M. A., H. R. Akçakaya, and S. S. Loew. 1988. The use of extinction models for species conservation. Biological Conservation. 43: 9–25.

Busby, M. W., and K. I. Darmer. 1970. A look at the Hudson River Estuary. Water Resources Bull. 6(5): 802–12.

Cairns, J., Jr., and K. L. Dickson (eds.). 1973. Biological methods for the assessment of water quality. American Society for Testing and Materials Spec. Publ. 528. Philadelphia. 256 pp.

Cairns, J., Jr., G. P. Patil, and W. E. Waters. (eds.). 1979. Environmental biomonitoring, assessment, prediction, and management—certain case studies and related quantitative issues. Burtonsville: International Cooperative Publishing House. 438 pp.

Calhoun, A. J. 1953. Distribution of striped bass fry in relation to major water diversions. Calif. Fish Game 39(3): 279–99.

Calhoun, A. (ed.). 1966. Inland fisheries management. Calif. Dept. Fish Game. 546 pp.

Cantelmo, F. R., C. Vale, T. Kelly, and B. Stewart. 1985. Importance of underpier areas in the lower Hudson River for striped bass. Coastal Zone (1): 706–15.

Canter, L. W. 1979. Water resources assessment—Methodology and technology sourcebook. Ann Arbor: Ann Arbor Science. 529 pp.

Canter, L. W., and L. G. Hill. 1979. Handbook of variables for environmental impact assessment. Ann Arbor: Ann Arbor Science. 203 pp.

Carlson, D. M. 1986. Fish and their habitats in the upper Hudson Estuary. New York Department of Environmental Conservation, Region 4 Fisheries.

Carr, W. E. S., and C. A. Adams. 1973. Food habits of juvenile marine fishes occupying seagrass beds in the estuarine zone near Crystal River, Florida. Trans. Am. Fish. Soc. 102(3): 511–40.

Carriker, M. R. 1967. Ecology of estuarine benthic invertebrates: a perspective. In Estuaries (G. H. Lauff, ed.) AAAS Publ. 83, Washington.

Chadwick, H. K., D. E. Stevens, and L. W. Miller. 1977. Some factors regulating the striped bass population in the Sacramento-San Joaquin Estuary, California. Pp. 18–35 in Proceedings of the conference on assessing the effects of power-plant-induced mortality on fish populations (W. Van Winkle, ed.). New York: Pergamon Press.

Chang, W. Y. B. 1982. A statistical method for evaluating the reproducibility of age determinations. Can. J. Fish. Aquat. Sci. 39: 1208–10.

Chen, C. W. 1987. Compensatory mechanisms in fish populations: Literature reviews. EPRI Report EA-5200. Palo Alto, Ca.

Christiansen, S. W., and R. J. Klauda. 1988. Two scientists in the courtroom: what they didn't teach us in graduate school. Am. Fish. Soc. Monogr. 4: 307–15.

Chubb, S. L., and C. R. Liston. 1986. Density and distribution of larval fishes in Pentwater Marsh, a coastal wetland on Lake Michigan. J. Great Lakes Res. 12(4): 332–43.

Clark, J. R., and S. E. Smith. 1969. Migratory fish studies of the Hudson Estuary. In Hudson River Ecology (G. P. Howells and G. I. Lauer, eds.). Second Symposium on Hudson River Ecology, HRES.

Clifford, H. F. 1972. Downstream movements of white sucker, *Catostomus commersoni*, fry in a brown-water stream of Alberta. J. Fish. Res. Bd. Can. 29: 1091–93.

Coastal Environmental Services, Inc. 1989. Hudson River striped bass stock assessment workshop—final report. Prepared for NYPA.

Coffey, D. S., J. C. Sprenger, D. T. Tingey, G. E. Neeley, and J. C. McCarty. 1988. National crop loss assessment network: Quality assurance program. Environmental Pollution 53: 89–98.

Colby, D. R. 1988. Null hypotheses, models, and statistical designs in the study of larval transport. Pp. 149–62 in Larval fish and shellfish transport through inlets (M. P. Weinstein, ed.). Am. Fish. Soc. Symp. 3.

Cole, J. J., S. Findlay, and M. L. Pace. 1988. Bacterial production in fresh and saltwater ecosystems: a cross-system overview. Mar. Ecol. Prog. Ser. 43: 1–10.

Colwell, R. K. 1974. Predictability, constancy, and contingency of periodic phenomena. Ecology 55: 1148–53.

Cook, E. R., and G. C. Jacoby, Jr. 1979. Evidence for quasi-periodic July drought in the Hudson Valley, New York. Nature 282 (5737): 390–92.

Cooper, J. C., F. R. Cantelmo, and C. E. Newton. 1988. Overview of the Hudson River Estuary. Am. Fish. Soc. Monogr. 4: 11–24.

Cormack, R. M., 1968. The statistics of capture-recapture methods. Oceanogr. Mar. Biol. Ann. Rev.: 405–506.

Cormack, R. M., G. P. Patil, and D. S. Robson. 1979. Sampling biological populations. Statistical ecology, vol. 5. Burtonsville: International Cooperative Publishing House. 392 pp.

Crecco, V. 1989. The environmental and stock-dependent effects of recruitment of Atlantic coast striped bass. Emergency striped bass study annual striped bass workshop abstracts.

Crowder, L. B., and W. E. Cooper. 1982. Habitat structural complexity and the interaction between bluegills and their prey. Ecology 63: 1802–13.

Cummins, K. W. 1979. The natural stream ecosystem. Pp. 7–24 in The ecology of regulated streams (J. V. Ward and J. A. Stanford, eds.). New York: Plenum Press.

Cuerrier, J. P. 1951. The use of pectoral fin rays to determine age of sturgeons and other fish species. Canadian Fish Cult. 11: 10–18.

Dadswell, M. J. 1975. Biology of the shortnose sturgeon *Acipenser brevirostrum* in the Saint John River Estuary, New Brunswick, Canada. St. Andrews, N.B.: Huntsman Marine Lab.

Dadswell, M. J. 1979. Biology and population characteristics of the shortnose sturgeon, *Acipenser brevirostrum* LeSueur 1818 (Osteichthys: Acipenseridae), in the Saint John River Estuary, New Brunswick, Canada. Canadian J. Zool. 57: 2186–2210.

Dadswell, M. J., B. D. Taubert, T. S. Squires, D. Marchette, and J. Buckley. 1984. Synopsis of biological data in shortnose sturgeon, *Acipenser brevirostrum* LeSueur 1818. Fish Synop. 140. Tech. rept. 14. National Marine Fisheries Service. 45 pp.

Dahlberg, M. D. 1972. An ecological study of Georgia coastal fishes. Fish. Bull. 70(2): 323–53.

Darmer, K. I. 1969. Hydrological characteristics of the Hudson River Estuary. Pp. 40–55 in Hudson River Ecology (G. P. Howells and G. I. Lauer, eds.). New York State Dept. Environ. Conserv.

Davis, J. C. 1973. Statistics and data analysis in geology. New York: John Wiley and Sons, Inc. 550 pp.

Dean, Bashford, and F. B. Sumner. 1897. Notes on the spawning habits of the brook lamprey (*Petromyzon wilderi*). Trans. New York Acad. Sci. 16: 321–24.

Derickson, W. K., and K. S. Price. 1973. The fishes of the shore zone of Rehoboth and Indian River bays, Delaware. Trans. Am. Fish. Soc. 102(3): 552–62.

Dew, C. B. 1988. Biological characteristics of commercially caught Hudson River striped bass, 1973–1975. North American Journal of Fisheries Management. 8: 75–83.

Dey, W. P. 1981. Mortality and growth of young-of-the-year striped bass *Morone saxatilis* in the Hudson River Estuary. Trans. Am. Fish. Soc. 110: 151–57.

Dickson, K. L., J. Cairns, Jr., and R. J. Livingston (eds.). 1977. Biological data in water pollution assessment: Quantitative and statistical analyses. Philadelphia: American Society for Testing and Materials Special Publication 652. 184 pp.

Dovel, W. L. 1964. An approach to sampling estuarine macroplankton. Chesapeake Sci. 5(1/2): 77–90.

Dovel, W. L. 1971. Fish eggs and larvae of the upper Chesapeake Bay. Nat. Res. Inst., Univ. Maryland, Spec. Sci. Rept. no. 4.

Dovel, W. L. 1973. An investigation of the population dynamics of Hudson River fishes found in the general area of the Tappan Zee and Haverstraw Bay with particular application to the Rockwood Hall property. Summary Report for NY State Office of Parks and Recreation, Albany. Yonkers: Boyce Thompson Inst. Plant Res., Inc.

Dovel, W. L. 1978. The biology and management of shortnose and Atlantic sturgeons in the Hudson River. Report to NYSDEC.

Dovel, W. L. 1979. The biology and management of shortnose and Atlantic sturgeons of the Hudson River. Final Report for the period October 1, 1975, to September 30, 1980. Yonkers: Boyce Thompson Institute for Plant Res., Inc.

Dovel, W. L. 1979. Atlantic and shortnose sturgeon in the Hudson River Estuary. Testimony of William Dovel prepared for the US Environmental Protection Agency, Region II. Stamford, Conn.: The Oceanic Society.

Dovel, W. L. 1981a. Ichthyoplankton of the lower Hudson Estuary, New York. N.Y. Fish Game J. 28(1): 21–39.

Dovel, W. L. 1981b. The endangered shortnose sturgeon of the Hudson Estuary: Its life history and vulnerability to the activities of man. The Oceanic Society. FERC Contract no. DE-AC 39–79 RC-10074. Stamford: The Oceanic Society. 133 pp.

Dovel, W. L., and T. J. Berggren. 1983. Atlantic sturgeon of the Hudson Estuary, New York. N.Y. Fish Game J. 30(2): 140–72.

Dovel, W. L., A. W. Pekovitch, and T. J. Berggren. This volume. Biology of the shortnose sturgeon (*Acipenser brevirostrum* Le Sueur 1818) of the Hudson River Estuary, New York. HRES, SUNY Press.

Duncan, A. J. 1974. Quality control and industrial statistics. 4th Edition. Homewood: Richard D. Irwin, Inc. 1047 pp.

Dunning, D. J., and Q. E. Ross. 1986. Parameters for assessing Hudson River striped bass stocking. Pp. 391–97 in Fish culture in fisheries management (R. H. Stroud, ed.). Am. Fish. Soc. Bethesda, Md.

Dunning, D. J., Q. E. Ross, B. R. Friedman, and K. L. Marcellus. In press. Coded wire tag retention by, and tagging mortality of, striped bass reared at the Hudson River hatchery. Proc. Int. Symp. and educational workshop on fish marking techniques. Bethesda: Am. Fish. Soc.

Dunning, D. J., Q. E. Ross, M. T. Mattson, P. Geoghegan, and J. R. Waldman. 1989. Reducing mortality of striped bass captured in seines and trawls. North Am. J. Fish. Manag. 9: 171–76.

Dunning, D. J., Q. E. Ross, J. R. Waldman, and M. T. Mattson. 1987. Tag retention by, and tagging mortality of, Hudson River striped bass. North Am. J. Fish. Manag. 7: 535–38.

Dunning, D. J., J. R. Waldman, D. G. Heimbuch, and M. T. Mattson. This volume. Postjuvenile striped bass studies after the Settlement Agreement.

EA. 1978. Thermal effects literature review for Hudson River representative important species. Prepared for CHGE, ConEd, and ORU.

EA. 1982. Roseton generating station entrainment abundance studies, 1981 report. Prepared for CHGE.

EA. 1983. Roseton and Danskammer Point generating stations entrainment abundance studies, 1982 report. Prepared for CHGE.

EA. 1984. Roseton and Danskammer Point generating stations entrainment abundance studies, 1983 report. Prepared for CHGE.

EA. 1985. Roseton and Danskammer Point generating stations impingement monitoring program, 1984 annual progress report. Prepared for CHGE.

EA. 1986. Roseton and Danskammer Point generating stations impingement monitoring program, 1985 annual progress report. Prepared for CHGE.

EA. 1987. Roseton and Danskammer Point generating stations entrainment abundance studies, 1986 report. Prepared for CHGE.

Edmondson, W. T., and G. C. Winberg. (eds.). 1971. A manual on methods for the assessment of secondary productivity in fresh waters. International Biological Programme Handbook no. 17. Oxford: Blackwell Scientific Publications. 358 pp.

Edwards, R. W., and M. Owens. 1962. The effects of plants on river conditions. IV. The oxygen balance of a chalk stream. J. Ecol. 50(1): 207–20.

EEA. 1988a. Report on aquatic studies—Hudson River site. Prepared for New York City Public Development Corporation.

EEA. 1988b. Hudson River center site: Aquatic environmental study. Final report. Prepared for New York City Public Development Corporation.

EIFAC (European Inland Fisheries Advisory Committee). 1975. Symposium on the methodology for the Survey, Monitoring, and Appraisal of fishery Resources in lakes and large rivers. EIFAC Technical Paper No 23. 747 pp.

Elliott, J. M. 1967. Invertebrate drift in a Dartmoor stream. Arch. Hydrobiol. 63: 202–37.

Ellis, D. 1985a. Environmental audits. Marine Pollution Bulletin 16: 171–72.

Ellis, D. 1985b. Taxonomic sufficiency in pollution assessment. Marine Pollution Bull. 16: 459.

Ellis, D. 1986. Identification centres. Marine Pollution Bull. 17: 479–80.

Ellis, D. V. 1988. Quality control of biological surveys. Marine Pollution Bull. 19: 506–12.

EML (Environmental Measurements Laboratory, Department of Energy). 1982. Environmental Report EML-405 (Prepared by E. P. Hardy and L. E. Toonkel). New York, N.Y.

EML. 1986. A compendium of the EML's research projects related to the Chernobyl nuclear accident (H. L. Volchok and N. Chieco, eds.). EML-460. New York, N.Y.

Epifanio, C. E. 1988. Transport of invertebrate larvae between estuaries and the continental shelf. Pp. 104–14 in Larval fish and shellfish transport through inlets (M. P. Weinsten, ed.). Bethesda: Am. Fish. Soc. Symp. 3.

Faber, D. J. 1980. Observations on the early life history of the golden shiner, *Notemigonus crysoleucas* (Mitchill), in Lac Henry, Quebec. Pp. 69–78 in

Proceedings of the fourth annual larval fish conference (L. A. Fuiman, ed.), FWS/OBS-80/43.

Faber, D. J. 1981. A light trap to sample littoral and limnetic regions of lakes. Verh. Int. Ver. Theor. Angew. Limnol. 21: 744–49.

Fabrizio, M. C. 1987. Contribution of Chesapeake Bay and Hudson River stocks of striped bass to Rhode Island coastal waters as estimated by isoelectric focusing of eye lens proteins. Trans. Am. Fish. Soc. 116(4): 588–93.

Fair, G. M., and J. C. Geyer, 1961. Water supply and waste-water disposal. New York: John Wiley and Sons, Inc.

Fallon, R. D., S. Y. Newell, and C. S. Hopkinson. 1983. Bacterial production in marine sediments: Will cell-specific measures agree with whole-system metabolism? Mar. Ecol. Prog. Ser. 11: 119–27.

Federal Water Pollution Control Administration. 1968. Report of the committee on water quality criteria. Prepared for the U.S. Department of the Interior. 234 pp.

Ferson, S., R. Akcakaya, L. Ginzburg, and M. Krause. In press. Applications of RAMAS to the analysis of ecological risk: examples from two species of fish. Palo Alto: EPRI Technical Report.

Ferson, S., L. R. Ginzburg, and A. Silvers. In press. Extreme event risk analysis for age-structured populations. Ecological Modeling.

Ferson, S., F. J. Rohlf, L. R. Ginzburg, and G. Jacquez, 1988. RAMAS/a user manual: Modeling fluctuations in age-structured populations. Setauket: Exeter Publishing.

Findlay, S. E. G., J. L. Meyer, and R. T. Edwards. 1984. Measuring bacterial production via rate of incorporation of [3H] thymidine into DNA. J. Microb. Meth. 2: 57–72.

Findlay, S., J. L. Meyer, and R. Risley. 1986. Benthic bacterial biomass and production in two blackwater rivers. Can. J. Fish. Aquat. Sci. 43(6): 1271–76.

Findlay, S., K. Limberg, and D. Strayer. 1988. Modelling carbon flow in Tivoli South Bay, Hudson River, N.Y. Section IX, 23 pp. in Polgar Fellowship Reports of the Hudson River National Estuarine Research Reserve Program. 1987 (J. R. Waldman and E. A. Blair, eds.). New York: Hudson River Foundation.

Fischer, H. B., E. J. List, R. C. Y. Koh, J. Imberger, and N. H. Brooks. 1979. Mixing in inland and coastal waters. Academic Press. 483 pp.

Fisher, A. K. 1891. Notes on the occurrence of a young crab-eater (*Elecate canada*) from the lower Hudson Valley, New York. Proc. U.S. Natl. Mus. (1890): 13: 195.

Fives, J. M., S. M. Warlen, and D. E. Hass. 1986. Aging and growth of larval bay anchovy, *Anchoa mitchilli*, from the Newport River Estuary, North Carolina. Estuaries 9(4B): 362–67.

Fofonoff, N. P., and S. Tabata. 1958. Program for oceanographic computations and data processing on the electronic digital computer, ALWAC II-E, PSW-1. Programs for properties of sea water. Manuscript report 25, Fish. Res. Bd. Can., Ottawa.

Foster, G. R., and T. E. Hakonson. 1987. Erosional losses of fallout plutonium. Pp. 225–54 in Environmental research on actinide elements (J. E. Pinder et al., eds.) CONF-841142. NTIS Springfield, Va.

Fritzsche, R. A. 1978. Development of fishes of the Mid-Atlantic Bight. Vol. 5. USDI Fish and Wildlife Service FWS/OBS-78/12. 340 pp.

Fuhrman, J., and F. Azam. 1980. Bacterioplankton secondary production estimates for coastal waters of British Columbia, Antarctica, and California. Appl. Environ. Microbiol. 39: 1085–95.

Fuhrman, J., and F. Azam. 1982. Thymidine incorporation as a measure of heterotrophic bacterial plankton production in marine surface waters: evaluation and field results. Mar. Biol. 66: 109–20.

Fuiman, L. A., J. V. Conner, B. F. Lathrop, G. L. Buynak, D. E. Snyder, and J. J. Loos. 1983. State of the art of identification for cyprinid fish larvae from eastern North America. Trans. Am. Fish. Soc. 112(2B): 319–32.

Geoghegan, P., M. T. Mattson, D. J. Dunning, and Q. E. Ross. In press. Improved data quality in a tagging program through quality assurance and quality control. In R. Kendall (ed.). International symposium and educational workshop on fish-marking techniques. Am. Fish. Soc., Bethesda, Md.

George, Carl J. 1981. The fishes of the Adirondack park. New York State Department of Environmental Conservation. 94 pp.

Geraghty and Miller, Inc. 1973. Investigations of ground-water conditions, Croton Point, Westchester County, N.Y. Report to Westchester County. 40 pp.

Geraghty and Miller, Inc. 1974. Phase II program of Hydrogeologic Investigations at the Croton Point landfill site, Westchester Co., N.Y. Report to Westchester County. 53 pp. plus appendices.

Gerking, S. D. 1962. Production and food utilization in a population of bluegill sunfish. Ecol. Monogr. 32:31–78.

Giese, G. L., and J. W. Barr. 1967. The Hudson River Estuary, a preliminary investigation of flow and water-quality characteristics. New York State Water Resources Comm., Bull 67. 39 pp.

Gilinsky, E. 1984. The role of fish predation and spatial heterogeneity in determining benthic community structure. Ecology 65(2): 455–68.

Ginzburg, L. R., L. B. Slobodkin, K. Johnson, and A. G. Bindman. 1982. Quasiextinction probabilities as a measure of impact on population growth. Risk Analysis 2: 171–81.

Gladden, J. B., F. R. Cantelmo, J. M. Croom, and R. Shapot. 1988. Evaluation of the Hudson River ecosystem in relation to the dynamics of fish populations. Am. Fish. Soc. Monogr. 4: 11–24.

Glass, N. R. 1971. Computer analysis of predation energetics in the largemouth bass. Pp. 325–63 in Systems analysis and simululation ecology (B. C. Patten, ed.). New York: Academic Press.

Goldhammer, A., and S. Findlay. 1988. Estimation of suspended material flux between a *Trapa natans* stand and the Hudson River estuary. Section VIII. 46 pp. in Polgar fellowship reports of the Hudson River national estuarine research reserve program, 1987 (J. R. Waldman and E. A. Balir, eds.). New York: Hudson River Foundation.

Goodyear, C. P. 1978. Management problems of migratory stocks of striped bass. Mar. Rec. Fish. 3: 75–84.

Goodyear, C. P. 1985. Relationship between reported landing and abundance of young striped bass in Chesapeake Bay, Maryland. Trans. Am. Fish. Soc. 114(1): 92–96.

Gotceitas, V., and P. Colgan. 1987. Selection between densities of artificial vegetation by young bluegills avoiding predation. Trans. Am. Fish. Soc. 116(1): 40–49.

Grabe, S. A. 1980. Food of age 1 and 2 Atlantic tomcod, *Microgadus tomcod*, from Haverstraw Bay, Hudson River, New York. Fish. Bull. 77: 1003–6.

Grant, B. F. 1979. Factors causing subtle changes in water quality and effects on fish habitat and populations (Aquatic Contamination: Search for water quality criteria), Proc. 3rd Ann. Meet., Potomac Chap. Am. Fish. Soc. (N. W. Prosser, ed.). 99 pp.

Greeley, John R. 1935. Fishes of the watershed with annotated list. Pp. 45–103 in A biological survey of the Mohawk-Hudson watershed. Supplement to 24th Annual Report for 1934, Albany. New York State Conservation Department.

Greeley, John R. 1937. Fishes of the area with annotated list. Pp. 45–103 in a biological survey of the lower Hudson watershed. Supplement to the 26th Annual Report for 1936. Albany: New York State Conservation Department.

Greeley, John R., and Sherman C. Bishop. 1933. Fishes of the upper Hudson watershed with annotated list. Pp. 64–101 in A biological survey of the upper Hudson watershed. Supplement to 22nd Annual Report for 1932, Albany: New York State Conservation+ Department.

Gregory, R. S., and P. M. Powles. 1985. Chronology, distribution, and sizes of larval fishes sampled by light traps in macrophytic Chemung Lake. Can. J. Zool. 63: 2569–77.

Griffith, J. S., Jr. 1974. Utilization of invertebrate drift by brook trout (*Salvelinus fontinalis*) and cutthroat trout (*Salmo clarki*) in small streams in Idaho. Trans. Am. Fish. Soc. 103(3): 440–47.

Gross, M. G. 1974. Sediment and waste disposition in New York Harbor. Ann. New York Acad. Sci. 250: 112–18.

Gross, M. G. 1976. Dredging and disposal of dredged materials in Hudson River Estuary and New York Bight—past, present, and future. Baltimore: Chesapeake Bay Institute.

Grove, T. L., T. J. Berggren, and D. A. Powers. 1976. The use of innate tags to segregate spawning stocks of striped bass, *Morone saxatilis*. Pp. 166–67 in Estuarine processes, vol. I (M. Wiley, ed.).

Gulland, J. A. 1966. Manual of sampling and statistical methods for fisheries biology. Part 1. Sampling methods. FAO Manuals in Fisheries Science 3. 87 pp.

Gulland, J. A. 1969. Manual of methods for fish stock assessment. Part 1. Fish population analysis. FAO Manuals in Fisheries Science 4. 154 pp.

Hairr, L. M. 1974. An Investigation of factors influencing radiocaesium cycling in estuarine sediments of the Hudson River. Ph.D. Dissertation, New York University, New York.

Hansen, B. L. 1963. Quality control: Theory and applications. Englewood Cliffs: Prentice-Hall. 498 pp.

Hansen, B. L., and J. S. Lebedeff. 1987. Global trends of measured surface air temperature. J. Geophys. Res 92: 13,345–13,372.

Hardy, E. P., and L. E. Toonkel. 1982. Environmental report EML–405. Department of Energy, Environmental Measurements Laboratory, New York.

Hardy, Jerry D., Jr. 1978. Development of fishes of the mid-Atlantic bight. Vol. III. USDI Fish and Wildlife Service FWS/OBS–78/12. 394 pp.

Harlemann, D. R. F., A. V. Quinlan, J. D. Ditmars, and M. L. Thatcher. 1972. Application of the MIT Transient Salinity Intrusion Model to the Hudson River Estuary. Technical report 153, Ralph M. Parsons Laboratory for Water Resources and Hydrodynamics. Massachusetts Institute of Technology. 61 pp.

Hartman, R. M. 1975. Development of guide for aquatic ecological surveys. Pp. 771–84 in Environmental effects of cooling systems at nuclear power plants. Vienna: International Atomic Energy Agency. 829 pp.

Hassell, M. P. 1986. Detecting density dependence. Trends in ecology and evolution 1: 90–93.

Hayes, D. F., G. L. Raymond, and T. N. McLellan. 1984. Sediment resuspension from dredging activities. In Dredging and dredge material disposal. Proc. Confer. on dredging, 1984. Am. Soc. Civil Engineers: 72–82.

Heck, K. L., and T. A. Thoman. 1984. The nursery role of seagrass meadows in the upper and lower reaches of the Chesapeake Bay. Estuaries 7: 70–92.

Heidt, A. R., and R. J. Gilbert. 1978. The shortnose sturgeon in the Altamaha River drainage, Georgia. Ms Report, Contract 03-7-043-35-165, NMFS, 16 pp.

Heimbuch, D. G., D. J. Dunning, H. Wilson, and Q. E. Ross. In press. Sample size determination for mark-recapture experiments: Hudson River case study. Proc. Int. Symposium and Educational Workshop on Fish Marking Techniques. Bethesda: Am. Fish. Soc.

Hildebrand, S. F. 1963. Family Engraulidae. pp. 152–249 in Fishes of the Western North Atlantic. Part 3. New Haven: Sears Foundation for Marine Research.

Hildebrand, S. F., and L. E. Cable. 1930. Development and life history of fourteen teleostean fishes at Beaufort, N.C. Bull. U.S. Bur. Fish. 46: 383–488.

Himchak, P. J. 1982. Monitoring of the status of the striped bass population in New Jersey. NOAA Project AFC-4-1. Nat. Marine. Fish. Serv. Quart. Rept. for N.J.

Hobbie, J. E., R. J. Daley, and S. Jasper. 1977. Use of nuclepore filters for counting bacteria by fluorescence microscopy. Appl. Environ. Microbiol. 33: 1225–28.

Hocutt, C. H., and J. R. Stauffer, Jr. 1980. Biological monitoring of fish. Lexington: D. C. Heath and Company. 416 pp.

Hoff, J. G. 1965. Two shortnose sturgeon, *Acipenser brevirostrum*, from the Delaware River, Scudder's Falls, New Jersey. Bull. N.J. Acad. Sci. 10: 23.

Hoff, J. G., and R. H. Klauda. 1979. Data on shortnose sturgeon (*Acipenser brevirostrum*) collected incidentally from 1969 through June 1979 in sampling programs conducted for the Hudson River Biological Study. TI, Nov. 30.

Hoff, J. G., R. J. Klauda, and B. S. Belding. 1977. Data on distribution and incidental catch of shortnose sturgeon (*Acipenser brevirostrum*) in the Hudson River Estuary 1969 to present. Buchanan, N.Y.: Texas Instruments, Inc.

Hoff, T. B., R. J. Klauda, and J. R. Young. 1988a. Contribution to the biology of shortnose sturgeon in the Hudson River estuary. Pp. 171–92 in Fisheries Research in the Hudson River (C. L. Smith, ed.). Albany: HRES, SUNY Press.

Hoff, T. B., J. B. McLaren, and J. C. Cooper. 1988b. Stock characteristics of Hudson River striped bass. Am. Fish. Soc. Monogr. 4: 59–68.

Hogman, W. 1968. Annulus formation scales of four species of coregonids reared under artificial conditions. J. Fish. Res. Bd. Canada 25(10).

Hollis, E. H. 1952. Variations in the feeding habits of the striped bass, *Roccus saxatilis* (Walbaum), in Chesapeake Bay. Bull. Bingham Ocean. Coll. 14(1): 111–31.

Hook, S. M. 1985. USAE Division/District presentation. Aquatic plant problems-operation activities; North Atlantic Division, New York District. Pp. 11–14 In Proceeding 19th Annual Meeting, Aquatic Plant Control Research Program, November 26–29, 1984, Galveston. Misc. Paper A-85-4, Vicksburg: Environmental Laboratory, U.S. Army Engineer Waterways Experimental Station.

Horrocks, D. L. 1977. The H number concept. Beckman Technical Report 1095. Fullerton: Beckman Instrument Company.

HRES. 1973. Hudson River Ecology. Printed in cooperation with New York State.

Humphreys, M., R. E. Park, J. T. Reichle, M. T. Mattson, D. J. Dunning, and Q. E. Ross. In press. Stocking checks as an internal tag for identifying hatchery striped bass in the Hudson River. Proc. Int. Symposium and Educational Workshop on Fish Marking Techniques. Bethesda: American Fisheries Society.

Hutchison, G. E. 1975. A treatise on limnology. Vol. 1, part 2. Chemistry of Lakes. Wiley Interscience. pp. 541–1015.

Hynes, H. B. N. 1970. The ecology of running waters. Toronto: University of Toronto Press. 555 pp.

Ikusima, I. 1965. Ecological studies on the productivity of aquatic plant communities: I. Measurements of photosynthetic activity. Botanical Magazine, Tokyo. 78: 202–11.

International Commission of Radiological Protection. 1979. Limits for intake of radionucleides by workers. ICRP Publication 30, part 1. New York: Pergamon Press.

Isaac, P. C. G. 1965. The contribution of bottom muds to the depletion of oxygen in rivers and suggested standards for suspended solids. Pp. 476–94 in Biological problems in water pollution. U.S.P.H.S. Pub. 999-wp-25.

Jinks, S. M. 1975. An investigation of the factors influencing radiocaesium concentrations of fish inhabiting natural aquatic systems. Ph.D. Dissertation. New York University, New York.

Jinks, S. M., and M. E. Wrenn. 1976. Radiocaesium transport in the Hudson River Estuary. Pp. 207–27 in Environmental Toxicity of Aquatic Radionucleides: Models and Mechanisms (M. W. Miller and J. N. Stannard, eds.) Ann Arbor: Ann Arbor Sci.

Jinks, S. M., M. E. Wrenn, B. J. Friedman, and L. M. Hairr. 1973. A critical pathway evaluation of the radiological impact resulting from liquid waste discharges at the Indian Point Unit 1 Nuclear Power Station. In Proc. 3rd. Symp on Hudson River Ecology. New York University Medical Center, New York.

Johnsen, J. H. 1966. The geology and mineral resources of the Hudson Estuary. Symposium on Hudson River Ecology, Hudson River Environmental Society.

Johnson, G. David. 1978. Development of fishes of the Mid-Atlantic bight. Vol. IV. USDI Fish and Wildlife Service FWS/OBS-78/12. 314 pp.

Johnson, B. H., M. J. Traule, and P. G. Kee. 1986. Discussion of a laterally averaged numerical model for computing salinity and shoaling with an application to the Savannah River. Proc. 3rd. Int. Symposium on River Sedimentation, ISRS. University of Mississippi.

Jones, Philip W., F. Douglas Martin, and Jerry D. Hardy, Jr. 1978. Development of fishes of the Mid-Atlantic bight. Vol. 1. USDI Fish and Wildlife Service FWS/OBS-78/12. 366 pp.

Kas'yanov, V. P., and V. N. Zlokazov. 1974. K metodike opredeleniya vozrasta sibirskogo osetra. Taz. Otchetnoy sessii Tsentr. n.-1.in-ta. psetr. rybn.kh-va. (On the method of determining age in the Siberian sturgeon. Abstracts from a review session of the Central Sturgeon Fisheries Institute. Astrakhan'.

Keast, A. 1984. The introduced aquatic macrophyte, *Myriphyllum spicatum*, as habitat for fish and their invertebrate prey. Canadian J. Zool. 62: 1289–1303.

Keeney, R. L., and H. P. Raiffa. 1976. Decisions with multiple objectives: preferences and value trade-offs. New York, N.Y. John Wiley and Sons.

Kemp, W. M., W. R. Boynton, and R. R. Twilley. 1984. Influences of submersed vascular plants on ecological process in upper Chesapeake Bay. Pp. 367–94 in The estuary as a filter (V. S. Kennedy, ed.). Orlando: Academic Press.

Kernehan, R. J., M. R. Headrick, and R. E. Smith. 1981. Early life history of striped bass in the Chesapeake and Delaware Canal and vicinity. Trans. Am. Fish. Soc. 110(1): 137–50.

Klauda, R. J., J. B. McLaren, R. E. Schmidt, and W. P. Dey. 1988a. Life history of white perch in the Hudson River. Am. Fish. Soc. Monogr. 4: 69–88.

Klauda, R. J., R. E. Moos, and R. E. Schmidt. 1988b. Life history of the Atlantic tomcod, *Microgadus tomcod*, in the Hudson River estuary, with emphasis on spatio-temporal distribution and movements. Pp. 219–51 in Fisheries Research in the Hudson River (C. L. smith, ed.). Albany: HRES, SUNY Press.

Klauda, R. J., P. H. Muessig, and J. A. Matousek. 1988c. Fisheries data sets compiled by utility-sponsored research in the Hudson River Estuary. Pp. 7–85 in Fisheries Research in the Hudson River (C. L. Smith, ed.). Albany: HRES, SUNY Press.

Kohlhurst, D. W., L. W. Miller, and J. J. Orsi. 1980. Age and growth of white sturgeon collected in the Sacramento-San Joaquin Estuary, California, 1961–1970 and 1973–1976. Calif. Fish Game 66(2): 83–95.

Koski, R. T., E. C. Kelly, and B. E. Turnborough. 1971. A record-sized shortnose sturgeon from the Hudson River. N.Y. Fish Game J. 18: 75.

Kushland, J. A. 1984. Sampling characteristics of enclosure fish traps. Trans. Am. Fish. Soc. 110(4): 557–62.

Lake, Thomas R. 1982. Fall fishing. Hudson River Fisherman, Autumn 1982: 3, 5.

Lake, Thomas R. 1983. Atlantic Needlefish. The Conservationist. Jul./Aug. 38(1): 32–37.

Lasalle, M. W. In press. Proceedings of the workshop on effects of dredging on anadromous fish of the Pacific Coast (C. Simenstad, ed.). Washington Seagrant Program, Seattle, Wa.

Lasalle, M. W., J. Homziak, J. D. Lunz, D. G. Clarke, and T. J. Fredette. In press. Seasonal restriction on dredging and disposal operations. Tech. Rept. Environmental Effects of Dredging. Vicksburg: U.S. Army Engineer Waterways Experiment Station.

Lascara, J. 1981. Fish predator-prey interactions in areas of eelgrass (*Zostera marina*). M.A. thesis, College of William and Mary. 81 pp.

Lavenberg, R. J., G. E. McGowen, and R. E. Woodsum. 1984. Preservation and curation. Pp. 57–59 in Ontogeny and Systematics of Fishes, ASIH Spec. Publ. no. 1.

Lee, S., and J. A. Fuhrman. 1987. Relationships between biovolume and biomass of naturally derived marine bacterioplankton. Appl. Environ. Microbiol. 53(6): 1298–1303.

Lentsch, J. W. 1974. The fate of gamma-emitting radionuclides released into the Hudson River Estuary and an evaluation of their environmental significance. PhD dissertation, New York University, N.Y.

Leopold, L. B., M. G. Wolman, and J. P. Miller. 1964. Fluvial processes in geomorphology. San Francisco: W. H. Freeman and Co.

Lepage, S., and R. G. Ingram. 1986. Salinity intrusion in the Eastmain River Estuary following a major reduction of freshwater input. J. Geophysical Res., AGU, 91(C1): 909–15.

Leslie, J. A., K. A. Abood, E. A. Maikich, and P. J. Keeser. 1988. Recent dissolved oxygen trends in the Hudson River. Pp. 287–303 in Fisheries Research in the Hudson River (C. L. Smith, ed.). Albany: HRES, SUNY Press.

Lesueur, C. A. 1818. Description of several species of Chondropterygious fishes of North America, with their varieties. Trans. Am. Philos. Soc. 1: 383–95.

Limburg, K. E. 1987. Studies of young-of-the-year river herring and American sahd in the Tivoli Bays, Hudson River, N.Y. Section VII. 62 pp. in Polgar Fellowship Reports of the Hudson River National Estuarine Research Reserve Program, 1987 (J. R. Waldman and E. A. Blair, eds.). New York: Hudson River Foundation.

Limberg, K. E., M. A. Moran, and W. H. McDowell. 1986. The Hudson River Ecosystem. New York: Springer-Verlag. 244 pp.

Linsalata, P. 1979. Plutonium in the Hudson River Estuary. M.S. thesis, New York University, N.Y.

Linsalata, P. 1984. Distribution and mobility of Plutonium and Radiocesium in soils, sediments and water in the water column of the Hudson River Estuary. Environ. Geol. Water Sci. 7(4): 193–204.

Linsalata, P., M. E. Wrenn, N. Cohen, and N. P. Singh. 1980. Pu-239, 240 and Pu-238 in sediments of the Hudson River Estuary. Environ. Sci. Technol. 14(12): 1519–23.

Linsalata, P., and N. Cohen. 1982. ^{95}Zr/Nb determined in Hudson River water. Health Physics 43: 742–44.

Linsalata, P., H. J. Simpson, C. R. Olsen, N. Cohen, and R. M. Trier. 1985. Plutonium and radiocaesium in the water column of the Hudson River Estuary. Environ. Geol. Water Sci. 7(4): 193–204.

Linsalata, P., D. Hickman, and N. Cohen. 1986. Comparative pathway analysis of radiocaesium in the Hudson Estuary: Environmental measurements and regulatory dose assessment models. Health Physics 51: 295–312.

Lippson, A. J., and R. L. Moran. 1974. Manual for identification of early developmental stages of fishes of the Potomax River Estuary. Power Plant Siting Prog. MD Dept. Nat. Res. PPSP-MP-13. 282 pp.

Lippson, A. J., M. S. Haire, A. F. Holland, F. Jacobs, J. Jensen, R. L. Moran-Johnson, T. T. Polgar, and W. A. Richkus. 1980. Environmental Atlas of the Potomac Estuary. Martin-Marietta Corp., Baltimore, MD. 279 pp.

LMS. 1972. Technical report on water quality. Part 1. Water quality and hydrodynamic effects. Prepared for Parsons, Brinckerhoff, Quade, and Douglas, Inc.

LMS. 1975. Environmental impact assessment Hudson River water quality analysis. Prepared for National Technical Information Service.

LMS. 1978a. Annual progress report, 1974. Prepared for CHGE.

LMS. 1978b. Annual progress report, 1975. Prepared for CHGE.

LMS. 1978c. Upper Hudson River PCB no action alternative study. Final report. Prepared for NYSDEC.

LMS. 1978d. Biological effects of Once-through cooling. Vol. 1. Prepared for the Utility Water Act Group.

LMS. 1979a. Annual progress report, 1976. Prepared for CHGE.

LMS. 1979b. Annual progress report, 1977. Prepared for CHGE.

LMS. 1979c. Changes in Hudson River water elevation resulting from Westway. Prepared for Parsons, Brinckerhoff, Quade and Douglas, Inc.

LMS. 1980a. Annual progress report, 1978. Prepared for CHGE.

LMS. 1980b. Annual progress report, 1979. Prepared for CHGE.

LMS. 1980. Biological and water quality data collected in the Hudson River near the proposed Water project during 1979–80. Vol. 1.

LMS. 1981. Annual progress report, 1980. Prepared for CHGE.

LMS. 1982. Impingement abundance at Roseton and Danskammer Point generating stations. Annual progress report, 1981. Prepared for CHGE.

LMS. 1983a. Water quality memo summarizing conditions within Westway project area from 1977 to 1983. Prepared for Parsons, Brinckerhoff, Quade, and Douglas, Inc.

LMS. 1983b. Impingement abundance sampling at Roseton and Danskammer Point generating stations. Annual progress report, 1982. Prepared for CHGE.

LMS. 1984a. Albany steam generating station (SPEDES) aquatic monitoring program. October 1982–Sept. 1983.

LMS. 1984b. Inpingement monitoring program at Roseton and Danskammer Point generating stations, 1983. Prepared for CHGE.

LMS. 1984c. Westway mitigation studies. Recommendations Rept. Phase I.

LMS. 1985a. Albany steam generating station (SPDES) Aquatic Monitoring Program. April 1984–April 1985.

LMS. 1985b. Entrainment abundance monitoring program at the Roseton and Danskammer Point generating stations, 1984 progress report. Prepared for CHGE.

LMS. 1986a. Entrainment abundance monitoring program at the Roseton and Danskammer Point generating stations, 1985 progress report. Prepared for CHGE.

LMS. 1986b. Hudson River estuary white perch adult and subadult assessment study, fall 1985. Prepared for ORU.

LMS. 1987a. Hudson River Estuary white perch adult and subadult stock assessment study, fall 1986. Prepared for ORU.

LMS. 1987b. Impingement monitoring program at the Roseton and Danskammer Point generating Stations, 1986 annual progress report. Prepared for CHGE.

LMS. 1988a. Hudson River Estuary white perch adult and subadult stock assessment study, Fall 1987. Prepared for ORU.

LMS. 1988b. Siltation in River Walk project area. Riverwalk DEIS. Prepared for Parish and Weiner, Inc.

LMS. 1989. 1986 and 1987 year class report for the Hudson River Estuary monitoring program. Prepared for Con Ed.

Logan, D. T. 1985. Environmental variation and striped bass population dynamics: a size-dependent mortality model. Estuaries 8(1): 28–38.

Lumia, R., R. J. Archer, P. M. Burke, and F. N. Dalton. 1984. Water resources data. New York. Water year 1983. Vol. 1. Eastern New York excluding Long Island. U.S. Geological Survey Water-Data Report, NY-83-1.

Lunz, J. D., M. W. Lasalle, and L. J. Houston. 1988. Predicting dredging impacts on dissolved oxygen. Proc. 1st. Ann. Meet. Puget Sound Res. Seattle, WA. Vol. 1: 331–36.

Makarewicz, J. C., and G. E. Likens. 1979. Structure and function of the zooplankton community of Mirror Lake, New Hampshire. Ecol. Monogr. 49(1): 109–27.

MPI. 1982. Hudson river estuary fish habitat study. Prepared for USACE-NYD.

MPI. 1983. Hudson River federal channel maintenance dredging. Prepared for USACE-NYD.

MPI. 1984a. Westway fisheries study, December 1983 to April 1984. New Jersey Marine Sciences Consortium. Vol. 1: Bottom trawl striped bass catch and bottom stratum water quality, May 1984. I. 1–1 to I. 3–79.

MPI. 1984b. Westway fisheries study, December 1983 to April 1984. New Jersey Marine Sciences Consortium. Vol. 2: Total catch (all species) and water quality by station: bottom and midwater trawl, December 29, 1983–March 1, 1984. II. 2–1 to II. 6–82.

MPI. 1984c. Westway fisheries study. December 1983 to April 1984. New Jersey Marine Sciences Consortium. Vol 3: Total catch (all species) and water quality by station; Bottom and Midwater Trawl, March 2, 1984–April 30, 1984. III. 3–1 to III. 12–127.

Mancini, E. R., M. N. Busdosh, and B. D. Steele. 1979. Utilization of autochonous macroinvertebrate drift by a pool fish community in a woodland stream. Hydrobiologia 62: 249–56.

Mansfield, P. J. 1984. Reproduction by Lake Michigan fishes in a tributary stream. Trans. Am. Fish. Soc. 113(2): 231–37.

Manteifel, B. P., I. I. Girsa, and D. S. Pavlov. 1978. On rhythms of fish behaviour. Pp. 215–24 in Rhythmic activity of fishes (J. E. Thorpe, ed.). New York: Academic Press.

Marcellus, K. L. 1979. Letter to Henry Gluckstern. Eng., USEPA May 7.

Marchette, D. E., and R. Smiley. 1982. Biology and life history of incidentally captured shortnose sturgeon, *Acipenser brevirostrum* in South Carolina. SC Wildl. Mar. Res. unpublished ms. 57 pp.

Marcy, B. C., Jr. 1976. Early life history studies of American shad in the lower Connecticut River and the effects of the Connecticut Yankee plant. Am. Fish. Soc. Monogr. 1: 141–68.

Markle, D. E., and G. C. Grant. 1970. The summer food habits of young-of-the-year striped bass in three Virginia Rivers. Chesapeake Sci. 11: 50–54.

Martin, F. Douglas. 1978. Development of fishes of the mid-Atlantic bight. Vol. VI. USDI Fish and Wildlife Service FWS/OBS-78/12. 416 pp.

MMES (Martin Marietta Environmental Systems). 1984. Draft report on the estimation of the fraction of striped bass population (1982 and 1983 year classes) located in the Westway Project area from January through April 1984. Vols. 1–3. Prepared for MPI.

MMES (Martin Marietta Environmental Systems). 1986a. 1984 year class report for the Hudson River Estuary monitoring program. Prepared for Con Ed.

MMES (Martin Marietta Environmental Systems). 1986b. Evaluating the effectiveness of outages. Objective I: Enumeration and review of statistical estimators. Prepared for CHGE, Con Ed, NYPA, NMPC, and ORU.

MMES (Martin Marietta Environmental Systems). 1986c. An overall study design for a hatchery evaluation and population assessment for Hudson River striped bass. Prepared for NYPA.

Massman, W. H. 1954. Marine fishes in fresh and brackish waters of Virginia rivers. Ecology 35(1): 75–78.

Massman, W. H. 1963. The "critical zone" in estuaries. Sport Fishing Inst. Bull. 141: 1–2.

Massman, W. H., J. J. Norcross, and E. B. Joseph. 1963. Distribution of larvae of the naked goby, *Gobiosoma bosci*, in the York River. Chesapeake Sci. 4(3): 120–25.

Mattson, M. T., J. R. Waldman, D. J. Dunning, and Q. E. Ross. In press. Internal anchor tag abrasion and protrusion in Hudson River striped bass. Proc. Int. Symp. and Educational Workshop on Fish Marking Techniques. Bathesda: American Fisheries Society.

Mauro, J. 1974. An investigation into the reasons for a lack of a trophic level effect of ^{137}Cs in *Fundulus heteroclitus* and its food in the Hudson River Estuary. Ph.D. Dissertation, New York University, N.Y.

May, R. M., and G. F. Oster. 1976. Bifurcations and dynamic complexity in simple ecological models. Am. Nat. 110: 573–99.

McCarron, E., and S. Findlay. In press. Sediment metabolism at Tivoli South Bay and a *Vallisneria* bed in the Hudson River. Polgar report to the Hudson River Foundation. In Reports of the Hudson River National Estuarine Research Reserve in 1988 (E. A. Blair and J. Waldman, eds.). New York: Hudson River Foundation.

McDonough, R. J., R. W. Sanders, K. G. Porter, and D. L. Kirchman. 1986. Depth distribution of bacterial production in a stratified lake with anoxic hypolimnion. Appl. Environ. Microbiol. 52(5): 992–1000.

McFadden, J. T., Texas Instruments, and Lawler, Matusky and Skelly, Engineers. 1977. Influence of Indian Point Unit 2 and other steam electric generating plants on the Hudson River Estuary, with emphasis on striped bass and other fish populations. Report to Con Ed.

McFadden, J. T. 1977. An argument supporting the reality of compensation in fish populations and a plea to let them exercise it. Pp. 153–83 in Proceedings of the Conference on Assessing the Effects of Power-plant-induced Mortality on Fish Populations. Pergamon Press.

McFadden, J. T. 1978. Influence of the proposed Cornwall pumped storage project and steam electric generating plants on the Hudson River Estuary with emphasis on striped bass and other fish populations. Prepared for Con Ed.

McGahee, C. F., and G. J. Davis. 1971. Photosynthesis and respiration in *Myriophyllum spicatum* L. as related to salinity. Limnol. Oceanogr. 16: 826–29.

McHugh, J. L. 1967. Estuarine nekton. Pp. 581–620 in Estuaries (G. H. Lauff, ed.). Washington: AAAS.

McLaren, J. B., J. C. Cooper, T. B. Hoff, and V. Lander. 1981. Movements of Hudson River striped bass. Trans. Am. Fish. Soc. 110(1): 158–67.

McLaren, J. B., T. H. Peck, W. P. Dey, and M. Gardinier. 1988a. Biology of the Atlantic tomcod in the Hudson River Estuary. Am. Fish. Soc. Monogr. 4: 102–12.

McLaren, J. B., J. R. Young, T. B. Hoff, I. R. Savidge, and W. L. Kirk. 1988b.

Feasibility of supplementary stocking of age-0 striped bass in the Hudson River. Am. Fish. Soc. Monogr. 4: 133–42.

Mearns, E. A. 1898. A study of the vertebrate fauna of the Hudson Highlands, with observations on the mollusca, crustacea, lepidoptera, and flora of the region. Bull. Am. Mus. Nat. Hist. 10: 311–22.

Meehan, W. E. 1910. Experiments in sturgeon culture. Trans. Am. Fish. Soc. 39: 85–91.

Menzie, C. A. 1980. The chironomid (Insecta: Diptera) and other fauna of a *Myriophyllum spicatum* L. plant bed in the lower Hudson River. Estuaries 3: 38–54.

Merriman, D. 1937. Notes on the life history of the striped bass (*Roccus lineatus*). Copeia (1): 15–36.

Merriman, D. 1941. Studies on the striped bass (*Roccus saxatilis*) of the Atlantic coast. Fish. Bull. 50(35): 1–77.

Mihursky, J. A., W. R. Boynton, E. M. Setzler, K. V. Wood, H. H. Zion, E. W. Gordon, L. Tucker, P. Pulles, and J. Leo. 1976. Final report on Potomac estuary fisheries study; ichthyoplankton and juvenile investigations. Univ. Md. Chesapeake Biol. Lab., Solomons, Md. (Ref. No. 76-12-CBL).

Mitchill, C. T., and J. R. Hunter. 1970. Fishes associated with drifting kelp, *Macrocystis pyrifera*, off the coast of southern California and northern Baja California. Calif. Fish Game 56: 288–97.

Mitchill, S. 1811. Collections of the New York Historical Society for the year 1809. Vol. 1. I. Riley.

Moeller, R. E. 1985. Macrophytes. Pp. 257–65 in An ecosystems approach to aquatic ecology (G. E. Likens, ed.). Springer-Verlag, N.Y.

Moriarty, D. J. 1986. Measurement of bacterial growth rates in aquatic systems from rates of nucleic acid synthesis. Pp. 245–92 in Advances in microbial ecology (K. C. Marshall, ed.). Plenum Publishing Corporation, N.Y.

Muenscher, W. C. 1937. Aquatic vegetation of the lower Hudson area. Suppl. 26th Ann. Rept., NY Conservation Dept., Biol. Surv. 11: 231–48.

Muller, K. 1978. Locomotor activity of fish and environmental oscillations. Pp. 1–19 in Rhythmic activity of fishes (J. E. Thorpe, ed.). Academic Press, N.Y.

Murphy, G. I. 1968. Pattern in life history and the environment. Am. Nat. 102: 391–403.

National Marine Fisheries Service. 1980. Consumer data for New York State. Sandy Hook: National Marine Fisheries Service.

National Ocean Service (NOAA). 1988a. Tabulation of monthly sea surface temperatures and densities, Station: The Battery (Months of May–September 1988). Rockville: NOAA Office of Oceanography.

National Ocean Service (NOAA). 1988b. Tides, high and low waters. Station: The Battery (Months of May–September 1988). Rockville: NOAA Office of Oceanography.

NAI. 1985a. 1982 year class report for the Hudson River Estuary monitoring program. Prepared for Con Ed.

NAI. 1985b. 1983 year class report for the Hudson River Estuary monitoring program. Prepared for Con Ed.

NAI. 1985c. Final report for the 1983–1984 Hudson River white perch stock assessment study. Report prepared for ORU.

NAI. 1986. Size selectivity and relative catch efficiency of a 3m beam trawl and a 1m epibenthic sled for sampling young of the year striped bass and other fishes in the Hudson River Estuary. Prepared for NYPA.

NAI. 1987. Hydrographic survey narrative. Prepared for Con Ed.

NAI. 1987. Water quality monitoring of Haverstraw Bay maintenance dredging, prepared for USACE-NYD. 40 pp.

NAI. 1988. 1987–1988 Hudson River striped bass hatchery evaluation. Report to NYPA.

NAI. 1989. Abundance and stock characterization of the Atlantic tomcod (*Microgadus tomcod*) spawning population in the Hudson River, winter 1988–89. Prepared for NYPA.

Neiheisel, J. 1966. Significance of clay minerals in shoaling problems. Tech. Bull. no. 10, U.S. Army Corps of Engineers.

New Jersey Mar. Sci. Consortium. 1984. Summary Report, Westway fisheries studies field and data program.

New York Electric and Gas Corp. and Long Island Light Co. 1978. Environmental Report. NYSE and G. 1 and 2. Stuyvesant Nuclear Station, Binghamton, NY. Part 2, vol. 1, Chapter 2.

New York University Medical Center. 1985. Radioecological studies of the Hudson River. Progress report to ConEd and NYPA. Tuxedo, N.Y.: NYU Institute of Environmental Medicine.

New York University Medical Center. 1988. Radioecological studies of the

Hudson River. Progress Report to NYPA. Tuxedo, N.Y.: Institute of Environmental Medicine.

Nielson, L. A., and D. L. Johnson. 1983. Fisheries techniques. Bethesda: American Fisheries Society. 468 pp.

Nikolsky, G. V. 1961. Special Ichthyology. (Translated by Israel Program for Scientific translations, Jerusalem). U.S. Dept. Comm. Office Tech. Serv. OTS 60-21817. 538 pp.

NRC (U.S. Nuclear Regulatory Commission). 1977. Calculation of Annual Doses to Man from routine releases of reactor effluents for the purposes of evaluating compliance with 10CFR Part 50, Appendix I., Rev. 1. Regulatory guide 1.109. Washington D.C.

Ocean Surveys, Inc. 1987. Field Investigations, Hudson River Center Site, N.Y. Prepared for EEA, Inc. 47 pp.

Odum, W. E. 1971. Pathways of energy flow in a South Florida estuary. Sea Grant Tech. Bull. no. 7. 162 pp.

Odum, W. E. 1988. Comparative ecology of tidal freshwater and salt marshes. Ann. Rev. Ecol. Syst. 19: 147-76.

Odum, W. E., M. L. Dunn, and T. S. Smith III. 1978. Habitat value of freshwater tidal wetlands. Pp. 248-55 in Wetland functions and values: The state of our understanding. Am. Water. Res. Assoc.

Olney, J. E. 1983. Eggs and early larvae of the bay anchovy, *Anchoa mitchilli*, and the weakfish, *Cynoscion regalis*, in lower Chesapeake Bay with notes on associated ichthyoplankton. Estuaries 6(1): 20-35.

Olsen, C. R. 1979. Radionucleides, sedimentation, and the accumulation of pollutants in the Hudson Estuary. Ph.D. Dissertation, Columbia University, N.Y.

Olsen, C. R., H. J. Simpson, T. H. Peng, R. F. Bopp, and R. M. Trier. 1981. Sediment mixing and accumulation rate effects on radionuclide depth profiles in Hudson Estuary sediments. J. Geophys. Res. 86: 11020-28.

Orth, R. J., and K. L. Heck, Jr. 1980. Structural components of eel grass (*Zostera marina*) meadows in the lower Chesapeake Bay fishes. Estuaries 3: 278-88.

Orth, R. J., K. L. Heck, Jr., and J. van Montfrans. 1984. Faunal communities in seagrass beds: a review of the influence of plant structure and prey characteristics on predator-prey relationships. Estuaries 7: 339-50.

Paller, M. H. 1987. Distribution of larval fish between macrophyte beds and open channels in a southeastern floodplain swamp. J. Freshwater Ecology 4(2): 191–200.

Panuzio, F. L. 1965. Lower Hudson River siltation. U.S. Army Corps of Engineers, New York District. Prepared for Federal Interagency Sedimentation Conference, Jackson, Ms.

Panuzio, F. L. 1965. Lower Hudson River siltation. Pp. 512–50 in Proc. Symp. Federal Interagency Sedimentation Conference. Misc. Publ. 970 Agricultural Research Service.

Park, R. E., M. Humphreys, J. T. Reichle, M. T. Mattson, and D. J. Dunning. In prep. Validation of the scale aging method for aging striped bass.

Paschoa, A. S., M. E. Wrenn, and M. Eisenbud. 1979. National radiation dose to *Gammarus* from Hudson River. Radioprot. 14: 99–115.

PBQD—Parsons, Brinkerhoff, Quades, and Douglas, Inc. 1984. Westway sedimentation studies in project area. Prepared for New York State Department of Transportation.

Pearson, J. L. 1938. The life history of the striped bass or rockfish *Roccus saxatilis*. Fish. Bull. 49: 825–51.

Peck, D. V., J. L. Engels, K. M. Howe, and J. E. Pollard. 1988. Aquatic effects research program episodic response project integrated quality assurance plan. EPA 600/X-88/274. U.S. Environmental Protection Agency, Las Vegas, Nevada.

Peierls, B., N. F. Caraco, and J. J. Cole. 1988. Primary productivity in the Hudson River. EOS 69(44): 1135.

Pekovitch, A. W. 1979. Distribution and some life history aspects of the shortnose sturgeon (*Acipenser brevirostrum*) in the upper Hudson River Estuary. Hazelton Environ. Sci Corp. 67 pp.

Polgar, T. T. 1977. Striped bass ichthyoplankton abundance, mortality, and production estimation for the Potomac River population. Pp. 110–26 in W. Van Winkle (ed.), Assessing the effects of powerplant-induced mortality on fish populations. New York: Pergamon Press.

Polgar, T. T., R. E. Ulanowicz, D. A. Payne, and G. M. Krainak. 1975. Investigations of the role of physical-transport processes in determining ichthyoplankton distribution in the Potomac River. Interim report for 1974 spawning season data. Maryland Power Plant Siting Program, PPRM-11 and PPRM-14 (combined).

Polgar, T. T., J. A. Mihursky, R. e. Ulanowicz, R. P. Morgan, and J. S. Wilson. 1976. An analysis of 74 striped bass spawning success in the Potomac Estuary. Pp. 151–65 in Estuarine Processes (M. L. Wiley, ed.). Vol. 1:

Uses, Stresses, and Adaptation to the Estuary. New York: Academic Press.

Posmentier, E. S., and J. M. Raymont. 1979. Variations of longitudinal diffusivity in the Hudson Estuary. Estuarine and Coastal Marine Science 8: 555–64.

Postma, H. 1967. Sediment transport and sedimentation in the estuarine environment. In Estuaries (G. H. Lauff, ed.). AAAS Publ. 83, Washington, D.C.

Pottle, R., and M. J. Dadsworth. 1979. Studies on larval and juvenile shortnose sturgeon. Rept. to N.E. Utilities, Hartford, Conn.

Priegel, G. R., and T. L. Wirth. 1971. The lake sturgeon, its life history, ecology, and management. Wisconsin Dept. Nat. Res. publ. 240–70.

Pritchard, D. W. 1967. What is an estuary: physical viewpoint. Pp. 3–5 in Estuaries (G. H. Lauff, ed.). Amer. Assoc. Adv. Sci.

QLM. 1970. Evaluation of flooding conditions at Indian Point Nuclear Generating Unit no. 3. Prepared for Con Ed.

QLM. 1974. Hudson River aquatic ecology studies at Bowline. Bowline Unit 1 preoperational studies, Vol. IV: Hudson River hydrodynamic characteristics and water quality. Prepared for ORU.

Raney, E. C. 1952. The life history of the striped bass *Roccus saxatilis* (Walbaum). Bull. Bingham Oceanogr. Coll. 14(1): 1–97.

Rathjen, W. F., and L. C. Miller. 1957. Aspects of the early life History of the striped bass (*Roccus saxatilis*) in the Hudson River. N.Y. Fish Game J. 4(1): 43–60.

Reider, Robert H. 1979. Occurrence of the silver lamprey in the Hudson River. N.Y. Fish Game J. 26(1): 93.

Reisen, W. K. 1972. The influence of organic drift on the food habits and life history of the yellowfin shiner, *Notropis lutipinnis* (Jordan and Brayton). Am. Midl. Nat. 88: 376–83.

Ricker, W. E. 1954. Stock and recruitment. J. Fish. Res. Bd. Canada 11: 559–623.

Ricker, W. E. 1975. Computation and interpretation of biological statistics of fish populations. Bull. Fish. Res. Bd. Canada. 191. 382 pp.

Ricker, W. E. 1979. Notes on certain of the testimonial documents that pertain to the effects of powerplants on striped bass in the lower Hudson River and Estuary. Appendix I: Appraisal of certain arguments, analyses, forecasts, and precedents contained in the utilities evidentiary studies on power plant insult to fish stocks of the Hudson Estuary. Submitted to EPA hearing no. c/II-WP-77-01, Exhibit 218.

Ritchie, D. E., Jr., and T. S. Y. Koo. 1968. Movements of juvenile striped bass in the estuary as determined by tagging and recapture. Univ. Maryland Chesapeake Biol. Lab. Rept. no. 68–31.

Ritchie, D. E., Jr., and T. S. Y. Koo. 1973. Movements of juvenile striped bass in the estuary as determined by tagging and recapture. In Proceedings of a workshop on egg, larval, and juvenile stages of fish in Atlantic coastal estuaries. Tech. Publ. 1 Natl. Mar. Fish. Serv. Atlantic Coastal Fisheries Center, Highlands, N.J.

Robson, D. S., and D. G. Chapman. 1961. Catch curves and mortality rates. Trans. Am. Fish. Soc. 90(2): 181–89.

Robson, D. S., and H. A. Regier. 1964. Sample size in Peterson mark-recapture experiments. Trans. Am. Fish. Soc. 93(3): 215–26.

Rogers, B. A., D. T. Westin, and S. B. Saila. 1977. Life stage duration studies on Hudson River striped bass, *Morone saxatilis* (Walbaum). Univ. Rhode Island Mar. Tech. Rep. no. 31.

Rohlf, F. James. 1988. Analysis of data on counts of fish found in underpier and interpier areas. Prepared for EEA. 23 pp.

Rozas, L. P., and W. E. Odum. 1987. Fish and macrocrustacean use of submerged plants in tidal freshwater marsh creeks. Mar. Ecol. Prog. Ser. 38: 101–8.

Rozas, L. P., and W. E. Odum. 1988. Occupation of submerged aquatic vegetation by fishes: testing the roles of food and refuge. Oecologia 77: 101–6.

Ryder, J. R. 1890. The sturgeons and sturgeon industries of the eastern coast of the United States, with an account of experiments bearing upon sturgeon culture. Bull. U.S. Fish. Comm. 8: 231–328.

Saila, S., and E. Lorda. 1977. Sensitivity analysis applied to a matrix model of the Hudson River striped bass population. Pp. 311–32 in Proceedings of the conference on assessing the effects of power-plant-induced mortality of fish populations (W. Van Winkle, ed.). Pergamon Press.

Saila, S., B. Martin, S. Feron, and L. R. Ginzburg. 1989. Demographic modeling of selected fish species, with results from RAMAS 3. EPRI Technical Report. Palo Alto, Ca.

Sandler, R., and D. Schoenbrod, eds. 1981. The Hudson River Power Plant Settlement. Conference sponsored by New York University School of Law and the Natural Resources Defense Council, Inc., New York, N.Y.

SAS Institute, Inc. 1982. SAS user's guide: Basics, 1982 edition. Cary, N.C. 923 pp.

SAS Institute, Inc. 1985. SAS user's guide: statistics, version 5 edition. Institute, Inc. Cary, N.C. 1292 pp.

SAS Institute, Inc. 1985. SAS/Stat Guide for Personal Computers, Version 6 Edition. Cary, N.C. 378 pp.

Sasaki, S. 1966. Distribution of juvenile striped bass, *Roccus saxatilis*, in the Sacramento-San Joaquin delta. Pp. 59–67 in Ecological studies of the Sacramento-San Joaquin delta (J. T. Turner and D. W. Kelly, eds.). Part II. Fishes of the Delta. Fish Bull. 136, Calif. Dept. Fish and Game.

Savidge, I. R., J. B. Gladden, K. P. Campbell, and J. S. Ziesenis. 1988. Development and sensitivity analysis of impact assessment equations based on recruitment theory. Am. Fish. Soc. Monogr. 4: 191–203.

Savino, J. F., and R. A. Stein. 1982. Predator-prey interaction between largemouth bass and bluegills as influenced by simulated, submersed vegetation. Trans. Am. Fish. Soc. 111(3): 255–66.

Schaffer, W. M. 1974. Optimal reproductive effort in fluctuating environments. Am. Nat. 108: 783–90.

Schaffer, W. M., and M. Kot. 1986. Differential systems in ecology and epidemiology. Pp. 158–78 in Chaos (A. V. Holden, ed.). Princeton: Princeton University Press.

Schilling, E. G. 1978. A lot sensitive sampling plan for compliance testing and acceptance inspection. Journal of Quality Technology 10: 47–51.

Schmidt, R. E. 1986. Fish community structure in Tivoli North Bay, a Hudson River freshwater tidal marsh. U.S. Dept. Commerce, National Oceanic and Atmospheric Administration Technical Report Series OCRM/SPD. 57 pp. (unpublished).

Schmidt, R. E. 1987. Fish survey of the Saw Kill at Montgomery Place, Annandal, New York (unpublished ms, 3 pp.).

Schmidt, R. E., and E. Kiviat. 1988. Communities of larval and juvenile fish associated with water-chestnut, watermilfoil, and water-celery in the Tivoli Bays of the Hudson River. A Report to the Hudson River Foundation. Annandale, N.Y.: Hudsonia, Ltd.

Schmidt, R. E., R. J. Klauda, and J. M. Bartels. 1988. Distribution and movements of the early life stages of three species of *Alosa* in the Hudson River, with comments on mechanisms to reduce interspecific competetion. Pp. 193–215 in Fisheries Research in the Hudson River (C. L. Smith, ed.). Albany: HRES, SUNY Press.

Schoeberl, K. L., and S. Findlay. 1988. Composition, abundance, and dynamics of macroinvertebrates in Tivoli South Bay, with emphasis on the *Chironomidae* (Diptera). Section V. 35 pp. in Polgar Fellowship Reports of the Hudson River National Estuarine Research Reserve Program, 1987 (J. R. Waldman and E. A. Blair, eds.). New York: Hudson River Foundation.

Schroeder, L. A. 1981. Consumer growth efficiencies: Their limits and relationships to ecological energetics. J. Theor. Biol. 93: 805–28.

Seber, G. A. F. 1973. The estimation of animal abundance and related parameters. New York: Hafner Press. 506 pp.

Seber, G. A. F. 1982. The estimation of animal abundance. 2nd ed. New York: MacMillian Publishing Co., Inc.

Serafy, J. E., R. M. Harrell, and J. C. Stevenson. 1988. Quantitative sampling of small fishes in dense vegetation: design and field testing of portable "pop-nets." J. Appl. Ichthyol. 4: 149–57.

Simpson, H. J., P. Linsalata, C. R. Olsen, and N. Cohen. 1987. Transport of fallout and reactor radionuclides in the drainage basin of the Hudson River Estuary. Pp. 273–98 in Environmental research on actinide elements (J. E. Pinder et al., eds.). CONF-841142. Springfield, Va.: NTIS.

Simpson, K. W., R. W. Bode, J. P. Fagnani, and D. M. DeNicola. 1984. The freshwater macrobenthos of the main channel, Hudson River. Part B. Biology, taxonomy, and distribution of resident macrobenthic species. Final Report to Hudson River Foundation. Grant #8/83a/39. 203 pp.

Simpson, K. W., J. P. Fagnani, R. W. Bode, D. N. DeNicola, and L. E. Abele. 1986. Organism-substrate relationships in the main channel of the lower Hudson River. J. North American Benthol. Soc. 5(1): 41–57.

Sorokin, Y. 1972. Biological productivity of the Rybinsk Reservoir. Pp. 493–503 in Productivity problems of freshwaters (A. Kajak and A. Hillbricht-Ilkowska, eds.). Warszawa, Krakow: PWN-Polish Scientific Publishers.

Sloan, R. J., and R. W. Armstrong. 1988. PCB patterns in Hudson River fish. II. Migrant/Marine species. Pp. 325–50 in Fisheries Research in the Hudson River (C. L. Smith, ed.). Albany: HRES SUNY Press.

Slobodkin, L. B., and H. L. Sanders. 1969. On the contribution of environmental predictability to species diversity. Brookhaven Symp. Biol. 22: 82–95.

Smith, C. Lavett. 1977. The Hudson River fish fauna. Fourth Symposium on Hudson River Ecology, Hudson River Environmental Society. 12 pp.

Smith, C. Lavett. 1986. Inland Fishes of New York State. Albany: New York State Department of Environmental Conservation. 522 pp.

Smith, L. D. 1970. Life history of striped bass, January 1, 1967, through June 30, 1970, in Final Report, Anadromous Fish Project. Fish. Sect., Dept. Nat. Resources, Brunswick, Ga. (as cited in Smith and Wells, 1977).

Smith, W. G., and A. Wells. 1977. Biological and fisheries data on striped bass, *Morone saxatilis*. Tech. Ser. Rept. 4, Sandy Hook Lab., NOAA.

Sokolov, L. I., and N. V. Akimova. 1976. Age determination of the Lena River sturgeon *Acipenser baeri*. Jour. Ichthyol. 16: 773–78 (translated from Russian).

Southwood, T. R. E. 1978. Ecological methods (second edition). New York: Halstead Press. 524 pp.

Squiers, T. S., and M. Smith. 1978. Distribution and abundance of shortnose sturgeon and Atlantic sturgeon in the Kennebec River Estuary. Prog. Rep. Project no. AFC-19-1. Dept. Mar. Res. Maine. 31 pp.

Stearns, S. C. 1981. On measuring fluctuating environments: predictability, constancy, and contingency. Ecology 62: 185–99.

Stevenson, R. A., Jr. 1958. The biology of the anchovies *Anchoa mitchilli mitchilli* Cuvier and Valenciennes, 1848, and *Anchoa hepsetus hepsetus* Linnaeus 1758, in Delaware Bay. M.A. Thesis, Univ. Delaware. 36 pp.

Stone, H. L., and P. L. T. Brian. 1963. Numerical solution of convective transport problems. American Institute of Chemical Engineers J. 9(5): 681–88.

Stone, W. B., A. M. Narahara, and W. L. Dovel. 1982. Giemsa stained sections of pectoral fin rays for determining the age of sturgeons. N.Y. Fish Game J. 29(1): 103–5.

Strong, D. R. 1986. Density-vague population change. Trends in Ecology and Evolution. 1: 39–42.

Sullivan, J. F., and G. J. Atchison. 1978. Predator-prey behavior of fathead minnows, *Pimephales promelas*, and largemouth bass, *Micropterus salmoides*, in a model ecosystem. J. Fish. Biol. 13: 249–53.

Tabery, M. A., A. P. Ricciardi, and T. J. Chambers. 1978. Occurrence of inshore lizardfish in the Hudson River Estuary. N.Y. Fish Game J. 25: 87–88.

Tagatz, M. E. 1961. Tolerance of striped bass and American shad to changes of temperature and salinity. U.S. Fish and Wildl. Serv. Spec. Sci. Rept., Fish 388.

Talbot, A. 1983. Settling things: six case studies in environmental mediation. The Conservation Foundation, Washington, D.C. 101 pp.

Taubert, B. D. 1980. Biology of the shortnose sturgeon, *Acipenser brevirostrum*, in the Holyoke Pool, Connecticut River, Massachusetts. PhD. Dissertation, University of Massachusetts, Amherst.

Taubert, B. D., and R. J. Reed. 1978. Observations of the shortnose sturgeon (*Acipenser brevirostrum*) in the Holyoke Pool of the Connecticut River, MA. Progress Rept. to NEUSC, Amherst: Massachusetts. Coop. Fish. Unit.

Taylor, G. I. 1954. The dispersion of matter in turbulent flow through a pipe. Proc. Royal Society of London. Ser. A. 223: 446–68.

Taylor, J. K. 1987. Planning for quality data. Marine Chemistry 22: 109–15.

Taylor, J. K., and T. W. Stanley (eds.). 1985. Quality assurance for environmental measurements. American Society for Testing and Materials Special Publication 867. 441 pp.

Tetra Tech, Inc. 1983. Assessment methodology for new cooling lakes. Vol. 1: Methodology to assess multiple uses for new cooling lakes. Prepared for Electric Power Research Institute.

Thatcher, M. L., and D. R. F. Harleman. 1972a. A mathematical model for the prediction of unsteady salinity intrusion in estuaries. Technical Report 144, Ralph M. Parsons Laboratory for Water Resources and Hydrodynamics. Massachusetts Institute of Technology. 232 pp.

Thatcher, M. L., and D. R. F. Harleman. 1972b. Prediction of unsteady salinity intrusion in estuaries: mathematical model and users manual. Tech. Rept. 159. Ralph M. Parsons Laboratory for Water Resources and Hydrodynamics. Massachusetts Institute of Technology. 117 pp.

Thatcher, M. L., and D. R. F. Harleman. 1978. Development and application of a deterministic time-varying salinity intrusion model for the Delaware Estuary (MIT-TSIM). Volume I: Main Report. Report prepared for the Delaware Basin Commission, West Trenton, N.J. 170 pp.

Thatcher, M. L., and D. R. F. Harleman. 1981. Long-term calculation of salinity intrusion in the Delaware Estuary. Journal of the Environmental Engineering Division, ASCE. 107(EE1): 11–27.

Thatcher, M. L., T. O. Najarian, and P-S Huang. 1981. Fifty-year analysis of salinity intrusion and associated average annual costs to water users in the Delaware Estuary. Report to U.S. Army Corps of Engineers, Philadelphia District Office, Philadelphia Pa. 158 pp.

TI. 1975. Indian Point impingement study report for the period 1 January 1974 through 31 December 1974. Prepared for Con Ed.

TI. 1975. First annual report for the multiplant impact study for the Hudson River Estuary. Prepared for Con Ed.

TI. 1976a. Liberty State Park ecological study: Final Report. Rept. to Port Authority of New York and New Jersey.

TI. 1976b. A synthesis of available data pertaining to major physiochemical variables within the Hudson River Estuary emphasizing the period from 1972 through 1975. Prepared for Con Ed.

TI. 1976c. Indian Point impingement study report for the period 1 January 1975 through 31 December 1975. Prepared for Con Ed.

TI. 1977. 1974 year-class report for the multiplant impact study of the Hudson River Estuary. Vols. I–III. Prepared for Con Ed.

TI. 1978a. 1975 year-class report for the multiplant impact study of the Hudson River Estuary. Prepared for Con Ed.

TI. 1978b. 1976 year-class report for the multiplant impact study of the Hudson River Estuary. Prepared for Con Ed.

TI. 1978c. Catch efficiency of 100-ft (30m) beach seine for estimating density of young-of-year striped bass and white perch in the shore zone of the Hudson River Estuary. Prepared for Con Ed.

TI. 1979a. Efficiency of a 100-ft beach seine for estimating shore densities at night of juvenile striped bass, juvenile white perch, and yearling and older (150mm) white perch. Prepared for Con Ed.

TI. 1979b. 1976 year-class report for the multiplant impact study of the Hudson River Estuary. Prepared for Con Ed.

TI. 1980a. 1977 year-class report for the multiplant impact study of the Hudson River Estuary. Prepared for Con Ed.

TI. 1980b. 1978 year-class report for the multiplant impact study of the Hudson River Estuary. Prepared for Con Ed.

TI. 1981. 1979 year-class report for the multiplant impact study, Hudson River Estuary. Prepared for Con Ed.

Tranter, D. J. (ed.). 1968. Zooplankton sampling. Paris: The UNESCO Press. 174 pp.

Tranter, D. J., and P. E. Smith. 1968. Filtration performance. Pp. 27–56 in Reviews on zooplankton sampling methods (D. J. Trantor, ed.). Monographs of Oceanographic Methodology. UNESCO.

Turner, J. L., and H. K. Chadwick. 1972. Distribution and abundance of young-of-the-year striped bass, *Morone saxatilis*, in relation to river flow in the Sacramento-San Joaquin Estuary. Trans. Am. Fish. Soc. 101(3): 442–52.

UEC. 1974a. The impact of consumptive use of water on the salinity distribution in the Delaware Estuary. Report to Delmarva Power and Light Company. Summit Power Station, Units 1 and 2. United Engineers and Constructors, Inc. Philadelphia, Pa.

UEC. 1974b. The impact of consumptive use of water on the salinity distribution in the Delaware Estuary. Report to Public Service Electric and Gas Company, Hope Creek Station, Units 1 and 2. United Engineers and Constructors, Inc. Philadelphia, Pa.

University of Washington. 1985. Sampling design for aquatic ecological monitoring. Vols. 1–5. Prepared for Electric Power Research Institute.

USACE-NYD (U.S. Army Corps of Engineers—New York District. 1985. Assessment of the impacts of maintenance dredging the Hudson River Federal Channel. Final EA.

USACE-NYD. 1988. Assessment of the impacts of maintenance dredging of the Hudson River Federal Channel. Final EA.

USACE-NYD and U.S. Dept. of Transportation, FHA. Region 1. 1984. Final Supplemental Environmental Impact Statement, Westway Highway Project. Vol. II: Fisheries Portion.

U.S. Department of Agriculture. 1974. Erosion and Sediment Inventory: New York. USDA Soil Conservation Service. Syracuse, N.Y. 100 pp.

U.S. Fish and Wildlife Service. 1985. Detailed Report for Kill Van Kull, Newark Bay Project. Prepared for USACE-NYD.

U.S. Geological Survey. 1977, 1978, 1979, 1980, 1981. Water resources data for New York (Vol. 1). Springfield, Va.: NTIS.

USEPA. 1974. Manual of methods for chemical analysis of water and wastes.

USEPA. 1983. Manual of methods for chemical analysis of water and wastes.

USNRC. 1977. Calculation of annual doses to man from routine releases of reactor effluents for the purposes of evaluating compliance with 10 CFR Part 50, Appendix I., Rev. 1. Regulatory Guide 1.109. U.S. Nuclear Regulatory Commission, Washington, D.C.

Van der Donck, A. 1841. Collections of the New York Historical Society. 2nd ser. Vol. 1.

Vannote, R. L., G. W. Minshall, K. W. Cummins, J. R. Sedell, and C. E. Cushing. 1980. The river continuum concept. Can. J. Fish. Aquat. Sci. 37: 130–37.

Van Winkle, W. (ed.). 1977. Assessing the effects of power-plant-induced mortality on fish populations. New York: Pergamon. 380 pp.

Van Winkle, W., D. S. Vaughan, L. W. Barnthouse, and B. L. Kirk. 1981. An analysis of the ability to detect reductions in year-class strength of the Hudson River white perch (*Morone americana*) population. Can. J. Fish. Aquat. Sci. 38: 627–32.

Vaughan, D. S., and W. Van Winkle. 1982. Corrected analysis of the ability to detect reductions in year-class strength of the Hudson River white perch (*Morone americana*) population. 1982. Can. J. Fish. Aquat. Sci. 39: 782–85.

Versar, Inc. 1987. 1985 year class report for the Hudson River Estuary monitoring program. Prepared for Con Ed.

Versar. 1988. Evaluation of Hudson River beach seine programs conducted by the New York utilities and the New York State Department of Environmental Conservation. Prepared for Con Ed.

Vladykov, V. D., and D. H. Wallace. 1938. Is the striped bass (*Roccus saxatilis*) of Chesapeake Bay a migratory fish? Trans. Am. Fish. Soc. Proc. 67th Annual Meeting (1937): 67–86.

Volchok, H. L., and N. Chieco (eds.). 1986. A compendium of the EML research projects related to the Chernobyl Nuclear Accident. EML-460. New York: Department of Energy, Environmental Measurements Laboratory.

Vouglitois, J. J., K. W. Able, R. J. Kurtz, and K. A. Tighe. 1987. Life history and population dynamics of the bay anchovy in New Jersey. Trans. Am. Fish. Soc. 116(2): 141–53.

Wade, J. C., and E. O. Heady. 1978. Measurements of sediment control impacts on agriculture. Water Resources Res. 14: 1–8.

Walburg, C. H., and P. R. Nichols. 1967. Biology and management of the American shad and status of the fisheries. Atlantic coast of the United States, 1960. U.S. Fish and Wildlife Service, Special Scientific Rept. Fish, 550. 105 pp.

Walters, C. J. 1985. Bias in the estimation of functional relationships from time series data. Can. J. Fish. Aquat. Sci. 42: 147–49.

Walters, C. 1986. Adaptive management resources of renewable resources. New York: MacMillan Publishing Co.

Waldman, J. R., D. J. Dunning, Q. E. Ross, and M. T. Mattson. 1990. Range dynamics of Hudson River striped bass along the Atlantic coast. Trans. Am. Fish. Soc. 119(5) 910–19.

Wang, J. C. S. 1974. A study of ichthyoplankton in the Delaware River in the vicinity of Artificial Island. Prog. Rept. for the Period January through December 1973. Ichthyological Associates, Inc. 571 pp.

Wang, J. C. S., and R. J. Kernehan. 1979. Fishes of the Delaware estuaries, a guide to the early life histories. Towson, Md. E.A. Communications, Ecological Analysts, Inc., 410 pp.

Ward, D. V. 1978. Biological environmental impact studies: theory and methods. New York: Academic Press. 157 pp.

Warren, C. E. 1971. Biology and water pollution control. W. B. Saunders Co. 434 pp.

Waters, T. F. 1962. Diurnal periodicity in the drift of stream invertebrates. Ecology 43(2): 316–20.

Waters, T. F. 1965. Interpretation of invertebrate drift in streams. Ecology 46(1): 316–20.

Weber, C. I. (ed.). 1973. Biological field and laboratory methods for measuring the quality of surface water effluents. Environmental Protection Agency 670/4–73–001.

Weinstein, M. P. 1979. Shallow marsh habitats as primary nurseries for fishes and shellfish, Cape Fear, North Carolina. Fish. Bull. 77(2): 339–58.

Welcomme, R. L. (ed.). 1975. Symposium on the methodology for the survey, monitoring, and appraisal of fishery resources in lakes and large rivers. European Inland Fisheries Advisory Commission Technical Paper no. 23. Supplement 1, Vols. 1 and 2. 747 pp.

Werner, E. E., J. F. Gilliam, D. J. Hall, and G. G. Mittelbach. 1983. An experimental test of the effects of predation risk on habitat use in fish. Ecology 64: 1540–48.

Westin, D. T., and B. A. Rogers. 1978. Synopsis of biological data on the striped bass, *Morone saxatilis* (Walbaum) 1792. Marine Technical Report 67. University of Rhode Island, Kingston.

Westlake, D. F. 1966. The light climate for plants in rivers. Pp. 99–119 in Light as an ecological factor (R. Bainbridge, G. C. Evans, and O. Rackham, eds.). Oxford: Blackwell Scientific Publications.

Wilbur, H. M., D. W. Tinkle, J. P. Collins. 1974. Environmental certainty, trophic level, and resource availability in life history evolution. Am. Nat. 108: 805–17.

Wilk, S. J., and M. J. Silverman. 1976. Summer benthic fish fauna of Sandy Hook, N.J. NOAA Tech. Rep. NMFS SSRF-698. 16 pp.

Winberg, G., V. Babitsky, S. Gavrilov, G. Gladky, I. Zakharenkov, R. Kovalevskaya, T. Mikheeva, P. Nevyadomskaya, A. Ostapenya, P. Petrovich, J. Potaenko, and O. Yakushko. 1972. Biological productivity of different types of lakes. Pp. 383–404 in Productivity problems of freshwaters (A. Kajak and A. Hillbricht-Ilkowska, eds.). Warszawa: PWN-Polish Scientific publishers.

Woodhead, P. M. J., and S. S. McAfferty. 1986. Report on the fish community of lower New York harbor in relation to borrow pit sites. Mar. Sci. Res. Center, SUNY Stony Brook. Prepared for USACE-NYD.

Worf, D. L. (ed.). 1980. Biological monitoring for environmental effects. Lexington: D. C. Heath and Company. 227 pp.

Wrenn, M. E., S. M. Jinks, N. Cohen, and L. M. Hairr. 1974. Cs-137 and Cs-134 distribution in sediment, water, and biota of the lower Hudson River and their dosimetric implications for man. Pp. 279–84 in Proc. 3rd. International Congress of the International Radiation Protection Association. Springfield, Va.: NYIS.

Wydoski, R., and L. Emery. 1983. Tagging and Marking. Pp. 215–37 in Fisheries Techniques (L. A. Neilsen and D. L. Johnson, eds.). Bethesda: American Fisheries Society.

Young, Byron H. 1979. A study of striped bass in the Marine District of New York. III. April 1, 1976, to March 31, 1979. NOAA Project AFC-9.

Young, Byron H. 1981. A study of striped bass in the Marine District of New York III. April 1, 1980, to March 31, 1981. NOAA Project AFC-9, Segment 2.

Young, B. H., I. H. Morrow, and S. R. Wanner. 1982. First record of the bluespotted cornetfish in the Hudson River. N.Y. Fish Game J. 29: 106.

Young, J. R., and T. B. Hoff. 1981. Age specific variation in reproductive effort in female Hudson River striped bass. Pp. 124–33 in Fisheries research in the Hudson River (C. L. Smith, ed.). Albany: HRES, SUNY Press.

Young, J. R., R. J. Klauda, and W. P. Dey. 1988. Population estimates for juvenile striped bass and white perch in the Hudson River Estuary. Am. Fish. Soc. Monogr. 4: 89–101.

Contributors

Karim A. Abood, Lawler, Matusky and Skelly Engineers, One Blue Hill Plaza, Pearl River, NY 10965

A. Barth Anderson, 538 Egremont Road, Great Barrington, MA 01230

Guy A. Apicella, Lawler, Matusky and Skelly Engineers, One Blue Hill Plaza, Pear River, NY 10965

Thomas J. Berggren, Fish Passage Center, Columbia Basin, Fishery Agencies and Tribes, 2501 S.W. First Avenue, Suite 230, Portland, OR 97201-4752

Edward H. Buckley, Boyce Thompson Institute, Cornell University, Tower Road, Ithaca, NY 14853

Norman Cohen, New York University Medical Center, Institute of Environmental Medicine, A. J. Lanza Research Laboratories, Tuxedo, NY 10987

Janet Collura, EEA, Inc., 55 Hilton Avenue, Garden City, NY 11530

Martin W. Daley, Central Hudson Gas and Electric Corporation, 284 South Avenue, Poughkeepsie, NY 12601

Contributors

William Dey, EA Engineering, Science, & Technology, Inc., The Maple Building, 3 Washington Center, Newburgh, NY 12550

William L. Dovel, Estuarine Fisheries Ecologist, 1300 North River Road, Venice, FL 34293

Dennis J. Dunning, New York Power Authority, 123 Main Street, White Plains, NY 10601

Phillip J. Fallon, Jr., Kemron Environmental Services, 33 Walt Whitman Road, Huntington Station, NY 11746

Scott Ferson, Applied Biomathematics, 100 North Country Road, Setauket, NY 11733-2852

Stuart E. G. Findlay, Institute of Ecosystem Studies, The New York Botanical Garden, Mary Flagler Carey Arboretum, Millbrook, NY 12545

Paul Geoghegan, Normandeau Associates, Inc., 25 Nashua Road, Bedford, NH 03102

Lev R. Ginzburg, Ecology and Evolution, State University of New York, Stony Brook, NY 11794-5245

Douglas G. Heimbuch, Coastal Environmental Services, Inc., 1099 Winterson Road, Linthicum, MD 21090

Leonard J. Houston, U.S. Army Corps of Engineers, Environmental Analysis Branch (NANPL-E), 26 Federal Plaza, New York, NY 10278

Jay B. Hutchison, Jr., Westinghouse Savannah River Co., Savannah River Site, Aiken, SC 29808

Roger G. Keppel, Consolidated Edison Company of New York, Inc., 4 Irving Place, New York, NY 10003

William L. Kirk, Consolidated Edison Company of New York, Inc., 4 Irving Place, New York, NY 10003

Ronald J. Klauda, The Johns Hopkins University, Applied Physics Laboratory, Environmental Sciences Group, Shadyside, MD 20764

Mark W. LaSalle, Marine Resources Specialist, Mississippi State University, Coastal Research and Extension Center, 2710 Beach Boulevard, Suite 1E, Biloxi, MS 39531

Karin Limburg, Cornell University, Ithaca, NY 14850

Paul Linsalata, American Cyanamid Company, Medical Research Division, Lederle Laboratories, Pearl River, NY 10965.

David Lints, Institute of Ecosystem Studies, The New York Botanical Garden, Mary Flagler Cary Arboretum, Millbrook, NY 12545

John D. Lunz, Science Application International, 18706 North Creek Parkway, Bothell, WA 98011

E. A. Maikish, Lawler, Matusky and Skelly Engineers, One Blue Hill Plaza, Pearl River, NY 10965

Wayne J. Mancroni, Central Hudson Gas and Electric Corporation, 284 South Avenue, Poughkeepsie, NY 12601

John A. Matousek, Lawler, Matusky and Skelly Engineers, One Blue Hill Plaza, Pearl River, NY 10965

Mark T. Mattson, Normandeau Associates, Inc., 25 Nashua Road, Bedford, NH 03102

M. U. McGowan, Lawler, Matusky and Skelly Engineers, One Blue Hill Plaza, Pearl River, NY 10965

Kim A. McKown, New York State Department of Environmental Conservation, Bldg. #40, SUNY, Stony Brook, NY 11790-2356

Susan G. Metzger, Lawler, Matusky and Skelly Engineers, One Blue Hill Plaza, Pearl River, NY 10965

Michael L. Pace, Institute of Ecosystem Studies, The New York Botanical Garden, Mary Flagler Carey Arboretum, Millbrook, NY 12545

Anthony W. Pekovitch, Minnesota Light and Power, 30 West Superior Street, Duluth, MN 55802-2093

Quentin E. Ross, New York Power Authority, 123 Main Street, White Plains, NY 10601

Robert E. Schmidt, Simon's Rock of Bard College, Great Barrington, MA 01230

C. Lavett Smith, Department of Ichthyology and Herpetology, American Museum of Natural History, Central Park West at 79th Street, New York, NY 10024

Roy R. Stoecker, EEA, Inc., 55 Hilton Avenue, Garden City, NY 11530

M. Llewellyn Thatcher, Department of Civil Engineering and Engineering Mechanics, S. W. Mudd Building, Room 610, Columbia University, New York, NY 10027

T. B. Vanderbeek, Lawler, Matusky and Skelly Engineers, One Blue Hill Plaza, Pearl River, NY 10965

John R. Waldman, Hudson River Foundation, 122 East 42nd Street, New York, NY 10168

Alan W. Wells, Lawler, Matusky and Skelly Engineers, One Blue Hill Plaza, Pearl River, NY 10965

Robert Will, U.S. Army Corps of Engineers, Planning Division, Environmental Analysis Branch, 26 Federal Plaza, New York, NY 10278-0090

Byron H. Young, New York State Department of Environmental Conservation, Bldg. #40, SUNY, Stony Brook, NY 11790-2356

John R. Young, Consolidated Edison Company of New York, Inc., 4 Irving Place, New York, NY 10003

Index

A

Abundance and survival, striped bass, 345
Acceptable Quality Level, 314
Acipenser brevirostrum. *See* Shortnose sturgeon
Acipenser oxyrhynchus. *See* Atlantic sturgeon
Adirondack Mountains, 13
Age determination: quality control, 316; shortnose sturgeon, 192
Age Structured Population Model, 396
Ageing, 344–345
Agrostris alba, 483
Albany Steam Generating Station, 194
Albany, 360, figure 2.6
Albemarle Sound, 266
Alewife, 415–417, 427, 432, 435–436, 438, 443, 466–467, 469, 470, 471–473
Alosa mediocris. *See* Hickory shad
Alosa pseudoharengus. *See* Alewife
Alosa sp., 470
Alosa aestivalis. *See* Blueback herring
Alosa sapidissima. *See* American shad
[241]Am, 156
American shad, 353, 360, 373, figure 17.3, 415, 416, 432
American eel, 154, 415–417, 426–427, 432
American Society for Testing and Materials, 304
American Society for Quality Control, 304
Anaerobic production, 455

543

Anchoa hepsetus. See Striped anchovy
Anchoa mitchilli. See Bay anchovy
Anchor tags, 343
Anguilla rostrata. See American eel
Annual precipitation, 13–14
Annual snowfall, 13
Annuli, 345
ANOVA, 356
Aquatic studies at Hudson River Center site, 407, 427
ARMA, 23, 32
Arrow arum, 461
Arthur Kill, 280
Ashokan Reservoir, 11
Atlantic cod, 441
Atlantic croaker, 416
Atlantic herring, 416–417, 431–432
Atlantic mackerel, 416
Atlantic menhaden, 416–417, 431–433, 435–436, 438, 442
Atlantic moonfish, 416
Atlantic silverside, 416–417, 432, 441, 444
Atlantic sturgeon, 216, 441
Atlantic tomcod, 58; predator of bay anchovy, 230; 323–338; population size, 330–332; CPUE index of abundance, 331; 353, 356, 373, 415–417, 427, 431–432, 436, 438, 443, 445
Autoregressive moving average (ARMA), 23, 32

B

Bacteria, as base resource, 457
Bacteria, pelagic biomass, 451
Bacterial production, 447
Banded killifish, 154, 467–469, 471–472, 480
Bathymetry, 414, 423
Battery, the, 20, figure 1.6, 328
Battery Park, 325

Bay anchovy: 353, 358, 360, 373, 426, 431–432, 434, 436, 438, 443, 444; food for Atlantic tomcod, 230; distribution of juveniles, 238; density isopleths of eggs and larvae, figure 10.3; distribution of postlarvae, 234–238; maximum size, 238–241; seasonal distribution of adults, 232–234; sexual maturity, 241; postlarvae, 236–238
Bay of Fundy, 345
Beach seine, 266
Beach seine sampling program, 380, figure 18.5, figure 18.6
Beach seine survey, 244, 246–247
Beam trawl, 353, 377
Benthic bacteria, 450
Benthic grab baseline study, 417; survey, 413
Benthic invertebrates, table 20.2
Benthic macroinvertebrates, 450, 453
Beverton-Holt function, 393, 396–397, 400, figure 19.1
Beverton-Holt compensation model, 398, 402
Biological monitoring program, 340
Biological Oxygen Demand model, 86, 98
Biomass and energetics of consumers, 446
Black sea bass, 441
Blueback Herring, 416, 432, 435, 436, 438, 443, 470–471, 472
Blueclaw crab: 178, 432, 440, 444; bioaccumulation of ^{137}Cesium, 179
Bluefish, 416, 432, 436–438, 443
Bluegill, 154, 441
Bottom trawls, 325
Bowline channel, 257–258
Bowline Point, 282
Bowline inlet discharge, 257–258

Box traps, 324–325
Brevoortia tyrannus. *See* Atlantic menhaden
Brooklyn, 285
Brown bullhead, 154
Butterfish, 416, 432

C

Cesium: bioaccumulation of, 178–179; migration in watershed soils, 164–168; accumulation in undisturbed soils, 168–175; ^{134}Cs, 153; ^{137}Cs, 169
Calibration procedures, table 14.2
Cape Hatteras, 345
Carassius auratus. *See* Goldfish
Carbon budgets, 447
Carbon model, 454
Carlin-Ritchie tags, 192
Carp, 154, 441, 467, 469, 470–472, 474, 493
Carrying capacity, 395
Catch per unit effort indices: Atlantic tomcod, 323–338; accuracy, 337
Catch per unit effort (CPUE): 323–338, 411
Catfish. *See* Brown bullhead, White catfish
Catostomus commersoni. *See* White sucker
Catskill, 280, 354, 356, 360, 362–363, 365
Catskill Aqueduct, 11
Catskill Mountains, 9
Channel maintenance dredging, impact on shortnose sturgeon, 212
Chapman modification of Peterson mark-recapture estimator, 327
Chelsea, 154, 175
Chemical Oxygen Demand model, 98
Chenopodium ambrosioides, 483

Chernobyl, 158
Chesapeake Bay, 266, 268, 275
Chironomid, 480
Chlorinity distribution, 146–150
Cladocera, 450
Clam. *See* Soft clam
Clark, George, Jr., 193
Climate, 13
Cluster analysis, 260
^{243,244}Cm, 156
^{58}Co, 153
^{60}Co, 153
Cod. *See* Atlantic cod
Cold Spring, 263
Colonization studies, benthic invertebrates, 413, 422
Commercial fishing, impact on shortnose sturgeon, 211
Communities, 495
Comparison trawl samples, 412, 417
Compensation, 392–403
Compensation models: Beverton-Holt, 398; Ricker, 398
Complexity of biological systems, 493
Conceptual model, of lower food web, 447, figure 22.1
Conductivity, 72–80, figures 3.10, 3.11, 3.12, 3.13, 3.14
Confidence intervals for mark/recapture estimates, 327
Conservation of salt equation, 137–138
Consolidated Edison Company, 277
Constitution Island, 264
Consumer biomass, 453
Continuity equation, 136–137
Cooling towers, 492
Copepoda, 451
Cornwall Pumped Storage Facility, 243, 492
Cornwall, 222, 379
Courant Criterion, 138
CPUE, 411
CPUE, bay anchovy, figure 10.2

Crab. *See* Blueclaw crab
Critical zone, 300
Croaker. *See* Atlantic croaker
Croton-Haverstraw, 222–223
Croton Bay/Croton River, 476, 477
Croton River, 479
Croton River Reservoir, 11
Cruger island, 461
Cunner, 441
Currents, 423
Cusk eel, 441
Cycles of freshwater flow, 21–23
Cyprinus carpio. See Carp

D

Danskammer Point, 282
Danskammer Point generating station, 258–259
Dart tag, 343
Darter. *See* Tessellated darter
Data analysis and reports, quality control, 318–320
Data management for Hudson River Utilities Ecological Study, 316–318
Delaware estuary, 136
Delaware River, 11
Delivery ratio, 163
Deming philosophy, 304
Density isopleths, figure 10.3
Detritus, as base resource for higher organisms, 457
Dip netting, 464
Dissolved oxygen: 66, figure 3.7, 71, 73, figure 3.9, 87–104, 88, figures 4.2, 4.4, tables 4.1, 4.2, 4.4, 4.5; effects on shortnose sturgeon, 213–214
Dissolved oxygen models, 98
Distichlis spicata, 483
DNA, synthesis, 447
Dose estimates, radionuclides, table 7.6
Dredging, 82–104, 108
Drift, fish larvae, 462
Dynamics, larval fish populations, 458–475

E

East River, 280, 285, 297
Eastmain River Estuary, 136
Echinochloa walteri, 483
Eel. *See* American eel
Electric generating plants, effect on shortnose sturgeon, 214–215
Eleocharis calva, 483
Eleocharis parvula, 483
Emmigration, striped bass, 280
Enrichment ration, 169
Entrainment, xi
Entrainment, larval white perch, 259
Entrainment, white perch eggs, 259
Epibenthic sled, 190, 218–219, 245, 354, 377
Equation of State, 138
Equilibrium concentrations, 170, table 7.4
Equilibrium depths, 112–114
Erosion estimates and sediment input, 158–164
Esopus Creek, 6, 263
Esopus Meadows, 175, 193–194, 204
Estimates of abundance and standing crop, assumptions, 349
Etheostoma olmstedi. See Tessellated darter
Eurasian watermilfoil, 461, 463, 464, 467, 474

F

Fall shoals sampling program, 380, figure 18.4
Fall shoals survey, 244, 246, 377

Fallout Inputs, 158
Federal Dam at Troy, 8
Federal Navigation Channel, 83
Fin clips, 325–326
Fin regeneration, 326
Financial support for research, 495
Fish: bioaccumulation of 137Cs, 178; distribution in Newark Bay, 428–445; species in Hudson estuary, 30; response to physical and chemical characteristics, 31
Fish and ichthyoplankton analysis, quality control, 314–316
Fisheries studies at Hudson River Center, 411
Fishkill Creek, 263
Flounder. *See* Four spot flounder, Smallmouth flounder, Smooth flounder, Windowpane, Winter flounder
Flow obstructions, 108
Flow histograms, figure 1.5
Food web: 446; data, table 22.1; in tidal freshwater, 447
Four spot flounder, 441
Fourspine stickleback, 470
Freshwater discharge, temporal patterns, 46–49, figures 2.9, 2.10, 2.11
Freshwater flow: at Green Island Dam, 64, figure 3.2; at Green Island in 1988, 135; in lower Hudson, 18; monthly mean, 16; seasonal average, 21, table 1.7; summary, 21
Freshwater wetlands, 459
Fudulus diaphanus. *See* Banded killifish
Fundulus heteroclitus. *See* Mummichog

G

Gaging stations: upper Hudson, 15; Green Island, 32

Gammarus, 462
George Washington Bridge, 106, 289, 325
Gillnet, 191, 429–431
Golden shiner, 154, 467, 469–472, 474
Goldfish, 467, 469–471, 493
Goosefish, 416
Gray literature, 320, 494
Great South Bay, 285
Green Island: 5, 8, 13; freshwater flow, 37, 135; average trends of Hudson River flow, figures 1.9, and 1.10; flow variance, 23; seasonal average freshwater flow, 21, 23, table 1.7
Groundwater from Croton landfill, 485
Growth patterns on scales of striped bass, identification of hatchery fish, 342
Growth: striped bass, 275; shortnose sturgeon, 199–202
Grubby, 416, 432, 436–437, 438, 442

H

Hackensack River, 285
Handling techniques for striped bass, 344
Hatchery fish, proportion in a cohort, 343
Haverstraw Bay, 82–104, 108, 266, 280
Hearings preparation, quality control, 320
Heavy metals, 484
Hempstead Bay, 285
Herring. *See* Atlantic herring, Blueback herring
Heterotrophic systems, 456
Hibiscus palustris, 481
Hickory shad, 441
Hogchoker, 415–417, 432

Holyoke Pool, 207
Hoosic River, 6
Hudson River basin: characteristics, 5; physiographic features, 8
Hudson River Center Associates, 408
Hudson River Center Site, 407–429
Hudson River Cooling Tower Settlement Agreement, 339–340
Hudson River Ecological Study: 491; definition, xi; field crew organization, 310; field sampling regions, frontispiece, 491; field and laboratory operations, 310–316; flowmeter calibration, 312–313; instrument calibration, 312; quality control inspections, 313–314; quality control program, 306–308; standard operating procedure, 311–312; training field crews, 311
Hudson River Environmental Society, xii
Hudson River Fishermen's Association, 487
Hudson River Foundation for Science and Environmental Research, xii, 345
Hudson River freshwater flow summary, 21
Hudson River freshwater flow trends, chapter 1
Hudson River longitudinal river survey, 244–246
Hudson River National Estuarine Research Reserve, 461
Hudson River Settlement Agreement, 339–341, 349
Hudson River Utilities entrainment and impingement programs, 251
Hudson River Utilities Environmental studies: quality assurance, 303–322; quality control, 303–322
Hudson River-Black River regulating district, 21
Hyde Park, 222, figure 2.6
Hydrology, 13, 414, 423

I

Ichthyoplankton: 354–356; American shad, 360; bay anchovy, 362; striped bass, 366–367; white perch, 362–366
Immature striped bass, movements of, 276–300
Impatiens capensis, 483
Impingement, white perch at Danskammer Point generating station, 258–259
Index of year-class strength, needed for striped bass, 347
Indian Lake Reservoir, 11
Indian Point: 280, 282; water temperature, figure 2.6
Indian Point cooling towers, 492
Indian Point Power Plant, 308
Indian Point Units 2 and 3, 340
Indian River, 6
Internal anchor tags, 344
Interpier areas, 407
Interpier gill nets, 412, 417
Interpier trawls, 415
Interpier trawl survey, 411
Invertebrate density in colonization samples, 422
Iona Island, 264

J

Jamaica Bay, 280
Juvenile fish: sample methods, 353–354; CPUE, 356

K

^{40}K, 160, table 7.2
Kill van Kull, 31, 285, 429
Killifish. *See* Banded killlifish, Mummichog
Kingfish. *See* Northern Kingfish
Kingston area, 222, 356, 449

Kingston/Saugerties region, 354

L

Lag time, 18–19
Lake Marion-Moultrie, 207
Lake Pleasant, 13
Larval fish: exchange between South Bay and the Hudson, 465; population dynamics, 458–475; transport, 461
Larval fish transport, 461
Lawler, Matusky and Skelly, Engineers, 5, 28
Leachate flow, 484
Length-weight measurements, quality control, 316
Length frequency: bay anchovy, figure 10.5; shortnose sturgeon, 223–224; striped bass YOY, figure 12.5
Lepomis macrochirus. See Bluegill
Lepomis gibbosus. See Pumpkinseed
Liberty Park, 285
Life history model, shortnose sturgeon, 225
Light intensity, 465
Light meter measurements, 469
Light transmission, 415, 425
Light traps, 463
Lined seahorse, 416, 432, 441
Longitudinal river program, 377
Longitudinal Momentum Equation, 137
Long River sampling program, 380
Long Island Sound, 280, 285
Lookdown, 441
Lot Tolerant Percent Defective Plan, 319
Lovett, 282
Lower Hudson: 8–9; freshwater flow history, figure 1.6; freshwater flow patterns, 18; seasonal freshwater flow average, 20–21
Lythrum salicaria, 461, 486

M

Macrophyte biomass, 450–451
Macrophytes, 447
Macrozooplankton, 449
Magdalen Island, 461
Magnetically coded wire tags, 268
Manhattan, 291–299, 407
Manning's "n", 141, 143
Marinas, 477
Mark-recapture estimates, assumptions of, 347
Mark-recapture estimates: tomcod, 326–327
Marking: coded wire tags, 341; anchor tags, 343
Martin Marietta Environmental Systems, 278–291
Menhaden. See Atlantic menhaden
Metro North, 296
Metro South, 296
Microgadus tomcod. See Atlantic tomcod
Microzooplankton, 449
Migrations, 206–208; summer and fall fish migrations, 203–206
Minisceongo Creek, 477
MIT Transient Salinity Intrusion Model: structure, 139; governing equations, 136–138; input-output requirements, 138
^{54}Mn, 156, table 7.1
Models: striped bass movements, 279; radionuclide migration, 165–167
Mohawk River, 6, 8–9, 13
Moonfish. See Atlantic moonfish
Morone americana. See White perch
Morone saxatilis. See Striped bass
Morphological deformity, 208
Morris Canal, 289

Index

Movements, immature striped bass, 276–300
Mummichog, 154, 479
Mya arenaria. See Soft clam
Myriophyllum beds: as fish habitat, 263, 463–464, 467–468, 474
Myriophyllum spicatum. See Eurasian watermilfoil

N

Nack, Everett, 193
Narrow-leaf cattail, 461
Narrows, the, 31
New York, a water state, 491
New York Bay, 31
New York City Public Development Corporation, 408
New York Harbor, 280
New York Harbor sedimentation: bathymetric observations, 120; deposition rates, 117; dredging records, 115; field observations, 115; mitigation measures, 129
New York State Conservation Department, Biological Survey, 491
New York State Department of Environmental Conservation: 266, 342; beach seine program, 244, 250, 258
New York University Institute of Environmental Medicine, monitoring program, 153
Newark Bay: 280, 285, 428–445; fish distribution in, 428–445; nursery for tomcod and winter flounder, 443, 445
Newburgh Bay, 60, 175
Northern kingfish, 417, 441
Northern pipefish, 416, 432
Northern puffer, 432, 441
Northern searobin, 416, 432, 441
Northwest Marine Technologies, 341

Notemigonus crysoleucas. See Golden shiner
Notropis hudsonius. See Spottail shiner
Nuclear test ban treaty, 158
Null point, 107
Nuphar advena, 461

O

Olympia and York Development Company, 116
Optical turbidity, table 4.3, figure 4.5
Otter trawl, 192, 429–431; sampling for shortnose sturgeon, 218
Outages and reduced flows, 349
Overwintering, of striped bass, 289
Oxygen saturation levels, table 4.2
Oyster toadfish, 416

P

Paleomonetes pugio, 480
Palmer Drought Severity Indices (PSDI), 28
Peekskill, 279
Peekskill Bay, 263
Pelagic zone, primary production, 449
Peterson mark-recapture estimates: 324, 327; for Atlantic tomcod, 332–333, 336, table 15.2
pH, 66, figure 3.6
Phragmites communis, 483, 485
Physical and chemical characteristics, long-term variability and predictability, 29–58
Physical parameters, Haverstraw Bay, 82–104
Phytoplankton: 447; biomass, 449, 451
Pier (Hudson River) No. 76, 408

Pinfish, 432, 441
Pipefish. *See* Northern pipefish
Piseco Lake, 13
Plankton nets, 190, 465
Pluchea purpurescens, 483
Plutonium: accumulation in undisturbed soil, 168–175; fallout, 169; migration in watershed soils, 164–168
Polgar Fellowship Program, 459
Polygonum hydropiperoides, 483
Polygonum pensylvanicum, 483
Polygonum punctatum, 483
Ponar bottom grab, 190, 413
Pop-nets, 480
Population estimates: shortnose sturgeon, 192–193, 208–210
Population model, 396
Population crash, 401
Port Newark, 437
Post-yolk-sac larvae: abundance as index of year class strength, 376–391
Potomogeton perfoliatus, 483
Potomogeton spp., 461
Poughkeepsie, 277, 324, 328, 354, 362–363, 365, 373, figure 17.5, figure 17.7
Poughkeepsie Water Works: temperatures, 20–31, 37; weekly mean water temperatures, figure 2.1
Power plants, impact on striped bass, 341
Precipitation, Hudson Basin, 14
Predation models, 492
Prespawning and spawning activities of shortnose sturgeon, 193
Primary producer biomass, 453
Probabilistic models, 392–403
Protozoans, pelagic, 455, 456
Puffer. *See* Northern puffer
Pumpkinseed, 154, 432, 441
Pure research, 495
Purple loosestrife, 461

Pushnet, 354
PYSL Index of Abundance, 345, 388–389

Q

Quality Assurance: definition, 306; Hudson River environmental studies, 303–322
Quality Control: definition, 306; hearings, 320; Hudson River environmental studies, 303–322; inspections, 313–314, table 14.3
Quality Assurance/Quality Control: cost of, 321; for striped bass studies, 346; in ecological and fisheries research, 304
Quasiextinction, 394, 399–402

R

^{226}Ra, 160, table 7.2
Radiocesium, longterm monitoring of, 175
Radiological studies: NYUIEM monitoring program, 153
Radionuclides: environmental dosimetry, 181–183; fallout inputs, 158–159; long term trends, 152–185; reactor inputs, 156–157; research, 152–185; sources to Hudson River, 156; watershed removal, 152–185; ^{241}Am, 156; ^{243,244}Cm, 156; ^{58}Co, 153; ^{60}Co, 153; ^{134}Cs, 153; ^{137}Cs; fallout, 169; ^{40}K, 160, table 7.2; ^{54}Mn, 156, table 7.1; ^{226}Ra, 160, table 7.2
Rainbow smelt, 416, 441
RAMAS population model, 396
Recruitment and year-class strength, anadromous fishes, 447
Red hake, 416, 432, 436–437, 438, 441–443

552 Index

Relative abundance index, YOY striped bass, 268, table 12.1, figure 12.2
Reservoirs, 11
Respiration, 451
Restoration, Croton Bay/Croton River, 476–487
Restoration of ecosystems, 495
Return rates, striped bass tags, 343
Ricker function, 393, 396–397, figure 19.2
Ricker model of compensation, 398, 402
Risk, of population decline, 394
River continuum concept, 456
River strata, 350, figure 17.1
Riverwalk Project, 125, 129, figures 5.9, 5.11
Roanoke River, 266, 275
Rock gunnel, 441
Rondout Creek, 6
Rose Bengal stain, 413
Roseton, 282
Roseton Generating Station: 60; entrainment of white perch eggs, 259; entrainment of white perch larvae, 260; impingement of white perch, 259
Rotifera, 450
Rumex mexicana, 483

S

Sacandaga reservoir, 11
Sacandaga River, 6
Sacremento San Joaquin: delta, 285; estuary, 299
Sagittaria, 461
Salinity: impact of withdrawals on, 134; spatial patterns, 52, figures 2.14, 2.15; temporal patterns, 49, figure 2.13; validation of calculated with observed values, 145, 147
Salt balance model, 140

Salt Equation, conservation, 137–138
Salt front, figure 2.12
Sampling gear, table 8.1
Sampling programs for striped bass postjuveniles, 342
Saratoga Lake, 13
SAS data sets, 317
SAS statistical package, 328
Saugerties, 222, 360
Saw Kill, 461–462, 473
Schoharie Reservoir, 11
Schroon Lake, 13
Scouring velocity, 111
Scup, 416, 432
Seabass. *See* Black sea bass
Seahorse. *See* Lined seahorse
Searobin. *See* Northern searobin
Seasonal average freshwater flows, 21, table 1.7
Seasonal distribution: bay anchovy, 232; shortnose sturgeon, 220–223
Seward movement of young striped bass, 290, figures 13.6, 13.9
Sediment chemistry, 414, 424
Sediment transport, 111
Sediment trap, 287
Sedimentation in Croton Bay, 485
Sedimentation: 110, 414, 424; bathymetric observations, 120; deposition rates, 117; evaluating rates of, 111; exponential decay model, 131; in New York Harbor, 105, 115; mitigation measures, 129; observations, 115; sources of, 106
Selene vomer. *See* Lookdown
Settlement Agreement, 1980, 353
Settlement Agreement, xi; *See also*: Hudson River Settlement Agreement
Shad, American: 154, 179; bioaccumulation of ^{137}Cesium in, 179
Shad. *See* Hickory shad
Shad beach seine program, 379
Shiner. *See* Golden shiner, Spottail shiner

Shortnose sturgeon: 187–216, 250–251; age, 201–203; disease and fin rot, 212–213; distribution in Hudson estuary 1984–1988, 217–227; early development and nursery area, 197–199; effects of power plants, 214–215; future research, 215–216; growth, 199; impact of human activities, 211–215; length frequency, 223; morphological abnormalities, 208–209; population estimates, 208; potential competition with Atlantic sturgeon, 216; prespawning and spawning activities, 193–197; rationale for basic migrations, 206–208; recaptures, table 8.2; sampling gear, 190–192; seasonal distribution, 220–223, figure 13.3; summer and fall migrations, 203–206; tagging methods, 192
Silver hake, 416, 432
Silverside. *See* American silverside
Site specific research, 493
Smallmouth flounder, 432, 441
Smooth flounder, 432, 441
Smelt. *See* Rainbow smelt
Soft clam, 420, 426
Soil loss estimates, table 7.3
South Oyster Bay, 285
Spartina alterniflora, 483
Spartina patens, 481
Spatterdock, 461
Species density, 425
Spier Falls, 5, 13, 21
Spotfin butterflyfish, 441
Spottail shiner, 154, 466–467, 469, 470–471, 472
Spotted hake, 416, 432, 436–437, 438, 442
^{90}Sr, 158
Standard station concept, 337–338
Standing crop estimates, 348–375
Staten Island, 285
Statistical methods, white perch abundance survey, 251

Stickleback. *See* Fourspine stickleback, Threespine stickleback
Stock assessment, 343
Stocking striped bass, evaluation of, 341
Stony Point, 477
Stratified random sampling design, 279
Striped mullet, 416
Striped searobin, 416, 432
Striped anchovy: 432, 441; uncommon in Hudson, 230
Striped bass: 154, 230, 340, 353, 356, 415, 416, 417, 426–427, 431, 432, 435, 436, 438, 442, 493; abundance of YOY, 269, 358; abundance of post-yolk-sac larvae, 373; bioaccumulation of ^{137}Cesium, 178; biweekly mean size, 268; biweekly mean size of YOY, 268; distribution of eggs and immatures, 280; eggs, 200; emigration from Hudson, 280; fall distribution of YOY, 282; fishery, 277; future research, 346; hatchery, 340; identification of hatchery fish, 342; immature stages, 278; influence of temperature and salinity, 55; marking with coded wire tags, 268, 341; monitoring populations of, 266; movement routes, 285; movements of immatures, 276–300; movements of yearling and age 2 fish, 294; postjuvenile studies after the Settlement Agreement, 339–347; predation on bay anchovy, 230; role of salinity in movements, 299–300; role of salinity in movements of immatures, 300; spring and fall distribution of young-of-the-year, 282; stock assessment, 343; summer distribution, 280–282; survival, 393; time of spawning, 280; vital rates, 397; winter distribution, 285; winter concentration areas, 289

554 Index

Striped killifish, 432, 441
Student-Neuman-Keuls groupings, 356
Sturgeon. *See* Atlantic sturgeon, Shortnose sturgeon
Submerged aquatic vegetation, 461, 474, 479; as food source, 480; as shelter for juvenile fish, 480; loss of, 481
Sucker. *See* White sucker
Summer flounder, 415, 416, 417, 432
Sunfish. *See* Bluegill, Pumpkinseed
Suspended solids, 100

T

Taconic Mountains, 245
Tagging: 192, 341, 343; cost for hatchery fish, 342; mortality, 343
Tag retention, 343
Taguchi method, 304
Tappan Zee, 266, 296, 328, 354, 362
Target species, 493
Tautog, 441
TdR(^{3}H-hymidine), 449
Temperature: mean at RM 66, 65, figure 3.3; spatial patterns, 39–46; temporal patterns, 33–39, 63, figure 3.4
Tessellated darter, 466–467, 471–472
Texas Instruments Science Services Division: 307, 308–310; project organization for Hudson River Ecological Study, 308–310
^{238}Th, table 7.2
Threespine stickleback, 441
Tidal current, effect on striped bass movement, 282
Tidal exchange, Tivoli South Bay, 466
Tidal marshes, 458–476
Tidal wetlands, 459
Title 10 Code of Federal Regulations Part 50, appendix B, 307

Tivoli Bays, 459
Tivoli South Bay, 459
Toadfish. *See* Oyster toadfish
Tomcod. *See* Atlantic tomcod
Trapa beds, 463, 464, 465, 467, 468, 473
Trapa natans, 263, 461, 463, 464, 467, 474, 475
Tree-ring-reconstructed drought indices, 28
Tributaries: Mohawk River, 9, table 1.1; Lower Hudson, 10–11; Upper Hudson, 9, table 1.1
Troy, 188
Troy dam, 207
Tucker trawl, 245, 354, 374, 377
Turbidity: Haverstraw Bay, 66, 68, figure 3.5; before dredging, 89, figure 4.3; during dredging, 91, figure 4.5
Two-layer system, 107
Typha angustifolia, 461, 481

U

"U-snout", 209
U.S. Fish and Wildlife Service, 429
U.S. Army Corps of Engineers, 83–85, 429
Underpier areas, 407
Underpier/interpier comparison sampling: 412; gill nets, 417
Unifying theoretical base for estuarine studies, lack of, 494
Unsampled shore zones, 351
Unsampled upriver shoals, 351
Utility-sponsored research after the Settlement, xii

V

Valisneria americana, 461, 463, 464, 467, 474, 483
Valisneria beds: 463, 464, 467, 468,

474; benthic respiration in, 480; loss of, 481
Vandenburgh cove, 193
Van Veen grab, 190
Variable speed pumps, 340
Verrazano Narrows, 8, 285

W

Wappinger Creek, 16
Water celery, 263, 461
Water Chestnut: 461; as fish habitat, 263; effects on population estimates of white perch YOY, 263–264
Water quality: recent trends and patterns, 59–81; 422; effects of toxic chemicals on shortnose sturgeon, 214; at Hudson River Center, 413
Water temperature: at Poughkeepsie waterworks, 1951–1987, figure 2.2; deviations from weekly average, 39, figure 2.5; effects on shortnose sturgeon, 225–227
Watermilfoil, 263
Waterside, 125, figures 5.9, 5.10
Waterways Experiment Station, 84–85
Weakfish, 416, 432
West Point, 280, 328, 356
West Side Highway Project, 491; see also: Westway
Westchester County, 487
Westchester County landfill, 481
Westway, 121–125, 278–279
White perch stock assessment program: 244, 247–250, 257; sampling stations, table 11.2
White hake, 416, 432
White catfish, 154
White, C., 195

White perch: 154, 243, 251, 256, 353, 358, 368–369, 372–373, 415, 416, 417, 426–427, 432, 435, 436, 438, 441, 442, 466–467, 471–472, 473, 493, figures 17.5, 17.7, 17.8, 17.9; abundance trends, 242–264; adult CPUE index, 257; entrainment of eggs, 259; entrainment of larvae, 260; impingement, 259; indicator of the effects of power plant operation, 243; combined standing crop index, 256; CPUE of young of year, 256; eggs standing crop, 251; estimates of standing crop, 386; fall regression index, YOY, 257; post-yolk-sac larvae standing crop, 256; summer regression index, 257; yolk-sac larvae standing crop, 251–256
White perch trawl, 219
White sucker, 466–467, 469–472, 473
Window pane, 416, 432
Winter flounder, 415, 416, 417, 426–427, 431, 432, 434, 436, 438, 442–443, 445

Y

Year class strength, 265–275
Yonkers, figure 2.6, 277, 296, 324, 328
YOY (young of year): striped bass, 268–269, 282; white perch, 257, 263–264

Z

Zooplankton: biomass in Kingston area, 453